Changing Poverty, Changing Policies

Changing Poverty, Changing Policies

Maria Cancian
and
Sheldon Danziger

Editors

Russell Sage Foundation ♦ New York

The Russell Sage Foundation

The Russell Sage Foundation, one of the oldest of America's general purpose foundations, was established in 1907 by Mrs. Margaret Olivia Sage for "the improvement of social and living conditions in the United States." The Foundation seeks to fulfill this mandate by fostering the development and dissemination of knowledge about the country's political, social, and economic problems. While the Foundation endeavors to assure the accuracy and objectivity of each book it publishes, the conclusions and interpretations in Russell Sage Foundation publications are those of the authors and not of the Foundation, its Trustees, or its staff. Publication by Russell Sage, therefore, does not imply Foundation endorsement.

Library of Congress Cataloging-in-Publication Data

Changing poverty, changing policies / Maria Cancian and Sheldon Danziger, editors.
   p. cm.
  Includes bibliographical references and index.
  ISBN 978-0-87154-310-3 (alk. paper)
  1. Poverty. 2. Economic assistance, Domestic. 3. Public welfare. I. Cancian, Maria. II. Danziger, Sheldon.
HC79.P6C4274 2009
362.5—dc22

2009011413

Text design by Suzanne Nichols.

RUSSELL SAGE FOUNDATION
112 East 64th Street, New York, New York 10065
10 9 8 7 6 5 4 3 2 1

To Robert H. Haveman and Elizabeth Evanson,
for their decades of leadership and dedicated service
to the Institute for Research on Poverty

Contents

Contents

Contributors

MARIA CANCIAN is professor of public affairs and social work and research affiliate of the Institute for Research on Poverty at the University of Wisconsin–Madison.

SHELDON DANZIGER is Henry J. Meyer Distinguished University Professor of Public Policy and director of the National Poverty Center at the Gerald R. Ford School of Public Policy at the University of Michigan.

MARY JO BANE is Thornton Bradshaw Professor of Public Policy and Management and academic dean at the John F. Kennedy School of Government at Harvard University.

REBECCA M. BLANK is Robert S. Kerr Senior Fellow at the Brookings Institution.

BENJAMIN COWAN is graduate student of economics and graduate research fellow of the Institute for Research on Poverty at the University of Wisconsin–Madison.

ROBERT HAVEMAN is John Bascom Professor of Economics and Public Affairs Emeritus and research affiliate of the Institute for Research on Poverty at the University of Wisconsin–Madison

HARRY J. HOLZER is professor of public policy at Georgetown University, institute fellow at the Urban Institute, and nonresident senior fellow at the Brookings Institution.

BRIAN A. JACOB is Walter H. Annenberg Professor of Education Policy, professor of economics, and director of the Center on Local, State, and Urban Policy (CLOSUP) at the Gerald R. Ford School of Public Policy at the University of Michigan.

MARKUS JÄNTTI is professor of economics at the Swedish Institute for Social Research at Stockholm University, Sweden.

JENS LUDWIG is McCormick Foundation Professor of Social Service Administration, Law, and Public Policy at the University of Chicago.

Contributors

KATHERINE MAGNUSON is assistant professor of social work and research affiliate of the Institute for Research on Poverty at the University of Wisconsin–Madison.

DANIEL R. MEYER is Mary C. Jacoby Distinguished Professor of Social Work and research affiliate of the Institute for Research on Poverty at the University of Wisconsin–Madison.

ROBERT MOFFITT is the Krieger-Eisenhower Professor of Economics at the Johns Hopkins University.

STEVEN RAPHAEL is professor of public policy at the Goldman School of Public Policy at the University of California–Berkeley.

DEBORAH REED is director of research for the Oakland office of Mathematica Policy Research, Inc.

JOHN KARL SCHOLZ is professor of economics and a research affiliate of the Institute for Research on Poverty at the University of Wisconsin–Madison.

EUGENE SMOLENSKY is emeritus professor of public policy at the Goldman School of Public Policy at the University of California–Berkeley.

KATHERINE SWARTZ is professor of health economics and policy at Harvard University.

ELIZABETH VOTRUBA-DRZAL is assistant professor of psychology at the University of Pittsburgh.

JANE WALDFOGEL is professor of social work and public affairs at the Columbia University School of Social Work and a visiting professor at the Centre for Analysis of Social Exclusion (CASE) at the London School of Economics.

GEOFFREY L. WALLACE is associate professor of public affairs and economics and research affiliate of the Institute for Research on Poverty at the University of Wisconsin–Madison.

Acknowledgments

Changing Poverty is the fifth in a series of edited volumes sponsored by the Institute for Research on Poverty that evaluate the nature of poverty and the scope of antipoverty polices. The first volume, *A Decade of Federal Antipoverty Programs: Achievements, Failures, and Lessons,* edited by Robert H. Haveman, appeared in 1977. It was followed by *Fighting Poverty: What Works and What Doesn't,* edited by Sheldon H. Danziger and Daniel H. Weinberger (1986); *Confronting Poverty: Prescriptions for Change,* edited by Sheldon H. Danziger, Gary Sandefur, and Daniel H. Weinberg (1994); and *Understanding Poverty,* edited by Sheldon H. Danziger and Robert H. Haveman (2001).

The chapters in this volume were initially presented at a conference held in May 2008 in Madison, Wisconsin; they have been revised to respond to the conference participants and two anonymous referees. The Institute for Research on Poverty at the University of Wisconsin–Madison and the Office of the Assistant Secretary for Planning and Evaluation in the U.S. Department of Health and Human Services jointly sponsored the conference, with additional support from the Russell Sage Foundation.

We gratefully acknowledge the support of Eric Wanner, president, and Suzanne Nichols, director of publications, of the Russell Sage Foundation, and the advice and encouragement of Bob Haveman and other members of the Executive Committee of the Institute for Research on Poverty. Institute staff, including Emma Caspar, Dawn Duren, Deborah Johnson, Robin Snell, Bill Wambach, and Coreen Williams provided essential editorial, technical, and logistical support for the project.

Additional resource materials for instructors, including presentation-ready charts and suggested supplemental readings, are available on the volume Web site at http://www.russellsage.org. Any views expressed in this book are those of the chapter authors and should not be construed as representing the official position or policy of any sponsoring institution, agency, or foundation.

M. M. C.
S. H. D.

Chapter 1

Changing Poverty and Changing Antipoverty Policies

Maria Cancian and Sheldon Danziger

It is not surprising that the severe economic downturn that began in late 2007 reduced employment and earnings and raised the official poverty rate. What many readers may find surprising, however, is that even during the long economic expansions of the 1980s and 1990s the official poverty rate remained higher than it was in 1973. Since the early 1970s, dramatic changes in the economy, in the social conditions that affect the demographic composition of the population, and in public policies have combined to reduce the antipoverty effects of economic growth. Even though gross domestic product (GDP) per capita has grown substantially since the early 1970s, the antipoverty effects of this growth were substantially lower than they were in the quarter-century that followed the end of World War II. Economic growth is now necessary, but not sufficient, to significantly reduce poverty. Antipoverty policies must be expanded and reformed to address these new demographic and economic realities.

This volume examines changing poverty and changing antipoverty policies in the United States since the early 1970s. The chapter authors consider both how economic and demographic changes have changed which individuals and families are poor and how antipoverty programs and policies have, and have not, changed in response. Poverty rates have declined for some demographic groups and increased for others. The authors address the range of economic, social, and public policy factors that have contributed to changing levels of poverty and examine how changes in existing programs and policies and the implementation of new programs and policies might reduce poverty in the future. Some of these policies would supplement the incomes of today's low-income families, while others aim to prevent poverty by raising employment and earnings—either in the near future or in the next generation.

Most analyses in this volume utilize the Census Bureau measure of poverty, adopted in the late 1960s, according to which an individual is counted as poor if his or her current money income from all sources and from all related family members falls below the official poverty line. In 2008 a family of four was considered poor if its money income before payment of taxes was less than $22,017; a single, non-elderly person was poor if his or her pretax money income was less than $11,201. Measuring poverty requires analysts to confront many conceptual and technical issues. As discussed in the chapters by Daniel Meyer and Geoffrey Wallace and by Robert Haveman, many researchers consider the current poverty measure outdated. The official poverty rate remains, however, one of our nation's most important social indicators. Despite its flaws, it provides valuable information on how far the nation still has to go to reach President Lyndon Johnson's goal, set out in 1964, when he declared "War on Poverty"—the elimination of income poverty.

How best to understand the range of factors that lead some people to become poor or to remain poor is contentiously debated. Some explanations suggest that poverty is primarily the consequence of an individual's own choices regarding investments in education, job search efforts, and motivation to work and his or her decisions about family formation and childbearing. Other explanations emphasize structural factors that shape the set of choices available to an individual and that differ systematically by, for example, parental socioeconomic status, race, and gender. Structural factors include changes in the nature of available jobs brought about by technological changes, globalization, and economic policies and unequal access to good schools and employment opportunities due to residential segregation or discriminatory practices.

Because so many complex interactions affect an individual's money income, a single poverty experience can reasonably be explained in different ways. Consider a single mother who did not graduate from high school and has now lost her minimum-wage service-sector job after missing a few days of work to care for a sick child with chronic asthma. Is her family now poor because of a short-term health crisis? If so, is the crisis due primarily to the mother's failure to make alternative child care arrangements and call her employer when she missed work, or is it primarily due to the nature of low-wage jobs, which usually do not provide workers with even unpaid sick leave or subsidized health insurance? Or is her family's economic vulnerability due to the personal choices she made when she dropped out of high school and gave birth to a child outside of marriage? To what extent does graduating from high school reflect an individual's own choices, efforts, and motivation, as opposed to the quality of his or her educational opportunities, which vary with property values in the local school district and other factors largely beyond individual choice or control? As these questions illustrate, the causes of poverty are varied and difficult to disentangle, and it is hardly surprising that poverty researchers and policy analysts disagree about which policy changes would most effectively reduce poverty.

To make recommendations about promising antipoverty policies, the authors here analyze how economic, demographic, social, and public policy changes since the early 1970s have shaped the choices and structural constraints that individuals face and the consequences of these changes for understanding changes in poverty. Several chapters discuss the changing economy and changing labor market, which have affected employment and earnings and, hence, changing patterns of poverty for men and women. Others examine the changing demographic composition of the population—particularly increases in single-mother families and increased immigration—and their effects on poverty. Others analyze the changing role of public policies relating to labor markets, income support programs, education and training programs, health insurance, and family policies in reducing poverty among today's adults and preventing poverty in the next generation.

Before we describe each chapter, we review three crosscutting factors that shape the extent and nature of poverty and the impact of those factors on prospects for reducing poverty: the changing role of race and ethnicity in the labor market and society; changing gender roles, which have influenced both trends in the labor force participation of women and patterns of family formation and child-bearing; and the recent history of social welfare programs and policies. Following the chapter reviews, we outline high priority elements of a new antipoverty agenda.

THE CHANGING ROLE OF RACE AND ETHNICITY: UNEVEN PROGRESS AND PERSISTENT DISPARITIES

The large and persisting differences in poverty rates between racial and ethnic groups are an enduring and troubling aspect of our nation's social and economic history. In 1950 three out of four black Americans had incomes below the level specified by the official poverty line; in contrast, about 35 percent of whites were poor.[1] Both the high absolute level of black poverty and the disparity between the economic status of whites and blacks challenged the American ideal of equal opportunity. The second half of the twentieth century was a period of great, but uneven and incomplete, progress. Although overt, legally sanctioned discrimination explicitly based on race and ethnicity has largely been eliminated, public policies and institutional practices continue to have effects that differ by race and ethnicity and that disadvantage minorities.[2] Moreover, the lingering effects of past discrimination in schooling, housing markets, and labor markets reduce the ability of racial and ethnic minorities to take full advantage of contemporary opportunities (Lin and Harris 2008). Although the absolute gap in poverty rates between whites and racial and ethnic minorities has narrowed since the 1960s, continuing large disparities raise challenges for antipoverty policies.

The 1950s and 1960s were decades of rapid economic growth that raised earnings for workers of all races, ethnicities, and educational groups. Changes in public policies and civil rights legislation increased access to educational and job opportunities and contributed to relative income growth and occupational gains for black Americans. By 1969 poverty rates had fallen to 31 percent for blacks and 8 percent for whites. Although blacks were more than three times as likely as whites to be poor, the racial gap in poverty rates had fallen from forty percentage points in 1949 to twenty-three in 1969.

The 1970s and 1980s saw additional progress in reducing discriminatory barriers based on race and ethnicity, but slow economic growth, coupled with higher unemployment rates and falling real wages for workers with no more than a high school diploma, brought progress against poverty to a halt for all racial and eth-nic groups. Minorities were overrepresented among workers with a high school diploma or less, a group whose wages and employment prospects fell relative to those of college graduates. Slow and unequal growth resulted in a unique period in recent American economic history—two decades over which the official poverty rate rose. In 1973 the official rate was 7.5 percent for white non-Hispanics, 31.4 percent for blacks, and 21.9 percent for Hispanics. In 1993 the rates for whites and blacks had increased modestly to 9.9 percent and 33.1 percent, respectively. The rate for Hispanics, however, had increased substantially to 30.6 percent—in part reflecting increased immigration (on immigration-related changes in the composition of the Hispanic population and their consequences for both the Hispanic and overall poverty rates, see Raphael and Smolensky, this volume).

The economic boom that started after the recession of the early 1990s resulted in the lowest unemployment rates since the late 1960s—4 percent in 2000—and the inflation-adjusted wages of less-educated workers, which had fallen between the early 1970s and the early 1990s, increased. Tight labor markets and rising real wage rates for less-educated workers had a larger positive effect on the incomes and poverty rates of black and Hispanic families than on those of white non-Hispanic families—both because black and Hispanic workers were more likely than whites to have less education and because, among less-educated workers, blacks and Hispanics made larger gains than whites. Between 1993 and 2000, the poverty rate for white non-Hispanics fell from 9.9 percent to 7.4 percent, while the poverty rate for minorities dropped dramatically. The rate for blacks declined from 33.1 percent to 22.5 percent, and the rate for Hispanics from 30.6 percent to 21.5 percent.

Poverty rates increased following the 2001 recession and the slow growth in employment in the subsequent six years. In 2007, 8.2 percent of white non-Hispanics, 24.5 percent of blacks, and 21.5 percent of Hispanics were poor. Among other racial and ethnic groups, poverty rates in 2007 were high among Native Americans (25 percent) and relatively low for Asian Americans (10 percent). Given the recession that started in December 2007 and the very large number of jobs lost since then, poverty rates will be even higher at the end of 2009 and are unlikely to reach the lower rates of 2000 for several years after that.

Absolute disparities in poverty rates fell over the latter decades of the twentieth century but remain large. The gap between whites and Hispanics was thirteen points in 2007 compared to twenty-one points in 1993. The black-white gap in poverty rates was sixteen percentage points in 2007, substantially smaller than the twenty-four-point gap in 1993 and the forty-point gap in 1950. However, the rates for blacks, Hispanics, and Native Americans in 2007 were higher than the 1959 rate for whites—18.1 percent. In 2007 blacks and Native Americans remained three times as likely as whites to be poor, with white-Hispanic differentials only slightly smaller.

The progress in reducing the official poverty rate and the narrowing of race-ethnic disparities reflect overall economic growth over the last half of the twenti-eth century, expanded income support policies (especially for the elderly), and the elimination of most explicit discriminatory policies and practices. Remaining disparities reflect the vulnerability engendered by a history of disadvantage as well as more subtle forms of discrimination—the institutional structures, policies, and attitudes that have been more resistant to change (Lin and Harris 2008).

The persistent disparity in poverty rates across racial and ethnic groups reflects both race-specific and race-neutral factors. Because about half of the 37 million poor Americans are either black or Hispanic, race-neutral economic changes and public policy changes that affect low-wage workers and low-income families disproportionately affect racial-ethnic minorities. But race and ethnicity, as well as other factors, also directly shape the context and content of public policies in ways beyond those associated with the disproportionate representation of minorities among the poor.

Consider, for example, recent trends in educational attainment and changes in wages for workers with differing educational attainments. One of the most powerful labor market changes since the 1970s has been increasing returns to education, owing primarily to increased employer demand for college-educated workers and decreased demand for high school dropouts and high school graduates, particularly among men. For example, many less-educated men with high-wage jobs worked in manufacturing industries in the quarter-century following World War II. The number of these jobs has decreased dramatically since the early 1970s, and that trend has accelerated in the first decade of the twenty-first century. As a result, the earnings of black and Hispanic men have fallen relative to those of white men; this decrease is largely a "mechanical" or "race-neutral" labor market effect due to the disproportionate representation of these minorities among less-educated workers.

On the other hand, the disproportionate share of blacks and Hispanics with low levels of education is due in part to continuing high levels of racial residential segregation and the related restricted educational opportunities available to children of color. For example, recent audit studies have documented continued high levels of housing discrimination, including reduced access to available units and racial steering (Turner et al. 2002). These discriminatory practices contribute to the tendency for racial and ethnic minorities, especially blacks, to live in areas of concentrated poverty (Stoll 2008). Because school quality is negatively correlated with the neighborhood poverty rate, even in the absence of discrimination in educational opportunity directly related to race or ethnicity, historical and persisting patterns of residential segregation restrict access to educational opportunities.

Another factor that has negatively affected the employment prospects of minority workers who are residentially concentrated in central cities is the movement of jobs from central cities to suburbs and the rapid expansion of employment outside of central cities in the last quarter of the twentieth century (Stoll and Raphael 2000). Moreover, some employers relocated their firms from the central cities to the suburbs in reaction to the "browning" of central cities. That is, the spatial mismatch between minority workers and jobs reflects both technological changes that made suburban location for some firms more efficient and racially motivated relocations by firms seeking a "whiter" workforce (Holzer 1996; Stoll 2006).

Less-educated minority men also have been disproportionately affected by the rapid increase in incarceration rates since the 1980s. In 2006 about 5 percent of all African American men were incarcerated—about six times the rate for whites, and more than twice the rate for Latinos. Steven Raphael (2007) notes that, in 2001, 2.6 percent of non-Hispanic white men, 16.6 percent of non-Hispanic black men, and 7.7 percent of Hispanic men had served time in prison. Among recent cohorts of less-educated men, incarceration rates are dramatically higher: for example, over two-thirds of black male high school dropouts, and one-third of those with less than a college education, had been incarcerated by the time they reached their early thirties (Western and Wildeman 2009). Racial and ethnic disparities in incarceration reflect both differences in criminal behaviors and differential treatment by the criminal justice system. That is, blacks and Hispanics are both more likely to engage in criminal behavior—in part, reflecting restricted employment opportunities—and more likely to face incarceration as a consequence—reflecting explicit and implicit discrimination within the criminal justice system (Wheelock and Uggen 2008).

Mass incarceration has negative consequences for incarcerated individuals and their families and for minority communities as a whole. For example, not only do individuals who have been incarcerated face reduced employment prospects, but some employers appear to discriminate against less-educated black men, regardless of the individual's history of incarceration, because they assume that minority men with sporadic employment histories have spent time in jail (Holzer, Raphael, and Stoll 2006; Pager 2007).

Finally, as we discuss further in the next section, differences in patterns of family structure across racial and ethnic groups contribute to racial-ethnic differences in poverty. Poverty is much lower for married-couple families than for other family types for all racial and ethnic groups. In 2006, 71 percent of black children, 50 percent of Hispanic children, and 27 percent of white children were born to unmarried mothers (Martin et al. 2009), the family structure with the highest poverty rate.

There is a long history of contentious debate among social scientists, policymakers, and the public about the factors that account for declines in marriage, increases in nonmarital childbearing, and racial and ethnic differences in these patterns (on racial and ethnic differences in marriage and childbearing, see Cancian and Reed, this volume). There have been dramatic changes in norms across racial, ethnic, and socioeconomic groups regarding premarital sexual activity, nonmarital fertility, cohabitation, and divorce that have reduced the stigma associated with nontraditional family formation. Changes in women's employment and related changes in the timing of marriage and childbearing have had differential effects by education level and therefore by race (Ellwood and Jencks 2004). Some analysts also attribute the relatively low rates of marriage and high rates of nonmarital childbearing among blacks to declines in the number of black men who earn enough to support a family (Wilson 1996). The relatively low proportion of black men with family-supporting earnings reflects the previously discussed decline in the relative wages of less-educated men, the declining availability of jobs, and higher incarceration rates. Moreover, the decline in the work and earnings of black men, especially young black men, stands in contrast to growing employment and earnings for black women (Holzer 2009). These changing economic realities have interacted with changing societal norms and expectations regarding marriage and parenting (Edin and Kefalas 2005).

Regardless of causal factors, large differences in family structure have implications for labor market behaviors and the receipt of government benefits, which have their own independent effects on the racial-ethnic disparity in poverty rates. Many programs and policies have eligibility criteria or benefit levels that are related to both marital status and economic status. These include cash welfare (now Temporary Assistance for Needy Families, TANF), the Earned Income Tax Credit (EITC), and Social Security, to name a few. As a result, these social policies differentially affect racial and ethnic groups owing to their family structure differences. Some scholars suggest that the racial and ethnic composition of the poor and of potential program beneficiaries influences the generosity of public programs. For example, Joe Soss and his colleagues (2001) find that the 1996 welfare reform was implemented in ways that were correlated with the racial composition of a state's welfare caseload. As a result, a greater proportion of blacks and Latinos than whites live in states that have stricter sanctions, work requirements, and other policies (see also Lieberman 2001; Soss, Fording, and Schram 2008; Quadagno 1994).

Because minorities account for more than half of all poor persons, reducing the overall poverty rate requires a reduction in the high rates of poverty among racial-ethnic minorities. Race-neutral antipoverty policies that increase labor market prospects for all less-educated workers and supplement the incomes of all workers with low earnings and that address the challenges faced by single-parent families can have a substantial effect. Given the lasting effects of discriminatory practices, however, additional policies will be needed to reduce racial and ethnic disparities in opportunities and outcomes.

CHANGING GENDER ROLES AND EXPECTATIONS

Since the 1960s, the United States and most other advanced economies have experienced dramatic changes in gender roles and expectations regarding women's choices in the domains of education, marriage, childbearing, and employment. Growth in women's employment reflects large increases in married mothers' work in the 1970s and 1980s and in the employment of single mothers in the 1990s. For example, in 1970 only 40 percent of married women with children under the age of eighteen worked outside the home; by 2006, 68 percent of such women worked for pay.

In part because of changing gender roles and in part because of increased labor market opportunities, women are staying in school longer, marrying at later ages, and having fewer children. For example, in 1964, among young adults between the ages of twenty-five and twenty-nine, 69 percent of men and 70 percent of women had completed at least a high school diploma, and 17 percent of men and 9 percent of women were college graduates. By 2007 young women in this age group were more likely to have graduated from both high school and college: 89 percent and

33 percent, respectively, compared to 85 percent and 26 percent, respectively, of men.

There has also been a large increase in the percentage of children who reside with only one parent. This reflects higher divorce rates after the 1960s, a delay in the age of first marriage, a decline in the percentage of women who marry, a lower birthrate for married women, and a somewhat higher birthrate for unmarried women. Maria Cancian and Deborah Reed (this volume) examine the complex relationships between increased women's work and earnings and decreased marriage and fertility. Declines in marriage and increases in nonmarital childbearing have increased women's risk of poverty, whereas increased educational attainment and employment and declines in the number of children per woman have contributed to reductions in poverty.

These profound changes in gender roles and market work have important implications for the design of public policies and employer practices. Issues of family leave, access to affordable child care, and child support payments from noncustodial parents have all become widespread concerns that affect the resources available to children and families across the distribution of income. But low-wage jobs generally offer few family-friendly benefits. Moreover, most public policies designed to help parents balance work and family responsibilities are not well designed for low-income families. For example, the $1,000 per child tax credit implemented by the George W. Bush administration provides additional resources that can be used for child care and other expenses. However, because the tax credit is not fully refundable, some low-income families that do not owe federal income taxes but do pay Social Security taxes have not received the credit.[3]

Another example of a policy that is not well designed for low-income families is the Family and Medical Leave Act (FMLA) of 1993. The act grants eligible workers up to twelve weeks of unpaid leave during any twelve-month period to care for a newborn or adopted child, to care for immediate family members with a serious health condition, or to take medical leave for the employee's own serious health condition. However, the FMLA exempts firms with fewer than fifty employees, and low-wage workers are more likely than higher-wage workers to be employed by small firms. FMLA also provides only unpaid leave, which is not a viable option for most low-income families, who cannot rely on savings or sufficient earnings from other family members (Waldfogel, this volume; Boots, Macomber, and Danziger 2008).

The increased employment of mothers and changes in family formation patterns have directly influenced changes in policies and programs focused on low-income women. Although Aid to Families with Dependent Children (AFDC) was designed in the 1930s to allow poor mothers (particularly, white widows) to stay home and care for their children, the Personal Responsibility and Work Opportunity Reconciliation Act (PRWORA) of 1996 ("welfare reform") mandated work requirements for almost all cash welfare recipients, even the mothers of infants. This change in expectations about the market work of welfare recipients in part reflects the increased work of mothers not receiving welfare. According to Ron Haskins (2006, 18), "that working mothers, millions of them single, should work to pay taxes so that other single mothers could stay home with their children proved to be a highly unstable political situation."

The 1996 welfare reform also reflected public concerns about declining marriage and increased nonmarital childbearing among the poor. Some analysts (for example, Murray 2001) advocated cutting income supports to make single-parent families less economically viable and to provide a greater incentive for single mothers to marry the fathers of their children or give the children up for adoption.

Most mothers of young children work for pay at some time during the year, but most do not work full-time, full-year. Nonetheless, many states have TANF work requirements that expect such mothers to work full-time (Cancian and Reed, this volume). Moreover, public policies do not adequately address the reality that many poor women, compared to their middle-class counterparts, live in less stable housing, in less safe neighborhoods, and have fewer options to purchase acceptable child care. This makes it more difficult for poor mothers to find and hold jobs. Thus, even though the poverty rate for single-mother families with children fell rapidly in the decade following the 1996 welfare reform, their poverty rate remains very high—36.5 percent in 2006, thirty percentage points higher than the rate for married-couple families. Effective antipoverty policy will need to better respond to the challenges associated with changes in family structure and the increasing employment of mothers.

CHANGING SOCIAL PROGRAMS AND POLICIES

In January 1964, President Lyndon Johnson declared:

> This administration today, here and now, declares unconditional war on poverty in America. Our chief weapons in a more pinpointed attack will be better schools, and better health, and better homes, and better training, and better job opportunities to help more Americans, especially young Americans escape from squalor and misery and unemployment rolls (Johnson 1964).

Johnson and his economic advisers thought that the programs and policies that the War on Poverty would launch, together with a growing economy that raised the wages of most workers and low unemployment rates, would eliminate poverty as officially measured within a generation. Their expectations were incorrect— poverty remained as high in 2007 as it had been in 1968. However, given the economic conditions of the 1960s, their optimistic projections were reasonable ones. As mentioned earlier, poverty had fallen in the 1950s and 1960s, and Johnson's economists were confident that their fiscal and monetary policies could moderate the business cycle and keep the economy growing (Tobin 1967).

They also expected that the enactment of the Economic Opportunity Act of 1964, which increased federal spending on education and training, and the implementation of additional policies to break down discrimination in schools and the labor market would raise the employment and earnings of the poor, especially racial-ethnic minorities and women. Among the many programs launched by the Economic Opportunity Act and the Higher Education Act of 1965 that still operate today are Head Start, the Job Corps, and Pell grants, subsidized Stafford loans, and the work-study program for college students. Johnson's advisers expected that these new programs and policies would increase the ability of future generations of high school graduates to earn enough to escape poverty and increase the likelihood that children from poor families would graduate from high school and enroll in college.

Many among the poor in the mid-1960s were not expected to work—the elderly, the disabled, and single mothers with young children—and many poor adults were too old for investments in their education and training to be productive. As a result, in the decade following declaration of the War on Poverty, there was rapid growth in Social Security and welfare benefits designed to raise the incomes of those not benefiting from economic growth.

A growing economy, expanding economic opportunities, and more generous public benefits all contributed to a rapid decline in poverty from 19.0 percent to 11.1 percent between 1964 and 1973. The rapid poverty declines came to an end in 1973, however, and since then the official poverty rate has never fallen below the 1973 level. The intervening decades have been characterized, for the most part, by slower economic growth. Real per capita GDP and real per capita personal income grew more rapidly in the quarter-century following World War II than they did in the last quarter of the twentieth century. Even this more modest economic growth would have reduced poverty had it not been accompanied by rising inequality in earnings and family income, with those at the bottom of the income distribution falling further behind those at the top.

For most groups at high risk of poverty (except the elderly), growth in government benefits also slowed after 1973. For some periods and some groups, there were significant contractions in benefits. For example, the inflation-adjusted value of the median monthly AFDC benefit, then the major cash assistance program for poor single-mother families with children, fell substantially after the mid-1970s, and the number of welfare beneficiaries fell dramatically after enactment of the 1996 welfare reform. As John Karl Scholz, Robert Moffitt, and Benjamin Cowan (this volume) document, growth in government benefits after the mid-1980s was targeted on low-income workers, primarily through the Earned Income Tax Credit.

The failure of poverty rates to fall below their 1973 level contributed to a backlash by policymakers and the public against antipoverty policies. Some critics blamed the growth of antipoverty programs themselves for poverty's failure to decline further (Murray 1984; Mead 1985). In a February 15, 1986, radio address, President Reagan expressed such a view:

> In 1964, the famous War on Poverty was declared. And a funny thing happened. Poverty, as measured by dependency, stopped shrinking and actually began to grow worse. I guess you could say "Poverty won the War." Poverty won, in part, because instead of helping the poor, government programs ruptured the bonds holding poor families together.

Other critics argued that the goal of eliminating income poverty should be replaced by the goal of changing the behaviors of the poor. An American Enterprise Institute (AEI) task force concluded:

> Money alone will not cure poverty; internalized values are also needed. The most disturbing element among a fraction of the contemporary poor is an inability to seize opportunity even when it is available and while others around them are seizing it. Their need is less for job training than for meaning and order in their lives. An indispensable resource in the war against poverty is a sense of personal responsibility. (Novak et al. 1987)

Our reading of the evidence presented by Rebecca Blank (this volume) and Sheldon Danziger and Peter Gottschalk (1995) is that poverty has not fallen below the 1973 level in large part because of economic changes that led the real annual earnings of working male high school graduates to fall in the three decades after 1973. The poverty rate would be somewhat lower today if fewer low-skilled men had withdrawn from the labor market and if marriage rates had not declined so much over these decades. These effects are small, however, compared to the poverty-increasing effects of a labor market that shifted from a quarter-century of rapid economic growth that benefited all workers to a quarter-century of declining wages and employment prospects for workers with no more than a high school diploma.

The impact of slow economic growth was exacerbated by a lack of public policies aimed at helping vulnerable workers and families adjust to the changing economic realities. The Johnson administration proposed a range of education and training opportunities and jobs programs and greatly increased federal subsidies to help the disadvantaged during a period of economic growth. In recent decades, however, government has provided less support at a time during which a changing labor market has increased the rewards for more years of schooling and during which the rising costs of college have made increased public support for students from low-income families more critical. Whereas the United States was a leader in investing in education in earlier decades, it has failed to keep pace with other countries in making the necessary skills and training broadly available. At a time when changing industrial organization has contributed to fewer opportunities to move up within a firm and less job security in many sectors, government spending on workforce retraining is much smaller than it was in the 1970s (Holzer, this volume).

Poverty persists, not because the ideas of the War on Poverty planners were fundamentally mistaken, but because the changing economy increased economic hardships for many workers and existing antipoverty policies did not respond sufficiently to offset market-generated increases in poverty. Policies also failed to respond adequately to largely unanticipated changes in family organization. Poverty need not remain high. The historical evidence and the new analyses in this volume document that certain antipoverty policies, if undertaken, can effectively reduce poverty far below its current level.

REVIEW OF THE CHAPTERS

The chapters of this book are organized into four sections. Current poverty levels and the contribution of economic and demographic changes to the lack of progress in reducing poverty since the early 1970s are discussed in part 1. Part 2 evaluates poverty mobility—the consequences of childhood poverty for later life outcomes and the chances that individuals with poor parents will escape poverty as adults. Antipoverty policies, including income support policies, family policies, education and workforce development policies, and health policy, are analyzed in part 3. Finally, part 4 assesses the politics of poverty and related policies and reconsiders how we define poverty and how new definitions of poverty and material hardships might support new policy solutions.

This volume analyzes changes in poverty and changes in antipoverty policies in the United States. However, a comparison of U.S. experiences with those of other advanced economies can illuminate some of the underlying causes of poverty and the prospects for change.[4] As Daniel Meyer and Geoffrey Wallace document in the next chapter, by a common measure, U.S. poverty rates are among the highest of all advanced economies.

Some readers may find it surprising that poverty is higher in the United States when our GDP per capita is higher, our unemployment rate is lower, and Americans work more hours per year than workers in most other rich countries. However, there is greater inequality in wages in the United States, lower unionization rates, and a lower minimum wage. Thus a greater proportion of American workers are poor than their counterparts in many European countries. In addition, government social programs in the United States provide lower benefits to fewer families than do government programs in other rich countries (Smeeding 2008; Scholz, Moffitt, and Cowan, this volume).

Economic Changes, Demographic Changes, and Trends in Poverty

In chapter 2, Daniel Meyer and Geoffrey Wallace review how poverty is currently measured and show how poverty differs among demographic groups—for instance, poverty rates are relatively high for children (compared to adults and the elderly), for blacks and Hispanics (compared to white non-Hispanics), and for families headed by women (compared to married couples). Because of their size in the overall population, however, white non-Hispanics account for about 40 percent of all poor persons. Fewer than half of all poor people live in female-headed households.

It is difficult to consistently measure poverty from the 1960s to the present because the official measure counts only cash income and is increased each year only to account for inflation. The official measure thus does not reflect the overall rise in living standards, which has led many analysts to advocate for a higher poverty line (Blank 2008). It also does not reflect the increase in government noncash benefits and tax credits that raise the well-being of the poor but are not counted as income by the official measure. Nonetheless, both the official measure and alternative measures presented by Meyer and Wallace reveal little progress against poverty for all persons for four decades—the official poverty rate was 12.8 percent in 1968, and 12.3 percent in 2006. While about one in eight people were poor in both 1968 and 2006, poverty among the elderly fell from 25.0 percent to 9.4 percent and child poverty rates increased from 15.4 percent to 17.4 percent. Poverty rates for blacks (32.8 percent versus 24.2 percent) and for female-headed families (40.6 percent versus 31.9 percent) were also lower in 2006 than in 1968.

Meyer and Wallace discuss recent estimates comparing poverty in the United States and ten other industrialized countries that show that the United States has the highest proportion of poor households when households in a country are counted as poor if they have incomes below 50 percent of the median income in that country.[5] Under this relative poverty measure, 17 percent of American households are poor. Of the other countries compared, only Ireland has a comparable poverty rate (16.5 percent). Among the other countries, Italy, the United Kingdom, and Canada have rates of poverty ranging between 11 and 13 percent, and Sweden (5 percent) and Finland (7 percent) have low rates of poverty. Meyer and Wallace also present comparative data from an absolute poverty measure that uses the value of the official U.S. poverty line and calculates equivalent values in these same countries. According to this measure, 8.7 percent of U.S. households are poor, a rate not much higher than the 5.2 to 7.6 percent in seven European countries, and below the 12.4 percent rate of the United Kingdom. Meyer and Wallace show that relative poverty in the United States is higher than in most other advanced economies primarily because workers earn relatively less in the United States and a smaller percentage of poor families receive government benefits than do poor families in those other countries.

Most non-elderly adults, including the poor, rely primarily on their own earnings and the earnings of other family members. In chapter 3, Rebecca Blank examines how recent changes in employment and labor market opportunities for less-educated workers have increased their risk of poverty. Blank shows that the number of jobs for less-educated workers has increased substantially, but that many jobs no longer pay wages sufficient to avoid poverty and that labor market outcomes for less-educated men and women have diverged.

Among non-elderly men with less than a high school diploma, labor force participation fell from 79 percent to 73 percent between 1979 and 2006. If incarcerated individuals are included, the decline in labor force participation is even greater, especially among less-educated black men. Also, inflation-adjusted, full-time weekly wages for high school dropouts fell from $548 to $388 between 1979 and 1994, then rose to $426 by 2006—still below their 1979 values.

Over the same period, women in all education categories worked more. Among less-educated women, growth in labor force participation was concentrated in the 1990s, when declines in the availability of cash welfare and expansions of the Earned Income Tax Credit made employment more attractive to single mothers.

Weekly wages for women high school dropouts who worked full-time grew modestly, from $300 to $334 between 1970 and 2006, but their standing improved substantially relative to male dropouts, whose real wages declined.

Blank emphasizes that low-income families have been more reliant on earnings since the 1996 welfare reform than in previous decades. She predicts that the recession that began in December 2007 will cause poverty to rise to about 15 percent, similar to the rates during the recession of the early 1980s and the recession of the early 1990s. The sensitivity of the poverty rate to the business cycle makes maintaining low unemployment rates and raising the earnings of less-educated workers central to any reforms of current antipoverty policies.

Poverty rates vary dramatically by family structure. In chapter 4, Maria Cancian and Deborah Reed explain that interrelated changes in family formation and in women's and men's employment since the 1960s have led to substantial changes in who is poor, and why. Over these decades, fewer people have married, more marriages have ended in divorce, and more unmarried women have had children. As a result, children are now much more likely to live with only one parent—usually their mother. Single-parent families generally rely on at most one adult worker and are much more likely to be poor than married-couple families. All else being equal, changes in family structure have been poverty-increasing.

However, related changes among women have been poverty-reducing. For example, their increased work effort—especially work by married mothers of young children and single mothers—has largely offset the poverty-increasing effects of changing family structure. As Waldfogel also notes in chapter 9, the increased antipoverty impacts of mothers' market work underscore the need to increase their labor market flexibility and provide parents with additional supports, such as access to subsidized child care and paid leave for caregiving, that promote both employment and caring for their children. These impacts also highlight the key role of jobs and the labor market in determining poverty rates. In the current economic and policy environment, recessions are likely to have larger poverty-increasing effects than in the past because families rely more on wages and less on government benefits.

The portion of U.S. residents who were born in another country has grown dramatically, from 4.8 percent in 1970 to 12.4 percent in 2003. In chapter 5, Steven Raphael and Eugene Smolensky show how poverty varies by race, ethnicity, and nativity, and they estimate the contribution of this increased immigration to the overall poverty rate. They examine the poverty status of recent immigrants and their children, as well as the effects of immigration on the wages of native workers.

Raphael and Smolensky show that in the 1980s and 1990s immigrants were more likely to be poor because the share of all immigrants who were from western Europe had declined and the shares from Mexico and Southeast Asia had increased. Their synthetic cohort analysis shows that the differential between immigrant and native poverty rates falls quickly with time in the United States since immigration, in part because some of the less successful immigrants return to their country of origin. About ten to twenty years after they arrive in the United States, most immigrants have poverty rates roughly similar to those of native-born residents. Thus, despite increased immigration, Raphael and Smolensky conclude that immigrants raise the overall poverty rate by only about one percentage point.

Does competition from immigrants in the labor market lower wages and increase poverty among native workers? Raphael and Smolensky show that the distribution of skills of immigrants and native workers differs substantially, and they suggest that increases in the supply of immigrants with few years of schooling might actually raise the wages of native workers with higher levels of education. They estimate a range of potential effects of immigration on wages and conclude that increased immigration has had at most modest effects on the poverty status of natives.

Mobility and Its Consequences

What are the consequences of poverty for future productivity and well-being, and how likely is it that poor children will become poor adults? The chapters in part 2 address these issues. In chapter 6, Katherine Magnuson and Elizabeth Votruba-Drzal review the evidence on the long-term consequences of childhood poverty. About one-third of all children will be poor at some point, and one in ten will spend more than half their childhood in poverty. Black children and children born to single mothers or mothers with low levels of education are much more likely to spend many years in poverty.

Children who grow up in poverty are more likely to experience poor outcomes in later life. However, measuring the causal effects of poverty itself is difficult. Magnuson and Votruba-Drzal review alternative theoretical perspectives and methodological approaches to identifying the enduring consequences of childhood poverty. They conclude that the causal impact of poverty on academic and labor market achievement is likely to be modest and that poverty has only small direct effects on negative child behaviors and health outcomes. They conclude that both increased government benefits for families with young children and expanded educational programs for poor children could improve poor children's life chances when they become adults.

In chapter 7, Markus Jäntti analyzes the extent to which poverty persists across months, years, and generations. If poverty were measured on a monthly, rather than annual, basis, the overall poverty rate would be much higher—about one in five Americans experience at least two months of poverty-level income in a given year. On the other hand, most families experiencing poverty this year will not be poor next year. Groups that are more likely to be poor this year, however—including single-mother families and families with less-educated heads—are also more likely to be persistently poor.

Persistent poverty is, by definition, less common than poverty measured over a shorter period of time. Jäntti provides comparable data on poverty dynamics in other developed countries. The United States has relatively high levels of poverty, but some contend that its competitive market system, although it makes individuals vulnerable to annual income fluctuations, also provides more opportunities to move up the economic ladder. Jäntti documents, however, that the United States has relatively high levels of persistent poverty and lower intergenerational mobility than other advanced nations. For example, sons of poor fathers in the United States are more likely to themselves be poor adults than is the case for sons of poor fathers in many European countries.

The Evolution and Scope of Antipoverty Policies

The chapters in part 3 analyze alternative policies to combat poverty. In chapter 8, John Karl Scholz, Robert Moffitt, and Benjamin Cowan examine trends in income support programs. They document important changes in the size and structure of programs that provide benefits for low-income families, including cash welfare (AFDC/TANF), Supplemental Security Income (SSI), the EITC, Medicaid, and food stamps. Since the early 1980s, total inflation-adjusted spending on low-income families has grown only modestly (except for spending on medical care), and the pattern of spending has changed, with increased spending on low-income workers and decreased benefits for those who are unwilling to work or who cannot find jobs. In addition, the share of antipoverty expenditures going to the poor has declined, as has the percentage of the poverty gap filled by transfers, signaling a shift in expenditures away from the very poor (who tend to be nonworkers) to the near-poor and nonpoor (who tend to be workers).

Social insurance programs are not specifically designed to reduce poverty because they provide benefits to people of all income classes who have made payroll contributions and/or whose employers have made contributions. However, social insurance programs, such as Social Security and Medicare, play an important role in reducing poverty and economic hardship, especially for the elderly. Inflation-adjusted spending on these programs has grown rapidly since the mid-1960s. Because social insurance programs are so large, they fill a greater share of the poverty gap than is filled by means-tested transfers.

Programs that target benefits to low-income families provide levels of support that vary by marital status, state of residence, and other circumstances. Current expenditures, amounting to about 1.8 percent of GDP in 2005, are low by historical standards, and as a share of GDP they are only one-third to one-half as large as such expenditures in other rich countries. Scholz, Moffitt, and Cowan advocate a renewed antipoverty effort that would continue to expand resources to reward work but also provide a more adequate safety net for needy nonworkers.

In chapter 9, Jane Waldfogel analyzes the challenges of balancing employment and family responsibilities and discusses how family policies could address these challenges. Because most poor children live in families that include a low-wage worker, reducing poverty requires programs and policies that facilitate increased parental work hours but also ones that allow parents to meet their caretaking obligations. Family leave, sick leave, flexible work schedules, and subsidized child care can all enhance a parent's ability to balance employment and caretaking.

Waldfogel reviews the evidence on the effects of these programs in the United States and other countries. While some employers provide these parental supports, limited and uneven coverage—especially for low-wage workers—suggests the need for public policy changes.

Low-wage working parents, especially single parents, need additional wage supplements, such as higher child tax credits and higher EITC benefits, and enhanced child support enforcement to increase payments from nonresident parents. Waldfogel also reviews the potential of pregnancy prevention and marriage promotion efforts to reduce the proportion of children living in single-parent families. She concludes that such policies cannot be expected to bring about a dramatic reduction in the number of single-parent families.

Improving the education and training of low-income children and adults has been a cornerstone of our long-term antipoverty strategy since the War on Poverty. In chapter 10, Brian Jacob and Jens Ludwig review what is known about how to improve educational outcomes for poor children who do not fare well in the current education system. For example, there are large disparities in achievement test scores between those who are eligible for free school lunch and those with incomes above the program cutoff, as well as large disparities by race, with white students outperforming black and Hispanic students.

Jacob and Ludwig document that many complex factors contribute to these achievement disparities—schools serving poor children often have fewer resources, are not always using resources optimally, and are limited in the extent to which they can make up for the disadvantages that poor students and their families face outside of school. They review recent education policy evaluation research that has identified several cost-effective interventions that can substantially reduce income and racial disparities in educational outcomes. These include interventions that require major public investments—expanded early childhood education and class-size reductions, for example—as well as less costly curriculum reforms and policies that improve school accountability.

Even though improving access to educational and labor market opportunities has been an important policy goal for decades, federal funding for education and training programs for adult workers has declined dramatically since the early 1980s, despite recent increases in rewards for skills. In chapter 11, Harry Holzer argues that there is compelling evidence for additional investments in workforce development as an antipoverty strategy designed to raise the employment and earnings of the workers who have been most negatively affected by the labor market changes of the last several decades.

In part, the decline in federal funding reflects dissatisfaction with the inability of many previous workforce development programs to raise the employment and earnings of disadvantaged adults. Holzer notes, however, that investments in some programs have produced modest, but cost-effective, results and that recent innovations are promising. These include training programs that consider the local labor market demand for certain types of workers, that coordinate worker training with employers or industries that offer well-paying jobs, and that provide additional support services to address potential employment barriers, such as child care or transportation. Holzer proposes a strategy for consolidating existing workforce development programs, increasing and better targeting investments, and continuing evaluation efforts to make workforce development programs more effective.

Katherine Swartz addresses the challenge of providing health care for the poor in chapter 12. Publicly provided health insurance is available through Medicare, Medicaid, and, since the late 1990s, the State Children's Health Insurance Program (SCHIP). Eligibility expansions in these public programs and reductions in employer provision of insurance, especially for low-wage workers, have led to a rising share of the population receiving coverage from public programs and concerns about rapidly rising costs. In 1970 Medicaid spending accounted for 1.4 percent of the federal budget and for 9.7 percent of state spending; by 2006 it accounted for 6.6 percent and 21.5 percent of federal and state expenditures, respectively. As Swartz details, rising costs have led the federal and state governments to pursue a variety of cost-cutting strategies.

There are also concerns about the quality of care provided by public health insurance programs, especially for the elderly and disabled, and about lack of coverage, especially for poor non-elderly adults, those with mental health and substance abuse problems, and immigrants. Another concern is the potential "crowding out" of employer-sponsored insurance, especially as Medicaid expansions and SCHIP have expanded eligibility for the children of most low-wage workers. These concerns, as well as pressures arising from increasing costs, require a serious reevaluation of the structure of public health insurance, its financing, and coverage.

Swartz concludes that a national system of health insurance is the best approach for resolving issues related to rising costs and access to care, because they cannot be adequately addressed by our current patchwork system of public insurance for certain groups, such as the elderly and poor children. She also recommends increased federal support for the training of primary care providers knowledgeable about the health care needs of low-income families and renewed efforts to provide low-income families with preventative health information.

The Politics of Poverty and Its Meaning in a Rich Country

The final part of the volume informs our understanding of poverty and the potential for policy changes. In chapter 13, Mary Jo Bane discusses changes in the politics of antipoverty policy and changes in public attitudes toward the poor following the 1996 welfare reform and suggests how political strategies might be changed to facilitate the adoption of new antipoverty policies. She concludes that "welfare as we know it has indeed ended" because of the dramatic decline in the cash-assistance caseload and because state and county welfare departments now play a smaller role in the lives of the poor. Many social services are being delivered instead by private for-profit and nonprofit agencies, including faith-based organizations.

Bane also shows that the 1996 welfare reform legislation removed negative comments about welfare recipients from political campaigns, but she also notes that this has not led the president and Congress to consider a post–welfare reform antipoverty agenda. (The major exception was John Edwards's unsuccessful campaign for the 2008 presidential nomination.) New antipoverty programs have been implemented, however, in some states and cities.

Bane notes several factors that limit the prospects for sustained antipoverty efforts. First, the federal budget deficit was dramatically increased by the recession that started in late 2007, the financial bailouts, and the 2009 stimulus bill. This deficit will at some point limit the ability of any presidential administration to make permanent increases in social spending. In addition, the increased influence of the affluent in politics and the contentious immigration policy debates make it difficult to change negative public perceptions about the "poor."

Bane suggests that policymakers should consider changing their language. Instead of "helping the poor," they should focus on "helping people who can't take care of themselves," "aiding struggling working families," and "guaranteeing food and shelter." She also suggests that American policy analysts pay more attention to the high poverty rates in developing countries, both because globalization has increased linkages between countries and because immigration to the United States would be likely to fall as living standards increase in sending countries, such as Mexico.

In the final chapter, Robert Haveman describes the history of the official poverty measure and offers a number of suggestions for how it might be revised. He also compares the official measure to alternative concepts of economic poverty, including relative poverty, which compares a family's income not to a fixed poverty line but to the society's overall living standard. He discusses poverty measures that are based on consumption or assets instead of family income. And he contrasts poverty measures with broader conceptions of poverty and deprivation, such as indicators of material deprivation and "social exclusion," a concept recently developed in the European Union and the United Kingdom.

Haveman endorses the European view that rich societies require measures that track progress in meeting many dimensions of the needs of their least-well-off citizens and that income alone fails to capture the complex situation in which the most deprived citizens find themselves. Additional dimensions of concern include indicators of educational attainment, such as having less than a high school diploma; labor force and employment status, such as living in a jobless household; housing status, such as living in poor-quality housing with overcrowding and a lack of plumbing or kitchen facilities; health and disability status, such as having a number of disabling conditions or a mental health problem; vehicle availability; and linguistic isolation.

Haveman suggests that these measures would provide important information on the effectiveness of programs that seek to reduce deprivations that are not reflected in measured income. For example, because U.S. policies are designed to increase access to food, housing, transportation, medical care, education and training, and employment, we should have direct measures that reflect our progress or lack of progress on these dimensions.

CHANGING POLICIES TO REDUCE POVERTY IN THE TWENTY-FIRST CENTURY

Given current economic, demographic, and public policy contexts, poverty is not likely to fall substantially in the near future. This was evident even before the severe recession that began in December 2007 and the world economic crisis that began in the fall of 2008. Although the chapter authors agree on this pessimistic forecast, they are optimistic that poverty can be reduced significantly in the long term if the public and policymakers muster the political will to pursue a range of promising antipoverty policies. The policies proposed by the authors would bring about changes in the labor market, family policies, schools, and the health care system that would raise the employment and earnings of low-income families, reduce their expenses, and increase opportunities for their children. Our own high-priority antipoverty policies, a subset of the policies discussed in the chapters that follow, are based on three fundamental assumptions about trends in work effort, patterns of family formation, and continuing changes in how the globalized economy affects the employment and earnings prospects of less-educated workers.

First, our proposals are based on the assumption that one's own earnings, not government cash benefits, will remain the primary source of family income for most adults who are not elderly and not disabled. Although some analysts have made the case for providing welfare benefits to single mothers who stay home to care for their young children, we do not anticipate that, for example, an income-tested cash entitlement program like AFDC will be reinstated. We also do not expect the adoption of a guaranteed annual income, such as a negative income tax, even though both President Richard Nixon and President Jimmy Carter proposed such programs in the late 1960s and mid-1970s (Moffitt 2004). Scholz, Moffitt, and Cowan (chapter 8) and Bane (chapter 13) note that, since the early 1980s, and especially in the aftermath of the 1996 welfare reform, public policy changes have increased the extent of income support for the working poor and reduced cash benefits for the nonworking poor who are not elderly or disabled. We see no evidence to suggest that this pattern will be reversed.

The elderly and persons with disabilities are generally not expected to work to support themselves.[6] However, the expectation of work has evolved to now include most adults. In 1969, in defending his proposed negative income tax, the Family Assistance Plan, President Nixon stated that "it is not our intent that mothers of preschool children must accept work" (Nixon 1969). In contrast, the 1996 welfare reform allowed states to set their own expectations for work; some states now require new mothers to participate in work-related activities once their child is three months old. Magnuson and Votruba-Drzal (chapter 6) and Waldfogel (chapter 9) document that requiring mothers to return to work shortly after giving birth has negative implications for child development; nevertheless, the evolution of public policy since the 1980s suggests that work will continue to be expected and exemptions from the work requirement will continue to be restricted. Thus, as we prioritize antipoverty policy proposals, we assume that most adults, including the parents of young children, will work for pay.

Our second assumption relates to changes in societal attitudes about marriage and childbearing and the changes in family structure that have occurred since the 1960s. We assume that many children will continue to be born to unmarried parents or will spend part of their childhood living with a divorced parent. Children who spend all or most of their childhood living with only one biological parent (usually their mother) have a much higher risk of poverty than children living with two parents. Reducing nonmarital births, especially teen births, is a long-standing social policy goal, and marriage promotion policies are a recent policy innovation. However, even if these public efforts to change family formation patterns and fertility behaviors have effects that are larger than we expect, as both Cancian and Reed (chapter 4) and Waldfogel (chapter 9) note, it is likely that they will only modestly reduce the total number of poor families with children. In part, this is because the noncustodial fathers of the children of unmarried mothers tend to have poor labor market prospects and low annual earnings. The poverty rate for such parents, even if married, is likely to be much higher than the rate for currently married couples (Carlson, McLanahan, and England 2004).

Our third assumption deals with the labor market prospects of workers with no more than a high school diploma. As Blank notes in chapter 3, even though the economy has produced a substantial increase in the number of jobs since the 1970s, the inflation-adjusted wages of the least-educated workers, especially men, were no higher in 2006 than in 1973, and their employment rates were lower. Thus, we assume that for the foreseeable future the labor market will not be characterized by the consistent wage growth or the number of high-wage jobs that became available in the quarter-century following World War II. As a result, we expect that many less-educated workers will continue to have difficulty earning enough on their own to support a family.

Economists have not been successful in making long-term macroeconomic projections. As noted earlier, in the early 1970s the nation's leading poverty researchers predicted that poverty would be eliminated within a generation. Their projections were based on assumptions that were reasonable at the time—they expected the economy to grow rapidly and to continue to raise real wages for less-educated workers, as had been the case for the previous quarter-century. Notwithstanding the difficulty of predicting future economic trends, we see little reason to expect dramatic growth in wages for workers at the bottom of the labor market. Indeed, the recession that began in December 2007 has already led to significant job losses and put downward pressure on wage rates. We thus assume that the uneven economic growth of the past thirty-five years will continue and hence, on its own, will not significantly reduce poverty.

Given these three assumptions about trends in work, family structure, and the antipoverty effects of economic growth, we conclude that an antipoverty policy agenda for the twenty-first century should pursue three fundamental goals. The first is "to make work pay"—or as David Ellwood (1988) wrote two decades ago, if you work hard and play by the rules, you should not be poor.[7] This requires that government regulations about wages and working conditions (such as the minimum wage or the ability of workers to unionize) and government benefits for low-wage workers (such as the Earned Income Tax Credit or subsidized child care) should allow most workers to avoid poverty. Because the 1996 welfare reform greatly reduced access to cash welfare, there is an additional need for policies to provide work opportunities for those who are willing to work but cannot find steady employment, either because of poor economic conditions or because they face substantial employment barriers (such as physical and mental health problems or learning disabilities) that make it difficult for them to work steadily.

The second goal has received less attention in the United States than in other industrialized nations—to provide sufficient support to parents so that those in both one-parent and two-parent families can work not only steadily but also flexibly. This would help working parents to devote sufficient time to parenting and caregiving. Balancing responsibilities as a parent and a worker is a challenge for all families, whether one- or two-parent families, low-income or high-income families. Work-family balance issues are particularly difficult, however, for single parents, who have less time for family responsibilities than married couples, and for most parents with limited financial or community resources.

The third goal reiterates a key goal of the War on Poverty—increased investments in education and training over the life course to raise employment and earnings. We need changes in our early childhood and K–12 educational policies to raise the educational attainment and abilities of poor children and policy changes in "second-chance" workforce development programs to raise the skills of disadvantaged young adults. Americans have always favored providing a "hand up" to promote labor market opportunities instead of a "hand-out" to reduce poverty. However, as Jacob and Ludwig document in chapter 10, disparities in educational opportunities persist, and spending for education and training programs for disadvantaged youth and adults, as Holzer details in chapter 11, has fallen dramatically since the early 1980s.

Making Work Pay

A work-centered antipoverty strategy requires a robust economy that provides high levels of employment and job growth. A growing economy on its own is not likely to do enough, however, to raise the earnings of many less-educated workers above the poverty line because, since the early 1970s, wage growth for less-educated workers was substantial only in the last half of the 1990s. Making work pay for today's adult workers thus requires policy changes to increase the proportion of jobs with wages sufficient to support a family and larger wage supplements and expanded work supports to "make work pay" for those who earn low wages.

A fundamental step in making work pay is a well-functioning labor market that rewards workers with the same skills equally, without regard to race, ethnicity, or gender. There has been substantial progress in reducing gender discrimination in access to occupations and in wages since the 1960s, as women's employment and earnings have increased relative to those of men. And compared to the situation in the 1960s, racial and ethnic earnings disparities have narrowed. In some domains, however, disparities in employment opportunities and wage gaps between white non-Hispanics and racial and ethnic groups have widened. For example, young black men face substantially reduced labor market opportunities relative to similar white men; this both reflects and contributes to high levels of incarceration (Pager 2007; Western and Wildeman 2009). Reducing labor market discrimination should be a higher priority for public policy than it has been in recent years.

Several other policy changes could raise the wages of less-educated workers. Between the early 1960s and early 1980s, the minimum wage in 2007 dollars ranged between about $7.00 and $8.50 per hour. Because Congress increased the minimum wage only a few times over the next twenty-five years, it has ranged between $6.00 and $7.00 (in 2007 dollars) in most years since the mid-1980s. The minimum wage was constant in nominal terms at $5.15 per hour from 1997 to 2007, when Congress passed a three-part increase: to $5.85 per hour in July 2007, to $6.55 in July 2008, and to $7.25 in July 2009. A higher minimum wage that maintains its real value by being indexed to inflation or to average wages would be an important step in making work pay. During the campaign, the candidate Obama proposed raising the minimum wage to $9.50 by 2011 and indexing it for inflation.[8]

Expanded income supplements for low-wage workers are needed. The Earned Income Tax Credit provides substantial support for low-income families with children, and as Scholz, Moffitt, and Cowan note in chapter 8, it does so without reducing work incentives. The EITC is available to both one- and two-parent families. In addition, almost half of all states have implemented a state EITC on top of the federal one. The maximum federal EITC for a family with two or more children (in current dollars) was $400 in 1975, $550 in 1986, $953 in 1991, and $4,824 in 2008. In 2008 the maximum EITC for a family with one child was $2,917; however, for a single person or a married couple without children, it was only $438.

Adam Carasso and his colleagues (2008) compare four recent proposals for EITC expansions that increase work incentives for childless workers. They highlight the trade-offs inherent in alternative designs: expanded credits for single individuals can increase marriage disincentives, but proposals that avoid marriage penalties are more expensive. While policymakers will have to balance competing goals in developing specific reforms, expanding the EITC to childless workers would broaden the commitment to encourage work and reduce poverty for those who are working but face low wages (see Berlin 2007).

Even before the economic downturn began in late 2007, there was a clear need for policies to increase the employment of those who want to work but cannot find steady employment. In addition to those affected by unemployment fluctuations over the business cycle, applicants for these jobs are likely to include those who have exhausted eligibility for cash welfare or who have difficulty getting and keeping jobs because of low skills or other employment barriers, such as a criminal record or physical or mental health problems.

Public service employment programs have not been politically popular since the Great Depression and have not operated since the early 1980s, when President

Reagan terminated the last such program (the Comprehensive Employment and Training Act, CETA). However, because the availability of government assistance has been linked with work, there is a need for a transitional jobs-of-last-resort program. Workers in last-resort jobs might be expected to perform socially beneficial tasks for which there is little effective labor demand, such as labor-intensive public services in disadvantaged communities that are generally provided in affluent ones—monitoring playgrounds after school hours, maintaining neighborhoods, and assisting the elderly. Jobs could be time-limited, and they could offer wages slightly less than the minimum wage, thereby providing an incentive for workers to accept available private-sector jobs. During the campaign, Obama endorsed transitional jobs programs as a way to help low-income Americans succeed in the workforce.[9]

Because the United States lacks universal national health insurance, work does not pay for some families that are eligible for Medicaid only if they do not work or if they work little. The State Children's Health Insurance Program implemented in the late 1990s and Medicaid expansions from the late 1980s to the mid-1990s have guaranteed access to subsidized health care coverage for all poor and low-income children. SCHIP could be extended to poor and near-poor adults who lack coverage. For example, Wisconsin has developed BadgerCare, which serves Medicaid and SCHIP beneficiaries and has effectively expanded subsidized coverage to the parents of low-income children.

Supporting Parents on the Job and at Home

An antipoverty strategy that assumes that most non-elderly, non-disabled adults will work must consider programs, provided by firms or governments, that enable working parents to properly care for their children and sick or disabled family members. Examples include access to affordable child care and to jobs that allow enough flexibility for workers to meet their family obligations. Single parents are more likely to need subsidized child care and workplace flexibility than married couples, since they are generally less able to rely on another adult for financial or logistical support. Also needed are policies that strengthen the incentives for, and capacity of, nonresident parents (typically fathers) to earn enough so that they can pay child support. Transitional jobs of last resort and "second-chance" training programs are two such programs that would help both custodial and noncustodial parents.

Magnuson and Votruba-Drzal (in chapter 6) and Jacob and Ludwig (in chapter 10) document that public investments in poor young children serve multiple purposes. Early childhood education enhances school-readiness and reduces disparities in later outcomes, such as high school graduation and the risk of becoming a teen parent or a delinquent. However, even if the long-term gains from early childhood programs were small, making adequate child care affordable for low-income families facilitates stable parental employment in the short run.

Public funding for child care increased substantially following the 1996 welfare reform, but many low-income parents still have difficulty finding adequate child care, especially for very young children. Such care is expensive, and there is a shortage of child care facilities, especially in low-income communities. Our assumptions about the need for parents to work to escape poverty and the fact that many children spend part of their childhood living with one parent strongly suggest the need for increased public subsidies for child care.

The Wisconsin experience after the 1996 welfare reform is instructive. The state implemented a demanding work requirement for welfare mothers and dramatically cut the welfare rolls. At the same time, it greatly expanded the number of low-income families that received child care subsidies as the reduced spending on cash benefits was shifted to child care. Other states also increased spending on subsidized child care after welfare reform, so that national spending on subsidized care increased from $5.3 billion to $12.0 billion between 1997 and 2006 (in constant 2006 dollars; U.S. Department of Health and Human Services 2008). Notwithstanding this growth, recent estimates suggest that only about one-third of eligible low-income families receive subsidies (Mezey, Greenberg, and Schumacher 2002; U.S. Department of Health and Human Services 2005). However, as discussed later, the American Recovery and Reinvestment Act (the 2009 economic stimulus package) provides for further expansions (U.S. Congress 2009).

Working parents also need flexibility at work so that they do not have to choose between keeping their jobs and adequately parenting their children. For example, because many low-income workers have limited sick leave and inflexible work hours, it is difficult for them to deal with the unexpected demands of child-rearing. As Waldfogel points out, the United States does not have paid parental leave—many low-income mothers give up their jobs to give birth.

Workplace flexibility is a key aspect of antipoverty policy for three reasons. First, single parents, who are overrepresented among the poor, are more likely to be the only adults available to manage their children's health, education, and other needs. They are more likely than married parents to need sick leave, family leave, and other flexible work policies. Second, low-wage workers are more likely than other workers to have jobs that lack fringe benefits, such as employer-subsidized health insurance, paid sick leave, and vacation days. Finally, compared to other families, low-income families are less able to buy market substitutes—from child care to prepared meals—and are more likely to have long commutes on public transportation and to live in neighborhoods where safety is an issue and more parental supervision of children is required.

Waldfogel advocates parental support policies that build on recent experience in the United Kingdom. In the U.S. context, such policies might include eight to twelve weeks of paid parental leave after birth or adoption for all workers, funded by a payroll tax and operated like other social insurance programs; an employer mandate to provide two weeks of annual paid leave for family illness or other family responsibilities; and the right for parents of young children to request part-time work or flexible hours.

As noted, most low-income children will spend a substantial part of their childhood in a single-parent family. This highlights the importance of child support system reforms that raise the support received by resident parents. Child support enforcement policies have been strengthened over the past several decades, and most children living with only one parent have a legally established nonresident parent who has been ordered to pay child support. However, even though both paternity establishment (for children born outside of marriage) and child support order establishment rates have grown over time, most poor single mothers do not receive the amount of child support that the courts have ordered (Cancian and Meyer 2006).

Making child support a consistent source of income for single parents requires several related efforts. Because nonresident parents cannot pay support if they do not have income, efforts to raise their employment and earnings are needed. When nonresident parents do pay support, their payments should benefit their children—not offset public welfare or medical assistance paid by the state (Cancian, Meyer, and Caspar 2008).

Investing over the Life Course

At the outset of the War on Poverty, President Johnson's economic advisers thought that because most high school graduates at that time could earn enough to support a family on their own, their task was to invest in young children to raise educational attainment and hence reduce poverty by raising employment and earnings in the next generation. Educational policies remain appealing to the public, but in the short term they are more expensive than policies that raise the annual incomes of poor families. For example, the target group for early childhood programs that increase the cognitive and noncognitive skills of young children from low-income families includes all children at high risk of becoming poor adults. And the payoffs from these programs—increased educational attainment, employment, and earnings and lower rates of incarceration and nonmarital births when these children reach adulthood—are not evident for many years.

As noted, economic changes since the 1970s have eroded the labor market prospects of workers who have no more than a high school diploma. Thus, if we are to reduce poverty among future labor force entrants, we must raise the high school graduation rate and the skills of these graduates and ensure that a greater percentage of graduates go on to earn two-year community college degrees and certificates and four-year college degrees. Although the provision of a high-quality public school education for all children is not a controversial policy goal, the current education system falls well short of providing low-income students with the skills they need to succeed in the twenty-first-century labor market.

Jacob and Ludwig (in chapter 10) and Magnuson and Votruba-Drzal (in chapter 6) document the importance of expanding the scope of early childhood education for low-income three-, four-, and five-year-old children. Head Start was a featured program of the War on Poverty. Yet, four decades later, many poor preschool children do not participate in early education programs. It is time to guarantee early childhood education to all poor children. The Obama administration has proposed such an expansion, including a comprehensive federal program for children from "zero to five." The American Recovery and Reinvestment Act of 2009 includes major expansions in funding for Head Start and Early Head Start (U.S. Congress 2009).[10]

Holzer documents in chapter 11 that workforce training programs, another highlight of the War on Poverty, have withered away since the 1980s. Given the increased employer demand for labor market skills, it is important to expand funding for Pell grants for low-income college students and to expand workforce development programs that have raised the employment and earnings of high school dropouts and high school graduates. The American Recovery and Reinvestment Act includes an increase in the maximum Pell grant and a new tax credit for college students (U.S. Congress 2009).

CONCLUSION

Taken as a whole, the chapters in this volume provide a careful review of the evidence concerning economic changes, demographic changes, and public policy changes since the 1964 declaration of War on Poverty. They demonstrate that, in the absence of a comprehensive expanded antipoverty strategy, there is little reason to expect substantial progress in reducing poverty. In the quarter-century following the election of Ronald Reagan in 1980, the public and policymakers were unwilling to spend more on antipoverty programs. In part because of dissatisfaction with the policies of the prior quarter-century and in part because the economic crisis of 2008 has justified increased government spending, the Obama administration has endorsed many of the policies that are analyzed in the chapters of this book. These include policies that can raise the employment and earnings of low-income parents, help parents better balance their work and family obligations, and raise the educational attainment and skills of the next generation. Despite the challenges created by the economic downturn that began in late 2007, there are reasons for optimism about prospects for reducing poverty in the United States.

We thank Laura Dresser, Harry Holzer, Jennifer Noyes, Joe Soss, and two anonymous reviewers for helpful comments, and Deborah Johnson for editorial assistance. Sheldon Danziger was supported in part by a John Simon Guggenheim Foundation Fellowship.

Additional resource material, including presentation-ready charts and suggested supplemental readings, are available on the volume Web site at http://www.russell sage.org.

NOTES

1. The Census Bureau has published the official poverty rate for each year since 1959. Poverty rates for whites and blacks are available since 1959, and poverty rates for Hispanics since 1972. Christine Ross, Sheldon Danziger, and Eugene Smolensky (1987) adjust the official poverty lines back to 1939 in the same manner as they are officially brought forward—that is, by adjusting them each year only for changes in the consumer price index (CPI). Robert Plotnick and his colleagues (2000) discuss the historical trend in poverty starting in the early twentieth century.

2. Measurement of racial discrimination and the distinction between explicitly discriminatory treatment and treatment that has a "differential effect" by racial group is addressed by a recent National Research Council report (Blank, Dabady, and Citro 2004).

3. The American Recovery and Reinvestment Act of 2009 lowered the threshold for refundability, but a family with two children, for example, would still need over $16,000 in earnings to qualify for the full credit (Center for Law and Social Policy 2009).

4. Robert Haveman (this volume) and Daniel Meyer and Geoffrey Wallace (this volume) discuss the difficulties that arise in cross-national comparisons of poverty. Nonetheless, by most widely accepted measures of poverty, the United States has higher poverty rates than most other rich countries.

5. Relative poverty lines, like 50 percent of the median, are widely used as poverty thresholds in European countries.

6. The Supplemental Security Income program, adopted in the early 1970s, provided a guaranteed monthly income of $627 for a single recipient with no other income in 2008. SSI recipients also automatically qualify for Medicaid. The program is an entitlement for the low-income elderly and qualifying disabled persons.

7. "People who are willing to work as much as society deems reasonable ought to be able to support their families at or above the poverty level without relying on welfare or welfare-like supports" (Ellwood 1988, 12).

8. See http://www.barackobama.com/2007/07/18/remarks_of_senator_barack_obam_19.php.

9. See http://www.barackobama.com/2007/07/18/remarks_of_senator_barack_obam_19.php.

10. See the website for the White House–President Barack Obama, "The Issues: Education," available at: http://www.whitehouse.gov/issues/education. See also the summary of provisions prepared by the Center on Law and Social Policy (2009).

REFERENCES

Berlin, Gordon. 2007. "Rewarding the Work of Individuals: A Counterintuitive Approach to Reducing Poverty and Strengthening Families." *The Future of Children* 17(2): 17–36.

Blank, Rebecca. 2008. "How to Improve Poverty Measurement in the United States." *Journal of Policy Analysis and Management* 27(2): 233–54.

Blank, Rebecca, Marilyn Dabady, and Constance Citro, eds. 2004. *Measuring Racial Discrimination: Panel on Methods for Assessing Discrimination.* Washington: National

Academies Press/Committee on National Statistics, Division of Behavior and Social Sciences and Education.

Boots, Shelley Waters, Jennifer Ehrle Macomber, and Anna Danziger. 2008. "Supporting Parents' Employment and Children's Development?" New Safety Net paper 3. Washington, D.C.: Urban Institute.

Cancian, Maria, and Daniel R. Meyer. 2006. "Child Support and the Economy." In *Working and Poor: How Economic and Policy Changes Are Affecting Low-Wage Workers*, edited by Rebecca Blank, Sheldon Danziger, and Robert Schoeni. New York: Russell Sage Foundation.

Cancian, Maria, Daniel R. Meyer, and Emma Caspar. 2008. "Welfare and Child Support: Complements, Not Substitutes." *Journal of Policy Analysis and Management* 27(2): 354–75.

Carasso, Adam, Harry J. Holzer, Elaine Maag, and C. Eugene Steuerle. 2008. "The Next Stage for Social Policy: Encouraging Work and Family Formation Among Low-Income Men." Discussion paper 28. Washington, D.C.: Urban Institute.

Carlson, Marcia J., Sara McLanahan, and Paula England. 2004. "Union Formation in Fragile Families." *Demography* 41(2): 237–62.

Center for Law and Social Policy. 2009. "Preliminary Summary of Key Provisions of the American Recovery and Reinvestment Act Aimed at Improving the Lives of Low-Income Americans." Available at: http://www.clasp.org/publications/preliminarysummary ofarra021309.pdf (accessed July 9, 2009).

Danziger, Sheldon, and Peter Gottschalk. 1995. *America Unequal.* Cambridge, Mass.: Harvard University Press.

Edin, Kathryn, and Maria Kefalas. 2005. *Promises I Can Keep: Why Poor Women Put Motherhood Before Marriage.* Berkeley: University of California Press.

Ellwood, David. 1988. *Poor Support: Poverty in the American Family.* New York: Basic Books.

Ellwood, David T., and Christopher Jencks. 2004. "The Spread of Single-Parent Families in the United States Since 1960." In *The Future of the Family,* edited by Daniel Patrick Moynihan, Timothy Smeeding, and Lee Rainwater. New York: Russell Sage Foundation.

Haskins, Ron. 2006. *Work over Welfare: The Inside Story of the 1996 Welfare Reform Law.* Washington, D.C.: Brookings Institution Press.

Holzer, Harry. 1996. *What Employers Want: Job Prospects for Less-Educated Workers.* New York: Russell Sage Foundation.

———. 2009. "The Labor Market and Young Black Men: Updating Moynihan's Perspective." *Annals of the American Academy of Political and Social Science* 621(1): 47–69.

Holzer, Harry, Steven Raphael, and Michael A. Stoll. 2006. "Perceived Criminality, Racial Background Checks, and the Racial Hiring Practices of Employers." *Journal of Law and Economics* 49(2): 451–80.

Johnson, Lyndon B. 1964. *State of the Union Address.* Available at: http://www.janda.org/ politxts/StateofUnionAddresses/1964-1969 Johnson/LBJ.64.html.

Lieberman, Robert C. 2001. *Shifting the Color Line: Race and the American Welfare State.* Cambridge, Mass.: Harvard University Press.

Lin, Ann Chih, and David R. Harris, eds. 2008. *The Colors of Poverty: Why Racial and Ethnic Disparities Persist.* New York: Russell Sage Foundation.

Martin, Joyce A., Brady E. Hamilton, Paul D. Sutton, Stephanie J. Ventura, Fay Menacker, Sharon Kirmeyer, and T. J. Mathews. 2009. "Births: Final Data for 2006." *National Vital Statistics Reports* 57(7, January 7). Hyattsville, Md.: National Center for Health Statistics. Available at: http://www.cdc.gov/nchs/data/nvsr/nvsr57/nvsr57_07.pdf (accessed July 9, 2009).

Mead, Lawrence. 1985. *Beyond Entitlement: The Social Obligation of Citizenship.* New York: Basic Books.

Mezey, Jennifer, Mark Greenberg, and Rachel Schumacher. 2002. "The Vast Majority of Federally Eligible Children Did Not Receive Child Care Assistance in FY2000." Policy report. Washington, D.C.: Center for Law and Social Policy.

Moffitt, Robert. 2004. "The Idea of a Negative Income Tax: Past, Present, and Future." *Focus* 23(2): 4–9.

Murray, Charles. 1984. *Losing Ground: American Social Policy 1950–1980.* New York: Basic Books.

———. 2001. "Family Formation." In *The New World of Welfare,* edited by Rebecca Blank and Ron Haskins. Washington, D.C.: Brookings Institution Press.

Nixon, Richard M. 1969. *Welfare Reform: A Message from the President of the United States.* House Document No. 91-146, Congressional Record, vol. 115, no. 136. The House of Representatives, 91st Congress, First Session, H7239-7241.

Novak, Michael, et al. 1987. *The New Consensus on Family and Welfare: A Community of Self-Reliance.* Milwaukee, Wisc.: Marquette University Press.

Pager, Devah. 2007. *Marked: Race, Crime, and Finding Work in an Era of Mass Incarceration.* Chicago: University of Chicago Press.

Plotnick, Robert, Eugene Smolensky, Erik Evenhouse, and Siobhan Reilly. 2000. "The Twentieth-Century Record of Inequality and Poverty in the United States." In *The Cambridge Economic History of the United States,* vol. 3, *The Twentieth Century,* edited by Stanley Engerman and Robert Gallman. Cambridge: Cambridge University Press.

Quadagno, Jill S. 1994. *The Color of Welfare: How Racism Undermined the War on Poverty.* New York: Oxford University Press.

Raphael, Steven. 2007. "Early Incarceration Spells and the Transition to Adulthood." In *The Price of Independence: The Economics of Early Adulthood,* edited by Sheldon Danziger and Cecilia Elena Rouse. New York: Russell Sage Foundation.

Ross, Christine, Sheldon Danziger, and Eugene Smolensky. 1987. "The Level and Trend in Poverty, 1939–1979." *Demography* 24(November): 587–600.

Smeeding, Timothy M. 2008. "Poverty, Work, and Policy: The United States in Comparative Perspective." In *Social Stratification: Class, Race, and Gender in Sociological Perspective,* 3rd ed., edited by David Grusky. Boulder, Colo.: Westview Press.

Soss, Joe, Richard Fording, and Sanford F. Schram. 2008. "The Color of Devolution: Race, Federalism, and the Politics of Social Control." *American Journal of Political Science* 52(3): 536–53.

Soss, Joe, Sanford F. Schram, Thomas P. Varnatian, and Erin O'Brien. 2001. "Setting the Terms of Relief: Explaining State Policy Choices in the Devolution Revolution." *American Journal of Political Science* 45(2): 378–95.

Stoll, Michael. 2006. "Job Sprawl, Spatial Mismatch, and Black Employment Disadvantage." *Journal of Policy Analysis and Management* 25(4): 827–54.

———. 2008. "Race, Place, and Poverty Revisited." In *The Colors of Poverty: Why Racial and Ethnic Disparities Persist,* edited by Ann Chih Lin and David R. Harris. New York: Russell Sage Foundation.

Stoll, Michael A., and Steven Raphael. 2000. "Racial Differences in Spatial Job Search Patterns: Exploring the Causes and Consequences." *Economic Geography* 76(3): 201–23.

Tobin, James. 1967. "It Can Be Done! Conquering Poverty in the U.S. by 1976." *New Republic* (June 3): 14–18.

Turner, Margery Austin, Stephen L. Ross, George Gaister, and John Yinger. 2002. "Discrimination in Metropolitan Housing Markets: National Results from Phase 1 of HDS 2000." Washington: Urban Institute/Metropolitan Housing and Communities Policy Center.

U.S. Congress. 2009. *American Recovery and Reinvestment Act of 2009.* Washington: U.S. Government Printing Office. Available at: http://frwebgate.access.gpo.gov/cgi-bin/get doc.cgi?dbname=111_cong_bills&docid=f:h1enr.pdf (accessed May 20, 2009).

U.S. Department of Health and Human Services. Administration for Children and Families. 2008. *Child Care and Development Fund Expenditure Data.* Available at: http://www.acf.hhs. gov/programs/ccb/data/index.htm#expenditure (accessed July 9, 2009).

U.S. Department of Health and Human Services. Assistant Secretary for Planning and Evaluation. Office of Human Services Policy. 2005. "Child Care Eligibility and Enrollment Estimates for Fiscal Year 2003." *Policy Issue Brief* (April).

Western, Bruce, and Christopher Wildeman. 2009. "The Black Family and Mass Incarceration." *Annals of the American Academy of Political and Social Science* 621(1): 221–42.

Wheelock, Darren, and Christopher Uggen. 2008. "Punishment, Crime, and Poverty." In *The Colors of Poverty: Why Racial and Ethnic Disparities Persist,* edited by Ann Chih Lin and David R. Harris. New York: Russell Sage Foundation.

Wilson, William Julius. 1996. *When Work Disappears.* New York: Alfred A. Knopf.

Part 1

Economic Changes, Demographic
Changes, and Trends in Poverty

Chapter 2

Poverty Levels and Trends in Comparative Perspective

Daniel R. Meyer and Geoffrey L. Wallace

In the 1964 State of the Union address, President Lyndon Johnson said, "This administration today, here and now, declares unconditional war on poverty in America. . . . It will not be a short or easy struggle, no single weapon or strategy will suffice, but we shall not rest until that war is won."[1] Yet, as we will show, total official poverty rates are not much different today than they were in the late 1960s. Even though Johnson predicted the struggle would not be "short or easy," why has it ended up being so long and so difficult?

In this chapter, we present basic information about poverty, believing that this can be useful in understanding why the eradication of poverty has been so difficult. For example, if groups that were the target of policy changes show declines in poverty, while other groups show increases, this suggests a key reason for the lack of progress. Alternatively, if targeted groups do not show improvements, this could hint toward policy ineffectiveness. More broadly, simple data on the level of poverty can help us understand the nature of disadvantage and provide information to test our ideas about the causes of poverty. For example, examining the percentage of those below the poverty level who are in families in which the head is not working can help us explore the extent to which poverty is primarily caused by nonwork. Or if one believes that poverty is primarily caused by discrimination, then a comparison of poverty rates between people of color and non-Hispanic whites can be informative (though not, of course, conclusive because many factors could be related).

This chapter begins with a review of how poverty is officially measured in the United States. We use this official definition to present poverty rates in 2006 and answer several questions about poverty: Which types of individuals and families have the highest risks of poverty? What are the characteristics of those who live in poverty? What types of income sources do they have? We then examine trends over the 1968 to 2006 period, examining which groups have made the most progress and looking for clues as to why. Finally, we try to put the U.S. story in perspective. Do our conclusions change if we use a different definition of poverty?

How do poverty rates in the United States compare to those of several other countries, and how do we explain these differences?

THE OFFICIAL U.S. POVERTY MEASURE

Because the substantial literature on conceptual issues in measuring poverty is discussed elsewhere in this volume (Haveman, chapter 14), we present only a summary here. A person or family is usually defined as "poor" if their resources fall below a particular level or threshold. This simple concept highlights three issues[2]:

- What should be counted as resources? For example, should we count only cash, or should "near-cash" sources like food stamps count? Should assets play a role? Should anything be subtracted from resources, such as taxes, expenses associated with gaining resources (child care, for example), health care expenses, or other nondiscretionary expenditures?

- Whose resources should count? Should we add up all the resources in a household or only those from individuals linked to each other by blood or marriage (the Census Bureau's definition of "family")? Or should we try to determine each individual's resources without considering other household members?

- What should the threshold be, and for whom should it vary? Should the threshold be higher for large families or for those living in more expensive locations? Considering trends in poverty adds another important dimension: How should the threshold vary over time? Only as prices change, or as the general standard of living changes, or by some other criteria?

The official Census Bureau definition answers these questions by including total pretax money income (ignoring near- and non-cash sources, assets, and all expenditures) for all individuals related by blood or marriage (a family) and comparing this to a threshold that varies by the family's size and age composition but not their geographic location. The threshold changes over time only with changes in prices.[3]

Originally constructed in 1963 to 1964 by Mollie Orshansky, the official poverty thresholds in the United States were based on the Department of Agriculture's Economy Food Plan (for a history of the development of the official threshold, see, for example, Fisher 1992). The Economy Food Plan summed the prices of specified amounts of different foods deemed necessary for low-income families to meet their *temporary* nutritional needs; this amount was then multiplied by three because some research showed that low-income families spent an average of one-third of their income on food.[4] Poverty thresholds were further differentiated by farm or nonfarm status, the number of children, the sex of the family head, and the age of persons in family units.

Other than annual inflation indexing and the elimination of the differential thresholds for farm families and female-headed families in 1980, there have been very few changes in the poverty thresholds since the mid-1960s. In 2008 the poverty line ranged from $10,326 for a single elderly person to a weighted average of $22,017 for a four-person family and $44,380 for a family of nine or more persons.[5]

Each year the Census Bureau reports the official poverty rate based on data gathered in the March Current Population Survey (CPS), which interviews over 50,000 U.S. households. Households are divided into families (those related by blood or marriage) and individuals, and an individual is poor if the income of his or her family is less than or equal to the poverty threshold for his or her family size.[6]

In the next two sections of this chapter, we primarily use this official measure of poverty and report our own calculations from the March CPS data.[7] The official poverty rate has been criticized along a number of dimensions (see, for example, Blank 2008; Citro and Michael 1995; Haveman, this volume; Ziliak 2008). A key criticism is that the official money income concept does not include receipt of in-kind transfers such as food stamps and housing subsidies, child care subsidies, or the Earned Income Tax Credit (EITC), all of which increase the economic well-being of the family; nor does the money income concept account for work expenses or taxes paid, which reduce well-being. In selected cases, we compare the results based on the official measure with an alternative poverty measure that addresses some short-comings on the resource side of the official measure. For this alternative, we use the official poverty thresholds but change the income concept by adding food stamps and subtracting net federal and state income and payroll taxes. Some individuals have a combination of food stamps and EITC payments that are higher than their tax liabilities, so for these individuals net income would be higher than gross pre-tax income. Because of data limitations, we show trends with this alternative measure only from 1980 on and are unable to account for assets, housing subsidies, work expenses, or other nondiscretionary expenses.[8]

The United States is unusual among developed countries in having a single official method of calculating poverty. Because the measure is widely used and allows for our calculations to be easily compared to official data, we use it here. However, because the measure is somewhat controversial, we also use selected alternative measures and discuss the extent to which conclusions vary by the measure selected.

POVERTY IN THE UNITED STATES IN 2006

In 2006, 12.3 percent of all persons living in the United States were poor by the official poverty measure—a measure that ignores noncash sources of income and taxes. If we were to use a more comprehensive measure of resources, including the cash value of food stamps and the EITC and subtracting an esti-mate of payroll, state, and federal income taxes paid, 11.4 percent of all persons would be below the poverty threshold. The alternative poverty rate declines because food stamps and the EITC provide more to the poor than the taxes they pay take away.

Table 2.1, which focuses on the official measure, shows that the official poverty rate varies dramatically for different demographic groups. The rate for children, 17.4 percent, is substantially higher than the rate for adults between the ages of eighteen and sixty-four, 10.8 percent, and the rate for the elderly, 9.4 percent.

The focus of this book is primarily on those below age sixty-five, so the remainder of the table includes only non-elderly individuals. People of color have particularly high poverty rates—the rate for both non-Hispanic African Americans and Hispanics is more than twice the rate of non-Hispanic whites.[9] Poverty rates are relatively similar across regions, with slightly higher rates in the South. Central-city residents have the highest rates, followed closely by rural residents; poverty is substantially lower among those residing in urban areas outside central cities.

Individuals who live in a married-couple family have very low poverty rates, less than 6 percent. We divide those not living in a married-couple family into four groups; individuals living in any one of these groups have poverty rates more than twice as high as those living in a married-couple family. Individuals in female-headed families have by far the highest poverty rates, at nearly 32 percent. Nonfamily individuals and individuals in families with six or more people also have high poverty rates.

The final panels demonstrate that poverty is closely tied to the education and employment levels of the primary person in the unit. (We define "primary person" as the family head for those living in families and as the individual for those not living in families.) Poverty rates for those units in which the primary person has less than a high school education (31 percent) are more than twice as high as those for units whose primary person has just a high school degree (15 percent). Those living in units in which the primary person has a college degree have particularly low rates, 3.5 percent. The differences in poverty rates by work status of the primary person are dramatic: fewer than 5 percent of those living in units in which the primary person works full-time, full-year are poor, but nearly half of those living in a unit in which the primary person did not work during the last year are poor.

The table reveals some well-known characteristics of the risks of poverty—people of color, central-city residents, those living in female-headed families, and those in units in which the primary person did not complete high school are substantially more likely to be poor. Thus far, we have examined characteristics only one at a time. However, if a person has more than one characteristic associated with disadvantage—for example, a person of color with little education—is poverty even higher than it would be based on the individual areas of disadvantage? Or does the risk of poverty increase for those with any one disadvantage, but the number of disadvantages does not matter? One approach to this issue would be to examine poverty rates for a variety of smaller subgroups. Alternatively, these rates can be captured in a simple descriptive regression of an indicator variable for family poverty status on indicators of characteristics of disadvantage (female-headed family, nonwhite, central city, and high school dropout) as well as each two-way interaction.[10]

In table 2.2, we show estimated poverty rates based on the coefficients that result from this simple regression. The model implies that the poverty rate for

TABLE 2.1   /   U.S. Poverty in 2006

	Poverty Rate	Share of the Poor	Average Gap
All	12.3%	100.0%	$8,113
Age group			
Children	17.4	35.3	9,919
Age eighteen to sixty-four	10.8	55.4	7,593
Elders	9.4	9.3	4,378
All younger than age sixty-five	12.7	90.7	8,496
Race			
White	8.4	42.2	7,748
Black	24.2	24.2	9,338
Hispanic	20.7	26.5	8,738
Other	13.0	7.1	9,175
Region			
Northeast	11.7	16.6	8,411
Midwest	11.7	20.3	8,373
South	14.1	40.3	8,578
West	12.2	22.7	8,523
Urban status			
Central city	16.7	35.7	8,967
Other metro	9.1	31.1	8,221
Rural	15.9	18.9	8,343
Unclassified	12.5	14.2	8,119
Family			
Family	11.3	75.9	9,240
Nonfamily	20.8	24.1	6,126
Family type			
Married-couple family	5.9	29.8	8,590
Male-headed family	14.7	5.4	8,301
Female-headed family	31.9	40.8	9,839
Male (nonfamily)	18.4	11.9	6,107
Female (nonfamily)	23.7	12.1	6,144
Family size			
One	20.8	24.1	6,126
Two	9.5	15.1	7,025
Three	10.8	16.8	7,988
Four	9.8	18.2	9,020
Five	12.0	12.1	10,022
Six or more	19.3	13.8	12,784

(Table continues on p. 40.)

TABLE 2.1 / *Continued*

	Poverty Rate	Share of the Poor	Average Gap
Education of primary person			
Less than high school diploma	31.4%	34.6%	$9,051
High school diploma	14.8	34.9	8,170
Some college	10.6	22.4	8,094
College degree	3.5	8.2	8,758
Work status of primary person			
Not working	47.2	46.0	10,320
Working, not full-time full-year	24.3	30.5	7,493
Working, full-time full-year	4.2	23.6	6,310

Source: Authors' calculations based on the 2007 Current Population Survey (U.S. Department of Commerce and U.S. Department of Labor, various years).

the base category (row A: primary individuals who are not single mothers, are non-Hispanic whites, live outside central cities, and have at least a high school education) would be 8.5 percent. Each characteristic associated with disadvantage is associated with an increase in the likelihood of poverty, as seen in rows B through E, and in some cases the likelihood is substantially higher. For example, if we change the family status to single mother while retaining all of the

TABLE 2.2 / Estimated Probability of Having Income Below Poverty

Row	Female Head?	Nonwhite?	Central City?	Education Less Than Twelve Years?	Estimated Simple Poverty Rate	Estimated Poverty Rate with Interactions
A	No	No	No	No	8.5%	
B	Yes	No	No	No	22.9	
C	No	Yes	No	No	14.5	
D	No	No	Yes	No	10.3	
E	No	No	No	Yes	26.7	
F	Yes	Yes	No	No	29.0	32.0%
G	Yes	No	Yes	No	24.8	20.4
H	Yes	No	No	Yes	41.1	51.4
I	No	Yes	Yes	No	16.4	18.5
J	No	Yes	No	Yes	32.7	38.4
K	No	No	Yes	Yes	28.5	NS

Source: Authors' calculations based on the 2007 Current Population Survey (U.S. Department of Commerce and U.S. Department of Labor, various years).
Notes: Estimates come from linear probability model on 68,537 non-elderly family heads and non-family individuals. All variables in the model are shown; all coefficients are statistically significant at $p < .01$, except for NS, which denotes that the interaction was not statistically significant.

other base-level characteristics (row B), the poverty rate jumps to 22.9 percent. Likewise, if we change the level of education to less than high school while retaining the other base-level characteristics, the poverty rate is even higher, at 26.7 percent.

In rows F through K, we examine those with two vulnerable characteristics. We show both the estimated simple poverty rate (which comes from merely adding the main coefficients and ignoring the interactions) and the estimated rate that includes the interaction terms to explore the extent to which risks accumulate. Row F shows that single mothers who are nonwhite (and who have other base characteristics) have predicted poverty rates of 32.0 percent, about 10 percent higher than the predicted 29.0 percent that would come from the simple sum. In two cases, having two vulnerable characteristics adds a large disadvantage. Female heads with low education (row H) have poverty rates that are not merely 41 percent (the rate that would result from the sum) but 51 percent. Similarly, poverty rates for nonwhite heads with low education (row J) are estimated to be 38 percent, not merely the 33 percent that would come from the sum of these characteristics. On the other hand, although both female-headed families and those in central cities have higher rates, a female head in a central city (row G) actually has lower rates of poverty than would be expected based on the individual characteristics. Thus, the risk of poverty is complicated: some risks accumulate, but in other cases the presence of multiple risks can be somewhat protective.

The "Face" of Poverty: The Characteristics of Those Below the Poverty Line

Poverty rates provide information on the risk of being poor. Examining the characteristics of those individuals living below the poverty level can provide a related, but different, story. For example, some small groups may be particularly likely to be poor, but because there are relatively few people in the group, the typical person below the poverty level (the "face" of poverty) does not belong to that risky group. Returning to table 2.1, the second column presents information on the composition of those below the poverty line, enabling us to examine the characteristics of a typical such person. For each panel, these numbers sum to 100 percent. Consider first the distribution of those below the poverty level by age: about one-third are children, more than half are adults below age sixty-five, and fewer than 10 percent are elderly.

The remainder of the table covers only those who are younger than sixty-five. The table shows that media images of poverty as the condition primarily of people of color and of those who live in central cities, female-headed families, or in families whose head is not working may reflect the risk of poverty but do not always reflect the characteristics of the typical person below the poverty level. Whites constitute a larger share of the poor than blacks or Hispanics. Only about one-third of the poor live in central cities, and fewer than half live in female-headed families.

Fewer than half of the poor live in a family in which the primary person did not work at all in the previous year. Some groups with relatively low poverty rates constitute a significant proportion of the poor: nearly one-third of the poor live in suburban areas; 30 percent live in married-couple families; and nearly one-quarter live in a family in which the head worked full-time, full-year. Nonetheless, the "feminization of poverty" is clear: more than half of the poor come from one of two groups: those who live in female-headed families (41 percent) or female nonfamily individuals (12 percent).

How Poor Are Those Below the Poverty Level?

The poverty rate is a relatively crude measure of disadvantage: individuals are either above or below the line. The public and policymakers may feel very differently about the extent to which poverty is a problem depending not only on how many people are classified as being poor but also on how close they are to the poverty line. The third column of table 2.1 shows the average poverty "gap," defined as the difference between the poverty line and income for those who are below the line. The first row shows that the average person below the poverty line in 2006 would have needed $8,113 in additional family income to come up to the poverty line, suggesting that most poor families are not clustered just below the line but would need a significant increase in their income to move over the line. The table shows that families in which the head is not working and families with five or more members have an average poverty gap of over $10,000.

Income Sources of the Poor

Table 2.3 shows the income sources of the poor, differentiating between those units in which the head is younger than sixty-five and those in which the head is sixty-five or older. Among non-elderly heads, half have earnings that average $3,874 (column 2). The median earnings for those with earnings is $7,000 (column 3). As discussed elsewhere (Blank, this volume), earnings are the main source of income for most non-elderly families, and key reasons for poverty among non-elderly heads are unemployment and low wages. Note that to the extent that earnings are the most important income source for low-income families, ignoring the expenses associated with earnings (as is done by the official measure) can be a significant problem. Governmental programs lessen the poverty gap. The role of social insurance and welfare programs in limiting or eliminating poverty is discussed in greater detail by Scholz, Moffitt, and Cowan (this volume). Here we simply note that none of the other cash income sources are common for the non-elderly who are poor—only 11.2 percent receive Social Security; 7.1 percent, public assistance; 6.7 percent, child support; and 10.7 percent, Supplemental Security Income

TABLE 2.3 / Income Sources for Those Below the Poverty Line, 2006

	Has an Income Source	Average Income	Median if Present
Non-elderly heads			
Earnings	50.1%	$3,874	$7,002
Social Security	11.2	869	8,022
Public assistance	7.1	223	2,507
Child support	6.7	190	2,400
Supplemental Security Income	10.7	656	7,200
Other	25.0	673	1,524
Family income	78.9	6,485	7,950
Poverty gap		7,197	
Food stamp value	29.4	725	1,860
Tax liability (excluding EITC)	48.2	−421	−536
EITC	35.6	653	1,225
Net family income	81.4	7,445	8,340
Poverty gap (net income)		6,240	
Elderly heads			
Earnings	6.2	239	3,500
Social Security	76.9	5,378	7,200
Public assistance	1.3	26	1,500
Child support	0.3	10	3,900
Supplemental Security Income	13.5	568	3,600
Other	32.5	613	877
Family income	91.3	6,834	7,934
Poverty gap		3,925	
Food stamp value	17.9	199	816
Tax liability (excluding EITC)	7.8	−420	−383
EITC	2.7	33	412
Net family income	91.2	6,646	8,082
Poverty gap (net income)		4,112	

Source: Authors' calculations based on the 2007 Current Population Survey (U.S. Department of Commerce and U.S. Department of Labor, various years).

(SSI, the cash program for low-income people with a disability and those age sixty-five or older). For those who receive them, Social Security (median $8,022) and SSI ($7,200) benefits are about as large as the median earnings for workers. Total income averages just under $6,500, though for the nearly 80 percent of families with income, the median is higher, nearly $8,000.[11] Still, on average these families below the poverty line would need to have about twice their current income to reach the line. The noncash income sources received and taxes paid that are not considered in the official poverty calculation are received by many of the poor— 29.4 percent receive food stamps, 35.6 percent receive the EITC, and 48.2 percent would have some federal or state tax obligation if the EITC were not in place. Accounting for these other sources increases mean and median incomes but still leaves most families far from the poverty line.

Not surprisingly, a much smaller percentage of elderly poor families have earnings (6.2 percent) and a much larger share receive Social Security (76.9 percent). The median Social Security benefit for poor recipients is about the same as median earnings for the non-elderly poor ($7,200). Mean and median family incomes are relatively close to the figures for non-elderly families, but because these families have fewer people in them, resulting in a lower poverty line, their average poverty gap is considerably smaller. A comparison of the panels shows that the income and expenditures that we can account for but that are ignored in the official measure—food stamps, the EITC, and taxes—are less important for poor seniors than for those below age sixty-five.

TRENDS IN POVERTY

About one in eight Americans were poor in 2006. As we have seen, poverty rates are not uniform, but they are substantially higher for children than for elders, for people of color than for non-Hispanic whites, and for those in single-parent families than for those in married-couple families. To better understand the issues of greatest concern and the individuals affected by them, we also consider the progress, or lack of progress, made in fighting poverty. Even in periods of fairly stable total poverty rates, we find that some groups have made remarkable progress, while others have lost ground.

Before examining recent trends, we comment on long-term patterns. There are several conceptual and measurement issues that make it difficult to calculate comparable poverty rates for previous generations.[12] A key difficulty is that research has shown that the public's ideas about what a family needs to escape poverty increase as the country's standard of living increases (Blank 2008; Citro and Michael 1995; Ruggles 1990).[13] This means that poverty measures that are based only on prices and that ignore the standard of living can become outdated, especially when comparisons are made over long periods. Notwithstanding these difficulties, some researchers have calculated historical poverty rates based on thresholds that changed only with prices. Robert Plotnick and his colleagues (2000) report a poverty rate in 1914 of 66.0 percent, a high of 78.1 percent in 1932, and a rapid decline in poverty during World War II to a level of 23.9 percent in 1944. Gordon Fisher's (1986) series begins in 1947 at 32.0 percent and declines during the post–World War II boom to 24.3 percent in 1958. The official governmental series then begins in 1959 with poverty at 22.4 percent, which declined to 12.8 percent by 1968, the year when our analyses begin and the first year for which we have consistent data.

FIGURE 2.1 / Poverty Trends, 1968 to 2006, by Two Measures of Poverty

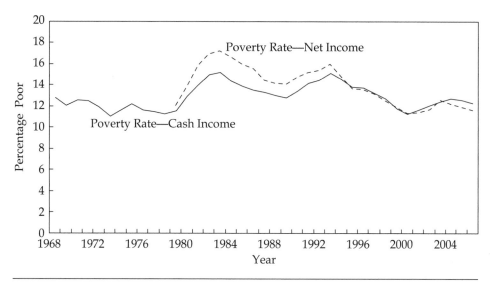

Source: Authors' calculations based on various years of Current Population Survey (U.S. Department of Commerce, various years).

Poverty Rates, 1968 to 2006

In figure 2.1, we show that the official poverty rate in 1968 was 12.8 percent. The official measure roughly follows the business cycle: poverty rose with the recession of the early 1980s, then declined during the improved economic times of the late 1980s. Poverty rose again in the downturn of the 1990s, but declined during the economic boom. Poverty rates increased again in the recession of 2001. A substantial body of research has concluded that although a variety of factors are related to poverty rates, they are strongly affected by the business cycle (see, for example, Blank, this volume; Freeman 2001; Hoynes, Page, and Huff Stevens 2006). Although this relationship still holds in general, the historical pattern changed somewhat in the 1970s and 1980s, when poverty was linked less closely to economic growth than it had been early in the period or since (Danziger 2007). Throughout these business cycles, however, the official poverty rate fluctuated between 11 and 15 percent, with the 2006 rate within half a percentage point of the 1968 rate (12.3 percent).

The figure also shows our adapted measure, a measure based on income that incorporates taxes paid and food stamps and EITC received. Because of data limitations, this series does not begin until 1979, when the rate was 12.0 percent (compared to the official rate of 11.6 percent). In the early part of the period, poverty rates for this measure were higher than the official measure because taxes on low-income families were higher than they now are and EITC payments were lower (Scholz 2007). For example, in 1984 the official rate was 14.4 percent, but our alternative measure was 16.6 percent. With the expansion of the EITC in 1986, 1990, and 1993, fewer low-income families paid net income taxes, and federal and state EITCs (and food stamps) generally offset taxes. Thus, poverty under the net income measure fell more than under the official measure, and the two rates were quite similar in the years after 1995. To the extent that there is a difference, poverty rates with the net income measure are now lower (11.6 percent to 12.3 percent) because in addition to the federal EITC, an increasing number of state EITCs (Levitis and Koulish 2008) provide income that more than offsets taxes.

Poverty Trends for Subgroups, Using the Official Measure

In table 2.4, we show poverty rates in 1968, 1990, and 2006. The first year for which we have consistent data is 1968, which is close to the peak of the late 1960s boom. The 1970s and 1980s brought stagflation and the most serious recession since the Great Depression. Moreover, during these decades there were several significant demographic and economic changes, with increasing rates of single-parent families, nonmarital births, cohabitation, female labor force participation (for example, Cancian and Reed 2001; Cancian and Reed, this volume), increased inequality (for example, Jones and Weinberg 2000), and increased life expectancy. We show poverty rates in 1990, which, again, was a year close to an economic peak (though at a rate of unemployment of 5.6 percent, higher than the 3.6 percent of 1968). After a recession in the early 1990s, there was a sustained economic boom, followed by recession with the period ending in better economic times (an unemployment rate of 4.6 percent in 2006). Some of the demographic trends flattened or even reversed directions during the 1990s, and others continued. For example, Cancian and Reed (this volume) show that the percentage of married mothers in the labor force increased from 1970 to 1990, then stabilized or declined from 1990 to 2006, and that the largest increases in single-parenthood for African American families were in the 1970 to 1990 period. In contrast, they show that the proportion of children born to unmarried parents increased throughout this period, as did the proportion of women who were not married. Moreover, life expectancy increased throughout this period (Arias 2007). As shown in more detail by Cancian and Reed (this volume), increases in employment would be expected to decrease poverty, and increases in single-parenthood would be expected to increase it.

Throughout the 1968 to 2006 period, there were several important social policy changes as well. As described in more detail by John Karl Scholz, Robert Moffitt, and Benjamin Cowan in this volume, spending on social insurance programs increased much faster than spending on means-tested programs (except for Medicaid) during this period, and spending on in-kind programs increased more rapidly than spending on cash programs. New programs in this period included the EITC, child care subsidy programs, and Temporary Assistance for Needy Families (TANF)—primarily work-focused programs and one newly federalized program for people not expected to work (SSI). The policy changes that provided additional in-kind benefits, benefits through the tax system, or other work supports do not

TABLE 2.4 / Poverty Rates in 1968, 1990, and 2006

	1968	1990	2006
All	12.8%	13.5%	12.3%
Age group			
Children	15.4	20.6	17.4
Age eighteen to sixty-four	9.0	10.7	10.8
Elders	25.0	12.1	9.4
	1968		
All younger than age sixty-five	11.5	13.7	12.7
Race	1970		
White	7.5	8.7	8.4
Black	32.8	31.6	24.2
Hispanic	23.8	28.3	20.7
Other	15.1	14.9	13.0
Region	1968		
Northeast	8.0	11.7	11.7
Midwest	8.1	12.5	11.7
South	18.9	15.7	14.1
West	9.3	13.5	12.2
Urban status			
Central city	12.2	20.0	16.7
Other metro	6.4	8.2	9.1
Rural	16.3	16.4	15.9
Unclassified		13.2	12.5
Family			
Family	10.9	13.0	11.3
Nonfamily	24.3	18.8	20.8
Family type			
Married-couple family	7.6	7.1	5.9
Male-headed family	16.7	12.4	14.7
Female-headed family	40.6	39.4	31.9
Male (nonfamily)	18.8	16.4	18.4
Female (nonfamily)	28.9	21.9	23.7
Family size			
One	24.3	18.8	20.8
Two	8.3	9.8	9.5
Three	6.8	11.8	10.8
Four	7.1	10.9	9.8
Five	9.4	14.7	12.0
Six or more	19.2	24.2	19.3

(*Table continues on p. 48.*)

TABLE 2.4 / *Continued*

	1968	1990	2006
Education of primary person			
Less than high school diploma	19.5%	33.3%	31.4%
High school diploma	6.8	13.3	14.8
Some college	5.5	8.8	10.6
College degree	3.1	3.2	3.5
Worker status of primary person			
Not working	42.9	55.5	47.2
Working, not full-time full-year	22.0	25.4	24.3
Working, full-time full-year	5.4	3.8	4.2

Source: Authors' calculations based on various years of the Current Population Survey (U.S. Department of Commerce, various years).

directly affect the official poverty rate, because these sources are not counted in gross cash income. Thus, although our focus in this section is on official poverty rates, we also discuss rates based on net income.

Did the economic, demographic, and policy changes over the period result in similar trends in poverty, or did they affect some groups differentially? The first panel of table 2.4 shows a substantially different trend by age group. In 1968 elders were by far the most vulnerable to poverty, with rates of 25 percent, but their poverty rates improved dramatically in the first period. Poverty continued to decline in the second period, so that by 2006 elderly poverty rates were the lowest of the three age groups. Because relatively few elders work, declines in elderly poverty are primarily the result of increases in unearned income (increases in Social Security and the introduction of the federal SSI program). Adults age eighteen to sixty-four had by far the lowest poverty rates of the three groups in 1968 and showed a relatively small increase, primarily in the first period. The rate for children, however, began relatively high (15 percent) and increased substantially during the first period, to more than one in five children being poor, before improving somewhat by 2006. In our view, the dramatic improvement for elders over this period is one of the most important stories in poverty trends in the forty-year period. Because the improvements among elders could obscure the trends for other subgroups, the remaining panels focus on those younger than sixty-five.

The poverty rate for non-Hispanic whites shows a slight increase over this period.[14] Poverty rates for people of color are substantially higher than those of non-Hispanic whites throughout this period and show some different patterns. Poverty rates for non-Hispanic blacks improved slightly between 1970 and 1990 and more substantially between 1990 and 2006. The rates for Hispanics increased during the first period before showing substantial improvements in the second. Poverty declines for Hispanics during the second period are particularly remarkable given the increase in immigration (for analysis, see Raphael and Smolensky, this volume). Thus, for both groups, poverty rates in 2006 were less than in 1970, and substantially less for African Americans.

Poverty rates for every region other than the South increased during the first period, reflecting the decline of the older industrial cities of the Northeast and Midwest. During the second period, poverty rates improved in every region except the Northeast. Similarly, poverty rates for those in central cities rose rapidly in the first period, but declined in the second. Poverty rates in rural areas were more stable. Poverty rates for those in married-couple families and in female-headed families improved during both periods, with the rate for female-headed families showing a marked decline in the second period. In contrast, rates for nonfamily individuals and those in male-headed families declined only in the first period.

Considering education, poverty rates among those living in a unit in which the primary person had less than a high school degree increased dramatically between 1968 and 1990, consistent with the decline in earnings and job availability for those without educational credentials and increased employer demand for skills (see Blank, this volume).[15] Somewhat surprisingly, poverty rates for this group made some improvement during the second period. Poverty rates for those living in a unit in which the primary person had only a high school degree increased sharply during the first period and continued to increase in the second period. Because of changes in the safety net (see Scholz, Moffitt, and Cowan, this volume), the rate for persons living in a unit in which the primary person was not working increased from 42.9 percent to 55.5 percent during the first period, before decreasing to 47.2 percent.

In summary, the trend analysis reveals a complicated picture. Some groups showed significant improvement in poverty rates over time. We have already highlighted those age sixty-five and over, whose poverty rates declined from 25 percent to less than 10 percent. Focusing on those younger than sixty-five, groups that showed an improvement of more than 20 percent included African Americans, those in the South, those in married-couple or female-headed families, and those in families whose heads worked full-time, full-year. Declines in the most recent period were particularly large for African Americans and those in female-headed families. These trends are related in that a larger proportion of African Americans live in female-headed families; these are also two groups that saw increases in labor force participation (Cancian and Reed, this volume). On the other hand, several groups showed a worsening of their poverty rates by 20 percent or more, including those in the Northeast, Midwest, and West, those in both central cities and suburban areas, those with a family size of two to five, and those living with a head who had any level of education less than a college degree.

Table 2.4 focuses only on changes in the poverty rates of different subgroups. These are important, but changes in the overall level of poverty are also a result of changes in the size of various subgroups (not shown on table). In this regard, some population trends among the non-elderly have been favorable. Notably, the proportion living in a family whose head had less than a high school education—families that typically have had high poverty rates—shrank dramatically over these thirty-eight years, from 40 percent of the population in 1968 to 14 percent in 2006. Similarly, the proportion of individuals living in large families, especially families of six or more people, declined from 26 percent of the population in 1968 to only 9 percent in 2006; thus, the high poverty rates of this group became less influential. On the other hand, two key trends would increase overall poverty rates, all else being equal. Non-Hispanic whites, who historically have had lower rates of poverty, shrank as a proportion of the population, from 83 percent to 64 percent. Similarly, as discussed in more detail by Cancian and Reed (this volume), the proportion living in married-couple families, another group with low poverty rates, also declined markedly, from 84 percent in 1968 to 64 percent in 2006.

Trends in the Characteristics of the Poor

Over the nearly forty-year period between 1968 and 2006, there have been some dramatic shifts in the composition of the poor. For example, Hispanics now make up a substantially larger share of the poor than they did in 1970 (27 percent, compared to 10 percent), with declines in shares for both non-Hispanic whites (from 55 percent to 42 percent) and African Americans (from 33 percent to 24 percent). However, much of this shift has been driven by changes in the population rather than by changes in poverty rates. A combination of population shifts and changes in poverty rates has also resulted in a larger fraction of the poor in 2006 living in central cities and other urban areas and a substantially smaller fraction living in rural areas (22 percent, compared to 49 percent in 1968).[16] Among the subgroups we study, there are three additional substantial differences in the composition of those below the poverty line in 1968 and 2006, but these all primarily reflect changes in the population rather than changes in poverty rates. First, in 1968, 43 percent of those below the poverty line lived in families of six or more individuals; the comparable figure for 2006 was 14 percent. Second, in 1968 more than half of those below the poverty line lived in married-couple families; by 2006 only 30 percent of those below the poverty line lived in such families. Finally, in 1968, 70 percent of those below the poverty line were living in families in which the head did not have a high school degree; by 2006 this group was only 35 percent of those below the poverty line. All of these changes reflect population shifts: toward smaller families, toward single-parent families and nonfamily individuals, and toward higher education. Regardless of the cause, the change in the "face" of poverty has been dramatic. In 1968 a non-Hispanic white individual living in a rural area and as part of a married-couple family whose head had less than a high school degree would have accurately presented characteristics associated with about half or more of those below the poverty line. By 2006, none of these characteristics would have accurately reflected the characteristics of more than half of those below the poverty line.

Trends in the Depth of Poverty

Earlier we showed that in 2006 the amount needed to bring an individual who was below the poverty line just up to the threshold (the poverty gap) was $8,113.

The comparable figure for 1968 was $8,067 (in 2006 inflation-adjusted dollars), so there have not been large changes over the period we study in how far the average poor individual is from the poverty threshold. However, the average masks substantial variation. The largest differences in the average poverty gap between 1968 and 2006 are for those in a family whose head worked full-time, full-year (their average gap declined by $2,378) and for those in a family of six or more people (their gap increased by $1,840). Note, however, that the decline in the gap for those working full-time, full-year is somewhat misleading to the extent that the current poverty measure ignores any expenses associated with working that have increased over this time period (child care, for example).[17]

Trends in Income Sources for the Poor

In these analyses, we examine two time points (1968 and 2006), use the official measure of poverty, and consider cash income sources. The proportion of non-elderly poor families with earnings decreased from 62 percent in 1968 to 50 percent in 2006. The share of income attributable to earnings also decreased over this time period: in 1968 earnings accounted for 67 percent of the income of the average poor family, while by 2006 earnings accounted for only 60 percent. The proportion of family units receiving public assistance declined from 20 percent in 1968 to 7 percent in 2006; this income accounted for 15 percent of total income for poor families in 1968, but only 3 percent in 2006. For poor elderly families, the percentage with earnings declined from 14 percent in 1968 to 6 percent in 2006. Thus, for both elderly and non-elderly poor families, earnings have become less important over time. This change, consistent with other research showing that the pretransfer poverty gap is growing (Ziliak 2008), means that governmental transfers would have had to become more generous over time to bring families above the poverty line. Yet the data show that this has not occurred: cash transfers have become substantially less important for non-elderly families as we have moved toward a policy system that focuses more on requiring and supporting work than on providing cash transfers.

PUTTING POVERTY IN PERSPECTIVE

Accounting for Changes in the Standard of Living, or, Comparisons with Others

An important criticism of the official poverty measure is that the poverty thresholds have not been updated since the 1960s to reflect increasing standards of living but instead are based on an absolute standard. Even in the eighteenth century, the father of economics, Adam Smith, pointed out that the standard of living of a society is closely related to how we think about what is necessary: "By necessaries I understand, not only the commodities which are indispensably necessary for the support of life, but whatever the customs of the country renders it indecent for creditable people, even the lowest order, to be without" (Smith 1852, 368). One traditional way to measure this construct is to take a particular percentage (often half) of median income as a measure that is more closely linked to the "customs of the country." This type of measure is often called a "relative" measure because the incomes of others matter in the setting of the poverty threshold. (Measures based only on what is "needed" to survive are typically called "absolute" measures.)

In this section, we use the expanded income concept that we introduced before (accounting for near-cash sources of income and taxes) and compare this measure of resources to a threshold based on half of the median income. This measure then reflects growth in standards of living over time. More specifically, we compare equivalized household income to 50 percent of equivalized median household income in that year.[18]

We use 50 percent of median household income in part because it is often used in other countries—though the European Union now recommends 60 percent of median income (European Union Social Protection Committee 2001)—and in part because the U.S. official measure was approximately half the median income when it was set in 1963. Because net incomes have risen substantially faster than prices over the last forty years, a poverty threshold based on half of median incomes is substantially higher than the official measure.[19] For example, the official threshold for a non-elderly adult living alone in 2006 was $10,488; the threshold measure based on median income was $12,982, or about 24 percent higher. Similarly, the official threshold for a married couple with two children in 2006 was $20,444; the threshold based on median income was $25,963, a difference of 27 percent. Because of these higher thresholds, poverty rates calculated using this relative measure will be higher than the official rates.

Indeed, our relative-income measure always shows higher poverty rates than the official measure or the measure that uses net income compared to the official threshold. Poverty under this measure is 14.4 percent in 1979, when the official rate was 11.6 percent; in 2006 this measure showed rates of 15.7 percent, compared to 12.3 percent for the official measure and 11.4 percent using the net income/official threshold measure. Like the official rate, it increased during the difficult economic times of the early 1980s, to 18 percent by 1983, and varied less with the business cycle after that. When the economy boomed after the mid-1990s, median income also rose, so the relative threshold increased, and the relative poverty measure fell less than the official measure. For example, between 1993 and 2000 the official measure fell 3.9 percentage points, while the relative measure fell only 1.6 percentage points.

Subgroups that have higher poverty rates using the official measure generally have higher poverty rates using the relative measure. One notable exception is age group. In 2006 the poverty rate for children, using the official measure, was 17.4 percent, followed by 10.8 percent for adults age eighteen to sixty-four and 9.4 percent for elders. The rates using our relative poverty measure are markedly different, especially for the elderly: 20.2 percent for children, 13.4 percent for adults age eighteen to sixty-four, and 18.7 percent for elders. This result occurs because many elders have resources that put them just above the official poverty threshold, so the increase in the threshold for the median income measure substantially increases their rate of poverty.

Similarly, conclusions about trends in poverty by subgroup are not particularly sensitive to whether we use an absolute or relative measure, with one exception: trends by age for the relative measure differ from the trends for the absolute measure. More specifically, the absolute rate for the elderly falls from 25.0 percent in 1968 to 9.4 percent in 2006, whereas a comparable (gross cash income) relative measure declines from 38.9 percent in 1968 to 28 percent in 2006.[20] Thus, this is a case in which poverty measurement may matter a great deal. If policymakers are considering whether to slow the increases in Social Security benefits, data based on the official measure could lead them to make such cuts, since elders are now at limited risk of poverty. Data based on the relative income measure, however, would suggest that they should proceed more cautiously: according to this measure, elders are still very vulnerable, and the rate of decline has not been as dramatic.

Poverty in the United States Compared to Selected Other Countries

The Luxembourg Income Study (LIS) allows researchers to compare poverty rates in the United States to those in other countries. The most recent data available from this source are from about 2000 (specific years of data vary somewhat across countries). The economist Timothy Smeeding (2006) has recently compared poverty rates in the United States with rates in ten other countries (Canada and nine European countries), using a measure of resources similar to our "net income" measure and a threshold based on half the median income in each country.[21] As shown in the first column of table 2.5, poverty in the United States is the highest of the countries examined, at 17 percent. Poverty rates in Canada are substantially lower, at 11.4 percent, and they are particularly low in the Scandinavian countries— 5.4 percent in Finland and 6.5 percent in Sweden. The next column shows that the United States has particularly high poverty rates for households with children, at 19 percent. Here the contrast with the Scandinavian countries is most stark: their poverty rates for households with children are much lower than their overall rate, at 4 percent in Sweden and 3 percent in Finland. The third column shows that the United States also does not compare favorably in poverty rates for the elderly, having the second-highest rate, though it is substantially lower than Ireland's.[22]

In the final column, we report Smeeding's analysis of a measure roughly comparable to the U.S. official poverty measure. Note that this analysis is substantially different from the earlier columns, in which the poverty threshold for each country is set based on its own income distribution in recognition that part of the concept of poverty is having less than what "the custom of the country" deems it needful to have. In the absolute measure, the approximate amount that could be purchased in the United States with an income just equal to the U.S. threshold is taken and the equivalent amount of income is calculated in other countries. Under this measure, poverty in the United States is lower than that in the United Kingdom and closer to other countries. Thus, the United States has higher poverty rates than other rich

TABLE 2.5 / Poverty Rates in Eleven Rich Countries

| | | Relative Measure | | Absolute Measure |
	All	Households with Children	Age Sixty-Five or Older	All
United States	17.0%	18.8%	28.4%	8.7%
Ireland	16.5	15.0	48.3	NA
Italy	12.7	15.4	14.4	NA
United Kingdom	12.4	13.2	23.9	12.4
Canada	11.4	13.2	6.3	6.9
Germany	8.3	7.6	11.2	7.6
Belgium	8.0	6.0	17.2	6.3
Austria	7.7	6.4	17.2	5.2
Netherlands	7.3	9.0	2.0	7.2
Sweden	6.5	3.8	8.3	7.5
Finland	5.4	2.9	10.1	6.7

Source: Reprinted from Smeeding (2006) with permission.
Notes: Data are from 2000 except for the United Kingdom and the Netherlands, where data are from 1999. The relative measure compares cash and near-cash household income to 50 percent of median equivalized household income. The absolute measure uses the U.S. poverty threshold, converted to each country's currency using purchasing power parities.

countries under both measures, but it has especially high rates when poverty is defined as having substantially less income than others in the country.

The LIS has data from some countries in the mid-1980s as well as around 2000, so trends can also be explored. Smeeding (2006) examines changes in relative poverty between approximately 1987 and 2000. Poverty in the United States declined from 17.8 percent to 17.0 percent during this period. The trends do differ by country: poverty rates in the United Kingdom, Belgium, and Ireland all increased by over three percentage points over a roughly comparable period, whereas the largest decline, one percentage point, was in Sweden, followed by the decline in the United States.

Why does the United States rank so poorly in comparisons with other wealthy nations? A substantial literature has explored this question (see, for example, Burtless 2007; Kim 2000; Osberg, Smeeding, and Schwabish 2004; Rainwater and Smeeding 2003). Because so few elders work, the primary factors related to their poverty are unearned income, primarily the generosity of public pensions and other governmental supports. Even though great strides have been made in reducing poverty among elderly Americans in the last forty years (see table 2.4), the United States still ranks second only to Ireland among the eleven countries surveyed by Timothy Smeeding using the relative measure of poverty. The United States does not fare any better in poverty among elders according to an absolute measure that applies the U.S. threshold adjusted for purchasing power to other countries. Here the United States ranks second only to the United Kingdom among the nine countries for which these calculations were made. These results suggest that while policy in the form of Social Security and SSI have been successful in reducing poverty, the generosity of these old-age retirement and insurance programs in the United States lags behind that of industrialized European countries.

Among the non-elderly, the story is somewhat more complicated, but explanations center on differences in taxes, social insurance (benefits that are not means-tested), and social assistance (means-tested benefits, including the EITC in the United States and the Working Tax Credit [WTC] in the United Kingdom), as well as differences in labor supply and differences in earnings in the United States compared with wealthy European countries.

One way to assess the poverty-reducing effects of taxes, social insurance, and social assistance is to compute poverty rates using gross market income, compute rates using net disposable income, and then compare the two measures. Both Smeeding (2006) and Janet Gornick and Markus Jäntti (forthcoming) have performed this exercise using LIS data from around 2000, for slightly different sets of countries. The results indicate that the tax and transfer policies of other countries do far more to reduce poverty than similar policies in the United States. Among the eleven countries for which Smeeding performed this exercise, the United States achieved the lowest poverty reduction as a result of tax and transfer policy, at 26.4 percent. The next-lowest country was Ireland, at 44.1. The remaining ten countries all had percentage-poverty-rate reductions due to tax and transfer policy of around 60 percent or more. Gornick and Jäntti also find that the United States ranks lowest in the poverty-alleviating effects of tax and transfer policy when a relative measure of poverty is used among the thirteen countries they survey. When they use an absolute standard of 1.25 times the U.S. poverty threshold, they find that the United States ranks above only the relatively poor countries of Israel and Poland.[23]

These results suggest that policy in the United States is doing far less to reduce poverty than in most other countries. The primary reason for the ineffectiveness of U.S. policy is the level of expenditures. Among the eleven countries surveyed by Smeeding, the United States ranks the lowest in non-elderly cash and near-cash social spending as a percentage of GDP, and it has the highest non-elderly poverty rate. The United States is not merely a special case: across the eleven countries, the correlation between the percentage of non-elderly poor and non-elderly social expenditures is very high, at 0.78.

To what extent do relatively high poverty rates in the United States have to do with differences in labor supply or wages? Smeeding also examines this question and finds that average annual hours worked by the head and spouse in poor households in the United States exceeds that of the six other countries for which there is comparable data. In most cases, the differences are quite striking. For instance, using a net-disposable-income measure and a relative (50 percent of median household income) poverty threshold, poor U.S. household heads and their spouses worked an average of over 1,200 hours per year in 2000, compared with only 489 in the Netherlands, 371 in Germany, and 463 in Belgium, all countries with dramatically lower poverty rates. Thus, high poverty rates in the United States are not merely the result of low levels of labor supply. In fact, quite the contrary is true: non-elderly poor in the United States work more hours than their coun-terparts in other wealthy nations.

While differences in labor supply do not explain the relatively high poverty rates in the United States, low wages do. As shown by Smeeding (2006), the correlation between the percentage of full-time workers earning less than 65 percent of median earnings and the non-elderly poverty rate among the eleven countries he surveyed is 0.92. Furthermore, the United States has the largest absolute and percentage dif-ferential between poverty rates for children with the least-educated parents and children with more-educated parents, suggesting that much of the U.S. problem is rooted in low earnings for the lowest-skilled workers.

CONCLUSION

In 2006, forty-two years after the War on Poverty was proclaimed, poverty accord-ing to the official measure was 12.3 percent—about the same as it was in the late 1960s. A poverty measure that incorporates additional income sources shows somewhat lower poverty, 11.4 percent, but if a relative measure (which incorpo-rates changes in the standard of living over time) is used, poverty in 2006 would be 15.7 percent.

Is the poverty rate, whether it is 11 percent or 16 percent, so high that it is a social problem, or is it at about the best one can expect? When the war was pro-claimed, its architects thought that poverty could be eradicated, but there were no real comparison points for a particular level of poverty. We can now compare the poverty level to two benchmarks: poverty in the United States in previous years, and poverty in other countries. On both comparisons, the United States fares poorly. Over the 1968 to 2006 period, even during the best economic times, with substantial governmental efforts, and with a poverty threshold that many con-sider too low, the official poverty rate has never been as low as 10 percent, and there is no strong trend toward lower poverty rates over time. Moreover, not only are U.S. poverty rates high compared to the recent historical record, but they are also quite high compared to rates in other developed countries.

In addition to being high, an examination of the trends in poverty shows that the level of overall poverty is remarkably and stubbornly stable. Over the years we analyze, over the business cycle, the poverty rate does not change a great deal even though living standards now are much higher than they were in the mid-1960s.

There are substantial differences in poverty rates across demographic groups that have persisted over the study period. Using the official measure, the highest poverty rates, all above 20 percent, are for those living in female-headed families, those living in a family whose head does not have a high school degree or was not working, and people of color. The first two characteristics highlight the critical importance of the labor market. Part of the reason single-parent families have higher rates of poverty is that there is only one adult available to work, and that adult must cover both economic support and nurturing.[24] Part of the reason indi-viduals with low education have such high poverty rates is that their earnings are low. In both these cases, those with low earnings (and especially those with no earnings) are at very high risk of poverty because in the United States programs to supplement low earnings are generally not generous enough to bring them above the poverty level (see Scholz, Moffitt, and Cowan, this volume). Finally, the fact that people of color have such high poverty rates highlights the extent to which race is still strongly connected to opportunity and outcome in the United States.

Yet we caution against making simplistic assumptions about who is poor or the causes of poverty. We have shown that poor people are represented among all groups in the population and include people of all ages, races and ethnicities, educational levels, and family and work statuses, living in all regions and urban and rural locations. Among the official poverty population, 55 percent are between the ages of eighteen and sixty-four. Among the non-elderly poor, 42 percent are non-Hispanic whites, 30 percent live in a married-couple family, and more than half have at least one worker in the family. Moreover, some of the groups with higher poverty rates in 2006 made substantial progress over the period we study. For example, poverty rates for those in female-headed families and for African Americans had fallen to about three-quarters of their 1970 level by 2006, and rates for Hispanics fell to less than three-quarters of their 1990 level. These success stories are also part of the overall picture of poverty trends.

A detailed examination of the causes of the level of poverty and its trends is beyond the scope of this chapter. Nonetheless, we do note that the boom in the 1990s was associated with increased willingness on the part of employers to hire minorities and other groups that had traditionally faced disadvantages (Holzer, Raphael, and Stoll 2006), and that there remains a strong link between macroeconomic performance and the poverty rates of various disadvantaged groups (see Blank, this volume). The trends also suggest that policy can make a difference in fighting poverty. The prime example is that most analysts credit increases in Social Security benefits as the primary cause of the dramatic declines in elderly poverty (see, for example, Burtless and Quinn 2001; Danziger 2007; Engelhardt and Gruber 2006). Researchers have found that increases in the employment rate among single mothers in the 1990s were due not merely to the economic boom but also to increases in the EITC and changes in welfare policy (see, for example, Meyer and Rosenbaum 2001; Ellwood 2000), and these increases in employment are part of the reason for the decline in poverty rates among single mothers. It is also instructive to consider the experience of the United Kingdom. In 1999 Prime Minister Tony Blair essentially declared war on child poverty, pledging to end it by 2020. The pledge led to a substantial review of policies affecting poverty and to significant policy change. The initial results were quite positive: 600,000 children were lifted out of poverty, although progress has slowed, and the intermediate goals have not yet been met (Minoff 2006; Palmer, MacInnes, and Kenway 2007).

As President Johnson predicted, the struggle against poverty has not been "short or easy." He also realized that no "single weapon or strategy" would be sufficient. Despite a variety of social policy changes, discussed in other chapters in this volume, the official measure, as well as our alternative measures, shows that very little progress has been made. Perhaps it is time for a renewed war on poverty, this time fought with new commitments and different policy weapons.

NOTES

1. Johnson's State of the Union speech, delivered on January 8, 1964, is available at: http://www.americanrhetoric.com/speeches/lbj1964stateoftheunion.htm.

2. We do not present much information on the depth of poverty; for a discussion of indices that include more than just dichotomous measures of whether an individual is poor, see, for example, Sen (1976) or Ziliak (2006). We focus here only on poverty in a single time period rather than on persistent or permanent poverty. For simplicity, we also ignore other issues, including whether income or consumption is the best measure of resources and whether there should be a single measure or multiple measures.

3. Through 1969, the thresholds were indexed using the price of food. Up until 1980, the poverty thresholds were indexed using the consumer price index (CPI) for urban wage earners and clerical workers. Since 1980, it has been indexed by the consumer price index for all urban consumers (CPI-U).

4. The percentage spent on food was based on the 1955 Household Food Consumption Survey (the latest available to Orshansky in the mid-1960s). The survey indicated that on average families of three or more persons spent an average of one-third of their weekly after-tax income on food. However, the same survey indicated that families of two persons and single individuals spent a lower fraction of their income on food, so for these units a higher multiple was applied to the Economy Food Plan to determine a poverty threshold.

5. See U.S. Census Bureau, *Poverty Thresholds,* available at: http://www.census.gov/hhes/www/poverty/threshld.html. The comparable figures for 2006, the year of the data we use here, are $9,669, $20,614, and $41,499.

6. In households containing two or more unrelated families, each family's poverty status is determined separately on the basis of its family-specific threshold and income. The poverty status of nonfamily individuals age fifteen and over, whether they are living with a family, by themselves, or with other nonfamily individuals, is assigned by comparing their personal income to the poverty line for one person. The poverty statuses of persons residing in institutional group quarters, college dormitories, military barracks, and living situations without conventional housing that is not a shelter are not computed. Also, because the CPS collects only income data for persons over the age of fourteen, the poverty status of nonfamily individuals under the age of fifteen is not computed.

7. We use our own calculations rather than the Census Bureau's published series for two reasons. First, we calculate the official poverty rate for subgroups that are not available in the published series (including, for example, family size and our division of family type). Second, the alternative poverty measures we report are not available from the Census Bureau. By using our own calculations, any differences in poverty rates among the series are not due to any differences in how we and the Census Bureau analyze the data.

8. The Inter-University Consortium for Political and Social Research (ICPSR) files of the March CPS do not provide information about food stamp receipt until 1980, and they do not provide estimated taxes until 1991. Thus, we impute federal, state, and payroll

taxes for years prior to 1991 using the TAXSIM model of the National Bureau of Economic Research (NBER) (Feenberg and Coutts 1993). We impute the values of missing variables when possible, but there is not enough information in the CPS to impute mortgage interest (and other itemized deductions), child care expenses, and capital gains and losses. We ignore these variables in our tax imputations. Our filing status imputations also differ from those published by the Census Bureau. In years in which both our imputations and those from the census are available, our average tax liability is higher, suggesting that we have omitted some income tax deductions. Our basic strategy when presenting information on poverty measures using net income is to use CPS imputations when discussing the level of poverty and to use our own imputations using TAXSIM when discussing trends, since this is a longer, more consistent series.

9. Our categories are focused on race and ethnicity but not on immigrant status because immigration is covered in more detail in the chapter by Steven Raphael and Eugene Smolensky.

10. Our goal with this descriptive regression is not to attempt a causal model but to examine heuristically whether disadvantage accumulates by estimating whether interaction terms are statistically significant. Using a linear probability model and measuring each characteristic as a dichotomous variable provides coefficients that are simple to interpret.

11. Underreporting of income may be a significant problem. For example, the amount of welfare income reported in surveys totals substantially less than the amount of benefits paid according to government accounts. This topic is the subject of a body of research and has led some to argue for consumption-based measures; for a discussion of these issues, see, for example, Bavier (2008), Meyer and Sullivan (2007), or Ziliak (2006).

12. The U.S. Census Bureau calculates official poverty rates back to 1959, using a threshold that is backdated for changes in prices. Gordon Fisher (1986) has back-cast the official threshold even further, to 1947, and Robert Plotnick and his colleagues (2000) have created a poverty series that dates back to 1914. All of these series are back-cast only for changes in prices and do not reflect increases in the general standard of living.

13. For example, in showing that responses to the minimum amount needed to "get along" track 50 percent of median income through the late 1980s, Rebecca Blank (2008) suggests that as the general standard of living increases, so does the amount reported as needed. Since the late 1980s, with increases in inequality, responses to the amount needed to get along have increased by more than median income and seem more closely related to half the mean income. Thus, if median or mean incomes are increasing, updating a poverty line by prices only will eventually underestimate what most people think of as the amounts needed to get by.

14. This panel uses 1970 as the base because Hispanics were not consistently identified in 1968.

15. Of course, the types of individuals who had less than a high school education probably also changed substantially over this time period.

16. The figures for 1968 examine only those whose status has been classified; 15 percent of the poor were not classified into central city, other urban, or rural.

17. Since large families have become less common, the types of individuals in these families may have become less typical, and this could result in increases in the poverty gap.

18. Unlike the official measure, poverty status is computed for all household members, regardless of their family membership. We thus assume that all household members, whether related or not, share their incomes. Because this assumption is not likely to hold for persons living in non-institutional group arrangements (such as college dormitories), we excluded these persons from this measure. We use the household rather than the family because this procedure is roughly equivalent in concept and construct to how many industrialized countries measure poverty. Income is equalized using the scale (Household Size)$^{0.5}$.

19. A higher poverty threshold is also appropriate given that food expenditures are now a much lower portion of overall expenditures, which suggests that food costs should be multiplied by a much larger multiplier than three to be consistent with the original methodology. Based on the 2006 Consumer Expenditure Survey, food expenditures for consumer units averaged slightly more than 10 percent of before-tax income.

20. Because our net income measure does not go back to 1968, for this long-term trend we compare gross cash income to the relative income threshold.

21. A key difference from our net income measure is that Smeeding's measure includes cash housing benefits.

22. Ireland experienced rapid growth in income during the 1990s, particularly among the young, but very little growth in pension income. This is the primary reason why Ireland's relative poverty rates are so high among elders. This rapid growth in incomes with a corresponding increase in inequality is also one of the reasons why Ireland shows an increase in relative poverty over the 1987 to 2000 period. Smeeding (2006) also computes changes in poverty using a measure where the threshold is anchored at 50 percent of equivalized household income in 1987 and only adjusted for inflation thereafter. According to this measure, Ireland's poverty rate decreased from 16.5 percent to 1.2 percent between 1987 and 2000.

23. When the 1.25 times the U.S. poverty threshold is applied to a net-disposable-income measure, Israel has a poverty rate of 29.3 percent and Poland has a poverty rate of 81.5 percent.

24. For most single-parent families, there is a living parent who does not reside with the child, making child support an important potential income source. In addition, in theory, single-parent families could live with other adults, which would lessen the burden on a single adult to provide both economic support and care (for information on the living arrangements of single parents, see Cancian and Reed, this volume).

REFERENCES

Arias, Elizabeth. 2007. "United States Life Tables, 2004." *National Vital Statistics Reports* 56(9, December 28). Washington: U.S. Department of Health and Human Services. Available at: http://www.cdc.gov/nchs/data/nvsr/nvsr56/nvsr56_09.pdf (accessed July 8, 2009).

Bavier, Richard. 2008. "Reconciliation of Income and Consumption Data in Poverty Measurement." *Journal of Policy Analysis and Management* 27(1): 40–62.

Blank, Rebecca M. 2008. "How to Improve Poverty Measurement in the United States." *Journal of Policy Analysis and Management* 27(2): 233–54.

Burtless, Gary. 2007. "What Have We Learned About Poverty and Inequality? Evidence from Cross-National Analysis." *Focus* 25(1): 12–17.

Burtless, Gary, and Joseph Quinn. 2001. "Retirement Trends and Policies to Encourage Work Among Older Americans." In *Ensuring Health and Income Security for an Aging Workforce,* edited by Peter Budetti, Richard Burkhauser, Janice Gregory, and Allan Hunt. Kalamazoo, Mich.: W. E. Upjohn Institute for Employment Research.

Cancian, Maria, and Deborah Reed. 2001. "Changes in Family Structure: Implications for Poverty and Related Policy." In *Understanding Poverty,* edited by Sheldon H. Danziger and Robert H. Haveman. New York and Cambridge, Mass.: Russell Sage Foundation and Harvard University Press.

Citro, Constance F., and Robert T. Michael. 1995. *Measuring Poverty: A New Approach.* Washington, D.C.: National Academies Press.

Danziger, Sheldon H. 2007. "Fighting Poverty Revisited: What Did Researchers Know Forty Years Ago? What Do We Know Today?" *Focus* 25(1): 3–11.

Ellwood, David T. 2000. "The Impact of the Earned Income Tax Credit and Social Policy Reforms on Work, Marriage, and Living Arrangements." *National Tax Journal* 53(4, pt. 2): 1063–1106.

Engelhardt, Gary V., and Jonathan Gruber. 2006. "Social Security and the Evolution of Elderly Poverty." In *Public Policy and the Distribution of Income,* edited by Alan Auerbach, David Card, and John Quigley. New York: Russell Sage Foundation.

European Union Social Protection Committee. 2001. "Report on Indicators in the Field of Poverty and Social Exclusion." Available at: http://ec.europa.eu/employment_social/ spsi/docs/social_protection_commitee/laeken_list.pdf (accessed July 8, 2009).

Feenberg, Daniel, and Elisabeth Coutts. 1993. "An Introduction to the TAXSIM Model." *Journal of Policy Analysis and Management* 12(1): 189–94.

Fisher, Gordon. 1986. "Estimates of the Poverty Population Under the Current Official Definition for Years Before 1959." Unpublished paper, Office of the Assistant Secretary for Planning and Evaluation, U.S. Department of Health and Human Services, Washington.

———. 1992. "The Development and History of the Poverty Thresholds." *Social Security Bulletin* 55(4): 3–14.

Freeman, Richard B. 2001. "The Rising Tide Lifts . . . ?" In *Understanding Poverty,* edited by Sheldon H. Danziger and Robert H. Haveman. New York and Cambridge, Mass.: Russell Sage Foundation and Harvard University Press.

Gornick, Janet C., and Markus Jäntti. Forthcoming. "Child Poverty in Upper-Income Countries: Lessons from the Luxembourg Income Study." In *From Child Welfare to Child Well-Being: An International Perspective on Knowledge in the Service of Making Policy,* edited by Sheila B. Kamerman, Shelley Phipps, and Asher Ben-Arieh. New York: Springer Publishing Company.

Holzer, Harry J., Steven Raphael, and Michael A. Stoll. 2006. "Employers in the Boom: How Did the Hiring of Less-Skilled Workers Change During the 1990s?" *Review of Economics and Statistics* 88(1): 283–99.

Hoynes, Hilary W., Marianne E. Page, and Ann Huff Stevens. 2006. "Poverty in America: Trends and Explanations." *Journal of Economic Perspectives* 20(1): 47–68.

Jones, Arthur F., Jr., and Daniel H. Weinberg. 2000. *The Changing Shape of the Nation's Income Distribution.* Current Population Reports P60-204. Washington: U.S. Department of Commerce, U.S. Census Bureau.

Kim, Hwanjoon. 2000. "Anti-Poverty Effectiveness of Taxes and Income Transfers in Welfare States." *International Social Security Review* 53(4): 105–29.

Levitis, Jason, and Jeremy Koulish. 2008. "State Earned Income Tax Credits: 2008 Legislative Update." Washington, D.C.: Center on Budget and Policy Priorities. Available at: http://www.cbpp.org/files/6-6-08sfp1.pdf (accessed July 8, 2009).

Meyer, Bruce D., and Dan T. Rosenbaum. 2001. "Welfare, the Earned Income Tax Credit, and the Labor Supply of Single Mothers." *Quarterly Journal of Economics* 116(3): 1063–1114.

Meyer, Bruce D., and James X. Sullivan. 2007. "Further Results on Measuring the Well-Being of the Poor Using Income and Consumption." Working paper W13413. Cambridge, Mass.: National Bureau of Economic Research.

Minoff, Elisa. 2006. "The U.K. Commitment: Ending Child Poverty by 2020." Washington, D.C.: Center for Law and Social Policy.

Osberg, Lars, Timothy M. Smeeding, and Jonathan Schwabish. 2004. "Income Distribution and Public Social Expenditure: Theories, Effects, and Evidence." In *Social Inequality*, edited by Kathryn Neckerman. New York: Russell Sage Foundation.

Palmer, Guy, Tom MacInnes, and Peter Kenway. 2007. *Monitoring Poverty and Social Exclusion 2007*. York, U.K.: Joseph Rowntree Foundation.

Plotnick, Robert D., Eugene Smolensky, Erik Evenhouse, and Siobhan Reilly. 2000. "The Twentieth-Century Record of Inequality and Poverty in the United States." In *The Cambridge Economic History of the United States*, vol. 3, edited by Stanley L. Engerman and Robert E. Gallman. Cambridge: Cambridge University Press.

Rainwater, Lee, and Timothy M. Smeeding. 2003. *Poor Kids in a Rich Country: America's Children in Comparative Perspective*. New York: Russell Sage Foundation.

Ruggles, Patricia. 1990. *Drawing the Line: Alternative Poverty Measures and Their Implications for Public Policy*. Washington, D.C.: Urban Institute.

Scholz, John Karl. 2007. "Taxation and Poverty: 1960–2006." *Focus* 25(1): 52–57.

Sen, Amartya K. 1976. "Poverty: An Original Approach to Measurement." *Econometrica* 44(2): 219–31.

Smeeding, Timothy. 2006. "Poor People in Rich Nations: The United States in Comparative Perspective." *Journal of Economic Perspectives* 20(1): 69–90.

Smith, Adam. 1852. *An Inquiry into the Nature and Causes of the Wealth of Nations*. London: T. Nelson and Sons. Available at: http://books.google.com.

U.S. Department of Commerce, Bureau of the Census. Various years. Current Population Survey: Annual Demographic Files, 1969–2002. Washington: U.S. Dept. of Commerce, Bureau of the Census [producer], 1969–2002. Ann Arbor, Mich.: Inter-university Consortium for Political and Social Research [distributor], 1969–2002.

U.S. Department of Commerce, Bureau of the Census, and U.S. Department of Labor, Bureau of Labor Statistics. Various years. Current Population Survey: Annual Social and Economic (ASEC) Supplement Surveys, 2003–2007. ICPSR21321-v1. Ann Arbor, Mich.: Inter-university Consortium for Political and Social Research [distributor], 2003–2007.

Ziliak, James P. 2006. "Understanding Poverty Rates and Gaps: Concepts, Trends, and Challenges." *Foundations and Trends in Microeconomics* 1(3): 127–99.

———. 2008. "Filling the Poverty Gap: Then and Now." In *Frontiers of Family Economics*, vol. 1, edited by Peter Rupert. Bingley, U.K.: Emerald Group.

Chapter 3

Economic Change and the Structure of Opportunity for Less-Skilled Workers

Rebecca M. Blank

The primary source of support for most non-elderly adults comes from their employment and earnings. Hence, understanding the jobs and wages available to less-educated workers is key to understanding changes in the well-being of low-income populations. Expansions and contractions in the macroeconomy influence unemployment rates, wages, and overall economic growth, all of which are important determinants of the economic circumstances facing low-income families.

This chapter focuses on the trends in labor market and macroeconomic circumstances that particularly affect less-educated and low-wage workers. The first section looks at changes in work behavior among individuals by skill level, the second at unemployment and job availability. The third section investigates trends in earnings and discusses the reasons behind substantial earnings shifts among less-educated men and women since 1980. The fourth section looks at the most disadvantaged families and investigates the relationship between macroeconomic and labor market factors and poverty rates. The final section discusses policy implications.

A primary finding is that low-income families are more reliant on jobs and earnings in the 2000s than they were in past decades. This is particularly true for less-skilled single mothers, who greatly increased their earnings following welfare reform in the mid-1990s. Maintaining a high-employment economy, with stable or growing wages and jobs that are readily available to less-educated workers, continues to be the most important antipoverty policy for this country. The deep recession that began in 2007 and has already brought unemployment rates to their highest levels in twenty-five years is likely to cause significant increases in poverty.

WORK BEHAVIOR AMONG LESS-EDUCATED PERSONS

The economy primarily affects individuals who are working or actively looking for work. Because trends in labor force participation since 1980 have differed between less-educated men and women, I discuss the factors influencing work behavior among men first.

FIGURE 3.1 / Male Labor Force Participation by Skill Level, 1979 to 2007

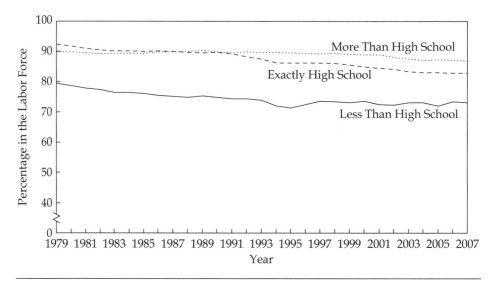

Source: Author's compilation based on Current Population Survey Outgoing Rotation Group data (U.S. Bureau of the Census, various years).
Note: Based on all non-institutionalized civilian adults age eighteen to sixty-five.

Changes in Work Among Less-Educated Men

Employment declined markedly among less-educated men between 1979 and 2007, although more of this decline occurred between 1979 and 1995 than in the more recent decade. Figure 3.1 shows the trends over this time period in the share of men between the ages of eighteen and fifty-four who reported themselves as either working or looking for work.[1] The solid line shows labor force participation among men who did not hold a high school diploma. The dashed line shows labor force participation among men who held only a high school diploma, while the dotted line represents men who had at least some schooling beyond high school.

Men with more than a high school diploma have always been highly likely to work, with about a 90 percent labor force participation rate throughout this time period. (The slight decline is due to growing years of school and earlier years of retirement within this group.) In contrast, men with only a high school diploma or less have seen substantial declines in labor market involvement. The participation rate among non-elderly men without a high school diploma fell from 79 percent to 73 percent between 1979 and 2007; among those with exactly a high school diploma it fell from 92 percent to 83 percent. These declines are particularly steep among African American men (data not shown).

Later I discuss wage declines for these men, particularly over the 1980s. Chinhui Juhn (1992) indicates that virtually all of the decline in less-skilled men's labor force participation over the 1980s can be explained by declining wages. More recent declines are less easily understood. While labor force participation has risen slightly among the least-educated, it continues to decline among those with just a high school education. This is true even though unemployment rates remained relatively low throughout the 1990s and early 2000s. Harry Holzer, Paul Offner, and Elaine Sorensen (2005) indicate that increased incarceration (making men less employable upon release) and increased child support enforcement (making work less lucrative) explain some, but not all, of the decline in labor force participation among young black men. There appears to have been a behavioral change in labor market involvement among less-skilled young men, especially black men, that was unrelated to measurable economic variables. It is unclear whether the deep recession that started in 2007 will exacerbate these trends as even fewer jobs are available.

Even more disturbing, these data underestimate the declining labor market involvement of less-skilled men because they exclude men in the armed forces and in prisons and jail. Over the past two decades, incarceration rates have risen rapidly, especially among lower-skilled black men (Western 2006). Thus, fewer less-skilled men are now in the non-institutionalized population used to measure labor force participation statistics.

Table 3.1 indicates the magnitude of this effect for selected years between 1980 and 2006. The number of men in jails or prisons under state or federal jurisdiction grew from around 420,500 in 1980 to just over 2 million in 2006, while the size of the armed forces shrank from 1.86 million to 1.17 million. The first two rows show the actual employment-to-population ratio for the non-institutionalized civilian population and the estimated ratio if one includes the armed forces in both the population and the employment numbers and the men in jails and prisons in the population (but not in employment). The net effect is to increase the employment-to-population ratio in 1980, from 72.0 percent to 72.3 percent, as the addition of the (employed) armed forces more than dominates the addition of (not employed) prisoners. By 2006 the growing prison population has a larger effect than the shrinking armed forces population, and the net effect is to decrease the employment-to-population ratio from 70.1 percent to 69.1 percent. This adjustment suggests that declines in labor force participation would have been even larger if a growing number of men had not been incarcerated.

The last three columns in table 3.1 present these same data by race for 2006. In this year, adding in the armed forces and the prison and jail populations would reduce the employment-to-population ratio by less than 0.4 percentage points for white men, by 3.4 percentage points for black men, and by 1.9 percentage points for Hispanic men. This reflects the much larger rate of incarceration among black and Hispanic men.

The bottom two rows of table 3.1 compare the actual unemployment rate with a simulated rate that includes the armed forces in the employed population and the prison population in the labor force. In this simulation, I count all armed forces personnel as employed. I assume that 80 percent of prisoners would be in

TABLE 3.1 / The Effect of Including Armed Forces Members and Men in Prisons and Jails
in Men's Labor Force Statistics, Based on All Men Age Sixteen and Older

					2006		
	1980	1990	2000	2006	White	Black	Hispanic
Employment-to-population ratio							
Actual	72.0%	72.0%	71.9%	70.1%	70.2%	60.3%	76.8%
Including armed forces and inmates[a]	72.3	71.8	71.0	69.1	69.8	56.9	74.9
Unemployment rate							
Actual	6.9	5.7	3.9	4.6	3.9	9.6	4.8
Simulated[b]	6.8	5.7	4.2	5.0	4.1	10.6	5.3

Sources: Author's compilation based on U.S. Department of Labor, Bureau of Labor Statistics, http://www.bls.gov/home.htm; "Unpublished Tables from the Current Population Survey, Annual Averages, 2006." U.S. Department of Defense, Defense Manpower Data Center, DRS 21811 as of September 30 for selected years. U.S. Department of Justice, Bureau of Justice Statistics, *Prisoners at Midyear 1995* and *Prison and Jail Inmates at Midyear 2000 and 2006,* http://www.ojp.usdoj.gov/bjs/prisons.htm; *Male Prisoners Under State or Federal Jurisdiction, 1977–2004* and *Jail Inmates by Sex, 1978–1993,* http://www.ojp.usdoj.gov/bjs/dtdata.htm#corrections.
a. Adds armed forces members into both employment and population; adds men in prisons and jails into population but not employment.
b. Unemployment rate estimated to include all armed forces personnel in the labor force. This simulation assumes that all men in prisons and jails were available to work and that 80 percent of inmates would be in the labor force if it were an option, but that the unemployment rate would be 25 percent among this population.

the labor force if they had this option, and that their unemployment rate would be 25 percent. While high, this unemployment rate is not unreasonable for those who have been incarcerated. This simulation has almost no effect on the overall unemployment rate in 1980 or 1990. By 2006, however, the simulated unemployment rate is 5.0 percent compared to the actual 4.6 percent rate, more than 8 percent higher. The simulations for 2006 by race raise unemployment among black non-elderly men by a full percentage point, from 9.6 percent to 10.6 percent, among Hispanics by 0.5 percentage points, and among whites by 0.2 percentage points.

In short, if we adjusted our labor force statistics to include the armed forces and to take into account the growing incarceration rates among men, our labor force statistics would look worse than they do. We would have seen even faster declines in labor force participation than were actually observed, because the share of men in prison has increased rapidly. This compositional effect has also lowered unemployment rates by removing young men, who are likely to have very high unemployment rates. And of course, it is worth noting that these high rates of incarceration also reduce future employment and earnings once these men are released (Western 2006; Holzer, Raphael, and Stoll 2007).

The share of the less-skilled labor force that is composed of immigrants rather than the native-born has also increased. Table 3.2, taken from Borjas (2006), shows

TABLE 3.2 / Immigrant Population Share by Skill Level, 1980, 1990, and 2000

	1980	1990	2000
Men: Percentage immigrant			
Less than high school	11.1%	23.6%	41.2%
Exactly high school	3.9	6.6	11.0
More than high school	6.2	7.8	10.6
Women: Percentage immigrant			
Less than high school	12.2	21.6	35.1
Exactly high school	4.5	6.2	9.8
More than high school	5.9	6.8	9.0

Source: Census data presented in Borjas (2006), table 2.1.

the percentage of men and women who were immigrants in three different education groups, using census data from 1980, 1990, and 2000. Among those without a high school diploma, the share of men who were immigrants increased from 11.1 percent to 41.2 percent between 1980 and 2000; among similar women, the immigrant share rose from 12.2 percent to 35.1 percent.[2] Although the groups with more education also show substantial increases in immigrant share, the numbers are much lower. For both men and women with a high school diploma or with higher levels of schooling, the immigrant share was around 10 percent in 2000. Most of these immigrants were Hispanic workers, with a much smaller share who were Asian, black, or white. All else being equal, rising immigration has helped to raise labor force participation over time. Of course, all else may not be equal. Labor force participation among natives may be reduced by immigration (see Raphael and Smolensky, this volume; Borjas, Freeman, and Katz 1997).

Changes in Work Among Less-Educated Women

Figure 3.2 shows labor force participation changes among women between 1979 and 2007, differentiating between the same three education groups as in figure 3.1. The trends in work behavior in the formal labor market are quite different for women versus men. In general, all women have increased their labor force involvement since 1979, although the patterns of change differ across groups. Women with post–high school training (the dotted line in figure 3.2) show steady increases in work, from 68.0 percent in 1979 to 78.8 percent in 1998, after which the rate falls slightly, to 76.6 percent, in 2007. High school graduates show a similar pattern, starting at 61.7 percent in 1979, peaking at 69.9 percent in 1997, and falling to 66.8 percent in 2007.

In contrast, women who were high school dropouts had labor force participation rates just over 44 percent from 1979 to 1994. Their rate increased to over 50 percent by 2000, then declined slightly to 47.8 percent by 2007. The increase in work among

FIGURE 3.2 / Female Labor Force Participation by Skill Level, 1979 to 2007

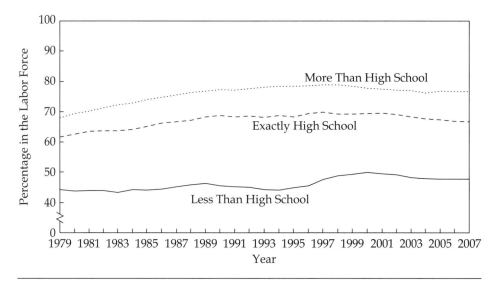

Source: Author's compilation based on Current Population Survey Outgoing Rotation Group data (U.S. Bureau of the Census, various years).
Note: Based on all non-institutionalized civilian adults age eighteen to sixty-five.

the least-educated women in the mid-1990s was related to the policy changes in welfare and in work subsidies enacted at that time. Cash welfare support became much less available, and those on welfare were required to participate in welfare-to-work programs. A very large number of single-mother families left welfare and increased their earnings. At the same time, expansions in the Earned Income Tax Credit (EITC) made work more attractive. Research has linked work expansions among less-skilled women with both the EITC expansions and the welfare reform changes (Blank 2002; Grogger and Karoly 2005; Cancian and Reed, this volume).

Increases in incarceration have had little net effect on women's overall labor force statistics. Although the share of incarcerated women has grown substantially, the total number remains quite low.

Of greater concern is the growing number of women who have left welfare but have not found employment. Rebecca Blank and Brian Kovak (2009) document increases in the number of "disconnected women"—single mothers who are neither working nor on welfare. A high share of these women face barriers to employment, such as learning disabilities, mental and physical health problems, past histories of domestic violence or sexual abuse, or other issues that limit their ability to hold full-time, steady employment. Much more extensive interventions are needed to move this population to economic self-sufficiency (Blank 2007).

Similar to less-skilled men, a growing share of women without a high school diploma are immigrants, as table 3.2 indicates. In 2000, 35.1 percent of these women were born outside the country. Immigrant shares remain lower among women than among men, in part because single men are more likely to immigrate. Immigrant women are also less likely to be in the labor force than are native-born women.

In sum, since 1979 men's labor force participation has fallen, but women's has risen. A primary reason for this is different wage trends among less-skilled men and women. We turn to that issue after a discussion of job availability.

JOB AVAILABILITY, UNEMPLOYMENT, AND THE BUSINESS CYCLE

Labor force participation measures the share of the population that is working or looking for work. If a high share of those in the labor force are without a job but searching, this indicates lower well-being than when employment is high. Hence, the overall unemployment rate is an important indicator of economic well-being, particularly for lower-wage workers, who generally face higher unemployment rates than more-skilled workers.

Changes in Unemployment

Figure 3.3 plots unemployment rates by education level between 1979 and 2007 for the three groups shown in figures 3.1 and 3.2. Data are not shown separately for men and women, in part because their unemployment rates move together very closely. Women's unemployment is slightly higher than men's in most years, particularly among high school dropouts.

Unemployment rates were relatively low from the mid-1990s to the mid-2000s, certainly in comparison to the early 1980s, when unemployment rose steeply. Among those with less than a high school diploma, unemployment was 16.4 percent in 1983. Even as overall unemployment fell, unemployment rates among the less skilled exceeded 8 percent in every year between 1979 and 2007, even during the booming years of the 1990s. Those with less than a high school diploma had an unemployment rate of 8.7 percent in 2007, well above the 5.2 percent for high school graduates and the 3.1 percent for those with post–high school training. While we do not yet have 2008 data available, unemployment rose sharply over this year as the economy moved into recession, and overall unemployment rates in 2009 are expected to rival or exceed those of the early 1980s. The historical pattern is clearly being repeated in the recession of the late 2000s, as unemployment among the least skilled is rising much more rapidly than unemployment among more highly skilled workers.

Changes in Jobs and Job Availability

Since the mid-1980s, the labor market has absorbed a large increase in less-skilled immigrant workers and a large increase in less-skilled native-born women workers,

FIGURE 3.3 / Unemployment Rates by Skill Level, 1979 to 2007

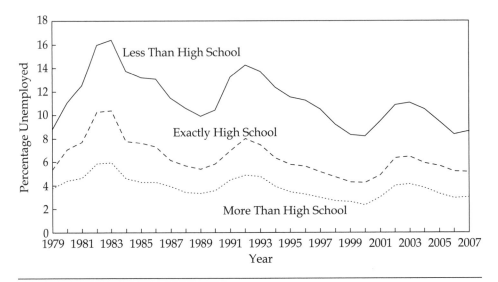

Source: Author's compilation based on Current Population Survey Outgoing Rotation Group data (U.S. Bureau of the Census, various years).
Note: Based on all non-institutionalized civilian adults age eighteen to sixty-five.

while experiencing relatively low and stable unemployment rates through most of this period. Even with some decline in male labor force participation among less-educated workers, the U.S. economy has been the envy of many other countries that have faced much higher unemployment and lower labor force participation over the past two decades. This reflects strong overall U.S. economic growth during these decades, which created a growing number of jobs.

There has been much concern about the declining number of "good jobs" that pay high wages and provide fringe benefits for less-educated workers. Figure 3.4 plots changes in manufacturing jobs from 1985 to 2007 among men and women.[3] The black bars show the percentage of all workers employed in manufacturing. The gray bars show the share of less-skilled workers (those with a high school diploma or less) working in manufacturing. Manufacturing jobs have declined dramatically—among all male workers, the share employed in manufacturing fell from 29.1 percent in 1985 to 16.8 percent in 2007. Among less-educated men, this decline has been even faster, from 33.5 percent in 1985 to 19.5 percent in 2007. Women have always been less likely to work in manufacturing; by 2007 fewer than 10 percent of women workers were in this industry. Less-educated women saw their manufacturing employment decline from 22.4 percent to 12.3 percent between 1985 and 2007.

The decline in manufacturing jobs has not meant that fewer jobs are available for less-skilled workers; rather, it has meant that different jobs are available. For instance, figure 3.5 shows the share of workers in retail trade and selected service

FIGURE 3.4 / Workers in Manufacturing Jobs by Gender and Skill, 1985 to 2007

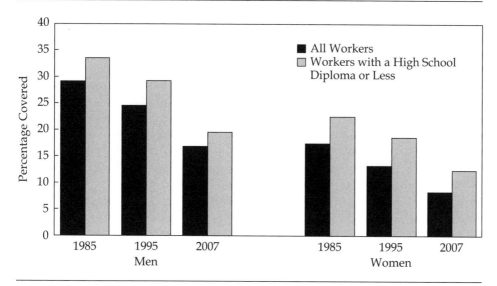

Source: Author's compilation based on the March Current Population Survey (U.S. Bureau of the Census, various years).
Note: Worker counts include all current employment in durable and nondurable manufacturing.

FIGURE 3.5 / Workers in Retail Trade and Selected Service Jobs by Gender and Skill, 1985 to 2007

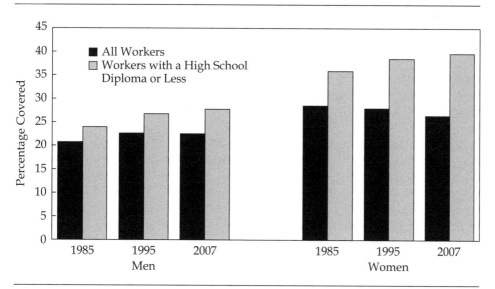

Source: Author's compilation based on the March Current Population Survey (U.S. Bureau of the Census, various years).
Note: Worker counts include all current employment in retail trade, arts and entertainment, recreation, accommodation, food and drinking places, and personal laundry services.

jobs, including hotels, restaurants, and entertainment and tourism. The share of less-educated men in these jobs grew from 23.9 percent to 27.7 percent between 1985 and 2007, and the share of less-educated women from 35.8 percent to 39.6 percent.

Figure 3.5 shows growth in a selected set of jobs. There has also been substantial employment growth among less-educated workers in health care and in clerical jobs. Such industry shifts, reducing manufacturing jobs but increasing other job opportunities, can cause severe short-term disruptions for individuals who find themselves seeking work in very different sectors of the economy. Particularly among less-educated men, the jobs they used to hold have become much less available. In aggregate, however, there have been jobs available to less-skilled workers over the past three decades. The problem has not been job availability, but the wages that these jobs pay, as we discuss later in this chapter.

The Effect of the Economic Cycle on Less-Skilled Workers

Less-educated workers are more affected by cyclical movements in economic growth than are more-educated workers. When unemployment rises, less-educated workers are more likely to lose their jobs, to move into part-time work, or to leave the labor force entirely. A glance at unemployment trends among more- and less-educated workers (figure 3.3) indicates that unemployment among the less-educated is much more cyclical than among more-educated workers (Hoynes 2000; Blank and Shierholz 2006).

An interesting question is whether the economic situation of less-educated workers has become more or less sensitive to changes in unemployment over time. One group that has become more vulnerable to economic fluctuations, in part as a result of welfare reform, is low-income, single-mother families. Prior to welfare reform, unmarried women with children were less affected by unemployment because they had ready access to cash assistance. As this has changed, their reliance on the labor market has risen, and hence their exposure to unemployment and economic cycles has grown.

A mild recession in 2001 appeared to have little effect on single mothers, but this recession was concentrated in manufacturing and traded goods industries, sectors where few less-skilled women are employed. In 2001 consumer spending remained strong, continuing to create demand for low-skilled workers in retail trade and in hotel and food services. Unfortunately, the recession that started in 2007 is much more widespread and has affected all sectors of the U.S. economy. By the end of 2008, unemployment among women had risen sharply and cash public assistance caseloads had begun to rise for the first time since the welfare reforms of the 1990s. Food stamp usage increased sharply as well. This recession will test whether states are able or willing to provide cash assistance to growing numbers of nonworking single mothers when unemployment is high, and it will also test the federal government's willingness to assist states in funding caseload increases during a recession.

FIGURE 3.6 / Real Median Weekly Wages Among Men by Skill Level, 1979 to 2007

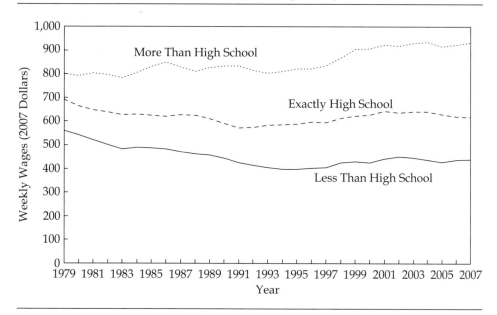

Source: Author's compilation based on Current Population Survey Outgoing Rotation Group data, 1979 to 2007 (U.S. Bureau of the Census, various years).
Notes: Adjusted to full-time equivalents. Inflation adjusted to 2007 dollars using the PCE deflator from the Bureau of Economic Analysis. Based on all non-institutionalized civilian adults age eighteen to sixty-five.

WHAT DO LESS-EDUCATED WORKERS EARN, AND WHY HAS THIS BEEN CHANGING?

The U.S. economy has long been praised for its very flexible labor market, which has led to substantial job creation and relatively low unemployment rates in comparison to many European nations. This flexibility has also created a larger number of lower-wage jobs. On the one hand, the United States has maintained relatively low unemployment rates. On the other hand, the wages paid in these jobs are low.

Wage Trends Among Less-Educated Men

Figure 3.6 graphs the trends in real median weekly wage rates among men between 1979 and 2007, by the same three education groups that were shown in figures 3.1, 3.2, and 3.3. The solid line plots weekly wages among those without a high school diploma; the dashed line shows wages among those with only a high school diploma; and the dotted line shows median weekly wages among men with

FIGURE 3.7 / Real Median Weekly Wages Among Women by Skill Level, 1979 to 2007

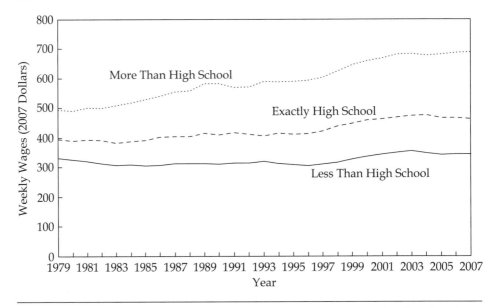

Source: Author's compilation based on Current Population Survey Outgoing Rotation Group data, 1979 to 2007 (U.S. Bureau of the Census, various years).
Notes: Adjusted to full-time equivalents. Inflation adjusted to 2007 dollars using the PCE deflator from the Bureau of Economic Analysis. Based on all non-institutionalized civilian adults age eighteen to sixty-five.

post–high school training. These data are in 2007 dollars, adjusted for inflation and expressed in "full-time equivalents," so that differences in hours of work over time do not affect them.[4]

As has been widely noted, wages for less-skilled men declined substantially after 1979. Those without a high school diploma saw their weekly wages for full-time work decline from $562 in 1979 to $398 in 1994; for those with a high school diploma, wages fell from $693 in 1979 to a low point of $572 in 1991. Among those with post–high school education, wages rose slightly, from $802 in 1979 to $812 in 1994. (There were much larger increases among men with a college education.) Since the early 1990s, wages have risen at all skill levels. By 2007 full-time weekly wages were $439 for high school dropouts, $619 for high school graduates, and $934 for those with more than a high school diploma. For the two less-educated groups, however, these levels are still well below where they were in 1979.

Wage Trends Among Less-Educated Women

In contrast to less-educated men, less-educated women experienced little drop in wages over the 1980s. Figure 3.7 shows trends in real median weekly wages for full-time work among women by education group between 1979 and 2007. High school graduate women saw significant wage increases over this period, while wages grew much less among those with less than a high school diploma. Female dropouts reported median weekly wages that increased from $331 to $344 between 1979 and 2007. Female high school graduates saw wages grow from $395 in 1979 to $463 in 2007. More skilled women experienced quite steep growth, from $494 in 1979 to $688 in 2007.

These changes narrowed the wage gap between less-educated women and men from 59 percent in 1979 to 78 percent in 2007. The wage gap among more-skilled men and women narrowed as well because more-skilled women's wages rose faster than equivalent men's wages.

Explaining the Wage Shifts

The period since 1979 has been a period of rising wage inequality. There is general agreement that the rise in inequality (and the decline in real wages) in the bottom half of the wage distribution occurred primarily in the 1980s. There was little change in relative wages in the bottom part of the distribution after that decade. In contrast, inequality in the top half of the wage distribution has risen steadily throughout this time period as wages among the highest-skilled workers have continued to rise rapidly (Lemieux 2008a; Autor, Katz, and Kearney 2008).

Figures 3.8 and 3.9 document these trends, using data from David Autor, Lawrence Katz, and Melissa Kearney (2008), who provide comparable numbers from the 1960s onward.[5] Figure 3.8 shows the log (50/20) wage ratio (that is, the log of wages at the median of the distribution divided by wages at the twentieth percentile of the distribution) from 1969 through 2006. The solid line shows the log (50/20) wage ratio among men, while the dashed line shows the ratio among women. The steep increase in male wage inequality in the late 1970s and early 1980s is clearly visible, with little change after the mid-1980s. Wages at the median and the twentieth percentile of the male wage distribution have moved together since that time. The log (50/20) wage ratio for women rose less rapidly in the 1980s and has also been largely flat since then.

In contrast, Figure 3.9 graphs the log (80/50) wage ratio for men and women, showing wage changes among higher-paid workers at the eightieth percentile of the distribution relative to those at the median. For both women and men, these wage ratios grew steadily from the mid-1970s onward. Autor, Katz, and Kearney (2008) note that much of the growth in high-end wages after 1990 occurred among workers with more than a college degree rather than among those with a four-year college degree.

In fact, the evidence suggests that wages among the least-skilled and the most-skilled have grown slightly faster over the past fifteen years, while wages in the middle have stagnated. Thomas Lemieux (2008a, 2008b) indicates that wages grew most rapidly below the twentieth percentile and above the sixtieth percentile of the wage distribution between 1989 and 2004. The result is a U-shaped curve in wage growth over the wage distribution. (The U "turns up" much more at the upper end

FIGURE 3.8 / Log 50/20 Wage Ratio by Gender, 1969 to 2006

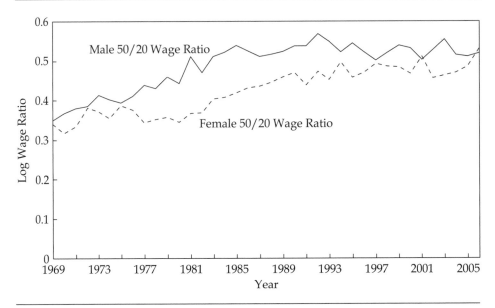

Source: Author's compilation based on data provided by David Autor (Autor, Katz, and Kearney 2008). Original data from the March Current Population Survey.
Note: Weekly wages calculated as annual earnings divided by weeks worked in the last year.

than at the bottom of the distribution because wage growth among high-wage earners was much larger than among lower-wage earners.) This U-shaped pattern in wage growth is particularly noticeable for men. Hence, while less-skilled men lost earnings power over the 1980s, they have experienced more wage growth in recent years, even if this more recent wage growth has not brought them back to the same level of real wages.

The wage losses among less-skilled workers in the 1980s appear to have been due to numerous forces.[6] A primary factor is what economists call skill-biased technological change (SBTC), which occurs when changes in technology increase labor demand for workers at higher skill levels.[7] Technological changes in the 1980s led to SBTC, with increased computer use in a growing number of applications, from robotics to just-in-time inventory systems. This increased demand for more-skilled workers outstripped supply increases, driving up wages. At the same time, demand for less-skilled workers fell. Autor, Levy, and Murnane (2003) and Autor, Katz, and Kearney (2008) indicate that SBTC has continued to affect the labor market in the 1990s and 2000s but is primarily driving widening wages in the top half of the wage distribution as information technology continues to increase demand for the most-skilled workers, while displacing moderately skilled workers who perform more routine tasks.

FIGURE 3.9   /   Log 80/50 Wage Ratio by Gender, 1969 to 2006

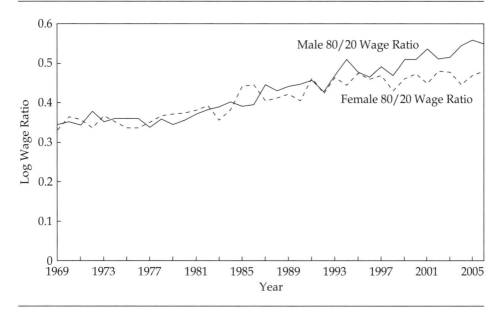

Source: Author's compilation based on data provided by David Autor (Autor, Katz, and Kearney 2008). Original data from the March Current Population Survey.
Note: Weekly wages calculated as annual earnings divided by weeks worked in the last year.

The popular discussion of stagnating wages often emphasizes growing trade and the internationalization of the economy. Less-skilled workers in less-developed countries typically earn much lower wages than less-skilled workers in the United States. Outsourcing production components that require only limited skill inputs can save a company money and reduce their demand for less-skilled labor in the United States. The research literature has downplayed the importance of trade in rising wage inequality and falling wages among less-skilled workers, suggesting that declining wages would have occurred even without the growth in global markets (Berman, Bound, and Griliches 1994). Recent work does suggest that trade in intermediate inputs, leading to changes in industrial organization, can be important (Feenstra and Hanson 2003). Paul Krugman (2008) provides reasons why trade shifts since the mid-1990s (particularly the rise of China) might make trade a more important factor for the evolution of less-skilled wages in the United States, although this effect is very difficult to measure.[8]

Some researchers have noted that institutional changes contributed to the declining wages of less-skilled workers, in addition to changes due to trade or technology. For instance, David Card (1996) notes that the rapid decline in unions over this period explains about 20 percent of the wage decline among the least skilled. Unions often raise wages at the bottom of the distribution, and the decline of unions has left less-skilled jobs that previously were somewhat protected by union bargaining efforts more open to market vicissitudes. Unionization declined rapidly among all workers between 1985 and 2007 but fell faster among the less-skilled. Among less-skilled men, collective bargaining coverage declined from 28 percent to 15 percent between 1985 and 2007. Fewer women are in jobs covered by bargaining—their coverage decline over the same period was from 14.1 percent to 8.5 percent by 2007.[9]

In addition, the minimum wage remained constant throughout the 1980s, and its declining real value was an important factor in pushing wages downward among the less skilled (Lee 1999). John DiNardo, Nicole Fortin, and Thomas Lemieux (1996) note that female workers were particularly affected, since a disproportionately large number of them work in minimum-wage jobs. Of course, changes in minimum wages and in unionization may not be exogenous forces independent from changes in technology or in trade. Increasing global competition in U.S. manufacturing was one cause of declining unionization. Falling demand for less-skilled workers may have strengthened resistance to minimum-wage increases over the 1980s.

The declines in minimum wages in the 1980s were partially made up by minimum-wage increases in 1989, 1996, and 2006 and, for workers with children, by increases in the Earned Income Tax Credit (EITC). The EITC was greatly expanded in 1993 so that a growing share of low-wage workers could receive tax refunds, even if they owed no taxes. Figure 3.10 shows pretax (solid line) and post-tax (dashed line) income, inflation-adjusted, for a single mother with two children working full-time at a minimum-wage job from 1979 through 2007. During the 1980s, her real wages fell steadily with inflation erosion in the minimum wage. The minimum-wage increases of 1989, 1996, and 2006 are clearly visible in the graph. Even more important, however, is the expansion in the EITC, which by 2007 had increased her income by over $3,000.[10] It is clear that policy (a non-inflation-indexed minimum wage) worked to lower wages in the 1980s, but that minimum-wage increases and EITC expansions helped raise earnings in the 1990s.

Lemieux (2008b) describes the 1980s as a "perfect storm" in which multiple technological, institutional, and policy factors resulted in an expansion in inequality across the wage distribution. These forces, however, appear to have been more quiescent in the past fifteen years. Since the early 1990s, demand and wage changes have benefited highly skilled workers and flattened wages for middle-range workers. Less-skilled workers have seen moderate wage gains.

Of course, wage changes have to be compared to price changes. If prices are falling, then lower wages may not leave families worse off. A recent paper by Christian Broda and John Romalis (2008) argues that increased trade over the past three decades has resulted in substantive price declines in the nondurable goods bought by lower-income families. This paper, however, does not look at the total market basket of goods. Housing prices, which constitute a substantial share of lower-income family budgets, have risen substantially over the past three decades in many areas, and the share of budgets going to housing has increased (Brennan and Lipman 2007).

It is interesting to compare the U.S. experience to the experience of many western European nations. As in the United States, unemployment rose steeply in Europe in

FIGURE 3.10 / Pretax and Post-Tax Income for a Single Mother Working at the Minimum Wage, 1979 to 2007

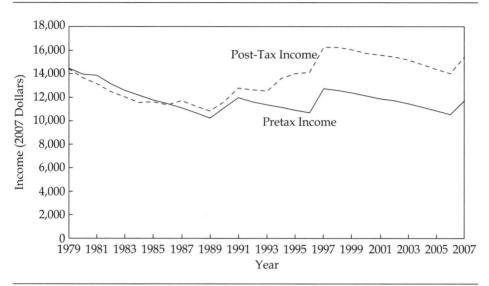

Source: Author's compilation based on minumum-wage data from the U.S. Department of Labor, *History of Federal Minimum Wage Rates Under the Fair Labor Standards Act, 1938–2007,* available at: http://www.dol.gov/esa/minwage/chart.htm. Tax liabilities and credits for all years calculated using the NBER TAXSIM model, version 8.0, available at: http://www.nber.org/~taxsim/.
Notes: This single-mother family is estimated to have one full-time worker at the minimum wage (for a total of 2,000 annual hours of work) and two children. Federal income tax, FICA payroll taxes, and EITC are included in post-tax calculations. Figures inflated to 2007 dollars using the PCE deflator.

the 1970s; unlike in the United States, it has remained very high in the decades since, although some countries have been more successful at lowering unemployment in recent years. An extensive research literature has focused on the flexibility of the U.S. labor market, which has fewer job protection policies, versus more rigid European labor markets, where it is expensive to hire or fire workers (see, for instance, Bean 1994; Freeman and Katz 1995). Indeed, most European countries have altered their labor market policies to create more labor market flexibility. This has involved changes such as shorter periods of unemployment benefit payments, more limited job severance payments, and fewer restrictions on part-time work.

Yet, while unemployment remained high in Europe, wage inequality in most European countries did not grow as it did in the United States. And only in the United States were there significant wage declines among less-educated workers. European countries appear to have developed a set of institutions that better protected less-educated workers, with higher minimum-wage levels, more centralized collective bargaining, and higher unemployment payments (Freeman and

Katz 1995). Hence, the flexible U.S. labor market allowed significant wage changes and widening inequality, particularly in the 1980s, but was able to offer an ongoing supply of low-wage jobs. In contrast, European labor markets were more rigid. This protected the incomes of less-educated workers but resulted in significant job loss. Reviewing this evidence, Olivier Blanchard (2006) concludes that the lesson is to protect workers but not jobs, allowing flexibility in job creation (and destruction) and assisting those who are displaced, but incentivizing workers to seek new employment.

Despite the positive changes since the mid-1990s, the long-term wage outlook for less-skilled workers is not rosy. All predictions for the future suggest that global demand for more-skilled workers will increase; it is hard to tell a story in which the demand for less-skilled workers will increase very much within the United States. The labor market for the less-skilled has been relatively robust for the past fifteen years, however, with low unemployment and slowly rising wages. At best, one can hope that demand remains stable and that a growing U.S. service sector continues to need workers in low-skill jobs.

Finally, it is worth commenting on the relationship between wage changes and family income changes. Difficulties in the low-wage labor market might be expected to translate into declining family incomes and rising poverty. Poverty is based on family incomes, which depend upon the composition of families, the number of earners, and the amount worked by each earner. For instance, the increase in single-parent families, all else held constant, has lowered family income.

While family incomes among lower-income families did not rise in the 1980s, neither did they fall as men's wages fell. This was the case among married couples because wives' labor force involvement expanded and wives' earnings offset the decline in male earnings (Cancian and Reed 1999). Adults in families, particularly women, were working more in order to maintain the same level of real income. As a result, family income growth has been stronger than wage growth. While it is good that the economic situation of families has not deteriorated, extra work hours have meant fewer hours spent at home in child care or home production. This has changed the composition of spending within households. Because families have to buy more of what used to be produced at home (for example, child care, food preparation, and other services), it is not clear what has happened to overall family well-being. A family at the same—or even a higher—income level in which the adults are working more hours in the market and buying more child care to support that work may have less disposable income and be worse off (see Meyer and Wallace, this volume). Family incomes also depend upon nonwage sources of income, and lower-income families are often affected by changes in public transfer policies (Scholz, Moffitt, and Cowan, this volume).

POVERTY AND THE MACROECONOMY

A family of four with an income below $21,000 was considered poor in 2007 in the United States. An ongoing literature has looked at the responsiveness of poverty to changing economic variables and found that the effects of unemployment on poverty appear to have shifted over time (see, for instance, Blank and Blinder 1986; Blank and Card 1993; Haveman and Schwabish 2000; Gunderson and Ziliak 2004). Analysis of data through the 1970s reveals a very large effect of rising unemployment on rising poverty; however, this relationship deteriorated in the 1980s, with unemployment and poverty becoming more disconnected. Recent evidence suggests that the unemployment-poverty link strengthened again in the 1990s.

Revisiting the question of how poverty is related to the macroeconomy, I have added data from the 2000s and also have tried to measure the effects of widening wage inequality with greater precision. I start with a comparison of two regressions:

$$P_t = \alpha + \rho P_{t-1} + \beta \times UR_t + \delta \times WR_t + \gamma \times X_t + \varepsilon_t \tag{3.1}$$

and

$$P_t = \alpha_1 + \alpha_2 \times D80 + \alpha_3 \times D90 + \alpha_4 \times D00 + \rho P_{t-1} + \beta_1 \times UR_t + \beta_2 \times UR_t \\ \times D80 + \beta_3 \times UR_t \times D90 + \beta_4 \times UR_t \times D00 + \delta \times WR_t + \gamma \times X_t + \varepsilon_t \tag{3.2}$$

The dependent variable, P, is a measure of poverty. I show regressions using a variety of different dependent variables: the percentage of all persons in poverty; adults (age eighteen to sixty-five), children, and elderly in poverty; whites, blacks, and Hispanics in poverty; and single individuals, single mothers with children, and married couples with children in poverty. Official poverty statistics start in 1959, but for many of these groups data are not available until 1966 or 1973. I use as much data as available for each group. I also include a lagged dependent variable, so that the coefficients on other variables measure the effect of those variables on changes in poverty.

Explanatory variables include the annual unemployment rate, UR. Because prior studies have noted that the unemployment rate had different effects after 1970, in equation 3.2, I interact UR with three dummy variables. $D80$ equals one in every year during the decade of the 1980s; $D90$ is a dummy variable covering the decade of the 1990s; and $D00$ is a dummy variable for the years 2000 to 2006. The coefficients on these interactive terms will tell us whether there are differential unemployment effects in the three most recent decades. In this specification, I also include the three dummy variables by themselves, to allow the intercept of the regression to shift in each decade. This is similar to regressions that others have run to look at the changing impact of unemployment on poverty over time.

I also include the log 50/10 wage ratio, WR, which controls for shifts in wages among the lowest-paid workers, relative to median workers.[11] The remaining explanatory variables, the vector X in equations 3.1 and 3.2, include the consumer price index (CPI) to measure inflation and a measure of government antipoverty spending, defined as federal expenditures on public assistance programs in each year (excluding medical care expenditures) as a share of GDP. This measure includes most means-tested transfer programs, including cash welfare, Supplemental Security Income (SSI), energy and food assistance programs, and the EITC.[12]

I also include a measure of where the poverty line sits in the overall income distribution, which is specified as the poverty line divided by median income. The poverty line has been adjusted only by inflation since the early 1960s, when it was defined. Hence, as real economic growth and distributional changes led to changes in the location and shape of the income distribution, the poverty line moved from 49 percent of median income in 1959 to 28 percent in 2005 (Blank 2008). This shift in the location of the poverty line should mechanically result in a change in poverty counts, as fewer people will be poor (that is, will lie below the line) when the line hits at a lower level in the income distribution.[13]

Table 3.3 presents the results of these regressions using the poverty rate for all persons as the dependent variable. Column 1 corresponds to equation 3.1. The coefficients in column 1 show a strong correlation between the current and lagged poverty rate, as expected. There is also a strong positive relationship between increases in unemployment and increases in poverty. Taking the lagged dependent variable into account, a 2-point rise in the unemployment rate leads to a 0.9-point rise in the poverty rate over time.[14] Rises in wage inequality in the bottom half of the income distribution also led to rising poverty over this time period. The coefficient on the log wage ratio suggests that the 10 percent increase in the 50/10 wage ratio that occurred over the decade of the 1980s would have raised poverty by 2.4 percentage points in the long term, all else being equal. Although this is a large effect, it is consistent with the unexplained rise in poverty, despite declining unemployment and declines in the poverty line relative to median income over the 1980s.

Changes in the consumer price index have little effect on poverty, as others have found. Although the share of government expenditures going to transfer programs has an unexpectedly positive effect on poverty, the coefficient is small and insignificant. The location of the poverty line in the income distribution is positively correlated with poverty, as expected. When the poverty line hits at a higher point in the income distribution, more people are below that point and poverty is higher.

The second column in table 3.3 adds dummy variables for the decades of the 1980s, 1990s, and 2000s and interacts these dummy variables with the unemployment rate, as described in equation 3.2. Consistent with earlier research, the positive effect of unemployment on poverty almost disappears over the 1980s. (The coefficient for the unemployment rate interacted with the D80 dummy variable is almost as large as, and of opposite sign to, the overall coefficient on unemployment.) After the 1980s, the strong poverty-unemployment relationship is reestablished and the interaction effects go to zero. With the inclusion of these dummy variables, however, the coefficient on the wage ratio also goes to zero and loses all significance.

Changes in the wage ratio are highly correlated with the decadal dummy variables, with wage inequality increasing most steeply in the 1980s. By including these dummy variables (by themselves and interacted with the unemployment rate), the regression in column 2 allows for different coefficients during the period when the wage ratio was changing rapidly. The flexible decadal coefficients in column 2 are essentially a more mechanical way of controlling for the same variation that the shifting wage ratio picks up in column 1. Or stated another way, the inclusion of

TABLE 3.3 / Determinants of Poverty Under Alternative Specifications

Variable	Dependent Variable: Poverty Rate Among All Persons		
	(1)	(2)	(3)
Lagged poverty rate	0.612**	0.386**	0.383**
	(0.100)	(0.093)	(0.096)
Unemployment rate	0.167*	0.305**	0.252*
	(0.078)	(0.110)	(0.110)
UnemploymentRate × D80		−0.245*	−0.269*
		(0.110)	(0.103)
UnemploymentRate × D90		−0.045	−0.090
		(0.122)	(0.121)
UnemploymentRate × D00		0.066	−0.042
		(0.193)	(0.197)
Log 50/10 Wage Ratio	10.031**	−0.215	
	(2.665)	(2.544)	
Consumer price index	0.030	0.001	−0.008
	(0.044)	(0.039)	(0.039)
Public assistance/GDP[a]	0.440	−1.068	−0.478
	(0.642)	(0.726)	(0.722)
Poverty line/median income	0.228**	0.346**	0.396**
	(0.075)	(0.071)	(0.067)
D80[b]		2.582**	2.788**
		(0.814)	(0.733)
D90[c]		2.116*	2.295**
		(0.840)	(0.803)
D00[d]		1.567	2.251*
		(1.092)	(1.068)
Constant	−12.906**	−6.728*	−9.119**
	(3.289)	(2.758)	(1.624)
Number of observations	44	44	48

Source: Author's regressions.
Note: Standard errors are in parentheses.
a. Public assistance spending includes federal payments to cash assistance, energy assistance, food assistance, foster care and adoption, black lung, SSI, and EITC, all as a percentage of GDP.
b. D80 is a dummy variable for the years 1980 to 1989.
c. D90 is a dummy variable for the years 1990 to 1999.
d. D00 is a dummy variable for the years 2000 to 2006.
**significant at 1 percent level; *significant at 5 percent level

the wage ratio in column 1 has essentially the same effect as including the dummy variables and their interactions for recent decades in column 2.[15] This is further confirmed in column 3, where I drop the wage ratio entirely and find essentially identical coefficients as in column 2. I interpret these results as confirming evidence that it is wage shifts that explain the puzzling change in the relationship between unemployment and poverty over the 1980s that others have documented.

Although unemployment fell in that decade, so did wages among low-wage workers, and the two effects offset each other.

In table 3.4, I use the specification in column 1 of table 3.3, including unemployment and the wage ratio, to investigate the determinants of poverty among various subgroups of the poor.[16] Column 1 repeats the estimates for "all persons," while columns 2 through 4 show the coefficients for the share of poor non-elderly adults (age eighteen to sixty-four), poor children, and poor elderly adults (sixty-five or older). Columns 5 through 7 show the coefficients for the share of poor whites, poor blacks, and poor Hispanics. Columns 8 through 10 show the effects for single-mother families, for married-couple families with children, and for single individuals.

The results in columns 2 through 10 emphasize the important impact of the economy on poverty among most of these groups. Unemployment rates and wage ratios have significant effects on all groups except the elderly poor, poor single individuals (of whom about one-quarter are elderly), and Hispanics (where the effect of wages is quite large but poorly determined owing to a smaller number of observations). Unemployment appears to have a particularly strong effect on poverty among children, among blacks, and among single mothers. A 2.0-point rise in the unemployment rate results in a rise in poverty of 0.9 points among all persons, but 3.2 points among blacks and over 4.0 points among single mothers. Rising wage inequality has had a relatively strong effect on increasing poverty among children, whites, Hispanics (although imprecisely estimated), and married parents.

Government expenditures have little effect on poverty, although the coefficients are larger (if poorly determined) among the elderly, single mothers, and blacks, all groups that have been major beneficiaries of expanded public assistance. Inflation, as measured by consumer prices, has little effect on any group (with the exception of children). A relatively higher poverty line is correlated with greater poverty for a variety of groups.

As many have noted, there are serious problems with the current official poverty measure (Citro and Michael 1995; Blank 2008; Haveman, this volume). The Census Bureau provides a variety of alternative poverty measures. In the last column in table 3.4, I utilize an alternative definition of poverty based on a more complete measure of disposable income among families, taking into account both in-kind transfers and taxes before calculating whether a family is poor or not.[17] This series is available only from 1980 on, so there are relatively few observations in this regression. The results with this alternative poverty definition are not strikingly different from the results in column 1. A 2.0-point rise in unemployment suggests a 1.1-point rise in poverty using this measure. The wage ratio is insignificant, but the shorter time period reduces the variation in this variable.

Overall, these regressions demonstrate that poverty remains very responsive to the economic cycle. Although falling unemployment in the mid- to late 1980s had little effect on poverty because of an offsetting decline in real wages, lower unemployment in the 1990s and 2000s significantly reduced poverty for most groups. In contrast, inflation has virtually no effect on poverty.

The recession that began in 2007 promises to be extremely deep. As this is written in early 2009, many economists are predicting that unemployment will reach

TABLE 3.4 / Determinants of Poverty Among Different Groups of Persons

| | Dependent Variable: Poverty Rate Among | | | | | | | | | | Alternative Poverty Rate |
Variable	All Persons (1)	Adults (Eighteen to Sixty-Four) (2)	Children (3)	Elderly (4)	Whites (5)	Blacks (6)	Hispanics (7)	Single Mothers (8)	Married Parents (9)	Single Individuals (10)	All Persons (11)
Lagged poverty rate	0.612** (0.100)	0.751** (0.094)	0.774** (0.062)	0.670** (0.090)	0.688** (0.109)	0.662** (0.102)	0.702** (0.156)	0.682** (0.095)	0.526** (0.176)	0.790** (0.077)	0.484** (0.121)
Unemployment rate	0.167* (0.078)	0.166* (0.071)	0.389** (0.118)	-0.253 (0.221)	0.125 (0.072)	0.548** (0.193)	-0.008 (0.457)	0.668** (0.287)	0.195 (0.141)	-0.122 (0.211)	0.293** (0.099)
Log 50/10 wage ratio	10.031** (2.665)	7.896** (2.573)	15.106** (4.274)	-5.717 (7.275)	9.879** (2.506)	-1.417 (6.163)	16.909 (8.770)	5.279 (9.617)	8.379** (2.987)	2.595 (7.113)	2.170 (2.071)
Consumer price index	0.030 (0.044)	0.047 (0.037)	0.137* (0.056)	0.060 (0.078)	0.054 (0.044)	0.090 (0.083)	0.101 (0.199)	0.146 (0.129)	0.038 (0.074)	0.031 (0.080)	0.072 (0.062)
Public assistance/GDP	0.440 (0.642)	0.398 (0.580)	0.551 (0.993)	-2.998 (1.493)	0.431 (0.603)	-1.585 (1.568)	1.316 (2.307)	-1.780 (2.397)	-0.446 (0.869)	-0.557 (1.403)	-0.056 (0.626)
GDP	0.228** (0.075)	0.079 (0.054)	0.157* (0.074)	0.361 (0.180)	0.154* (0.063)	0.299 (0.228)	0.706 (0.469)	0.226 (0.189)	0.228 (0.167)	0.290* (0.131)	0.112 (0.123)
Poverty line/median income											
Constant	-12.906** (3.289)	-8.024* (3.039)	-16.797** (4.818)	-0.459 (7.216)	-11.598** (2.986)	-2.266 (8.299)	-34.064* (13.004)	-2.023 (10.578)	-12.284** (4.216)	-7.278 (6.631)	-2.412 (2.998)
Number of Observations	44	40	44	40	44	40	34	44	32	44	26

Source: Author's regressions.

Note: Standard errors are in parentheses.

a. Public assistance spending includes federal payments to cash assistance, energy assistance, food assistance, foster care and adoption, black lung, SSI, and EITC, all as percentage of GDP.

**significant at 1 percent level; *significant at 5 percent level

10 percent. The most recent poverty data we have available are for 2007, when the poverty rate for all persons was 12.5 percent and the average unemployment rate was 4.6 percent. If the unemployment rate rises from 4.6 percent to 10.0 percent and everything else remains unchanged, poverty could increase from 12.5 percent to 14.8 percent over the long term. This would be just below the high poverty rates that followed the recessions of 1980 to 1982 and 1990 to 1991. Although many other factors could limit such a sharp rise in poverty, this estimate provides evidence of how important the labor market is to the economic well-being of low-income families.

Finally, it is worth commenting that growth in the macroeconomy alone will not eliminate poverty. Even when the economy recovers, unemployment is not likely to fall below its level in the late 1990s and early 2000s, when it was between 4 and 5 percent. Hence, rises in unemployment above this level will increase poverty, but unemployment is not likely to fall to a level that pushes poverty down substantially below where it was in 2000 at 11.3 percent. Declines in poverty below this level are likely to require targeted efforts to expand resources for those who cannot work and to expand earning opportunities for less-skilled workers.

CONCLUSION

There is both good news and bad news regarding the effects of the economy on the earnings opportunities of less-skilled workers. The good news is that low unemployment rates continue to benefit low-income persons. Poverty in the 2000s appears to have been highly responsive to lower unemployment. Unemployment has been relatively low over the past two decades. Furthermore, at least since the early 1990s, wages have not fallen among less-skilled workers and have even risen somewhat. Wages among less-skilled women are higher than at any previous point in history.

The bad news is that wages among less-skilled men remain below where they were in the 1970s. And overall wage growth among all less-skilled workers has been limited. Although the economy has been in a period of sustained growth, this has benefited higher-skilled workers much more than less-skilled workers. And a serious economic recession has brought that period of growth to an end, with much worse economic prospects for low-income families, especially female-headed families, who now rely more heavily on earnings and less on cash welfare.

These results suggest several important policy issues in the years ahead. Maintaining a strong economy and low unemployment is most important for the long-term economic well-being of low-wage workers. As I have written elsewhere and document in this chapter, the best policy we can pursue for the poor is to keep unemployment low and the economy strong (Blank 2000).

Given the forces that have shifted demand toward higher-skilled workers, however, economic growth by itself may not be enough to reduce poverty or substantially improve the economic well-being of low-income families. Maintaining a reasonable level of the minimum wage is also important. When the minimum wage deteriorated in the 1980s, the real earnings of less-skilled workers declined.

The decline of unions has also accelerated wage losses among lower-wage workers, suggesting that effective forms of worker organization in a global economy may also prevent wage losses for some groups of workers.

We must also maintain the level of the Earned Income Tax Credit as a subsidy to lower-wage workers in low-income families. At present the EITC is primarily available to families with children. Expanding the EITC to other low-wage workers in low-income families without children would help reduce poverty, as others have noted (Berlin 2007; Scholz 2007). Such an EITC expansion might help reverse the falling labor force participation of less-skilled men, as shown in figure 3.1. Other chapters in this volume discuss other relevant policies, such as making child care and health insurance more widely available or revising the unemployment insurance system.

Finally, any long-term solution to these problems will require increasing skill levels. Reforming and improving the public school system is critical, as is increasing opportunities for postsecondary education (Jacob and Ludwig, this volume; Holzer, this volume). Given the rapidly growing immigrant population among the less-skilled, the educational achievements of the children of these immigrants will be quite important for the future of the economy. Intergenerational mobility will increase if these children are able to reach higher educational levels than their parents, and these families will be in a better position to escape poverty over time.

The labor market has had a plentiful supply of low-wage jobs available, but the long-term outlook for jobs is uncertain. At best, there will continue to be a large low-wage employment sector; at worst, depending on broader trends in technology and economic globalization, the number of these jobs could shrink relative to the supply of low-wage workers. Or the wages for these jobs could fall, as they did in the 1980s. There is little prospect, however, that there will be substantial wage gains in low-skill jobs. Shifts in demand away from less-skilled work, combined with the large supply of less-skilled workers, will keep wages down.

Nonetheless, most families headed by less-skilled adults rely primarily on earnings. Assuring these families of stable and sufficient incomes is important in order to keep poverty low and to keep these families attached to the labor market rather than idle or engaged in less socially desirable activities. This requires ongoing public subsidies to less-skilled workers and ongoing attention to the problems faced by low-wage workers.

Thanks are due to Victoria Finkle and Howard Lempel for excellent research assistance.

NOTES

1. The data in figures 3.1 and 3.2 come from the Outgoing Rotation Groups (ORG) in the monthly Current Population Survey (CPS), a representative national sample of the

population. The ORG includes data from one-fourth of the CPS in each month. The monthly samples are combined to produce annual averages.

2. It is widely believed that these data do not fully count undocumented immigrants, many of whom are working. If undocumented workers are more likely to be less skilled, then the numbers in table 3.2 undercount the effects of immigration in the low-skilled labor market.

3. Figures 3.4 and 3.5 are calculated with March CPS data. The industry definitions change each decade, so constructing a consistent series is not straightforward. The data start in 1985 because it is hard to reconcile these numbers with the industry definition used prior to that year. Figure 3.4 includes workers in durable and nondurable manufacturing. Figure 3.5 includes workers in retail trade, arts entertainment and recreation, accommodation, food and drinking places, and personal laundry services.

4. The data are deflated using the GDP deflator for personal consumption expenditures (PCE). To adjust for differences in hours of work, I took average hours of work among full-time men (those working more than thirty-five hours per week) in each year and scaled up wages among men who did not work full-time, using the ratio of average full-time hours to their actual hours. Figure 3.7 makes the same calculation for women.

5. I thank David Autor for making this data available for use here and in the regressions later in this chapter.

6. Although they were affected by all the same forces, less-educated women did better than less-educated men in the labor market over the past twenty-five years. Blank and Shierholz (2006) have investigated why this happened. Women's accumulating labor market experience and increasing returns to experience offset declines in the returns to education. Furthermore, the negative effects of children and marriage on women's wages appear to have abated over this period.

7. For a summary, see Acemoglu (2002). One criticism of SBTC is that it is a hard theory to prove since technological change is a difficult concept to measure (see Card and DiNardo 2006).

8. Krugman's empirical work, however, suggests that trade remains a relatively less important factor in the determination of U.S. wages, although the increasing complexity of intermediate component outsourcing makes it difficult to measure this effect.

9. These numbers were tabulated by the author from the March Current Population Survey.

10. The pattern in figure 3.10 is not unique to a single mother. If we plot the equivalent lines for a married-couple family with children in which the father works full-time at the minimum wage and the mother works part-time, the pattern looks very similar.

11. These data are provided by David Autor from Autor, Katz, and Kearney (2008). They are available from 1963 to 2006, and these dates determine the number of observations for many of the regressions.

12. The full list includes food stamps, black lung payments, SSI, direct relief assistance, energy assistance, cash welfare, WIC (Women, Infants, and Children) programs, foster care and adoption payments, payments to nonprofit welfare institutions, and the EITC. These expenditures are taken as a share of GDP.

13. I experimented with a variety of other variables as well, such as employment-to-population ratios or overall GDP growth rates. These variables, as well as wage mea-

sures, are sometimes significant in other papers that utilize state-by-year variation and have far more observations, such as Gunderson and Ziliak (2004).

14. The coefficient of 0.167 tells you the expected effect in the next year. But the presence of the lagged dependent variable suggests that there are lagged effects; hence, the long-term coefficient is larger at 0.430 (which is .0167/[1 − 0.612]). I report here the long-term effects of unemployment and wage inequality changes.

15. Indeed, the estimated impact of unemployment on poverty, adjusting for the lagged dependent variable, is virtually identical whether one uses the unemployment coefficient from column 1 (controlling for the wage ratio changes) or the base unemployment coefficient from column 2 (allowing a shift effect in the 1980s). This is because the coefficient on the lagged dependent variable is much smaller when separate dummy variables are included for recent decades. In both regressions, except for the 1980s, a 2.0-point rise in unemployment leads to a rise in poverty of 0.9 to 1.0 points.

16. This specification includes seven variables and has more than thirty degrees of freedom in every regression. This is more than earlier research had available, but the small number of observations does mean that significance levels are likely to be low.

17. These data are available (through 2003) at the Census Bureau's website on alternative poverty estimates: http://www.census.gov/hhes/www/income/reports.html; I use series 14. Data for 2004 and 2005 can be found in table 2 at: http://www.census.gov/hhes/www/poverty/detailedpovtabs.html.

REFERENCES

Acemoglu, Daron. 2002. "Technical Change, Inequality, and the Labor Market." *Journal of Economic Literature* 40(1): 7–72.

Autor, David H., Lawrence F. Katz, and Melissa S. Kearney. 2008. "Trends in U.S. Wage Inequality: Revising the Revisionists." *Review of Economics and Statistics* 90(2): 300–23.

Autor, David H., Frank Levy, and Richard J. Murnane. 2003. "The Skill Content of Recent Technological Change: An Empirical Investigation." *Quarterly Journal of Economics* 118(4): 1279–1333.

Bean, Charles. 1994. "European Unemployment: A Survey." *Journal of Economic Literature* 32(2): 573–619.

Berlin, Gordon L. 2007. "Rewarding the Work of Individuals: A Counterintuitive Approach to Reducing Poverty and Strengthening Families." *The Future of Children* 17(2): 17–42.

Berman, Eli, John Bound, and Zvi Griliches. 1994. "Changes in the Demand for Skilled Labor Within U.S. Manufacturing: Evidence from the Annual Survey of Manufactures." *Quarterly Journal of Economics* 109(2): 367–97.

Blanchard, Olivier. 2006. "European Unemployment: The Evolution of Facts and Ideas." *Economic Policy* 21(45): 5–59.

Blank, Rebecca M. 2000. "Fighting Poverty: Lessons from Recent U.S. History." *Journal of Economic Perspectives* 14(2): 3–19.

———. 2002. "Evaluating Welfare Reform in the U.S." *Journal of Economic Literature* 40(4): 451–68.

———. 2007. "Improving the Safety Net for Single Mothers Who Face Serious Barriers to Work." *The Future of Children* 17(2): 183–97.

———. 2008. "How to Improve Poverty Measurement in the United States." *Journal of Policy Analysis and Management* 27(2): 233–54.

Blank, Rebecca M., and Alan S. Blinder. 1986. "Macroeconomics, Income Distribution, and Poverty." In *Fighting Poverty,* edited by Sheldon H. Danziger and Daniel H. Weinberg. Cambridge, Mass.: Harvard University Press.

Blank, Rebecca M., and David Card. 1993. "Poverty, Income Distribution, and Growth: Are They Still Connected?" *Brookings Papers on Economic Activity* 1993(2): 285–339.

Blank, Rebecca M., and Brian Kovak. 2009. "The Growing Problem of Disconnected Single Mothers." In *Making the Work-Based Safety Net Work Better,* edited by Carolyn J. Heinrich and John Karl Scholz. New York: Russell Sage Foundation.

Blank, Rebecca M., and Heidi Shierholz. 2006. "Exploring Gender Differences in Employment and Wage Trends Among Less-Skilled Workers." In *Working and Poor: How Economic and Policy Changes Are Affecting Low-Wage Workers,* edited by Rebecca M. Blank, Sheldon H. Danziger, and Robert F. Schoeni. New York: Russell Sage Foundation.

Borjas, George J. 2006. "Wage Trends Among Disadvantaged Minorities." In *Working and Poor: How Economic and Policy Changes Are Affecting Low-Wage Workers,* edited by Rebecca M. Blank, Sheldon H. Danziger, and Robert F. Schoeni. New York: Russell Sage Foundation.

Borjas, George J., Richard B. Freeman, and Lawrence F. Katz. 1997. "How Much Do Immigration and Trade Affect Labor Market Outcomes?" *Brookings Papers on Economic Activity* 1: 1–67.

Brennan, Maya, and Barbara J. Lipman. 2007. *The Housing Landscape for America's Working Families, 2007.* Washington, D.C.: Center for Housing Policy.

Broda, Christian, and John Romalis. 2008. "Inequality and Prices: Does China Benefit the Poor in America?" Unpublished paper, University of Chicago.

Cancian, Maria, and Deborah Reed. 1999. "The Impact of Wives' Earnings on Income Inequality: Issues and Estimates." *Demography* 36(2): 173–84.

Card, David. 1996. "The Effects of Unions on the Structure of Wages: A Longitudinal Analysis." *Econometrica* 64(4): 957–80.

Card, David, and John DiNardo. 2006. "The Impact of Technological Change on Low-Wage Workers: A Review." In *Working and Poor: How Economic and Policy Changes Are Affecting Low-Wage Workers,* edited by Rebecca M. Blank, Sheldon H. Danziger, and Robert F. Schoeni. New York: Russell Sage Foundation.

Citro, Constance F., and Robert T. Michael. 1995. *Measuring Poverty: A New Approach.* Washington, D.C.: National Academies Press.

Dinardo, John, Nicole M. Fortin, and Thomas Lemieux. 1996. "Labor Market Institutions and the Distribution of Wages, 1973–1992: A Semiparametric Approach." *Econometrica* 64(5): 1001–46.

Feenstra, Robert C., and Gordon H. Hanson. 2003. "Global Production Sharing and Rising Inequality: A Survey of Trade and Wages." In *Handbook of International Trade,* edited by E. Kwan Choi and James Harrigan. Oxford: Blackwell Publishing.

Freeman, Richard B., and Lawrence F. Katz. 1995. *Differences and Changes in Wage Structures.* Chicago: University of Chicago Press.

Grogger, Jeffrey, and Lynn A. Karoly. 2005. *Welfare Reform: Effects of a Decade of Change.* Cambridge, Mass.: Harvard University Press.

Gunderson, Craig, and James P. Ziliak. 2004. "Poverty and Macroeconomic Performance Across Space, Race, and Family Structure." *Demography* 41(1): 61–86.

Haveman, Robert, and Jonathan Schwabish. 2000. "Has Macroeconomic Performance Regained Its Antipoverty Bite?" *Contemporary Economic Policy* 18(4): 415–27.

Holzer, Harry J., Paul Offner, and Elaine Sorensen. 2005. "Declining Employment Among Young, Black, Less-Educated Men: The Role of Incarceration and Child Support." *Journal of Policy Analysis and Management* 24(2): 329–50.

Holzer, Harry J., Steven Raphael, and Michael A. Stoll. 2007. "The Effect of an Applicant's Criminal History on Employer Hiring Decisions and Screening Practices." In *Barriers to Reentry?* edited by Shawn Bushway, Michael A. Stoll, and David F. Weiman. New York: Russell Sage Foundation.

Hoynes, Hilary W. 2000. "The Employment, Earnings, and Income of Less-Skilled Workers over the Business Cycle." In *Finding Jobs: Work and Welfare Reform,* edited by David E. Card and Rebecca M. Blank. New York: Russell Sage Foundation.

Juhn, Chinhui. 1992. "Decline of Male Labor Market Participation: The Role of Declining Market Opportunities." *Quarterly Journal of Economics* 107(1): 79–121.

Krugman, Paul R. 2008. "Trade and Wages, Reconsidered." *Brookings Papers on Economic Activity* 1: 103–43.

Lee, David S. 1999. "Wage Inequality in the U.S. During the 1980s: Rising Dispersion or Falling Minimum Wage?" *Quarterly Journal of Economics* 114(3): 977–1023.

Lemieux, Thomas. 2008a. "The Changing Nature of Wage Inequality." *Journal of Population Economics* 21(1): 21–48.

———. 2008b. "What Do We Really Know About Changes in Wage Inequality?" Unpublished paper. University of British Columbia.

Scholz, John Karl. 2007. "Employment-Based Tax Credits for Low-Skilled Workers." Hamilton Project discussion paper 2007-14. Washington, D.C.: Brookings Institution.

U.S. Bureau of the Census. Various years. Current Population Survey data. Washington: U.S Bureau of the Census and Bureau of Labor Statistics. Available at: http://www.census.gov/cps.

Western, Bruce. 2006. *Punishment and Inequality in America.* New York: Russell Sage Foundation.

Chapter 4

Family Structure, Childbearing, and Parental Employment: Implications for the Level and Trend in Poverty

Maria Cancian and Deborah Reed

Changes in family structure and changes in poverty are closely related. Single-mother families are about five times as likely to be poor as married-parent families.[1] While they are less likely to be poor than they were fifty years ago, single-parent families are more common now, accounting for a larger share of all poor families. Moreover, eligibility for income support programs, including cash welfare, food stamps, and the Earned Income Tax Credit (EITC), is tied to family composition. In recent years, policymakers have sought not only to respond to family changes but also to influence the decisions that people make about marriage, divorce, and childbearing. Thus, poverty policies and family policies are also increasingly tied.

If the strength of the link between poverty and family structure seems obvious, its nature is less clear. For example, having a child before getting married is associated with an increased likelihood of poverty. However, living in poverty also increases the likelihood of nonmarital childbearing.[2] Thus, neither nonmarital childbearing nor poverty on its own can account for the high rates of poverty among single-mother families. In addition, decisions about work, marriage, and childbearing are increasingly disconnected (Schoen, Landale, and Daniels 2007; Edin and Kefalas 2005; Ellwood and Jencks 2004; Spain and Bianchi 1996). Women are now more likely to work, regardless of marital or parental status, and children are increasingly likely to spend time in families that do not include both biological parents and that may include half-siblings or step-siblings. There is greater variety in family forms, and the members of any given family are increasingly likely to experience changes in household structure over time (Bumpass and Lu 2000; Manning, Smock, and Majumdar 2004; Cancian, Meyer, and Cook 2009).

In addition to its relationship to economic well-being, family structure is of interest because children who do not live with both biological parents may be more vulnerable to other risks, even after taking economic factors into account (Amato 2005;

McLanahan and Sandefur 1994). Recent discussions have emphasized the potential importance of fathers, who are less likely to be part of their children's lives when parents are divorced or were never married (Hofferth 2006; Tamis-LeMonda and Cabrera 2002). Moreover, poverty creates challenges that may be difficult to manage with only one available parent (Oliker 1995; Edin and Lein 1997), especially as more single mothers work outside the home (Waldfogel, this volume). Thus, changes in family structure not only place more individuals at greater risk of poverty but also may increase their vulnerability to the challenges associated with poverty.

Poverty reflects insufficient resources relative to needs. Income poverty in the United States is measured by comparing cash income (for low-income families, largely earnings and cash benefits) to a needs standard (which adjusts for the number of individuals in the household). For example, a single woman (or man) in 2008 was considered poor if her income was below $11,201. If she had two children, becoming a single mother and part of a family of three, she would have been considered poor if her family income was below $17,346. Thus, even putting aside the demands of motherhood and the potential reduction in hours worked and earnings, the increased financial needs of a larger family increase the chance of poverty. If she married, becoming a married-couple family of four, the needs standard would have risen to $21,834. However, with a second adult in the household, there is likely to have been a second earner—potentially reducing poverty. The potential poverty reduction associated with a second adult also reflects the relatively modest increase in the needs standard with each person added to the household. Economies of scale mean that each additional person adds less than proportional needs (see Meyer and Wallace, this volume).

We use this simple model of income and needs to help structure the discussion that follows. The implications for poverty of changes in marriage, childbearing, and work depend on how these changes are related, and the net effects of these changes on income and on needs. As we will show, the decline in marriage has increased poverty, all else being equal. But all else has not remained equal: although women are less likely to be married, they are also more likely to be working. Because these two changes are related, measuring the effect of changes in marriage on poverty is complex.

This chapter examines changes since 1970 in family structure and their implications for poverty and income support policy. We discuss changes in marriage and childbearing and their implications for the living situations of children, such as the increasing proportion of children living with a single mother. We also highlight differences in work and earnings by marital and parental status, such as the substantial increase in the employment rates of single mothers with young children. Notwithstanding the growing interest in men and fathers, much of our analysis focuses on women's marriage rates, fertility, living arrangements, and employment. This focus follows from the concern for children and reflects the persistent presumption that women have the primary responsibility for both fertility decisions and child well-being, as well as the reality that most children live with their mother (and less often with their father).

TRENDS IN FAMILY STRUCTURE SINCE 1970

Changing patterns of poverty, prospects for the future, and the potential of alternative policy interventions all depend on the interrelationships between poverty and marriage, childbearing, family living arrangements, and employment status. In the current policy context, with limited cash income supports designed to reduce poverty, poverty status largely depends on the number of adults in the household, their hours of work and wage rates, and the number of children they have to support. We highlight changes over time and across racial and ethnic groups. We analyze demographic trends for all families—not just for families at greatest risk for poverty. However, the trends are qualitatively similar if, for example, we restrict our analysis to less-educated women.[3]

Marriage, Divorce, and Cohabitation

Households that include two adults generally have greater opportunities to avoid poverty—since the second adult on average adds more to potential income (through earnings) than to needs (given economies of scale). Thus, both declines in marriage and increases in divorce add to poverty. Cohabitating couples may capture the same benefits, though the implications of cohabitation for official poverty measures, as well as for actual economic well-being, are complex; we discuss these implications further later in the chapter.

Family composition changes reflect changes in the proportion of individuals who marry, the stability of marriages, and, for those who divorce, the probability of remarriage. Cohabitation as a prelude to, or substitute for, marriage has also increased (Bumpass and Lu 2000; Raley 2001). Figure 4.1 shows that the proportion of women married at any age declined steadily between 1970 and 2006.[4] The first line shows that in 1970 almost 80 percent of women between the ages of twenty-five and twenty-nine were married, with the share married remaining stable through the forty- to forty-four-year-old category. By 2006 only about 45 percent of women were married by age twenty-five to twenty-nine, and even by age forty to forty-four only 64 percent were married. The steepest declines in age-specific marriage percentages occurred between 1970 and 1980 and between 1980 and 1990, with more modest declines after 1990.[5] A similar decline and delay in marriage is apparent for men (data not shown). But because men on average marry at older ages, the proportion married compared to women is lower at ages twenty-five to twenty-nine, similar by ages thirty-five to thirty-nine, and slightly higher at forty to forty-four.[6]

The declining proportion of individuals who are currently married reflects growth in the proportion of women and men who never marry and changes in divorce, remarriage, and cohabitation. In 1970 only 5 percent, or one in twenty, women had never been married by age forty to forty-four, a figure that tripled, to 15 percent, by 2006. The proportion married at a point in time fell more dramati-

FIGURE 4.1 / Married Women by Age, 1970 to 2006

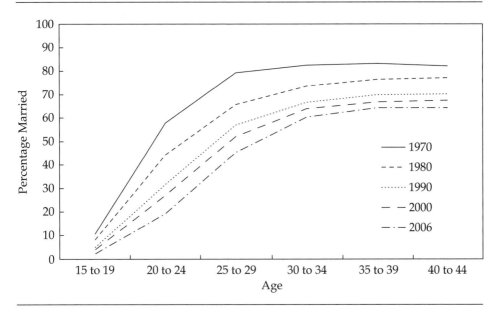

Sources: Authors' calculations from the decennial census (U.S. Bureau of the Census 1970, 1980, 1990, 2000) and the American Community Survey (U.S. Bureau of the Census 2006).

cally because of increased divorce rates. In 1970 about 6 percent of women in their early forties were divorced; this doubled to 12 percent by 1980 and rose to 16 percent in 2006.

The trends in marital status for all individuals obscure variation across racial and ethnic groups. Figure 4.2 shows the percentage of women married and cohabiting at ages forty to forty-four for whites, blacks, Hispanics, Asian and Pacific Islanders, and American Indians.[7] With the exception of Asians and Pacific Islanders, the proportion married fell substantially for every group. Between 1970 and 2006, the percentage of women age forty to forty-four who were married declined from 61 percent to 39 percent for blacks and from 76 percent to 53 percent for American Indians. Thus, the two groups with the lowest proportion married in 1970 also experienced the sharpest declines in the 1970s and 1980s, increasing the gap in marriage rates by race and ethnicity. More recently, the decline in marriage for black women has slowed somewhat.

Figure 4.2 also shows that rates of cohabitation increased dramatically, especially in the 1980s and 1990s.[8] Calculations of the proportion of women who are married *or* cohabiting show a smaller decline than the decline in marriage. For example, while the proportion of white women married at age forty to forty-four declined from 85 percent to 68 percent between 1970 and 2006, the proportion married or cohabiting fell only from 85 percent to 74 percent. Increases in cohabitation

FIGURE 4.2   /   Married and Cohabiting Women, Age Forty to Forty-Four, by Race and Ethnicity, 1970 to 2006

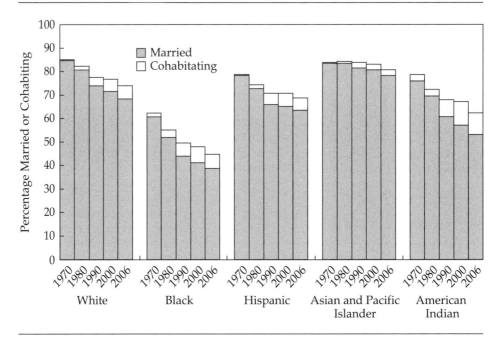

Sources: Authors' calculations from the decennial census (U.S. Bureau of the Census 1970, 1980, 1990, 2000) and the American Community Survey (U.S. Bureau of the Census 2006).

account for an even greater part of the decline in marriage at younger ages (Bumpass, Sweet, and Cherlin 1991; Raley 2000).

Differences in marriage patterns by race and ethnicity are also affected by the inclusion of cohabitation. As already noted, blacks and American Indians experienced large declines in the proportion married. For American Indians, more than for blacks, much of this decline coincided with substantial increases in cohabitation. The percentage of American Indian women age forty to forty-four who were married or cohabiting fell twelve percentage points (from 79 percent to 67 percent) between 1970 and 2000—compared to the nineteen-percentage-point decline in marriage alone (from 76 percent to 57 percent).

In sum, marriage rates have fallen over time, increasing the proportion of people living in households that depend on one adult for both earnings and caretaking. Although cohabitation has increased, most cohabiting unions are relatively short-lived, and the sharing of resources within such unions is less certain. Marriage rates have fallen relatively rapidly for blacks and American Indians, who began the period with relatively low rates, contributing to increasing racial and ethnic disparities in family structure.

FIGURE 4.3 / Average Number of Children by Age of Woman, 1970 to 2006

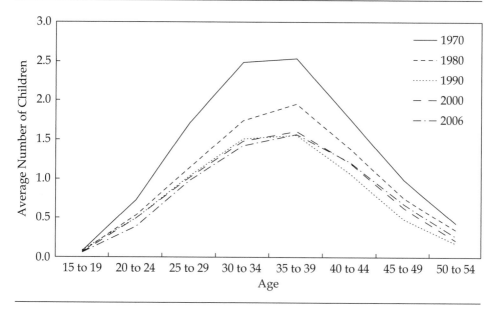

Sources: Authors' calculations from the decennial census (U.S. Bureau of the Census 1970, 1980, 1990, 2000) and the American Community Survey (U.S. Bureau of the Census 2006).

Childbearing

Changes in marriage patterns interact with changes in childbearing and affect both poverty and the composition of the poor. As declining marriage rates and increasing divorce rates reduce the number of adults available to provide income to households, poverty increases. To the extent that declines in marriage coincide with women having fewer children, reductions in the size of families reduce the resources needed to avoid poverty. Figure 4.3 shows that the average number of children present in the household has declined over time, falling especially in the 1970s and 1980s.[9] In 1970 women age thirty-five to thirty-nine had an average of 2.4 children; by 1990 they had an average of only 1.3 children. All other things being equal, women are more likely to be poor the more children they have, both because larger families need more income to avoid poverty and because greater parenting responsibilities restrict women's work hours in the paid labor market. Thus, the declining numbers of children per woman can be expected to reduce poverty, all else being equal. The decline in the number of children is apparent for all racial and ethnic groups (not shown).[10]

Although fertility declines tend to reduce poverty, growth in the proportion of children born outside of marriage has had the opposite effect. In 1960, 5 percent of all births were to unmarried mothers. As shown by the dashed line in figure 4.4,

FIGURE 4.4 / Fertility Rates by Marital Status, 1960 to 2006

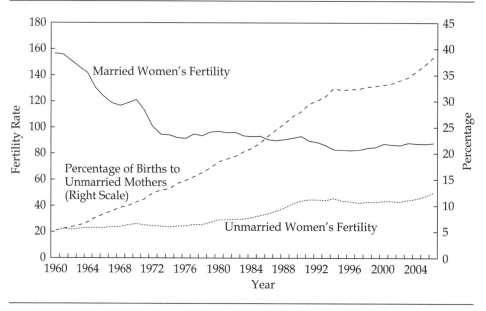

Sources: Authors' compilation. Measures for the period 1960 to 1979 are from U.S. Department of Health and Human Services (1995); measures for 1980 to 2006 are from Martin et al. (2009).

by 2006 that share had risen to 39 percent. Many authors have focused on the social, economic, and policy changes responsible for these trends and on their implications.[11] To understand the trends one must recognize that the *proportion* of births to unmarried mothers depends on the marriage rate and the fertility patterns of all women, not just those of unmarried women. The tendency for married women to have children, the tendency for unmarried women to have children, and the proportion of women of childbearing age who are married, all determine the proportion of births to unmarried women.[12]

Figure 4.4 shows that the increase in the proportion of children born to unmarried mothers in the 1960s and early 1970s resulted from sharp declines in fertility among married women (solid line) rather than from increases in the fertility of unmarried women (dotted line). The declining proportion of women who were married, shown in figure 4.1, also contributed. During the late 1970s and 1980s, birthrates among married women stabilized, and the continued increase in the proportion of births to unmarried women reflected increases in birthrates for unmarried women and the reduction in marriage, which left more women unmarried and therefore at risk for an unmarried birth. During the 1990s and the early years of the new century, unmarried women's fertility stabilized, but a decline in married women's fertility in the early 1990s and continued declines in the proportion of married women contributed to relatively modest increases in the proportion of children born to unmarried mothers. The proportion married continued to decline, and increases in unmarried women's fertility accelerated after 2002. By 2006 almost two in five children in the United States were born to an unmarried mother.

Patterns of marital and nonmarital births vary substantially by race and ethnicity, though detailed time-series information is available principally for whites and blacks. Between 1980 and 2006, the nonmarital birthrate more than doubled for whites, from 18.1 to 46.1 children per 1,000 unmarried women, while for blacks it fell from 81.1 to 66.2 percent in 2002, before rising somewhat to 71.5 percent in 2006 (Martin et al. 2009).[13] Thus, for blacks, increases in the proportion of children born to unmarried mothers are largely due to declines in marriage rates and in marital fertility rather than to increases in the likelihood that an unmarried woman will have a baby. In 2006 the proportion of children born to unmarried mothers was 17 percent for Asian and Pacific Islanders, 27 percent for whites, 50 percent for Hispanics, 65 percent for American Indians, and 71 percent for blacks (Martin et al. 2009).

Understanding the origins of the growing proportion of children born outside of marriage is important in evaluating potential causes and policy responses. Although empirical evidence for a causal connection is mixed (Moffitt 1998a, 2003), there are some theoretical reasons to expect that increased welfare benefits might provide incentives to increase nonmarital births. However, to the extent that the increased proportion of births to unmarried women is due to changes in *marital* fertility, as was the case through the mid-1970s, a causal role for welfare policy becomes questionable. There is also little evidence that the major 1996 welfare reforms had a substantial effect on marriage and childbearing (Grogger and Karoly 2005, 2007).

Although less than one-quarter of nonmarital births are to teen mothers, most teen mothers—over 80 percent in recent years—are unmarried when their child is born (Martin et al. 2009). Teen mothers are more likely to drop out of school and to face other poverty-increasing barriers to employment, and their children face elevated risks of poor outcomes (Maynard 1997; Child Trends 2008). Because teen mothers often faced disadvantages prior to pregnancy, however, it is difficult to disentangle the causal effect of teen births (Furstenberg 2007; Fletcher and Wolfe, forthcoming).

Between 1991 and 2005, teen birthrates fell dramatically—from 61.8 to 40.5 per 1,000 women between the ages of fifteen and nineteen. The most recent figures suggest a significant increase in 2006, to 41.9 births per 1,000, but teen birthrates still remain low by historic standards. In 1991 teen birthrates were highest for black teens (116.2 per 1,000), followed by Hispanic teens (100.3 per 1,000) and whites (42.5 per 1,000). Rates have fallen for all groups, but black teens' birthrates have fallen most dramatically, such that by 2006 they had a substantially lower birthrate (63.7) than Hispanic teens (83.0), though still much higher than the rate for whites (26.6) (Martin et al. 2009).

The increased proportion of births to single mothers increases children's vulnerability to poverty as more children (and mothers) live in households that include only one potential earner. On the other hand, declines in the number of children per family have tended to reduce poverty. In other words, contemporary women are less likely to have a husband to contribute economic support, but they are also less likely to need to support large families. Furthermore, declines in teen births mean that young women are less likely to face motherhood before they have had a chance to finish high school.

Family Living Arrangements

The implications of changes in marriage and fertility for children's living arrangements and poverty rates can be complex, especially when we consider the presence of unmarried partners or other adults. Figure 4.5 shows changes in the living arrangements of children. The top panel shows that, in 1970, 86 percent of all children lived in a married-couple family—though the couple may have included stepparents or adoptive parents.[14] The share had dropped to only 69 percent in 2006. Most children living in a single-parent household lived with a single mother, though by 2006 more than one in five children not living with a married couple lived with their father. Figure 4.5 also shows great variation in family structure across different racial and ethnic groups.[15] Living with a married couple was most common for Asian and Pacific Islander children (90 percent in 1970 and 85 percent in 2006) and white children (90 percent in 1970 and 76 percent in 2006). Black children were least likely to live with a married-couple family: only 35 percent lived with a married couple in 2006, a substantial decline from 64 percent in 1970. The proportion of Hispanic children living with a married couple fell from 82 percent to 64 percent between 1970 and 2006, and the percentage of American Indian children from 78 percent to 50 percent. A relatively high rate of single-father households (11 percent) is also evident for this group. Many children who live with an unmarried mother or unmarried father also live with another adult in the household—their grandparent, another relative, or, increasingly, their parent's cohabiting partner.

Figure 4.6 shows the living arrangements of single mothers, distinguishing those who are cohabiting with a partner, living with their parent or other relatives, living with other unrelated adults, or living alone. We observe a steady increase in cohabitation; in 1970, 2 percent of single mothers lived with a cohabiting male partner, 17 percent lived with a grandparent, and 18 percent lived with another adult relative.[16] The remaining 62 percent did not live with another adult. By 2006, 12 percent were cohabiting, 21 percent lived with a grandparent, 10 percent lived with another relative, and only 55 percent were living alone.

Although the proportion of all single mothers living alone fell from 62 percent to 55 percent overall, there was a substantially larger decline for Hispanic mothers (from 65 percent to 45 percent) and Asian mothers (from 64 percent to 47 percent), while among black mothers the proportion living alone actually rose slightly (from 57 percent in 1970 to 60 percent in 2006). Cohabitation rose in each decade between 1970 and 2000 for all groups. However, in the most recent period cohabitation among single mothers stabilized, and it declined for blacks from 9 percent to 6 percent between 2000 and 2006.

FIGURE 4.5   /   Family Structure for Families with Children, 1970 to 2006

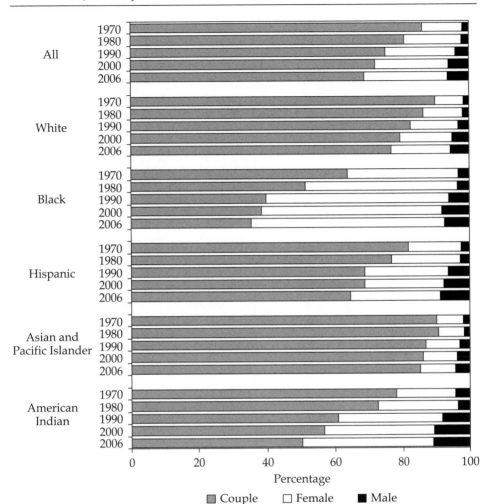

Sources: Authors' calculations from the decennial census (U.S. Bureau of the Census 1970, 1980, 1990, 2000) and the American Community Survey (U.S. Bureau of the Census 2006).

The living arrangements of single fathers are quite different from those of single mothers. In 2006 only 30 percent of single fathers (compared to 55 percent of single mothers) lived with no other adult. Thirty-one percent of single fathers cohabited, and an additional 34 percent lived with an adult relative. White single fathers were more likely to live alone (38 percent) than American Indian (30 percent), black (26 percent), Asian (22 percent), and especially Hispanic (15 percent) fathers.

The increase in single parents who live with an unmarried partner or related adult has consequences for the economic and social resources available to these parents

FIGURE 4.6 / Living Arrangements of Single Mothers, 1970 to 2006

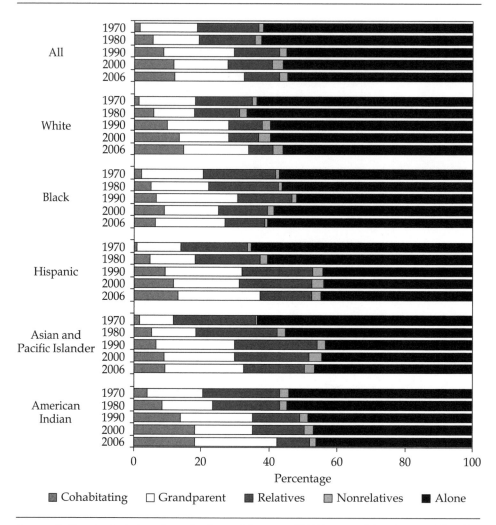

Sources: Authors' calculations from the decennial census (U.S. Bureau of the Census 1970, 1980, 1990, 2000) and the American Community Survey (U.S. Bureau of the Census 2006).

and their children. In determining poverty status, official poverty statistics include the income of related adults as part of total family income and include them as family members supported by that income. In contrast, the income and needs of "unrelated" cohabitants are not considered. If an unrelated cohabitant is a part of the same economic unit, household income needs are greater (given larger household size) and household resources may be greater (if the cohabiting adult has income).

The technical issues related to household membership and poverty measures reflect important substantive challenges in defining economic units and assessing their resources and needs. Ideally, additional adults, such as grandparents, increase the financial and social resources available to vulnerable families. A grandparent or other adult may also provide formal or informal child care and other supports. On the other hand, additional adults may increase family stress and the responsibilities of a single parent. For example, an elderly grandparent may require care, or a single mother may feel the need to supervise her children more closely because of the potential for physical or emotional abuse from an additional adult.[17] Even the assumption that parents and their biological children share resources to maximize some measure of family well-being is a simplification (Bergstrom 1997).

Employment

Changes in labor market opportunities are discussed in greater detail elsewhere in this volume (Blank, chapter 3). Here we examine women's increased employment, declines in male employment, and how these are related to changes in family structure and their implications for poverty. All else being equal, families are less likely to be poor the greater the number of adults and the fewer the number of children. Households that include adult males are less likely to be poor than those that include only adult females, both because men work more hours on average and because they earn more per hour on average. Since 1970, however, women's labor force participation has increased, especially for women with children, and gender gaps in labor market outcomes have declined (Blau 1998; Blau and Kahn 2000). These changes affect the level and distribution of income among families headed by married couples as well as among families with single female heads (Blau 1998; Cancian and Reed 1999). They also reflect changes in gender roles and contemporary expectations regarding the caretaking and employment responsibilities of mothers and fathers, which interact with the public policy context. As the relationship between family structure and work has changed, so too has the relationship between family structure and poverty. An accounting of changes in family and poverty must therefore account for the dramatic growth in women's labor force participation and the declining opportunities for men, especially those with less education (Toossi 2002; Blau and Kahn 2007; Moffitt 2000).

Figure 4.7 shows the proportion of men and women who worked at least one week in the previous year, by age. Female labor force participation increased substantially in the 1970s and 1980s. In the 1970s, women's labor force participation was lower during prime child-rearing ages, but by 1990 there was no longer a substantial shift in the proportion working between the ages of twenty and forty-five. In 1970, about 50 percent of all women age thirty to thirty-four worked; from 1990 onward, almost 80 percent did.

Changes in labor force participation vary substantially by gender and across education groups. While women's work hours increased, men's declined somewhat, especially among men with lower levels of education. Between 1970 and 2006, the proportion of all non-elderly women working at all increased from 57 percent to

FIGURE 4.7 / Annual Labor Force Participation Rates by Gender and Age, 1970 to 2006

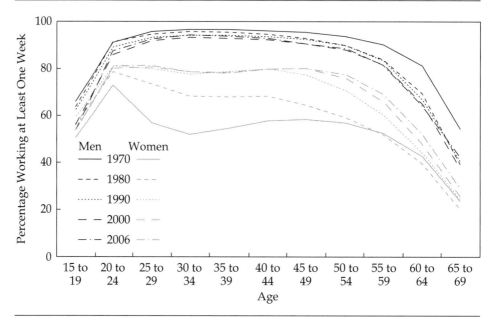

Sources: Authors' calculations from the decennial census (U.S. Bureau of the Census 1970, 1980, 1990, 2000) and the American Community Survey (U.S. Bureau of the Census 2006).

76 percent, while the proportion who work full-time, full-year grew from 25 percent to 44 percent. Absolute levels of employment were lower for women with less education, but trends were similar.[18] Among all men, the proportion working full-time, full-year fell from 70 percent to 67 percent. In 2006 only 60 percent of men between the ages of eighteen and sixty-four with a high school diploma or less worked full-time, full-year.

Although women's employment rates increased in most periods for most groups, the patterns varied substantially by family structure. Figure 4.8 shows increases in the proportion working at some point in the previous year among women between the ages of eighteen and sixty-four by marital status and the presence of preschool children (under age six) or school-age children (age six to seventeen). In the 1970s and 1980s, the increase was more pronounced for married women, especially married mothers. Between 1970 and 1990, the proportion of married women with children under age six who worked in the paid labor force increased from 41 percent to 68 percent, while employment rates for married women with older children increased from 54 percent to 77 percent. In contrast, there was little change in employment among married women from 1990 to 2006. The timing of changes in work was quite different for single women, and especially for single mothers relative to married mothers. The greatest increase in work for single mothers with young children occurred between 1990 and 2000, a period of slow growth for mar-

FIGURE 4.8 / Annual Labor Force Participation Rates, Women Age 18 to 64, by Marital Status and Motherhood, 1970 to 2006

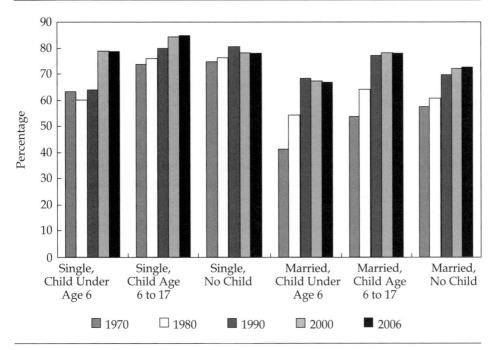

Sources: Authors' calculations from the decennial census (U.S. Bureau of the Census 1970, 1980, 1990, 2000) and the American Community Survey (U.S. Bureau of the Census 2006).

ried mothers and falling employment rates for single women without children. The increased employment for single mothers of young children began in 1993 and was strong in the late 1990s, partially coinciding with more restrictive welfare policies that reduced the availability of cash assistance.[19]

As shown in figure 4.7, there is less change over time in employment patterns for men, though there have been modest declines over time in male employment rates—in contrast to the increases apparent among women. When we disaggregate male employment patterns by family structure, we find that in all years married men and resident fathers are more likely to work, but there is little evidence of systematic difference in the time trend by marital or parental status (figure not shown).

Although it remains an important cultural reference point, the "traditional" family—an employed father, a homemaker mother, and children—is increasingly uncommon. In 2006 only 12 percent of all families fit this model, down from 36 percent in 1970.[20] In part, this decline reflects a growing disconnect between marriage and childbearing and childrearing. At the same time that single-mother families are more prevalent, increases in women's own earnings mean they are less vulnerable to economic hardship. We consider explanations for these countervailing changes in the next section, and then turn to an assessment of their importance in explaining changes in the level of poverty over time.

EXPLAINING CHANGES IN MARRIAGE, CHILDBEARING, AND EMPLOYMENT

We have documented substantial declines in marriage, a reduction in the average number of children per family, and a dramatic increase in the proportion of children born outside of marriage since 1970. Over the same period, women's employment has increased, especially for mothers. In contrast, men, especially those with less education, have experienced stagnant or declining rates of employment. These changes in family structure and employment are interrelated. For example, delays in marriage may reduce fertility, thereby reducing demands for work in the home and facilitating women's market work. On the other hand, as labor market opportunities for women improve—in absolute terms, or relative to men's—women face higher opportunity costs of leaving employment to have (additional) children, as well as reduced economic incentives to marry. Decisions to have children outside of marriage may reflect both women's increasing ability to support a family independently and a short supply of men with family-supporting earnings.

Understanding the factors that underlie changes in family formation and how these changes have been affected by economic and policy changes is complicated by the interdependence of economic, social, and demographic changes. Although few factors can accurately be viewed as independent, an assessment of the causes of family structure and employment changes can inform policy discussions. First, to the extent that social policy attempts to alter certain behaviors—for example, to encourage employment—understanding the factors underlying current behavior is an important starting point. Second, concerns that current (undesired) patterns of behavior are the *result* of policy have motivated policy change. For example, the emphasis of the 1996 welfare reform on reducing nonmarital childbearing reflected concerns that increases in the proportion of children born outside of marriage were the result of the incentives created by the availability of welfare benefits for single mothers. The 2005 Deficit Reduction Act (DRA) reauthorizing the 1996 reform further emphasized policies designed to promote marriage and reduce nonmarital births.

The decline in the proportion of married people results from people marrying at older ages or not at all. It also reflects higher rates of divorce, which are only somewhat offset by increases in remarriage. What accounts for these trends? The standard economic model of marriage emphasizes gains from a specialized division of labor in a context where one spouse (generally the husband) commands a substantially higher wage (Becker 1991). In this case, marriage creates a context in which the lower-wage spouse can devote herself to home production—raising children, preparing meals, maintaining the home—and leave the higher-wage spouse to specialize in earning wages. As men's advantage in the labor market relative to women has declined (Blau and Kahn 2000; Bowler 1999), so have the potential gains from marital specialization, reducing women's incentive to marry.

In addition, over the same period, increased marital instability increased the risks to women of interrupting their wage employment. As divorce has become more common, the probability that a woman will have to be the primary provider for herself and her children has increased. At the same time, as labor force participation has increased, so has the feasibility of leaving an undesirable marriage. Thus, women's increasing economic independence may be both a cause and a consequence of greater marital instability.

The past three decades have seen increased inequality in the distribution of wages for men and stagnant or declining wages, especially for younger men with low education (Blank, this volume). Thus, men's labor market advantage, and the consequent potential gains from marriage, have been particularly eroded for low-income individuals. William Julius Wilson (1987) argues that industrial restructuring and changes in the organization and location of jobs substantially reduced men's employment and earnings prospects, especially for urban black men with low education. High rates of incarceration also limit the pool of "marriageable" men with access to family-supporting employment, especially for African Americans (Blau, Kahn, and Waldfogel 2000; Lopoo and Western 2005; Holzer 2007).

Together with women's increased economic prospects and the availability of birth control, changes in social norms have made it easier to have sexual relationships and cohabit outside of marriage, to establish households independent of parents or spouses, and to rear children outside of marriage. Thus, as the economic advantage of marriage has declined, so has the importance of marriage as a precursor to parenthood (Edin and Kefalas 2005). The independent causal role of social norms is difficult to disentangle. In any case, economically stable marriage remains the normative goal, even among demographic groups with low rates of marriage (Gibson-Davis, Edin, and McLanahan 2004). Nonetheless, cohabitation, nonmarital childbearing, and divorce are increasingly accepted (Thornton and Young-DeMarco 2001).

Changes in contraceptive technology and reduced fertility also contribute to women's increased labor force participation. Of course, it is difficult to distinguish cause and effect; mothers may be more likely to work in the market because they have fewer children, or they may be having fewer children because of the demands of greater labor force participation.

Another focus of public debate and research has been the role that policy plays in facilitating changes in marriage, childbearing, and employment among low-income women. With regard to marriage policy, there are concerns about the disincentives to marriage embedded in the welfare system, as well as the vulnerability of the low-income population to policies aimed at altering family behaviors. Critics of welfare argued that the availability of financial support and the structure of eligibility rules that targeted single-parent families discouraged marriage and parental responsibility (Murray 1984). The generosity of welfare cannot fully explain changes in marriage because AFDC (Aid to Families with Dependent Children) benefits declined substantially after the mid-1970s, over the same period that marriage rates declined. And the decline in marriage was also evident among higher-income individuals who never received welfare. Estimates of the magnitude of any negative impact of welfare on marriage vary quite substantially but generally suggest at most modest effects (Moffitt 1998b, 2003; on recent welfare reforms, see Grogger and Karoly 2005, 2007). Some research suggests that income supports may *increase* marriage rates, possibly by helping low-income couples achieve the financial stability seen by some as a prerequisite for marriage (Gassman-Pines and Yoshikawa 2006; Gibson-Davis, Edin, and McLanahan 2004).

The impact of child support enforcement on marriage is another area of debate. Policy changes over the past thirty years have substantially increased the proportion of nonmarital births for which paternity is established and contributed to more fathers of children born to unmarried mothers being ordered to pay child support and making payments (Cancian and Meyer 2006). Although child support enforcement and paternity establishment are primarily aimed at increasing the formal economic support provided by nonresident fathers, improved enforcement may also change incentives to marry and have children. The increasing probability of paying and receiving child support might be expected to have offsetting effects on the financial incentives to have children outside of marriage—increasing the costs of nonmarital births for nonresident fathers and decreasing them for resident mothers. For some single men who might otherwise provide few resources to their children, increased child support enforcement may raise the expected costs of fatherhood. In contrast, despite receiving child support or cash welfare, single mothers typically bear most of the responsibility and costs associated with raising children. Changes in welfare benefit levels (or child support payments) may thus have a relatively minor impact on the benefits and costs faced by a single woman considering motherhood.[21] Research suggests that increased child support enforcement is associated with reductions in nonmarital births (Garfinkel et al. 2003; Plotnick et al. 2004, 2006).

Because many nonmarital births are to cohabiting or romantically involved parents, child support enforcement may negatively affect these "fragile families." Although child support provides financial resources, the requirements to establish paternity and to issue a formal child support order and the efforts to enforce that order may increase conflict between parents. Noncompliant fathers face enforcement actions that may reduce their willingness and ability to support their children (Waller and Plotnick 2001; Waller 2002; Pate and Johnson 2000; Garfinkel and McLanahan 2000).

Over the last three decades, several policy changes have sought to encourage employment and to "make work pay" for low-income parents, including an expanded Earned Income Tax Credit and expansions of Medicaid and the State Children's Health Insurance Program (SCHIP). The EITC provides a substantial earnings subsidy for low-income earners with children (Scholz, Moffitt, and Cowan, this volume; Meyer and Rosenbaum 2001), and the expanded availability of public health insurance for low-income children supports the move from welfare to work (Swartz, this volume). Child care policies, particularly recently expanded subsidies for some low-income families, also facilitate employment (Waldfogel, this volume).

TABLE 4.1 / Poverty Rates and Population Shares by Family Type, 1969 to 2006

	2006		1969		Change	
	Poverty Rate	Population Share	Poverty Rate	Population Share	Poverty Rate	Population Share
Single female	17.3%	9%	19.8%	4%	−2.5%	5%
Single female, with children	39.9	13	47.7	8	−7.8	6
Single male	14.0	8	15.0	3	−1.0	5
Single male, with children	19.0	4	17.1	2	1.9	2
Married couple	2.8	20	4.3	17	−1.5	3
Married couple, with children	7.5	46	8.6	67	−1.1	−21
Overall	12.6	100	11.5	100	1.1	—

Source: Authors' calculations from the decennial census (U.S. Bureau of the Census 1970) and American Community Survey (U.S. Bureau of the Census 2006).
Note: Data include families with heads age eighteen to sixty-four.

THE IMPACT OF CHANGES IN FAMILY STRUCTURE AND WOMEN'S EMPLOYMENT ON POVERTY

The preceding analysis revealed substantial changes in family structure and growth in female employment since 1969. How have the changes affected poverty rates? We decompose changes in poverty to show that, on their own, changes in family structure would have led to a substantial increase in poverty. However, the growth of female employment had important poverty-reducing effects.

Table 4.1 reports poverty rates and population shares for non-elderly persons classified by six mutually exclusive family types, defined by headship (single female, single male, or married couple) and presence of children.[22] The first column shows poverty rates in 2006. Persons living in families headed by single women raising children had the highest poverty rate, at 39.9 percent, and married couples had the lowest—2.8 percent for those with no children residing with them and 7.5 percent for those with children. Most persons (66 percent) lived in married-couple families, either with (46 percent) or without (20 percent) children (column 2). Poverty rates in 1969 (column 3) showed the same pattern, with high rates for single mothers with children and low rates for married couples.

Between 1969 and 2006, the poverty rate grew by 1.1 percentage points, from 11.5 percent to 12.6 percent. However, the poverty rate within five family types declined (column 5); the only exception was single males with children, who accounted for only 4 percent of persons in 2006. This suggests that an important factor in the growth of the overall poverty rate may have been the shift in population shares by family type. As we have shown earlier in this chapter, marriage and child-rearing rates declined over this period, and the share of children raised in single-parent families increased. As a result of these changes, the share of persons living in married-couple families fell by twenty-one percentage points, whereas the share of people in families without children grew by thirteen percentage points, and the share in single-parent families grew by eight percentage points (column 6). With the exception of married couples without children, all of the growing family types have higher poverty rates than do married couples with children. In other words, the population shifted from a relatively low-poverty group (married couples with children) to family types with higher risks of poverty.

By how much would overall poverty have increased if there had been a change in family structure but no change in poverty rates for each type of family? One approach to this question is to construct a counterfactual level of poverty with the 2006 shares of persons by family type and the 1969 poverty rates. This method is known as a "shift-share" analysis because we are shifting the population shares while holding poverty rates constant. Applying this approach to the numbers in table 4.1, we find that the poverty rate in 2006 would have been 14.6 percent. Therefore, if all else remained the same as in 1969, the change in family structure would have increased the poverty rate by 3.1 percentage points, from 11.5 percent in 1969 to 14.6 percent in 2006.[23]

The shift-share analysis provides a simple way of gauging the possible magnitude of the impact of family structure changes. However, this approach may overestimate the impact of family structure changes by implicitly assuming that poverty rates would remain the same within each family type. For example, the decline in poverty among single women may result from a change in family structure if the decline in marriage was disproportionately among high-education, high-resource women. We improve on the estimates by conducting the shift-share analysis separately by education and age. This analysis implicitly assumes that within an education-age category, if nothing beyond family structure had changed, single mothers in 2006 would face the same poverty rate faced by single mothers in 1969.[24] As we discuss later, this analysis is an improvement on the simple shift-share, but it also has some limitations. Using the shift-share analysis that controls for education and age, we find that changes in family structure increased poverty, but that the impact was smaller when controlling for education and age: 2.6 percentage points as compared to 3.1 percentage points (table 4.2).[25]

Over this same period, there was substantial growth in female employment. Including women's labor force participation in the shift-share analysis, we find that growth in women's work reduced poverty by 1.4 percentage points.[26] Taken together, changes in family structure and women's work led to a 1.2-percentage-point increase in poverty, which is comparable to the actual increase in poverty over this period (table 4.2, row 1).

We see a similar pattern across racial and ethnic groups: changes in family structure put upward pressure on poverty, but this was mitigated by growth in female employment. Poverty among blacks fell substantially, in part owing to growth in

TABLE 4.2 / Shift-Share Estimates of the Expected Impact of Changes in Family
Structure and Employment on Poverty Rates by Demographic Group
and by Time Period

| | Expected Change | | | |
	Family Structure	Female Work	Total	Actual Change
1969 to 2006				
All	2.6%	−1.4%	1.2%	1.1%
White	1.8	−1.2	0.6	0.5
Black	3.2	−2.7	0.5	−8.8
Hispanic	1.2	−3.3	−2.1	−3.1
Children	4.6	−2.2	2.5	3.0
1969 to 1989				
All	0.6	−1.1	−0.5	0.4
White	0.6	−1.1	−0.5	0.0
Black	1.2	−1.3	−0.2	−5.5
Hispanic	0.2	−2.2	−2.0	−0.4
Children	1.6	−1.4	0.2	2.3
1989 to 2006				
All	2.4	−0.6	1.9	0.6
White	1.6	−0.2	1.4	0.5
Black	2.2	−2.2	0.0	−3.3
Hispanic	1.1	−1.2	−0.1	−2.7
Children	3.5	−1.2	2.4	0.7

Sources: Authors' calculations from decennial census (U.S. Bureau of the Census 1970, 1990, 2000)
and American Community Survey (U.S. Bureau of the Census 2006).
Notes: Data include families with heads age eighteen to sixty-four. Table shows estimates of the
impact in percentage points. "Total" is the sum of the three preceding columns. Reported number may not add to the total due to rounding.

female employment. In addition, black women had stronger growth in education
over this period, with the share in our low-education group falling from 60 percent
in 1969 to 46 percent in 2006.[27] Not surprisingly, the change in family structure had
a more substantial impact on poverty among children, although this too was mitigated by the growth in female employment.

When we separately analyze the early decades and the late decades, we find similar patterns in both periods, with changes in family structure increasing poverty
and growth in women's work decreasing poverty. Interestingly, although family
structure changes were very substantial over the period 1969 to 1989, they had a relatively small impact on poverty. During this period, the growth in single-mother
families was more substantial for high-education women, resulting in an overall
impact on poverty that was smaller than would otherwise be expected.[28]

Shift-share analysis within education-age groups improves on the simple shift-share analysis. These counterfactual calculations, however, do not measure the causal effects of changes in family behaviors on poverty because the analysis ignores the relationship between family behaviors and poverty rates. The shift-share calculations rely on the unrealistic assumption that family structure and female employment could change to 2006 levels while poverty rates within each type of family could remain at 1969 levels after controlling for education, age, and race-ethnicity—that is, the "all else remained the same" assumption. In addition, we cannot properly account for the impact of changes that affect both family structure and poverty rates within given family types. For example, the growth in women's labor market opportunities may directly affect family structure (reducing marriage and fertility) and at the same time reduce vulnerability to poverty within single-mother families.[29] In practice, as discussed earlier in this chapter, decisions about family structure and labor force participation are interconnected, and many unobservable characteristics influence these behaviors.

CONCLUSION

We have shown that changes in family structure and changes in the implications of family structure for poverty reflect a complex set of interrelated factors. Fewer people are marrying, and those who are married are on average older and more likely to divorce. This smaller number of married couples are having fewer children, while the birthrates for the growing number of unmarried women have increased. Together these trends result in a greater proportion of families headed by single mothers—because of growth both in the proportion of births that take place outside of marriage and in the proportion of children born within marriage whose parents divorce.

Single-mother families, generally relying on the earnings of only one adult, are more than five times as likely to be poor as married-couple families. On its own, the change in family structure has increased poverty. However, a number of factors have had countervailing impacts. First, the increase in single-female households has coincided with a major increase in the employment of women. Although fewer women and children can depend on regular support from a husband or resident father, more women, especially mothers, are working, and many are earning enough to raise their families out of poverty. Employment rates for single mothers with young children—a particularly vulnerable group— grew substantially in the 1990s. In addition, women are having fewer children, reducing the total family income needed to avoid poverty. Moreover, almost half of recent births to unmarried women were to cohabiting parents. Treating cohabiting adults as partners and including their income as a family resource substantially reduces the increase in poverty due to changes in family structure.

Thus, changes in employment, the number of children, and cohabitation have reduced the growth in poverty otherwise associated with the declining proportion of married-couple families. However, while increased employment has made women and single mothers less economically vulnerable, it has presumably come at the cost of (unpaid) time spent supporting their family and community (Waring 1999; Sandberg and Hofferth 2001). In addition, the standard measure of income poverty used here neglects the nondiscretionary personal *costs* of employment, such as transportation and child care, and thus overstates the poverty-reducing effects of employment (Iceland and Kim 2000). Similarly, while many unmarried mothers may live with the fathers of their children or other men, cohabiting relationships provide less economic security than marriage, in part because of their relative instability (Bumpass and Lu 2000; Manning, Smock, and Majumdar 2004; Kenney 2004; DeLeire and Kalil 2005).

There are several types of public policy responses to the increased diversity and instability of family forms. Some policies explicitly aim to *change* family structure, for example, to promote marriage or reduce nonmarital births. Although it is too early to know whether recent efforts to promote healthy marriage will be successful (Dion 2005; Dion et al. 2008), some have argued that even small changes in marriage patterns could produce substantial returns on fairly modest investments (Amato 2005; Amato and Maynard 2007). Nonetheless, it seems unlikely that current policy options will dramatically alter the marriage and fertility patterns of the last four decades, most of which generally apply across income groups within the United States as well as in other countries. Although some policies to encourage marriage and, especially, reduce unplanned and teen pregnancy may prove effective, declines in marriage and increases in nonmarital childbearing are unlikely to be reversed by feasible public policies.

Other policies aim to *respond* to changes in family forms—for example, to reduce the negative consequences of nonmarital births and divorce through policies such as child support, or to encourage or facilitate employment, especially among single mothers. These policies, discussed in Jane Waldfogel's chapter in this volume, will be critical in determining the consequences of family change for the well-being of children.

As we have documented, the past forty years have been a period of increasing diversity in family structures and changing relationships between marriage, fertility, and employment. Children are more likely to spend some time living outside a married-couple family. Regardless of whether their mother is married or single, children, especially younger children, are also more likely to live with a mother who is working in the paid labor market. To reduce the economic vulnerability of children and families, public policy must respond to the diversity and instability of family forms. Even if effective policy interventions to reduce divorce and nonmarital childbearing are developed, many children will live with only one parent, and many parents will face challenges in meeting the economic and social needs of their families. Recognizing these challenges, public policy must respond in ways that support the increasing complexity of family arrangements and the growing proportion of workers who also have primary responsibility for parenting their children.

Earlier versions of this chapter were presented at the Association for Public Policy Analysis and Management Research Conference in Washington, D.C., November 2007. The authors gratefully acknowledge helpful discussions and comments on an earlier draft from Sheldon Danziger, Sanders Korenman, Rebecca Maynard, Isabel Sawhill, conference participants, and two anonymous referees; the research assistance of Qian Li and Eunhee Han; and the editorial assistance of Deborah Johnson. Deborah Reed acknowledges financial support from the Public Policy Institute of California.

NOTES

1. In 2006 about 8 percent of married couples with children and 40 percent of single-mother families were poor, according to the authors' calculations from the American Community Survey (ACS) for families with prime-age heads between the ages of eighteen and sixty-four.
2. On the causes and consequences of teen pregnancy, see Maynard (1997), Hotz, McElroy, and Sanders (2005), Fletcher and Wolfe (forthcoming), and Furstenberg (2007). On nonmarital births, see Upchurch, Lillard, and Panis (2002).
3. We evaluated trends for women with "low education" defined as less than a high school diploma in 1970 and no more than a high school diploma in 2006. In both years, about 40 percent of all women between the ages of eighteen and sixty-four were in these categories. This definition uses a changing cutoff point but includes the equivalent part of the distribution in both years, in contrast to one that uses a constant education level (such as less than high school) but reflects a relatively more disadvantaged group as the educational distribution improves over time. These calculations are available from the authors.
4. Unless otherwise noted, all statistics come from authors' calculations from the decennial census (1970, 1980, 1990, 2000) and the American Community Survey (U.S. Bureau of the Census 2006).
5. The most recent period shown spans six rather than ten years because the 2006 data were the latest available when this chapter was written.
6. Heterosexual marriage rates for men and women are, by definition, related. Nonetheless, somewhat different patterns do emerge. In addition to differences in age at first marriage, differences by gender reflect the higher probability of remarriage for divorcing men relative to divorcing women.
7. Hispanics of any race are included only in the Hispanic race-ethnicity group.
8. It is difficult to measure cohabitation, both because, until recently, few surveys asked respondents about nonmarital partners and because social stigma and the lack of a formal legal status make self-reports of nonmarital partners difficult to interpret. We use the Adjusted POSSLQ measure developed by Lynne Casper, Philip Cohen, and Tavia Simmons (1999). Beginning with the 1990 census, household heads were able to identify individuals as their "unmarried partner," providing a "direct" measure of partners. The Adjusted POSSLQ measure captured 95 percent of all self-identified

"partners"; however, almost 40 percent of those identified by the Adjusted POSSLQ measure were not self-identified as partners. The Adjusted POSSLQ does not take into account same-sex partners.

9. The decennial census and American Community Survey data do not provide sufficient information to study family relationships for people who are not related to the household head. In 2006 unrelated household members made up 7 percent of adults and 2 percent of children.

10. Between 1970 and 2006, the number of co-resident children of their own for women age thirty-five to thirty-nine declined from 2.5 to 1.5 for whites; from 2.6 to 1.4 for blacks; from 2.8 to 1.8 for Hispanics; from 2.3 to 1.4 for Asians; and from 3.4 to 1.4 for American Indians.

11. See Ellwood and Jencks (2004) for a recent review. On the role of policy and other factors in explaining nonmarital birth rates, see Murray (1984), McLanahan and Sandefur (1994), Moffitt (1998b, 2000), and Raley (2001); on the implications for economic status and child outcomes, see Carlson and Corcoran (2001), Kenney (2004), Amato (2005), Manning and Brown (2006), and Osborne, Manning, and Smock (2007).

12. Assume that the only change between two periods is a decline in the portion of women who marry—that is, that there are no changes in the likelihood that a married or single woman will have a child. In that instance, change in the relative number of married and unmarried women, by itself, will increase the proportion of births to unmarried women. Similarly, a decline in the fertility of married women, with no change in the fertility of unmarried women, will increase the proportion of births to unmarried women (see McLanahan 1985).

13. The trends in fertility statistics for whites and blacks cited in this paragraph include Hispanics of either race.

14. Figure 4.5 includes only children under age eighteen living with at least one biological parent, stepparent, or adoptive parent. Persons under eighteen who are heads of families, institutionalized, living in households not headed by a relative, or not living with a parent are excluded. In 1970 this excluded 1 percent of people under eighteen; in 2006, 1.6 percent were excluded.

15. Race and ethnicity is determined by the race and ethnicity of the female head, if present, and otherwise by the male head.

16. The data only distinguish mothers who are household heads or related to their household head. Note that we cannot distinguish the relationship between children of the household head and adults unrelated to the head. Thus, some "cohabiting male partners" may be the fathers of children in the household, and some of the children living with their unmarried mother may also be living with their (unmarried) father. The parallel situation exists in the case of single-father households and unmarried female partners.

17. On mutual obligations and family support, see Oliker (1995). On resource allocation within cohabiting couples, see Kenney (2004), Brown (2004), and DeLeire and Kalil (2005). On complicated families and social fathers, see Hofferth and Anderson (2003), Hofferth (2006), Gibson-Davis (2008), and Berger et al. (2008). There is a growing literature on the role of grandparents, including DeLeire and Kalil (2002), Park (2006), and Dunifon and Kowaleski-Jones (2007).

18. For women in the lower 40 percent of the education distribution—those with less than a high school diploma in 1970 or no more than a high school diploma in 2006 (see note 3)—the proportion working full-time, full-year grew from 21 percent to 37 percent.

19. Trends in the 1990s are based on authors' calculations from the Current Population Survey (CPS) and are not shown in figure 4.8.

20. Authors' calculations for people under age fifty-five. Employment is defined as working at least one week in the previous year.

21. The state government typically retains all or most of the child support paid to welfare recipients (all but the first $50 per month) to offset the costs of providing welfare. Thus, mothers receiving welfare receive very limited formal child support. The DRA of 2005 encouraged states to allow mothers to receive up to $200 per month in child support while maintaining their full welfare eligibility. These provisions took effect in 2008. As of this writing, however, most states retain 100 percent of child support paid on behalf of children of cash welfare recipients.

22. Poverty rates differ from the official Census Bureau statistics because we use the census and the American Community Survey rather than the Current Population Survey and because we limit the analysis to families with heads in the age range of eighteen to sixty-four. We standardize the poverty thresholds over time by using the 2006 thresholds. For consistency with official poverty thresholds, we adjust income to 2006 dollars using the CPI-U (consumer price index for all urban consumers) before 1983 and the CPI-U-X1 (consumer price index for all urban consumers, X1 series) in 1983 and later. As in the official poverty calculation, all related persons living in the same household are grouped as a single family. Families are classified into types based on the marital status of the family heads. For example, a single woman heading a household that includes her married daughter, son-in-law, and grandchild is classified as "single female, with children."

23. We do not attempt to separately identify the poverty-increasing effects of the decline in marriage from the poverty-reducing effects of the decline in childbearing.

24. We distinguish between low and high education as described in note 3. Women age forty or younger make up the low-age group. Interacting two education groups and two age groups, we conduct four shift-share analyses. We also divide families with children into families with one child and those with two or more children.

25. As an alternative counterfactual, we conduct all shift-share analyses using 2006 poverty rates and shifting population shares in each group from 2006 levels to 1970 levels. This analysis, available from the authors, provides substantively similar results.

26. Within education-age groups, we divide the population into families where the female head or female spouse of the head had earnings in the past year and those where she did not have earnings.

27. Education statistics are for black women who were the head of household or the spouse of the head of household.

28. Without controls for education-age groups, the shift-share analysis suggests that the impact of changes in family structure on poverty would have been of similar magnitude in both periods at just over 1 percent.

29. Although it is not possible to derive causal estimates, alternative methods of estimating the counterfactual also show a substantial effect of family structure changes.

Adam Thomas and Isabel Sawhill (2002) simulate marriages in 1998 to match marriage patterns in 1970 and find that the decline in marriage had a substantial effect on child poverty. Mary Daly and Robert Valletta (2006) use a model-based approach and find that changes in family structure increased poverty while growth in women's employment reduced poverty.

REFERENCES

Amato, Paul R. 2005. "The Impact of Family Formation Change on the Cognitive, Social, and Emotional Well-Being of the Next Generation." *The Future of Children* 15(2): 75–96.

Amato, Paul R., and Rebecca A. Maynard. 2007. "Decreasing Nonmarital Births and Strengthening Marriage to Reduce Poverty." *The Future of Children* 17(2): 117–41.

Becker, Gary S. 1991. *A Treatise on the Family*. Cambridge, Mass.: Harvard University Press.

Berger, Lawrence, Marcia J. Carlson, Sharon H. Bzostek, and Cynthia Osborne. 2008. "Parenting Practices of Resident Fathers: The Role of Marital and Biological Ties." *Journal of Marriage and Family* 70(3): 625–39.

Bergstrom, Theodore C. 1997. "A Survey of Theories of the Family." In *Handbook of Population and Family Economics,* edited by Mark R. Rosenzweig and Oded Stark. New York: Elsevier.

Blau, Francine. 1998. "Trends in the Well-Being of American Women, 1970–1995." *Journal of Economic Literature* 36(1): 112–65.

Blau, Francine, and Lawrence M. Kahn. 2000. "Gender Differences in Pay." *Journal of Economic Perspectives* 14(4): 75–99.

———. 2007. "Changes in the Labor Supply Behavior of Married Women: 1980–2000." *Journal of Labor Economics* 25(3): 393–438.

Blau, Francine D., Lawrence M. Kahn, and Jane Waldfogel. 2000. "Understanding Young Women's Marriage Decisions: The Role of Labor and Marriage Market Conditions." *Industrial and Labor Relations Review* 53(4): 624–47.

Bowler, Mary. 1999. "Women's Earnings: An Overview." *Monthly Labor Review* 122(12): 13–21.

Brown, Susan L. 2004. "Family Structure and Child Well-Being: The Significance of Parental Cohabitation." *Journal of Marriage and the Family* 66(2): 351–67.

Bumpass, Larry L., and Hsien-Hen Lu. 2000. "Trends in Cohabitation and Implications for Children's Family Context in the United States." *Population Studies* 54(1): 29–41.

Bumpass, Larry L., James A. Sweet, and Andrew J. Cherlin. 1991. "The Role of Cohabitation in Declining Rates of Marriage." *Journal of Marriage and the Family* 53(4): 913–27.

Cancian, Maria, and Daniel R. Meyer. 2006. "Child Support and the Economy." In *Working and Poor: How Economic and Policy Changes Are Affecting Low-Wage Workers,* edited by Rebecca M. Blank, Sheldon H. Danziger, and Robert F. Schoeni. New York: Russell Sage Foundation.

Cancian, Maria, Daniel R. Meyer, and Steven Cook. 2009. "The Evolution of Family Complexity from the Perspective of Children: Siblings, Half-Siblings, and Step-Siblings." Madison: University of Wisconsin, Institute for Research on Poverty.

Cancian, Maria, and Deborah Reed. 1999. "The Impact of Wives' Earnings on Income Inequality: Issues and Estimates." *Demography* 36(2): 173–84.

Carlson, Marcia J., and Mary E. Corcoran. 2001. "Family Structure and Children's Behavioral and Cognitive Outcomes." *Journal of Marriage and the Family* 63(3): 779–92.

Casper, Lynne M., Philip N. Cohen, and Tavia Simmons. 1999. "How Does POSSLQ Measure Up? Historical Estimates of Cohabitation." Working paper 36. Washington: U.S. Government Printing Office for U.S. Bureau of the Census, Population Division (May).

Child Trends. 2008. "Teen Births." *Child Trends Data Bank.* Available at: http://www.child trendsdatabank.org/indicators/13TeenBirth.cfm (accessed July 10, 2009).

Current Population Survey, March file. 1967–2006. CPS Utilities, Unicon Research Corporation. Available at: www.unicon.com.

Daly, Mary C., and Robert G. Valletta. 2006. "Inequality and Poverty in the United States: The Effects of Rising Dispersion of Men's Earnings and Changing Family Behavior." *Economica* 73(289): 75–98.

DeLeire, Thomas, and Ariel Kalil. 2002. "Good Things Come in Threes: Single-Parent Multigenerational Family Structure and Adolescent Adjustment." *Demography* 39(2): 393–413.

———. 2005. "How Do Cohabiting Couples with Children Spend Their Money?" *Journal of Marriage and Family* 67(2): 285–94.

Dion, Robin M. 2005. "Healthy Marriage Programs: Learning What Works." *Future of Children* 15(2): 139–56.

Dion, Robin M., Alan M. Hershey, Heather H. Zaveri, and Sarah A. Avellar. 2008. *Implementation of the Building Strong Families Program.* MPR Reference 8935–134. Washington, D.C.: Mathematica Policy Research.

Dunifon, Rachel, and Lori Kowaleski-Jones. 2007. "The Influence of Grandparents in Single-Mother Families." *Journal of Marriage and Family* 69(2): 465–81.

Edin, Kathryn, and Maria Kefalas. 2005. *Promises I Can Keep: Why Poor Women Put Motherhood Before Marriage.* Berkeley: University of California Press.

Edin, Kathryn, and Laura Lein. 1997. *Making Ends Meet: How Single Mothers Survive Welfare and Low-Wage Work.* New York: Russell Sage Foundation.

Ellwood, David T., and Christopher Jencks. 2004. "The Spread of Single-Parent Families in the United States Since 1960." In *The Future of the Family*, edited by Daniel Patrick Moynihan, Timothy Smeeding, and Lee Rainwater. New York: Russell Sage Foundation.

Fletcher, Jason M., and Barbara L. Wolfe. Forthcoming. "Education and Labor Market Consequences of Teenage Childbearing: Evidence Using the Timing of Pregnancy Outcomes and Community Fixed Effects." *Journal of Human Resources.*

Furstenberg, Frank F. 2007. *Destinies of the Disadvantaged: The Politics of Teen Childbearing.* New York: Russell Sage Foundation.

Garfinkel, Irwin, Chien-Chung Huang, Sara S. McLanahan, and Daniel S. Gaylin. 2003. "The Roles of Child Support Enforcement and Welfare in Nonmarital Childbearing." *Population Economics* 16(1): 55–70.

Garfinkel, Irwin, and Sara S. McLanahan. 2000. "Fragile Families and Child Well-Being: A Survey of New Parents." *Focus* 21(1): 9–11.

Gassman-Pines, Anna, and Hirokazu Yoshikawa. 2006. "Five-Year Effects of an Anti-Poverty Program on Marriage Among Never-Married Mothers." *Journal of Policy Analysis and Management* 25(1): 11–30.

Gibson-Davis, Christina. 2008. "Family Structure Effects on Maternal and Paternal Parenting in Low-Income Families." *Journal of Marriage and Family* 70(2): 452–65.

Gibson-Davis, Christina, Kathryn Edin, and Sara McLanahan. 2004. "High Hopes but Even Higher Expectations: The Retreat from Marriage Among Low-Income Couples." Working paper 2003-06-FF. Princeton, N.J.: Princeton University, Center for Research on Child Well-Being.

Grogger, Jeffrey, and Lynn A. Karoly. 2005. *Welfare Reform: Effects of a Decade of Change.* Cambridge, Mass.: Harvard University Press.

———. 2007. "The Effects of Work-Conditioned Transfers on Marriage and Child Well-Being." Working paper WR 531. Santa Monica, Calif.: RAND Corporation.

Hofferth, Sandra L. 2006. "Residential Father Family Type and Child Well-Being: Investment Versus Selection." *Demography* 43(1): 53–77.

Hofferth, Sandra L., and Kermyt G. Anderson. 2003. "Are All Dads Equal? Biology Versus Marriage as a Basis for Paternal Investment." *Journal of Marriage and Family* 65(1): 213–32.

Holzer, Harry J. 2007. "Collateral Costs: The Effects of Incarceration on the Employment and Earnings of Young Workers." Discussion paper 3112. Bonn: Institute for the Study of Labor (IZA).

Hotz, V. Joseph, Susan Williams McElroy, and Seth G. Sanders. 2005. "Teenage Childbearing and Its Life Cycle Consequences: Exploiting a Natural Experiment." *Journal of Human Resources* 40(3): 683–715.

Iceland, John, and Joshua Masnick Kim. 2000. "Poverty Among Working Families: New Insights from an Improved Poverty Measure." Paper presented to the annual meeting of the Population Association of America. Los Angeles, Calif., March 23–25, 2000.

Kenney, Catherine. 2004. "Cohabiting Couple, Filing Jointly? Resource Pooling and U.S. Poverty Policies." *Family Relations* 53(2): 237–47.

Lopoo, Leonard M., and Bruce Western. 2005. "Incarceration and the Formation and Stability of Marital Unions." *Journal of Marriage and the Family* 67(3): 721–34.

Manning, Wendy D., and Susan Brown. 2006. "Children's Economic Well-Being in Married and Cohabiting Parent Families." *Journal of Marriage and Family* 68(2): 345–62.

Manning, Wendy D., Pamela J. Smock, and Debarun Majumdar. 2004. "The Relative Stability of Cohabiting and Marital Unions for Children." *Population Research and Policy Review* 23(2): 135–59.

Martin, Joyce A., Brady E. Hamilton, Paul D. Sutton, Stephanie J. Ventura, Fay Menacker, Sharon Kimeyer, and T. J. Matthews. 2009. "Births: Final Data for 2006." *National Vital Statistics Reports:* 57(7, January 7). Hyattsville, Md.: National Center for Health Statistics. Available at: http://www.cdc.gov/nchs/data/nvsr/nvsr57/nvsr57_07.pdf (accessed July 10, 2009).

Maynard, Rebecca A. 1997. *Kids Having Kids: Economic Costs and Social Consequences of Teen Pregnancy.* Washington, D.C.: Urban Institute Press.

McLanahan, Sara. 1985. "Charles Murray and the Family: *Losing Ground:* A Critique." Special Report Series 38. Madison: University of Wisconsin, Institute for Research on Poverty.

McLanahan, Sara, and Gary Sandefur. 1994. *Growing Up with a Single Parent: What Hurts, What Helps.* Cambridge, Mass.: Harvard University Press.

Meyer, Bruce D., and Dan T. Rosenbaum. 2001. "Welfare, the Earned Income Tax Credit, and the Labor Supply of Single Mothers." *Quarterly Journal of Economics* 116(3): 1063–1114.

Moffitt, Robert A. 1998a. "Beyond Single Mothers: Cohabitation and Marriage in the AFDC Program." *Demography* 35(3): 259–78.

———. 1998b. "The Effect of Welfare on Marriage and Fertility." In *Welfare, the Family, and Reproductive Behavior,* edited by Robert A. Moffitt. Washington, D.C.: National Academies Press.

———. 2000. "Welfare Benefits and Female Headship in U.S. Time Series." *American Economic Review* 90(2): 373–77.

———. 2003. "The Temporary Assistance for Needy Families." In *Means-Tested Transfer Programs in the United States,* edited by Robert A. Moffitt. Chicago: University of Chicago Press.

Murray, Charles. 1984. *Losing Ground: American Social Policy, 1950–1980.* New York: Basic Books.

Oliker, Stacey J. 1995. "The Proximate Contexts of Workfare and Work: A Framework for Studying Poor Women's Economic Choices." *Sociological Quarterly* 36(2): 251–72.

Osborne, Cynthia, Wendy D. Manning, and Pamela J. Smock. 2007. "Married and Cohabiting Parents' Relationship Stability: A Focus on Race and Ethnicity." *Journal of Marriage and Family* 69(5): 1345–66.

Park, Hwa-Ok Hannah. 2006. "The Economic Well-Being of Households Headed by Grandmother as Caregiver." *Social Service Review* 80(2): 264–96.

Pate, David, and Earl S. Johnson. 2000. "The Ethnographic Study for the W-2 Child Support Demonstration Evaluation: Some Preliminary Findings." *Focus* 21(1): 18–22.

Plotnick, Robert D., Irwin Garfinkel, Daniel S. Gaylin, Sara S. McLanahan, and Inhoe Ku. 2004. "Better Child Support Enforcement: Can It Reduce Teenage Premarital Childbearing?" *Journal of Family Issues* 25(5): 634–57.

———. 2006. "The Impact of Child Support Enforcement Policy on Nonmarital Childbearing." *Journal of Policy Analysis and Management* 26(1): 79–98.

Raley, Kelly R. 2000. "Recent Trends and Differentials in Marriage and Cohabitation: The United States." In *The Ties That Bind: Perspectives on Marriage and Cohabitation,* edited by Linda J. Waite. New York: Aldine de Gruyter.

———. 2001. "Increasing Fertility in Cohabiting Unions: Evidence for the Second Demographic Transition in the United States?" *Demography* 38(1): 59–66.

Sandberg, John F., and Sandra L. Hofferth. 2001. "Changes in Children's Time with Parents: United States, 1981–1997." *Demography* 38(3): 423–36.

Schoen, Robert, Nancy S. Landale, and Kimberly Daniels. 2007. "Family Transitions in Young Adulthood." *Demography* 44(4): 807–20.

Spain, Daphne, and Suzanne M. Bianchi. 1996. *Balancing Act: Motherhood, Marriage, and Employment Among American Women.* New York: Russell Sage Foundation.

Tamis-LeMonda, Catherine S., and Natasha Cabrera, eds. 2002. *Handbook of Father Involvement: Multidisciplinary Perspectives.* Mahwah, N.J.: Lawrence Erlbaum Associates.

Thomas, Adam, and Isabel Sawhill. 2002. "For Richer or for Poorer: Marriage as an Antipoverty Strategy." *Journal of Policy Analysis and Management* 21(4): 587–99.

Thornton, Arland, and Linda Young-DeMarco. 2001. "Four Decades of Trends in Attitudes Toward Family Issues in the United States: The 1960s Through the 1990s." *Journal of Marriage and the Family* 63(4): 1009–37.

Toossi, Mitra. 2002. "A Century of Change: The U.S. Labor Force, 1950–2050." *Monthly Labor Review* 125(5): 15–28.

Upchurch, Dawn M., Lee A. Lillard, and Constantijn W. A. Panis. 2002. "Nonmarital Childbearing: Influences of Education, Marriage, and Fertility." *Demography* 39(2): 311–29.

U.S. Bureau of the Census. Various years. U.S. Census, Public Use Microdata Sample. Washington: U.S. Bureau of the Census. Available at: http://www.census.gov/main/www/pums.html.

———. 2006. *American Community Survey.* Washington: U.S. Bureau of the Census. Available at: http://www.census.gov/acs/www (accessed July 8, 2009).

U.S. Department of Health and Human Services. 1995. Report to Congress on Out-of-Wedlock Childbearing. Washington: U.S. Government Printing Office. Available at: http://www.cdc.gov/nchs/data/misc/wedlock.pdf (accessed July 9, 2009).

Waller, Maureen R. 2002. *My Baby's Father: Unmarried Parents and Paternal Responsibility.* Ithaca, N.Y.: Cornell University Press.

Waller, Maureen R., and Robert Plotnick. 2001. "Effective Child Support Policy for Low-Income Families: Evidence from Street-Level Research." *Journal of Policy Analysis and Management* 20(1): 89–110.

Waring, Marily. 1999. *Counting for Nothing: What Men Value and What Women Are Worth.* Toronto: University of Toronto Press.

Wilson, William Julius. 1987. *The Truly Disadvantaged: The Inner City, the Underclass, and Public Policy.* Chicago: The University of Chicago Press.

Chapter 5

Immigration and Poverty in the United States

Steven Raphael and Eugene Smolensky

Between 1970 and 2003, the proportion of U.S. residents born in another country increased from 4.8 percent to 12.4 percent. This relative increase corresponded to a sizable absolute increase in the number of foreign-born. Net international migration accounted for over one-quarter of net population growth during this period. Moreover, recent international migrants are heavily concentrated among groups with either extremely low or relatively high levels of formal educational attainment, with the group at the low end being particularly large. Many have conjectured that this large flow of immigrants has had adverse effects on the economic well-being of the least-skilled native-born and hence the poverty rate.

The potential contribution of international migration to the official poverty rate in the United States is likely to operate through two avenues. First, migrants may have a direct effect on the poverty rate. Since the poverty rates observed among the foreign-born are high, an increase in the proportion of foreign-born will, as a matter of arithmetic, increase the national poverty rate. This direct compositional effect can be either exacerbated or mitigated over time depending on the extent to which immigrants acquire experience in U.S. labor markets and progress through the earnings distribution.

Second, international immigration alters the relative supplies of workers with different levels of education and other labor market skills, a factor that may influence the wages and employment of both migrants and natives. In particular, recent immigration has increased the number of workers with very low levels of educational attainment. The impact of this change on poverty depends on the sensitivity of native employment and earnings to the influx of competing immigrant labor. Moreover, the effects on poverty rates are likely to vary across racial and ethnic groups. In particular, African Americans, native-born Hispanics, and the native-born children of prior immigrants tend to be less educated on average and thus are perhaps most likely to be affected by competition with immigrants.

In this chapter, we assess the contribution of immigration over the past three and a half decades to poverty in the United States. We first document trends in poverty rates among the native-born by race and ethnicity and poverty trends among all immigrants, recent immigrants, and immigrants by their region and (in some instances) country of origin. Next, we assess how poverty rates among immigrants change with time in the United States. By measuring poverty rates over time among immigrant cohorts defined by when they arrived, we are able to track how the poverty rates of immigrants change as their time in the United States increases.

Having documented these basic facts, we turn to a discussion of the likely impact of immigration on poverty rates operating through (1) a shift in the composition of the population and (2) an impact of immigration on the earnings and employment of natives. We first assess what the nation's poverty rate would have been if there had been no change in the proportion of immigrants between 1970 and 2005, assuming no labor market effects of immigration. Next, we provide a simple theoretical discussion of labor market competition between immigrants. Finally, we simulate what native poverty rates would be under alternative estimates of the effects of immigrants on native earnings and employment.

To summarize our findings, poverty in the United States declined modestly between 1970 and 2005. Declines were notable for the native-born, while poverty among immigrants increased absolutely. Within country-of-origin groupings, poverty declined for most groups. The distribution of the U.S. immigrant population by region of origin, however, has shifted decisively toward source countries that generate immigrants who are more likely to be poor.

We find that poverty rates among immigrants groups decline quite quickly with time in the United States. Moreover, while the initial level of poverty among recent arrivals has increased in recent decades, the declines in poverty observed in subsequent censuses suggests that even the poorer immigrants of the most recent wave either exit poverty at a fairly rapid rate or emigrate out of the country. Interestingly, the immigrant-native disparity in the incidence of poverty declines with immigrants' time in the United States when immigrants are compared to native birth cohorts of similar age at similar points in time. This pattern is consistent with either real income growth for immigrant households that propels immigrants out of poverty or the selective return migration of those immigrants most likely to be poor.

Our analysis reveals that immigration patterns had a modest impact on poverty. Overall poverty declined by a modest amount between 1970 and 2005. Decomposing this change into a component attributable to changing population shares across groups by nativity and country of origin indicates that, had the composition of the U.S. population not changed, the poverty rate would have fallen by an additional percentage point. Thus, while immigration certainly has contributed to overall poverty rates, the contribution through this direct channel is modest. Our estimates that account for the effects of immigration on native wages suggest modest effects of immigration over this time period on the least-educated natives (those with less than a high school diploma) and no or slightly

FIGURE 5.1 / Proportion of All U.S. Residents, Native-Born Residents, and Immigrants in Poverty, 1970 to 2005

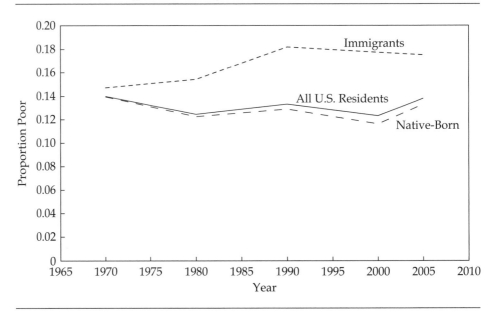

Source: Authors' tabulations based on the Public Use Microdata Samples (PUMS) (U.S. Bureau of the Census, various years) and the 2005 American Community Survey (ACS) (U.S. Bureau of the Census 2005).

positive effects on the earnings of most other skill groups.[1] The simulation results suggest that labor market competition with immigrants has had little to no effect on overall native poverty levels or on those for specific racial and ethnic groups.

DATA DESCRIPTION AND BASIC POVERTY TRENDS

We analyze data from the 1970, 1980, 1990, and 2000 U.S. censuses and the 2005 American Community Survey (ACS).[2] Poverty is imputed from total household income (not inclusive of transfer payments), with the federal poverty line adjusted for family size in each census year (and in 2005 for the ACS sample). We restrict the sample to all non-institutionalized residents of the United States.

First we document the poverty trends. Figure 5.1 displays the poverty rates measured for each census year and 2005 for all U.S. residents, the native-born, and immigrants. Since the native-born constitute the majority of the U.S. population in each year (from a high of 95 percent in 1970 to a low of 87 percent in 2005), the

TABLE 5.1 / Poverty Among the Native-Born by Race-Ethnicity, 1970 to 2005

	1970	1980	1990	2000	2005	Change 1970 to 2005
Non-Hispanics						
White	10.3%	8.8%	9.1%	7.9%	9.3%	−1.0%
Black	36.2	30.1	30.6	25.2	26.7	−11.0
Asian	9.4	8.4	11.2	12.3	12.5	3.1
Other	37.1	27.0	30.8	22.1	24.3	−12.8
Hispanic	27.0	23.9	25.4	22.1	23.5	−3.1

Sources: Authors' compilation based on the Public Use Microdata Samples (PUMS), 1970 through 2000 (U.S. Bureau of the Census, various years), and the 2005 American Community Survey (U.S. Bureau of the Census 2005).

overall poverty rate closely mirrors the poverty rate among the native-born. Poverty increases notably among immigrants, however, from roughly 15 percent to 18 percent over the time period depicted.

Table 5.1 displays the percentage of natives in poverty for five mutually exclusive race-ethnicity groupings in all decennial census years since 1970 and in 2005. Several changes are notable. First, with the exception of native-born Asians, poverty declines for all groups, with particularly large declines for non-Hispanic blacks (from 36 percent to 27 percent) and non-Hispanic others (from 37 percent to 24 percent). More modest declines are observed for whites and Hispanics. For blacks and Hispanics, poverty rates decline monotonically between 1970 and 2000 and then increase slightly in 2005.

Table 5.2 presents similar tabulations for all U.S. resident immigrants in all decennial census years since 1970 and in 2005, by region of origin.[3] We provide separate country-of-origin estimates for Mexico given the disproportionate importance of immigrants from this country. Immigrants from Mexico have the highest poverty rates: between 26 and 29 percent of Mexican immigrants were poor in each year. Immigrants from Central and South America and from Asia also have relatively high poverty rates. On the other hand, western European immigrants and immigrants from other North American countries have low poverty rates, with percentages in poverty that are fairly stable across census years. Interestingly, there are few notable increases in poverty within country- or region-of-origin groups, and many instances where poverty rates decline.

We also tabulated comparable poverty rates where immigrants within each group and year are further subdivided into immigrants who arrived within five years prior to the census (recent immigrants) and immigrants who arrived earlier (nonrecent immigrants). Figure 5.2 displays these tabulations. Poverty rates are much higher among recent immigrants within all country-of-origin groupings.

TABLE 5.2 / Poverty Among Immigrants by Region of Origin, 1970 to 2005

	1970	1980	1990	2000	2005	Change 1970 to 2005
North America	9.0%	8.0%	8.1%	7.6%	8.0%	−1.0%
Latin America						
Mexico	29.2	26.4	29.4	26.5	26.1	−3.2
Central America	15.9	20.6	22.4	19.9	17.9	2.0
Caribbean	14.7	16.4	18.6	17.5	17.9	3.2
South America	14.5	15.3	14.6	15.5	12.2	−2.3
Europe						
Western[a]	12.6	8.5	8.1	7.8	8.2	−4.4
Eastern[b]	14.3	8.9	9.2	11.7	10.9	−3.4
Russian Empire	16.1	14.9	19.7	19.6	16.9	0.8
Asia						
East	13.4	12.7	15.6	15.1	15.0	1.6
Southeast	16.2	19.8	18.4	12.2	11.4	−4.8
India and Southwest	14.6	17.2	12.4	11.0	9.8	−4.8
Middle East	14.3	20.1	19.5	18.3	19.3	5.0
Africa	12.5	20.4	14.9	17.6	20.4	7.9
Oceania	11.9	15.9	16.1	12.1	10.5	−1.4
Other	20.8	23.1	24.7	—	17.4	−3.4

Sources: Authors' compilation based on the Public Use Microdata Samples (PUMS), 1970 through 2000 (U.S. Bureau of the Census, various years), and the 2005 American Community Survey (U.S. Bureau of the Census 2005).
a. Excludes Warsaw Pact countries and the components of the former Yugoslavia.
b. Includes former Warsaw Pact countries and the components of the former Yugoslavia.

This pattern is consistent with either a strong negative effect of time in the United States on poverty or increasing poverty rates among cohorts of more recent arrivals. We investigate this issue in more detail in the next section.

The poverty trends in figure 5.1 reveal increases in poverty among immigrants, while the tabulations in table 5.2 suggest that within-group poverty rates have been relatively stable. Taken together, these two trends suggest that the distribution of immigrants across country-of-origin groupings must have shifted toward higher-poverty immigrant groups. Indeed, this is the case. Table 5.3 displays the distribution of the U.S. resident population by nativity, by race-ethnicity among natives, and by region of origin among immigrants. The tabulations for immigrants reveal several stark changes in the region-of-origin distribution for immigrants. Western Europeans constituted 41 percent of the immigrant population in 1970 but only 10 percent in 2005. By contrast, Mexican immigrants constituted 8 percent of

FIGURE 5.2 / Poverty Rates Among Recent Immigrants (Arrived Within Past Five Years) and Nonrecent Immigrants (Arrived More Than Five Years Before)

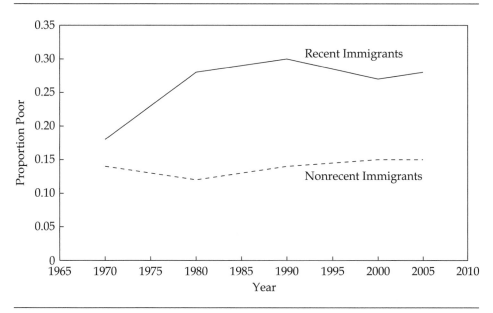

Sources: Authors' tabulations based on the Public Use Microdata Samples (PUMS) (U.S. Bureau of the Census, various years) and the 2005 American Community Survey (ACS) (U.S. Bureau of the Census 2005).

immigrants in 1970 and 27 percent of immigrants in 2005. Sizable increases are also observed in the proportion of immigrants from other Latin American countries and Asian countries. Thus, we observe a sizable shift toward immigrant groups with higher U.S. poverty rates.

HOW IMMIGRANT POVERTY RATES CHANGE WITH TIME IN THE UNITED STATES

We noted that poverty rates among recent immigrants are considerably higher than poverty rates among immigrants from the same regions who arrived in the more distant past. This cross-sectional pattern suggests that, with time in the United States, immigrant poverty may decline and perhaps converge to the lower levels experienced by the native-born.

In more recent years, however, new immigrants are increasingly likely to come from regions that supply poorer immigrants. Moreover, it is possible that there have been comparable shifts in the composition of immigrants from the same nation (from lower-poverty to higher-poverty co-nationals). Thus, more recent immigrants may be fundamentally different from previous immigrants, with higher propensities to

TABLE 5.3 / Distribution of the U.S. Resident Population by Nativity, by Race-
Ethnicity Among the Native-Born, by Time in the United States Among
Immigrants, and by Region of Origin Among Immigrants

	1970	1980	1990	2000	2005	Change 1970 to 2005
All U.S. residents	100.00%	100.00%	100.00%	100.00%	100.00%	—
Native-born	95.18	93.82	92.03	88.82	87.60	−7.58
Immigrant	4.82	6.18	7.97	11.18	12.40	7.58
All natives	100.00%	100.00%	100.00%	100.00%	100.00%	—
Non-Hispanic white	84.50	81.61	81.52	76.67	78.25	−6.25
Non-Hispanic black	11.43	11.94	10.50	11.71	10.00	−1.43
Non-Hispanic Asian	0.50	0.69	1.07	2.11	2.47	1.97
Non-Hispanic other	0.42	0.74	0.99	1.39	1.10	0.68
Hispanic	3.15	5.02	5.91	8.10	8.19	5.04
All immigrants	100.00%	100.00%	100.00%	100.00%	100.00%	—
Recent	82.46	76.15	75.15	75.63	82.54	0.08
Nonrecent	17.54	23.85	24.85	24.37	17.46	−0.08
All immigrants	100.00%	100.00%	100.00%	100.00%	100.00%	—
North America	9.60	6.13	4.12	2.90	3.03	−6.57
Latin America						
Mexico	8.22	15.82	22.77	30.74	27.45	19.23
Central America	1.21	2.54	5.52	6.46	6.10	4.89
Caribbean	7.05	9.12	9.08	9.09	8.25	1.2
South America	2.71	4.08	5.18	5.93	6.56	3.85
Europe						
Western[a]	40.94	26.27	16.37	9.99	9.77	−31.17
Eastern[b]	11.36	6.58	4.22	3.48	3.46	−7.9
Russian Empire	6.09	3.51	1.99	2.79	3.14	−2.95
Asia						
East	4.31	6.84	8.90	8.63	9.78	5.47
Southeast	1.74	6.60	10.13	9.89	10.43	8.69
India and Southwest	0.92	2.79	4.13	5.45	6.57	5.65
Middle East	1.33	2.02	1.95	1.71	1.76	0.43
Africa	0.63	1.35	1.54	2.50	3.16	2.53
Oceania	0.43	0.58	0.53	0.53	0.48	0.05
Other	3.45	5.77	3.57	0.00	0.06	−3.39

Sources: Authors' compilation based on the Public Use Microdata Samples (PUMS), 1970 through
2000 (U.S. Bureau of the Census, various years) and the 2005 American Community Survey (ACS)
(U.S. Bureau of the Census 2005).

experience poverty in the United States. Observing higher poverty among recent immigrants in a given year is also consistent with a decline in the average earnings potential of more recent immigrants relative to immigrants from times past.

This difficulty in interpreting the difference in socioeconomic status between recent immigrants and nonrecent immigrants is a central point of contention in the research regarding the degree to which immigrant wages assimilate upward toward the higher earnings of the native-born. In a series of papers, Barry Chiswick (1978, 1980) argues that the strong cross-sectional relationship between immigrants' time in the United States and earnings is indicative of the speed with which immigrants assimilate into the U.S. labor market.

In a series of articles, George Borjas (1986, 1995) contests this interpretation of the cross-sectional earnings data. Borjas argues that to the extent that more recent immigrants have discretely lower earnings potential than immigrants from previous years, comparing immigrants of different ages in a given year provides a distorted picture of the future earnings paths of recent immigrants. Borjas constructs "synthetic cohorts" across census years to investigate this possibility. A synthetic cohort compares the earnings of a specific arrival cohort at different points in time (across census years), thereby providing an alternative characterization of the age-earnings profile. For example, the average earnings of immigrants who arrived between 1965 and 1970 as measured in the 1970 census, the 1980 census, and so on are compared. In this comparison, changes between years would pertain to the same cohort and might be attributable to time in the United States. When estimated in this fashion, the age-earnings profiles of immigrants look considerably less steep than those implied by the cross-sectional patterns. That is to say, earnings growth appears to be no faster than that of comparable natives, immigrant earnings do not overtake native earnings, and native-immigrant income convergence occurs at a slower rate than is implied by a cross-sectional analysis comparing the earnings of immigrants of different ages at a given point in time (such as a census year).

In table 5.4, we apply the synthetic cohort analysis of Borjas to the measurement of poverty. Specifically, using census data from 1970 through 2005, we define immigrant cohorts by their year of arrival and measure their poverty rates in successive census years. Assuming that the composition of the cohort does not change over time through selective emigration or measurement error (a big assumption that we will discuss further), changes in poverty rates across census years for fixed arrival cohorts provide estimates of how immigrant poverty changes with immigrants' time in the United States.

We present results for immigrants from all source countries and for all ages in the top panel. These initial results reveal several distinct patterns. First, the poverty rates of recent immigrants (shown along the diagonal) increased notably between 1970 and 1990. In 1970, 18 percent of recent immigrants (defined as those who had arrived within the past five years) had incomes below the federal poverty line. This increased to 28 percent in 1980, and to 30 percent in 1990, but then declined to 28 percent in 2000. The top panel also reveals that poverty rates decline quite quickly with time in the United States. Moreover, these declines are more pronounced for more recent cohorts relative to past cohorts. For example,

TABLE 5.4 / Synthetic Cohort Analysis of Immigrant Poverty Rates by Census Year and by Year of Arrival

	1970	1980	1990	2000	2005
Year of first arrival					
All immigrants					
1965 to 1970	18.0%	12.3%	10.8%	10.3%	9.5%
1975 to 1980	—	27.9	16.3	13.1	10.7
1985 to 1990	—	—	30.3	17.9	14.5
1995 to 2000	—	—	—	27.8	17.8
Immigrants eighteen to thirty-four in census year immediately following arrival					
1965 to 1970	16.8	10.4	9.5	9.5	8.6
1975 to 1980	—	27.0	14.8	12.0	9.3
1985 to 1990	—	—	29.6	17.5	13.6
1995 to 2000	—	—	—	28.5	16.8
Natives age eighteen to thirty-four in:					
1970	10.7	8.3	7.2	7.4	8.1
1980	—	11.4	8.9	7.1	8.1
1990	—	—	13.4	8.5	9.3
2000	—	—	—	13.8	12.2

Sources: Authors' compilation based on the Public Use Microdata Samples (PUMS), 1970 through 2000 (U.S. Bureau of the Census, various years), and the 2005 American Community Survey (ACS) (U.S. Bureau of the Census 2005).

considering the first row of the panel, between 1970 and 1980 the poverty rate of immigrants who arrived between 1965 and 1970 declined by 5.7 percentage points (from 18.0 percent to 12.3 percent). The comparable ten-year change for recent immigrants in the 1980 census was 11.3 percentage points (27.9 percent to 16.3 percent), while the comparable change for recent immigrants in the 1990 census was 12.4 percentage points (30.3 percent to 17.9 percent). Even for the five-year period following the 2000 census, the poverty rate among recent immigrants declined by a full 10.0 percentage points.

To address whether the decline over time in poverty rates represents convergence between immigrants and natives, we need to compare changes in poverty for comparable age groups. The middle panel reproduces the top panel for immigrants who were between eighteen and thirty-four years of age in the census year following their arrival (excluding children and older immigrants from each arrival cohort).[4] The patterns are quite similar, with poverty declining during the first ten years in the United States by ten percentage points or more in most instances. The bottom panel presents comparable cross-census comparisons of poverty rates among the native-born who were age eighteen to thirty-four in each of the decennial census years. For example, the figures in the first row present poverty rates for those natives who were age eighteen to thirty-four in 1970, twenty-eight to forty-four in 1980, thirty-eight to forty-four in 1990, and so

FIGURE 5.3 / Immigrant Poverty Rate Minus Native Poverty Rate by Arrival Cohort, Immigrants Age Eighteen to Thirty-Four at First Census Year After Arrival

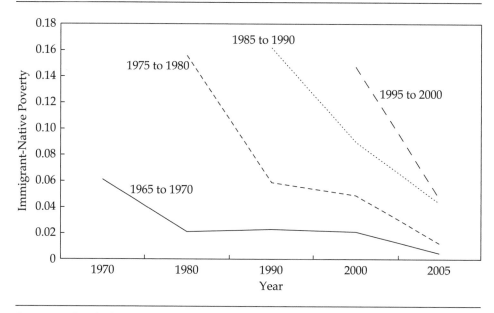

Sources: Authors' tabulations based on the Public Use Microdata Samples (PUMS) (U.S. Bureau of the Census, various years) and the 2005 American Community Survey (ACS) (U.S. Bureau of the Census 2005).

on. We can assess the degree to which immigrant poverty rates converge toward those of the native-born by comparing the corresponding immigrant-native poverty rates (using the figures in the middle and bottom panels) and their change over time.

Figure 5.3 graphs the corresponding differences between immigrant and native poverty rates in the middle and bottom panels of table 5.4 for each arrival cohort. For example, the left-most point in figure 5.3 shows the six-percentage-point gap between immigrant and native-born poverty for recent immigrants and natives who were age eighteen to thirty-four in 1965 to 1970 (corresponding to the difference between 16.8 percent and 10.7 percent shown in the first column of the middle and bottom panels of table 5.4). The figure reveals the rapid convergence of native and immigrant poverty rates. For example, over the thirty-five-year period between 1970 and 2005, the immigrant-native poverty rate differential between the 1965 to 1970 arrival cohort and the comparably aged natives declined from about six percentage points to half a percentage point. Between 1980 and 2005, the relative poverty rate differential for the 1975 to 1980 cohort declined from 15.6 percentage points to 1.2 percentage points. Among the most recent arrivals in the 2000 census (the 1995 to 2000 arrival cohort), the immigrant-native poverty differential declined from 14.7 percentage points to 4.6 percentage points over a relatively short five-year period. Thus, in contrast to the wage results discussed earlier, the poverty rates of immigrants did indeed assimilate for the better compared to native outcomes.[5]

We also tabulated comparable synthetic cohort analyses of the relationship between time in the United States and poverty rates among immigrants for select region-of-origin groups. Here we summarize these additional results.[6] Although there are large differences in starting poverty rates for recent immigrants (with Mexican immigrants experiencing the highest initial poverty rates and Asian immigrants the lowest), poverty declines with time in the United States for all groups. For example, between 1980 and 2005, the percentage in poverty among the 1975 to 1980 arrival cohort declined by 14.5 percentage points among Mexican immigrants, 19.8 percentage points among Central American immigrants, 19.4 percentage points among South American immigrants, 16.1 percentage points among East Asian immigrants, and 22.6 percentage points among Southeast Asian immigrants.

To provide an alternative set of metrics of poverty assimilation among immigrants, we also compared the poverty rates for Mexican, Central American, and South American immigrants to those of native-born Hispanics. Similarly, we compared the poverty rates for East Asian and Southeast Asian immigrants to those of native-born Asians. These comparisons also reveal substantial narrowing of the immigrant-native poverty rate disparity with time in the United States. The slowest narrowing is observed for Mexican immigrants, while for Central American and South American immigrants, poverty rates fall below native-born Hispanic poverty rates in several instances. For East Asian and Southeast Asian immigrants, nearly all of the immigrant-native poverty disparity is eliminated within ten years, while the remaining disparity disappears within twenty years in most instances.

The results from this section strongly suggest that with time in the United States the poverty rates of specific immigrant cohorts defined by year of arrival decline sharply and, for the most part, converge to the lower poverty rates of the native-born. Since these results are based on synthetic cohorts rather than on analysis of longitudinal data on actual cohorts, they are open to several alternative interpretations. One clear possibility is that as immigrants acquire experience in the United States, labor market earnings increase sufficiently to propel many out of poverty. An alternative interpretation is that those immigrants who are the most likely to remain poor selectively migrate out of the United States and back to their home countries. In other words, the arrival cohort observed near the time of arrival may differ in composition from the same arrival cohort observed a decade or two later.

We cannot distinguish between these two possibilities with census data, but recent research by Darren Lubotsky (2007) speaks directly to this issue. Lubotsky hypothesizes two sources of upward bias to synthetic cohort estimates of earnings growth among immigrants. First, selective emigration of the least successful leaves a positively selected, higher-earning group of immigrants remaining in the United States. Less successful immigrants leave the United States and are not included in estimates of later earnings. Second, since the census basically asks immigrant respondents when they arrived in the United States "to stay," immigrants who cycle in and out of the United States, and who are perhaps more likely to be low earners, are overrepresented among recent immigrants. By comparing longitudinal earnings records from the U.S. Social Security Administration with synthetic cohort estimates from the census and other sources, Lubotsky shows that both sources of bias tend to exaggerate the degree to which immigrant earnings increase with time in the United States.

What are the implications of these findings for the analysis here? Clearly, any upward bias in synthetic cohort estimates of immigrant earnings assimilation is likely to lead us to overstate the degree to which an immigrant who enters the United States today will climb out of poverty in future years. However, the extent of this bias in the current application is perhaps less severe than in studies of income growth. Since progressing out of poverty simply requires that household income cross the poverty line, income growth beyond this threshold (even if exaggerated) has no impact on the incidence of poverty. The second source of bias resulting from misclassification suggests that our estimates of poverty among recent immigrants are likely to be too high, while the estimates of the poverty rates for nonrecent immigrants are likely to be low. Again, this bias is perhaps less important when the poverty count is at issue. What is clear, however, is that with time in the United States income growth and selective migration result in sharply declining poverty rates among specific time-of-arrival cohorts of immigrants.

THE CONTRIBUTION OF IMMIGRATION TO THE NATIONAL POVERTY RATE: COUNTRY-OF-ORIGIN COMPOSITIONAL EFFECTS

The descriptive statistics indicate that poverty among the U.S. immigrant population has increased and that this increase has been driven largely by shifts in the composition of the immigrant population toward higher-poverty source countries. Moreover, the figures in table 5.3 indicate that a larger proportion of the nation's population is foreign-born (increasing from 4.8 percent to 12.4 percent over the period studied). Increasing poverty among immigrants, coupled with a higher proportion of immigrants in the population, must add to the national poverty rate. In this section, we assess by how much.

To be sure, the results thus far suggest that this composition effect cannot be large. Immigrants still constitute a minority of the U.S. population, with poor immigrants being a minority of this minority. Thus, their contribution to the national weighted average poverty rate is dwarfed by the contribution of the lower poverty rate of the native-born. Of course, native poverty may be higher as a result of labor market competition with immigrants (an issue we analyze in detail in the next section). Nonetheless, the pure compositional effect is limited in size by the size of the overall foreign-born population.

To analyze this question more formally, here we calculate a simple decomposition of the change in the national poverty rate between 1970 and 2005. The decomposition allows us to assess the contribution to changes over time in the poverty rate of two components: the change due to the change in the internal composition

TABLE 5.5 / Decomposition of Changes in National Poverty Rates into a Component Due to Changing Population Composition and a Component Due to Changes in Poverty Rates

	Percentage-Point Change in National Poverty Rate	Change Due to Changes in Population Shares	Change Due to Changes in Group-Specific Poverty Rates
1970 to 2005	−0.94	1.15	−2.09
1980 to 2005	0.56	0.63	−0.07
1990 to 2005	−0.01	0.54	−0.56
2000 to 2005	0.90	−0.28	1.18

Sources: Authors' compilation based on the Public Use Microdata Samples (PUMS), 1970 through 2000 (U.S. Bureau of the Census, various years) and the 2005 American Community Survey (ACS) (U.S. Bureau of the Census 2005).

Notes: These decompositions are calculated as follows. Let w_{it} be the proportion of the U.S. population at time t accounted for by group i, where the index i encompasses the native-born and each of the country-of-origin groups listed in table 5.2. In addition, define $poverty_{it}$ as the corresponding poverty rate for group i in year t. The national poverty rate for 1970 and 2005 can be expressed as a weighted sum of the group-specific poverty rates:

$$poverty_{1970} = \sum_{i=1}^{I} w_{i1970} poverty_{i1970}, \quad poverty_{2005} = \sum_{i=1}^{I} w_{i2005} poverty_{i2005}. \tag{5.1}$$

The change in poverty rates can be expressed by

$$\Delta Poverty = \sum_{i=1}^{I} w_{i2005} poverty_{i2005} - \sum_{i=1}^{I} w_{i1970} poverty_{i1970}. \tag{5.2}$$

Adding and subtracting the term $\sum_{i=1}^{I} w_{i1970} poverty_{i2005}$ to equation 5.2, then factoring, gives the decomposition

$$\Delta Poverty = \sum_{i=1}^{I} \left(w_{i2005} - w_{i1970} \right) poverty_{i2005} + \sum_{i=1}^{I} w_{i1970} \left(poverty_{i2005} - poverty_{i1970} \right).$$

The first component on the right-hand side shows the contribution to the poverty change associated with the shift in population shares between 1970 and 2005. This component is reported in the second column of the table. The second component represents the contribution of changes in group-specific poverty rates between 1970 and 2005, holding the population shares constant at 1970 levels. This component is reported in the third column of the table.

of the U.S. resident population across native and immigrant groups, and a component driven by changes in poverty rates occurring within these groups.[7]

Table 5.5 presents these decompositions for various time periods. In nearly all comparisons, the shift in population shares away from the native-born, and within the immigrant population, toward immigrants from poorer source countries has tended to increase poverty in the United States. However, declines in poverty within groups have for the most part more than offset the partial increases in poverty driven by changes in the national-origin population shares. For example, between 1970 and 2005, poverty declined slightly (by 0.94 percentage points). The changes in the population distribution between 1970 and 2005 increased poverty by 1.15 percentage points. This suggests that the composition effect of immigration has increased the national poverty rate by 1.15 percentage points above what it would otherwise be had the population shares not changed between 1970 and 2005. These decompositions are similar for all periods compared in table 5.5, with the exception of the 2000 to 2005 decomposition. During this period, the poverty rate increased slightly. Here, compositional changes were such that they tended to reduce poverty holding all else constant, while changes in poverty rates within groups increased poverty during this latter period. These decompositions suggest that the direct compositional effects of immigration on poverty are modest, especially during the later periods.[8]

POVERTY AMONG NATIVES DUE TO LABOR MARKET COMPETITION WITH IMMIGRANTS

The contribution of immigration to poverty analyzed in the previous section is purely arithmetic. To the extent that immigrants have higher poverty rates and immigrants are an increasing proportion of the resident population, the national poverty rate increases. Beyond this compositional effect, immigrants may also affect national poverty through labor market competition with natives. To the extent that immigrants drive down the wages of natives with similar skills, increased immigration contributes to native poverty. Moreover, this effect may be exacerbated if natives respond to lower wage offers by working fewer hours.

In this section, we begin with a theoretical discussion of the potential impact of immigrants on the earnings and employment of natives. We then present upper- and lower-bound estimates of the effects of immigration on native poverty operating through an impact of immigrant competition on the national wage distribution.[9]

Plainly stated, an influx of immigrants lowers the wages of those native-born workers with whom immigrants are in direct labor market competition. To the extent that wage suppression is sufficient to push these natives below the poverty line, immigration contributes to native poverty. The economic forces behind this proposition are best illustrated with a simple model of wage determination in the overall economy. Suppose that all workers in the economy are exactly the same in that employers can perfectly substitute one employee—immigrant or native—for another. Also assume that the stock of productive capital (machinery, plant, and equipment used in the production of goods and services) is fixed. Under these conditions, an increase in immigration increases the supply of labor in the national economy and lowers the wages and employment of native workers who now compete with immigrant workers.[10] At the same time, total employment (immigrant plus native) increases, raising national output. In conjunction with lower wages, increased output translates into higher incomes accruing to the owners of capital.[11]

This is a relatively straightforward story. Immigration increases national output, harms native labor, but enriches the owners of capital. Stated in an alternative manner using terminology that we define more clearly momentarily, immigration harms those "factors of production" with which it directly competes, while benefiting those factors that it complements. Given the large increases in immigration in recent decades and the clear predictions of these simple theoretical arguments, one may wonder what there is to debate.

Of course, the actual economy and the likely impacts of immigration operate within a far more complex model. Most conspicuously, in telling our simple story we assumed that employers could perfectly substitute the average immigrant worker for the average native worker (and vice versa). This is clearly unrealistic. Immigrants and natives differ along a number of dimensions that are likely to be of value to employers. Immigrants tend to have less formal education on average; levels of educational attainment are particularly low among Hispanic immigrants and many Southeast Asian immigrants. Immigrant and native-born workers are likely to differ in their ability to converse in English, and immigrants also tend to be younger than natives, a fact suggesting that the average immigrant worker may have less labor market experience than the average native-born worker.[12]

Given such differences in skills, it is more likely that immigrants and natives are imperfect substitutes in production—that is, substituting immigrant for native workers is possible, but limited by differences in skills. Moreover, the substitution possibilities are likely to vary across jobs according to the skill content of various occupations. In some instances, certain subgroups of natives are likely to complement immigrant labor in production. That is to say, certain native workers are likely to be hired in conjunction with the hiring of immigrant workers. For example, Spanish-speaking laborers on a construction site may increase the demand for native-born bilingual Hispanics with enough education to serve in supervisory positions. As another example, an increase in the supply of low-skilled construction labor may increase the demand for architects, structural and civil engineers, skilled craftsmen, and workers in other such occupations whose labor constitutes important inputs in the construction industry.

The imperfect substitutability between immigrant and native workers in the United States is most readily demonstrated by comparing their distributions across educational attainment groups. Table 5.6 presents the distributions of immigrants and native men and women, ages eighteen to sixty-four, across formal educational attainment levels for the year 2000. The share of immigrant workers with extremely low levels of educational attainment is quite high relative to all native groups. For example, roughly 22 percent of immigrant men left school before the ninth grade, compared with 2 percent of native-born white men, 4 percent of native-born black men, 2 percent of native-born Asian men, and 8 percent of native-born Hispanic men. Similar patterns are observed when comparing immigrant and native-born women. Immigrants are also more likely to hold advanced degrees relative to most of the native-born groups.

We can further characterize the degree of overlap between the skill distributions of immigrants and natives by incorporating the effects of age as well as education on skills and earnings. We do so by defining fifty-four age-education groups, ranking the groups by average earnings and identifying those age-education groups that

TABLE 5.6 / Distribution of Educational Attainment by Immigration States and by Race-Ethnicity for Adults, Age Eighteen to Sixty-Four, 2000

Educational Attainment	Foreign-Born		Native-Born American Citizens							
			Non-Hispanic White		Non-Hispanic Black		Non-Hispanic Asian		Hispanic	
	Men	Women	Men	Women	Men	Women	Men	Women	Men	Women
Less than ninth grade	21.61%	19.57%	2.32%	1.63%	4.18%	2.93%	2.09%	1.63%	8.15%	7.22%
Ninth to twelfth grade, no diploma	17.48	15.70	10.02	8.47	23.14	18.73	7.72	6.00	23.29	19.56
High school graduate	19.02	20.76	29.04	28.99	33.90	30.18	18.67	17.43	29.80	28.70
Some college	18.43	22.05	31.37	34.66	28.16	33.81	36.60	36.94	28.10	32.37
Bachelor's degree	12.62	14.09	17.80	17.81	7.60	9.89	24.18	27.04	7.45	8.78
Master's degree or higher	10.84	7.83	9.45	8.43	3.02	4.47	10.74	10.96	3.21	3.37

Source: Authors' compilation based on 1 percent 2000 Public Use Microdata Samples (PUMS) (U.S. Bureau of the Census, various years).

FIGURE 5.4 / Distribution of Immigrant and Native-Born Men Across Earnings
Groups Based on Native Population Quartiles

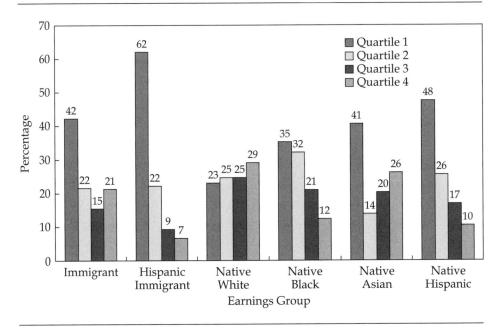

Sources: Authors' tabulations based on the Public Use Microdata Samples (PUMS) (U.S. Bureau
of the Census, various years) and the 2005 American Community Survey (ACS) (U.S. Bureau of
the Census 2005).

account for the bottom 25 percent, or first quartile, of the skill distribution for natives;
the next 25 percent of natives, or the second quartile; the middle-upper 25 percent of
natives, or the third quartile; and the top 25 percent of the native skill distribution, or
the fourth quartile.[13] With this breakdown, we then calculated the percentage of each
immigrant and native group that falls within each skill quartile. To the extent that the
percentage for a given group and quartile exceeds 25 percent, the group is overrepresented in this portion of the skill distribution. Conversely, to the extent that the percentage falls below 25 percent, the group is underrepresented.

Figure 5.4 presents these skill distributions for immigrant and native men. In
addition to all immigrants, we also present the distribution for Hispanic immigrants. Immigrants are heavily overrepresented in the least-skilled quartile and
underrepresented in the remainder of the skill distribution. Fully 42 percent of all
immigrant men and 62 percent of Hispanic immigrant men lie in the bottom quartile of the overall native skill distribution. For the native-born, by contrast, 23 percent of white men, 35 percent of black men, 41 percent of Asian men, and 48 percent
of Hispanic men fall in this low-skilled group. Furthermore, immigrants are underrepresented in the middle of the skill distribution, with 37 percent of all immigrants

FIGURE 5.5 / Distribution of Immigrant and Native-Born Women Across Earnings Groups Based on Native Population Quartiles

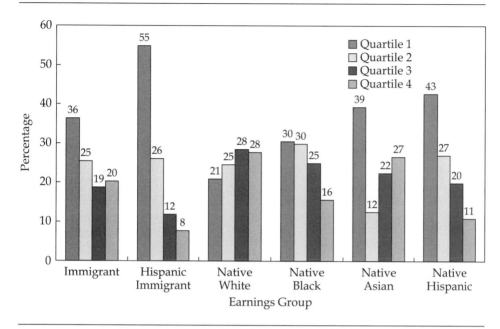

Sources: Authors' tabulations based on the Public Use Microdata Samples (PUMS) (U.S. Bureau of the Census, various years) and the 2005 American Community Survey (ACS) (U.S. Bureau of the Census 2005).

and 31 percent of Hispanic immigrants in the second and third quartiles; for the native-born, the comparable figures are 50 percent for white men, 53 percent for black men, 34 percent for Asian men, and 43 percent for Hispanic men. Figure 5.5 presents comparable distributions for women. Here we also see fairly large differences between the skill distributions of immigrant and native women.

These figures suggest that immigrants and natives differ considerably in terms of their skills, a fact that complicates our analysis. Allowing for imperfect substitution between immigrant and native labor driven by differences in skills alters our theoretical predictions regarding the economic effects of immigrants on native labor market outcomes. Those natives whose skills are most like those of immigrants are most likely to be harmed. On the other hand, those natives groups with sufficiently different skill sets are likely to be the least harmed or may even benefit in the form of higher wages and greater employment as a result of an increase in immigrant labor. The educational attainment figures presented in table 5.6 and the skill distributions depicted in figures 5.4 and 5.5 indicate that there are substantial differences in skills between immigrants and natives. Perhaps the greatest degree of similarity is between immigrants and native-born Hispanics. Nonetheless, one cannot predict a priori the average impact on immigration of each of these groups, since immigrant skills distributions clearly differ in each case. The ultimate effect of immigrants on natives—positive or negative—is an empirical rather than a theoretical question.

In our simple model of the effect of immigration on native wages and employment, we also assumed that the stock of productive capital is held fixed—in other words, that an immigration-induced increase in the nation's endowment of labor does not spur additional net investment on the part of domestic and foreign producers. Capital investment involves the deliberate allocation of resources toward activities that augment the future productive capacity of the economy—for example, the addition of a machine or a factory. Whether the economy makes sufficient investments to, on net, increase the stock of productive capital depends on the return to capital, with increasing returns spurring net capital accumulation.

The connection between immigration and capital accumulation is driven by the effect of immigration on these returns. To the extent that immigration increases the nation's labor supply, each unit of existing capital has more labor to work with. This increased relative scarcity of capital makes each unit more productive, which in turn increases the return to capital investment and the incentive to invest in future productive capacity. The resulting net capital accumulation partially offsets the negative effects of immigration on native wages and employment by increasing labor productivity (and, in turn, wages) and by creating new employment opportunities. The degree of this offset depends on the responsiveness of the capital supply to changes in return, as well as on the underlying technological relationships governing production in the economy. Nonetheless, capital accumulation dulls the wage and employment effects of immigration on natives.

Thus, we began with a simple story in which immigration unambiguously lowers the wages and reduces the employment of native workers and then finished with a more nuanced description in which the theoretical predictions are more ambiguous and varied. In our more complex yet more realistic theoretical discussion, the potential adverse labor market effects of immigration should be greatest for those native-born workers who are most similar in their skills to immigrants. Workers who are sufficiently different may even benefit from immigration insofar as immigrants complement such natives in producing goods and services. In addition, capital accumulation in response to an immigrant inflow, in isolation, benefits all workers by making them more productive. This partially offsets the wage declines for workers who are most similar to immigrants and accentuates the wage increases for natives with complementary skills.

Because the theoretical predictions regarding the magnitude and size of the effects of immigrants on native wages and employment are ambiguous (as is, therefore, the theoretical prediction regarding poverty), whether immigration increases or decreases poverty is ultimately an empirical issue. To estimate the contribution of immigration to poverty through labor market competition with natives, we simulate the hypothetical wages that workers of various skill groups would have earned in the year 2005 if the supply of immigrant labor had been held to 1970 levels. Using a range of alternative wage estimates, we then simulate what personal income, total family income, and poverty rates would have been had the immigrant population been held at 1970 levels.[14]

Table 5.7 presents lower- and upper-bound estimates of the effects of immigration on the national wage structure between 1970 and 2005. Each set of estimates provides the proportional effect of immigration during this time period on the weekly wages of the native-born by educational attainment and the level of labor market experience (in years). Note that the range of wage effects in these simulations spans the existing range of estimates in the empirical literature (see, for example, Borjas 2005; Ottaviano and Peri 2005, 2007).[15]

The lower-bound estimates assume that immigrants and natives within each skill group are imperfectly substitutable for one another, and they also assume a fairly high degree of substitutability between workers at different levels of educational attainment. Imperfect substitutability between immigrants and natives concentrates the negative wage effect of immigration on immigrants themselves, while the greater the degree of substitutability between workers of different levels of educational attainment, the more evenly the effect of the immigrant supply increases concentrated among the least skilled is diffused across all native-born workers. In conjunction, these two factors lead to estimates of the impact of immigration on native wages that are relatively modest, with small negative effects for high school dropouts only and zero to slightly positive effects for all other groups of workers. The upper-bound results in the second column of table 5.7 assume considerably less substitutability between workers in different education groups, thus concentrating the effect of immigration on those groups that are most affected. Not surprisingly, the predicted negative effects on the wages of high school dropouts increase (in absolute value), while the positive impacts on the wages of high school graduates and those with some college increase.

The final wage simulation assumes limited substitutability between workers of different levels of educational attainment (as in the simulation presented in the second column of table 5.7), but perfect substitutability between immigrants and natives within skill groups. This simulation yields the largest adverse wage effects for high school dropouts: perfect substitutability between similarly skilled immigrants and natives transmits a greater share of the supply shock to native workers, while the limited substitutability between workers with different education levels prohibits the shock from spreading out of the skill groups most affected by immigration. In all simulations, capital is allowed to accumulate in response to immigration-induced changes in the return to capital.

With these wage simulations, we are able to calculate hypothetical family income for households with a native-born household head and alternative poverty rates for all such households in 2005. The results of this exercise are presented in tables 5.8 and 5.9. In table 5.8, we present actual poverty rates and simulated poverty rates for those residing in households headed by a native-born person by the race-ethnicity

TABLE 5.7 / Simulated Proportional Effects of Immigration Between 1970 and 2005 on Native Weekly Wages by Level of Educational Attainment and Potential Years of Work Experience

Years of Experience of Native Skill Group	Assumes Immigrants and Natives Are Imperfect Substitutes Within Skill Group		Assumes Immigrants and Natives Are Perfect Substitutes Within Skill Group
	Lower Bound	Upper Bound	Upper Bound 2
Less than high school			
0 to 4	−0.00	−0.05	−0.07
5 to 9	−0.02	−0.07	−0.09
10 to 14	−0.02	−0.07	−0.09
15 to 19	−0.02	−0.07	−0.09
20 to 24	−0.02	−0.07	−0.09
25 to 29	−0.01	−0.06	−0.08
30 to 34	−0.01	−0.06	−0.08
35 to 40	−0.00	−0.06	−0.07
High school graduate			
0 to 4	0.01	0.01	0.01
5 to 9	0.00	0.01	0.00
10 to 14	0.00	0.01	0.00
15 to 19	0.00	0.01	0.00
20 to 24	0.01	0.01	0.01
25 to 29	0.01	0.02	0.01
30 to 34	0.01	0.02	0.01
35 to 40	0.01	0.02	0.01
Some college			
0 to 4	0.01	0.02	0.02
5 to 9	0.01	0.02	0.02
10 to 14	0.01	0.02	0.01
15 to 19	0.01	0.02	0.01
20 to 24	0.01	0.02	0.01
25 to 29	0.01	0.02	0.02
30 to 34	0.01	0.02	0.02
35 to 40	0.01	0.02	0.02
College graduate			
0 to 4	0.01	0.00	0.00
5 to 9	0.00	0.00	−0.01
10 to 14	0.00	0.00	−0.01
15 to 19	0.00	0.00	−0.01
20 to 24	0.00	0.00	0.00
25 to 29	0.00	0.00	0.00
30 to 34	0.01	0.00	0.00
35 to 40	0.01	0.00	0.00

Sources: Authors' tabulations based on the Public Use Microdata Samples (PUMS) (U.S. Bureau of the Census, various years) and the 2005 American Community Survey (ACS) (U.S. Bureau of the Census 2005).
Note: See text for description of wage simulations.

TABLE 5.8 / Actual Poverty Rates in 2005 Among Persons in Households Headed by Natives and Simulated Poverty Rates Holding Immigrant Labor Supply to 1970 Levels

	Actual Poverty Rate	Using Lower-Bound Wage Effects and Assuming Immigrants and Natives Are Imperfect Substitutes		Using Upper-Bound Wage Effects and Assuming Immigrants and Natives Are Imperfect Substitutes		Using Upper-Bound Wage Effects and Assuming Immigrants and Natives Are Perfect Substitutes	
		Elastic Labor Supply	Inelastic Labor Supply	Elastic Labor Supply	Inelastic Labor Supply	Elastic Labor Supply	Inelastic Labor Supply
Race-ethnicity of household head							
Non-Hispanics							
White	7.9%	7.9%	7.8%	7.8%	7.9%	7.8%	7.8%
Black	26.0	25.8	25.8	25.8	25.7	25.5	25.6
Asian	8.0	8.0	7.9	7.9	7.9	7.8	7.8
Other	19.6	19.5	19.5	19.5	19.5	19.2	19.3
Hispanic	19.3	19.0	19.1	18.7	18.9	18.4	18.8
Educational attainment of household head							
Less than high school	29.1	28.4	28.6	27.6	28.2	27.2	27.9
High school	14.0	13.9	13.9	13.9	13.9	13.8	13.8
Some college	9.9	9.9	9.9	10.0	9.9	10.0	9.9
College or higher	3.0	2.9	2.9	2.9	2.9	2.9	2.9

Sources: Authors' tabulations based on the Public Use Microdata Samples (PUMS) (U.S. Bureau of the Census, various years) and the 2005 American Community Survey (ACS) (U.S. Bureau of the Census 2005).
Notes: Actual and simulated poverty rates pertain to persons in households where the household head is native-born. Simulations with elastic labor supply assume a weeks-worked labor supply elasticity of one. Simulations with inelastic labor supply assume a weeks-worked labor supply elasticity of zero. See the text for a complete discussion of the calculations of the simulated poverty rates.

of the household head and by the level of educational attainment of the household head. Table 5.9 presents similar comparisons for groups defined by the interaction between the race-ethnicity of household heads and the heads' educational attainment. For each of the three wage simulations, we present two sets of hypothetical poverty rates. The first assumes that higher wages induce an increase in weeks worked—that is, that labor supply is elastic—thus yielding higher hypothetical family income (and lower hypothetical poverty rates) for those adversely affected by competition with immigrants. The second assumes that labor supply is unresponsive

TABLE 5.9 / Actual Poverty Rates in 2005 Among Persons in Households Headed by Natives and Simulated Poverty Rates Holding Immigrant Labor Supply to 1970 Levels by Race-Ethnicity and Household Head Level of Educational Attainment

	Actual Poverty Rate	Using Lower-Bound Wage Effects and Assuming Immigrants and Natives Are Imperfect Substitutes		Using Upper-Bound Wage Effects and Assuming Immigrants and Natives Are Imperfect Substitutes		Using Upper-Bound Wage Effects and Assuming Immigrants and Natives Are Perfect Substitutes	
		Elastic Labor Supply	Inelastic Labor Supply	Elastic Labor Supply	Inelastic Labor Supply	Elastic Labor Supply	Inelastic Labor Supply
Non-Hispanic white							
Less than high school	21.2%	20.6%	20.8%	20.0%	20.4%	19.8%	20.3%
High school	10.0	9.9	9.9	10.0	9.9	9.9	9.9
Some college	7.6	7.6	7.5	7.7	7.6	7.6	7.5
College or higher	2.5	2.5	2.5	2.5	2.5	2.4	2.4
Non-Hispanic black							
Less than high school	45.3	44.5	44.6	43.4	44.1	43.0	43.8
High school	29.7	29.6	29.5	29.8	29.6	29.5	29.4
Some college	19.9	20.0	19.9	20.3	20.0	20.1	19.9
College or higher	6.2	6.1	6.1	6.0	6.0	6.0	6.0
Non-Hispanic Asian							
Less than high school	25.0	24.8	24.8	24.6	24.8	23.7	24.7
High school	10.9	10.8	10.8	11.0	10.9	10.7	10.7
Some college	8.7	8.7	8.7	8.7	8.7	8.7	8.7
College or higher	4.4	4.4	4.4	4.3	4.3	4.3	4.3
Non-Hispanic other							
Less than high school	41.3	40.3	40.8	39.1	40.1	38.7	39.7
High school	23.4	23.5	23.4	23.7	23.5	23.4	23.4
Some college	16.8	17.0	16.9	17.4	17.0	17.1	16.8
College or higher	5.7	5.7	5.7	5.6	5.6	5.6	5.6

TABLE 5.9 / *Continued*

	Actual Poverty Rate	Using Lower-Bound Wage Effects and Assuming Immigrants and Natives Are Imperfect Substitutes		Using Upper-Bound Wage Effects and Assuming Immigrants and Natives Are Imperfect Substitutes		Using Upper-Bound Wage Effects and Assuming Immigrants and Natives Are Perfect Substitutes	
		Elastic Labor Supply	Inelastic Labor Supply	Elastic Labor Supply	Inelastic Labor Supply	Elastic Labor Supply	Inelastic Labor Supply
Hispanic							
Less than high school	36.6%	35.7%	36.0%	34.3%	35.5%	33.5%	35.1%
High school	19.7	19.6	19.6	19.5	19.6	19.2	19.5
Some college	13.2	13.2	13.2	13.4	13.2	13.3	13.2
College or higher	4.6	4.6	4.5	4.5	4.5	4.5	4.5

Source: Author's tabulations based on the Public Use Microdata Samples (PUMS) (U.S. Bureau of the Census, various years) and the 2005 American Community Survey (U.S. Bureau of the Census 2005).

Notes: Actual and simulated poverty rates pertain to persons in households where the household head is native-born. Simulations with elastic labor supply assume a weeks-worked labor supply elasticity of one. Simulations with inelastic labor supply assume a weeks-worked labor supply elasticity of zero. See the text for a complete discussion of the calculations of the simulated poverty rates.

to changes in weekly wages—that is, that supply is inelastic. When the simulated poverty rate is below the actual poverty rate, the simulation suggests that the 2005 poverty rate for the group in question would have been lower had the immigrant population been held to 1970 levels.

The simulation results by race-ethnicity suggest that immigration over this time period had negligible effects on poverty overall. For example, for black households the simulation using the largest adverse wage effects for high school dropouts suggests that had immigration been held to 1970 levels, the black poverty rate in 2005 would have been 25.5 percent, compared with actual poverty rates for this group of 26 percent. Among households headed by a native-born Hispanic, the lowest hypothetical poverty rate is 18.4 percent, compared to an actual poverty rate of 19.3 percent. By level of educational attainment, we find that the largest potential effects are on the poverty rates of households headed by someone with less than a high school diploma. The simulations suggest a hypothetical 2005 poverty rate between 27.2 and 28.6 percent for this group, compared to an actual poverty rate of 29.1 percent. Again, this is a relatively small impact. For households headed by a native-born person with a high school diploma or greater (the overwhelming majority of U.S. households), the effects of immigration on poverty are essentially equal to zero.

The poverty simulation results for households defined by both the race and educational attainment level of the household head (presented in table 5.9) lead to very similar conclusions. Again, the lowest simulated poverty rates imply only modest impacts of labor market competition with immigrants on native poverty rates for households headed by someone with less than a high school diploma, and there are virtually no effects of such competition for all other groups. Among the lowest-skilled households, African Americans and Hispanics experience the largest poverty effects. For example, the lowest simulated poverty rate for black households headed by someone with less than a high school diploma is 43 percent, 2.3 percentage points lower than the actual poverty rate for this group in 2005 (45.3 percent). The comparable figures for low-skilled Hispanic households are 33.5 percent and 36.6 percent.

CONCLUSION

In this chapter, we explored three possible connections between international immigration to the United States between 1970 and 2005 and the nation's poverty rate. First, we documented the increased poverty incidence among immigrants and the connections between the changing national-origin mix of the immigrant population and immigrant poverty. Second, we estimated how poverty rates change within immigrant arrival cohorts as time in the United States increases. Finally, we discussed in detail the avenues through which immigration may have an impact on the wages of the native-born; we simulated the likely wage effects of immigration between 1970 and 2005; and we simulated the consequent effects on native poverty rates.

In the end, it appears that the only substantive contribution of immigration to the national poverty rate occurs through the compositional effects of recent immigrants on the national poverty rate. Recent immigrants from Latin America and Asia tend to experience high initial poverty rates, which certainly increases the overall poverty rate relative to what it would otherwise be. This effect, however, is small. Moreover, through wage growth and selective out-migration, immigrant poverty declines quickly with time in the United States.

We find much less evidence of an impact of immigration on native poverty through immigrant-native labor market competition. Despite adverse wage effects on high school dropouts and relatively small effects on the poverty rates of high school dropouts, the effects on native poverty rates are negligible. This last result is largely driven by the fact that even most native-born poor households have at least one working adult with at least a high school education.

We thank Maria Cancian, Sheldon Danziger, and Cordelia Reimers for their valuable input into an earlier draft of this chapter.

NOTES

1. As discussed later in the chapter, these estimates are based on a model of wage determination that allows for imperfect substitutability of workers with different skill levels and allows for the accumulation of capital in response to changes in the supply of labor.
2. We analyze data from the Integrated Public Use Microdata Samples (IPUMS) collected and maintained by the University of Minnesota. We use the 1 percent samples from the 1970, 1980, 1990, and 2000 U.S. Censuses of Population and Housing and the 2005 American Community Survey.
3. Note that the census does not ask whether foreign nationals are legal residents in the United States. The census does collect information on whether the foreign-born are naturalized citizens. Thus, noncitizens include both legal residents and illegal residents who are captured in the sampling universe (all addresses that receive mail) of the census.
4. We also tabulated synthetic cohort estimates restricting the cohorts to those age eighteen to thirty-four at the time of arrival who were not enrolled in school. These estimates are quite close to those presented for all recent arrival age eighteen to thirty-four presented in table 5.4.
5. Similar positive assimilation is observed for homeownership rates (see Borjas 2002; Greulich, Quigley, and Raphael 2004). Rubén Rumbaut (1999) documents the downward assimilation of immigrants in health and behavioral outcomes; recent immigrants perform better than the native-born in these outcomes—that is, immigrant outcomes worsen over time to reflect more closely the comparable outcomes for natives.
6. Readers interested in these additional findings are referred to Raphael and Smolensky (this volume).
7. The technical details of the decomposition are presented in the notes to table 5.5.
8. Immigration may have indirect compositional effects on the national poverty rate if the native-born children of immigrants are more likely to experience poverty than the native-born children of the native-born. In other words, immigration may shift the internal composition of the native-born in a manner that tends to increase poverty rates. Indeed, the distributional patterns in table 5.3 show that the native population of Hispanic and Asian origin increased notably between 1970 and 2005, a change that, holding group poverty rates constant, tended to increase native poverty rates. The results in table 5.5 accounts for changes in the composition of the native-born, and thus our decomposition accounts for this indirect effect.
9. The discussion in this section draws heavily on the discussion in Raphael and Ronconi (2007).
10. Native employment declines if the propensity of the native-born to work depends positively on wages. That is to say, an immigration-induced decline in wages may cause some natives to withdraw from the labor force. Note, this need not be the case, theoretically. Existing empirical research on labor supply, however, suggests that labor supply increases with wages, especially for women.
11. For a more detailed discussion of the theoretical model briefly summarized here, see the working paper version of this chapter in Raphael and Smolensky (2008).

12. Of course, if immigrants enter the labor market earlier in life because they left school at a younger age, the relative youth of immigrant workers may not translate into lower average years of work experience relative to natives.

13. We first defined fifty-four groups based on age and educational attainment. We use the six educational attainment groups defined in table 5.1 and the nine age groups: eighteen to twenty-five, twenty-six to thirty, thirty-one to thirty-five, thirty-six to forty, forty-one to forty-five, forty-six to fifty, fifty-one to fifty-five, fifty-six to sixty, and sixty-one to sixty-four. The interaction of these six educational groups and nine age grouping define fifty-four age-education cells. We then use the 2000 Public Use Microdata Samples (PUMS) data to rank these groups from lowest to highest average earnings among those employed within each group. We use average earnings among native-born, non-Hispanic white men to do these rankings. We use this group to rank age-education groupings into apparent skills groups since white men are the largest subgroup in the labor market. We exclude other groups and women to abstract from the effects of race, ethnicity, and gender on wages. In other words, we wish to identify a ranking that is more likely to provide a pure reflection of average differences in skills. This ranking serves as an indication of skill endowments as they are valued by the market.

14. We simulate the effects of competition with immigrants on native poverty rates in the following manner. First, we estimate the parameters of a theoretical model that ties the wages of workers of various skill groupings to their own supply and the supply of all other workers. We then use the calibrated theoretical model to simulate the hypothetical wages that workers of various skill groups would earn if the supply of immigrant labor were held to 1970 levels. Using these alternative wage estimates, we simulate hypothetical personal income and total family income with restricted immigrant labor supply. Finally, we use these simulated family income levels to simulate what native poverty rates would have been had the immigrant population been held at 1970 levels. Note that these simulations take household composition as given. To the extent that lower wages affect household formation, our simulations may understate the impact on poverty. The theoretical model of wage determination posits that the wages of workers in a given skill level depend inversely on the supply of workers at that skill level. In addition, a given group's wages also depend on the supply of other workers. The supply of other types of workers can either suppress (when these workers are close substitutes) or increase (when these workers are complementary) the wages for a given skill group, depending primarily on the ease with which employers can substitute workers of different skill levels in producing goods and services. See Raphael and Smolensky (2008) for details on the formal model; a description of the data that we use to estimate the parameters of the model; and our alternative estimates of the impact of immigration between 1970 and 2005 on the wages of natives of different skills groups, defined by their level of educational attainment and potential years of work experience. For additional research employing these simulation methods, see Borjas (2003, 2005), Borjas, Grogger, and Hanson (2008), Card and Lemieux (2001), and Ottaviano and Peri (2005).

15. For relatively large effects, see Borjas, Grogger, and Hanson (2008); for estimates suggesting relatively small effects, see Raphael and Ronconi (2008).

REFERENCES

Borjas, George. 1986. "Assimilation, Changes in Cohort Quality, and the Earnings of Immigrants." *Journal of Labor Economics* 3(4): 463–89.

———. 1995. "Assimilation and Change in Cohort Quality Revisited: What Happened to Immigrant Earnings in the '80s?" *Journal of Labor Economics* 13(2): 201–45.

———. 2002. "Homeownership in the Immigrant Population." *Journal of Urban Economics* 52(3): 448–76.

———. 2003. "The Labor Demand Curve Is Downward Sloping: Reexamining the Impact of Immigration on the Labor Market." *Quarterly Journal of Economics* 118(4): 1335–74.

———. 2005. "Wage Trends Among Disadvantaged Minorities." Working paper 05-12. Ann Arbor: University of Michigan, National Poverty Center.

Borjas, George J., Jeffrey Grogger, and Gordon H. Hanson. 2008. "Imperfect Substitution Between Immigrants and Natives: A Reappraisal." Working paper 13887. Cambridge, Mass.: National Bureau of Economic Research.

Card, David, and Thomas Lemieux. 2001. "Can Falling Supply Explain the Rising Return to College for Younger Men? A Cohort-Based Analysis." *Quarterly Journal of Economics* 116: 705–46.

Chiswick, Barry. 1978. "The Effect of Americanization on the Earnings of Foreign-Born Men." *Journal of Political Economy* 86(5): 897–921.

———. 1980. "The Earnings of White and Colored Immigrants in Britain." *Economica* 48(185): 897–921.

Greulich, Erica, John Quigley, and Steven Raphael. 2004. "The Anatomy of Rent Burdens: Immigration, Growth, and Rental Housing." In *The Brookings-Wharton Papers on Urban Economic Affairs,* vol. 5, edited by William G. Gale and Janet Rothenberg Pack. Washington, D.C.: Brookings Institution.

Lubotsky, Darren. 2007. "Chutes or Ladders? A Longitudinal Analysis of Immigrant Earnings." *Journal of Political Economy* 115(5): 820–67.

Ottaviano, Gianmarco I. P., and Giovanni Peri. 2005. "Rethinking the Gains from Immigration: Theory and Evidence from the U.S." Working paper 11672. Cambridge, Mass.: National Bureau of Economic Research.

———. 2007. "Rethinking the Gains from Immigration: Theory and Evidence from the U.S." Working paper. Davis: University of California.

Raphael, Steven, and Lucas Ronconi. 2007. "The Effects of Labor Market Competition with Immigrants on the Wages and Employment of Natives." *Du Bois Review* 4(2): 413–32.

———. 2008. "Reconciling National and Regional Estimates of the Effect of Immigration on U.S. Labor Markets: The Confounding Effects of Native Male Incarceration Trends." Unpublished paper, University of California, Berkeley.

Raphael, Steven, and Eugene Smolensky. 2008. "Immigration and Poverty in the United States." Discussion paper 1347-08. Madison: University of Wisconsin, Institute for Research on Poverty.

Rumbaut, Rubén G. 1999. "Assimilation and Its Discontents: Ironies and Paradoxes." In *The Handbook of International Immigration: The American Experience,* edited by Charles Hirschman, Philip Kasinitz, and Josh DeWind. New York: Russell Sage Foundation.

U.S. Bureau of the Census. Various years. Public Use Microdata Samples (PUMS). Washington: U.S. Bureau of the Census. Available at: http://www.census.gov/main/www/pums.html (accessed May 13, 2009).

————. 2005. American Community Survey. Washington: U.S. Bureau of the Census. Available at: http://www.census.gov/acs/www (accessed May 13, 2009).

Part 2

Mobility and Its Consequences

Chapter 6

Enduring Influences of Childhood Poverty

Katherine Magnuson and Elizabeth Votruba-Drzal

Poverty is a common experience for children growing up in the United States. Although only about one in five children are in poverty each year, roughly one in three will spend at least one year living in a poor household. Child poverty is a significant concern to researchers and policymakers because it is linked to a multitude of worse outcomes, including reduced academic attainment, higher rates of nonmarital childbearing, and a greater likelihood of health problems. Moreover, childhood poverty, especially when it is deep and persistent, increases the chances that a child will grow up to be poor as an adult, thereby giving rise to the intergenerational transmission of economic disadvantage (Jäntti, this volume).

In this chapter, we review research on the dynamics of child poverty and the influences of poverty on well-being during childhood and early adulthood in the United States. We begin by describing trends in child poverty. Then we present three dominant frameworks for understanding the influences of poverty on families and discuss the challenges faced by researchers interested in measuring causal effects. That discussion is followed by a review of studies that estimate childhood poverty's influence on development in three domains: educational attainment and achievement, behavior, and physical health. We conclude by discussing policies that show promise in attenuating the links between childhood poverty and development across the life course.

CHILD POVERTY DYNAMICS

In the United States, child poverty rates are higher than rates for the adult and elderly populations (Meyer and Wallace, this volume). In 2006 nearly 17.4 percent of children lived in families with incomes below the official poverty threshold, compared with only 10.8 percent of adults. Another 22 percent of children lived in families with incomes between 100 and 200 percent of the poverty threshold. Although it is difficult to make international comparisons, research suggests that

TABLE 6.1 / Fifteen-Year Poverty Experiences of Children in the PSID Born Between
1975 and 1987, by Race and Maternal Characteristics at Birth

	Average Number of Years Poor	Never Poor	Poor for at Least Five Years	Poor for at Least Eight Years
Total sample	1.81	65%	15%	10%
African American	5.53	30	46	37
White	0.93	75	7	4
Unmarried mother	5.39	24	46	33
Mother has less than a high school diploma	5.03	31	44	33

Source: Calculations based on the Panel Study of Income Dynamics (PSID) analyzed by Kathleen
Ziol-Guest, Harvard University.
Note: Figures in this table are based on weights that adjust for differential sampling and response
rates.

the United States has one of the highest rates of child poverty among Western
industrialized nations (Bradbury and Jäntti 2001).

Young children have higher rates of poverty than older children—the 2005
poverty rate for children under age three was 21 percent, while it was 15 percent
for children ages twelve to seventeen (Douglas-Hall, Chau, and Koball 2006). The
parents of young children do not earn as much as parents of older children
because those with young children tend to be younger themselves and to have
less work experience. It is also possible that the higher cost of child care for young
children reduces parents' employment.

Poverty rates are also higher among racial and ethnic minority children. In
2006 the poverty rate for children under age eighteen was 33 percent for African
Americans, 28 percent for Hispanics, 15 percent for Asians, and 12 percent for
whites. Children of immigrants also experience higher rates of poverty than children of native-born parents—24 percent versus 12 percent (Fass and Cauthen 2007).

These annual poverty rates provide only a snapshot of the number of children
in poverty. With child poverty rates remaining relatively stable over time, it
would be easy to come to the mistaken conclusion that the population of children
experiencing poverty also changes little. Yet analysis of longitudinal data reveals
substantial turnover among the poor as events like unemployment and divorce
push families into poverty and reemployment, marriage, and career gains pull
them out. Building on the research of Greg Duncan and Willard Rodgers (1988),
Kathleen Ziol-Guest (2008) calculated that on average children experience 1.8 of
their first 15 years of life in poverty. Of course, this average masks considerable
heterogeneity (table 6.1). About 65 percent of children never experience poverty,
whereas 15 percent of children are poor for at least five of fifteen years.

African American children are considerably more likely than white children to
experience chronic poverty. Ziol-Guest found that the average African American

child is poor for nearly 5.5 years, whereas the average white child is poor for less than a year. Moreover, only 30 percent of African American children never experience poverty, compared with 75 percent of white children. Children born to unmarried mothers and mothers with less than a high school diploma are also more likely to experience chronic poverty, with an average of 5.4 and 5.0 childhood years spent in poverty, respectively.

Childhood poverty can also be characterized by the number of poverty spells that individuals experience. Most poverty spells are relatively short, ending within two years (Gottschalk, McLanahan, and Sandefur 1994). About half of poor individuals who escape poverty, however, experience another spell of poverty within four years (Stevens 1999). Recurrent poverty spells are also evident among children: more than half of children who are ever poor experience more than one spell of poverty (Ashworth, Hill, and Walker 1994).[1] Children who are in poverty for longer periods of time are more likely to experience deep poverty (Ashworth, Hill, and Walker 1994).

THEORETICAL FRAMEWORKS FOR UNDERSTANDING HOW POVERTY MIGHT AFFECT FAMILIES AND CHILDREN

Three main theoretical frameworks describe the pathways through which child poverty may affect development: family and environmental stress, resource and investment, and cultural theories. We begin our discussion of the consequences of child poverty by summarizing these approaches. Each framework is grounded in a different disciplinary background, but they share similarities and may be complementary. Although developed primarily in the U.S. context, these theories have cross-national and cross-cultural applications.

Family and Environmental Stress Perspective

Economically disadvantaged families experience high levels of stress in their everyday environments, and such stress may affect human development. The family stress model was developed first by Glen Elder to document the influence of economic loss during the Great Depression (Elder 1974; Elder, Nguyen, and Caspi 1985). According to this perspective, poor families face significant economic pressure as they struggle to pay bills and are forced to cut back on daily expenditures. This economic pressure, coupled with other stressful life events that are more prevalent in the lives of poor families, creates high levels of psychological distress, including depressive and hostile feelings, in poor parents (Kessler and Cleary 1980; McLeod and Kessler 1990). Psychological distress spills over into marital and co-parenting relationships. As couples struggle to make ends meet, their interactions become more hostile and conflicted, and they tend to withdraw from each other (Brody et al. 1994; Conger and Elder 1994). Parents' psychological distress and conflict, in turn, are linked with parenting practices that, on average, are more punitive, harsh, inconsistent, and detached as well as less nurturing, stimulating, and responsive to children's needs. Such lower-quality parenting may be harmful to children's development (Conger et al. 2002; McLoyd 1990).

An understanding of environmental stress as a pathway through which poverty may affect individuals must extend beyond the family environment to consider other sources of stress that poor children encounter in daily life. Compared to their more affluent peers, poor children are more likely to live in housing that is crowded, noisy, and plagued by structural defects such as leaky roofs, rodent infestation, and inadequate heating (Evans, Saltzman, and Cooperman 2001; Evans 2004). Poor families are more likely to reside in neighborhoods with high rates of crime and risk factors such as boarded-up houses, abandoned lots, and inadequate municipal services (Evans 2004). The schools that poor children attend are more likely to be overcrowded and to have structural problems, such as inadequate lighting and ventilation and excessive noise, compared with the schools that more affluent children attend (Evans 2004). Economically disadvantaged children also tend to be exposed to greater air pollution from parental smoking, traffic, and industrial emissions (Evans 2004). These environmental conditions create physiological and emotional stress in the lives of impoverished children, which may have harmful effects in turn on their socioemotional, physical, cognitive, and academic development. For example, childhood poverty heightens children's risk for lead poisoning, which has been linked to health, behavior, and neurological problems that may endure into adolescence and adulthood (Cecil et al. 2008; Shonkoff and Phillips 2000).

The field of cognitive neuroscience provides related evidence that stress may harm poor children's development. Researchers have documented the negative effects of stress on animal brain development. Stress exposure and the elevation of stress hormones, such as cortisol, negatively influence animals' cognitive functioning, leading to impairments in brain structures such as the hippocampus, which is of central importance for memory (McEwen 2000). For obvious ethical reasons, these studies have not been replicated in humans. However, non-experimental studies have found that children of low socioeconomic status (SES) have significantly higher levels of stress hormones than their more advantaged counterparts (Lupien et al. 2001; Turner and Avison 2003). Thus, disparities in stress exposure and stress hormones may at least partially explain why poor children have lower levels of cognitive ability and achievement (Farah et al. 2006). Although this explanation is compelling, to date studies have not established a clear causal sequencing of these associations or isolated the role of poverty per se in these processes.

Resource and Investment Perspective

Household production theory has played a central role in how economists view child development. Gary Becker's *A Treatise on the Family* (1991) posits that child development is affected by a combination of endowments and parental investments. Endowments include genetic predispositions and the values and preferences that parents instill in their children. Parents' preferences, such as the importance they place on education and their orientation toward the future, combined with their resources, shape parental investments. Economists argue that time and money are the two basic resources that parents invest in children. For example, investments in high-quality child care and education, housing in good neighborhoods, and rich learning experiences enhance children's development, as do nonmonetary investments of parents' time. Links between endowments, investments, and development probably differ for achievement, behavior, and health outcomes. Children's own characteristics also affect the level and type of investments that parents make in them (Becker 1991; Foster 2002). For example, if a young child is talkative and enthusiastic about learning, parents are more likely to purchase children's books or take the child to the library (Raikes et al. 2006).

Household production theory suggests that children from poor families trail behind their economically advantaged counterparts because parents have fewer resources to invest in their children (Becker 1991). Compared with more affluent parents, poor parents are less able to purchase inputs for their children—including books and educational materials at home—enroll their children in high-quality child care settings and schools, and live in safe neighborhoods. The higher prevalence of single parents, nonstandard work hours, and less flexible work schedules among poor families may also leave these economically disadvantaged parents with less time to invest in their children (Smolensky and Gootman 2003), and this lack of time may also have negative consequences for their children.

Investments in cognitively stimulating and enriching home environments reflect familial investments of time and money into the materials and experiences that promote learning. Children from poor households tend to experience lower-quality home environments than their advantaged peers, and these differences explain some of the influence of poverty's effects on child educational achievement (Duncan and Brooks-Gunn 2000). The central role of home learning environments in accounting for poverty's effects is perhaps not surprising given the known influence of environmental enrichment on the structure and functioning of a wide range of brain areas in animals (van Praag, Kempermann, and Gage 2000). Disparities in the cognitive development of low- and middle-SES children are most pronounced in the brain regions that are important for language, memory, and cognitive control (Farah et al. 2006; Kishiyama et al., forthcoming; Noble, McCandliss, and Farah 2007). These differences may stem in part from differences in exposure to enriching environments and corresponding effects on brain development (Farah et al. 2008).

Cultural Perspectives

Sociological theories about how the norms and behavior of the poor affect children began with the "culture of poverty" theory put forth by Oscar Lewis (1969). Based on his fieldwork with poor families in Latin America, he argued that the poor are economically marginalized and have no opportunity for upward mobility. Individuals respond to their marginalized position by adapting their behavior and values. The resulting culture of poverty is characterized by little impulse control and an inability to delay gratification, as well as feelings of helplessness and inferiority. These adaptations manifest in poor communities' high levels of female-headed households, sexual promiscuity, crime, and gangs. Although Lewis (1969) acknowledged that these behaviors emerge in response to structural factors, he argued that over time these values and behaviors are transmitted to future generations and therefore become a cause of poverty. He wrote: "By the time slum children are age six or seven they have usually absorbed the basic values and attitudes of their subculture and are not psychologically geared to take full advantage of changing conditions or increased opportunities" (Lewis 1966, xlv).

Cultural explanations for the effects of poverty on children were prevalent in the mid-1980s through the 1990s. These approaches suggested high levels of non-marital childbearing, joblessness, female-headed households, criminal activity, and welfare dependency among the poor are likely to be transmitted from parents to children. Theorists agreed that behavioral differences exist, but they did not agree on the origins of these differences. For example, Lawrence Mead (1986) emphasized the role of individual characteristics and the liberal welfare state's perverse incentives that reward single-mother households and joblessness among men. Douglas Massey (1990) and William Julius Wilson (1987, 1996) stressed the importance of structural and economic factors: the concentration of neighborhood poverty, the social isolation of poor inner-city neighborhoods, and the deindustrialization of urban economies. They contended that these structural factors negatively influence the behavior of inner-city adults and their children.

A common criticism of "culture of poverty" explanations is that they fail to differentiate the behavior of individuals from their values and beliefs (Lamont and Small 2008). Evidence suggests that disadvantaged individuals hold many middle-class values and beliefs. Unlike the middle class, however, the poor face circumstances that make it difficult for them to behave in accordance with their values and beliefs. For example, as Kathryn Edin and Maria Kefalas (2005) show, poor women value marriage and recognize the benefits of raising children in a two-parent household. However, their low wages, as well as the high rates of unemployment and incarceration of poor men, lead many poor women to conclude that marriage is out of their reach. Traditional notions of a culture of poverty do not account for this sort of disconnect between values and behaviors.

Recently, sociologists have developed more sophisticated approaches to examine the intersection of culture and poverty, drawing on cultural concepts, including repertoires, frames, narratives, and social and cultural capital, to understand how poor adults experience, perceive, and respond to their economic position (Lamont and Small 2008). For example, studies suggest that poverty is related to smaller and less supportive social networks (Tigges, Browne, and Green 1998). The notion that norms and behaviors are passed down from generation to generation is implicit in cultural theories, even if it has not been well documented.

One exception is Annette Lareau (2003), who identifies differences in cultural child-rearing repertoires. Lareau finds that middle-class parents engage in "concerted cultivation" by providing stimulating learning activities and social interactions. As parents, they believe that they should do everything possible to promote their children's social and cognitive development. In contrast, she reports that working-class and poor parents view child development as unfolding naturally and believe that it is unnecessary to do more than provide basic supports, including food, shelter, and comforts. These differences in cultural repertoires provide a distinct advantage to middle-class children and contribute to the intergenerational transmission of social class.

CHALLENGES OF STUDYING THE CAUSAL EFFECTS OF CHILD POVERTY

In the sections that follow, we document associations between childhood poverty and academic achievement and attainment, social functioning, and physical health. In doing so, we differentiate studies that are more descriptive in nature from those that are more methodologically rigorous and thus more conducive to making causal claims. Researchers interested in identifying the causal influences of child poverty face formidable challenges. They must take seriously threats to internal validity from a variety of sources, including simultaneity considerations and potential omitted variables as well as genetic explanations. They also must contend with possible heterogeneity in poverty effects. We touch briefly on each issue before reviewing the literature.

Simultaneity Bias

Despite the abundance of research documenting links between childhood poverty and later outcomes, it is difficult to determine whether these outcomes are consequences or causes of poverty. Evidence suggests that causal pathways exist in both directions between child poverty and child outcomes. For example, consistent associations have been found between childhood poverty and a wide range of health outcomes, and evidence suggests that these associations reflect, in part, the causal effects of child poverty on health (Case, Lubotsky, and Paxson 2002; Currie and Stabile 2003). At the same time, mothers of children in poor health are less likely to be involved in the paid labor force, tend to work fewer hours, and have a greater likelihood of experiencing job loss (Earle and Heymann 2002; Gould 2004; Kuhlthau and Perrin 2001; Powers 2001, 2003). Researchers face considerable challenges in ruling out this type of simultaneity bias, but the failure to do so may result in an overestimation of poverty's effects.

Omitted Variables

A second challenge is isolating the effects of poverty from other disadvantages that poor families face. Children who live in poverty often have parents with lower levels of education and ability, as well as mental health issues, and they are more likely to live with only one parent. All of these factors may have an independent negative effect on children. Thus, to ascribe a causal effect to poverty per se requires ruling out other explanations for the association between poverty and children's development.

Some researchers have argued that income effects are largely specious and the result of unmeasured differences that are correlated with both income and child outcomes (Mayer 1997). In other words, unmeasured characteristics that contribute to greater earnings, such as parental mental health or motivation, may also enhance child development, leading to a spurious correlation between income and child development. This threat of omitted variable bias remains of significant concern in most research. Studies that use rigorous statistical techniques to clarify issues of causality tend to uncover smaller effect sizes than studies that do not attempt to reduce omitted variable biases (Duncan 2006).

Some researchers argue that trying to isolate the causal effects of poverty is misguided because it is difficult to know the extent to which related disadvantages, such as low levels of education or impaired mental health, are themselves caused by poverty (Gershoff, Aber, and Raver 2003). Separating the effects of related dimensions of disadvantage from those of poverty is likely to present a distorted or incomplete view of the extent to which economic disadvantage affects children. Nevertheless, to answer the question of whether a policy that increases family incomes will improve children's outcomes, it is important to know whether childhood poverty per se affects children.

Genes

Genetic explanations for the transmission of social and cognitive capacities represent a specific form of omitted variable bias in poverty research. Many skills, characteristics, and traits are in some part inherited by children from their parents. This has led some to argue that differences between poor and nonpoor children are primarily determined by genes (Rowe and Rodgers 1997). Yet efforts to parse out genetic or environmental determinants of development have been questioned as recent evidence indicates that gene expression is the result of a complex interplay between genetic endowments and environmental experiences (Collins et al. 2000; Lerner 2003). Nevertheless, because genetic processes are probably linked to both children's outcomes and parents' economic resources, researchers face the challenge of gene-environment correlations (Jencks and Tach 2006; Scarr 1992).

How genetics should be incorporated into poverty research is not obvious. One simple approach might be to try to determine how much of the correlation between poverty and an outcome is due to genetics.[2] In a recent review of genetic studies, Christopher Jencks and Laura Tach (2006) conclude that at most 40 percent of the correlation between parents' income and their adult children's incomes might be due to genes, suggesting that the bulk of the associations between parents' income and their children's outcomes cannot be attributed solely to genes. This tactic, however, ignores the fact that heritability may vary substantially in low- and high-SES families and is typically strongest in advantaged families (Guo and Stearns 2002; Rowe, Jacobson, and van den Oord 1999; Turkheimer et al. 2003). Individual differences in achievement in higher-SES environments appear to be driven more by genetic processes, whereas individual differences in low-SES environments appear to be more closely linked to environmental influences. Whether this is also the case for other skills and traits is uncertain. However, the differential heritability of cognitive ability in high- and low-SES environments suggests that any simple approach to addressing genetic bias in estimating the role of poverty may be misguided.

The Heterogeneity of Effects: Age, Gender, Race, and Immigration Status

In seeking to understand the effects of child poverty, researchers face theoretical and empirical questions about whether the effects of poverty differ by social categories or other individual characteristics. In this section, we briefly discuss why poverty's influence may depend on a child's age, gender, race, ethnicity, and immigrant status. Poverty's effects may also be contingent on other characteristics of individuals, such as personality or temperament, but this has generally not been the focus of research.

Both economic and psychological perspectives suggest that poverty may be more harmful to preschool-age children than it is to children who experience poverty during middle childhood or adolescence. Infancy and early childhood are times of rapid cognitive and socioemotional development, and young children are particularly sensitive to environmental influences (Shonkoff and Phillips 2000). The foundation of children's capacity to learn and regulate their emotions develops during this time through children's reciprocal interactions with the environment. Insensitive, inattentive, or unstimulating caregiving, which is more common in economically disadvantaged households, may be especially harmful to child well-being. The salience of poverty in early childhood is also consistent with economic theory that highlights the importance of early investments by arguing that early investments maximize returns as "skills beget skills" (Cunha et al. 2006). Empirical support for the importance of early poverty is especially strong for educational achievement and attainment, which is reviewed in our discussion of the consequences of child poverty that follows.

The influences of child poverty may also differ by child gender, but few studies have considered whether girls or boys fare worse. Glen Elder's early work on families during the Great Depression suggested that the influence of economic loss on children's well-being is complex and may depend not only on children's gender but also their stage of development. Among early adolescents, financial loss threatened girls' psychological well-being, but not boys' (Elder, Nguyen, and Caspi 1985). The disproportionate effects on girls may reflect their greater psychosocial vulnerability in early adolescence, as well as gender roles that lead them to take on greater household responsibilities, thereby increasing their exposure to the family stress that accompanies economic decline. Among younger children, however, boys were more likely than girls to be affected by economic loss during the Great Depression (Elder 1979). This pattern may be explained by the fact that young boys tend to be more reactive and vulnerable to environmental stress than young girls (Zaslow and Hayes 1986). Nevertheless, more studies are needed to identify systematically the gender differences in poverty's effects.

The disproportionate representation of immigrant children and children of color among the poor raises the question of whether the effects of poverty are similar for these groups. Theories about how poverty influences development provide little direct guidance on this question. Poverty may be more detrimental to children of color and immigrant children because their families face multiple sources of disadvantage, including discrimination and segregation, and have fewer resources to draw on when coping with poverty (Raver, Gershoff, and Aber 2007). Alternatively, the extreme challenges associated with living in poverty may overwhelm any ethnic, racial, or cultural specificity (Mistry et al. 2002). To date, this question has received little systematic theoretical or empirical treatment in the literature.

CONSEQUENCES OF CHILD POVERTY

Academic Achievement and Attainment

Does poverty affect children's achievement and educational attainment? Income gaps in achievement are present when children enter school and as they grow during the school years (Maldonado and Votruba-Drzal 2007). The magnitude of the gaps differs across studies and measures, but typically amounts to a modest difference of about one-third of a standard deviation (Blau 1999; Smith, Brooks-Gunn, and Klebanov 1997). Effects on educational attainment are larger, with the mean differences amounting to over one year of schooling (Duncan, Kalil, and Ziol-Guest 2008). Differential rates in high school completion and college attendance are also large—poor children are one-third as likely to complete high school (Corcoran 2001), and the gap in college attendance between the lowest and highest quintiles of income is nearly fifty percentage points (Haveman and Wilson 2007). These differences in children's achievement and attainment probably contribute to differences in job opportunities and later earnings (Jäntti, this volume).

Despite theoretical predictions and correlational evidence, whether family income and poverty are causal determinants of children's achievement and education behavior remains a controversial issue. As noted earlier, some scholars argue that both low family incomes and low achievement are the by-products of genetic, psychological, and social differences between poor and nonpoor families, and that these differences are the true causes of poor achievement and attainment (Mayer 1997).

Greg Duncan (2006) describes a continuum for evaluating the methodological rigor of studies aimed at estimating the influence of poverty and income on child development. On one end are correlational studies that analyze associations between concurrent measures of family income and child outcomes and make few adjustments for confounding factors. These studies are common, but probably plagued by biases. On the other end are experiments in which families are randomly assigned to receive additional income, without any strings attached. If implemented correctly, such experiments provide unbiased estimates of income effects, but such studies are exceptionally rare. Between these two extremes, ranging from more to less rigorous, are natural experiments, studies that employ econometric techniques to reduce omitted variable bias (such as fixed effects), instrumental variables regression, and longitudinal studies.

The only randomized interventions to consider "pure" income effects on children are the Negative Income Tax Experiments, which were conducted between 1968 and 1982 to identify the influence of guaranteed income on labor force participation. Some sites collected data on a limited set of child outcomes. Researchers found that elementary school children in the experimental group exhibited higher levels of early academic achievement and school attendance in some sites, but the result was not evident for adolescents. Youth in the experimental group did, however, have higher rates of high school completion and educational attainment in the two sites where these outcomes were assessed (Salkind and Haskins 1982). This suggests that income's effects may be causal, but the data were limited. In addition, it is impossible to distinguish the effect of income from the reduction in parental work effort that accompanied the income increase (Moffitt 2003).

Researchers have analyzed longitudinal data to better understand the effects of family income on children's achievement and education. Greg Duncan and Jeanne Brooks-Gunn (1997) coordinated the analyses of researchers working with ten different longitudinal data sets and seeking to isolate the effects of permanent income from other SES components. The researchers used statistical controls to hold constant confounds such as family structure and maternal education. They found, first, that the effects of household income appear to be nonlinear, with larger associations between income and achievement for families in the lower end of the income distribution. Second, family income in early childhood appears to be more important for shaping ability and achievement than income during middle childhood or adolescence. Finally, they discovered that experiences of persistent poverty and deep poverty are particularly detrimental to children's achievement.

Susan Mayer (1997) employed a rigorous study design because she was concerned that controlling for the effects of maternal education and family structure was an insufficient correction for biases associated with the omission of unmeasured factors, such as parental ability or mental health. She used income measured later in life as a proxy for unmeasured parental characteristics. When later income is held constant, she argued, the estimated effect of early income is likely to be less biased. She also analyzed components of parental income that are somewhat independent of the actions of the family, including income from family investments such as interest and stock dividends. When Mayer found that these methods lead to large reductions in the estimated impact of parental income, she concluded that much of the association between income and child and adolescent outcomes is spurious rather than causal.

Mayer's strategy, as she pointed out, has potential flaws. If families anticipate future income changes and adjust their consumption accordingly, and the consumption changes affect their children, then future income does indeed causally affect earlier child outcomes. In addition, measurement error in income from dividends and interest imparts a downward bias in their coefficients. Moreover, because interest and dividend income is almost nonexistent among poor families, these income sources are not useful for estimating income effects among these families.

David Blau's (1999) study used family fixed-effect models that relate sibling differences in test scores to sibling differences in the individual children's income histories during middle childhood. He employed two alternative measures of parental income: income (or wage rates) during the calendar year prior to the measurement of the child outcome, and average household income (of the mother) over all years in which the data were available. He found small and insignificant effects of current income on achievement and larger (though still modest) effects of long-run income. A limitation of this study, however, was the assumption that families can smooth consumption perfectly and that income effects in early childhood are equivalent to the effects of income received in other stages of childhood.

Experimental welfare reform evaluation studies undertaken during the 1990s provided a unique opportunity to consider how increases in family income affect poor children's development (Morris, Duncan, and Clark-Kauffman 2005). Although all of the experimental programs increased parental employment, only some increased family income. Comparing the effects of programs that boosted only parental employment with those that boosted both employment and income provides some indication of the extent to which increases in family income benefit children, although the comparison across the studies is non-experimental. Preschool and elementary-school children's academic achievement was improved when income increased, but not by programs that increased only parental employment (Morris, Duncan, and Clark-Kauffman 2005). Such benefits were not apparent for adolescents. These findings suggest that income plays a causal role in children's achievement, although these programs increased both income and parental employment.

Gordon Dahl and Lance Lochner (2005) capitalized on a natural experiment to identify income's effect. Between 1993 and 1997, the maximum Earned Income Tax Credit (EITC), which provides a tax credit to working-poor families, increased from $1,801 to $3,923 for a family with two children, thus creating an unexpected exogenous increase in income. Dahl and Lochner found that such increases in income predicted improvements in low-income children's achievement.[3]

Robust associations have also been found between childhood poverty and later educational attainment. Both Mary Campbell and her colleagues (2004) and Greg Duncan, Ariel Kalil, and Kathleen Ziol-Guest (2008) used regression-based approaches and longitudinal data to relate average household income to completed schooling. Their analyses allowed for differential effects of income according to when it was experienced (early childhood, middle childhood, or adolescence) and to deal with omitted variable bias, controls for differences in family structure, parental education, and other background characteristics. These studies suggest that parental income in early childhood and adolescence affects educational attainment, although they focus on income rather than poverty status per se. Campbell and her colleagues (2004) found that family income in both early childhood and adolescence affects educational attainment. In addition, they discovered that college attendance is affected only by income during adolescence, pointing to the possible financial barriers to higher education imposed by increasing college tuitions and credit constraints (Belley and Lochner 2007; Kane 2007).[4] Duncan, Kalil, and Ziol-Guest (2008) found that an increase of $10,000 averaged over the first five years of life would lead to an increase of four-tenths of a year in completed schooling for families earning less than $25,000. The same increase in income experienced during adolescence, however, was linked to increases in educational attainment for children only among families with incomes of $25,000 or more.

Erik Plug and WimVijverberg (2005) analyzed a sample of adoptees and found that parental income is associated with educational attainment among both adoptees and biological children.[5] Moreover, because the estimates are quite similar across these groups, the authors concluded that family income plays a causal role in determining educational attainment.

Additional studies relating changes in income during childhood to changes in child development to isolate income effects from unmeasured—and unchanging—parent and child characteristics further highlight the importance of income in early childhood for children's achievement (Dearing, McCartney, and Taylor 2001; Votruba-Drzal 2006). Thus, poverty probably matters for children's achievement and later educational attainment, although not as much as some of the early and less rigorous studies suggested. No study has been able to rule out all sources of bias or threats to internal validity, but taken together, the robust links between early childhood poverty and later achievement and attainment, as well as adolescent income and later educational attainment, suggest that parental economic resources play a modest causal role.

Behavior

Poor children are typically rated by their parents and teachers as having more behavior problems than their peers. In childhood, problematic behavior is reflected in elevated levels of externalizing problems, such as aggression and acting out, and internalizing problems, such as depression and anxiety; in adolescence and later adulthood, these problems manifest in higher rates of nonmarital fertility and criminal activity. Again, the extent to which these associations reflect causal associations remains uncertain.

Many studies have found links between poverty and behavior problems, antisocial behavior, inadequate self-regulation, and poor mental health (Blau 1999; Mistry et al. 2002; Votruba-Drzal 2006; Yeung, Linver, and Brooks-Gunn 2002). For example, 7.8 percent of poor parents versus 4.6 percent of nonpoor parents rated their children as having difficulties with emotions, concentration, behavior, or getting along with others (Simpson et al. 2005). Yet such differences have sometimes failed to be replicated in studies that hold constant important confounds, such as family structure and parental education (Duncan and Brooks-Gunn 1997; Duncan, Kalil, and Ziol-Guest 2008; Mayer 1997). For example, Eric Dearing, Kathleen McCartney, and Beck Taylor (2006) examined within-child associations between changes in income and changes in young children's behavior and found significant negative effects of lower family income on externalizing behavior, especially for children who live in chronically poor households, but not on internalizing behavior.

Using a natural experiment whereby a casino opening on an Indian reservation gave families an income supplement that increased annually, Jane Costello and her colleagues (2003) found that children whose families moved out of poverty experienced reductions in symptoms of conduct and oppositional defiance disorder. Reports of anxiety and depression, however, were unaffected.

These studies suggest that although poverty is associated with children's socio-emotional well-being, to the extent that the effects are causal, they are likely to be selective. Accumulating evidence suggests that, for example, poverty may be more strongly associated with externalizing problem behavior, such as aggression, rather than internalizing behavior, such as depression. The fact that family income may be more strongly linked with some types of behavior than others is not surprising. However, discrepancies across studies may also be attributable to differences in study design. Studies vary considerably in the ages of the children in their samples and the timing of the poverty or income measures they use. There is little evidence to indicate whether current or permanent income is a stronger predictor of children's behavior. Nor is there clear evidence on whether the age at which poverty is experienced or the timing of poverty is salient in understanding associations between income and children's behavior.

Some studies show that children raised in low-income households have higher rates of arrest and incarceration than their affluent counterparts (Bjerk 2007; Duncan, Kalil, and Ziol-Guest 2008). Duncan, Kalil, and Ziol-Guest (2008) found that boys living in poverty during the first five years of life were more than twice as likely to be arrested as boys who had family incomes over twice the poverty threshold (28 percent versus 13 percent). Taking into account the variety of ways in which poor families differ from wealthier families, however, reduced the associations to statistical insignificance. Consequently, the extent to which criminal activity can be attributed to poverty per se, rather than the range of social disadvantages associated with poverty, is uncertain.[6]

Nonmarital births are more prevalent among women who experienced poverty as children. Duncan, Kalil, and Ziol-Guest (2008) found that more than half of girls who experienced poverty for the first five years of their life had a nonmarital birth by age twenty-eight, compared to 21 percent for those with family incomes between 100 and 200 percent of the poverty threshold, and only 8 percent for those with household incomes over 200 percent of the poverty level. Attempting to isolate a causal effect of income, Mayer (1997) reduced associations by more than half but still found a significant association between income during adolescence and nonmarital fertility. In contrast, Robert Haveman, Barbara Wolfe, and Kathryn Wilson (1997) argue that the association between childhood poverty and subsequent nonmarital childbearing is not due to poverty per se, but to the fact that many poor children are raised in single-parent families.

Physical Health

Growing up in poverty is associated with a variety of worse health outcomes. Compared with children in nonpoor households, poor mothers report that their children have worse overall health. Janet Currie and Wanchuan Lin (2007) found that only 70 percent of poor children were reported to be in excellent or very good health, compared with 87 percent of nonpoor children. In Western industrialized nations, economic disparities in health tend to grow from early childhood through adolescence (Case, Lubotsky, and Paxson 2002; Currie and Stabile 2003), in part because income seems to protect children's health at the onset of early chronic conditions (Case, Lubotsky, and Paxson 2002).

In the United States, children from poor households also have higher rates of chronic conditions, such as asthma, diabetes, and hearing, vision, and speech problems, with 32 percent of poor children compared with 27 percent of nonpoor children reporting at least one such condition. Asthma is the most common chronic condition among poor children, followed by mental health conditions; attention deficit hyperactivity disorder is the largest diagnosis within this category (Currie and Lin 2007). Finally, poor children suffer from higher rates of health-related activity limitations and acute illness (Currie and Lin 2007).

Associations between childhood poverty and health extend into adulthood. Economic disadvantage in childhood has been linked to worse overall health status and higher rates of mortality in adulthood (Case, Fertig, and Paxson 2005; van den Berg, Lindeboom, and Portrait 2005). Rucker Johnson and Robert Schoeni (2007a) found that childhood poverty is linked to heightened risk for several chronic diseases in adulthood. By age fifty, individuals who have experienced poverty in childhood are 46 percent more likely to have asthma, 75 percent more likely to be diagnosed with hypertension, 83 percent more likely to have been diagnosed with diabetes, 2.25 times more likely to have experienced a stroke or heart attack, and 40 percent more likely to have been diagnosed with heart disease, in comparison to individuals whose incomes are 200 percent of the poverty line or greater. Adult disparities in chronic health problems by poverty status tend to become more pronounced with age.

Unadjusted differences in physical health by childhood poverty status probably overstate the true causal effect of childhood poverty on physical health. Possible omitted variable and simultaneity biases, along with the failure of most studies to account for the role of genes, make it difficult to draw causal conclusions. Some researchers have used more rigorous analytic approaches to deal with these sources of bias. Gerard van den Berg, Maarten Lindeboom, and France Portrait (2005) used business cycle conditions as a source of exogenous variation in family income during early childhood. They discovered a robust effect of economic conditions in early life on individual mortality rates at all ages—being born during a recession was associated with an 8 percent increase in the mortality rate after the first year of life. Johnson and Schoeni (2007a, 2007b) uncovered large and significant links between childhood poverty and a variety of health outcomes in adulthood. However, comparing siblings who experienced different economic conditions greatly reduced these associations. The association between childhood poverty and adult health status was robust in sibling models, but associations between childhood poverty and a variety of diseases in adulthood, including asthma, hypertension, and stroke or heart attack, were not. This raises questions about the extent to which basic correlations between childhood poverty status and adult health are causal.

With so few studies directly considering the effect of childhood poverty on later health, it is worth considering other sources of evidence that may shed light on this question. Research examining policies aimed at reducing poverty-related material hardships may provide additional information about poverty's influence on health. For example, the food stamp program, designed to reduce food insufficiency, has been shown to increase birthweight and reduce prematurity (Almond, Hoynes, and Schanzenbach 2007). Furthermore, Women, Infants, and Children (WIC) participation has been linked to improved birth outcomes and reductions in childhood obesity (Bitler and Currie 2005). Unfortunately, rigorous research on programs such as these has not yet been extended to consider physical health benefits beyond the very early years of childhood. To the extent that programs like food stamps and WIC lead to improvements in the health of the economically disadvantaged, one can infer that at least some of the influence of poverty on physical health may be causal.

SUMMARY

About one in three American children experience poverty during childhood. For most, poverty is transient; however, for some, poverty persists for many years. About 10 percent of children will spend more than half of their childhood in poverty (at least eight out of the first fifteen years). Children experiencing such chronic poverty are more likely to be born into single-parent families, to have mothers with low levels of education, and to be African American.

Theories suggest that experiencing poverty during childhood affects one's life chances by increasing family stress and reducing parental investments. Families may also adapt their behaviors when facing diminished economic opportunities, and these adaptations may lower the quality of parenting, leading to detrimental effects on children.

Studies confirm that children who experience persistent poverty are at risk of experiencing poor outcomes across important domains later in life. Because identifying the unique effect of poverty on child and adult outcomes is challenging, the extent to which these associations are causal is uncertain. Because poor and non-poor families differ in a variety of ways that may also affect individuals' outcomes, it is difficult to isolate the causal effect of income from that of other related disadvantages and family characteristics.

Cumulative research suggests that deep and early poverty is linked to lower levels of achievement, holding constant other family characteristics. Low family income during adolescence is likewise linked to lower levels of educational attainment. Despite such robust associations, it is difficult to provide a precise estimate of the magnitude of poverty's causal effects on achievement or attainment, owing to the differing measures and methods used in studies. Duncan's (2006) review of rigorous studies concluded that a $3,000 annual increment increase during the preschool years results in a standard deviation improvement in achievement of between 0.05 and 0.18 (an average effect of 0.11 of a standard deviation improvement). Yet, given accumulated evidence, it is much less clear that increased income would result in improved achievement for school-age children.

The associations between child and young adult behaviors, such as problem behavior, crime, and nonmarital childbearing, and poverty are more selective. Some evidence suggests that effects on externalizing behavior may be causal, although probably small. More research is necessary to better understand the associations between poverty and behavior, with particular attention to the age and timing of poverty as well as the particular type of behavior under consideration.

Although correlations between child poverty and health are well documented, there is little indication of whether these associations persist after adjustments are made for observable and unobservable differences across families. Theory and related literature provide good reasons to suspect that poverty is detrimental to children's health. Yet the base of rigorous research is inadequate for drawing any firm conclusions about the magnitude of causal effects.

POLICY IMPLICATIONS

Before discussing concrete policies for addressing child poverty, we briefly highlight key issues for policymakers and researchers to consider when weighing the merits of different strategies. First, we remind readers that poverty experienced during early childhood, deep poverty, and persistent poverty appear to be especially harmful to children's achievement and may have enduring effects on health and social functioning as well. Thus, early, deep, and persistent childhood poverty should be of particular concern to policymakers. Research suggests that children who experience economically disadvantaged circumstances are particularly likely to benefit from additional financial resources.

Second, meaningful improvements in poor children's achievement, and perhaps health or behavior, can be accomplished with modest financial investments. The income increases experienced by families from increases in the EITC during the 1990s and the income gains experienced as part of antipoverty programs appear to have been sufficient to bring about measurable gains in children's achievement. Put another way, a few thousand dollars for several years can make a meaningful difference in children's lives.

Third, the United States has a long history of differentiating eligibility for social benefits based on factors such as labor force attachment, immigrant status, and family structure. Yet the consequences of child poverty cannot be alleviated without giving all poor children and families access to benefits. If some families are excluded, for example, by making antipoverty programs dependent on employment, the children who are in greatest need may receive the least support. Finally, policymakers should consider the relative costs and benefits of differing programs and policies when deciding how to allocate limited public resources. Although it is often difficult to put a precise value on program outcomes, when choosing between strategies it is important to consider whether the benefits of programs and policies exceed their costs, and whether funds spent on a particular program would be better directed to an alternative program or policy with a larger net benefit (Kilburn and Karoly 2008).

Strategies for improving the life chances of poor children focus on boosting family economic resources directly, either by providing cash supplements and in-kind benefits, which offset the costs of basic necessities, or by increasing the earnings of poor workers. Interventions aimed directly at children and families provide an additional policy lever for enhancing the development of poor children. Next we prioritize these strategies for confronting the harmful consequences of child poverty.

First, income support policies, including child allowances and cash supplements, provide a basic minimum level of support to families with children (Waldfogel, this volume). Such benefits are common in advanced welfare states but have not been prominent in U.S. policy discussions. Instead, the U.S. tax system has been used to redistribute cash to low-income families. The child tax credit, a partially refundable tax credit, and the Earned Income Tax Credit, a fully refundable tax credit, are two mechanisms that direct economic resources to working-poor families with children. The EITC, which provides cash support to low-income workers, has been heralded by many policy analysts for its ability to boost family incomes and promote employment (Scholz, Moffitt, and Cowan, this volume). Making the child tax credit fully refundable and more generous would provide more help to poor families; this policy change is currently under consideration as part of President Barack Obama's economic stimulus plan. Another way to boost family income would be to increase the minimum wage (Blank, this volume) or to allow for generous earnings disregards in calculating cash welfare benefits, enabling recipients to keep a larger portion of their welfare benefits as their earnings increase.

Given the links between early poverty and development, targeting additional income support to families with young children may be particularly valuable. Expansions in cash support could be targeted to families with children under age six. Currently, the maximum child care tax credit is up to $1,000 for each child under the age of seventeen. An expansion that increased the credit to $2,000 for all children under the age of six would channel needed resources to poor families with young children. Likewise, the EITC schedule of benefits could be revised to provide larger benefits to parents of young children.

Second, means-tested benefits such as food stamps, WIC, housing assistance, and children's health insurance provide poor families with valuable in-kind support and hence raise disposable income. Child care subsidies are especially important to supporting low-income working mothers by offsetting the high costs of nonparental care (Waldfogel, this volume). In-kind benefits may be effective in attenuating the effects of child poverty if they reduce economic hardship and increase investments in poor children. Benefits that are not tethered to work supports may be particularly important ways of supporting families during economic downturns and rising unemployment.

Third, some interventions aimed directly at enhancing the educational experiences of poor children have been shown to be cost-effective. Jacob and Ludwig (this volume) discuss the range of successful educational programs and policies that may benefit poor children and increase the odds that they will develop into successful adults. High-quality early education programs for low-income three- and four-year-olds, including Head Start and prekindergarten programs, top the list of proven interventions. State and federal investments in Head Start and preschool programs operated by local school districts or nonprofit organizations could go a long way toward addressing developmental disparities related to child poverty by enhancing access to high-quality early childhood education.

If some of the association between poverty and child development is due to poorer-quality parenting by economically disadvantaged parents, parenting programs may offer another opportunity for improving the life chances of poor children. These diverse programs typically seek to improve parents' ability to provide enriching, stimulating, and sensitive caregiving. A review of parenting program evaluations suggests that although many programs can improve some dimensions of parenting, few can improve child outcomes, particularly cognitive development (see Magnuson and Duncan 2004; Brooks-Gunn and Markman 2005). Two important exceptions should be noted: parent management programs—such as the Incredible Years Program (Webster-Stratton 1990), designed specifically for parents with young children who exhibit high levels of problem behaviors such as aggression—and intensive nurse home-visitation programs for disadvantaged new mothers, which have been shown to be cost-effective means to reduce abuse and neglect as well as improve child outcomes well into adolescence (Olds, Sadler, and Kitzman 2007). Although parenting interventions may have effects on selective populations, on balance it seems unlikely that existing programs can significantly improve the life chances of poor children.

Finally, in recent years place-based antipoverty strategies, such as the Harlem Children's Zone (HCZ), have garnered much attention as a promising approach to improving the outcomes of poor families and children. Place-based interventions provide comprehensive programs and services throughout childhood to families in low-income urban neighborhoods. The HCZ, for example, begins with Baby College, which provides parenting education and services to new and expectant parents, and continues through the College Success Office, which supports adolescents as they prepare for college and career decisions. Preschool and after-school enrichment programs, charter schools, and health, fitness, and nutrition initiatives are also provided. By engaging an entire community, place-based initiatives seek to transform the culture of economically disadvantaged communities (Tough 2008). Yet, to date, these types of programs have not been rigorously evaluated. A main component of the Obama administration's antipoverty agenda is the establishment of twenty "Promise Neighborhoods," modeled after HCZ. If these programs come to fruition, it will be important to evaluate the extent to which they improve children's lives.

There are many programs and policies that may succeed in reducing poverty among families with young children or limiting the harmful effects of poverty. Children who experience chronic and deep poverty face many threats to their healthy development, only some of which are directly attributable to poverty per se. Given the heterogeneity of circumstances across poor families, no single policy response will be sufficient to break the link between poverty and child outcomes. Although the effect of poverty on any particular outcome is uncertain, alleviating childhood poverty would almost certainly improve children's life chances.

We would like to thank Greg Duncan and Kathleen Ziol-Guest for their help in conducting the analysis of the prevalence and persistence of childhood poverty in the PSID included in this chapter. We would also like to thank Maria Cancian, Sheldon Danziger, and IRP conference participants for their helpful comments. Remaining errors are, of course, our own.

NOTES

1. Some entries and exits from poverty reflect no more than slight fluctuations of family income above or below the poverty threshold, suggesting that transitions into or out of poverty may not reflect a significant change in economic resources.
2. Despite limitations, researchers have turned to twin and adoption studies in an attempt to disentangle the relative contributions of parental genes and environments to children's development. If siblings who are identical twins are more similar than fraternal twins, then this suggests a role for genes. Likewise, if biological children are more similar to their parents than adopted children are, this too might indicate a role for genes. These studies, however, involve small and unrepresentative samples and rest on tenuous assumptions about the independence of genetic and environmental influences on development (Bouchard and McGue 2003; Stoolmiller 1999).
3. One concern with this analysis is that other policy changes that occurred in the 1990s, such as expansions of Head Start, might be confounded with expansions in the EITC (for a discussion of this concern, see Jacob and Ludwig 2007).
4. Pedro Carneiro and James Heckman (2002) argue, however, that borrowing constraints have little impact on poor adolescents' college attendance.
5. Several adoption studies have considered the intergenerational transmission of socioeconomic status, more broadly defined than income (see Björklund, Jäntti, and Solon 2007).

6. Brian Jacob and Jens Ludwig's (2007) study of the Chicago Housing Voucher Program provides preliminary evidence that the housing voucher, which would increase a household's disposable income, is associated with reductions in male adolescent crime.

REFERENCES

Almond, Douglas, Hilary W. Hoynes, and Diane Whitmore Schanzenbach. 2007. "The Impact of the Food Stamp Program on Infant Outcomes." Working paper. Davis: University of California, Department of Economics.

Ashworth, Karl, Martha Hill, and Robert Walker. 1994. "Patterns of Childhood Poverty: New Challenges for Policy." *Journal of Policy Analysis and Management* 13(4): 658–80.

Becker, Gary Stanley. 1991. *A Treatise on the Family.* Cambridge, Mass.: Harvard University Press.

Belley, Philippe, and Lance Lochner. 2007. "The Changing Role of Family Income and Ability in Determining Educational Achievement." Working paper no. 13527. Cambridge, Mass.: National Bureau of Economic Research.

Bitter, Marianne P., and Janet Currie. 2005. "Does WIC Work? The Effects of WIC on Pregnancy and Birth Outcomes." *Journal of Policy Analysis and Management* 24(1): 73–91.

Bjerk, David. 2007. "Measuring the Relationship Between Youth Criminal Participation and Household Economic Resources." *Journal of Quantitative Criminology* 23(1): 23–39.

Björklund, Anders, Markus Jäntti, and Gary Solon. 2007. "Nature and Nurture in the Intergenerational Transmission of Socioeconomic Status: Evidence from Swedish Children and Their Biological and Rearing Parents." IZA discussion paper 2665. Ann Arbor: University of Michigan.

Blau, David M. 1999. "The Effect of Income on Child Development." *Review of Economics and Statistics* 81(2): 261–76.

Bouchard, Thomas J., and Matthew McGue. 2003. "Genetic and Environmental Influences on Human Psychological Differences." *Journal of Neurobiology* 54(1): 4–45.

Bradbury, Bruce, and Markus Jäntti. 2001. "Child Poverty Across the Industrialized World: Evidence from the Luxembourg Income Study." In *Child Well-Being, Child Poverty, and Child Policy in Modern Nations,* edited by Koen Vleminckx and Timothy Smeeding. Bristol, U.K.: Policy Press.

Brody, Gene H., Zolinda Stoneman, Douglas Flor, Chris McCrary, Lorraine Hastings, and Olive Conyers. 1994. "Financial Resources, Parent Psychological Functioning, Parent Co-Caregiving, and Early Adolescent Competence in Rural Two-Parent African American Families." *Child Development* 65(2): 590–605.

Brooks-Gunn, Jeanne, and Lisa B. Markman. 2005. "The Contribution of Parenting to Racial and Ethnic Gaps in School Readiness." *The Future of Children* 15(1): 139–68.

Campbell, Mary, Robert Haveman, Gary Sandefur, and Barbara Wolfe. 2004. "What Does Increased Economic Inequality Imply About the Future Level and Dispersion of Human Capital?" Working paper. Madison: University of Wisconsin.

Carneiro, Pedro, and James J. Heckman. 2002. "The Evidence on Credit Constraints in Postsecondary Schooling." *Economic Journal* 112(482): 989–1018.

Case, Anne, Angela Fertig, and Christina Paxson. 2005. "From Cradle to Grave? The Lasting Impact of Childhood Health and Circumstances." *Journal of Health Economics* 24(2): 365–89.

Case, Anne, Darren Lubotsky, and Christina Paxson. 2002. "Economic Status and Health in Childhood: Origins of the Gradient." *American Economic Review* 92(5): 1308–34.

Cecil, Kim M., Christopher J. Brubaker, Caleb M. Adler, Kim N. Dietrich, Mekibib Altaye, John C. Egelhoff, Stephanie Wessel, Ilayaraja Elangovan, Kelly Jarvis, and Bruce P. Lanphear. 2008. "Decreased Brain Volume in Adults with Childhood Lead Exposure." *PLoS Medicine* 5(5): 741–50.

Collins, W. Andrews, Eleanor E. Maccoby, Laurence Steinberg, E. Mavis Hetherington, and Marc H. Bornstein. 2000. "Contemporary Research on Parenting: The Case for Nature and Nurture." *American Psychologist* 55(2): 218–32.

Conger, Rand D., and Glen H. Elder Jr. 1994. *Families in Troubled Times: Adapting to Change in Rural America.* New York: Aldine de Gruyter.

Conger, Rand D., Vonnie C. McLoyd, Lora Ebert Wallace, Yumei Sun, Ronald L. Simons, and Gene H. Brody. 2002. "Economic Pressure in African American Families: A Replication and Extension of the Family Stress Model." *Developmental Psychology* 38(2): 179–93.

Corcoran, Mary. 2001. "Mobility, Persistence, and the Consequences of Poverty for Children: Child and Adult Outcomes." In *Understanding Poverty,* edited by Sheldon Danziger and Robert Haveman. New York and Cambridge, Mass.: Russell Sage Foundation and Harvard University Press.

Costello, E. Jane, Scott N. Compton, Gordon Keeler, and Adrian Angold. 2003. "Relationships Between Poverty and Psychopathology: A Natural Experiment." *Journal of the American Medical Association* 290(15): 2023–29.

Cunha, Flavio, James J. Heckman, Lance Lochner, and Dimitriy V. Masterov. 2006. "Interpreting the Evidence on Life Cycle Skill Formation." In *Handbook of the Economics of Education,* edited by Eric A. Hanushek and Finis Welch. Amsterdam: Elsevier.

Currie, Janet, and Wanchuan Lin. 2007. "Chipping Away at Health: More on the Relationship Between Income and Child Health." *Health Affairs* 26(2): 331–44.

Currie, Janet, and Mark Stabile. 2003. "Socioeconomic Status and Child Health: Why Is the Relationship Stronger for Older Children?" *American Economic Review* 93(5): 1813–23.

Dahl, Gordon B., and Lance Lochner. 2005. "The Impact of Family Income on Child Achievement." Working paper no. 11279. Cambridge, Mass.: National Bureau of Economic Research.

Dearing, Eric, Kathleen McCartney, and Beck A. Taylor. 2001. "Change in Family Income-to-Needs Matters More for Children with Less." *Child Development* 72(6): 1779–93.

———. 2006. "Within-Child Associations Between Family Income and Externalizing and Internalizing Problems." *Developmental Psychology* 42(2): 237–52.

Douglas-Hall, Ayana, Michelle Chau, and Heather Koball. 2006. "Basic Facts About Low-Income Children: Birth to Age Three." National Center for Children in Poverty (September). Available at: http://www.nccp.org/publications/pub_679.html (accessed June 25, 2008).

Duncan, Greg J. 2006. "Income and Child Well-Being." 2005 Geary Lecture. Dublin: Economic and Social Research Institute.

Duncan, Greg J., and Jeanne Brooks-Gunn, eds. 1997. *Consequences of Growing Up Poor.* New York: Russell Sage Foundation.

———. 2000. "Family Poverty, Welfare Reform, and Child Development." *Child Development* 71(1): 188–96.

Duncan, Greg J., Ariel Kalil, and Kathleen Ziol-Guest. 2008. "The Economic Costs of Early Childhood Poverty." Working paper no. 4. Washington, D.C.: Partnership for America's Economic Success.

Duncan, Greg J., and Willard L. Rodgers. 1988. "Longitudinal Aspects of Child Poverty." *Journal of Marriage and the Family* 50(4): 1007–1021.

Earle, Alison, and S. Jody Heymann. 2002. "What Causes Job Loss Among Former Welfare Recipients: The Role of Family Health Problems." *Journal of the American Medical Women's Association* 57(1): 5–10.

Edin, Kathryn, and Maria Kefalas. 2005. *Promises I Can Keep: Why Poor Women Put Motherhood Before Marriage.* Berkeley: University of California Press.

Elder, Glen H. 1974. *Children of the Great Depression.* Chicago: University of Chicago Press.

———. 1979. "Historical Change in Life Patterns and Personality." In *Life Span Development and Behavior,* edited by Paul B. Baltes and Orville G. Brim. New York: Academic Press.

Elder, Glen H., Tri van Nguyen, and Avshalom Caspi. 1985. "Linking Family Hardship to Children's Lives." *Child Development* 56(2): 361–75.

Evans, Gary W. 2004. "The Environment of Childhood Poverty." *American Psychologist* 59(2): 77–92.

Evans, Gary W., Heidi Saltzman, and Jana L. Cooperman. 2001. "Housing Quality and Children's Socioemotional Health." *Environment and Behavior* 33(3): 389–99.

Farah, Martha J., Laura Betancourt, David M. Shera, Jessica H. Savage, Joan M. Giannetta, Nancy L. Brodsky, Elsa K. Malmud, and Hallam Hurt. 2008. "Environmental Stimulation, Parental Nurturance, and Cognitive Development in Humans." *Developmental Science* 11(5): 793–801.

Farah, Martha J., David M. Shera, Jessica H. Savage, Laura Betancourt, Joan M. Giannetta, Nancy L. Brodsky, Elsa K. Malmud, and Hallam Hurt. 2006. "Childhood Poverty: Specific Associations with Neurocognitive Development." *Brain Research* 1110(1): 166–74.

Fass, Sarah, and Nancy Cauthen. 2007. "Who Are America's Poor Children? The Official Story." National Center for Children in Poverty (November). Available at: http://www.nccp.org/publications/pub_787.html (accessed June 25, 2008).

Foster, E. Michael. 2002. "How Economists Think About Family Resources and Child Development." *Child Development* 73(6): 1904–14.

Gershoff, Elizabeth Thompson, J. Lawrence Aber, and C. Cybele Raver. 2003. "Child Poverty in the United States: An Evidence-Based Conceptual Framework for Programs and Policies." In *Promoting Positive Child, Adolescent, and Family Development: A Handbook of Program and Policy Innovations,* edited by Francine Jacobs, Richard M. Lerner, and Donald Wertlieb. Thousand Oaks, Calif.: Sage Publications.

Gottschalk, Peter, Sara McLanahan, and Gary D. Sandefur. 1994. "The Dynamics and Intergenerational Transmission of Poverty and Welfare Participation." In *Confronting Poverty: Prescriptions for Change,* edited by Sheldon H. Danziger, Gary D. Sandefur, and Daniel H. Weinberg. Cambridge, Mass.: Harvard University Press.

Gould, Elise. 2004. "Decomposing the Effects of Children's Health on Mother's Labor Supply: Is It Time or Money?" *Health Economics* 13(6): 525–41.

Guo, Guang, and Elizabeth Stearns. 2002. "The Social Influences on the Realization of Genetic Potential for Intellectual Development." *Social Forces* 80(3): 881–910.

Haveman, Robert, and Kathryn Wilson. 2007. "Economic Inequality in College Access, Matriculation, and Graduation." In *Higher Education and Inequality,* edited by Stacy Dickert-Conlin and Ross Rubenstein. New York: Russell Sage Foundation.

Haveman, Robert, Barbara Wolfe, and Kathryn Wilson. 1997. "Childhood Poverty and Adolescent Schooling and Fertility Outcomes: Reduced-Form and Structural Estimates." In *Consequences of Growing Up Poor,* edited by Greg J. Duncan and Jeanne Brooks-Gunn. New York: Russell Sage Foundation.

Jacob, Brian, and Jens Ludwig. 2007. "The Effects of Housing Vouchers on Children's Outcomes." Working paper. Chicago: University of Chicago.

Jencks, Christopher, and Laura Tach. 2006. "Would Equal Opportunity Mean More Mobility?" In *Mobility and Inequality: Frontiers of Research from Sociology and Economics,* edited by Stephen L. Morgan, David B. Grusky, and Gary S. Fields. Palo Alto, Calif.: Stanford University Press.

Johnson, Rucker C., and Robert F. Schoeni. 2007a. "Early-Life Origins of Adult Disease: The Significance of Poor Infant Health and Childhood Poverty." Unpublished paper. Goldman School of Public Policy, University of California, Berkeley.

———. 2007b. "The Influence of Early-Life Events on Human Capital, Health Status, and Labor Market Outcomes over the Life Course." Working paper no. 07-05. Ann Arbor: University of Michigan, National Poverty Center.

Kane, Thomas J. 2007. "Public Intervention in Postsecondary Education." In *Handbook of the Economics of Education,* edited by Eric A. Hanushek and Finis Welch. Amsterdam: Elsevier.

Kessler, Ronald C., and Paul D. Cleary. 1980. "Social Class and Psychological Distress." *American Sociological Review* 45(3): 463–78.

Kilburn, Rebecca, and Lynn Karoly. 2008. "The Economics of Early Childhood Policy: What the Dismal Science Has to Say About Investing in Children." RAND occasional paper. Available at: http://www.rand.org/pubs/occasional_papers/OP227 (accessed August 11, 2008).

Kishiyama, Mark M., William T. Boyce, Amy M. Jimenez, Lee M. Perry, and Robert T. Knight. Forthcoming. "Socioeconomic Disparities Affect Prefrontal Function in Children." *Journal of Cognitive Neuroscience.*

Kuhlthau, Karen A., and James M. Perrin. 2001. "Child Health Status and Parental Employment." *Archives of Pediatrics and Adolescent Medicine* 155(12): 1346–50.

Lamont, Michele, and Mario Luis Small. 2008. "How Culture Matters for the Understanding of Poverty: Enriching Our Understanding." In *The Colors of Poverty: Why Racial and Ethnic Disparities Persist,* edited by Ann Chih Lin and David Harris. New York: Russell Sage Foundation.

Lareau, Annette. 2003. *Unequal Childhoods: Class, Race, and Family Life.* Berkeley: University of California Press.

Lerner, Richard M. 2003. "What Are SES Effects Effects Of? A Developmental Systems Perspective." In *Socioeconomic Status, Parenting, and Child Development,* edited by Marc H. Bornstein and Robert H. Bradley. New York: Routledge.

Lewis, Oscar. 1966. *La Vida: A Puerto Rican Family in the Culture of Poverty—San Juan and New York.* New York: Random House.

———. 1969. "The Culture of Poverty." In *On Understanding Poverty: Perspectives from the Social Sciences,* edited by Daniel P. Moynihan. New York: Basic Books.

Lupien, Sonia J., Suzanne King, Michael J. Meaney, and Bruce S. McEwen. 2001. "Can Poverty Get Under Your Skin? Basal Cortisol Levels and Cognitive Function in Children from Low and High Socioeconomic Status." *Development and Psychopathology* 13(3): 653–76.

Magnuson, Katherine, and Greg Duncan. 2004. "Parent- vs. Child-Based Intervention Strategies for Promoting Children's Well-Being." In *Family Investments in Children: Resources and Behaviors That Promote Success,* edited by Ariel Kalil and Thomas DeLeire. Mahwah, N.J.: Lawrence Erlbaum Associates.

Maldonado, Carolina, and Elizabeth Votruba-Drzal. 2007. "Socioeconomic Disparities in Achievement Trajectories from Kindergarten Through Third Grade: The Role of Learning-Related Parenting Practices." Paper presented to the biennial meeting of the Society for Research in Child Development, April 2007, Boston.

Massey, Douglas S. 1990. "American Apartheid: Segregation and the Making of the Underclass." *American Journal of Sociology* 96(2): 329–58.

Mayer, Susan E. 1997. *What Money Can't Buy: Family Income and Children's Life Chances.* Cambridge, Mass.: Harvard University Press.

McEwen, Bruce S. 2000. "The Neurobiology of Stress: From Serendipity to Clinical Relevance." *Brain Research* 886(1–2): 172–89.

McLeod, Jane D., and Ronald C. Kessler. 1990. "Socioeconomic Status Differences in Vulnerability to Undesirable Life Events." *Journal of Health and Social Behavior* 31(2): 162–72.

McLoyd, Vonnie C. 1990. "The Impact of Economic Hardship on Black Families and Children: Psychological Distress, Parenting, and Socioemotional Development." *Child Development* 61(2): 311–46.

Mead, Lawrence M. 1986. *Beyond Entitlement: The Social Obligations of Citizenship.* New York: Free Press.

Mistry, Rashmita S., Elizabeth A. Vandewater, Aletha C. Huston, and Vonnie C. McLoyd. 2002. "Economic Well-Being and Children's Social Adjustment: The Role of Family Process in an Ethnically Diverse Low-Income Sample." *Child Development* 73(3): 935–51.

Moffitt, Robert A. 2003. *Means-Tested Transfer Programs in the United States.* Chicago: University of Chicago Press.

Morris, Pamela, Greg J. Duncan, and Elizabeth Clark-Kauffman. 2005. "Child Well-Being in an Era of Welfare Reform: The Sensitivity of Transitions in Development to Policy Change." *Developmental Psychology* 41(6): 919–32.

Noble, Kimberly G., Bruce D. McCandliss, and Martha J. Farah. 2007. "Socioeconomic Gradients Predict Individual Differences in Neurocognitive Abilities." *Developmental Science* 10(4): 464–80.

Olds, David, Lois Sadler, and Harriet Kitzman. 2007. "Programs for Parents of Infants and Toddlers: Recent Evidence from a Randomized Trial." *Journal of Child Psychology and Psychiatry* 48: 355–91.

Plug, Erik, and Wim P. M. Vijverberg. 2005. "Does Family Income Matter for Schooling Outcomes? Using Adoptees as a Natural Experiment." *Economic Journal* 115(506): 879–906.

Powers, Elizabeth T. 2001. "New Estimates on the Impact of Child Disability on Maternal Employment." *American Economic Review* 91(2): 135–39.

———. 2003. "Children's Health and Maternal Work Activity: Estimates Under Alternative Disability Definitions." *Journal of Human Resources* 38(3): 522–56.

Raikes, Helen, Gayle Luze, Jeanne Brooks-Gunn, H. Abigail Raikes, Barbara Alexander Pan, Catherine S. Tamis-LeMonda, Jill Constantine, Louisa Banks Tarullo, and Eileen T. Rodriguez. 2006. "Mother-Child Book Reading in Low-Income Families: Correlates and Outcomes During the First Three Years of Life." *Child Development* 77(4): 924–53.

Raver, Cybele, Elizabeth Gershoff, and J. Lawrence Aber. 2007. "Testing Equivalence of Mediating Models of Income, Parenting, and School Readiness for White, Black, and Hispanic Children in a National Sample." *Child Development* 78(1): 96–115.

Rowe, David C., Kristen C. Jacobson, and Edwin J. C. G. van den Oord. 1999. "Genetic and Environmental Influences on Vocabulary IQ: Parental Education Level as Moderator." *Child Development* 70(5): 1151–62.

Rowe, David C., and Joseph L. Rodgers. 1997. "Poverty and Behavior: Are Environmental Measures Nature and Nurture?" *Developmental Review* 17(3): 358–75.

Salkind, Neil J., and Ron Haskins. 1982. "Negative Income Tax: The Impact on Children from Low-Income Families." *Journal of Family Issues* 3(2): 165–80.

Scarr, Sandra. 1992. "Developmental Theories for the 1990s: Development and Individual Differences." *Child Development* 63(1): 1–19.

Shonkoff, Jack P., and Deborah Phillips. 2000. *From Neurons to Neighborhoods: The Science of Early Childhood Development.* Washington, D.C.: National Academies Press.

Simpson, Gloria A., Barbara Bloom, Robin A. Cohen, Stephen Blumberg, and Karen Bourdon. 2005. "U.S. Children with Emotional and Behavioral Difficulties: Data from the 2001, 2002, and 2003 National Health Interview Surveys." *Advance Data from Vital Health Statistics* 360 (June 23). Washington: U.S. Department of Health and Human Services, Centers for Disease Control and Prevention, National Center for Health Statistics.

Smith, Judith R., Jeanne Brooks-Gunn, and Pamela K. Klebanov. 1997. "Consequences of Living in Poverty for Young Children's Cognitive and Verbal Ability and Early School Achievement." In *Consequences of Growing Up Poor,* edited by Greg J. Duncan and Jeanne Brooks-Gunn. New York: Russell Sage Foundation.

Smolensky, Eugene, and Jennifer A. Gootman, eds. 2003. *Working Families and Growing Kids: Caring for Children and Adolescents.* Washington, D.C.: National Academies Press.

Stevens, Ann Huff. 1999. "Climbing Out of Poverty, Falling Back In: Measuring the Persistence of Poverty over Multiple Spells." *Journal of Human Resources* 34(3): 557–88.

Stoolmiller, Mike. 1999. "Implications of the Restricted Range of Family Environments for Estimates of Heritability and Nonshared Environment in Behavior-Genetic Adoption Studies." *Psychological Bulletin* 125: 392–409.

Tigges, Leann M., Irene Browne, and Gary P. Green. 1998. "Social Isolation of the Urban Poor: Race, Class, and Neighborhood Effects of Social Resources." *Sociological Quarterly* 39(1): 53–77.

Tough, Paul. 2008. *Whatever It Takes: Geoffrey Canada's Quest to Change Harlem and America.* New York: Houghton Mifflin Harcourt.

Turkheimer, Eric, Andreana Haley, Mary Waldron, Brian D'Onofrio, and Irving Gottesman. 2003. "Socioeconomic Status Modifies Heritability of IQ in Young Children." *Psychological Science* 14(6): 623–28.

Turner, R. Jay, and William R. Avison. 2003. "Status Variations in Stress Exposure: Implications of Research on Race, Socioeconomic Status, and Gender." *Journal of Health and Social Behavior* 44(4): 488–505.

Van den Berg, Gerard J., Maarten Lindeboom, and France Portrait. 2005. "Economic Conditions Early in Life and Individual Mortality." *American Economic Review* 96(1): 290–302.

Van Praag, Henriette, Gerd Kempermann, and Fred H. Gage. 2000. "Neural Consequences of Environmental Enrichment." *Nature Reviews: Neuroscience* 1(3): 191–98.

Votruba-Drzal, Elizabeth. 2006. "Economic Disparities in Middle Childhood: Does Income Matter?" *Developmental Psychology* 42(6): 1154–67.

Webster-Stratton, Carolyn. 1990. "Long-Term Follow-up of Families with Young Conduct Problem Children: From Preschool to Grade School." *Journal of Clinical Child Psychology* 19(2): 144–49.

Wilson, William Julius. 1987. *The Truly Disadvantaged: The Inner City, the Underclass, and Public Policy*. Chicago: University of Chicago Press.

———. 1996. *When Work Disappears: The World of the New Urban Poor*. New York: Alfred A. Knopf.

Yeung, W. Jean, Miriam R. Linver, and Jeanne Brooks-Gunn. 2002. "How Money Matters for Young Children's Development: Parental Investment and Family Processes." *Child Development* 73(6): 1861–79.

Zaslow, Martha J., and Cheryl D. Hayes. 1986. "Sex Differences in Children's Responses to Psychosocial Stress: Toward a Cross-Context Analysis." In *Advances in Developmental Psychology*, vol. 4, edited by Michael Lamb and Barbara Rogoff. Hillsdale, N.J.: Lawrence Erlbaum Associates.

Ziol-Guest, Kathleen. 2008. Personal communication. March 28, 2008.

Chapter 7

Mobility in the United States in Comparative Perspective

Markus Jäntti

The United States has a much more unequal distribution of income than most developed nations. Even though it has one of the highest standards of living on average, as measured by its gross domestic product per capita, its more unequal income distribution translates into comparatively high rates of both relative poverty (50 percent of median disposable income) and absolute poverty (the official U.S. poverty thresholds) (see, for example, Meyer and Wallace, this volume; Bradbury and Jäntti 2001). Some analysts suggest that high inequality and poverty in any one year are of little public policy concern if rates of mobility are also high. For example, assume that the poverty rate measured in terms of a single year's income is 20 percent in each of two societies. In one, every person has a one-in-five chance of being poor in any given year, but poverty in one year does not foretell being poor in the next year. In the other society, the same individuals are poor every single year. Because the first society has complete mobility and the second has no mobility, the latter society has a more serious poverty problem.

Income mobility and poverty mobility are closely related to notions of equality of opportunity, whereas annual measures of inequality and poverty are related to notions of equality of outcomes. One traditional explanation for the inequality of the U.S. income distribution is that Americans value equality of opportunity more highly than equality of outcomes (Corcoran 2001, citing Turner 1960). However, Lars Osberg and Timothy Smeeding (2006) find that Americans are very similar to residents in other countries in their attitudes about inequality and about the factors that justify large economic rewards. American attitudes are more sharply divided than is the case in other countries, with a larger minority being against equalization of annual incomes. Somewhat surprisingly, Americans are just as often in favor of reducing inequality at the top of the distribution as are citizens of other countries, but they are less concerned with reducing differentials at the bottom of the distribution. Therefore, it may be that higher American inequality and poverty are not so much an expression of a preference for inequality as a phenomenon driven, at least in part, by a failure to see the relationship between equality of opportunity and equality of outcomes. This chapter discusses both poverty mobility over time and intergenerational mobility, emphasizing the relationship between long- and short-run measures of economic outcomes.

I examine whether poverty is a persistent problem of a small group in society that does not enjoy equal opportunities or a problem that afflicts many, but for only brief periods of time. Because many individuals experience income fluctuations from year to year, poverty measured over longer periods is lower than poverty measured over short periods. One way of assessing the level of poverty mobility in the United States is to compare it to poverty mobility in other advanced economies.

This chapter begins by examining poverty mobility in the United States based on monthly incomes. The proportion of those who are poor in two or more months is much greater than the poverty rate based on annual income, so the experience of poverty is more common than is suggested by the official poverty rate, which is based on annual figures. Similar background factors—belonging to a racial minority or living in a female-headed household—are associated with higher short-term, annual, and long-term poverty. Next, I examine poverty dynamics based on annual income over a long period of time in the United States, Canada, Germany, and the United Kingdom. There is considerable mobility into and out of poverty in all of these countries, so in each country a much higher fraction of the population is poor at least once during the period than is poor in any given year, and far fewer are poor across all of the years. Germany and the United Kingdom have lower rates of poverty persistence than Canada and the United States.

In the fourth section, I analyze cross-national evidence on the extent of intergenerational income persistence. Recent research has shown that intergenerational persistence is higher than previously thought, and higher in the United States than in several other developed countries. Part of the reason for the high level of intergenerational income persistence in the United States is the income disadvantage of African Americans. Despite increases in the number and size of changes in income inequality since the mid-1970s, there is not much evidence that intergenerational income persistence has changed over the years. The final section discusses some policy implications of the findings.

SHORT-TERM POVERTY

Official U.S. poverty statistics, like those in most other countries, are based on annual income. For persons with low or no savings, income shortfalls during shorter periods may be highly distressing. Changes in household income from month to month can be part of normal economic activity. For instance, in industries such as agriculture, where activity levels are seasonally variable, laborers may earn income during short periods of the year to provide for consumption during the rest of the year. To the extent, however, that income changes within the year affect families who earn low wages and experience periods of unemployment, short-term income fluctuations may be associated with substantial drops in living standards.

TABLE 7.1 / Monthly and Annual Poverty Rates and Poverty Mobility
in the United States, 1996 to 1999

	1996	1997	1998	1999	1996 to 1999
Poor two or more months	23.3%	21.7%	20.4%	19.5%	34.2%
Annual poverty rate	12.5	11.4	10.5	10.1	NA
Average annual poverty rate[a]	15.5	14.3	13.5	12.8	NA
Poor in 1996 but not poor in 1997, 1998, or 1999	NA	34.9	44.5	49.5	NA
Not poor in 1996 but poor in 1997, 1998, or 1999	NA	2.9	3.3	3.5	NA

Source: Author's compilation based on Iceland (2003), figure 1.
a. Based on monthly poverty.

Income measured over any period reflects both true income and random measurement errors. Some of the changes in income from period to period reflect changes in measurement errors. Most analysts believe that there is more such "noise" in measured income over very short periods. Thus, not all of the short-term changes in poverty reflect true changes in poverty status. Unfortunately, it is very difficult to assess how much of the measured short-term movements reflect changes in measurement errors. Despite the potentially greater relative importance of measurement errors, it is instructive to examine short-term poverty dynamics.

In this section, I examine trends in short-term poverty, measured on a monthly basis. Because poverty rates for periods shorter than one year are unavailable for other countries, I focus solely on the United States.

Table 7.1 shows the official poverty rates of all persons for different time periods between 1996 and 1999 (Iceland 2003). The first row shows the rate of *episodic* poverty, defined as the proportion of the population that was poor in two or more months in every year from 1996 to 1999 as well as the proportion that was poor for two or more months between 1996 and 1999.[1] The rate of within-year episodic poverty declined from 23.3 percent in 1996 to 19.5 percent in 1999. That is, in 1999, one in five persons lived in a household with below-poverty-level income for at least two months of the year; over the four-year period, 34.2 percent experienced at least two months of poverty-level income. The second row shows the annual poverty rates, which also suggest that poverty declined from 1996 to 1999, but at a substantially lower level—from 12.5 percent in 1996 to 10.1 percent in 1999. The annual poverty rate is then compared with the average monthly poverty rate (third row), which ranged from 15.5 percent to 12.8 percent from 1996 to 1999. Thus, a higher fraction of persons experienced at least one month of poverty than were counted as officially poor.

John Iceland (2003) also reports trends in poverty for different time periods for selected population groups. The first column in table 7.2 shows the episodic poverty rate in 1999 by race, age, family type, and area. White non-Hispanics had the lowest rate of episodic poverty, 13.9 percent, while 34.5 percent of blacks and

TABLE 7.2 / Monthly and Annual Poverty Rates and Poverty Mobility
in the United States by Select Population Groups

| | Short-Term Poverty | | Longer-Term Poverty | |
| | Episodic Poverty— Poor in Two or More Months 1999 | Average Monthly Poverty Rate 1999 | Poor in Every Month 1996 to 1999 | Median Poverty Spell 1996 to 1999 |
	(1)	(2)	(3)	(4)
All persons	19.5%	12.8%	2.0%	4.0%
Race				
White	16.8	10.7	1.5	3.9
White non-Hispanic	13.9	8.7	1.0	3.8
Black	34.5	24.8	5.1	4.9
Hispanic	37.1	24.7	5.6	4.6
Age				
Zero to seventeen	26.8	18.3	2.6	4.4
Eighteen to sixty-four	17.2	10.9	1.4	3.9
Sixty-five and older	15.4	10.7	3.8	4.0
Family type				
Married-couple family	12.8	7.0	0.6	3.7
Female householder	41.7	30.4	5.7	5.8
Male householder	21.9	12.4	0.8	4.1
Unrelated individuals	28.2	21.0	5.2	4.4
Other[a]	NA	NA	NA	NA
Area				
Central city	24.8	16.8	2.9	4.2
Suburbs	14.0	8.9	1.1	3.8
Nonmetropolitan area	25.2	16.3	2.7	4.5

Source: Author's compilation based on Iceland (2003), figures 5, 6, 7, 9–11.
Note: Based on annual incomes and poverty thresholds.
a. "Other" includes both female and male householders.

37.1 percent of Hispanics experienced episodic poverty. Children (26.8 percent) had a much higher risk of episodic poverty than persons of working age (17.2 percent) or the elderly (15.4 percent). Households with a female householder had an episodic poverty risk of more than twice that of the average person in 1999. Finally, episodic poverty affected one in four persons living in either a central city or a nonmetropolitan area, while that rate was 14 percent in suburban areas.

The second column of table 7.2 reports group-specific average monthly poverty rates. The patterns by group are similar to those in column 1. Blacks and Hispanics had a much higher risk of being poor in any given month than white non-Hispanics—about one in four for each minority group, compared to 8.7 percent for white non-Hispanics.

In sum, by shortening the period over which poverty is measured, we find substantial changes in poverty status. Although some part of the short-term dynamics of poverty probably reflects measurement errors rather than actual changes in income, examining short-term dynamics is informative all the same. The episodic poverty rate—defined as the proportion of the population with below-poverty-level income in two or more months within the year—is about twice the poverty rate based on annual income. However, racial minorities and female-headed households are at greatest risk of both annual poverty and short-term poverty.

LONG-TERM POVERTY

The study of poverty dynamics typically examines poverty across longer periods than a single year rather than taking the shorter perspective discussed in the previous section. One way to approach this analysis is to choose a period of, say, four years and examine how many persons were poor *during the whole period*—so-called *persistent poverty*. We can also examine the fraction of the population that was poor at *any one time* during the period; this would be *episodic poverty*. It is also interesting to look at *entries into* and *exits out of* poverty, along with the distribution of *poverty spells*. In this section, I analyze comparable evidence for the United States and other countries on patterns of long-term poverty and poverty dynamics over periods longer than one year.

John Iceland (2003) measures long-term poverty in the United States based on monthly incomes, so I first review his results.[2] The third and fourth columns in table 7.2 show different aspects of long-term poverty. We start by asking: what proportion of the population was poor in every period? Column 3 in table 7.2 shows that 2.0 percent of all persons were *persistently* poor—that is, poor in every one of the forty-eight months from 1996 to 1999. As also reported in columns 1 and 2, the risk of persistent poverty varied substantially by race and ethnicity: both blacks and Hispanics had more than a 5 percent risk of chronic poverty, compared to 1 percent for white non-Hispanics. Female-headed households and unrelated individuals were also at high risk of persistent poverty. Children were at a higher risk than the average person of persistent poverty, as were the elderly.

Persistent poverty as defined in column 3 of table 7.2 considers only a portion of the overall experience of poverty—those who were poor in every one of forty-eight months. Another way to examine poverty dynamics is to focus on the length of a spell of poverty. Figure 7.1 shows the distribution of poverty spells according to how many months a spell had lasted, given that it lasted two months or more. More than half of all spells were of relatively brief duration, lasting two to four months. Overall, 79.6 percent of all poverty spells lasted for twelve months or less. On the other hand, 9.2 percent of all poverty spells were quite long, lasting more than two years.

Column 4 in table 7.2 shows the median spell length in months for all persons and for population groups. The median poverty spell for all persons lasted 4.0 months. Hispanics' median spell lasted 4.6 months, and that of blacks 4.9 months. The median spell of persons in female-headed households was

FIGURE 7.1 / Duration of Poverty Spells in the United States, 1996 to 1999

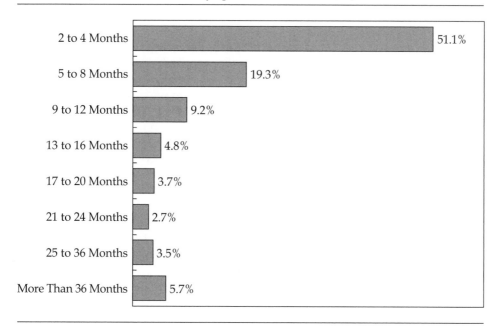

Source: U.S. Bureau of the Census, 1996 Survey of Income and Program Participation, reprinted from Iceland (2003).
Note: Excludes spells that were under way during the first interview month.

5.8 months, which contrasts with 3.7 months for married-couple families. Children's median poverty spell was 4.4 months. Again, the characteristics that are associated with greater annual poverty rates are also associated with longer poverty spells.

INTERNATIONAL EVIDENCE

The annual poverty rate in the United States is high compared to the rates in other nations, especially poverty that is based on a relative definition, as is customary in international comparisons. When poverty is based on an absolute definition by converting the official U.S. poverty line into an equivalent value in other countries, the comparison is more complicated. However, countries that have very low levels of relative poverty and reasonably high average income levels, such as the Nordic countries, tend to have much lower levels of poverty even when the U.S. poverty line is used (Smeeding, Rainwater, and Burtless 2001). How do poverty dynamics compare across countries? Answering this question is difficult because it requires having comparable data sets for many countries.[3]

Robert G. Valletta (2006) estimates poverty dynamics across six years for Canada, Germany, the United Kingdom, and the United States. Poverty in the United States is measured in terms of annual income and using both a relative definition (50 percent of median disposable income) and the official U.S. definition, but in the other countries only the relative definition is used.[4]

Table 7.3 summarizes for these four countries different aspects of poverty dynamics for the working-age population (household head between the ages of sixteen and sixty-four). Columns 1 to 3 show poverty rates based on both pretax, pretransfer (market) income and post-tax, post-transfer (disposable) income based on average annual rates (column 1); on having been poor in at least one of the six years (column 2); and on having been poor in every year (column 3). In all four countries, the episodic disposable income poverty rate in column 2 is substantially higher than the average annual rate. That is, about twice as many people experience poverty during a six-year period than are poor in any given year, which suggests substantial mobility into and out of poverty in all four countries. By contrast, the proportion of those who are poor in every one of the six years (column 3) is substantially smaller than the annual rate. For instance, the U.S. annual average poverty rate is 17 percent (column 1), which compares to 3.9 percent for those who are poor in all six years. In Germany, 9.7 percent, on average, are poor in any given year, but only 1.4 percent are poor in all six years.

Column 4 of table 7.3 also shows poverty rates based on income averaged across the six years, which Valletta (2006) calls *chronic* poverty. These rates, which measure those whose income is persistently low, vary substantially across countries. In Canada and the United States, the rate of chronic poverty is lower than the annual rate, but still quite substantial at 9.1 percent and 10.6 percent, respectively. In Germany and the United Kingdom, the chronic poverty rates are less than one-half of the annual rates, at 4.4 percent and 2.9 percent, respectively. This suggests that poverty mobility in Germany and the United Kingdom is associated with larger increases in income than is the case in Canada and the United States.

Table 7.3 also provides information about differences in the antipoverty effectiveness of government transfers by comparing the change in poverty on moving from a market income–based definition to one based on disposable income. For the most part, the differences in market income poverty rates and disposable income poverty rates are of the same order of magnitude. For instance, in Canada, market income poverty is reduced by five to seven percentage points for all four poverty definitions. For the relative poverty definition in the United States, poverty is not reduced very much by government transfers. Using the official definition (the last two rows of the table) reduces the persistent poverty rate from 4.1 percent to 2.3 percent (column 3); using a relative line reduces the persistent poverty rate from 5.5 percent to 3.9 percent.

Table 7.3 shows entry (column 5) and exit (column 6) rates into and out of poverty; column 7 shows the mean duration of poverty spells. The entry rates are quite similar across countries, with 3.1 percent of the German nonpoor and 5.5 percent of the U.S. nonpoor being at risk of entering relative poverty in any year. There is much more variation in exit rates from poverty—31.9 percent of the Canadian

TABLE 7.3 / Annual, Episodic, Persistent, and Chronic Poverty Rates in Canada, Germany, the United Kingdom, and the United States

Country and Income	Annual Poverty Rate (1)	In Poverty at Least Once (2)	Always in Poverty (3)	Chronic Poverty (4)	Yearly Rate of Entry (5)	Yearly Rate of Exit (6)	Mean Duration (7)
Canada							
Market income	19.5%	32.7%	8.0%	14.5%	5.1%	24.4%	3.1%
Disposable income	12.6	25.3	3.5	9.1	4.5	31.9	2.6
Germany							
Market income	16.2	27.6	3.6	9.1	4.9	26.9	2.4
Disposable income	9.7	18.1	1.4	4.4	3.1	42.0	1.9
United Kingdom							
Market income	15.9	26.1	2.5	7.0	4.3	34.8	2.2
Disposable income	9.9	21.2	0.4	2.9	3.8	55.2	1.6
United States							
Market income	18.3	30.7	5.5	12.2	5.3	31.4	2.3
Disposable income	17.0	30.5	3.9	10.6	5.5	37.3	2.1
U.S. official threshold							
Market income	15.0	25.7	4.1	8.8	4.3	32.8	2.3
Disposable income	11.8	22.2	2.3	6.0	3.9	41.7	2.0

Source: Author's compilation based on Valletta (2006), tables 3 and 4.
Note: Poverty is measured from 1991 to 1996 in all countries except Canada, where poverty is measured from 1993 to 1998.

poor exit poverty in any given year, compared to 55.2 percent in the United Kingdom. Exits out of U.S. official poverty, 41.7 percent, are more prevalent than exits out of relative poverty, 37.3 percent, suggesting that many U.S. exits leave individuals only a small distance from the official poverty line. The mean duration of poverty spells varies between the low of 1.6 years in the United Kingdom and the high of 2.6 years in Canada; for the United States it is 2.1 years.

Patterns of poverty dynamics exhibit similarities, but also some differences, across countries. What about the factors associated with poverty transitions? Table 7.4 reports the fraction of poverty entries and exits of the working-age population that are associated with different family- and job-related events. Changes in family structure (such as divorce, birth of a child, or death of a spouse) are very important for both entries into and exits out of poverty in all four countries. Roughly two in five poverty entries in every country are associated with a change in family structure (column 1, top panel). Family structure changes are also associated with between one-fourth and two-fifths of exits out of poverty (column 1, bottom panel). Changes in the number of full-time workers for those who had no change in family structure (column 2), while less important, are also related to both poverty entries and exits. For instance, a reduction in full-time workers in the United States is associated with 9 to 10 percent of all entries into poverty, and an increase in full-time workers is associated with 14 to 16 percent of all exits out of poverty. Holding constant family structure and the number of full-time workers, reductions (increases) in labor earnings (column 3) as opposed to other income sources (columns 4, 5, and 6) are associated with the most entries into (exits out of) poverty. Changes in government transfers (column 4) are reasonably important for poverty entries and exits in Germany and the United Kingdom, but less so in Canada and the United States.

Bruce Bradbury, Stephen Jenkins, and John Micklewright (2001) compare the poverty dynamics of children in several countries, including Germany, the United Kingdom, and the United States. They find that the persistence of child poverty is high in those countries where the annual child poverty rate is high. For instance, 7.7 percent of German children were poor in the first year of the data, and 1.5 percent of children were poor in all of the five years they were followed. In the United States, 24.7 percent of children were poor in the first year, and 13.0 percent were poor in all five years (Bradbury, Jenkins, and Micklewright 2001, 121).

Has the Persistence of Poverty Changed over Time?

Lloyd Grieger and Jessica Wyse (2008) estimate long-term child poverty rates based on post-tax, post-transfer income plus food stamps averaged across several years. Their measure, similar to what Valletta (2006) calls *chronic poverty*, increased for cohorts born in the 1970s from 5.9 percent to 10 percent for cohorts born in the 1980s, and decreased again, to about 7.3 percent, for those born in the 1990s. The chronic poverty rate was substantially higher and increased more and decreased less for black children.

TABLE 7.4 / Frequency of Family and Job-Related Events Associated with Poverty Transitions—Working–Age Households, Disposable Income Poverty

Country	Total Entries into Poverty Associated with Largest Decrease in:[b]					
	Change in Family Structure	Full-Time Workers[a]	Labor Earnings	Government Transfers	Capital and Other Income	Other
	Entries					
Canada	46.9%	6.4%	27.3%	13.3%	6.0%	0.2%
Germany	38.8	10.4	31.1	14.5	5.0	0.3
United Kingdom	41.5	8.1	33.6	12.8	3.7	0.3
United States	39.0	10.4	40.9	4.0	5.2	0.5
U.S. official threshold	38.7	9.2	39.2	6.1	5.9	0.9

Country	Total Exits out of Poverty Associated with Largest Increase in:[b]					
	Change in Family Structure	Full-Time Workers[a]	Labor Earnings	Government Transfers	Capital and Other Income	Other
	Exits					
Canada	39.1	15.8	28.3	11.5	5.2	0.1
Germany	24.4	14.2	32.2	24.2	4.7	0.3
United Kingdom	28.3	12.2	35.5	18.3	5.5	0.2
United States	29.3	16.4	42.8	5.3	5.5	0.7
U.S. official threshold	27.7	14.4	42.6	8.8	5.8	0.6

Source: Author's compilation based on Valletta (2006), table 5.
a. No change in family structure. "Full-time" defined as at least 1,750 hours per year for head and spouse only.
b. No change in family structure or in full-time work by the head and spouse.

In sum, while only about 2 percent of all Americans were poor in every month in the four years from 1996 through 1999, the risk of such long-term poverty was higher for groups that were at higher risk of both short-term and annual poverty. Differences in the length of poverty spells and exits out of and entries into poverty across the years show similar patterns. The same groups—racial and ethnic minorities, single-parent families—have above-average annual poverty rates and higher short- and long-term poverty rates.

Also, even though the United States has poverty rates that are higher than those in some other major economies, poverty dynamics are similar across countries. Episodic poverty over a period of six years occurs at a rate that is roughly twice the annual poverty rate, and the proportion of those who are poor in every single year is substantially smaller than the annual rate. The duration of poverty is also quite similar across countries, with Canada having the longest durations. Finally, in all four countries, poverty dynamics are most closely associated with changes in family structure, changes in the number of full-time workers in the household, and changes in labor earnings. The importance of public transfers in accounting for poverty dynamics, by contrast, varied quite a bit.

INTERGENERATIONAL MOBILITY

Do poor children become poor adults? In this section, I discuss what the U.S. and comparative literature have found to be the patterns of overall income persistence and persistence at the low end of the distribution. I also review differences in income persistence for men and for women and racial differences in income persistence in the United States.

Answering the question of whether poor children become poor adults requires that we confront many substantive and measurement issues (Björklund and Jäntti 2009). Cross-country comparisons of intergenerational income mobility are difficult because they are sensitive to many assumptions about measurement that the researcher must make.[5] The most common way to examine how closely related children's economic status is to that of their parents is to estimate the intergenerational elasticity—that is, the regression coefficient obtained from regressing the natural logarithm of offspring income on that of the parent. This elasticity is a measure of the number of percentage points by which a child's income will increase if a parent's income increases by a certain percentage. A larger dependence means children's adult economic status is more highly dependent on that of their parents.

Basing his study on work by Nathan Grawe (2004), Miles Corak (2006) identifies as many as twenty-six estimates of intergenerational income mobility in the United States. These range from a high of 0.61 (suggesting that a 1 percent increase in long-term parental income is associated, on average, with a 0.6 percent increase in the long-term adult income of offspring) to a low of 0.09.[6] One way to think of the estimated elasticity of children's income with respect to their parents' is to ask how much of a given income advantage observed in the parental generation is preserved in the children's generation. Corak (2006) exem-

TABLE 7.5 / Intergenerational Income Persistence for Fathers and Sons in Selected
Countries—Elasticity Estimates

Country	Elasticity
Australia	0.25
Canada	0.27
Denmark	0.12
Finland	0.28
France	0.42
Germany	0.25
Italy	0.44
Norway	0.25
Sweden	0.24
United Kingdom	0.29
United States	0.45

Source: Author's compilation of comparable estimates by Björklund and Jäntti (2009).

plifies this for the difference observed in the United States in families with children under the age of eighteen. The top fifth of such families have about twelve times as much income as the bottom fifth. If the intergenerational persistence of income is equal to one, that income advantage will be transferred in whole to the next generation. That is, the children of the richest fifth will have twelve times as much income as the children of the poorest fifth. If the intergenerational persistence of income is equal to zero, none of that advantage will be present among the children of these groups. Corak (2006) reports U.S. estimates of this elasticity that vary from 0.4 to 0.6, corresponding to an inherited income advantage of between 2.70 and 4.44 for the richest fifth compared to the poorest fifth.

Table 7.5 shows a set of the most comparable elasticity estimates for selected countries from Björklund and Jäntti (2009). The United States, Italy, and France all have high persistence, at 0.45, 0.44, and 0.42, respectively, which, with a twelvefold income advantage in the parental generation, translates to incomes among the children of the richest fifth that are roughly three times higher than those of the poorest. Denmark has the lowest persistence, at 0.12, and most other countries are quite close to 0.25. These numbers translate to incomes among the richest fifth of offspring that are 1.35 and 1.86 times higher, holding constant the parental income advantage.

Differences in Intergenerational Persistence Among Those with the Lowest- and Highest-Earning Fathers

The overall intergenerational persistence discussed in the previous section does not tell us about persistence at the low end of the income distribution. It is the outcomes of the worst-off children that are of greatest policy concern (see Magnuson

TABLE 7.6 / Intergenerational Mobility Matrix for the United States

	Son's Quintile Group				
Father's Quintile Group	First	Second	Third	Fourth	Fifth
First	42.2%	24.5%	15.3%	10.2%	7.9%
Second	19.4	28.3	20.8	17.4	14.0
Third	19.4	18.6	25.6	20.2	16.2
Fourth	12.5	18.2	19.8	25.2	24.3
Fifth	9.5	12.2	18.9	23.4	36.0

Source: Jäntti et al. (2006), based on the National Longitudinal Survey (NLS).
Notes: Sons' earnings are measured at ages thirty-three and forty-two. Fathers' income is measured as their family income in 1979. Each cell is the probability that the son of a father in the quintile group indicated by the row ends up as an adult in the quintile group indicated by the column. Each row sums to 100 percent.

and Votruba-Drzal, this volume). An earnings mobility matrix, such as table 7.6 for the United States (Jäntti et al. 2006), compares the economic status of fathers and their sons when the sons are between the ages of thirty-three and forty-four. The fathers' earnings quintiles are shown in the rows; each cell in the matrix gives the probability that the son with a father in a given quintile group will end up in the quintile group indicated by the column. If there were no relationship between a father's income and that of his son, the value in every cell in the matrix would be 20 percent (since each quintile group includes 20 percent of the fathers).

In contrast, the top-left cell shows that 44.2 percent of the sons who had a father in the lowest quintile of earners in that generation will end up in the lowest quintile of earners in their generation. The next cell in the first row is the likelihood that a lowest-quintile father's son will be in the second quintile of earners in his generation—24.5 percent. The main diagonal tends to have the highest numbers—that is, sons are most likely to end up in the same group as their fathers. The lowest and the highest groups have the largest probabilities on this main diagonal. Also, note that only 7.9 percent of the sons who have the poorest fathers end up as top earners in their generation, and that only 9.5 percent of the sons who have the richest fathers end up as the lowest earners in their generation.

Jäntti et al. (2006) estimate such mobility matrices for the United States, the United Kingdom, Sweden, Norway, Finland, and Denmark. Interesting differences can be found in the four "corners" of the mobility matrices, which give the probabilities that the son of a rich (poor) father will end up at the top (bottom) of the distribution, and the probabilities that a poor (rich) father's son will end up in the top (bottom) quintile group.

The United States and the United Kingdom have a somewhat lower probability that the son of a father in the highest-quintile group will end up in the bottom-quintile group (about 10 percent, relative to 15 percent for the other countries), and the likelihood that the son of a father who is a top earner will also be a top earner is about 35 percent in each country except the United Kingdom, where it is

30 percent. The United States is most different from other countries by having the highest probability that the son of a father who earns the least will also end up in the lowest quintile of earners—42 percent compared to about 30 percent in the United Kingdom and around 25 percent in the four Nordic countries. The United States also has the lowest probability that the son of a lowest-quintile group father will make it to the top-quintile group, although this difference is not very large— 7.9 percent in the United States, about 15 percent in Denmark, and 11 to 12 percent in the other four countries.

The Intergenerational Mobility of Women

Most studies of intergenerational mobility focus on the relationship between sons and their fathers. This focus on men is due in large part to the difficulties in measuring the economic status of women over time and across countries. The labor force participation rates of women have increased quite substantially in the past few decades, and the timing of these increases varies across countries. While most studies assume that the permanent income of men can be reliably measured between the ages of thirty-five and forty, this is the age at which many women are rearing young children and have either reduced their work hours or withdrawn from the labor force. Thus, comparing estimates of intergenerational mobility across countries with different labor market institutions for women may be problematic.

Laura Chadwick and Gary Solon (2002) examine the intergenerational income persistence of women in the United States using data on family income or the combined earnings of couples (for those who are married). Their estimates suggest that women's family incomes are also highly correlated with those of their parents, although slightly less strongly than for men—the elasticity is 0.429 for women and 0.535 for men.

Oddbjörn Raaum and his colleagues (2007) compare the intergenerational income persistence of women and men in the United States with that of women in the United Kingdom and the Nordic countries. They compile their cross-country evidence on the intergenerational persistence based both on a person's own annual earnings and on the combined earnings of their partners (if present) and themselves. Their main results for women are shown in table 7.7. The differences across countries in the persistence of a woman's own earnings, shown in row 1, with respect to the earnings of her parents are quite small, although such persistence is higher in the United Kingdom (0.270) and the United States (0.252) than in the Nordic countries (between 0.186 and 0.197). Once the combined earnings of women and their spouses (if present) are considered, in row 2, the persistence is greater in all countries, ranging from 0.359 in the United States and 0.325 in the United Kingdom to only about 0.21 in the three Nordic countries. The large differences in the persistence between own earnings and combined earnings, especially in the United States, suggest that positive marital sorting—that is, the extent to which high-wage women marry high-wage men—is quite strong.

TABLE 7.7 / Intergenerational Income Persistence for Women in Denmark, Finland, Norway, the United Kingdom, and the United States

	Denmark	Finland	Norway	United Kingdom	United States
All women: elasticity of own earnings in relation to her parents' earnings	0.190	0.197	0.186	0.270	0.252
Couples: combined earnings in relation to her parents' earnings	0.192	0.226	0.210	0.325	0.359

Source: Author's compilation based on Raaum et al. (2007), table 2.
Note: Combined earnings per adult are set equal to combined earnings divided by two for couples and own earnings for singles.

Intergenerational Mobility by Race in the United States

We documented earlier that annual and longitudinal poverty rates in the United States are higher for racial and ethnic minorities. There also are differences in intergenerational income persistence across racial groups (Hertz 2005). The rates of persistence in family income for both men and women among whites separately (0.393) and blacks separately (0.317) are lower than for both groups pooled together (0.534). This is due to the fact that differences in the average incomes of the two groups contribute to the high overall level of intergenerational income persistence. Note, however, that these results suggest that across the whole distribution there is more, not less, intergenerational mobility among blacks than whites.

This is not the case for persistence of low income. Tom Hertz (2005) also reports the likelihood that a child in a family in the lowest 25 percent of the income distribution will end up as an adult in the same part of the distribution as their parents. About 47 percent of children of parents who are in the lowest fourth of the income distribution are among the poorest 25 percent of their generation when they are young adults. Among African American children, 62.9 percent will be among the poorest quarter of the population when they are adults, compared to 32.3 percent of white children.

The sample sizes used in Jäntti and others (2006) to examine the likelihood that the son of a poorest-fifth father will remain in the poorest fifth are not large enough to yield reliable estimates by race, but when the sample is restricted to include only sons of white non-Hispanic fathers, the probability of remaining in the poorest fifth is 38 percent. This is lower than the 42 percent for all sons. Thus, the presence of minorities accounts for part of the higher U.S. low-income persistence, but even among white non-Hispanic Americans, low-income persistence is much higher than in the comparison countries.

The United States has high levels of immigration compared to many other countries, and recent immigrants might have high rates of intergenerational mobility.

As Abdurrahman Aydemir, Wen-Hao Chen, and Miles Corak (2006) report, however, the intergenerational mobility among immigrants in Canada, Sweden, and the United States tends to be quite close to that of the natives in each country. Thus, while immigration to a rich country is often associated with a large improvement in living standards, the offspring of the immigrants have incomes whose persistence is very close to that of native offspring.

Changes in Intergenerational Mobility

The United States has experienced large increases in income and earnings inequality since the late 1970s. In light of such changes, it is interesting to ask how intergenerational persistence has changed over time. Has the importance of family background decreased, reflecting more equally distributed opportunities to all? Or has the increase in inequality enhanced the importance of family background? Several researchers have examined this question and found somewhat conflicting results. Susan Mayer and L. M. Lopoo (2005) have studied the income persistence of men born between 1949 and 1965 and found that the persistence increased for cohorts born between 1949 and 1956, after which the persistence declined. Using more recent data and older children, for whom earnings more accurately measure lifetime income, neither Thomas Hertz (2007) nor Chui-In Lee and Gary Solon (forthcoming) find much of a trend in the intergenerational persistence for either women or men. Hertz (2007) finds that, if anything, persistence has been trending upward.

There are only a few countries apart from the United States where data allow an examination of changes in intergenerational mobility. Jo Blanden and her colleagues (2004) find that income persistence among men in the United Kingdom is greater for the cohort born in 1970 than the cohort born in 1958. Espen Bratberg, Øivind Anti Nielsen, and Kjell Vaage (2007) find that for Norwegian men and women born between 1950 to 1960, income persistence declined somewhat. Sari Pekkala and Robert Lucas (2007) similarly find that income persistence among Finnish men and women declined for cohorts born between 1930 and 1956, after which they remained at roughly the same level.

The evidence suggests that the U.S. persistence has either not changed by much or increased a little, that the U.K. persistence has increased, and that intergenerational persistence in Norway and Finland has decreased. David Levine and Bhashkar Mazumder (2007) suggest that the increased U.S. income persistence may be related to increased earnings gaps by educational attainment; however, precise explanations for why persistence has changed are not available.

What Accounts for the Intergenerational Persistence in Income?

It is important to know why income position is to some extent inherited, since some reasons might be more amenable than others to policy interventions to decrease persistence. Some policy interventions, if effective, might also be more likely than others to gain political support. In particular, interventions that occur early in life, such as intensive preschool education for disadvantaged children, tend to be popular. It would be good to know whether they are effective in decreasing persistence.

Economic explanations for why incomes are correlated across generations tend to emphasize that educational attainment, skills, and ability, all of which affect income levels, are transmitted from parents to children (Becker and Tomes 1986; Solon 2004). Sociological accounts of persistence tend to emphasize the intergenerational similarity of occupation and class (Erikson and Goldthorpe 1992). Some scholars emphasize the genetic transmission of traits (Jencks and Tach 2006). Although the exact mechanisms that explain income persistence are unknown, it seems that policies aimed at reducing inequalities in the quality of schooling and meritocratic selection into higher education might promote mobility and reduce intergenerational persistence. If income persistence and income inequality are positively related, as suggested by Anders Björklund and Markus Jäntti (2009), then policies aimed at reducing inequality might also decrease intergenerational persistence.

In sum, incomes are highly intergenerationally persistent in many countries, and this persistence is greater in countries with greater inequality and poverty. The income persistence of women is slightly less than men's, but once we examine family income, the levels of persistence are similar. The intergenerational income persistence of African Americans and of whites is lower when examined separately than when combined, which suggests that black-white income difference accounts for part of the high level of persistence in the United States. Income persistence in the United States seems not to have changed by much in recent decades, while persistence appears to have increased in the United Kingdom but decreased in the Nordic countries. Finally, developing effective policy interventions to reduce persistence would require that we know why incomes are intergenerationally persistent, but such knowledge eludes us.

CONCLUSION

Some policy analysts call attention to poverty dynamics to point out that the rate of persistent poverty is much smaller than the annual poverty rate, suggesting that poverty is less prevalent than is commonly believed. Analysis of poverty dynamics, however, also calls attention to the fact that more individuals are affected by poverty over a period of a few years than are poor in a single year, so the risk of poverty is quite widespread. Moreover, even if many people exit poverty each year, they do not exit very far from the poverty line and are at substantial risk of reentry. This suggests that the economically vulnerable population is quite large.

Focusing on poverty dynamics rather than the annual poverty rate is often associated with different kinds of policies to combat poverty. While annual poverty, or even persistent long-term poverty, suggests the use of income support programs to alleviate poverty, the examination of poverty spells and entries and exits leads policy analysts to consider what factors are associated with changes in poverty status. Work-based benefits, such as the Earned Income Tax Credit (EITC) in the United States and the Working Tax Credit (WTC) in the United Kingdom, are examples of the kinds of policies that are more closely associated with changes in poverty status, since they respond to declines in income.

We also documented that similar background factors are associated with long- and short-term as well as persistent poverty. Thus, a policy that reduces annual poverty risks might also reduce persistent poverty. Moreover, policies that are aimed at increasing the likelihood of poverty exit for families with children by providing strong work incentives risk reducing the living standards of children unless the policies result in substantially increased income.

Intergenerational income persistence in the United States is quite high com-pared to other countries, and that persistence has not changed much across the years. While economic and sociological theories suggest several reasons why we might expect intergenerational income differences to be quite persistent, cross-national research has yet to suggest which policy responses are likely to be effec-tive in reducing income persistence. However, reduced inequalities in schooling, especially for very young children, and more meritocratic selection into higher education would quite likely increase equality of opportunity and reduce inter-generational persistence.

This chapter was written while the author was a visiting scholar at the Russell Sage Foundation. The author would like to thank Steven Haider, Deborah Reed, and the editors of this volume for helpful comments and suggestions. The usual disclaimers apply.

NOTES

1. John Iceland (2003) calculates poverty rates and poverty dynamics from the Survey of Income and Program Participation (SIPP) for the years 1996 to 1999.
2. The requirement that a person be poor in every month across the years 1996 to 1999 is more stringent than the requirement that a person be poor in every year during that time, since many who are poor in terms of annual income will have some months with above-poverty-level income. Thus, chronic poverty defined in terms of monthly poverty is bound to be lower, or at least not higher, than chronic poverty defined in terms of annual incomes across the same number of years.
3. Richard Burkhauser and Kenneth Couch (2009) survey international evidence on income mobility and discuss many measurement issues. Peter Gottschalk and Sheldon Danziger (1998) examine evidence on levels and changes in income mobility in the United States.
4. Cross-national evidence on poverty dynamics for earlier years is provided in Duncan et al. (1993) and Nolan and Marx (2009).

5. Gary Solon (1999, 2002) also provides an overview of the evidence on intergenerational income persistence.

6. Much of the variation in estimates appears to be related to the age at which fathers' incomes are measured (see Jenkins 1987; Grawe 2006). Recent work on intragenerational income mobility in the United States by Steven Haider and Gary Solon (2006) suggests that measuring incomes around the age at which fathers are typically observed—the early forties—does not yield unbiased estimates of their permanent income. The large differences across different U.S. studies suggest that estimates obtained from different countries should be treated with considerable caution.

REFERENCES

Aydemir, Abdurrahman, Wen-Hao Chen, and Miles Corak. 2006. "Intergenerational Earnings Mobility Among the Children of Canadian Immigrants." Discussion paper 2085. Bonn: Institute for the Study of Labor (IZA).

Becker, Gary S., and Nigel Tomes. 1986. "Human Capital and the Rise and Fall of Families." *Journal of Labor Economics* 4(3): S1–39.

Björklund, Anders, and Markus Jäntti. 2009. "Intergenerational Income Mobility and the Role of Family Background." In *Oxford Handbook of Economic Inequality*, edited by Wiemer Salverda, Brian Nolan, and Timothy M. Smeeding. Oxford: Oxford University Press.

Blanden, Jo, Alissa Goodman, Paul Gregg, and Stephen Machin. 2004. "Changes in Intergenerational Mobility in Britain." In *Generational Income Mobility in North America and Europe*, edited by Miles Corak. Cambridge: Cambridge University Press.

Bradbury, Bruce, and Markus Jäntti. 2001. "Child Poverty Across Twenty-five Countries." In *The Dynamics of Child Poverty in Industrialized Countries*, edited by Bruce Bradbury, Stephen P. Jenkins, and John Micklewright. Cambridge: Cambridge University Press.

Bradbury, Bruce, Stephen P. Jenkins, and John Micklewright, eds. 2001. *The Dynamics of Child Poverty in Industrialized Countries*. Cambridge: Cambridge University Press.

Bratberg, Espen, Øivind Anti Nielsen, and Kjell Vaage. 2007. "Trends in Intergenerational Mobility Across Offspring's Earnings Distribution in Norway." *Industrial Relations* 46(1): 112–28.

Burkhauser, Richard, and Kenneth Couch. 2009. "Intragenerational Inequality and Intertemporal Mobility." In *Oxford Handbook of Economic Inequality*, edited by Wiemer Salverda, Brian Nolan, and Timothy M. Smeeding. Oxford: Oxford University Press.

Chadwick, Laura N., and Gary Solon. 2002. "Intergenerational Income Mobility Among Daughters." *American Economic Review* 92(1): 335–44.

Corak, Miles. 2006. "Do Poor Children Become Poor Adults? Lessons for Public Policy from a Cross-Country Comparison of Generational Earnings Mobility." *Research on Economic Inequality* 13(1): 143–88.

Corcoran, Mary. 2001. "Mobility, Persistence, and the Consequences of Poverty for Children: Child and Adult Outcomes." In *Understanding Poverty*, edited by Sheldon. H. Danziger and Robert H. Haveman. New York and Cambridge, Mass.: Russell Sage Foundation and Harvard University Press.

Duncan, Greg, Björn Gustafsson, Richard Hauser, Günther Shmauss, Hans Messinger, Ruud Muffels, Brian Nolan, and Jean-Claude Ray. 1993. "Poverty Dynamics in Eight Countries." *Journal of Population Economics* 6(3): 215–34.

Erikson, Robert, and John H. Goldthorpe. 1992. *The Constant Flux: A Study of Class Mobility in Industrial Societies.* Oxford: Clarendon Press.

Gottschalk, Peter, and Sheldon Danziger. 1998. "Family Income Mobility: How Much Is There and Has It Changed?" In *The Inequality Paradox: Growth of Income Disparity*, edited by James A. Auerbach and Richard S. Belous. Washington, D.C.: National Policy Association.

Grawe, Nathan D. 2004. "Intergenerational Mobility for Whom? The Experience of High- and Low-Earnings Sons in International Perspective." In *Generational Income Mobility in North America and Europe*, edited by Miles Corak. Cambridge: Cambridge University Press.

———. 2006. "Life Cycle Bias in Estimates of Intergenerational Earnings Persistence." *Labor Economics* 13(5): 519–664.

Grieger, Lloyd D., and Jessica J. Wyse. 2008. "Long-Term Poverty Among Black and White Children and Its Demographic Correlates: 1973–1999." Unpublished paper. Ann Arbor: University of Michigan, Gerald R. Ford School of Public Policy.

Haider, Steven J., and Gary Solon. 2006. "Life-Cycle Variation in the Association Between Current and Lifetime Earnings." *American Economic Review* 96(4): 1308–20.

Hertz, Thomas. 2005. "Rags, Riches, and Race: The Intergenerational Economic Mobility of Black and White Families in the United States." In *Unequal Chances: Family Background and Economic Success*, edited by Samuel Bowles, Herbert Gintis, and Melissa Osborne Groves. New York: Russell Sage Foundation.

———. 2007. "Trends in the Intergenerational Elasticity of Family Income in the United States." *Industrial Relations* 46(1): 22–50.

Iceland, John. 2003. "Dynamics of Economic Well-Being: Poverty 1996–1999." Current Population Reports P70-91. Washington: U.S. Government Printing Office, U.S. Census Bureau.

Jäntti, Markus, Bernt Bratsberg, Knut Røed, Oddbjorn Raaum, Robin Naylor, Eva Österbacka, Anders Björklund, and Tor Eriksson. 2006. "American Exceptionalism in a New Light: A Comparison of Intergenerational Earnings Mobility in the Nordic Countries, the United Kingdom, and the United States." Discussion paper 1938. Bonn: Institute for the Study of Labor (IZA).

Jencks, Christopher, and Laura Tach. 2006. "Would Equal Opportunity Mean More Mobility?" In *Mobility and Inequality: Frontiers of Research in Sociology and Economics*, edited by Stephen L. Morgan, David B. Grusky, and Gary S. Fields. Palo Alto, Calif.: Stanford University Press.

Jenkins, Stephen P. 1987. "Snapshots Versus Movies: 'Life Cycle Biases' and the Estimation of Intergenerational Earnings Inheritance." *European Economic Review* 31(5): 1149–58.

Lee, Chui-In, and Gary M. Solon. Forthcoming. "Trends in Intergenerational Income Mobility." *Review of Economics and Statistics.*

Levine, David, and Bhashkar Mazumder. 2007. "The Growing Importance of Family: Evidence from Brothers' Earnings." *Industrial Relations* 46(1): 7–21.

Mayer, Susan E., and L. M. Lopoo. 2005. "Has the Intergenerational Transmission of Economic Status Changed?" *Journal of Human Resources* 40(1): 170–85.

Nolan, Brian, and Ive Marx. 2009. "Economic Inequality, Poverty, and Social Exclusion." In *Oxford Handbook of Economic Inequality*, edited by Wiemer Salverda, Brian Nolan, and Timothy M. Smeeding. Oxford: Oxford University Press.

Osberg, Lars, and Timothy Smeeding. 2006. "'Fair' Inequality? Attitudes Toward Pay Differentials: The United States in Comparative Perspective." *American Sociological Review* 71(3): 450–73.

Pekkala, Sari, and Robert E. B. Lucas. 2007. "Differences Across Cohorts in Finnish Intergenerational Income Mobility." *Industrial Relations* 46(1): 81–111.

Raaum, Oddbjörn, Bernt Bratsberg, Knut Røed, Eva Österbacka, Tor Eriksson, Markus Jäntti, and Robin N. Naylor. 2007. "Marital Sorting, Household Labor Supply, and Intergenerational Earnings Mobility Across Countries." *BE Journal of Economic Analysis and Policy* 7(2 [advances]), article 7.

Smeeding, Timothy M., Lee Rainwater, and Gary Burtless. 2001. "United States Poverty in a Cross-National Context." In *Understanding Poverty,* edited by Sheldon Danziger and Robert Haveman. New York and Cambridge, Mass.: Russell Sage Foundation and Harvard University Press.

Solon, Gary. 1999. "Intergenerational Mobility in the Labor Market." In *Handbook of Labor Economics,* vol. 3, edited by Orley Ashenfelter and David Card. New York: Elsevier Science B.V.

———. 2002. "Cross-Country Differences in Intergenerational Earnings Mobility." *Journal of Economic Perspectives* 16(3): 59–66.

———. 2004. "A Model of Intergenerational Mobility Variation over Time and Place." In *Generational Income Mobility in North America and Europe,* edited by Miles Corak. Cambridge: Cambridge University Press.

Turner, Ralph H. 1960. "Sponsored and Contest Mobility and the School System." *American Sociological Review* 25(6): 855–67.

Valletta, Robert G. 2006. "The Ins and Outs of Poverty in Advanced Economies: Government Policy and Poverty Dynamics in Canada, Germany, Great Britain, and the United States." *Review of Income and Wealth* 52(2): 261–84.

Part 3

The Evolution and Scope
of Antipoverty Policies

Chapter 8

Trends in Income Support

John Karl Scholz, Robert Moffitt, and Benjamin Cowan

A ntipoverty programs are designed to mitigate the most pernicious aspects of market-based economic outcomes—unemployment, disability, low earnings, and other material hardship. These programs compose society's "safety net," and each has different eligibility standards and benefit formulas. While the programs can be aggregated and categorized to summarize trends in coverage and generosity, a consequence of their patchwork nature is that the safety net may appear different to a family in one set of circumstances than it does to a family in another.

Social insurance programs—Social Security, Medicare, unemployment insurance, and workers' compensation—are costly programs with much larger numbers of recipients. Despite the fact that they are not antipoverty programs per se, they have had a significant effect on poverty, particularly among the elderly. The antipoverty programs that constitute the safety net are collectively much smaller and have had varied support over time.

As noted in previous work (Burtless 1986, 1994; Scholz and Levine 2002), there has been a sharp reduction in cash entitlements for poor families and a very large increase in social insurance payments, particularly for the elderly, in past decades. The nature of programs has changed as well. Cash welfare benefits, for example, have been linked with work requirements, partly in response to evolving views about the nature of the poverty problem. Responsibility for antipoverty policy has broadened from the antipoverty agencies of the federal government (the Department of Health and Human Services and the Department of Labor) to the states (through their administration of Temporary Assistance for Needy Families [TANF] and Medicaid) and the tax code, as evidenced by the Earned Income Tax Credit (EITC) and the refundable child credit.

We have three primary goals in this chapter. First, we provide updated information on expenditures and recipients for a range of antipoverty programs, describing the evolution of the safety net over the past thirty-five years. Second, we use data from the Survey of Income and Program Participation (SIPP) to calculate the antipoverty effectiveness of federal programs for families and individuals in different circumstances. Third, we explore changes in the characteristics of recipients of means-tested transfers, tax credits, and social insurance. Robert Moffitt (2003a,

2007) documents a large increase in total per capita means-tested transfers, even in the decade following the 1996 welfare reform. He notes, based on aggregate data, that the shift in expenditures for different programs suggests that more transfers now go to workers and fewer to nonworkers, more to married couples and fewer to single mothers. Because aggregate transfers have increased, one can argue that society has become more generous over time. But as the safety net has evolved, some families have lost benefits while others have gained benefits.

SOCIAL INSURANCE

Social insurance programs provide near-universal coverage since any individual (or his or her employer) who makes the required contributions to finance the programs can receive benefits when specific eligibility requirements are met. These programs have dedicated funding mechanisms through which, at least in an accounting sense, social insurance taxes are remitted to trust funds from which benefits are paid.

It is often inefficient for individuals to self-insure for contingencies like an unexpectedly long life, end-of-life health shocks, or extended unemployment spells. Because of adverse selection problems—the tendency for the riskiest individuals and families to seek insurance, which makes the pricing of products unattractive to less risky families and individuals—private insurance markets are unlikely to work well. Social insurance programs, which are government-run, near-universal, and uniform in their rules and benefits, provide the welfare-enhancing benefits of insurance while overcoming the problems (through mandatory pooling) that arise in private insurance markets.

Social Security and Medicare

The largest social insurance program is Social Security, formally known as the Old-Age, Survivors, and Disability Insurance (OASDI) program. Founded in 1935 as one of President Franklin Roosevelt's New Deal programs, Social Security was designed to meet the unmet social needs of older workers leaving the workforce without sufficient postretirement income to be self-supporting.[1] Figure 8.1 plots the time series of real (inflation-adjusted) Social Security (OASI) payments from 1970 to 2006. (Disability insurance benefits are not included in this series but are discussed later.) Real Social Security payments tripled between 1970 and 2006, to $474 billion, because of three factors. First, the number of retired workers covered by Social Security has steadily increased as the aged population has grown over the years and state and local government workers, clergy, and other groups have been brought into the system. Second, the Social Security taxable wage base has grown steadily, as have real earnings. Third, legislated benefit increases frequently exceeded the cost of living into the early 1970s; benefits were indexed to inflation beginning in 1974. Aggregate real Social Security benefits increased 5.6 percent annually in the 1970s and 3.0 percent in the 1980s. Aggregate annual real benefits increased 1.8 percent in the 1990s and by the same amount between 2000 and 2006.

FIGURE 8.1 / Total Benefit Payments on Social Security (OASI), Unemployment Insurance (UI), Disability Insurance (DI), and Workers' Compensation and Outlays for Medicare, 1970 to 2007 (in Constant 2007 Dollars)

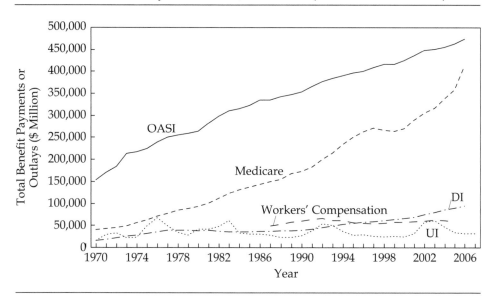

Sources:
OASI (total benefits): Social Security Online, "Old-Age and Survivors Insurance Benefit Payments: Annual Benefits Paid from OASI Trust Fund, by Type of Benefit, 1937–2006," at: http://www.ssa.gov/OACT/STATS/table4a5.html.
Medicare: U.S. Department of Health and Human Services, Centers for Medicare and Medicaid Services, "NHE Historical and Projections, 1965 to 2017: National Health Expenditure (NHE) Amounts by Type of Expenditure and Source of Funds: Calendar Years 1965–2017 in PROJECTIONS Format," at: http://www.cms.hhs.gov/NationalHealthExpendData/03_NationalHealth AccountsProjected.asp.
UI: Office of Management and Budget, "Historical Tables, Budget of the United States Government, Fiscal Year 2009: Table 8.5—Outlays for Mandatory and Related Programs, 1962–2013," at: http://www.whitehouse.gov/omb/budget/fy2009.
Workers' compensation (total benefits): National Academy of Social Insurance, "Full Report: Workers' Compensation: Benefits, Coverage, and Costs, 2005: Table 4—Workers' Compensation Benefits, by Type of Insurer, 1987–2005 (in million)," at: http://www.nasi.org/publications2763/publications_show.htm?doc_id=516615.
DI (total benefits): Social Security Online, "Disability Insurance Benefit Payments: Annual Benefits Paid from DI Trust Fund, by Type of Benefit, 1957–2006," at: http://www.ssa.gov/OACT/STATS/table4a6.html.
Medicaid (federal plus state and local Medicaid, including SCHIP): U.S. Department of Health and Human Services, Centers for Medicare and Medicaid Services, "NHE Historical and Projections, 1965 to 2017: National Health Expenditure (NHE) Amounts by Type of Expenditure and Source of Funds: Calendar Years 1965–2017 in PROJECTIONS Format," at: http://www.cms.hhs.gov/NationalHealthExpendData/03_NationalHealthAccountsProjected.asp.
SSI (total): House Ways and Means Committee, "Prints: 105-7, 1998 Green Books: Section 3, Supplemental Security Income: Table 3.24—Federal and State Benefit Payments Under SSI and Prior Adult Assistance Programs, Calendar Years 1970–1987 and Fiscal Years 1988–2002," at: http://www.gpoaccess.gov/wmprints/green/1998.html; "Table 3.23—Federal and State Benefit Payments Under SSI and Prior Adult Assistance Programs, Selected Years 1970–2005,"

at: http://www.gpoaccess.gov/wmprints/green/2004.html; and "Table 7.A4—Total Federally Administered Payments, by Eligibility Category, Selected Years 1974–2006," at: http://www.ssa.gov/policy/docs/statcomps/supplement/2007/7a.html#table7.a4.

AFDC/TANF (total benefits plus administrative): House Ways and Means Committee, "Prints: 105-7, 1998 Green Books: Section 7, Aid to Families with Dependent Children and Temporary Assistance for Needy Families (Title IV-A): Table 7.4—Total, Federal, and State AFDC Expenditures, Fiscal Years 1970–1996," at: http://www.gpoaccess.gov/wmprints/green/1998.html.

AFDC/TANF (total): House Ways and Means Committee, "Prints: 105-7, 1998 Green Books: Section 7, Temporary Assistance for Needy Families (TANF): Table 7.18—Total, Federal, and State Expenditures for TANF and Predecessor Programs (AFDC, EA, and Jobs), Fiscal Years 1990–2001," at: http://www.gpoaccess.gov/wmprints/green/2004.html.

AFDC/TANF (total federal funds): U.S. Department of Health and Human Services, Administration for Children and Families, "TANF Financial Data: Table A—Spending from Federal TANF Grant, FY 2001–2006," at: http://www.acf.hhs.gov/programs/ofs/data/index.html.

EITC (total amount of credit): Tax Policy Center (Urban Institute and Brookings Institution), "Tax Facts: Historical EITC Recipients: Earned Income Tax Credit: Number of Recipients and Amount of Credit, 1975–2005," at: http://www.taxpolicycenter.org/taxfacts/displayafact.cfm?Docid=37.

Food Stamps (total benefits): U.S. Department of Agriculture, Food and Nutrition Service, "Supplemental Nutrition Assistance Program Participation and Costs, 1969–2007," at http://www.fns.usda.gov/pd/SNAPsummary.htm.

Housing Aid (housing assistance): "Historical Tables: Budget of the United States Government, Fiscal Year 2009: Table 8.7—Outlays for Discretionary Programs, 1962–2009," at: http://www.whitehouse.gov/omb/budget/fy2009.

School Food Programs (total federal costs—cash payments plus commodity costs): U.S. Department of Agriculture, Food and Nutrition Service, "Federal Cost of School Food Programs, 1969–2007," at: http://www.fns.usda.gov/pd/cncosts.htm.

WIC (total program costs): U.S. Department of Agriculture, Food and Nutrition Service, WIC Program Participation and Costs, 1974–2007," at http://www.fns.usda.gov/pd/SNAPsummary.htm.

Head Start (appropriations): U.S. Department of Health and Human Services, Administration for Children and Families, Head Start Program Fact Sheet Fiscal Year 2008, "Head Start Enrollment History, 1965–2006," at: http://www.acf.hhs.gov/programs/ohs/about/fy2008.html.

Because many retired elderly workers have little labor market and capital income, pre–tax and transfer poor families receive a substantial share of Social Security benefits. The official poverty rate for people age sixty-five and older was 9.4 percent in 2006.[2] It was 17.4 percent for children under age eighteen, and 12.3 percent for all persons. The elderly poverty rate is the lowest largely because of Social Security benefits, which averaged $11,566.[3]

The elderly also receive substantial benefits from Medicare, which provides hospital insurance and supplementary medical and prescription drug coverage for most people over age sixty-five and for most Social Security disability recipients under age sixty-five.[4] Real Medicare outlays increased more than tenfold from $41 billion in 1970 (the program started in 1967) to $413 billion in 2006. Real expenditures per Medicare enrollee increased almost five times over the same time period, to $9,378 in 2006. In the late 1990s and early 2000s, Medicare growth slowed as efforts were made to reduce Medicare hospital spending and control fraud and abuse. Spending increased sharply in 2006 with the implementation of Medicare Part D, a prescription drug benefit that is projected to cost more than $40 billion annually.

A substantial portion of Medicare benefits go to elderly families whose pre-transfer incomes are below the poverty line. The official poverty measure does not account for Medicare benefits because they are in-kind (via the provision of health care and insurance) rather than in the form of cash. Hence, Medicare benefits are difficult to value. They could be valued at their cost to the government, at the cost a recipient would have to pay in the private market to acquire comparable benefits, or at the amount a person would be willing to pay for such benefits (which would be less than the cost to the government for many low-income recipients).[5] It is also difficult to determine which individuals in a given family receive benefits. In this chapter, when we assess the antipoverty effectiveness of spending, we make illustrative calculations of the degree to which Medicare reduces poverty.

The effect of Social Security on poverty is clear: as the Social Security system has grown, elderly poverty has fallen precipitously. The sharpest decline in the elderly poverty rate occurred between 1959 and 1974, a period that coincides with rapid growth in Social Security spending.[6]

Social Insurance for Prime-Age Workers

Although Social Security and Medicare also provide benefits for non-elderly people through disability insurance (DI) and survivor benefits, 84.7 percent of Medicare recipients were elderly in 2004 and 71.9 percent of Social Security recipients were elderly in March 2008.[7] Three smaller social insurance programs—unemployment insurance (UI), workers' compensation, and disability insurance—target prime-age workers; real expenditures on these programs are also shown in figure 8.1.

Unemployment insurance is a state-level program that provides temporary and partial wage replacement to workers who become involuntarily unemployed and who have a recent history of continuous employment at moderately high wages.[8] Although UI allows families to maintain their consumption during periods of involuntary layoffs (Gruber 1997), it has relatively small antipoverty effects because so many unskilled individuals do not have the necessary employment history at high enough wages to collect UI benefits. The Government Accountability Office (GAO 2000) reports that in the 1990s low-wage workers were twice as likely to be unemployed but less than half as likely to receive UI benefits as other unemployed workers.[9] Unemployment insurance is highly cyclical. Real UI benefits paid out in 2003, a year of slow economic growth, came to $61 billion, while real payments were $25 billion in 2000, a year with low unemployment.

Workers' compensation is a state-level program that provides cash and medical benefits to some persons with job-related disabilities or injuries and provides survivor benefits to dependents of workers whose death resulted from a work-related accident or illness. Benefit levels vary widely across states. Workers' compensation payments were $59 billion in real terms in 2005; Bruce Meyer, Wallace Mok, and James Sullivan (2007) note that roughly half of total program costs are for medical care. Because there is little federal involvement in this system, there is little information on its antipoverty effects. We speculate that any such effects are likely to be small, however, for the same reasons that UI has limited antipoverty effectiveness.

Disability insurance, a federal program that is part of the Social Security program, provides benefits when a covered worker is unable to engage in "substantial gainful activity" by reason of a physical or mental impairment that is expected to last for more than twelve months or that results in death.[10] Workers must have a minimum period of covered employment before being eligible; depending on the age at which a disability occurs, this ranges from six to forty covered quarters. The average annual growth rate in real DI expenditures was 9.0 percent in the 1970s, 0.1 percent in the 1980s, 5.3 percent in the 1990s, and 6.2 percent between 2000 and 2006. Despite program growth, the DI rules are stringent, with fewer than 40 percent of all applications being granted benefits; roughly 5.4 awards are made per 1,000 covered workers. Around 8.6 million people (including children) receive disability benefits, which cost $95 billion in 2006. Most DI recipients are pre–tax and transfer poor.[11]

Summary of Social Insurance

Social Security, Medicare, unemployment insurance, workers' compensation, and disability insurance are the major social insurance programs. Over time, the enormous increase in their benefits has been driven largely by increases in Social Security and Medicare. Social insurance benefits are predicated on events that are salient for most Americans—retirement, unemployment, a disability or work-related injury—and receipt of benefits does not depend on an individual's current total income but rather on past employment and earnings experience. All have dedicated financing mechanisms. And while Social Security may reduce national saving and hasten retirement, and while unemployment insurance may alter the intensity with which the unemployed search for jobs, there is no evidence that these programs encourage individuals not to marry or to have children out of wedlock, and with the possible exception of DI, they do not encourage individuals to spend extended periods out of the paid labor market (UI benefits are time-limited). Thus, the rationale and incentives of the programs do not appear at odds with societal norms of personal responsibility. In addition, Social Security and Medicare lessen adult children's caregiving responsibilities for their parents, a feature that is popular with both generations.

MEANS-TESTED TRANSFERS

Means-tested programs are financed by general tax revenues rather than through dedicated financing mechanisms; all limit benefits to those whose incomes and/or assets fall below some threshold. Some are entitlements—all who satisfy the stipulated eligibility requirements receive benefits, regardless of the total budgetary cost (for example, Medicaid, food stamps). Other means-tested programs provide benefits only until the funds that Congress or a state has allocated are spent, even if some eligible participants are not served (for example, the State Children's Health Insurance Program [SCHIP], Section 8 housing vouchers, and TANF). Means-tested programs have explicit antipoverty goals. Together, they account for a smaller share of government budgets than the social insurance programs.

FIGURE 8.2 / Total Supplemental Security Income (SSI) Benefits and Medicaid Program Costs, 1970 to 2007 (in Constant 2007 Dollars)

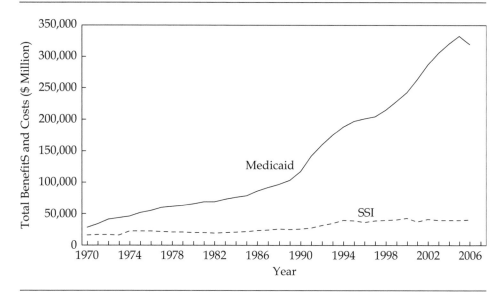

Source: Refer to source notes for figure 8.1.

Health Care and the Disabled

Medicaid, the largest means-tested transfer program (Swartz, this volume), funds medical assistance to persons who are aged, blind, or disabled and to certain pregnant women and dependent children. Recipients must meet asset and income tests that are set by states. Medicaid was expanded between 1986 and 1991 as Congress required states to cover pregnant women and children living in families with incomes up to 133 percent of the poverty level and allowed the expansion of coverage to families with incomes of up to 185 percent of the poverty level.[12] These expansions led to a large increase in the number of Medicaid recipients. About 23 million people received Medicaid in 1977 and 1988, but this number climbed steadily to 55 million in 2004. About 10 percent of Medicaid beneficiaries were sixty-five or older in 2005; they received about 26 percent of Medicaid expenditures.

The trend in Medicaid spending is shown in figure 8.2. Total real Medicaid spending increased from $28 billion to $320 billion between 1970 and 2006. After growing rapidly through the mid-1970s, Medicaid grew at annual rates between −0.5 percent and 8.8 percent between 1976 and 1989. The expansions of the late 1980s increased growth rates to 12.8, 21.4, and 12.1 percent in 1990, 1991, and 1992. Spending fell in 2006, owing largely to shifts in prescription drug costs to Medicare

Part D and to a reduction in the growth of enrollments (Holahan, Cohen, and Rousseau 2007; Swartz, this volume). Attempts to assess the antipoverty effectiveness of Medicaid face the same difficulties that arise with valuing Medicare benefits: it is not clear whether Medicaid benefits should be valued at the cost to the recipient, at the cost a recipient would have to pay in the private market to obtain similar benefits, or at the amount a person would be "willing to pay," which itself is difficult to know.

Supplemental Security Income (SSI) is a means-tested, federally administered, cash assistance program for the aged, blind, and disabled. The disabled make up nearly 80 percent of recipients. The program began in 1974 with the consolidation of several smaller programs.[13] An individual who meets the income, asset, and categorical eligibility standards receives a cash transfer of up to $637 per month; couples can receive up to one and a half times that amount, and children can receive half that amount, although states are allowed to supplement these amounts. SSI (figure 8.2) grew very slowly, from $22 billion to $26 billion, between 1974 and 1990 (in 2007 dollars).

Between 1990 and 1994, SSI costs grew by 55 percent, making it one of the fastest-growing entitlement programs. A factor driving this growth was the Zebley decision, a Supreme Court case that revised the childhood mental health impairment eligibility criterion to be consistent with the criterion that applies to adults. The Green Book (1998) reports that three groups accounted for nearly 90 percent of SSI's growth during this time: adults with mental impairments, children, and noncitizens. Since the mid-1990s, efforts have been made to reduce the growth in the number of children and immigrants covered by SSI, so real spending in 2006 was roughly equal to spending in 1994. In 2006, 7.2 million people received $40 billion in benefits.

Cash Means-Tested Transfers for Able-Bodied Families

Aid to Families with Dependent Children (AFDC) was the central safety net program for poor families with children from 1936 to 1996 (Moffitt 2003b). This program was directed primarily at single-parent families, though some two-parent families with an unemployed parent received benefits. AFDC was a means-tested entitlement, meaning that all applicants whose income and assets were below the stipulated levels could receive benefits. State-determined benefit generosity varied widely; funds were provided according to an uncapped federal matching formula.

The Personal Responsibility and Work Opportunity Reconciliation Act (PRWORA) of 1996 abolished AFDC and created Temporary Assistance for Needy Families (TANF), which provides block grants to states with few restrictions. States are required to spend at least 75 percent of their "historic" level of AFDC spending; a five-year lifetime limit has been imposed on receipt of federally supported cash assistance, though some hardship exemptions are allowed; and states have to meet targets for moving recipients into work activities. A combination of these AFDC-TANF changes, the longest economic expansion in history, sharp

FIGURE 8.3 / Total AFDC-TANF and EITC Benefits, 1970 to 2007
(in Constant 2007 Dollars)

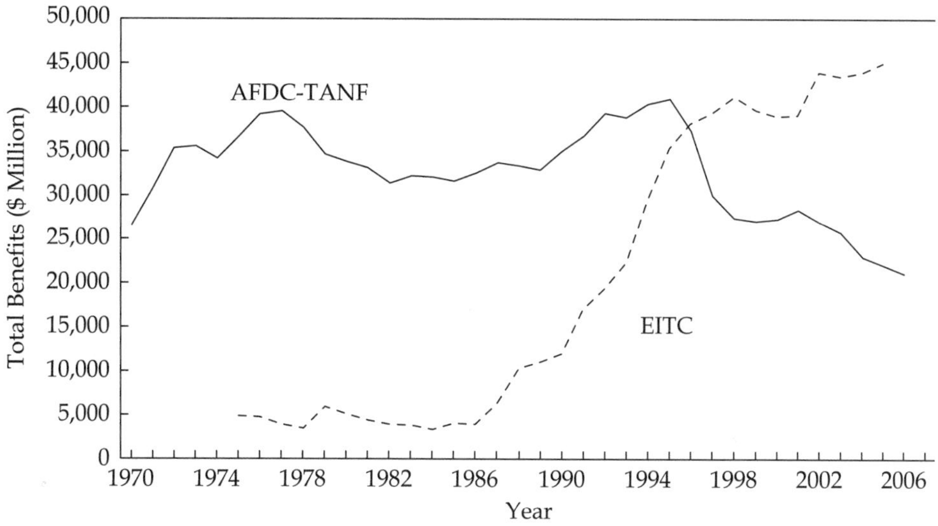

Source: Refer to source notes for figure 8.1.

increases in the Earned Income Tax Credit, and other factors contributed to a 52 percent decline in welfare caseloads between January 1993 and December 1999. Despite the weak economy in the years after the recession in 2001, TANF caseloads did not increase substantially from their historic lows.

Several commentators feared that TANF might set off a "race to the bottom"— that is, that the states, fearful of attracting low-income families from other states, might lower benefits, causing other states, in turn, to lower theirs. In fact, total AFDC-TANF spending on cash benefits declined from a peak of about $40 billion in 1995 to about $20 billion in 2006 (figure 8.3), but this reduction is roughly proportional to the welfare caseload reduction. In some jurisdictions, spending on other ancillary services for welfare recipients and other low-income families (for example, child care and transportation) has also increased since the mid-1990s.

The Deficit Reduction Act (DRA) of 2005 reauthorized the TANF program and increased work requirements—50 percent of all adults in single-parent families receiving TANF benefits in a state and 90 percent of the two-parent households receiving such benefits must now work. These percentages are lower for states if their welfare caseloads fall below 2005 levels, but caseloads in that year were at historically low levels, so this provision is unlikely to relax substantially the work requirement constraint. It is likely that states will place even greater emphasis on increasing employment among TANF recipients, divert potential TANF applicants from the program, or both.

Real spending on AFDC-TANF grew by an annual rate of 0.3 percent in the 1980s and fell by 2.5 percent in the 1990s. It fell by 4.2 percent a year from 2000 to 2005, despite a weak economy. In contrast, expenditures on the EITC grew sharply, from $5 billion in 1975 to $45 billion in 2006 (figure 8.3).[14] Most of this growth occurred after 1987; real EITC expenditures grew at an annual rate of 9.1 percent in the 1980s (owing to legislated increases in 1986), 12.5 percent in the 1990s (owing to legislated increases in 1990 and again in 1993), and 3.0 percent from 2000 to 2005. No other federal antipoverty program has grown so rapidly since the mid-1980s. The EITC is now the nation's largest cash or near-cash antipoverty program.

The incentives embedded in the EITC differ from those in AFDC-TANF. AFDC recipients with no earnings received the largest welfare payments. In contrast, the EITC encourages low-skilled workers to enter the labor market, since non-earners do not receive the credit, and the EITC amount rises with earnings up to about the poverty line.

A child tax credit was created in the 1997 Taxpayer Relief Act. Until 2001, the credit provided little financial benefit for poor and near-poor families because of limits on its refundability. Beginning in 2002, the child credit was made at least partially refundable for taxpayers with children and with earned income exceeding $10,750 (indexed for inflation). In 2004, a year we focus on later, the credit was a maximum of $1,000 per child. For taxpayers with no other federal income tax liability, 10¢ of child credit is paid (as a refundable credit) for every dollar earned in excess of $10,750, up to the total available child credit.

In-Kind Means-Tested Transfers for Able-Bodied Individuals

The safety net for low-income families includes in-kind benefit programs, the largest of which are food stamps, housing assistance, Head Start, school nutrition programs, and the special supplemental nutrition program for women, infants, and children (WIC).[15] The evolution of expenditures for these programs is shown in figure 8.4.

Food stamps are designed to enable low-income households to purchase a nutritionally adequate low-cost diet. It is the single, almost-universal entitlement for those with low income and assets. The maximum monthly food stamp benefit for a family of four was $542 in 2008.[16]

After food stamp benefits were made uniform across the country and indexed for inflation in 1972, real spending grew sharply. Legislative changes in 1981 and 1982 cut spending between 1982 and 1985 by nearly 13 percent ($7 billion) below what would have been spent under prior law. The liberalization of the program in 1985, 1986, and 1987, together with the early 1990s recession, led to a sharp increase in total food stamp spending between 1988 and 1992. Between 1994 and 2000, real food stamp expenditures fell to $18 billion from $32 billion, even though only modest changes to food stamp program rules were made by the 1996 welfare reform (primarily affecting immigrant households). The General Accounting Office (1999) concluded that participation fell "faster than related economic indicators

FIGURE 8.4 / Total Benefits or Program Costs for Various In-Kind Programs, 1970 to 2007 (in Constant 2007 Dollars)

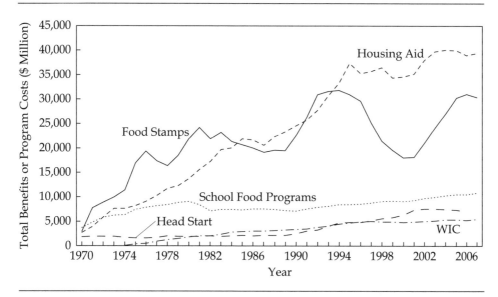

would predict" and speculated that some former cash welfare recipients thought they were also no longer eligible for food stamps.

Food stamp participation and spending increased sharply between 2000 and 2005: the caseload increased from around 18 million to 30 million, and spending increased from $18 billion to $31 billion (Rosenbaum 2006). Factors affecting these developments include increases in the number of poor people over this period, the use of food stamps as federal disaster aid for Hurricanes Katrina, Rita, and Wilma and other natural disasters, and changes in the 2002 farm bill that restored food stamp benefits to some legal immigrants, allowed states to provide benefits to households that own a reliable car, and simplified application procedures.

The Department of Housing and Urban Development (HUD) is primarily responsible for safety net housing assistance programs. Because these programs have never been entitlements, waiting lists are common. Aid comes in two principal forms: project-based aid (subsidies are tied to units constructed for low-income households) and household-based subsidies (renters choose housing units in the existing private housing stock). Since 1982, project-based aid has been curtailed in favor of rental subsidies. Housing assistance grew from $3 billion in 1970 (in 2007 dollars) to $37 billion in 1995, and then fluctuated, reaching $39 billion in 2007 (figure 8.4). The number of housing assistance recipients rose from 3.2 million in 1997 to a peak of 5.8 million in 1995, before declining to 5.1 million in 2007. Federal housing subsidies provide roughly $7,720 in annual benefits per recipient.

The school lunch and breakfast programs—entitlements funded by the Department of Agriculture—provide federal support for meals served by public and private nonprofit elementary and secondary schools and residential child care institutions that enroll and offer free or reduced-price meals to low-income children. Participation in the school breakfast program grew from about 800,000 in 1971 to 10 million in 2007. The school lunch program is larger but has grown more gradually, from 24 million children in 1971 to 31 million in 2007. Combined expenditures in 2007 were around $11 billion.

The special supplemental nutrition program for women, infants and children (WIC) provides vouchers for food purchase, supplemental food, and nutrition-risk screening and related nutrition-oriented services to low-income pregnant women and low-income women and their children (up to age five). WIC is not an entitlement. In 2007 roughly 8 million women, infants, and children received benefits from WIC, at a cost of almost $6 billion.

Head Start, an early childhood education program launched as part of the War on Poverty, seeks to improve social competence, learning skills, and the health and nutrition status of low-income children so that they can begin school on an equal basis with their more advantaged peers (Jacob and Ludwig, this volume). In real dollars, Head Start grew at an annual 9.9 percent rate in the 1990s. Program growth slowed considerably between 2000 and 2006, averaging 1.6 percent. Spending in 2006 was $7 billion for around 900,000 children.

Child Care

Several federal child care subsidy programs target low-income families. Because child care expenses are often seen as a deterrent to mothers entering the workforce (Waldfogel, this volume), the emergence of child care subsidy programs reflects the trend toward work-based assistance rather than cash welfare (Blau 2003). In 1988 the Family Support Act created the Aid to Families with Dependent Children Child Care, which served AFDC parents who participated in job training, and Transitional Child Care, which served former welfare recipients.[17] Two more programs were implemented in 1990: At-Risk Child Care, which served families at risk of going on welfare, and the Child Care Development Block Grant, which funds working, low-income families and provides funding to improve the quality of child care. In 1996 PRWORA consolidated all of these programs into the Child Care and Development Fund (CCDF).

According to Douglas Besharov, Caeli Higney, and Justus Myers (2007), the Child Care Development Block Grant more than doubled, from $4 billion to about $9 billion (in 2007 dollars), between 1996 and 2000, then rose to $10 billion in 2005. After the 1996 welfare reform, states could spend TANF block grant money on child care; by 2000 they had spent $3 billion. In 2005, 1.75 million children were served by the Child Care and Development Fund. The antipoverty effects of subsidized child care are not well known.

FIGURE 8.5 / Total Social Insurance, Cash, and In-Kind Means-Tested Transfers, 1970 to 2007 (in 2007 Dollars)

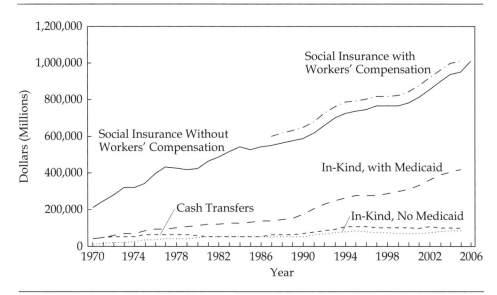

Source: Refer to source notes for figure 8.1.

Summary

Figure 8.5 summarizes the evolution of social insurance and means-tested (antipoverty) spending. Table 8A.1 presents spending by program, and table 8A.2 the numbers of recipients by program. Spending on all social insurance programs now exceeds $1 trillion annually. These expenditures (in real dollars, excluding workers' compensation owing to data limitations) rose at an annual rate of 7.2 percent in the 1970s, 3.3 percent in the 1980s, 2.9 percent in the 1990s, and 4.3 percent (in part because of Medicare Part D) between 2000 and 2006.

The bottom two lines of figure 8.5 show total spending on in-kind transfers (without Medicaid) and cash transfers. Means-tested in-kind transfers (the sum of school nutrition programs, WIC, Head Start, housing assistance, and food stamps) grew at an annual rate of 16.0 percent in the 1970s, 2.1 percent in the 1980s, 2.0 percent in the 1990s, and 5.1 percent between 2000 and 2005.[18] Means-tested cash transfers (the sum of AFDC-TANF, SSI, and the EITC) grew at an annual rate of 3.4 percent in the 1970s, 2.1 percent in the 1980s, and 4.2 percent in the 1990s, and they fell for the first time in thirty-five years between 2000 and 2005, despite a weak economy.

The growth rates of both cash and in-kind safety net spending increased significantly in the 1990s relative to the 1980s. In-kind programs continued to increase in the 2000s, while cash programs shrank. Spending on cash and in-kind antipoverty programs excluding Medicaid was around $200 billion in 2005; Medicaid was an additional $333 billion. In the following section, we discuss the degree to which these programs alleviate poverty.

EFFECTS OF ANTIPOVERTY POLICIES

In this section, we address the complex question: how do the social insurance and means-tested programs we have described affect the poverty rate and the depth of poverty among poor people? We examine the antipoverty effectiveness of these programs by measuring the degree to which they reduce the aggregate poverty gap, which is defined as the sum of the differences between market income and the poverty line for all families with incomes below the poverty line.[19] We measure the poverty gap using data from the first waves of the 1984, 1993, and 2004 Surveys of Income and Program Participation (SIPP), a nationally representative survey conducted by the U.S. Census Bureau. Each interview elicited information for the four months prior to the interview month. These surveys were conducted at similar business cycle points—October 1983 was eleven months, February 1993 twenty-three months, and February 2004 twenty-seven months following the trough of the prior recession.

We emphasize four questions. First, how large is the poverty gap, and how did it change between 1984 and 2004? Second, how has the antipoverty effectiveness of the tax and transfer system changed? Third, how effective are current programs in filling the poverty gap? And fourth, how do the effects of public policies differ across demographic groups—for example, among the elderly, one- and two-parent families, and families without children?

Behavioral Responses

Our analysis does not take into account behavioral responses to different programs, so before beginning our discussion of the preceding questions, we briefly discuss labor market, saving, and family formation responses to changes in the safety net for prime-age workers and their likely effect on our results.[20] These responses have been at the heart of the policy debates shaping the evolution of antipoverty policy.[21] The rapid increase in the Earned Income Tax Credit since 1986, for example, reflects the fact that the credit is widely perceived as being "pro-work." The momentum to "end welfare as we know it" in the early 1990s was fueled by a concern that AFDC had created a cycle of dependency, encouraging some women to not work and to have children.

All open-ended, means-tested transfer programs—that is, those that provide more benefits the lower the family income is—provide a disincentive to work because additional work necessarily reduces the benefits received. Economists have put most of their emphasis on the importance of the "tax rate" in these programs— defined as the fraction of benefits lost as income rises—and have recommended that the tax rate be kept low to minimize work disincentives. Historically, tax rates have been very high for low-income families. For example, as Stacy Dickert, Scott

Houser, and John Karl Scholz (1995) show, in 1990 cumulative *average* tax rates (that is, tax rates summed over all the programs in which a family participated) exceeded 85 percent for some low-wage, single-parent families from New York working anywhere from eight to thirty-five hours per week. This implies that an extra dollar of earnings would increase take-home income by only fifteen cents.

Since 1990, however, tax rates have been greatly reduced in the TANF program, and the EITC expansion has lowered them even further. Tax rates for those with very low earnings are usually less than 30 percent, and often they are negative (that is, benefits actually increase with earnings) because of the EITC (Coe et al. 1998).[22] These tax rate reductions increased employment rates over the late 1980s and 1990s (Meyer and Rosenbaum 2001). A series of classical experiments testing the effect of increased financial incentives on the work effort of low-income families also showed that families respond positively to such incentives (Berlin 2000).

Savings among low-income families can also be affected by antipoverty programs because eligibility requires low income and assets, which means that families will lose eligibility if they save enough to exceed these levels. Glenn Hubbard, Jonathan Skinner, and Steven Zeldes (1995) construct a simulation model that predicts, in the absence of asset testing, that low-income families would save considerably more than they actually do in the presence of asset testing, regardless of whether they ever draw program benefits. Nevertheless, the empirical evidence that asset tests discourage wealth accumulation is scant, at least for prime-age individuals (Hurst and Ziliak 2006; Engelhardt et al. 2008).[23]

Antipoverty programs often provide greater resources to single-parent families than to two-parent families and so may provide incentives to delay marriage, divorce, or not marry. Program benefits and the EITC also generally increase with family size and hence provide incentives to have additional children. Many studies have addressed the question of whether antipoverty programs affect behavior in the ways just described, and the results suggest that low-income individuals do indeed respond to these incentives, but that the magnitude of the response is small (Moffitt 1998).

We conclude that the tax and transfer system has measurable effects on the behavior of low-income families, with the strongest effects on reducing work effort. This implies that our estimates of the effect of antipoverty programs on the incomes of the poor, given later in the chapter, are overstatements of their initial impact, because those programs may cause incomes to fall even further as work effort is reduced. Our impact estimates should consequently be regarded as upper bounds.

The Evolution of the Poverty Gap, 1984 to 2004

Our market income measure aggregates wage and salary income, self-employment income, capital income (interest, dividends, and rents), and defined benefit pension income.[24] We do not consider the effects of the individual income tax, aside from the refundable EITC and child tax credits. Omitting the federal individual income tax has little consequence for poverty gap calculations because in recent years most poor families with children have not paid positive income taxes because of personal

TABLE 8.1 / Antipoverty Effectiveness of the Transfer System, 1984, 1993, and 2004

	Number of Families (Million)	Percentage Poor, Pretransfer[a]	Average Monthly Market Income per Poor Family	Monthly Pretransfer Poverty Gap ($ Million)	Monthly Pretransfer Poverty Gap per Poor Family	Total Monthly Transfers ($ Million)	Average Monthly Transfer per Recipient Family
2004 SIPP	124.5	30.3%	$326	$30,151	$800	$65,002	$844
1993 SIPP	106.4	30.5	354	26,276	809	54,005	1,086
1984 SIPP	90.7	29.7	360	21,402	793	40,430	1,002

Source: Authors' calculations from wave 1 of the 1984, 1993, and 2004 SIPP (U.S. Bureau of the Census, various years).

Notes: Dollar amounts are in 2007 dollars, using the CPI-U. The transfers reflected in the calculations include those listed in table 8.2, except Medicare and Medicaid.

a. This poverty rate is for families and unrelated individuals: it reflects the fraction of families (including single-person "families") in poverty rather than the fraction of the total population in poverty; the latter is the more traditional measure, emphasized in other chapters of this volume.

and child exemptions and the standard deduction. Low-income taxpayers without children and with incomes near the poverty line pay small amounts of federal income taxes. In contrast, because all workers are subject to the payroll tax, we reduce reported earnings by 7.65 percent (the employee OASDI tax rate) when measuring the poverty gap and the percentage of the population who are poor.

We include the following programs in table 8.1, which shows the evolution of the poverty gap between 1984 and 2004: Social Security (OASDI), unemployment compensation, workers' compensation, SSI, AFDC-TANF, the EITC, the child tax credit, general assistance, other welfare, foster child payments, veterans' benefits, food stamps, WIC, and housing assistance.[25]

SIPP and other nationally representative household surveys underreport aggregate transfers (Meyer, Mok, and Sullivan 2007). However, the number of recipients and the aggregate benefits for veterans' benefits, general assistance, other welfare, foster child payment, and OASI fairly closely match the administrative totals (or the programs are small, in cases where administrative totals are not readily available).[26] Because noncompliance biases the administrative totals for the EITC, we do not adjust our SIPP-based EITC calculations, nor do we adjust our child credit calculations in 2004. We do not have good administrative data on the number of worker's compensation recipients, so we adjust reported benefits in the SIPP to match the cash receipts reported in Meyer, Mok, and Sullivan (2007). For housing (and Medicaid in tables 8.2 and 8.3), we impute recipients based on the income, education, marital status, number of children, race-ethnicity, gender (of the family reference person), region, age (of the family reference person), age of children, and participation in other programs. In brief, we assign a propensity score to each nonrecipient SIPP household and impute average benefits to the nonrecipients with the highest probability of receiving benefits, until

Total Transfers to Poor ($ Million)	Average Monthly Transfer per Poor Family	Percentage of Total to Pretransfer Poor	Percentage of Total Used to Alleviate Poverty	Percentage of Poverty Gap Filled	Monthly Poverty Gap, Post-Transfer ($ Million)	Monthly Poverty Gap per Poor Family, Post-Transfer	Percentage Poor, Post-Transfer[a]
$35,103	$932	54.0%	30.7%	66.2%	$10,198	$580	14.1%
32,175	991	59.6	35.4	72.7	7,175	496	13.6
24,493	908	60.6	37.5	70.9	6,227	479	14.3

we match the number of recipients in the administrative data. For AFDC-TANF, food stamps, WIC, disability insurance, SSI, and UI, we do the same, and then once we match the number of recipients in the administrative data, we adjust household benefits in the SIPP to match the aggregate benefits reported in the administrative data. Hence, for each program we consider, we (roughly) match both the number of recipients and aggregate (and average) benefits in the administrative data.

We exclude Medicare and Medicaid in table 8.1 for two reasons. First, it is technically difficult to estimate the value of Medicare and Medicaid. Second, medical benefits and insurance are only imperfectly fungible with other expenditures. Hence, if resources are not available for food, shelter, and clothing, it is not clear that it would be appropriate to suggest that the insurance value of health benefits is sufficient to move an otherwise poor family above the poverty line. We do value Medicare and Medicaid when we focus on the effects of specific programs in 2004 in tables 8.2 and 8.3.

All programs considered in table 8.1 deliver cash benefits, except for food stamps and housing benefits. Because the value of food stamps does not exceed the food needs of the typical family, we value them at the cost to the government. We use fair market rent (FMR) data from the Department of Housing and Urban Development and value in-kind housing benefits as the difference between rents paid by housing assistance recipients and the FMR in the state.[27]

The first row of table 8.1 shows that the 2004 SIPP, when weighted, represented 124.5 million families (including unrelated individuals as one-person families). Using our after-payroll-tax, pretransfer income concept, 30.3 percent were poor. The pretransfer poverty gap, in 2007 dollars, was $30.2 billion a month, or $800 per poor family, suggesting that a perfectly targeted transfer of exactly that

TABLE 8.2 / Effect of Transfers on Poverty, 2004 SIPP—All Families and Individuals

	Total Monthly Transfers ($ Million)	Average Monthly Transfer per Recipient Family	Percentage of Total Transfers To Pretransfer Poor	Percentage of Total Transfers Used to Alleviate Poverty	Percentage of Poverty Gap Filled	Monthly Poverty Gap, Post-Transfer ($ Billion)	Percentage Poor, Post-Transfer[a]
No transfers						$30.2	30.3%
All transfers	$95,895	$1,238	54.9%	22.8%	72.5%	8.3	12.0
All social insurance	65,750	1,524	50.6	22.0	47.9	15.7	18.8
All cash transfers[b]	59,478	790	51.2	29.9	59.1	12.3	16.3
All in-kind transfers[c]	36,416	1,411	61.1	31.4	37.9	18.7	22.5
All means-tested transfers (except child care credit and foster child payments)	26,167	814	73.5	41.2	35.8	19.4	23.5
Social insurance							
Social Security (OASI)	33,115	1,224	46.4	25.1	27.6	21.8	22.3
Disability insurance	7,153	946	71.8	53.3	12.7	26.3	28.3
Medicare	17,074	2,131	47.7	16.9	9.6	27.3	27.2
Unemployment compensation	3,877	472	60.8	52.1	6.7	28.1	29.5
Workers' compensation	2,654	3,909	52.4	13.7	1.2	29.8	30.0
Veterans' benefits	1,876	682	46.8	27.9	1.7	29.6	29.9

Means-tested transfers

Medicaid	13,818	1,167	68.2	46.3	21.2	23.7	26.9
SSI	3,299	478	80.4	74.5	8.2	27.7	29.8
AFDC-TANF	922	435	87.1	83.3	2.5	29.4	30.2
EITC	2,326	120	65.4	57.9	4.5	28.8	29.2
Child tax credit	3,910	139	3.9	3.5	0.5	30.0	30.0
General assistance	76	234	61.5	61.3	0.2	30.1	30.3
Other welfare	201	493	53.2	35.7	0.2	30.1	30.2
Foster child payments	68	741	23.9	13.1	0.0	30.1	30.2
Food stamps	2,252	241	87.0	83.7	6.3	28.3	29.9
Housing assistance	2,825	547	86.6	79.8	7.5	27.9	29.7
WIC	447	106	58.5	56.7	0.8	29.9	30.2

Source: Authors' calculations from wave 1 of the 2004 SIPP (U.S. Bureau of the Census, various years).

Note: Dollar amounts are in 2007 dollars, using the CPI-U.

a. This poverty rate is for families and unrelated individuals: it reflects the fraction of families (including single-person "families") in poverty rather than the fraction of the total population in poverty; the latter is the more traditional measure, emphasized in other chapters of this volume.

b. Cash transfers include all programs listed under social insurance and the means-tested transfers headings, except housing, food stamps, Medicare, Medicaid, and WIC.

c. In-kind transfers are housing, food stamps, Medicare, Medicaid, and WIC.

TABLE 8.3 / Antipoverty Effectiveness of the Transfer System for Different Family Types, 2004 SIPP

	Number of families (Million)	Percentage Poor, Pretransfer[a]	Monthly Poverty Gap ($ Million)	Monthly Poverty Gap per Poor Family
Elderly families and individuals	23.2	55.2%	$8,905	$696
Non-elderly				
Single-parent families	10.6	47.8	5,123	1,014
Two-parent families	26.0	15.0	4,118	1,055
Childless families and individuals	64.7	24.6	12,005	754
White families and individuals	75.8	21.3	13,519	837
Black families and individuals	12.8	35.4	3,997	883
Hispanic families and individuals	12.8	32.8	3,729	891
Employed families	95.6	17.3	11,965	724
Unemployed, non-elderly families	12.1	83.0	10,290	1,029

Source: Authors' calculations from wave 1 of the 2004 SIPP (U.S. Bureau of the Census, various years).
Note: Dollar amounts in 2007 dollars, using the CPI-U.
a. This poverty rate is for families and unrelated individuals: it reflects the fraction of families (including single-person "families") in poverty rather than the fraction of the total population in poverty; the latter is the more traditional measure, emphasized in other chapters of this volume.

amount could have eradicated poverty, assuming no other behavioral responses. Total transfers measured in SIPP (excluding Medicare and Medicaid) were $65.0 billion per month, or $844 per recipient family; of these transfers, 54.0 percent were received by pretransfer poor families and 30.7 percent reduced the poverty gap.[28] The tax and transfer system closed 66.2 percent of the poverty gap, leaving 14.1 percent of families poor after the full effects of the safety net (excluding the value of medical benefits and insurance).

Rows 2 and 3 of table 8.1 show the same results for 1993 and 1984. The fraction of all families with income below the poverty line was about 30 percent in each year. The poverty gap per family was also about $800 per month in each year. And in each year, between 66 percent and 73 percent of the poverty gap was filled by safety net programs.

Although the pretransfer poverty rates across years are similar, the percentage of total transfers received by pretransfer poor families and the percentage of total transfers used to fill the poverty gap have been falling over time. In 1984, 38 percent of transfers filled the poverty gap, while only 31 percent did in 2004. For families who remained poor after transfers, the monthly poverty gap (of $580) in 2004 was larger than the monthly poverty gap (of $480) in 1984. This raises the possibility that transfers in 2004 moved more near-poor families over the poverty line, per-

Total Monthly Transfers ($ Million)	Average Monthly Transfer per Recipient Family	Percentage of Total to Pretransfer Poor	Percentage of Total Used to Alleviate Poverty	Percentage of Poverty Gap Filled	Percentage Poor, Post-Transfer[a]
$48,606	$2,151	52.6%	17.4%	95.0%	7.8%
11,276	1,119	76.1	37.3	82.1	13.8
15,137	631	43.4	20.5	75.5	5.1
20,876	1,005	57.2	29.1	50.7	16.0
30,121	779	51.5	25.9	57.7	12.3
8,906	1,118	70.7	33.9	75.6	15.0
8,262	1,004	63.9	31.1	69.0	15.4
47,450	901	38.9	15.8	62.7	8.4
13,973	1,681	90.2	49.0	66.6	44.1

haps leaving those further away from the poverty line with even less assistance than before. We explore this possibility later in the chapter.

The Antipoverty Effectiveness of Specific Programs

Table 8.2 shows the antipoverty effectiveness of specific safety net programs in 2004 (in 2007 dollars). For this portion of the analysis, we also value Medicare and Medicaid. We assume that for most families, Medicaid was worth the cost of a typical HMO policy (for a discussion of ways in which Medicaid is more valuable than private insurance and ways in which it is less valuable, see Gruber 2003); for elderly or disabled families, we increase this by a factor of 2.5 to account for the greater medical needs of these groups. We value Medicare using 2.5 times the average cost of a fee-for-service plan, adjusting for regional cost differences.[29]

Reading across the "all transfers" row (the sum of all social insurance and means-tested transfers shown in the table), the first entry shows $95.9 billion of benefits, or $1,238 per recipient family. Of these payments, 54.9 percent went to pretransfer poor families, and 22.8 percent reduced the poverty gap. These transfers filled 72.5 percent of the total poverty gap, which resulted in an after-tax and transfer poverty rate of 12.0 percent (down from 30.3 percent) and a monthly poverty gap of $8.3 billion.[30]

The next rows show these effects for various programs and groups of programs. "All in-kind transfers" includes housing, food stamps, Medicare, Medicaid, and WIC. "All cash transfers" includes all other means-tested transfers. The "all social insurance" and "all means-tested transfers except the child credit and foster child payments" entries are self-explanatory. We focus on the effects of three sets of programs—all social insurance, all means-tested transfers (excluding child care credit and foster child payments), and the combined effects of all programs. If there were no means-tested transfers in place, 51 percent of social insurance would go to the pretransfer poor, these payments would close 48 percent of the poverty gap, and they would reduce the poverty rate from 30.3 percent to 18.8 percent. Similarly, if there were no social insurance programs in place, 74 percent of means-tested transfers would go to the pretransfer poor, these payments would close 36 percent of the poverty gap, and they would reduce the poverty rate from 30.3 percent to 23.5 percent. The *combined* effect of social insurance and means-tested transfers can be seen from the top (complete) line of table 8.2. The effect of all transfers was to close 73 percent of the poverty gap and reduce the poverty rate from 30.3 percent to 12.0 percent.

As expected, given their universality, the major social insurance programs—Social Security (OASI), disability insurance (DI), Medicare, unemployment insurance (UI), and workers' compensation—are not sharply targeted at pretransfer poor households. Disability insurance and unemployment insurance are the exceptions: 72 percent of DI benefits and 61 percent of UI benefits went to the pretransfer poor. Around half of the other social insurance program benefits went to individuals or families with incomes below the poverty line. About half of DI and UI benefits and 14 to 28 percent of the other benefits reduced the poverty gap. Given the large size of the programs, however, they filled a substantial part of the poverty gap. For example, about half of all Social Security benefits went to the pretransfer poor; if we include disability insurance (looking at OASDI), they reduced the poverty gap by 40 percent.

Means-tested programs typically provided a larger share of their benefits to the pretransfer poor than did social insurance programs. For example, 87 percent of food stamp benefits went to the pretransfer poor, and 84 percent of these benefits reduced the poverty gap. But because food stamps is a much smaller program than Social Security, it filled only about 6.3 percent of the poverty gap. Medicaid, SSI, housing assistance, and the EITC also closed the poverty gaps by 4.5 to 8.2 percentage points.

The Effects of the Safety Net Programs by Family Type

Table 8.3 compares differences in the effects of safety net programs on elderly families and eight non-elderly family types: (1) single-parent, (2) two-parent, (3) childless, (4) white, (5) black, (6) Hispanic, (7) employed, and (8) unemployed. The top row shows that $48.6 billion in transfers per month, primarily Social Security and Medicare benefits, filled 95 percent of the poverty gap of the elderly, leaving them with a 7.8 percent post-transfer poverty rate. The second row shows that $11.3 billion in transfers were received by non-elderly single-parent families—76 percent went to poor families and 37 percent reduced the poverty gap. Although these transfers filled 82 percent of the poverty gap, 13.8 percent of non-elderly single-parent families remained poor. The $15 billion in monthly transfers for non-elderly two-parent families reduced their poverty gap by 76 percent, resulting in a poverty rate of 5.1 percent.

Non-elderly black and Hispanic families and individuals had higher pretransfer poverty rates than non-elderly white families, received (on a per capita basis) more transfer payments, and, for those who were poor, had a similar depth of poverty (as measured by the poverty gap). Despite receiving more in average transfers, black and Hispanic families and individuals had post-transfer poverty rates that were around three percentage points higher than those of white families and individuals.

Table 8.3 calls attention to several holes in the safety net. First, the tax and transfer system filled only 50.7 percent of the poverty gap for non-elderly childless families in 2004, compared to 75.5 percent for two-parent families with children, and 82.1 percent for single-parent families with children. Other than food stamps, these families had few public assistance programs they could access in the absence of a disability, though, as discussed earlier, strengthening their safety net runs the risk of creating incentives to not work or not invest in skills that could lead to greater self-sufficiency. Second, post-transfer poverty rates remained high for single-parent families with children (13.8 percent) as well as for black and Hispanic families (15.0 percent and 15.4 percent, respectively). Third, non-elderly families with no employed individuals had an exceptionally high post-transfer poverty rate, 44.1 percent. As we discuss in the next section, changes in the nature of the safety net over the past twenty years have increased the economic vulnerability of family heads who are unable or unwilling to work.

The Changing Nature of U.S. Antipoverty Programs

The safety net has changed in striking ways for the non-elderly. The changes are evident, in part, in figure 8.3, which shows the reduction from 1970 to 2007 in AFDC-TANF expenditures, which historically went to nonworkers, and the increase in EITC benefits, which go overwhelmingly to low-income workers with children. Other than food stamps and housing benefits, non-elderly families or individuals with very low or no earnings and patchy employment histories had no safety net to draw on.

We illustrate changes in the safety net for different groups of families with a series of figures that illustrate the average monthly benefits available to low- and moderate-income families. Figure 8.6 shows the trend in average benefits (over all programs but excluding Medicare and Medicaid) received by non-elderly,

FIGURE 8.6   /   Average Monthly Benefits for Single-Parent Families, 1984, 1993, 2004

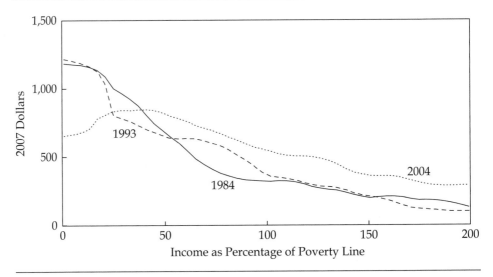

Source: Authors' calculations based on wave 1 of the 1984, 1993, and 2004 SIPP (U.S. Bureau of the Census, various years).

nondisabled, single-parent families. On the horizontal axis, we classify families by their pretransfer income, restricting the sample to families with incomes between zero and 200 percent of the poverty line.[31] On the vertical axis, we plot average transfer program benefits, excluding Medicare and Medicaid but including all other transfers enumerated in table 8.2. The three lines show average benefits (in 2007 dollars) for families in the 1984, 1993, and 2004 SIPP surveys.[32] Focusing first on the two lines for 1984 and 1993, we note that the largest benefits were received by those with no income and that average benefits fell as income as a percentage of the poverty line rose. This accords with the traditional structure of a transfer program, where benefits are phased out as income rises. In fact, the negative slope of the lines in figure 8.6 reflects the fact that benefits are phased out as income increases, as we discussed earlier. The steepness of the line in 1984 and 1993 vividly highlights the weak incentives that single parents faced to earn income in the paid labor market. In 1993, for example, families with no market income received around $1,200 of benefits, but as income increased to roughly 25 percent of the poverty line, average benefits fell to around $800.

The situation in 2004 was quite different, for the slope of the benefit line below 25 percent of the poverty line was actually positive, implying a subsidy to work (or a negative tax rate) on average. We noted that development earlier and traced it to the EITC and reductions in TANF tax rates. At the same time, however, average benefits received by a single parent with no income were 45 percent lower than in 1993. This was, in some sense, the "price" of increasing work incentives (namely, making things relatively worse off for those at the bottom). We also note that the

FIGURE 8.7 / Average Monthly Benefits for Two-Parent Families, 1984, 1993, and 2004

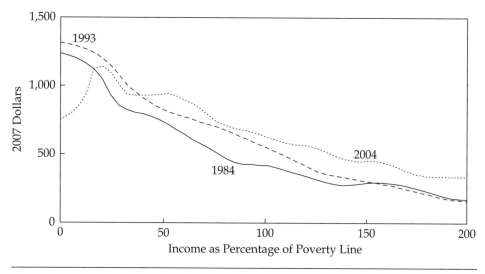

Source: Authors' calculations based on wave 1 of the 1984, 1993, and 2004 SIPP (U.S. Bureau of the Census, various years).

increases in benefits for higher-income families, that is, the work incentives provided, extended all the way up through the highest income level shown in the figure (200 percent of the poverty line). The income increases were driven almost solely by the Earned Income Tax Credit and, as income got higher, the refundable child credit.[33]

Figure 8.7 shows a similar pattern for married couples with children.[34] Average benefits for nondisabled, non-elderly married couples with children in 2004, with no income, were about 48 percent of the average benefits available in 1993. Once income exceeded roughly 40 percent of the poverty line, average benefits in 2004 were larger than comparable families received in earlier years.

Figure 8.8 shows average benefits for nondisabled, non-elderly childless families and individuals. Again, average benefits for those with very low or zero income were lower in 2004 than they were in earlier years. The EITC available to childless taxpayers, which was initiated in 1994, is evident in the figure. Otherwise, few benefits were available, and this fact had not changed for twenty years.

There are substantial numbers of families or individuals reflected in figures 8.6 through 8.8 with incomes below 25 percent of the poverty line.[35] The education of the "deep poor" rose over time, the number of children fell over time, and the fraction of employed families (defined as at least one person in the family being employed in all four months of the reference period) went from 15 percent in 1984 to 10 percent in 1993, to 36 percent in 2004. Thus, it appears that the incidence of regular, but sporadic and poorly compensated, work was much greater in the

FIGURE 8.8 / Average Monthly Benefits for Childless Families, 1984, 1993, and 2004

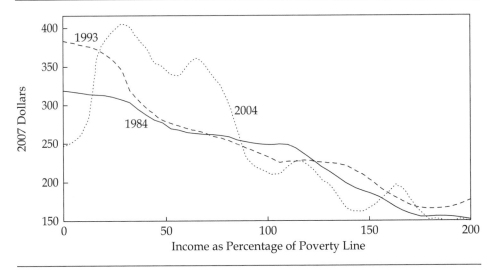

Source: Authors' calculations based on wave 1 of the 1984, 1993, and 2004 SIPP (U.S. Bureau of the Census, various years).

2004 SIPP. This conclusion is tempered, however, by three considerations. First, the SIPP employment question changed in 2004. Second, surely families and individuals with incomes below 25 percent of the poverty line supplemented public transfers with "off-the-books" resources, but the SIPP provides no insight into this phenomenon. Third, market income may also have been underreported by low-income individuals, and the magnitude of this underreporting may have changed over time in the SIPP.

The sample for figure 8.9 is restricted to elderly families (or unrelated individuals). Unlike the striking changes for the poorest non-elderly families, the average benefits received by poor elderly families in 2004 were similar or slightly higher than those received in 1993 (and larger than those received in 1984). This is largely due to the fact that Social Security was stable over this period. In contrast, the changes for non-elderly households were consistent with the changing incentives embodied in the safety net: as greater emphasis was placed on work, fewer benefits were available to those who, for one reason or another, were unwilling or unable to work.

THE FUTURE OF ANTIPOVERTY POLICY

Between 1975, the first year the EITC existed, and 2005, total spending on all means-tested cash and in-kind transfers (excluding Medicaid) averaged 2.0 percent of GDP, ranging between 1.8 percent and 2.5 percent. In 2005 it was 1.8 percent of

FIGURE 8.9 / Average Monthly Benefits for Elderly Families, 1984, 1993, and 2004

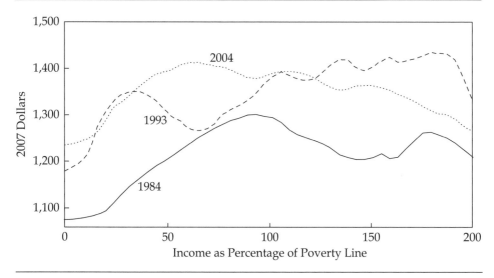

Source: Authors' calculations based on wave 1 of the 1984, 1993, and 2004 SIPP (U.S. Bureau of the Census, various years).

GDP, near its thirty-one-year low. Transfers now do less to close the poverty gap than they did before. As shown in table 8.1, transfers reduced the poverty gap by 66.2 percent in 2004, while the comparable figures were 72.7 percent in 1993 and 70.9 percent in 1984. The difference between pre- and post-transfer poverty rates was 16.2 percentage points in 2004, 16.9 percentage points in 1993, and 15.4 percentage points in 1984. But the depth of poverty for those remaining poor appears to have increased substantially—the after-transfer poverty gap in 2004 (all in 2007 dollars) was $580, compared to $496 in 1993 and $479 in 1984. These patterns are driven by substantial changes in the antipoverty policy mix, which has resulted in large changes in the resources available to families and individuals in different circumstances.

The contrast in levels and, to a lesser extent, trends in social expenditures between the United States and other industrialized countries is striking. Smeeding (2008) calculates a consistent set of social expenditures (including cash, near-cash, and housing expenditures) as a percentage of GDP for five groups of countries—Scandinavia, northern Continental Europe, central and southern Europe, "Anglo" (Australia, Canada, and the United Kingdom), and the United States—between 1980 and 1999. Spending ranges between 2.7 percent to 3.6 percent of GDP in the United States, a far lower level than in every other country group. The other Anglo countries averaged between 4.8 percent and 7.8 percent of GDP, similar to the central and southern European countries. Northern Europe and the Scandinavian countries averaged between 8.1 percent and 15.3 percent of GDP.

The trends across country groups vary, though most country groups increased expenditures as a share of GDP between 1980 and 1999. The United States did not.

Why has U.S. antipoverty spending been low and relatively stable given the nation's persistent and high poverty rates, at least by international standards? A number of factors are relevant. There may be indifference or antipathy to the poor on the part of the public (Bane, this volume). Voters and policymakers may be skeptical that we know what works and may believe that some well-intentioned policies have counterproductive consequences. Lastly, the fiscal policy climate over much of the previous thirty years, with a respite in the 1990s, has been difficult.

Developments in 2008 promise both continuation and possible change in these trends. The recession that began in 2008 may be long and deep, leading to both increases in pretransfer poverty and declines in government revenue, causing further fiscal distress at the federal and state levels. On the other hand, the voters in the 2008 election, with their election of President Obama and his progressive agenda, signaled a desire for social policy change that, among other features, is likely to promote a more equitable distribution of income and public benefits. How the twin pressures of increased economic contraction and fiscal stringency, on the one hand, and greater desire for activist government intervention, on the other, play out remains to be seen.

Given the severity of the economic downturn that began in 2008 and the magnitude of the likely fiscal policy response, it is an unusually difficult time to speculate on the evolution of antipoverty and social insurance programs. The policy agenda of many will be to broaden health insurance coverage, improve education access, expand tax credits for some groups of low-skilled workers, and extend (and possibly enhance) unemployment insurance benefits. But there nevertheless appears to be little appetite for tax increases among the population or political leadership, so the potential for widespread, durable change in social policy is not clear at this point.

To the extent that durable change occurs, we hope policymakers will be influenced by the large and growing body of evidence that work-based antipoverty strategies like the Earned Income Tax Credit, the Canadian Self-Sufficiency Project, the Wisconsin TANF program (W-2), and the Minnesota Family Investment Program can both increase work and the after-tax incomes of poor families. These policies require that the poor work to receive benefits but are structured so that greater work effort increases disposable income. Although such a work-based safety net aligns assistance with the fundamental values of Americans, we have not effectively struck a balance between supporting work and sensibly treating those families (and the children therein) who, for one reason or another, are unable or unwilling to work (Blank and Kovak 2009).

Also, while the 1996 welfare reform increased work, the earnings of most individuals who left welfare were still well below the poverty line, even many years after their exit. Hence, the degree to which work can be the primary antidote to poverty depends on the ability of low-skilled people to maintain employment that, over time, leads to higher incomes that allow families to be self-sufficient. More work is needed to develop effective ways of increasing the earnings of disadvantaged workers (Holzer, this volume; Heinrich and Scholz 2009).

Major changes in poverty will not be achieved by simply reshuffling the 1.8 percent of GDP that is spent on cash and in-kind means-tested transfers (excluding Medicaid). If antipoverty spending as a fraction of GDP simply increased to its *average* level over the last thirty-one years of 2.0 percent, there would be an additional $26.5 billion for new initiatives. These funds could be used to (1) expand successful state-level welfare reforms and provide new funding sources for child care and health insurance benefits that increase the attractiveness of work; and (2) augment the safety net, pursue effective human capital development, expand rental housing subsidies, and ensure that states have sufficient resources to handle families affected by TANF time limits in the way they see fit.

In the absence of a renewed antipoverty effort, many households will continue to be unable to afford adequate food, housing, and shelter. Our high poverty rate contributes to an erosion of social cohesion, a waste of the human capital of a portion of our citizenry, and the moral discomfort of condoning poverty amid affluence.

APPENDIX

Please see following page for table 8A.1, *Social Insurance and Antipoverty Spending by Program, 1970 to 2007.*

APPENDIX

TABLE 8A.1 / Social Insurance and Antipoverty Spending by Program, 1970 to 2007 (in Constant 2007 Dollars, Millions)

| | Social Insurance | | | | | Means-Tested Transfers | | | | | | | | |
Year	OASI	Medicare	UI	Workers' Compensation	DI	Medicaid	SSI	AFDC-TANF	EITC	Food Stamps	Housing Aid	School Food Programs	WIC	Head Start
1970	$153,882	$40,998	$16,427		$16,390	$28,264	$15,706	$26,522		$2,938	$2,693	$3,631		$1,740
1971	171,060	43,224	29,432		19,239	34,281	16,413	30,728		7,796	3,922	4,711		1,843
1972	184,138	46,255	32,937		22,188	41,235	16,825	35,337		8,915	5,734	5,784		1,867
1973	213,604	50,108	22,822		26,702	44,004	15,962	35,552		9,953	7,710	6,251		1,871
1974	217,091	56,474	23,506		29,032	46,574	22,063	34,113		11,432	7,671	6,350	$44	1,699
1975	225,490	62,958	49,354		32,427	51,820	22,653	36,589	$4,817	16,901	8,197	7,405	344	1,557
1976	239,405	71,764	67,650		36,316	55,348	22,104	39,154	4,719	19,410	9,125	7,879	520	1,607
1977	250,155	78,321	49,033		39,220	59,753	21,576	39,569	3,856	17,337	10,288	8,245	876	1,625
1978	255,527	84,807	34,618		39,792	61,904	20,836	37,649	3,333	16,343	11,700	8,484	1,207	1,988
1979	258,623	88,312	28,094		39,149	63,779	20,206	34,640	5,860	18,507	12,292	8,834	1,501	1,942
1980	264,396	93,556	42,498		38,844	65,504	19,982	33,806	4,997	21,944	13,789	9,101	1,831	1,849
1981	282,375	101,604	41,785		39,231	69,132	19,601	33,058	4,361	24,247	15,650	8,459	1,988	1,867
1982	298,229	111,905	47,867		37,253	68,780	19,297	31,398	3,814	21,934	17,326	7,043	2,039	1,959
1983	311,225	123,366	61,553		36,493	73,413	19,577	32,136	3,737	23,216	19,670	7,419	2,344	1,899
1984	315,028	131,424	33,963		35,721	76,297	20,698	32,067	3,269	21,345	20,052	7,414	2,770	1,987
1985	322,498	137,670	30,531		36,296	78,884	21,312	31,523	4,024	20,703	21,971	7,274	2,870	2,072
1986	334,557	144,525	30,524		37,547	85,856	22,855	32,530	3,801	20,063	21,644	7,488	2,995	1,968
1987	335,186	150,779	28,245	$49,859	37,438	91,878	23,638	33,686	6,189	19,165	20,585	7,570	3,066	2,063
1988	342,687	155,088	23,908	53,813	38,019	96,538	25,195	33,329	10,334	19,541	22,306	7,415	3,150	2,114
1989	347,761	168,276	23,309	57,380	38,246	103,592	24,592	32,869	11,028	19,513	23,374	7,192	3,195	2,065
1990	353,755	173,717	27,172	60,659	39,347	116,856	25,533	34,929	11,965	22,436	24,559	7,054	3,367	2,462
1991	366,024	183,630	38,229	64,223	42,111	141,898	27,370	36,739	16,906	26,360	25,816	7,503	3,503	2,971
1992	376,761	200,981	54,679	66,001	45,948	159,884	31,416	39,320	19,253	30,895	27,748	7,929	3,843	3,254
1993	384,270	215,182	50,883	61,593	49,644	175,594	34,686	38,795	22,294	31,576	30,702	8,089	4,059	3,984
1994	390,505	234,580	36,991	60,834	52,769	188,054	39,577	40,369	29,527	31,827	33,303	8,384	4,434	4,653
1995	396,837	250,869	28,986	57,307	55,642	197,086	38,263	40,939	35,313	30,971	37,330	8,469	4,675	4,808
1996	400,298	262,644	29,843	55,450	58,376	201,091	36,247	37,257	38,092	29,654	35,231	8,577	4,883	4,717
1997	408,627	271,773	26,606	54,220	58,985	204,730	38,911	29,944	39,258	25,254	35,775	8,766	4,966	5,142
1998	415,723	266,125	24,914	55,953	61,278	214,967	39,629	27,365	41,138	21,485	36,490	9,055	4,949	5,530
1999	416,224	264,856	26,579	57,639	63,884	229,230	40,016	27,042	39,702	19,626	34,406	9,187	4,901	5,797
2000	424,685	270,147	24,975	57,433	66,150	242,736	42,689	27,221	38,887	18,041	34,663	9,099	4,795	6,342
2001	435,957	289,596	32,675	59,506	69,751	263,782	36,856	28,284	39,075	18,202	35,201	9,297	4,863	7,259

Year														
2002	447,382	305,527	58,391	60,412	75,659	287,003	41,456	26,920	44,026	21,041	38,087	9,722	5,002	7,534
2003	450,622	317,178	61,304	62,052	79,901	306,092	39,094	25,756	43,561	24,120	39,785	9,979	5,098	7,513
2004	455,606	339,535	46,522	61,548	85,837	320,552	39,586	22,900	43,931	27,022	40,145	10,335	5,364	7,436
2005	462,218	358,862	34,304	58,717	90,659	332,818	39,532	21,972	45,025	30,329	40,035	10,589	5,301	7,265
2006	473,572	412,721	31,932		95,015	319,476	39,997	21,052		31,047	39,084	10,542	5,217	6,979
2007			32,454							30,373	39,436	10,891	5,450	

Sources:

OASI (total benefits): Social Security Online, "Old-Age and Survivors Insurance Benefit Payments: Annual Benefits Paid from OASI Trust Fund, by Type of Benefit, 1937–2006," at: http://www.ssa.gov/OACT/STATS/table4a5.html.

Medicare: U.S. Department of Health and Human Services, Centers for Medicare and Medicaid Services, "NHE Historical and Projections, 1965 to 2017: National Health Expenditure (NHE) Amounts by Type of Expenditure and Source of Funds: Calendar Years 1965–2017 in PROJECTIONS Format," at: http://www.cms.hhs.gov/NationalHealthExpendData/03_NationalHealthAccountsProjected.asp.

UI: Office of Management and Budget, "Historical Tables: Budget of the United States Government, Fiscal Year 2009: Table 8.5—Outlays for Mandatory and Related Programs, 1962–2013," at: http://www.whitehouse.gov/omb/budget/fy2009.

Workers' compensation (total benefits): National Academy of Social Insurance, "Full Report: Workers' Compensation: Benefits, Coverage, and Costs, 2005: Table 4—Workers' Compensation Benefits, by Type of Insurer, 1987–2005 (in million)," at: http://www.nasi.org/publications2763/publications_show.htm?doc_id=516615.

DI (total benefits): Social Security Online, "Disability Insurance Benefit Payments: Annual Benefits Paid from DI Trust Fund, by Type of Benefit, 1957–2006," at: http://www.ssa.gov/OACT/STATS/table4a6.html.

Medicaid (federal plus state and local Medicaid, including SCHIP): U.S. Department of Health and Human Services, Centers for Medicare and Medicaid Services, "NHE Historical and Projections, 1965 to 2017: National Health Expenditure (NHE) Amounts by Type of Expenditure and Source of Funds: Calendar Years 1965–2017 in PROJECTIONS Format," at: http://www.cms.hhs.gov/NationalHealthExpendData/03_NationalHealthAccountsProjected.asp.

SSI (total): House Ways and Means Committee, "Prints: 105-7, 1998 Green Books: Section 3, Supplemental Security Income: Table 3.24—Federal and State Benefit Payments Under SSI and Prior Adult Assistance Programs, Calendar Years 1970–1987 and Fiscal Years 1988–2002," at: http://www.gpoaccess.gov/wmprints/green/1998.html; "Table 3.23—Federal and State Benefit Payments Under SSI and Prior Adult Assistance Programs, Selected Years 1970–2005," at: http://www.gpoaccess.gov/wmprints/green/docs/statcomps/supplement/2007/7a.html#table7.a4.

AFDC-TANF (total benefits plus administrative): House Ways and Means Committee, "Prints: 105-7, 1998 Green Books: Section 7, Aid to Families with Dependent Children and Temporary Assistance for Needy Families (Title IV-A): Table 7.4—Total, Federal, and State AFDC Expenditures, Fiscal Years 1970–1996," at: http://www.gpoaccess.gov/wmprints/green/1998.html.

AFDC-TANF (total): House Ways and Means Committee, "Prints: 105-7, 1998 Green Books: Section 7, Temporary Assistance for Needy Families (TANF): Table 7.18—Total, Federal, and State Expenditures for TANF and Predecessor Programs (AFDC, EA, and Jobs), Fiscal Years 1990–2001," at: http://www.gpoaccess.gov/wmprints/green/2004.html.

AFDC-TANF (total federal funds): U.S. Department of Health and Human Services, Administration for Children and Families, "TANF Financial Data: Table A—Spending from Federal TANF Grant, FY 2001–2006," at: http://www.acf.hhs.gov/programs/ofs/data/index.html.

EITC (total amount of credit): Tax Policy Center (Urban Institute and Brookings Institution), "Tax Facts: Historical EITC Recipients: Earned Income Tax Credit: Number of Recipients and Amount of Credit, 1975–2005," at: http://www.taxpolicycenter.org/taxfacts/displayafact.cfm?Docid=37.

Food Stamps (total benefits): U.S. Department of Agriculture, Food and Nutrition Service, "Supplemental Nutrition Assistance Program Participation and Costs, 1969–2007," at http://www.fns.usda.gov/pd/SNAPsummary.htm.

Housing Aid (housing assistance): "Historical Tables: Budget of the United States Government, Fiscal Year 2009: Table 8.7—Outlays for Discretionary Programs, 1962–2009," at: http://www.whitehouse.gov/omb/budget/fy2009.

School Food Programs (total federal costs—cash payments plus commodity costs): U.S. Department of Agriculture, Food and Nutrition Service, "Federal Cost of School Food Programs, 1969–2007," at: http://www.fns.usda.gov/pd/cncosts.htm.

WIC (total program costs): U.S. Department of Agriculture, Food and Nutrition Service, WIC Program Participation and Costs, 1974–2007," at http://www.fns.usda.gov/pd/SNAPsummary.htm.

Head Start (appropriations): U.S. Department of Health and Human Services, Administration for Children and Families, Head Start Program Fact Sheet Fiscal Year 2008, "Head Start Enrollment History, 1965–2006," at: http://www.acf.hhs.gov/programs/ohs/about/fy2008.html.

TABLE 8A.2 / Number of Recipients by Program, 1970 to 2007 (Thousands)

	Social Insurance				Means-Tested Transfers									
Year	OASI	Medicare	UI	DI	Medicaid	SSI	AFDC-TANF[a]	EITC	Food Stamps[a]	Housing Aid	School Breakfast[b]	School Lunch[b]	WIC	Head Start
1970	23,035	20,491	6,397	2,666			8,466		4,340		450	22,400		477
1971	23,888	20,915	6,627	2,930			10,241		9,368		800	24,100		398
1972	24,804	21,332	5,713	3,271	17,606		10,947		11,109		1,040	24,400		379
1973	25,953	23,545	5,329	3,561	19,622		10,949		12,166		1,190	24,700		379
1974	26,664	24,201	7,730	3,912	21,462	3,996	10,864		12,862		1,370	24,600	88	353
1975	27,509	24,959	11,161	4,352	22,007	4,314	11,346	6,215	17,064		1,820	24,900	344	349
1976	28,212	25,663	8,560	4,624	22,815	4,236	11,304	6,473	18,549		2,200	25,600	520	349
1977	29,069	26,458	7,985	4,854	22,832	4,238	11,050	5,627	17,077	2,398	2,490	26,200	848	333
1978	29,584	27,164	7,568	4,869	21,965	4,217	10,570	5,192	16,001	2,643	2,800	26,700	1,181	391
1979	30,236	27,859	8,075	4,777	21,520	4,150	10,312	7,135	17,653	2,842	3,320	27,000	1,483	388
1980	30,844	28,478	9,992	4,682	21,605	4,142	10,774	6,954	21,082	3,032	3,600	26,600	1,914	376
1981	31,474	29,010	9,407	4,456	21,980	4,019	11,079	6,717	22,430	3,431	3,810	25,800	2,119	387
1982	31,804	29,494	11,648	3,973	21,603	3,858	10,258	6,395	21,717	3,619	3,320	22,900	2,189	396
1983	32,221	30,026	8,907	3,813	21,554	3,901	10,761	7,368	21,625	3,857	3,360	23,000	2,537	415
1984	32,617	30,455	7,743	3,822	21,607	4,029	10,831	6,376	20,854	4,081	3,430	23,400	3,045	442
1985	33,120	31,083	8,372	3,907	21,814	4,138	10,855	7,432	19,899	4,225	3,440	23,600	3,138	452
1986	33,690	31,750	8,361	3,993	22,515	4,269	11,038	7,156	19,429	4,336	3,500	23,700	3,312	452
1987	34,126	32,411	7,203	4,045	23,109	4,385	11,027	8,738	19,113	4,461	3,610	23,900	3,429	447
1988	34,539	32,980	6,861	4,074	22,907	4,464	10,915	11,148	18,645	4,530	3,680	24,200	3,593	448
1989	35,012	33,579	7,369	4,129	23,511	4,593	10,993	11,696	18,806	4,632	3,810	24,200	4,119	451
1990	35,559	34,203	8,629	4,266	25,255	4,817	11,695	12,542	20,049	4,710	4,070	24,100	4,517	541
1991	36,074	34,870	10,075	4,513	28,280	5,118	12,930	13,665	22,625	4,786	4,440	24,200	4,893	583
1992	36,614	35,579	9,243	4,890	30,926	5,566	13,773	14,097	25,407	4,830	4,920	24,600	5,403	621
1993	36,990	36,306	7,884	5,254	33,432	5,984	14,205	15,117	26,987	4,959	5,360	24,900	5,921	714
1994	37,298	36,935	7,959	5,584	35,053	6,296	14,161	19,017	27,474	5,035	5,830	25,300	6,477	740
1995	37,529	37,535	8,035	5,858	36,282	6,514	13,418	19,334	26,619	5,130	6,320	25,700	6,894	751
1996	37,664	38,064	7,990	6,072	36,118	6,614	12,321	19,464	25,543	5,104	6,580	25,900	7,186	752
1997	37,818	38,445	7,325	6,153	34,872	6,495	10,376	19,391	22,858	5,132	6,920	26,300	7,407	794

Year														
1998	37,911	38,825	7,332	6,335	40,649	6,566	8,347	20,273	19,791	5,082	7,140	26,600	7,367	822
1999	38,072	39,140	6,951	6,524	40,300	6,557	6,824	19,259	18,183	5,154	7,370	27,000	7,311	826
2000	38,741	39,620	7,033	6,673	42,887	6,602	5,778	19,277	17,194	5,104	7,550	27,300	7,192	858
2001	38,964	40,026	9,877	6,913	46,164	6,688	5,359	19,593	17,318	5,123	7,790	27,500	7,306	905
2002	39,223	40,489	10,093	7,221	49,329	6,788	5,064	21,703	19,096	5,268	8,150	28,000	7,491	912
2003	39,443	41,087	9,935	7,595	51,971	6,902	4,929	22,024	21,259	5,231	8,430	28,400	7,631	910
2004	39,738	41,693	8,369	7,949	55,002	6,988	4,745	22,270	23,858	5,172	8,900	29,000	7,904	906
2005	40,120	42,342	7,917	8,314		7,114	4,492	22,752	25,718	5,139	9,360	29,600	8,023	907
2006	40,503	43,252	7,351	8,619		7,236			26,672	5,192	9,770	30,100	8,088	909
2007	40,945	44,010		8,920					26,466	5,108	10,160	30,600	8,285	

Sources:

OASI: http://www.ssa.gov/OACT/STATS/OASDIbenies.html, Number of beneficiaries receiving benefits on December 31, 1970–2007.

Medicare: http://www.cms.hhs.gov/MedicareEnrpts/, The HI-SMI Trend Table. The HI-SMI Trend Table shows the unduplicated count of persons enrolled in either or both parts of the program (HI and/or SMI) [PDF, 23 KB]. Medicare Aged and Disabled Enrollees as of July 1, 1966–2007, Hospital and/or Supplementary Medical Insurance.

UI: http://www.ows.doleta.gov/unemploy/hb394.asp. Taxable and Reimbursable Claims Data, Ordered by year, 1970–2007. Number of First Payments.

DI: http://www.ssa.gov/OACT/STATS/OASDIbenies.html, Number of beneficiaries receiving benefits on December 31, 1970–2007.

Medicaid: http://www.gpoaccess.gov/wmprints/green/2000.html, Section 15—Other Programs, TABLE 15–14.—UNDUPLICATED NUMBER OF MEDICAID RECIPIENTS BY ELIGIBILITY CATEGORY, FISCAL YEARS 1972–98. Total recipients. http://www.cms.hhs.gov/MedicaidDataSourcesGenInfo/02_MSISData.asp#TopOfPage, MSIS Tables FY 1999–2004, Table 01: Medicaid Eligibles, Beneficiaries, and Payments. Beneficiaries.

SSI: http://www.ssa.gov/policy/docs/statcomps/supplement/2007/7a.html#table7.a9, Table 7.A9: Number of recipients of federally administered payments, by eligibility category and age, December 1974–2006. Total.

AFDC-TANF: http://www.census.gov/compendia/statab/cats/social_insurance_human_services/supplemental_security_income_temporary_assistance_to_needy_families.html, Table 546. Temporary Assistance for Needy Families (TANF)—Families and Recipients: 1936 to 2006. Recipients.

EITC: http://www.taxpolicycenter.org/taxfacts/displayafact.cfm?Docid=37, Earned Income Tax Credit: Number of Recipients and Amount of Credit, 1975–2005. Number of recipient families.

Food Stamps: http://www.fns.usda.gov/pd/SNAPsummary.htm, Food Stamp Program Participation and Costs, 1969–2007. Average monthly participation.

Housing Aid: http://www.gpoaccess.gov/wmprints/green/2000.html, Section 15—Other Programs, TABLE 15–30.—TOTAL HOUSEHOLDS RECEIVING DIRECT HOUSING ASSISTANCE ADMINISTERED BY HUD, BY TYPE OF SUBSIDY, 1977–2000. Total assisted renters and homeowners.

School Food Programs: http://www.fns.usda.gov/pd/sbsummar.htm, School Breakfast Program Participation and Meals Served, 1969–2007. Average (9 month) participation. http://www.fns.usda.gov/pd/slsummar.htm, National School Lunch Program: Participation and Lunches Served, 1969–2007. Average (9 month) participation.

WIC: http://www.fns.usda.gov/pd/wisummary.htm, WIC Program Participation and Costs, 1974–2007. Total participation.

Head Start: http://eclkc.ohs.acf.hhs.gov/hslc/About%20Head%20Start/dHeadStartProgr.htm, Head Start Enrollment History, 1965–2006. Enrollment.

a. Average monthly number of recipients.

b. Average monthly number of recipients, based on nine-month average.

We are grateful to Mark Duggan, Jon Gruber, Bob Plotnick, Chad X. Ruppel, the conference organizers Maria Cancian and Sheldon Danziger, and conference participants for providing helpful advice.

NOTES

1. In 2008 the OASDI program was financed by a 6.2-percentage-point payroll tax levied on employers and employees (for a combined 12.4 percent tax) on earnings up to $102,000. These tax receipts are credited to the Social Security trust fund. To receive benefits, a worker must have at least forty quarters of employment in jobs covered by the Social Security system. (Most jobs are now covered.) Workers (who are not disabled) can begin drawing reduced benefits as early as age sixty-two; the normal retirement age is sixty-seven for workers born after 1959. Benefit payments increase (nonlinearly) as retirement is delayed until age seventy-two, at which point benefits no longer increase with age of retirement.

2. The census money income concept to measure poverty is pretax and includes earnings, unemployment compensation, workers' compensation, Social Security, Supplemental Security Income (SSI), public assistance, veterans' payments, survivor benefits, pension or retirement income, interest, dividends, rents, royalties, income from estates, trusts, educational assistance, alimony, child support, assistance from outside the household, and other miscellaneous sources. See Meyer and Wallace (this volume) for more details.

3. All dollar amounts are given in 2007 dollars unless otherwise noted. Descriptions of statutory program rules refer to the year in question (in this example, 2008).

4. Medicare is financed by a 1.45 percent payroll tax on uncapped earnings levied on employers and employees (for a total tax of 2.9 percent).

5. Timothy Smeeding (1982) discusses these issues. Gary Burtless and Sarah Siegel (2004) discuss the issues that arise in accounting for health care spending and insurance when measuring poverty.

6. From 1959 to 1974, real Social Security spending increased 210 percent, a much sharper growth rate than in other fifteen-year periods. For example, real Social Security spending increased 110 percent between 1970 and 1985, and 29 percent between 1991 and 2006.

7. Authors' calculations from data provided by the Center for Medicare and Medicaid Services and the Social Security Administration.

8. The federal portion of unemployment insurance is financed by a 0.8 percent tax levied on employers on the first $7,000 of wages paid to each covered employee. The states levy additional, modest taxes to finance their programs.

9. Although UI eligibility varies by state, typically one must have worked for at least two quarters of the previous year in covered employment, be actively seeking work, and have lost one's job through no fault of one's own. A worker can generally receive a maximum of twenty-six weeks of benefits, and these benefits generally replace between 50 and 70 percent of the individual's average weekly pretax wage up to some state-determined maximum.

10. "Substantial gainful activity" is defined as work that involves significant physical or mental effort and is done for pay or profit. Complex regulations promulgated by the Commissioner of the Social Security Administration define disabilities and substantial gainful activity, though average monthly earnings above some threshold ($940 in 2008) demonstrate substantial gainful activity for people with an impairment other than blindness.

11. David Autor and Mark Duggan (2003) examine the factors affecting DI caseloads over time.

12. Throughout this chapter, figures on Medicaid recipients and expenditures include those for SCHIP.

13. In 2008 the SSI income test restricted countable income to less than the federal benefit rate of $637 a month. Countable income excluded $20 a month, the first $65 a month from earnings, 50 percent of earnings exceeding $65 per month, and food stamps. This implies that a person could have earned income of up to $1,359 per month and still be eligible for SSI. A couple with only wage income could have had earnings of $1,997. An individual also cannot have assets exceeding $2,000 ($3,000 for couples), though houses and generally automobiles are not counted. An applicant is expected to first file for all other available benefits, including DI if they are eligible.

14. The EITC is a refundable credit that taxpayers can receive after filing their tax returns. It seeks to encourage individuals with low earnings to increase their work hours. In 2008 low-income working families with two or more children could get a credit of 40 percent of income up to $12,060, for a maximum credit of $4,824, which stays at this level as earnings increase from $12,060 to $15,740. Their credit is reduced by 21.06 percent of earnings between $15,740 and $38,646. Those with one child can get a credit of 34 percent on income up to $8,580, for a maximum credit of $2,917. Childless taxpayers can get a credit of 7.65 percent on income up to $5,720, for a maximum credit of $438. See Hotz and Scholz (2003) for further discussion.

15. Programs designed to enhance human capital are discussed in Jacob and Ludwig (this volume) and Holzer (this volume).

16. Families receiving SSI or TANF also receive food stamps. Others must have incomes below the poverty line after subtracting a $134 per month standard deduction, 20 percent of earnings, dependent care and large shelter expenses, and child support payments. Total income cannot exceed 133 percent of the poverty line. A family must have less than $2,000 in assets ($3,000 if a member is elderly). Vehicles (under $4,650 in value) and houses do not count for the asset tests. PRWORA disqualified most permanent resident aliens and mandated work activities for able-bodied adults without dependents, who are now generally eligible for only three months of benefits in a thirty-six-month period if they are not working.

17. The Dependent Care Tax Credit, enacted in 1954, is a nonrefundable tax credit. However, it provides no benefit to families with incomes at or below the poverty line because these families do not have positive federal income tax obligations.

18. Medicaid is considerably larger than the combined value of the other in-kind transfers in recent years. In-kind transfers including Medicaid grew at an annual rate of 11.2 percent in the 1970s, 4.5 percent in the 1980s, 6.0 percent in the 1990s, and 6.2 percent between 2000 and 2005.

19. The poverty lines are the official Census Bureau thresholds for each year. For the 2004 thresholds, see U.S. Census Bureau, "Poverty," available at: http://www.census.gov/hhes/www/poverty/threshld/thresh04.html (last updated August 29, 2006).

20. Martin Feldstein and Jeffrey Liebman (2002) survey the behavioral effects of Social Security. Medicare is discussed in Swartz (this volume).

21. In addition to the chapters in this volume and work cited elsewhere in this chapter, see, for example, reviews by Sheldon Danziger, Robert Haveman, and Robert Plotnick (1981) and by Robert Moffitt (1992). Recent surveys on specific programs include Currie (2003) on food and nutrition programs, Olsen (2003) on housing assistance, and Daly and Burkhauser (2003) on SSI.

22. Families with somewhat higher earnings can still face high tax rates if they begin to pay federal and state income taxes and payroll taxes, have the EITC phased out, and perhaps have other benefits phased out.

23. It is also not clear that increasing saving for precautionary motives—that is, saving "for a rainy day"—should be encouraged, since such saving takes away from current consumption.

24. James Ziliak (2005) provides a wide-ranging discussion of the issues that arise in measuring poverty and calculates the evolution of the aggregate poverty gap over time. Using data from the Current Population Survey (CPS) (Ziliak 2008), he calculates the effects of various safety net programs on the poverty gap in 1979, 1982, 1989, 1991, 1999, and 2001, broken out by a wide range of household demographic characteristics. While Ziliak's conclusions differ from ours in some respects—he finds modest declines in poverty gaps over time where we find increases—he, like us, finds that a declining fraction of the poverty gap is being filled by transfers and that there have been marked changes in the distribution of inequality within subgroups (for example, single mothers).

25. The child credit was enacted in 1997, so it is only reflected in 2004.

26. The same is true for Medicare, which is reflected in tables 8.2 and 8.3.

27. The state FMRs are population-weighted averages by county (or major metropolitan area). We adjust by the number of bedrooms needed for families of different sizes, assuming that childless individuals or couples live in a one-bedroom dwelling and families with one or two children live in a two-bedroom dwelling. An extra bedroom is added for each child over two.

28. If a family has a poverty gap of $100 and the program provides $1,000 of benefits, only $100 would be included in the "percentage of total used to alleviate poverty" column.

29. The data come from the Kaiser Family Foundation and Health Research and Educational Trust, "Employee Health Benefits: 2005 Summary of Findings," averaging figures from the 2003 and 2005 Annual Employer Health Benefits Surveys, available at: http://www.kff.org/insurance/7315/sections/upload/7316.pdf; Kaiser Family Foundation, "Employer Health Benefits: 2003 Annual Survey: Cost of Health Insurance," available at: http://www.kff.org/insurance/upload/Kaiser-Family-Foundation-2003-Employer-Health-Benefits-Survey-Section-1.pdf; and Kaiser Family Foundation, "Employer Health Benefits: 2005 Annual Survey: Cost of Health Insurance," available at: http://www.kff.org/insurance/7315/sections/upload/7315Section1.pdf (accessed April 27, 2008). For 1984 and 1993, we used similar information from Kaiser Family Foundation and Health Research and Educational Trust, "Employee Health Benefits: 1999 Annual Survey," available at: http://www.kff.org/insurance/upload/The-1999-Employer-Health-Benefits-Annual-Survey.pdf (all accessed September 2, 2008).

30. The difference between the "all transfers" row in table 8.2 and the 2004 data in table 8.1 simply reflects the valuation of Medicare and Medicaid (in table 8.2), which reduce poverty by 2.1 additional percentage points—from 14.1 to 12.0 percent.
31. Among all families with incomes below twice the poverty line in 2004, about 29 percent had almost no reported income (zero to 25 percent of poverty), and 39 percent had incomes below 50 percent of poverty. The remaining 61 percent were fairly evenly distributed between 50 and 200 percent of the poverty line.
32. The data are smoothed with a Stata-supplied local polynomial function that uses an Epanechnikov kernel.
33. Given the sharp increases in health care costs over time, the magnitude of the cross-year differences in figures 8.6 through 8.9 are smaller, but the qualitative patterns are similar if Medicare and Medicaid are included. For this discussion, we prefer the figures without health care spending because they aptly characterize the transfers that households receive to provide food, shelter, clothing, and other nonmedical necessities.
34. For clarity, the Y-axis scales differ in figures 8.6 through 8.9.
35. For two-parent families in 1984 and 1993, 11 percent of those with incomes below 200 percent of poverty had incomes below 25 percent of the poverty line. For childless individuals in 2004, 32 percent of those with incomes below 200 percent of the poverty line had incomes below 25 percent of the poverty line.

REFERENCES

Autor, David, and Mark G. Duggan. 2003. "The Rise in Disability Recipiency and the Decline in Unemployment." *Quarterly Journal of Economics* 118(1, February): 157–205.

Berlin, Gordon L. 2000. "Encouraging Work, Reducing Poverty: The Impact of Work Incentive Programs." New York: Manpower Demonstration Research Corporation (March). Available at: http://www.mdrc.org/Reports2000/EWORK-RPOVERTY.pdf (accessed September 2, 2008).

Besharov, Douglas J., Caeli A. Higney, and Justus A. Myers. 2007. "Federal and State Child Care and Early Education Expenditures (1997–2005)." Unpublished paper, American Enterprise Institute, Washington; University of Maryland, College Park (September 4). Available at: http://www.welfareacademy.org/pubs/childcare_edu/Child_care_and_early_education_expenditure.pdf (accessed May 9, 2008).

Blank, Rebecca M., and Brian Kovak. 2009. "Providing a Safety Net for the Most Disadvantaged Families." In *Making the Work-Based Safety Net Work Better*, edited by Carolyn J. Heinrich and John Karl Scholz. New York: Russell Sage Foundation.

Blau, David M. 2003. "Child Care Subsidy Programs." In *Means-Tested Transfer Programs in the United States*, edited by Robert A. Moffitt. Chicago: University of Chicago Press.

Burtless, Gary. 1986. "Public Spending for the Poor: Trends, Prospects, and Economic Limits." In *Fighting Poverty: What Works and What Doesn't*, edited by Sheldon H. Danziger and Daniel H. Weinberg. Cambridge, Mass.: Harvard University Press.

———. 1994. "Public Spending on the Poor: Historical Trends and Economic Limits." In *Confronting Poverty: Prescriptions for Change*, edited by Sheldon H. Danziger, Gary Sandefur, and Daniel H. Weinberg. Cambridge, Mass.: Harvard University Press.

Burtless, Gary, and Sarah Y. Siegel. 2004. "Medical Spending, Health Insurance, and Measurement of American Poverty." In *Race, Poverty, and Domestic Policy*, edited by C. Michael Henry. New Haven, Conn.: Yale University Press.

Coe, Norma B., Gregory Acs, Robert I. Lerman, and Keith Watson. 1998. "Does Work Pay? A Summary of the Work Incentives Under TANF." Washington, D.C.: Urban Institute. Available at: http://www.urban.org/UploadedPDF/anf28.pdf.

Currie, Janet. 2003. "Food and Nutrition Programs." In *Means-Tested Transfer Programs in the United States,* edited by Robert A. Moffitt. Chicago: University of Chicago Press.

Daly, Mary, and Richard Burkhauser. 2003. "SSI." In *Means-Tested Transfer Programs in the United States,* edited by Robert A. Moffitt. Chicago: University of Chicago Press.

Danziger, Sheldon, Robert Haveman, and Robert Plotnick. 1981. "How Income Transfer Programs Affect Work, Savings, and Income Distribution: A Critical Assessment." *Journal of Economic Literature* 19(3, September): 975–1028.

Dickert, Stacy, Scott Houser, and John Karl Scholz. 1995. "The Earned Income Tax Credit and Transfer Programs: A Study of Labor Market and Program Participation." In *Tax Policy and the Economy,* edited by James M. Poterba. Cambridge, Mass.: National Bureau of Economic Research and MIT Press.

Engelhardt, Gary, Gregory Mills, William G. Gale, Rhiannon Patterson, Michael Erikson, and Emil Apostolov. 2008. "Effects of Individual Development Account on Asset Purchases and Saving Behavior: Evidence from a Controlled Experiment." *Journal of Public Economics* (92): 1509–30.

Feldstein, Martin, and Jeffrey Liebman. 2002. "Social Security." In *Handbook of Public Economics,* vol. 4, edited by Alan J. Auerbach and Martin Feldstein. New York: Elsevier.

General Accounting Office (GAO). 1999. "Food Stamp Program: Various Factors Have Led to Declining Participation." GAO/RCED-99-195 (July). Available at: http://www.gao.gov/archive/1999/rc99185.pdf.

———. 2000. "Unemployment Insurance: Role as Safety Net of Low-Wage Workers Is Limited." GAO-01-181 (December). Available at: http://www.gao.gov/new.items/d01181.pdf (accessed July 10, 2009).

Green Book. 1998. "Background Material and Data on Programs Within the Jurisdiction of the Committee on Ways and Means." Washington: U.S. Government Printing Office (May 18).

Gruber, Jonathan. 1997. "The Consumption Smoothing Benefits of Unemployment Insurance." *American Economic Review* 87(1, March): 192–205.

———. 2003. "Medicaid." In *Means-Tested Transfer Programs in the United States,* edited by Robert A. Moffitt. Chicago: University of Chicago Press.

Heinrich, Carolyn, and John Karl Scholz. 2009. "Making the Work-Based Safety Net Work Better." In *Making the Work-Based Safety Net Work Better,* edited by Carolyn J. Heinrich and John Karl Scholz. New York: Russell Sage Foundation.

Holahan, John, Mindy Cohen, and David Rousseau. 2007. "Why Did Medicaid Spending Decline in 2006?" Kaiser Commission on Medicaid and the Uninsured (October). Available at: http://www.kff.org/medicaid/upload/7697.pdf (accessed May 9, 2008).

Hotz, V. Joseph, and John Karl Scholz. 2003. "The Earned Income Tax Credit." In *Means-Tested Transfer Programs in the United States,* edited by Robert A. Moffitt. Chicago: University of Chicago Press.

Hubbard, R. Glenn, Jonathan Skinner, and Steven P. Zeldes. 1995. "Precautionary Saving and Social Insurance." *Journal of Political Economy* 103(April): 360–99.

Hurst, Erik, and James P. Ziliak. 2006. "Do Welfare Asset Limits Affect Household Saving? Evidence from Welfare Reform." *Journal of Human Resources* 41(1): 46–71.

Meyer, Bruce D., and Dan T. Rosenbaum. 2001. "Welfare, the Earned Income Tax Credit, and the Labor Supply of Single Mothers." *Quarterly Journal of Economics* 116(3): 1063–1114.

Meyer, Bruce D., Wallace K. C. Mok, and James X. Sullivan. 2007. "The Underreporting of Transfers in Household Surveys: Comparisons to Administrative Aggregates." Unpublished paper, University of Chicago.

Moffitt, Robert A. 1992. "The Incentive Effects of the U.S. Welfare System." *Journal of Economic Literature* 30(1, March): 1–61.

———. 1998. "The Effect of Welfare on Marriage and Fertility." In *Welfare, the Family, and Reproductive Behavior,* edited by Robert A. Moffitt. Washington, D.C.: National Academies Press.

———. 2003a. "Introduction." In *Means-Tested Transfer Programs in the United States,* edited by Robert A. Moffitt. Chicago: University of Chicago Press.

———. 2003b. "The Temporary Assistance for Needy Families Program." In *Means-Tested Transfer Programs in the United States,* edited by Robert A. Moffitt. Chicago: University of Chicago Press.

———. 2007. "Four Decades of Antipoverty Policy: Past Developments and Future Directions." *Focus* 25(1, spring–summer): 39–44. Available at: http://www.irp.wisc.edu/publications/focus/pdfs/foc251f.pdf (accessed May 9, 2008).

Olsen, Edgar. 2003. "Housing Assistance." In *Means-Tested Transfer Programs in the United States,* edited by Robert A. Moffitt. Chicago: University of Chicago Press.

Rosenbaum, Dorothy. 2006. "The Food Stamp Program Is Growing to Meet Need." Center for Budget and Policy Priorities (July 12). Available at: http://www.cbpp.org/6-6-06fa.htm (accessed May 9, 2008).

Scholz, John Karl, and Kara Levine. 2002. "The Evolution of Income Support Policy in Recent Decades." In *Understanding Poverty,* edited by Sheldon H. Danziger and Robert Haveman. New York and Cambridge, Mass.: Russell Sage Foundation and Harvard University Press.

Smeeding, Timothy M. 1982. "Alternative Methods of Valuing Selected In-Kind Transfer Benefits and Measuring Their Effect on Poverty." Technical paper 50. Washington: U.S. Census Bureau (March).

———. 2008. "Poverty, Work, and Policy: The United States in Comparative Perspective." In *Social Stratification: Class, Race, and Gender in Sociological Perspective,* 3rd ed., edited by David Grusky. Boulder, Colo.: Westview Press.

U.S. Bureau of the Census. Various years. Survey of Income and Program Participation. Washington: U.S. Bureau of the Census. Available at: http://www.census.gov/sipp.

Ziliak, James P. 2005. "Understanding Poverty Rates and Gaps: Concepts, Trends, and Challenges." *Foundations and Trends in Microeconomics* 1(3): 127–99.

———. 2008. "Filling the Poverty Gap, Then and Now." *Frontiers in Family Economics* 1: 39–114.

Chapter 9

The Role of Family Policies in Antipoverty Policy

Jane Waldfogel

F amilies are changing. In 1975 two-thirds of American children had a stay-at-home parent. Today only about one-quarter of children do: 20 percent live with two parents only one of whom works, while 6 percent live with single or married parents who do not work (see table 9.1). Fully half live with two parents who both work, while one-quarter (24 percent) live with a single parent who works.[1]

Low-income families are changing too. Today most children in low-income families have working parents, like their more affluent peers. Only 38 percent of children in families with incomes below 200 percent of the poverty line have a stay-at-home parent; about one-quarter (23 percent) live with two working parents who both work, and 39 percent live with a single parent who works (see table 9.1). As we move further down the income distribution, the share of children with non-working parents rises. But even among families with incomes below 100 percent of the poverty line, only half have a parent who is not in the labor market; the other half are headed by a single working parent (40 percent of the total) or two working parents (10 percent) (see table 9.1).[2]

The challenges facing working families become even more difficult during times of financial crisis and economic downturn, such as the United States has experienced with the recession that began in 2008. In past recessions, traditional male bread-winner families could send their second earner into the labor market to compensate for the loss of earnings from the main breadwinner's job. But that strategy is not available to families today, since many already have all their available earners working to full capacity.

So, as families change, and in turbulent economic times, family policies need to change too. To prevent child poverty in a context where most low-income parents work but many have insufficient earnings requires, first of all, work-family policies to address conflicts between the demands of employment and the demands of caring for children, thus allowing parents to take up employment and work more hours. Preventing poverty also requires income support policies to help parents supplement low incomes and cover periods when they are out of work. And preventing

TABLE 9.1 / Distribution of Children's Living Arrangements, by Family Structure and Parental Employment

	All Children	Low-Income	Poverty
Two parents, both work	50%	23%	10%
Single parent who works	24	39	40
Two parents, only one works	20	23	20
Single parent who does not work	5	12	25
Two parents, neither works	1	3	5

Source: Author's compilation based on U.S. Bureau of the Census (2007).
Notes: "Low-income" includes children with family incomes below 200 percent of the poverty line; "poverty" includes children with family incomes below 100 percent of the poverty line.

poverty requires that policies address the disproportionate risk of poverty faced by families with only one parent.

This chapter considers the role that these various types of family policies might play in reducing poverty among families with children.[3] In each case, I review evidence on current policies both in the United States and overseas (where relevant) and draw lessons for future reforms.

The first section focuses on work-family policies that help parents address the conflict between the demands associated with working and those associated with caring for children. These work-family policies, which include family leave, other types of paid leave, flexible work arrangements, and child care, could reduce child poverty by helping parents take up employment and work more hours when employed.

Even with such policies, however, low earnings or periods out of employment will leave some families poor. Low-paid work tends to be less stable than higher-paid employment, and the low-skilled are the most affected during economic downturns. Also, a small but growing share of low-income families are disconnected from the labor market, often because the parent has a disability or other barrier to work. For this reason, the second section discusses several types of income support policies, including universal child allowances that raise incomes for all families with children and child-focused earnings supplements targeted to low-income families (such as the Earned Income Tax Credit [EITC]). Such policies provide a safety net for families who have low-paid work or experience periods out of work.

The third section considers policies that address the disproportionate risk of poverty facing single-parent families. Making ends meet in low-wage employment, while also taking care of children, is difficult even when there are two parents sharing the load. But today an increasing share of children are living with a single parent who must be both breadwinner and caregiver (see Cancian and Reed, this volume). Addressing child poverty, therefore, also means doing what we can to reduce the elevated risk of poverty faced by children in single-parent families or to discourage the formation of such families in the first place. Three policies that have received a great deal of attention in this regard are child support enforcement, pregnancy prevention, and marriage promotion.

WORK-FAMILY POLICIES

What work-family policies have in common is that they address the potential conflict faced by parents, in particular mothers, in meeting the demands of working and caring for their children. In theory, work-family policies can help parents stay employed more continuously and work more hours when employed, thus leading to higher earnings in the short term and to better earnings growth in the future. In practice, however, such policies are often lacking, particularly in the low-wage jobs that parents in low-income families are likely to hold.

Several recent ethnographic studies provide compelling evidence about how difficult it is for parents to manage family responsibilities while working low-wage jobs (see, for example, Heymann 2000; Shipler 2004; DeParle 2004). They also document how the challenges are compounded when a child or other family member has a disability or chronic health condition. The fact that many low-wage workers have a nonstandard or irregular work schedule can also wreak havoc with parents' ability to balance low-wage work and family life. Currently, about 15 percent of the U.S. workforce (approximately 15 million people) work evenings, nights, rotating shifts, or irregular schedules or hours (U.S. Bureau of Labor Statistics 2005). Those who are low-educated or low-skilled are more likely than others to work nonstandard hours, as are parents in married-couple families, in families with young children (under age six), and in single-mother families (Presser 2003).

Here I consider four major types of work-family policies: parental leave, other types of paid leave, flexible work arrangements, and child care. I review the evidence on the share of low-income workers with access to these policies as well as the evidence on how the availability of such policies affects parents' employment and earnings. I conclude with suggestions for how such policies might be strengthened to be more effective in reducing poverty among families with children, drawing on evidence from pioneering states as well as overseas.

A common theme in this section is that, although employers are a potentially important source of work-family benefits, such benefits remain limited and are unequally distributed, with the lowest-wage workers and part-time workers the least likely to have access to them (Bernstein and Kornbluh 2005; Heymann 2000; Shipler 2004; Waldfogel 2007).[4] This suggests that if low-income parents are to be covered, public policy will have to play a role, whether by mandating or providing incentives for employer policies or by providing such policies directly.

Parental Leave

Parental leave provides new mothers and fathers with a period of job-protected leave after the birth or adoption of a child. Typically, the leave is paid, since otherwise many parents would not be able to afford to take it. However, the United States is anomalous. Not only does the United States not have a national policy guaranteeing parental leave, but the limited policy it does have (the federal Family and Medical Leave Act, or FMLA, of 1993) provides only unpaid leave. Moreover, the FMLA

TABLE 9.2 / Workers Covered and Eligible Under FMLA

Less than a high school education	44.2%
High school graduate	57.1
Some college	62.2
College graduate	65.3
Graduate school	73.8

Source: Author's compilation based on Cantor et al. (2001).

covers only select workers (those who have worked at least 1,250 hours in the prior year and who work in firms with 50 or more employees), so that fewer than half of new working parents are actually covered and eligible (Cantor et al. 2001). Low-income workers are less likely to be covered and eligible under FMLA than their higher-income peers (see table 9.2).

A handful of states (California, Hawaii, New Jersey, New York, and Rhode Island) provide some limited access to paid maternity leave for new mothers under their Temporary Disability Insurance (TDI) programs (Brusentsev and Vroman 2007; Han, Ruhm, and Waldfogel 2007). And a few states have recently enacted paid parental leave or family leave programs that provide some paid leave to all new parents.[5] These programs are generally funded through mandatory employee contributions and tend to provide proportionally more generous benefits to lower-earning parents.

Employer provision of parental leave varies a good deal, and the lowest-paid workers are least likely to have access to job-protected leave and to paid leave (see, for example, Waldfogel 2007). Only 44 percent of high school dropouts are covered and eligible under the FMLA, as compared to 74 percent of those with graduate degrees (Cantor et al. 2001). Moreover, although many workers are able to use paid vacation time or other paid leave time, about one-third of all employees who take leave for family reasons receive no pay at all during their leave, and the share of workers who receive no pay during family or medical leave is much higher among the low-income than among those with higher incomes, with about 75 percent of those with annual incomes below $10,000 receiving no pay during their family or medical leave as compared to only about 20 percent of those with annual incomes of $75,000 or more (Cantor et al. 2001). In addition, there is disparity by gender, with women less likely to be covered than men because they are less likely to work full-time or to have sufficient tenure, and there is also disparity by race-ethnicity, with Hispanic workers in particular less likely to be covered because they tend to be employed in lower-paid jobs (Cantor et al. 2001).

The low level of leave coverage is regrettable, since the evidence shows that parents who have leave rights tend to use them and then return to work for their pre-birth employer, thus maintaining their employment and building their stock of firm-specific human capital (Han, Ruhm, and Waldfogel 2007). Parental leave also has been shown to improve maternal health (Chatterji and Markowitz 2005) and child health and development, reducing infant mortality and increasing the share of children who are taken for well baby visits and receive immunizations (Berger, Hill, and Waldfogel 2005; Ruhm 2000; Tanaka 2005).

What do other countries do? Our peer nations in the Organization for Economic Cooperation and Development (OECD) provide an average of eighteen months of job-protected parental leave (Waldfogel 2006b). Moreover, in every country in the OECD, with the exception of the United States and Australia, at least some portion of the leave is paid.[6] While it is often thought that generous leave policies are unique to the Nordic countries, this is not the case. Canada, our neighbor to the north, recently extended its period of paid parental leave to one year, while the United Kingdom has extended paid maternity leave to nine months and plans to extend it to one year. Another misconception is that these policies operate by requiring employers to pay employees' salaries while they are out on leave. For the most part, this is not the case. Instead, most OECD countries fund their leave benefits through social insurance programs, to which employees and employers contribute. In Canada, for instance, the federal system of paid parental leave is administered through the unemployment system.

Enacting a minimum period of paid and job-protected leave for all workers in the United States would ensure that parents are able to stay home for the first weeks and months of a child's life and that they have some income protection while they do so. Such programs can build on existing TDI programs (as California did), set up new social insurance funds (as Washington State did), or use the unemployment system (as Canada does). With regard to how long such leaves should last, a bare minimum would be eight to twelve weeks to allow time for new mothers to recover from childbirth and to allow time for both parents to bond with their new child. Longer leaves would produce additional benefits in terms of child health and development, but of course would also generate costs (Waldfogel 2006a). It is not clear what the optimal leave length would be in the U.S. context. Most of our peer nations are converging to at least a year of paid leave, and this seems sensible given the evidence about the potential adverse effects of full-time maternal employment in the first year of life (for a review, see Waldfogel 2006a). Some parents would prefer even longer periods of leave, such as those found in several Nordic and Continental European countries, but those risk harming parents' labor market position by removing them from the labor market for an extended period of time.[7] Moreover, the health and developmental benefits of having a parent home full-time after the first year of life are not clear. For those reasons, I think moving toward a period of a year's parental leave, paid through a social insurance mechanism, would be a reasonable target for U.S. policy.

Other Types of Paid Leave

The United States also stands out from other peer countries in not providing paid time off that parents can use to care for sick children or take them to doctor's appointments, recover from their own illnesses, take family vacations, or attend to other personal or family needs. As with parental leave, employer provision of other types of paid leave time is voluntary, and that provision varies widely. As shown in table 9.3, fully half of workers whose incomes are below the poverty line

TABLE 9.3   /   Workers with Paid Leave of Zero Weeks, One Week or Less, or More Than One Week

Income	Zero Weeks	One Week or Less	More Than One Week
Less Than 100 percent of the poverty line	54	16	30
100 to 200 percent of the poverty line	39	18	43
More Than 200 percent of the poverty line	16	8	76

Source: Author's compilation based on Ross Phillips (2004).

have no paid leave time at all. Of particular concern, given evidence that sick children recover more quickly and receive better follow-up care if a parent can stay home with them (Heymann 2000), a substantial share of workers have no paid sick leave, and again, the lowest-paid workers are most likely to lack such coverage. One recent study found that 58 percent of low-income working parents had no paid sick leave, in contrast to only 17 percent of higher-income working parents (Clemans-Cope et al. 2008).

In the absence of paid and job-protected leave, parents who need to take time off to be with a sick child or to meet other pressing family needs may have their pay docked, face disciplinary action, or lose their job. In the context of today's living arrangements, with few children having the luxury of a stay-at-home parent, providing some minimal amount of paid and job-protected sick leave is an essential component of antipoverty policy. Elsewhere, I have proposed guaranteeing all American workers the right to take at least two weeks off work each year with pay, and specifically guaranteeing that parents have the right to take that time to meet important family needs, including the need to care for a sick child (Waldfogel 2006a). This could be accomplished by enacting an employer mandate, as in legislation currently under discussion in Congress that would require employers to provide a minimum number of paid sick days per year for all full-time employees.[8]

Flexible Work Arrangements

The United States is renowned for the flexibility of its labor market, and a growing share of the labor force has access to flexible work hours or work locations. From 1992 to 2002, the proportion of U.S. workers with access to traditional flextime rose from 29 percent to 43 percent (Galinsky, Bond, and Hill 2004).[9] But low-income workers are still much less likely to have access to flextime than their higher-income peers (Bond and Galinsky 2006; Waldfogel 2007). Again, this is an area where the United States lags other countries. Sweden, for instance, has since 1978 had a right for parents to work shorter hours, and the European Union since 1997 has directed its member countries to strengthen the rights of parents to work part-time or flexible hours on a voluntary basis (Gornick and Meyers 2003; Gornick, Heron, and Eisenbrey 2007).

Flexible work hours are one of the most valued benefits among working parents and can be particularly important for low-income single parents who may be juggling work and caregiving responsibilities on their own (Christensen 2005). Such hours also seem to be relatively easy for employers to provide. The United Kingdom's experience with the "right to request" is instructive here (Waldfogel 2006a). In 2003, to comply with the European Union directive, the United Kingdom implemented a right for parents with young children to request part-time or flexible hours. Employers were not obligated to comply with these requests, but were required to consider them. In the first year alone, one million parents (one-quarter of those eligible) requested reduced or flexible hours, and nearly all these requests were granted. Several evaluations have found that employers are quite content with the new policy, which was to be extended to parents with older children in April 2009 (Walsh 2008), and many would support it being extended to other employees, not just parents. The positive experience of the United Kingdom suggests that we might be able to do something similar in the United States. As in the United Kingdom, it may not be a mandate on employers that is needed, but simply a message to both employers and employees that parents have the right to request part-time and flexible hours and have the right to have those requests seriously considered.

Child Care

In the United States, children do not start school until about age five, and even then, they are in school for only about six hours a day. This leaves a substantial amount of time when children need care if their parents are working, and the situation is made even more complicated for parents who work nonstandard or irregular hours (many of whom are low-income). But child care is more than just a work support—if it is of good quality, it can also play an important developmental role, particularly for low-income children (whose parents are least able to afford such care on their own).[10] This tension between availability, affordability, and quality creates numerous challenges for child care policy.

Unlike our peer nations in the OECD, the United States relies primarily on the private market for child care (Kamerman and Waldfogel 2005). Thus, although public funding for child care has been expanded over the past decade, it still remains fairly limited relative to the levels of support in other peer countries (Gornick and Meyers 2003; Waldfogel 2006a). Middle-income families with working parents receive some support through the federal child and dependent care tax credit as well as the dependent care assistance plan and, in many states, through supplemental state child care tax credits (Donahue and Campbell 2002; Smolensky and Gootman 2003). Low-income families typically do not benefit from these tax credits (as most are not refundable), though they may be eligible for assistance through child care subsidies or through Head Start. But neither of these programs is an entitlement program. Child care subsidies reach only about 15 percent of eligible families, while Head Start reaches only about half of eligible three- and four-year-olds—and the services provided are often only part-day and part-year, although this is rapidly changing (Smolensky and Gootman 2003; Meyers et al. 2004; Winston 2007; Boots, Macomber, and Danziger 2008).

Employer involvement remains relatively uncommon, with only about 15 percent of employers providing any type of assistance, and as with other employee benefits, this assistance is more likely to be provided to higher-income workers than to their low-income counterparts (Waldfogel 2007). Most of the assistance provided by employers takes the form of programs allowing employees to pay for child care with pretax dollars or programs providing information and referral; direct provision of child care slots or assistance paying for care is rare (Waldfogel 2007).

Given the limited public funding available to offset child care costs, the minimal role of employers, and the heavy reliance on the private market, low-income families end up paying more for child care as a share of their income than do more affluent families (Meyers et al. 2004). Their children receive care that is of lower quality, on average, and they are also less likely than more affluent children to be enrolled in school- or center-based programs (Bainbridge et al. 2005). Hispanic children and children of immigrants have lower levels of enrollment than other children, in large part because their families tend to have lower incomes, but black children, in contrast, are, if anything, more likely than comparable white children to be enrolled in school- or center-based care (Magnuson, Lahaie, and Waldfogel 2006; Magnuson and Waldfogel 2005; Meyers et al. 2004).

Proposals to improve child care supports for low-income families—so that they are able to work and to place their children in affordable, good-quality care while they do so—include several elements: guaranteeing child care subsidy assistance to families with incomes below 200 percent of the poverty line; instituting mechanisms to improve the quality of care, coordinate child care with other early childhood programs, and ensure that payment rates are high enough to cover quality care; and making the federal dependent care tax credit refundable (Greenberg 2007). Others have proposed expanding funding for Head Start so that this program can serve more low-income children (Ludwig and Phillips 2007).

There is also a good deal of interest at the state level in moving toward universal provision of prekindergarten for three- and four-year-olds (Kirp 2007). This is the model used in most OECD countries, where universal public provision of preschool in the year or two prior to school entry is the norm (Waldfogel 2006a). Proponents of universal provision argue that it is the only way to ensure strong public support for these programs and to ensure that lower-income children are not isolated in separate and poorer-quality programs. Universal provision is costly, however, and for this reason some have argued instead for programs that are more targeted to low-income children (see, for example, Duncan, Ludwig, and Magnuson 2007).

If the priority is to support parental employment, particularly in low-income families, then the most important reforms to pursue are those that would make good-quality child care more affordable for low-income families. However, child care also plays a developmental role, which has implications for efforts to reduce child poverty in the next generation. For this reason, expansions in programs such as prekindergarten and Head Start are also important. Business groups are increasingly coming to appreciate the role that stable, good-quality, and affordable child care can play not just in helping their employees get to work but also in preparing the next generation of workers, but given the limited role of employers in the child care sector to date (and the pressures of other costs such as health care and pensions), it is probably not realistic to expect them to do much more in the foreseeable future. It seems clear that government (at both the state and federal level) will have to play a larger role here.

INCOME SUPPORT POLICIES

In this section, I consider three types of income support policies: child allowances, which raise incomes for all families with children; child-focused earnings supplements, such as the EITC, which are targeted to low-income families with an employed parent; and other types of income support for families with children.

Universal Child Allowances

Universal child allowances (sometimes known as child benefits) are cash grants that go to all families with children and that increase with the number of children. They provide a basic income floor and also a cushion for families when parents are out of work. The closest thing the United States has to a universal child allowance is its child tax credit.[11] Although originally nonrefundable, the child tax credit is now partially refundable (so that some low-income families can receive a credit even if it exceeds what their tax liability would have been), and its amount was raised to $1,000 per child in 2003 (Carasso and Steuerle 2005). A low-income family with two children could therefore expect to receive up to $2,000 in child tax credits.

In contrast to the United States, most of our peers in the OECD have some form of universal child allowance (Waldfogel 2006b). For example, in Canada all families with children are entitled to a universal child benefit, with supplemental payments available for low-income families. In 2008 the basic child benefit for a family with two children was $2,813 per year, rising (through the national child benefit supplement) to a maximum of $6,630 per year for low-income families (Canada Revenue Agency 2008).[12] The United Kingdom also has a universal child benefit, supplemented for low-income families. In 2008 the basic child benefit for a family with two children was £1,630.20 per year, rising (through the child tax credit, which is means-tested but not conditioned on work) to a total of £6,345.20 per year for low-income families (HM Revenue and Customs 2008).[13]

Many countries provide a higher allowance to families with a new baby, through some form of maternity grant or baby allowance.[14] These grants can be particularly important for families in which the mother was not working prior to the birth and is therefore not eligible for maternity or parental leave benefits. In addition, two OECD countries provide "early childhood benefits"—supplemental cash grants (beyond the universal child allowance) for families with young children. In Finland the grant is available to all families with a child under the age of three who are not using publicly funded child care (Kamerman 1994; Salmi and Lammi-Taskula 1999), while in Norway the benefit is available to parents of all children age twelve to thirty-six months (Leira 1999). In the absence of a universal child allowance, several authors have called for an early childhood benefit for low-income families in the United States to help offset the costs of caring for infants and toddlers and to help reduce poverty among families with young children.[15] It is important to acknowledge, however, that because it would not be conditioned on work, such a program would probably reduce employment among low-income families with young children. For this reason, in the U.S. context, expansions in child-focused earnings supplements (discussed next) seem more feasible.

Child-Focused Earnings Supplements

Child-focused earnings supplements are used in many countries as a way to create incentives for low-income parents to work and to raise incomes for such families when parents do work. In the United States, the major child-focused earnings supplement is the Earned Income Tax Credit. Expanding the EITC was an important part of the agenda to "make work pay" during the U.S. welfare reforms of the 1990s (Ellwood 2000; Blank 2002). The EITC is now the nation's largest cash assistance program for low-income families (Hotz and Scholz 2003; Scholz, Moffitt, and Cowan, this volume), and it is estimated that this program moves more than 4 million people out of poverty each year, including more than 2 million children (Blumenthal, Erard, and Ho 2005). Robert Greenstein (2005) concludes that the EITC moves more children out of poverty than any other single program or category of programs.

The EITC has been criticized on the grounds that it provides a disincentive to marriage by providing higher benefits to most parents if they are not married (see, for example, Horn 1998; but see also Primus and Beeson 2002).[16] As David Ellwood (2000) has pointed out, however, the marriage effects are complex (see also Carasso and Steuerle 2005; Edin and Reed 2005). On the one hand, if both of the potential partners have labor market income (or both are eligible for significant credits from the EITC), then there can be a large marriage penalty (particularly if the two partners' earnings are relatively equal). On the other hand, because EITC benefits are very low for those without children, a single mother's eligibility for EITC could be a significant attraction for a potential male partner who is not employed or has uncertain employment prospects; moreover, if a woman has children and does not work and the man has low earnings, then there is an incentive to marry, since marriage would make the couple eligible for the EITC.

Perhaps because the marriage penalties (or subsidies) associated with the EITC are complex and vary across families, studies have generally found few strong effects of the EITC on family formation (see, for example, Baughman and Dickert-Conlin 2003; Dickert-Conlin and Houser 2002; Ellwood 2000; see also the review in Hotz and Scholz 2003). Nevertheless, to the extent that marriage penalties in the

EITC do exist for some families and influence some recipients' behavior, they are counterproductive and should be corrected. Doing so, however, is not simple. Some of the problems with marriage disincentives are inherent in the basic design of the U.S. system of taxation (with its progressive tax rates and joint taxation for married couples). Perhaps the United States could learn some lessons from other countries (for instance, moving toward more individual taxation or toward some universal child benefits).

Recent reforms to the EITC have reduced the marriage penalties for low-income families (those with incomes below 200 percent of the poverty line), but as Gordon Berlin (2007) has pointed out, penalties remain for families with incomes between $20,000 and $30,000 per year. Berlin has proposed a new individual EITC (for low-wage, prime-age individuals who work full-time) that those who marry would still be able to claim even if their spouse was receiving the usual EITC. This proposal is marriage-neutral because the family would receive the same amount of EITC whether the parents were married, cohabiting, or living separately. However, unless benefits for other recipients were cut back to fund it—which would probably not be desirable—it would also be costly. Adam Carasso and Eugene Steuerle (2005) discuss other possible reforms to address the marriage penalties in the EITC (and other tax and transfer programs), including a maximum tax rate for low- and moderate-income families, individual wage subsidies (similar to what Berlin has proposed), universal child benefits, and individual (rather than joint) filing for married couples.[17]

Other Types of Income Support

Although it is beyond the scope of this chapter to provide an extensive discussion of the range of other types of income supports (see Scholz, Moffitt, and Cowan, this volume), it is important to note the role played by policies such as cash assistance, food assistance, TDI, and unemployment compensation, which supplement low incomes (associated with low earnings or hours) or provide replacement income during periods when parents are out of work. With welfare reform, the number of families receiving benefits through the major federal cash assistance program (formerly Aid to Families with Dependent Children [AFDC], now Temporary Assistance for Needy Families [TANF]) has fallen sharply, but low-income families still rely heavily on the other major income support programs, in particular, food stamps, which serves 22 million low-income people each month, about half of whom are children (U.S. Department of Agriculture 2008).[18] One challenge is that a much larger share of recipients in such programs are working now than in the past, and thus program rules and procedures (in particular, rules regarding application and reporting requirements and office opening hours) may have to change to enable them to access benefits without facing undue barriers (see also the discussion in Bane, this volume).

Rebecca Blank (2007) has documented that an increasing share of low-income mothers are disconnected from the labor market and traditional cash welfare programs (see also Acs and Loprest 2004; Blank, this volume; Turner, Danziger, and Seefeldt 2006; Zedlewski and Nelson 2003). She estimates that this group makes up 20 to 25 percent of low-income single mothers (that is, those with incomes below 200 percent of the poverty line). There is also a smaller group that is disconnected from the labor market and relies on welfare benefits for extended periods of time. What both groups have in common is that they face serious barriers to employment and yet do not qualify for disability programs such as Supplemental Security Income (SSI). Blank estimates that nearly 4 million children live with such mothers. She has called for a temporary and partial work waiver program that would combine temporary income support with active case management to help assess and address work barriers and other family needs, while also ensuring that children in these families have access to resources that provide them at least a minimum standard of living.

POLICIES TO REDUCE SINGLE-PARENT POVERTY

In this section, I discuss policies that have the potential to reduce poverty in single-parent families by raising the incomes of children living with single parents or by discouraging the formation of such families in the first place. The policies examined include: child support enforcement, pregnancy prevention, and marriage promotion. Such policies have drawn increasing attention in social policy discourse in the United States but, with the exception of child support enforcement, have received little attention in other countries. A common theme in this section is that, as others have emphasized, such policies may be useful but should not be seen as a cure-all for child poverty or as a replacement for other components of the safety net, since it is unlikely that, on their own, they could fully eliminate single-parent family poverty (see, for example, McLanahan, Donahue, and Haskins 2005).

Child Support Enforcement

Child support enforcement (CSE) policies have been successively strengthened over the past thirty years at both the federal and state levels (Garfinkel et al. 1998). In theory, tighter enforcement of child support should reduce family poverty by raising incomes for children in single-parent families. CSE might also reduce family poverty by discouraging the formation of single-parent families. What do we know about how successful such policies have been, and what does the research to date tell us about the ways in which such policies could be strengthened if they are to be more effective in reducing poverty?

As several authors have detailed (see, for example, Freeman and Waldfogel 2001; Huang, Garfinkel, and Waldfogel 2004), getting more income from absent fathers is a multistep process. Before any money reaches the child, the father's paternity must be established, a child support order must be entered, the father must be located, and the money must be collected. As CSE programs have been strengthened, agencies have achieved improvements in each of these steps. Yet the amount of money being transferred to children from their absent fathers remains disappointingly low. The reason for this is that, as Ronald Mincy and Elaine Sorenson (1998) famously pointed out, there are both "deadbeats and turnips" in child support. Deadbeats have the ability to pay but try to evade their obligation, unless forced to do so. But turnips do not have much ability to pay, no matter how hard they are squeezed. The implication is that if CSE programs are to get more money from low-income noncustodial fathers, they must not only pursue the four-step child support process but also take steps to raise the employment and earnings of low-income men. One promising policy in this regard is an earnings subsidy or tax credit for noncustodial fathers (Primus 2006). Another promising direction is to develop and expand programs to raise the skills of low-income men (Haskins 2006; see also Mincy 2006; Holzer, this volume).

The other way in which CSE programs might reduce poverty is by discouraging the formation of single-parent families in the first place. In theory, by raising the costs to men of having an out-of-wedlock birth and by sending a strong message about the responsibility of fathers to support their children, strong CSE programs should deter such births. However, the incentives for women should work in the opposite direction, if tougher CSE reduces the costs to women of having an out-of-wedlock birth. Thus, the effects of CSE on family formation are theoretically ambiguous (Nixon 1997; Willis 1999). Which effect dominates? In recent years, a great deal of attention has been devoted to this question. The evidence indicates that tougher CSE does seem to be associated with reductions in single parenthood (see, for example, Acs and Nelson 2004; Aizer and McLanahan 2006; Garfinkel et al. 2003; Huang 2002; Plotnick et al. 2004), suggesting that the deterrent effect for men is somewhat stronger than the incentive effect for women. Thus, as Irwin Garfinkel and his colleagues have pointed out, tougher CSE is a potential "win-win"—reducing poverty by raising the incomes of single-mother families and by discouraging the formation of such families (see, for example, Garfinkel et al. 1998).

It is also important to note that the poverty-reducing role of CSE should be larger now than in the past, when a substantial share of child support receipts for low-income families went to reimburse welfare costs. With fewer families on welfare, and for shorter lengths of time, more single-parent families are directly benefiting from the child support payments that absent fathers are making. Maria Cancian, Daniel Meyer, and Emma Caspar (2008) find, for example, that after reforms in Wisconsin that allowed mothers to keep all of their child support payments, paternity establishment occurred more quickly, fathers were more likely to pay support, and mothers and children received more support. Such outcomes signal improvement, but much more could be done to raise the share of payments that actually go to families. And it is still the case that to the extent that absent fathers' earnings are low, there is a limit to the role such payments can play in the lives of their children.[19]

Pregnancy Prevention

More than one-third of U.S. births each year occur to unmarried women (Martin et al. 2007), and such families have much higher poverty rates than married-couple families (U.S. Bureau of the Census 2007). Although it cannot be assumed that marriage would fully eliminate the excess risk of poverty for these families, there is nevertheless a great deal of interest in programs that would prevent pregnancies among unmarried women, and particularly among young unmarried women (see, for example, Thomas and Sawhill 2005). Some programs focus on encouraging young people to delay the onset of sexual activity or to abstain from sex until marriage, while others focus on encouraging the use of contraception among those who are sexually active.

Although these approaches are often viewed as competing, many analysts now believe that the most effective approach is likely to be one that combines them (see, for example, Amato and Maynard 2007). A more critical question is which specific types of programs are effective at preventing pregnancy. The evidence base in the pregnancy prevention area is not strong, and more work needs to be done to establish which programs are the most effective. It is likely that the answer to this question will depend on the age group targeted and possibly on other factors as well.

Marriage Promotion

Over the past decade, state and federal policymakers have directed increased attention to the potential role of marriage promotion policies in reducing poverty among families with children. Prior to 1996, when federal welfare reform legislation allowed states to use a portion of their block grant to promote marriage, the term "marriage promotion" rarely appeared on the national scene, and even under welfare reform there were no federal funds specifically allocated to it. This changed under the George W. Bush administration, which in 2001 began the Healthy Marriage Initiative and in 2004 proposed spending $1.5 billion over the next five years on marriage promotion programs (Dion 2005; McLanahan, Donahue, and Haskins 2005). Marriage promotion programs take several different forms, but most provide education for couples aimed at promoting marriage or preventing divorce.

Although these programs have expanded rapidly, it is still too soon to tell how effectively they promote marriage (or prevent marital breakup) among low-income parents. Until very recently, such programs have served mainly middle-class parents; the evidence base on their effects on low-income parents, who often face different relationship issues, is still very thin (Dion 2005). Experts differ on how large they expect the effects of such programs to be. Some analysts project fairly large impacts on reducing divorce (see, for example, Amato and Maynard 2007), while others argue that many factors influence divorce and marriage and such programs are likely to have only a limited impact (see, for example, Cherlin 2005; Thomas and Sawhill 2005). Firmer conclusions must await the results of several large-scale randomized trials (for a description of these studies, see Dion 2005).

While awaiting evidence on the efficacy of marriage promotion programs, we can, however, consider the underlying assumption behind these programs, which is that low-income families with children would be financially better off if their parents were married (see, for example, Amato and Maynard 2007; Scafidi 2008; Thomas and Sawhill 2005; but see also Stevenson and Wolfers 2008). While at first glance this proposition seems obvious (since having the father in the household would contribute something to the family's overall economic well-being and would also allow the family to benefit from economies of scale), it is actually not that straightforward. To determine their potential contribution, we need to know the characteristics of the unmarried fathers. To understand the implications for family poverty levels, we also need to know the counterfactual—that is, what the children's living arrangements would be if the parents were not married.

The best available evidence on the characteristics and capabilities of unmarried fathers comes from the Fragile Families and Child Well-Being Study, which interviewed mothers and fathers in nearly five thousand families who had a new birth in urban areas in the late 1990s. The data suggest just how disadvantaged unmarried fathers are, even relative to married fathers in the same urban areas (see McLanahan 2003, 2007, 2009). In terms of education, nearly 60 percent of married fathers have at least some college, 20 percent have a high school education, and only about 20 percent have not completed high school; in contrast, roughly 40 percent of unmarried fathers have not completed high school, 40 percent have only a high school education, and fewer than 20 percent have any college. Unmarried fathers are younger than married fathers but are more likely to have children from previous relationships. In addition, more than one-third of unmarried fathers have been incarcerated, as compared to only one in twenty married fathers. Unmarried fathers are also much more likely to have health, mental health, and substance abuse problems. Not surprisingly, given their many disadvantages, unmarried fathers earn on average only half as much as married fathers. Although there is some evidence that these men would earn more if they were married (for a review, see Lerman 2002), the evidence also suggests that a good part of the reason men who are married earn more is that they tend to be positively selected (see, for example, Mincy, Hill, and Sinkewicz 2008). Thus, even if these fathers (or other unmarried men) were to marry the mothers, family incomes would not rise to the average level of family income in married-couple families.[20]

Another factor to consider is that in only a minority of single-mother families are the fathers truly absent. Instead, a sizable share of low-income single-mother families already have a cohabiting or visiting adult male who is probably already contributing something financially to the household. In the Fragile Families survey, fully half of unmarried parents were cohabiting at the time of the birth, and another one-third were in a visiting relationship where the father spent some time at the mother's home (McLanahan 2003). It is not clear how much better off such families would be if the parents were married instead of cohabiting or visiting. Although it is true that cohabiting couples tend to have lower incomes than married couples and are less likely to share their income or accumulate wealth together (Amato and Maynard 2007; Thomas and Sawhill 2005), research has not established that these differences reflect causal effects of cohabitation. The evidence from Fragile Families suggests that preexisting differences between men who cohabit and those who marry are large and likely to play an important role in explaining the lower incomes of cohabiting families (see, for example, McLanahan 2003, 2007, 2009). Thus, even if these couples married, their incomes (and income-sharing) might not rise substantially. For those families where the father is just visiting, the income gains to marriage are likely to be greater, as they would benefit from greater economies of scale if the father joined the household (although it is unknown how much spouses would share incomes in such families). It must also be noted, however, that visiting fathers are the ones whose relationships with mothers are most tenuous and least likely to result in marriage.

Thus, if marriage promotion policies are to reduce poverty among low-income families, they will have to do more than just encourage marriage—they will also have to do something to raise the employment and earnings of the fathers in these families. As discussed earlier, some promising options in this regard include providing an EITC or other form of earnings supplement for noncustodial fathers or for single men, ensuring that the structure of the EITC does not penalize cohabiting or married fathers, and investing in programs to improve the employment and earnings prospects of disadvantaged young men (see Holzer, this volume).

Policies to improve the employment and earnings prospects of disadvantaged young women may play a role here too, both in encouraging them to delay pregnancy and in providing them with incomes sufficient to support a family. It is also possible that higher incomes for women could promote marriage among low-income couples by making them more financially secure and more confident about their ability to enter into marriage (see, for example, Edin and Reed 2005).

CONCLUSION

Changes in gender roles, alongside changes in family structure, mean that more children than ever before are living with working parents. Given these changes, work-family policies that address conflicts between employment and caregiving and allow parents to work more hours and gain higher earnings will be increasingly important in the prevention of child poverty. There is also a continued need for other types of income support policies that supplement low earnings or cover periods of no earnings. And there is a good deal of interest in policies to reduce the risk of poverty in single-parent families, whether by raising the income of such families through tougher child support enforcement or by discouraging their formation in the first place.

What can we conclude about the future contribution of these policies and the role that public policy should play? In the work-family arena, it is clear that, with more parents working and with cutbacks in cash welfare for nonworking families, work-supporting benefits such as paid parental leave, other types of paid leave, flexible work arrangements, and child care supports will be increasingly important to family economic security. It is also clear that voluntary employer provision will not address the low levels of benefits and inequality in access. There is there-fore a role for public policies that mandate some employer benefits and provide other work-supporting benefits directly.

It is apparent that the role of income support policies continues to be important. The fact that more low-income parents are working does not eliminate the need for this part of the safety net. It does require that we review how these supports are administered and make sure that they can be accessed by people who are working. We also need to address the problem of income support for parents who cannot work, whether temporarily or in the long term.

Finally, while policies to reduce poverty in single-parent families or to dis-courage the formation of these families certainly have a role to play, it is impor-tant to reiterate that such policies cannot be expected to eliminate single-parent poverty and should therefore not be seen as replacements for the other types of antipoverty strategies discussed in this chapter and elsewhere in this volume (see, for example, Cherlin 2005; McLanahan, Donahue, and Haskins 2005; Thomas and Sawhill 2005).

It is also apparent that the major stumbling block to family economic security for many low-income families is not the absence of the father but rather the father's low skills, employment, and earnings. This suggests that policies such as tougher CSE and marriage promotion can play only a limited role in reducing child poverty unless they are paired with programs to address the low levels of employment and earnings among low-skilled men. It is perhaps ironic that having moved so far away from the male breadwinner model, we find ourselves coming back to the impor-tance of men's earnings. But the truth is that it is very difficult now to raise children on a single paycheck, whether that check is a man's or a woman's. Thus, we need to put priority on policies that help families have all their adults working in the labor market and earning a decent wage, alongside policies that provide support to families that are not able to do so.

The world financial crisis and economic downturn in 2008 make this all the more urgent. Accordingly, in addition to the policies highlighted in Rebecca Blank's chapter in this volume (that is, maintaining a strong economy, a reasonable min-imum wage, and an adequate EITC for all low-income workers, as well as increas-ing skill levels), I would stress the following four policy reforms: (1) guaranteeing all American workers the right to at least eight to twelve weeks of paid parental leave after the birth or adoption of a new child (funded through a social insurance mechanism), at least two weeks paid leave time for family illness or other family responsibilities (paid by employers), and the right to request part-time or flexible hours; (2) making child care more affordable for low-income families by guaran-teeing subsidies to families with incomes up to 200 percent of poverty, making the federal dependent care tax credit fully refundable, and expanding funding for high-quality early education programs such as Head Start and universal prekinder-garten; (3) raising the guaranteed level of income support for low-income families by making the child tax credit more generous and fully refundable; and (4) reform-ing child support policies to raise the share of payments that go directly to fami-lies. The increased investments included in the February 2009 economic stimulus bill for Early Head Start, Head Start, the Child Care Development Block Grant (CCDBG), and the child tax credit are steps in the right direction.

NOTES

1. The source for these statistics is Waldfogel (2006a) and U.S. Bureau of the Census (2007).
2. The source for these statistics is U.S. Bureau of the Census (2007).
3. Thus, I do not consider policies that address poverty regardless of the presence of children (such as the minimum wage) or policies targeted to those with responsibility for caring for adults (such as policies regarding elder care or care for a disabled spouse). I also do not discuss health insurance policies, even though these are a key part of the social safety net for families with children; these policies are covered in detail by Katherine Swartz (this volume).
4. There are also disparities by gender, race, and ethnicity, as might be expected given that female workers are particularly likely to be found in part-time jobs and that racial and ethnic minority workers are more likely to be found in low-wage jobs.
5. California was the first state to pass paid family leave; its legislation was enacted in 2002 and came into effect in 2004. Washington State enacted similar legislation in 2007 (to take effect in 2009), followed by New Jersey in 2008. At the time of this writing (spring 2008), legislation was pending in several other states.
6. In late 2008, Australia's government was considering a plan to implement eighteen weeks of paid maternity leave.
7. Being out of the labor market for extended periods harms employees by reducing their work experience as well as their firm-specific tenure. Long absences also might lead employers to view women (who are most likely to take leave) as less stable employees and therefore to refrain from hiring them or to hire them only in particular jobs or sectors.
8. This policy could be accomplished through a social insurance mechanism, as is currently the case with unemployment and disability insurance, but this seems less practical in the U.S. context.
9. "Traditional flextime" refers to an employee's ability to obtain approval to switch to an alternative work schedule (involving a different starting or ending time, or sometimes a compressed work week) on a permanent basis. This contrasts with "daily flextime," in which employees can alter their hours on a day-to-day or as-needed basis. Many fewer employees have daily flextime than have traditional flextime, and access is uneven, with 12 percent of low-wage employees reporting access to daily flextime versus 26 percent of mid- and high-wage employees (Bond and Galinsky 2006).
10. The developmental role of child care was recognized by Barack Obama when, as president-elect, he pledged to invest an additional $10 billion in early education (Dillon 2008).
11. Enacted as part of the Taxpayer Relief Act of 1997, the federal child tax credit provides a modest credit to taxpayers for each qualifying child in the household. Its initial level in 1998 was $400 per child (see Tax Policy Center 2008).

12. These figures reflect child benefit only and do not take into account the other forms of income support and child care support available to low-income families in Canada.
13. These figures reflect child benefit and child tax credit only and do not take into account the Working Tax Credit (WTC) or other forms of income support and child care support available to low-income families in the United Kingdom.
14. In the United Kingdom, for instance, families with a child under age one receive double the family component of the child tax credit (worth an extra £545 in 2008) along with various types of maternity benefits (HM Revenue and Customs 2008).
15. See, for example, Duncan and Magnuson (2003) and Waldfogel (2006a), who propose a benefit of $2,400 per year per child.
16. The EITC is not the only program to have marriage penalties, but the EITC penalties have received more attention than those in other programs. For a detailed discussion of the penalties and subsidies inherent in other tax and transfer programs, see Acs and Maag (2005) and Carasso and Steuerle (2005).
17. See also Weinstein (1999), who reports on a proposal by the economist Alan Auerbach to simply eliminate the phaseouts and to pay for this by raising the statutory tax rate on wealthier families.
18. This is not to say that TANF is unimportant for working parents. TANF reduces family economic insecurity for working parents by providing support after the birth of a new child and during periods of non-employment. In addition, TANF is now an important source of child care funding as well as a source of funding for other types of family support programs.
19. One possible remedy for the low level of payments from absent fathers is to institute a government-guaranteed minimum payment for single-parent families, as some OECD countries do. However, such a policy runs the risk of providing an incentive for single parenthood (since couples would not receive such payments). For this reason, I prefer approaches (such as those discussed in the prior section) that are conditioned on the presence of children or low income, but not family structure.
20. This is confirmed by several studies that have conducted simulations to project what the incomes of unmarried mothers would be if they married the men available to them (for a review, see Thomas and Sawhill 2005).

REFERENCES

Acs, Gregory, and Pamela Loprest. 2004. "Leaving Welfare: Employment and Well-Being of Families That Left Welfare in the Post-Entitlement Era." Kalamazoo, Mich.: W. E. Upjohn Institute for Employment Research.

Acs, Gregory, and Elaine Maag. 2005. "Irreconcilable Differences? The Conflict Between Marriage Promotion Initiatives for Cohabiting Couples with Children and Marriage Penalties in Tax and Transfer Programs." Washington, D.C.: Urban Institute. Available at: http://www.urban.org/UploadedPDF/311162_B-66.pdf.

Acs, Gregory, and Sandi Nelson. 2004. "Changes in Living Arrangements during the Late 1990s: Do Welfare Policies Matter?" *Journal of Policy Analysis and Management* 23(2): 273–90.

Aizer, Anna, and Sara McLanahan. 2006. "The Impact of Child Support Enforcement on Fertility, Parental Involvement, and Child Well-Being." *Journal of Human Resources* 41(1): 28–48.

Amato, Paul R., and Rebecca A. Maynard. 2007. "Decreasing Nonmarital Births and Strengthening Marriage to Reduce Poverty." *The Future of Children* 17(2): 117–41.

Bainbridge, Jay, Marcia Meyers, Sakiko Tanaka, and Jane Waldfogel. 2005. "Who Gets an Early Education? Family Income and the Gaps in Enrollment of Three- to Five-Year-Olds from 1968 to 2000." *Social Science Quarterly* 86(4): 724–45.

Baughman, Reagan, and Stacy Dickert-Conlin. 2003. "Did Expanding the EITC Promote Motherhood?" *American Economic Review Papers and Proceedings* 93(2): 247–51.

Berger, Lawrence, Jennifer Hill, and Jane Waldfogel. 2005. "Maternity Leave, Early Maternal Employment, and Child Health and Development in the U.S." *Economic Journal* 115(February): F29–47.

Berlin, Gordon. 2007. "Rewarding the Work of Individuals: A Counterintuitive Approach to Reducing Poverty and Strengthening Families." *The Future of Children* 17(2): 17–41.

Bernstein, Jared, and Karen Kornbluh. 2005. "Running Faster to Stay in Place: The Growth of Family Work Hours and Incomes." Washington, D.C.: New America Foundation. Available at: http://www.newamerica.net/files/archive/Doc_File_2437_1.pdf.

Blank, Rebecca M. 2002. "Evaluating Welfare Reform in the United States." *Journal of Economic Literature* 40(December): 1105–66.

———. 2007. "Improving the Safety Net for Single Mothers Who Face Serious Barriers to Work." *The Future of Children* 17(2): 183–97.

Blumenthal, Marsha, Brian Erard, and Chih-Chin Ho. 2005. "Participation and Compliance with the Earned Income Tax Credit." *National Tax Journal* 58(2): 189–213.

Bond, James T., and Ellen Galinsky. 2006. "What Workplace Flexibility Is Available to Entry-Level, Hourly Employees?" New York: Families and Work Institute. Available at: http://fourhourworkweek.com/reports/fw-workplaceflex.pdf.

Boots, Shelley Waters, Jennifer Macomber, and Anna Danziger. 2008. "Family Security: Supporting Parents' Employment and Children's Development." In *A New Safety Net for Low-Income Families,* edited by Sheila Zedlewski, Ajay Chaudry, and Margaret Simms. Washington, D.C.: Urban Institute.

Brusentsev, Vera, and Wayne Vroman. 2007. "Compensating for Birth and Adoption." Washington: Urban Institute.

Canada Revenue Agency. 2008. "Canada Child Benefits." Available at: http://www.cra-arc.gc.ca/E/pub/tg/t4114/t4114-08e.pdf (accessed July 8, 2008).

Cancian, Maria, Daniel R. Meyer, and Emma Caspar. 2008. "Welfare and Child Support: Complements, Not Substitutes." *Journal of Policy Analysis and Management* 27(2): 354–75.

Cantor, David, Jane Waldfogel, Jeffrey Kerwin, Mareena McKinley Wright, Kerry Levin, John Rauch, Tracey Hagerty, and Martha Stapleton Kudela. 2001. *Balancing the Needs of Families and Employers: Family and Medical Leave Surveys.* Rockville, Md.: Westat.

Carasso, Adam, and C. Eugene Steuerle. 2005. "The Hefty Penalty on Marriage Facing Many Households with Children." *The Future of Children* 15(2): 157–75.

Chatterji, Pinka, and Sara Markowitz. 2005. "Does the Length of Maternity Leave Affect Maternal Health?" *Southern Economic Journal* 72(1): 16–41.

Cherlin, Andrew J. 2005. "American Marriage in the Early Twenty-First Century." *The Future of Children* 15(2): 33–56.

Christensen, Kathleen. 2005. "Achieving Work-Life Balance: Strategies for Dual-Earner Families." In *Being Together, Working Apart,* edited by Barbara Schneider and Linda Waite. Cambridge: Cambridge University Press.

Clemans-Cope, Lisa, Cynthia Perry, Genevieve Kenney, Jennifer E. Pelletier, and Matthew Pantell. 2008. "Access to and Use of Paid Sick Leave Among Low-Income Families With Children." *Pediatrics* 122(2): 480–86.

DeParle, Jason. 2004. *American Dream: Three Women, Ten Kids, and a Nation's Drive to End Welfare.* New York: Penguin Books.

Dickert-Conlin, Stacy, and Scott Houser. 2002. "EITC and Marriage." *National Tax Journal* 55(1): 25–39.

Dillon, Sam. 2008. "Obama's $10 Billion Promise Stirs Hope in Early Education." *New York Times,* December 17.

Dion, M. Robin. 2005. "Healthy Marriage Programs: Learning What Works." *The Future of Children* 15(2): 139–56.

Donahue, Elisabeth Hirschhorn, and Nancy Duff Campbell. 2002. "Making Care Less Taxing: Improving State Child and Dependent Care Tax Provisions." Washington, D.C.: National Women's Law Center.

Duncan, Greg J., Jens Ludwig, and Katherine A. Magnuson. 2007. "Reducing Poverty Through Preschool Interventions." *The Future of Children* 17(2): 143–60.

Duncan, Greg J., and Katherine A. Magnuson. 2003. "Promoting the Healthy Development of Young Children." In *One Percent for the Kids: New Policies, Brighter Futures for America's Children,* edited by Isabel Sawhill. Washington, D.C.: Brookings Institution Press.

Edin, Kathryn, and Joanna M. Reed. 2005. "Why Don't They Just Get Married? Barriers to Marriage Among the Disadvantaged." *The Future of Children* 15(2): 117–37.

Ellwood, David T. 2000. "The Impact of the Earned Income Tax Credit and Social Policy Reforms on Work, Marriage, and Living Arrangements." *National Tax Journal* 53(4): 1065–1106.

Freeman, Richard, and Jane Waldfogel. 2001. "Dunning Delinquent Dads: The Effects of Child Support Enforcement Policy on Child Support Receipt by Never Married Women." *Journal of Human Resources* 36(2): 207–225.

Galinsky, Ellen, James T. Bond, and E. Jeffrey Hill. 2004. "When Work Works: A Status Report on Workplace Flexibility." New York: Families and Work Institute. Available at: http://familiesandwork.org/3w/research/downloads/status.pdf (accessed January 11, 2005).

Garfinkel, Irwin, Chien Chung Huang, Sara McLanahan, and Daniel Gaylin. 2003. "Will Child Support Enforcement Reduce Nonmarital Childbearing?" *Journal of Population Economics* 16(1): 55–70.

Garfinkel, Irwin, Sara McLanahan, Daniel Meyer, and Judith Seltzer, eds. 1998. *Fathers Under Fire: The Revolution in Child Support Enforcement.* New York: Russell Sage Foundation.

Gornick, Janet C., Alexandra Heron, and Ross Eisenbrey. 2007. "The Work-Family Balance: An Analysis of European, Japanese, and U.S. Work-Time Policies." EPI working paper no. 189. Washington, D.C.: Economic Policy Institute.

Gornick, Janet C., and Marcia K. Meyers. 2003. *Families That Work: Policies for Reconciling Parenthood and Employment.* New York: Russell Sage Foundation.

Greenberg, Mark. 2007. "Next Steps for Federal Child Care Policy." *The Future of Children* 17(2): 73–96.

Greenstein, Robert. 2005. "The Earned Income Tax Credit: Boosting Employment and Aiding the Poor." Washington, D.C.: Center on Budget and Policy Priorities. Available at: http://www.stateeitc.com/research/CBPP_EITC_071905_Report.pdf (accessed August 17, 2007).

Han, Wen-Jui, Christopher Ruhm, and Jane Waldfogel. 2007. "Parental Leave Policies and Parents' Employment and Leave-Taking." Working paper 13697. Cambridge, Mass.: National Bureau of Economic Research.

Haskins, Ron. 2006. "Poor Fathers and Public Policy: What Is to Be Done?" In *Black Males Left Behind,* edited by Ronald B. Mincy. Washington, D.C.: Urban Institute.

Heymann, Jody. 2000. *The Widening Gap: Why America's Working Families Are in Jeopardy and What Can Be Done About It.* New York: Basic Books.

HM Revenue and Customs. 2008. "Child Benefit." Available at: http://www.hmrc.gov.uk/childbenefit/index.htm (accessed July 8, 2008).

Horn, Wade. 1998. "Government Punishes Marriage, Pushes Cohabitation." *Washington Times,* October 20.

Hotz, V. Joseph, and John Karl Scholz. 2003. "The Earned Income Tax Credit." In *Means-Tested Transfer Programs in the United States,* edited by Robert A. Moffitt. Chicago: University of Chicago Press.

Huang, Chien Chung. 2002. "The Impact of Child Support Enforcement on Nonmarital and Marital Births: Does It Differ by Race and Age Groups?" *Social Service Review* 76(2): 275–301.

Huang, Chien Chung, Irwin Garfinkel, and Jane Waldfogel. 2004. "Child Support and Welfare Caseloads." *Journal of Human Resources* 39(1): 108–134.

Kamerman, Sheila B. 1994. "Family Policy and the Under-Threes: Money, Services, and Time in a Policy Package." *International Social Security Review* 47(3–4): 31–43.

Kamerman, Sheila B., and Jane Waldfogel. 2005. "Market and Nonmarket Institutions in Early Childhood Education and Care." In *Market and Nonmarket Institutions,* edited by Richard Nelson. New York: Russell Sage Foundation.

Kirp, David. 2007. *The Sandbox Investment: The Preschool Movement and Kids First Politics.* Cambridge, Mass.: Harvard University Press.

Leira, Arnlaug. 1999. "Cash-for-Child Care and Daddy Leave." In *Parental Leave: Progress or Pitfall? Research and Policy Issues in Europe,* edited by Peter Moss and Fred Deven. Brussels: CBGS Publications.

Lerman, Robert I. 2002. "Marriage and the Economic Well-Being of Families with Children: A Review of the Literature." Washington, D.C.: Urban Institute.

Ludwig, Jens, and Deborah Phillips. 2007. "The Benefits and Costs of Head Start." *Social Policy Report* 21(3): 1–18.

Magnuson, Katherine, Claudia Lahaie, and Jane Waldfogel. 2006. "Preschool and School Readiness of Children of Immigrants." *Social Science Quarterly* 87(S1): 1241–62.

Magnuson, Katherine, and Jane Waldfogel. 2005. "Child Care, Early Education, and Racial-Ethnic Test Score Gaps at the Beginning of School." *The Future of Children* 15(1): 169–96.

Martin, Joyce A., Brady Hamilton, Paul D. Sutton, Stephanie Ventura, Fay Menacker, Sharon Kimeyer, and Martha Munson. 2007. "Births: Final Data for 2005." *National Vital Statistics Reports* 56(6): 1–104.

McLanahan, Sara. 2003. "Fragile Families and the Marriage Agenda." Working paper 2003-16-FF. Princeton, N.J.: Princeton University, Center for Research on Child Well-Being.

———. 2007. "Single Mothers, Fragile Families." In *Ending Poverty in America*, edited by John Edwards, Marion Crain, and Arne L. Kalleberg. New York: New Press.

———. 2009. "Fragile Families and the Reproduction of Poverty." *Annals of the American Academy of Political and Social Sciences* 621(1): 111–31.

McLanahan, Sara, Elisabeth Donahue, and Ron Haskins. 2005. "Introducing the Issue." *The Future of Children* 15(2): 3–12.

Meyers, Marcia, Dan Rosenbaum, Christopher Ruhm, and Jane Waldfogel. 2004. "Inequality in Early Childhood Education and Care: What Do We Know?" In *Social Inequality*, edited by Kathryn Neckerman. New York: Russell Sage Foundation.

Mincy, Ronald, ed. 2006. *Black Males Left Behind*. Washington, D.C.: Urban Institute.

Mincy, Ronald, Jennifer Hill, and Marilyn Sinkewicz. 2008. "Marriage: Cause or Mere Indicator of Future Earnings Growth?" Unpublished paper. New York: Columbia University.

Mincy, Ronald, and Elaine Sorenson. 1998. "Deadbeats and Turnips in Child Support Reform." *Journal of Policy Analysis and Management* 17(1): 44–51.

Nixon, Lucia. 1997. "The Effect of Child Support Enforcement on Marital Dissolution." *Journal of Human Resources* 32(1): 159–81.

Plotnick, Robert, Irwin Garfinkel, Sara McLanahan, and Inhoe Ku. 2004. "Better Child Support Enforcement: Can It Reduce Teenage Childbearing?" *Journal of Family Issues* 25(5): 634–57.

Presser, Harriet B. 2003. *Working in a 24/7 Economy: Challenges for American Families*. New York: Russell Sage Foundation.

Primus, Wendell E. 2006. "Improving Public Policies to Increase the Income and Employment of Low-Income Nonresident Fathers?" In *Black Males Left Behind*, edited by Ronald B. Mincy. Washington, D.C.: Urban Institute.

Primus, Wendell E., and Jennifer Beeson. 2002. "Safety Net Programs, Marriage, and Cohabitation." In *Just Living Together: Implications of Cohabitation for Families, Children, and Social Policy*, edited by Alan Booth and Ann C. Crouter. Mahwah, N.J.: Lawrence Erlbaum Associates.

Ross Phillips, Katherine. 2004. "Getting Time Off: Access to Leave Among Working Parents." Washington: Urban Institute.

Ruhm, Christopher. 2000. "Parental Leave and Child Health." *Journal of Health Economics* 19(6): 931–60.

Salmi, Minna, and Johanna Lammi-Taskula. 1999. "Parental Leave in Finland." In *Parental Leave: Progress or Pitfall? Research and Policy Issues in Europe*, edited by Peter Moss and Fred Deven. Brussels: CBGS Publications.

Scafidi, Benjamin. 2008. "The Taxpayer Costs of Divorce and Unwed Childbearing: First-Ever Estimates for the Nation and All Fifty States." New York: Institute for American Values.

Shipler, David. 2004. *The Working Poor: Invisible in America*. New York: Alfred A. Knopf.

Smolensky, Eugene, and Jennifer Gootman, eds. 2003. *Working Families and Growing Kids: Caring for Children and Adolescents*. Washington, D.C.: National Academies Press.

Stevenson, Betsey, and Justin Wolfers. 2008. "How Should We Think About the Taxpayer Consequences of Divorce?" Available at Council on Contemporary Families (April 15):

http://bpp.wharton.upenn.edu/jwolfers/Papers/TaxpayerConsequencesofDivorce (CCF).pdf (accessed July 10, 2009).

Tanaka, Sakiko. 2005. "Parental Leave and Child Health Across OECD Countries." *Economic Journal* 115(February): F7–28.

Tax Policy Center, Urban Institute and Brookings Institution. 2008. "Child Tax Credit." Washington, D.C.: Tax Policy Center.

Thomas, Adam, and Isabel Sawhill. 2005. "For Love and Money? The Impact of Family Structure on Family Income." *The Future of Children* 15(2): 57–74.

Turner, Lesley J., Sheldon Danziger, and Kristin Seefeldt. 2006. "Failing the Transition from Welfare to Work: Women Chronically Disconnected from Employment and Cash Welfare." *Social Science Quarterly* 87(2): 227–49.

U.S. Bureau of Labor Statistics (BLS). 2005. "Workers on Flexible and Shift Schedules in May 2004." Washington: U.S. Department of Labor. Available at: http://www.bls.gov/news.release/flex.toc.htm (accessed January 5, 2007).

U.S. Bureau of the Census. 2007. "Current Population Survey: 2006 Poverty Tables." Available at: http://pubdb3.census.gov/macro/032007/pov/toc.htm (accessed September 28, 2007).

U.S. Department of Agriculture. Food and Nutrition Service. 2008. "Supplemental Nutrition Assistance Program (SNAP)." Available at: http://www.fns.usda.gov/fsp (accessed April 17, 2008).

Waldfogel, Jane. 2006a. *What Children Need.* Cambridge, Mass.: Harvard University Press.

———. 2006b. "Early Childhood Policy: A Comparative Perspective." In *The Handbook of Early Childhood Development,* edited by Kathleen McCartney and Deborah Phillips. London: Blackwell.

———. 2007. "Work-Family Policies." In *Workforce Policies for a Changing Economy,* edited by Harry Holzer and Demetra Nightingale. Washington, D.C.: Urban Institute Press.

Walsh, Imelda. 2008. "A Review of How to Extend the Right to Request Flexible Working to Parents of Older Children." London: Department for Business, Enterprise, and Regulatory Reform.

Weinstein, Michael. 1999. "The Tax Bite Comes with Saw Teeth." *New York Times,* April 15.

Willis, Robert. 1999. "A Theory of Out-of-Wedlock Childbearing." *Journal of Political Economy* 107(6): S33–64.

Winston, Pamela. 2007. "Meeting Responsibilities at Work and Home: Public and Private Supports." Washington, D.C.: Urban Institute. Available at: http://www.urban.org/UploadedPDF/411537_meeting_responsibilities.pdf.

Zedlewski, Sheila R., and Sandi Nelson. 2003. "Families Coping Without Earnings or Government Cash Assistance." Assessing the New Federalism occasional paper 64. Washington, D.C.: Urban Institute.

Chapter 10

Improving Educational Outcomes
for Poor Children

Brian A. Jacob and Jens Ludwig

One of the best ways to avoid being poor as an adult is to obtain a good education. As Katherine Magnuson and Elizabeth Votruba-Drzal's chapter in this volume notes, people who have higher levels of academic achievement and more years of schooling earn more than those with lower levels of human capital. This is not surprising in light of the belief by economists that schooling makes people more productive and that wages are related to productivity.

Yet in modern America poor children face an elevated risk for a variety of adverse educational outcomes. In the 2007 National Assessment of Educational Progress (NAEP), only 16 percent of fourth-grade students eligible for free lunch scored at proficient levels in reading, compared with 44 percent of fourth graders whose family incomes were above the eligibility cutoff for free lunch; the disparity in math scores was even larger, 21 percent versus 53 percent (NCES 2007a; NCES 2007b). Equally large disparities in achievement test scores are observed between whites and minority racial or ethnic groups, with test score gaps that show up as early as three or four years of age (Jencks and Phillips 1998).[1] In fact, the black-white test score gap among twelfth-graders may not be all that different in magnitude from the gap observed among young children when they first start school (Phillips, Crouse, and John 1998; Ludwig 2003).

Understanding *why* children's outcomes vary so dramatically along race and class lines in America is central to formulating effective education policy interventions. Disagreements about how to improve schooling outcomes for poor children stem in part from different beliefs about the problems that underlie the unsatisfactory outcomes in many of our nation's public schools. Broadly speaking, critics tend to invoke, at least implicitly, one of the following reasons why children in high-poverty schools are not performing as well as we would like:

1. Schools serving poor and minority students have fewer resources than they need. In this case, a potential solution would be to provide more money to disadvantaged schools.

2. High-poverty schools lack the capacity to make substantial improvements in student learning, independent of financial resources. Under this perspective, the teachers and administrators in highly disadvantaged school districts are thought to lack the skills or knowledge necessary to improve the quality of instruction on their own. Potential solutions to this problem would involve helping schools improve the quality of their standard operating practices, for example, by helping to implement specific new instructional or organizational practices (that is, curriculum, instruction, school organization) or by increasing the instructional capacity of staff in these schools through professional development or more selective hiring. The success of this approach depends critically on whether there exist particular instructional, organizational, human resources, or other practices that are known to be effective and on how easily these practices could be implemented across different contexts.

3. High-poverty schools do not have sufficient incentives and/or flexibility to improve instruction. High-poverty schools underperform because teachers and administrators are not working hard enough, they are not working toward the right goal, or they have good local knowledge about what would work best but are unable to implement these ideas because of centralized authority. Proponents of this perspective often claim that without clarifying the key objectives of schools and holding key actors accountable, additional spending is simply squandered. Their solution is to enhance incentives and provide local actors with more flexibility through policies such as school choice or accountability.

4. Schools matter only so much. The real problem rests with the social context in which schools operate—namely, the family, neighborhood, and peer environments that under this perspective make it difficult for low-income children to take advantage of educational opportunities. Adopting accountability or market-oriented reforms without changing social policy more broadly simply punishes educators for factors beyond their control and may drive the most able teachers toward schools that serve less disadvantaged students.

For some reason, current education policy debates often seem to be argued as if these problems are mutually exclusive. In contrast, we believe that there is probably some truth to each of these major explanations—in other words, there is no single problem with our schools (and so potentially no single solution). Identifying the optimal policy response to the mix of problems that plague our public schools is complicated by the possibility that these problems might interact with each other. For example, it may be the case that certain curriculum reforms are effective only if they are accompanied by an increase in resources such as student support services, or by an increase in teacher quality generated by reforms to hiring and tenure policies. Social science theory and common sense are likely to carry us only so far in identifying the most effective—and most cost-effective—mix of education policy changes. For almost every education intervention that some theory suggests might be effective, there is another plausible theory suggesting that the intervention will be ineffective or even harmful. Education policy also needs to be guided by rigorous evaluation evidence about what actually works in practice.

Evaluation research in education has typically focused on easily measured and relatively short-term student outcomes, such as achievement test scores or school attainment. For this reason, most of the evidence we discuss here emphasizes these outcomes. In general, we expect these outcomes to be positively correlated with other important but harder-to-measure educational outcomes that society cares about, such as a student's interest in school or classroom behavior. But in some cases interventions could have different types of impacts on easy-to-measure versus harder-to-measure outcomes, as might occur, for example, with current proposals to shift Head Start's emphasis from comprehensive services to more academically oriented instruction. In these cases, understanding impacts on test scores or attainment may not be sufficient, but is still useful since these educational outcomes are associated with both a child's chances of becoming poor as an adult and other life outcomes that society cares about. More generally, in principle there is no reason why education research could not track other outcomes, such as a student's interest in school or a student's classroom behavior.

Research over the past four decades has unfortunately fostered the impression that when it comes to improving schools for poor children, "nothing works." One of the first studies to contribute to this sense of pessimism was the landmark report by the sociologist James Coleman and his colleagues (1966). Drawing on a large, nationally representative sample, the so-called Coleman Report found that most of the variation in student test scores occurred within rather than across schools, that family background was the strongest predictor of academic achievement, and that most measurable school inputs, like student-teacher ratios, were only weakly correlated with student outcomes. Subsequent evaluation studies of different educational interventions also tended to be disappointing and contributed to the pessimism about the ability of schools to increase poor children's life chances (Levin 1977; Glazer 1986; Jencks 1986).

In contrast, our chapter offers a message of tempered optimism. In the past few decades, dramatic improvements in the technology of education policy evaluation have enhanced our ability to uncover moderately sized program impacts within the complex environment that determines schooling outcomes. The available evidence reveals a number of potentially promising ways to improve the learning outcomes of low-income children. This is not to say that *everything* works: many current and proposed education policies either enjoy no empirical support for their effectiveness or in some cases enjoy strong empirical evidence for their ineffectiveness. But a careful sifting of the empirical evidence identifies a selected set of interventions that seem to be promising.

Our optimism is tempered by the recognition that the most successful educational interventions reduce, but do not eliminate, racial and social class disparities in educational outcomes. This is not a reason for either despair or inaction. The appropriate standard of success for policy interventions is that they generate net benefits, not miraculous benefits. Education policies that are capable of improving poor children's schooling outcomes by enough to justify the costs of these policies are worth doing, even if these policies or programs by themselves are not enough to equalize learning opportunities for all children in America.

The remainder of the chapter is organized as follows. In the next section, we review three areas in which we believe that increased resources may yield important benefits for poor children: early childhood interventions, class size reductions in the early grades implemented in ways that hold the quality of teachers constant, and initiatives to attract and retain the highest-quality teachers in disadvantaged schools. We then examine reforms that do not require a large investment of resources but instead seek to change how schools operate, from curriculum and instruction changes to changes in teacher hiring and promotion policy. There have been relatively few rigorous evaluations of specific school practices; we suggest that enacting meaningful federal or state mandates that schools use "evidence-based" methods would increase the supply of rigorous evaluations (Jacob and Ludwig 2005). In the next section, we review the literature on school accountability and school choice policies, which aim to change the goals, incentives, and organizational structure within which schools and families operate. The evidence on school accountability is moderately encouraging, though recent findings suggest that the design of accountability policies matters a great deal. There is less evidence that current public or private school choice plans improve student outcomes, but we argue that states and districts should continue to experiment with and evaluate a variety of choice options. In the next section, we discuss the extent to which student socioeconomic background influences the effectiveness of educational interventions. We pay particular attention to the role played by residential segregation with respect to race and social class, since schooling has a clear place-based character. We conclude by summarizing what we believe are the most promising education policies for improving the life chances of disadvantaged children.

SCHOOL RESOURCES

The question of whether "money matters" has been the subject of contentious debate in the research literature for the past forty years. Isolating the causal effects of extra school funding is complicated by the possibility that compensatory spending may be directed toward those schools serving the most disadvantaged students and that adequately controlling for all aspects of student disadvantage is quite difficult in practice. A few recent studies have used policy changes that generate sharp changes in school funding and find some impact on student outcomes (Figlio 1997; Card and Payne 2002; Guryan 2004). Nevertheless, the weight of the evidence provides fairly weak support for the idea that increases in unrestricted school funding on average improve student outcomes (see, for example, Hanushek 1997). In contrast, there is stronger evidence that some targeted increases in specific school inputs can improve student outcomes. This apparent paradox can be reconciled by noting that schools need not dedicate any unrestricted funding increases to those uses that are most effective in improving children's learning outcomes.

In this section, we discuss three specific areas in which we believe increased resources may yield important benefits for poor children: increased investments in early childhood education, class size reductions in the early grades, and targeted salary bonuses to help disadvantaged schools recruit and retain better teachers.

Early Childhood Education

Disparities in academic achievement by race and class are apparent as early as ages three and four, well before children enter kindergarten. Recent research in neuroscience, developmental psychology, economics, and other fields suggests that the earliest years of life may be a particularly promising time to intervene in the lives of low-income children (Shonkoff and Phillips 2000; Carniero and Heckman 2003; Knudsen et al. 2006). Studies show that early childhood educational programs can generate learning gains in the short run and, in some cases, improve the long-run life chances of poor children. Moreover, the benefits generated by these programs are large enough to justify their costs.

The Perry Preschool and Abecedarian programs are commonly cited as examples of high-quality preschool services that can change the lives of low-income children. A small group of children who participated in these programs in the 1960s and 1970s have been followed for many years and on average have better outcomes in a range of domains compared to a randomly assigned group of control children (Schweinhart et al. 2005; Ramey and Campbell 1979; Campbell et al. 2002; Barnett and Masse 2007). Despite the high cost of these programs, these studies suggest that their total economic benefit exceeded their costs (Belfield et al. 2006; Barnett and Masse 2007). Although these results are encouraging, it is important to keep in mind that these are model programs that were unusually intensive and involved small numbers of children in just two sites.

Nevertheless, the evidence on publicly funded early education programs, illustrating what can be achieved for large numbers of children in programs of variable quality, is also very encouraging. A recent random assignment evaluation of Head Start found positive short-term effects of program participation on a variety of cognitive skills on the order of 0.2 to 0.4 standard deviations, with typically positive effects on noncognitive outcomes as well (though they are usually not statistically significant).[2] A rigorous evaluation of Early Head Start, a program serving children under age three in a mix of home- and center-based programs, found positive effects on some aspects of parent practices and children's development, but the effects were generally smaller than for Head Start (Love et al. 2002).

Vivian Wong and her colleagues (2008) find that several recent state-initiated universal pre-K programs have even larger impacts on short-term cognitive test scores than does Head Start (see also Gormley et al. 2005; Gormley and Gayer 2005). Why might the new state pre-K programs generate larger gains than does Head Start? One explanation is that pre-K programs hire more qualified teachers, pay them more, and offer a more academically oriented curriculum than do Head Start programs. Another explanation is that the Head Start comparison group received more center-based care than did children in the pre-K comparison group.[3] A third possible explanation is that the recent Head Start study relies on a rigorous randomized experimental design, while the research design of the new state pre-K studies is more susceptible to bias from selection problems (see Ludwig and Phillips 2007).[4]

Although these short-run achievement gains from both Head Start and newer state pre-K programs are impressive, the crucial question is whether these effects persist over time. To explore longer-run impacts, we must rely on non-experimental studies of children who participated in Head Start decades ago and control for potential confounding factors (Currie and Thomas 1995; Garces, Thomas, and Currie 2002; Ludwig and Miller 2007; and Deming 2007). These studies suggest lasting effects on schooling attainment and perhaps criminal activity, although test score effects appear to fade out over time for many children. Nonetheless, the positive long-term effects seem large enough to generate benefits that outweigh program costs.

It is possible that the long-term effects of Head Start on more recent cohorts of children are different from those for previous cohorts of program participants because program quality changes over time, or because the developmental quality of the environments that children would experience as an alternative to Head Start changes. But the short-term test score impacts that have been estimated for recent cohorts of Head Start participants appear to be similar to what we see for earlier cohorts of children for whom we also now have evidence of long-term benefits. So there is room for cautious optimism that Head Start might improve the long-term outcomes for recent waves of program participants as well, even though this hypothesis cannot be directly tested for many years (Ludwig and Phillips 2007).

Preschool interventions represent a promising way to improve the life chances of poor children, but their success is not well reflected in federal government budget priorities, which allocate nearly seven times as much money per capita for K–12 schooling as for prekindergarten (pre-K), other forms of early education, and child care subsidies for three- to five-year-olds (Ludwig and Sawhill 2007). Most social policies attempt to make up for the disadvantages that poor children experience early in life. But given the substantial disparities that already exist between very young poor children and very young nonpoor children, it is perhaps not surprising that many disadvantaged children never catch up. For this reason, we believe that efforts to improve young children's school readiness with proven, high-quality programs should play a much more prominent role in our nation's antipoverty strategy than they do today.

Class Size Reduction

Reducing average class sizes may enable teachers to spend more time working with individual students, to tailor instruction to match children's needs, and to monitor classroom behavior more easily. But class size reductions are expensive. Additional teachers must be hired, and in some cases a school's physical space must be expanded. Nonetheless, the best available evidence suggests that class size reduction, holding teacher quality constant, can improve student outcomes by enough to justify these additional expenditures, with benefits that are particularly pronounced for low-income and minority children.

The evidence in favor of class size reduction comes mainly from Tennessee's Project STAR, which randomly assigned 11,600 students in grades K–13 and 1,330 teachers to small classes (thirteen to seventeen students), regular-size classrooms (twenty-two to twenty-five students), or regular-size classrooms that also included a teacher's aide.[5] The random assignment of teachers to different classroom environments in this study ensured that the average quality of teachers in small versus regular-size classrooms would be the same, a critical point to which we return in the context of policy efforts to take class size reduction to scale. Class size reductions of around one-third during these early grades increased Stanford-9 reading and math scores by around 0.12 standard deviations for whites and 0.24 standard deviations for blacks. Impacts were larger for students attending mostly black schools, although even within such schools, black students benefited somewhat more than did whites (Krueger and Whitmore 2002). Similarly, impacts were somewhat larger for students who were eligible for the free lunch program.

Follow-up evaluations of STAR find long-term benefits of attending a small elementary school class—the test score impacts seem to persist through eighth grade, although they decline by one-half to two-thirds (Achilles et al. 1993; Nye et al. 1995; Krueger and Whitmore 2001). As with the short-term effects, the eighth-grade test scores reveal larger gains among low-income and minority students. Moreover, black students in the treatment group were roughly five percentage points (or 15 percent) more likely to take a college entrance exam (the SAT or ACT) during high school (Krueger and Whitmore 2001, 2002).[6] The test score gains induced by smaller classes in STAR are probably large enough to justify the costs, even when we focus just on the benefits that arise from test scores on future earnings alone (Krueger 2003; Krueger and Whitmore 2001; Schanzenbach 2007).

The results from Project STAR are encouraging, but they come from a controlled experiment that held the quality of teachers constant by randomly assigning teachers as well as students across classrooms. A sobering example of the challenges of taking class size reduction to scale comes from the California experience. California introduced a statewide initiative to reduce primary grade class sizes in 1998–1999, which required schools to not only hire a large number of new teachers but also find additional physical space for the new classrooms (Borhnstedt and Stecher 2002; Jepsen and Rivkin 2002). The policy was implemented over a short time period. Many low-income school districts found it difficult to hire qualified teachers and had trouble arranging for adequate classroom space. Christopher Jepsen and Steven Rivkin (2002) argue that much of the benefit from smaller classes in California was lost due to reductions in average teacher quality, particularly in lower-income urban school districts.

California's experience illustrates the complexity of taking education policy reforms to a large scale. It suggests the potential value of focusing class size reductions in low-income districts or schools, as well as the importance of careful implementation of the program so as to minimize any adverse effects on teacher quality or physical capital. As long as these implementation efforts did not raise costs too much relative to STAR, it still seems plausible that a large-scale program to reduce class sizes might pass a benefit-cost test.

Bonuses for Teaching in High-Needs Schools or Subjects

Research has identified substantial variation across teachers in the ability to raise student achievement. These studies estimate teacher effectiveness by comparing changes in student achievement scores across classrooms, controlling for student, classroom, and school characteristics that influence achievement regardless of the teacher. Because these studies attempt to isolate the value that a teacher adds to student achievement, they are referred to as "teacher value-added" studies. These studies document substantial variation in teacher effectiveness, both within and across schools. According to a recent analysis of New York City elementary school math teachers, for example, students whose teacher falls in the top quarter of effectiveness learn roughly 0.33 test score standard deviations more in a single year than students whose teachers are in the bottom quarter (Kane, Rockoff, and Staiger 2006).[7] If disadvantaged children were taught by the most effective teachers, disparities in schooling outcomes might be narrowed.

Value-added measures of teacher effectiveness are not very strongly correlated with the easiest-to-observe characteristics of teachers. Novice teachers are less effective than more experienced ones, but this experience premium disappears after the first few years of teaching (Rockoff 2004). Teachers who have higher scores on the SAT or various teaching exams are generally more effective than others (Harris and Sass 2007; Clotfelter, Ladd, and Vigdor 2006), but many other observable teacher characteristics—such as whether they hold traditional teacher certifications or advanced degrees—are not systematically correlated with student learning (Kane, Rockoff, and Staiger 2006; Boyd et al. 2005; Hanushek 1997).

Hence, the policy challenge in this domain is to induce more effective teachers to teach in schools serving the most disadvantaged children, knowing that effectiveness cannot easily be measured by those teacher characteristics that can be observed at the hiring stage. Given the relationship between wages and teacher labor supply (see, for example, Hanushek, Kain, and Rivkin 2004; Stinebrickner 2002; Scafidi, Sjoquist, and Stinebrickner 2007), one strategy is to entice teachers who have shown to be effective to work in hard-to-staff schools or subjects through financial incentives such as targeted salary increases or bonuses. Although many states have adopted some sort of financial assistance program (such as loan forgiveness, mortgage assistance, salary supplements), there has been little systematic evaluation (Imazeki 2007; Guarino, Santibañez, and Daley 2006; Glazerman et al. 2006).

Evaluation of a targeted teacher bonus in North Carolina suggests that the program was successful in reducing teacher turnover rates in low-income or low-performing schools (Clotfelter et al. 2006). In California, from 2000 to 2002, the Governor's Teaching Fellowship Program offer to academically talented teaching candidates of $20,000 bonuses to work in low-performing schools increased the rate at which such teachers started working in disadvantaged schools but did not seem to influence subsequent retention rates (Steele, Murnane, and Willet 2008). Key questions remain: Do such programs successfully lure new teachers into the profession who would not otherwise have taught? Or do these programs simply resort a fixed pool of teachers across schools? How long do any talented new teachers drawn into teaching by incentive programs remain in the classroom? And do financial incentives that are not tied to teacher performance induce ineffective teachers to locate in hard-to-staff schools? Despite these uncertainties, the dramatic variation in effectiveness that we observe among teachers highlights the great value of policies that entice more effective teachers to work in schools that serve disproportionately poor student bodies.

CHANGING SCHOOL PRACTICES

In the previous section, we argued that there are targeted ways of spending money on schooling that can improve long-term outcomes for children even without fundamentally restructuring how our school system currently operates. Yet all of these policy changes are expensive and so must compete for scarce government resources with a variety of other pressing societal concerns. Some observers of the U.S. schooling system remain skeptical that additional spending is needed to improve the learning outcomes of poor children. They argue that improving the ways in which schools are organized, including the ways in which they deliver instruction, could improve student achievement with few additional resources. This line of reasoning assumes there is good evidence on which practices are most effective, but that school personnel simply do not have the capacity to identify or implement these programs on their own.

In this section, we discuss some low-cost changes in school operating practices that seem to improve student outcomes, including changes to school organization, classroom instruction, and teacher hiring and promotion. What remains unclear is why these "best practices" have not been more widely adopted. Presumably the obstacle has been some combination of lack of information, political resistance, bureaucratic inertia, and other factors.

Curricular and Instructional Interventions

In 2002 the Institute for Education Sciences (IES) within the U.S. Department of Education created the What Works Clearinghouse (WWC) in order to collect and disseminate scientific evidence on various educational interventions. A brief review of the WWC website highlights the lack of convincing evidence on curricular interventions. For example, the Everyday Mathematics curriculum was introduced in 1983 and has been used in 175,000 classrooms by around 2.8 million students (WWC 2007a). Yet WWC has found only four studies of Everyday Mathematics that meet its minimal standards of evidence "with reservations." This lack of success is not limited to traditional "paper and pencil" curricula. There is also little evidence that educational software programs have significant impacts on student learning, despite their growing popularity (Dynarski et al. 2007). WWC found only one program with strong evidence of improving reading achievement among beginning readers (Reading Recovery), one program for elementary school math (Everyday Mathematics), and two programs for middle school math (I Can Learn Algebra/ Pre-Algebra and Saxon Middle School Math). WWC excludes many studies that do not meet a minimal standard of evidence, but even the programs for which there is strong evidence of success according to WWC show a disappointingly low level of rigorous research.

A more recent approach to school improvement known as comprehensive (or whole) school reform (CSR) attempts to improve many different aspects of the school simultaneously and in a fashion that makes the changes complementary and reinforcing. For example, a CSR model might combine curriculum materials, professional development, teacher mentoring, reorganization of the school day (for example, block scheduling) and school structure (for example, schools-within-a-school). CSR examples include Success for All (Borman and Hewes 2003), Comer Schools (Cook, Hunt, and Murphy 2000), Direct Instruction (CRSQ 2006), Accelerated Schools (Bloom et al. 2001), America's Choice (CRSQ 2006), Career Academies (Kemple and Scott-Clayton 2004), Project GRAD (Snipes et al. 2006), First Things First (Quint et al. 2005), and Talent Development (Kemple, Herlihy, and Smith 2005). Unfortunately, as with curricular reforms, the evaluation evidence about the effectiveness of CSR programs is quite limited.

Nevertheless, at the elementary school level a few models have been shown to improve student outcomes. One of the more promising interventions seems to be Success for All (SFA), a comprehensive whole-school reform model that operates in more than 1,200 mostly high-poverty Title I schools.[8] SFA focuses on reading, with an emphasis on prevention and early intervention. Children receive ninety minutes each day of reading instruction in groups that are organized across grade levels based on each child's current reading level, enabling teachers to target instruction. Cooperative learning exercises in which students discuss stories and learn from each other reinforce what is being taught and build students' social skills. Both formal measures of reading competency and teacher observations are used to assess children at eight-week intervals. Children who fall behind are given extra tutoring or help with other problems, such as health or behavior problems. The program utilizes regular classroom teachers who receive brief initial training, ongoing coaching, and other forms of support and professional development.

A random assignment evaluation of SFA documented that at the end of three years students in the treatment schools scored roughly 0.2 standard deviations higher than students in the control schools on a standardized reading assessment. These effects were equivalent to about one-fifth the gap between low- and high-socioeconomic-status children (Borman et al. 2007).

SFA costs about $950 per student per year (Borman and Hewes 2003), with about two-thirds of this cost associated with the program's tutoring component. Current spending under the federal government's Title I program is around $880 per eligible student; there is little evidence that Title I funding as typically deployed by public schools translates into much gain in student learning (Gordon 2004; van der Klaauw 2008). One implication is that in schools serving predominantly poor students, SFA could be implemented mostly by just redeploying existing Title I funds. If the experimental evaluation of SFA is correct and the program's impact is anything like 0.2 standard deviations, this type of funding shift would easily pass a benefit-cost test, since, as Alan Krueger (2003) shows, test score increases of this magnitude would increase the present value of each student's lifetime earnings profile by thousands of dollars.

At the high school level, CSR models tend to incorporate some common features, often involving a reorganization of the larger high school into smaller learning communities, referred to as "small schools," "schools within a school," or "learning academies." Small learning communities aim to provide a more personalized learning environment that better engages and motivates students and prevents at-risk students from "falling through the cracks." Other common reform features include work-based learning opportunities, such as internships, and assistance for students who enter high school with poor academic skills (Herlihy and Quint 2006).

To date, however, there is little evidence that, as currently implemented, these high school CSR approaches improve student outcomes. The most rigorous evaluation of a high school CSR is MDRC's random assignment study of Career Academies, which are organized as small learning communities of between 150 and 200 high school students (often housed within larger, comprehensive high schools) that focus on a specific occupation or industry. Unlike the vocational education programs that were popular in the 1970s and 1980s, Career Academies combine academic and technical curricula, often using the technical curricula relevant to a particular industry to motivate students. One hallmark of these programs is establishing connections with employers in the field through mentoring and internships.

Early results of the Career Academy evaluation indicated that students in the program reported that their school provided a more personalized learning environment relative to what students in the control group experienced. The program raised attendance and completion of course credits in the early years of high school. A later follow-up found no differences in high school completion rates between program and control groups, but did find a substantial impact on earnings among high-risk students (Kemple and Willner 2008). It is worth noting that the schooling attainment levels of both the treatment and control groups in the Career Academy study are higher than what we see for other urban public school samples. More research is needed to assess this approach and answer remaining questions: Do the positive effects documented in the prior research generalize to students who do not volunteer for the program? And are the career academies that have already been evaluated of higher quality than the typical career academy?

The federal government can and should do more to improve the quality of research and development of curricular improvements and comprehensive school reform efforts by, for example, holding "design competitions." Federal, state, and local governments could provide curriculum developers with incentives to do more rigorous evaluation of their products by requiring that schools devote resources to only those products proven to be effective in randomized trials (see Jacob and Ludwig 2005). The Institute for Education Sciences has already been moving in this direction. But comparing the IES initiatives with the Food and Drug Administration's (FDA) requirement that new drugs be subject to at least three phases of clinical trials highlights how far we are from providing parents with similar assurances about the value of their children's learning experiences at school.

Teacher Labor Markets

A key policy challenge for school districts is to induce more effective teachers to teach in high-poverty schools. As discussed earlier in this chapter, one strategy is to offer targeted financial incentives to individuals to teach in hard-to-staff schools or subjects. But there are also a variety of potential inefficiencies in schools' hiring, promotion, and dismissal practices. At least some of these problems might be addressed without a substantial increase in resources.[9]

One promising approach is to promote alternative pathways into teaching. Traditional certification requirements impose a high cost (in terms of both money and time) on individuals interested in teaching, particularly on those with the best outside labor market options. As a result, certification requirements may help dissuade some highly skilled people from entering the teaching profession. Many studies have explored the relative effectiveness of teachers with traditional versus alternative (or no) certification. The emerging consensus is that differences between the groups are relatively small and that in certain grades and subjects teachers with alternative certification may actually outperform those with traditional certification (Boyd et al. 2005; Kane, Rockoff, and Staiger 2006; Glazerman et al. 2006). Hence, alternative certification may improve the supply of teachers without reducing quality.

Given the wide variation in effectiveness, policies that help school officials identify and hire the best applicants could have an important impact on student outcomes. For example, staffing rules, late state budgets, and inefficient human resource procedures dissuade many qualified applicants from teaching in urban schools (Levin and Quinn 2003; Levin, Mulhern, and Schunck 2005). This suggests that changing collective bargaining agreements to reform staffing rules and taking a more efficient, customer-focused approach to HR might help improve teacher quality.[10]

Whatever system is used to hire teachers, it is inevitable that some teachers will not perform well in the classroom. Recognizing that the hiring process is imperfect, virtually all school systems place new teachers on probation for several years, subjecting them to an up-or-out tenure review. In practice, however, public schools typically do not take advantage of the probationary period to obtain additional information about teacher effectiveness and weed out lower-quality teachers.[11] In New York City, for example, only about 50 out of roughly 75,000 teachers were dismissed for performance-related reasons in recent years.[12] In the Chicago Public Schools, only 15 out of 11,621 teachers who were evaluated in 2007 received a rating of unsatisfactory, and only 641 out of those 11,621 (roughly

5.5 percent) received a rating of satisfactory. The remaining teachers were rated excellent or superior.[13]

One possible solution is to raise the tenure bar for new teachers and to deny tenure to those who are not effective at raising student achievement. Some have suggested that this type of evaluation should be based at least in part on teacher value-added scores (see, for example, Gordon, Kane, and Staiger 2006). We concur with the general recommendation to institute rigorous and meaningful tenure reviews, but would suggest that this type of high-stakes decision should be based on a variety of teacher performance measures that include, but are not limited to, measures of effectiveness at raising student test scores. Given the concerns about the reliability and validity of value-added measures discussed earlier, these indicators should not be the only criteria used in making high-stakes decisions such as teacher dismissal.

Although commonly measured teacher characteristics have little correlation with student achievement, principals do recognize which teachers are most effective. Brian Jacob and Lars Lefgren (2007) compare principal ratings of teacher effectiveness with "objective" measures of teacher effectiveness calculated using student achievement gains. They find that principals can identify the best and worst teachers, but have little ability to distinguish between teachers in the middle of the ability distribution. This suggests that principal evaluations should be included as one factor in teacher tenure ratings, both because they may add additional information beyond student test scores and because they reduce potential negative effects of relying solely on an output-based measure (for example, teachers either cheating or teaching narrowly to the test in order to maximize short-run student test scores at the cost of skills that would maximize long-term learning).

One might still be concerned that principals would be hesitant to deny tenure to many teachers. Several years ago, the Chicago Public Schools and the Chicago Teachers' Union signed a collective bargaining agreement that gave principals considerable latitude to dismiss untenured teachers. Brian Jacob (2008) finds that the teachers selected for dismissal did have more absences and lower value-added scores than other probationary teachers in the same school who were not selected for dismissal, suggesting that principals consider productivity in making their decisions. He reports, however, that 30 to 40 percent of principals—including many at very low-performing schools—did not dismiss *any* teachers, suggesting that some administrators may be reluctant to remove poorly performing employees. One reason may be that it is difficult to hire high-quality replacements, and so principals might be reluctant to risk the chance of getting an even worse replacement. It is also possible that principals are reluctant to incur the social and political costs associated with dismissal. In either case, policies to raise the tenure bar must incorporate some system to ensure that difficult decisions actually get made.

INCENTIVES AND ACCOUNTABILITY

Class size reduction is an "input-based" educational intervention, based on the assumption that schools perform better with additional resources. Comprehensive school reform is based on the assumption that schools are not utilizing optimal pedagogical practices, and therefore it seeks to improve schooling outcomes by prescribing a more effective instructional approach. Both strategies assume that educators are willing to work as hard as they can, given their resource constraints. In addition, prescriptive approaches that push schools to adopt specific practices also assume that it does not make sense for individuals to "reinvent the wheel," and thus these approaches rely on centralized decisionmakers who presumably have better information about "best practices" for any given school than local principals and teachers.

An alternative approach to school reform focuses on enhancing both the incentives and the flexibility enjoyed by school personnel. Although the theories underlying school choice and school accountability differ in important ways, both strategies rely on the core notions of incentives and flexibility. In this section, we review the existing empirical work on the impact of accountability and choice reforms on student outcomes. The available evidence to date is probably strongest on behalf of the ability of school accountability systems to change the behavior of teachers and principals, although one lesson from that body of research is the great importance of getting the design of such policies right.

Teacher Merit Pay

The issue of teacher compensation often arises in discussions of school reform. Most public school teachers are paid according to strict formulas that incorporate years of service and credits of continuing education, including master's and doctorate degrees, despite the fact that research consistently finds that advanced degrees are not associated with better student performance and that experience matters only in the first few years of teaching. For this reason, reformers have suggested that a teacher's compensation should be tied directly to his or her productivity as measured by student performance or supervisor evaluation. Proponents of "pay for performance," also known as "merit" or "incentive" pay, argue that not only would it provide incentives for current teachers to work "harder" or "smarter," but also that it could alter the type of people who enter the teaching force and then choose to remain.

Critics of merit pay emphasize that teaching is a collaborative venture and that incentive pay for individuals could harm the teamwork necessary for effective schools. They note that it is difficult to monitor teachers and that because teachers are asked to achieve multiple objectives, a system that focuses on one easily observable outcome, such as student test scores, is likely to distort teacher behavior in ways that would harm other outcomes. For example, teachers may focus attention more on the subjects that "count" under the performance system, or they may neglect students they view as too far behind (or even too far ahead). Proponents counter that pay-for-performance systems can focus on teams of teachers or schools, and that distortions could be mitigated by incorporating principal evaluations as well as test scores.

As Richard Murnane and David Cohen (1986) note, incentive pay has a long history in American education, though few systems that directly reward teachers on the basis of student performance have lasted very long. Although many teachers indicate that their compensation incorporates some aspect of incentive pay, there are few examples of pay that is tied very closely to student performance. One prominent example is the Teacher Advancement Program (TAP), which incorporates incentive pay along with pay for additional professional development activities and other services. TAP began in 1999 and, as of the 2008–2009 academic year, served 6,200 teachers nationwide who together taught 72,000 students (TAP 2009). This program is more popular than many old-style merit pay programs, and there is some evidence that it may improve student performance on standardized tests (Springer, Ballou, and Peng 2008). Given this tentative but positive evidence, we believe that it is worthwhile for schools and districts to continue experimenting with, and evaluating, pay for performance.

School Accountability Systems

Recent studies suggest that accountability reforms can foster positive changes in behavior by school administrators, teachers, and students. At the same time, research provides some warnings that incentive-based reforms often generate unintended negative consequences, such as teachers neglecting certain students, cutting corners, or even cheating to raise student test scores artificially. The fact that actors within the school system do respond to changes in incentives highlights both the promise and the pitfalls of accountability reform and underscores the importance of the specific design details of accountability policies.

Although studies of school-based accountability policies in the 1980s and 1990s found mixed results (Jacob 2005), two major accountability reforms from the late 1990s—in Chicago and Florida—demonstrated positive results. In 1996 the Chicago Public Schools (CPS) introduced a comprehensive accountability policy designed to raise academic achievement. One component of the CPS reform was to place low-performing schools on probation, a process that entailed the expenditure of a modest amount of additional resources along with enhanced monitoring and the threat of future closure. Importantly, unlike the federal No Child Left Behind (NCLB) accountability reform, the CPS policy focused on holding students as well as school staff accountable for learning by ending a practice commonly known as "social promotion"—advancing students to the next grade regardless of ability or achievement level.

Jacob (2005) has found that math and reading achievement increased sharply following the introduction of this accountability policy, in comparison to both prior achievement trends in the district and changes experienced by other large urban districts in the Midwest. For younger students, however, the policy did not increase performance on a state-administered, low-stakes exam. Jacob's analysis suggests that the observed achievement gains were driven by increases in test-specific skills and student effort. This finding is consistent with prior work suggesting that the test preparation associated with high-stakes testing may artificially inflate achievement, producing gains that are not generalizable to other exams (see, for example, Koretz et al. 1991; Koretz and Barron 1998). Note that the policy did lead to substantial achievement gains for older students and that, for these students, the test-specific gains most likely represented real learning of the skills found on the high-stakes tests.

David Figlio and Cecilia Rouse (2006) studied Florida's A+ Plan for Education, a school-based accountability system implemented several years before the introduction of No Child Left Behind. In 1999 schools received "grades" based on their students' test scores on the Florida Comprehensive Achievement Test (FCAT). Under the A+ Plan, schools that received a failing grade ("F") in two consecutive years were required to offer their students vouchers to enroll in private schools. Schools that faced declining enrollments were subject to staff cuts and additional sanctions. It was hoped that the stigma associated with the highly visible failing grade, coupled with the threat of competition induced by the vouchers, would provide low-performing schools with an incentive to improve.

Figlio and Rouse (2006) found that the designation of a school as failing led to a significant increase in student math performance, on the order of five scale score points, or roughly 0.1 standard deviations. The impact of receiving an "F" on a low-stakes math test is about half as large. Researchers studying later versions of Florida's accountability system found similar effects (Chiang 2007; Rouse et al. 2007). Moreover, they found that many of these learning gains were sustained in the following few years.

Although these studies suggest that accountability policies can improve student achievement, other studies show that educators respond strategically to test-based accountability in many unintended ways, some of which may have negative consequences for students. Jacob (2005) found that educators in Chicago responded to the accountability program by placing a larger fraction of low-performing students in special education (thus removing them from the test-taking pool[14]), retaining a larger fraction of students before they reached the grades where they would be subject to accountability mandates (that is, in kindergarten through second grade), and shifting attention away from subjects, such as science and social studies, that were not used to determine student or school sanctions under the accountability policy. Each of these responses increased a school's measured performance, even though they seem inappropriate and detrimental to student learning. However, it is also possible that some, and perhaps most, educators viewed these steps as appropriate responses that would benefit students.[15] A growing body of research also suggests that accountability systems generate larger improvements among students who are relatively closer to the passing threshold used to reward schools (Chakrabarti 2008; Neal and Schanzenbach 2007). Finally, Jacob and Levitt (2003) found that the prevalence of teacher cheating rose sharply in low-achieving classrooms following the introduction of Chicago's accountability policy.

Two recent studies utilized data from the National Assessment of Educational Progress (NAEP) to assess the impact of standards-based accountability across a variety of states, rather than focusing on case studies of a single jurisdiction's policy. These studies are important because the NAEP data were not used by any state as part of its accountability program; thus, educators had no incentive to manipulate test scores in the way that prior studies document has occurred for high-stakes exams in individual states. Both studies find positive achievement effects overall, although they do not find evidence that accountability policies have consistently reduced the racial achievement gap (Carnoy and Loeb 2003; Hanushek and Raymond 2005).

A review of simple national time trends in the recent NAEP data suggests that NCLB may have improved student achievement, particularly the math performance of younger children. To our knowledge, however, there has been no systematic investigation of the impact of NCLB at a national level that attempts to account for prior achievement trends or the presence of other policies.

Yet even without any direct evaluation evidence about NCLB, the available accountability research suggests a number of modifications to NCLB that, in our view, would seem likely to do some good. First, we would encourage the adoption of a single achievement standard for all districts in the country. The provision that allowed states to choose the tests they use for measuring student performance has resulted in vast disparities in the academic rigor of accountability requirements across states. Knowing the political difficulty in imposing a uniform national standard, we support the recent voluntary efforts by national associations of state officials and educators to adopt common standards. Second, we recommend moving away from a single proficiency level—that is, holding schools accountable for the share of students with scores above some single cutoff value—since this provides schools with an incentive to neglect students who are far above or below this threshold. Instead, schools should be held accountable for the *gains* that all students make each year. Third, if the current level of federal funding is not increased substantially, we suggest that states and districts be given the flexibility to focus on the schools most in need of improvement.

School Choice

Another way to clarify goals or change incentives is to give parents a greater choice of schools for their children through public magnet schools, charter schools, or vouchers for private schools. Choice proponents suggest that by creating a marketplace where parents can select schools, a choice-based system might generate competition that would improve the quality of schools throughout the marketplace. This theory rests on several assumptions, including the assumption that the degree of choice would be large enough to generate meaningful competition. For example, a handful of charter schools with limited enrollment capacity is unlikely to generate meaningful competition in a large district. This suggests that a choice system must permit relatively easy entry into the market by potential suppliers, including individuals and organizations wishing to open schools. There must also be an easy "exit" from the market that allows (and indeed forces) unsuccessful schools to close.[16]

The second set of assumptions involves the information available to parents and their preferences for their children's education. Parents must have sufficient information to make an informed choice. Data on school performance must be transparent, accessible, and easily understood by parents with varying degrees of sophistication. The effects of choice also depend in large part on the nature of the preferences themselves. Expanded choice is only likely to increase student academic outcomes if achievement is a central concern for parents.

The most rigorous studies assessing parental preferences typically find that parents place a high value on proximity and student racial composition (Glazerman 1998; Calvo 2006; Hastings, Kane, and Staiger 2006a). On average, parents place limited value on the "academic quality" of the school according to measures like student test scores, though parents with higher income tend to place a higher priority on test scores (Hastings, Kane, and Staiger 2006b). Although these results suggest that choice plans do not lead to higher performance among poor children, there is some evidence that providing poor families with more transparent information about school quality does lead parents to select "better" schools in terms of academic performance (Hastings, van Weelden, and Weinstein 2007).

Even if school choice does not foster competition that increases the productivity of schooling overall, the opportunity to choose may still have a positive effect on students. Choice might allow a student to attend a school with better teachers, more resources, or more studious peers. Whether this re-sorting of children across schools improves average outcomes for all children or simply changes the distribution of academic achievement across children depends on whether some children gain more from "better" peer settings than others. Of course, if the goal is to reduce inequity in schooling opportunities and outcomes and school choice provides choices to disadvantaged students who would not have them otherwise, then choice may still have served a worthwhile purpose. Some argue that choice gives low-income parents the opportunities that wealthier parents have always had.

The availability of choice may also improve student outcomes if it allows parents to find schools that are a better "match" for their individual child's needs, a possibility that, in principle, could allow most students to benefit from choice.[17] Some would argue that if choice allows parents to select the type of schools they want for their children, the system should be considered a success. While this may be true from the parents' perspective, if society values certain outcomes more than others, then free choice on the part of parents may not maximize social welfare.

There are hundreds of studies on school choice that cover everything from charter schools to private voucher plans. However, the vast majority of research in this area suffers from a critical limitation, which researchers refer to as selection bias. Students who utilize school choice—whether it is to attend a public magnet school, a charter school, or a private school—differ from students who do not, both in terms of easily observable ways, such as race, income, and achievement level, and of more subtle ways such as personal motivation or family support. If researchers do not account for such differences when comparing, for example, charter schools with neighborhood public schools, then the results can be misleading.

The best studies of the impact on student achievement of attending a public school of choice overcome the problem of selection bias by focusing on choice schools that are oversubscribed and use random lotteries to determine admission. By comparing the outcomes of students who win and lose lotteries, the researchers can estimate the causal impact of attending a public school of choice. Looking at elementary and high schools in Chicago, Julie Berry Cullen, Brian Jacob, and Steven Levitt (2006) find that winning a choice lottery has no effect on a wide range of academic outcomes.[18] In a study of school choice lotteries in the Charlotte-Mecklenburg School District in North Carolina, Justine Hastings and her colleagues (2006b) find that, on average, students do not benefit from winning one of the lotteries and attending their preferred school. However, when they examine children whose parents seemed to place a greater value on academics (based on the type of schools they chose), these authors find that these students do experience higher test scores from winning the public school choice lottery. Finally, as noted earlier, there is some evidence that career academies, one prominent type of public choice school, have positive effects on student outcomes (Cullen, Jacob, and Levitt 2005; Kemple and Willner 2008).

A parallel literature that analyzes the effect of attending a charter school on academic outcomes yields similarly mixed outcomes. Several studies find small negative or zero effects (Hanushek et al. 2005; Bifulco and Ladd 2006; Sass 2006). A recent random evaluation of New York City charters uses a lottery-based research design, comparing students who win and lose lotteries to oversubscribed charter schools, and finds robust positive effects (Hoxby and Murarka 2007). This approach removes concerns about selection bias but has the drawback of focusing on a small number of particularly successful (or at least popular) charter schools.

Perhaps the most contentious form of school choice involves vouchers that allow students to attend private schools. Voucher experiments in Milwaukee, New York, Dayton, and Washington, D.C., have been evaluated. These studies typically focus on comparing outcomes between students who are offered the chance to attend private schools and those who are not. The results in most cities were discouraging, but the evaluation in New York City pointed to some modest test score gains for African American children, even if the magnitude of these results has been debated (Howell, Peterson, and Wolf 2002; Krueger and Zhu 2004).

The most difficult area of school choice to analyze empirically is the claim that choice will foster competition that will, in turn, improve the productivity of all schools. Caroline Hoxby (2000) compared geographic areas and found that those areas with more school choice for largely historical reasons (for example, streams and rivers made transportation difficult in earlier times and thus encouraged areas to divide themselves along the boundary of such waterways) had more productive schools, suggesting that greater choice is associated with greater efficiency in schooling. Others have argued, however, that these results are not particularly robust (Rothstein 2007a; Hoxby 2007). Miguel Urquiola (2005) finds evidence of sorting—the "best" public school students leaving for the private sector. Areas with greater district choice tend to have a smaller fraction of students attending private schools, but these districts also have schools that are more racially homogenous.

In summary, there is mixed evidence on whether the opportunity to attend a choice school—public magnet, charter, or private—has substantial academic benefits for poor children, and the question of whether large-scale choice programs improve the productivity of schools in general also remains unresolved. It is premature to make strong claims about whether such policies can have substantial benefits for disadvantaged children. In our view, the main risk associated with expanded choice opportunities is the possibility of exacerbating the segregation of poor, minority, or low-performing students within a subset of schools. This seems to have happened to some degree in New Zealand and Chile under the large-scale choice plans adopted in those countries (Fiske and Ladd 2000; Ladd and Fiske 2001; Hsieh and Urquiola 2006). As both Derek Neal (2002) and Helen Ladd (2002) point out, however, the effects of any choice plan are likely to depend crucially on the details of key design questions, such as whether schools are allowed to select the best students from their applicant pools. Many of the current public school choice plans require oversubscribed schools to admit students on the basis of lotteries, providing some guard against this type of sorting. Recognizing these concerns, we would encourage states and districts to continue experimenting and evaluating different forms of public school choice (for example, magnet or charter schools) to learn more about their potential impacts.

THE ROLE OF STUDENT BACKGROUND

Some people believe that the disappointing performance of our public schools, particularly those serving a low-income population, is due in large part to the challenges that poor children face outside of school. At some level this is clearly true. Going back at least to the Coleman Report in 1966, we have known that differences in family background help explain a large share of the variation in academic achievement outcomes across children. Poor children have substantially lower achievement test scores than nonpoor children as young as ages three or four—before they even start school.

More relevant for present purposes is whether the challenges of living in poverty cause poor children to *benefit less* than nonpoor children from similar types of schooling experiences. Our reading of the available evidence suggests that improving the quality of academic programs is at the very least sufficient to make noticeable improvements in poor children's educational outcomes. In fact, studies of different early childhood education programs, as well as of Tennessee's STAR class size reduction experiment, typically find that disadvantaged children benefit even *more* from these interventions than do nonpoor children.

This finding by itself does not resolve the long-standing debates about whether education and other social policies should be targeted at poor families or instead made universal, since political-economy considerations are also relevant. Nor are we arguing against the value of social policies that seek to improve children's life chances by lifting them out of poverty (such as the policies reviewed by Katherine Magnuson and Elizabeth Votruba-Drzal in this volume). Our point instead is that social policy changes that reduce child poverty in the United States, as desirable as they may be on their own merits, are not a necessary precondition for enacting education reforms that improve poor children's outcomes by enough to justify the costs of these reforms.

At the same time, the geographic concentration of poor children in neighborhoods that are segregated by race and social class presents special challenges for education policy, given that children have traditionally attended neighborhood schools. For example, research suggests that, all else being equal, teachers tend to prefer to work in schools that serve more affluent and less racially diverse student bodies (Hanushek, Kain, and Rivkin 2004). So the quality of the teachers available to poor children depends in part on whether they attend school mostly with other poor children or have a more socioeconomically diverse set of schoolmates. As another example, accountability policies must isolate the contribution of teachers and principals to student learning. Accountability systems that fail to account adequately for the confounding influence of family background may help drive the most effective teachers out of high-poverty schools. Peer characteristics may matter directly for student learning; teachers may set the level or pace of instruction to match the average student ability in their classroom. And students may learn from one another, or they may exert a negative influence on each other by disrupting classroom instruction. While empirical identification of peer effects has proven to be quite challenging in practice, the available research provides at least suggestive evidence that peer influences may be relevant (for an extensive review, see Vigdor and Ludwig 2008).

In theory, education policies could overcome the burden that concentrated poverty imposes on poor children by breaking the link between place of residence and school assignment. Some evidence suggests that earlier school desegregation efforts did improve the schooling outcomes of disadvantaged children. For example, Jonathan Guryan (2004) finds that dropout rates for blacks declined by around 25 percent when the largest urban school districts in the United States were forced by local federal court order to racially desegregate in the period from the late 1960s through the early 1980s, despite the fact that some white families responded by attending private schools or moving to other public school districts (for an extensive review of the segregation literature, see Vigdor and Ludwig 2008).

However, the potential for contemporaneous desegregation policies to achieve large gains in student outcomes remains unclear. First, there are substantial barriers—both logistical and political—to further integrating schools along race or class lines. Although there was some decline in residential segregation by race after

1970, neighborhoods remained more segregated by household income in 2000 than in 1970 (Jargowsky 2003; Watson 2006; Vigdor and Ludwig 2008). The substantial amount of residential segregation by race and social class that remains in the United States limits how much school desegregation can be accomplished, since the U.S. Supreme Court made it very difficult to enact across-district desegregation plans in the Milliken v. Bradley decision (418 US 717, 1974). More generally, the majority of Supreme Court decisions on school desegregation since the early 1970s have restricted the ability of districts to promote integration (Kahlenberg 2001), including two decisions in 2007 striking down desegregation plans in Seattle and Louisville (Meredith v. Jefferson County Board of Education and Parents Involved in the Community Schools v. Seattle School District No. 1). Second, the substantial change in both schooling and social conditions for poor children since the initial desegregation efforts may limit the effectiveness of desegregation efforts today. For example, while still far from equal, the difference in resources across poor and nonpoor schools has greatly narrowed since the early 1970s.

A different approach to addressing the problem of concentrated poverty is to use housing policy to help poor families move into different neighborhoods. In practice, data from the Experimental Housing Allowance Program in the 1970s and a more recent randomized housing voucher lottery in Chicago indicate that the provision of housing subsidies to families who are already living in private-market housing does little to change their neighborhood environment (Olsen 2003; Jacob and Ludwig 2009). Housing policy does seem to be able to help public housing families move into less disadvantaged neighborhoods, although it should be noted that only a modest share of all poor families with children currently live in public housing (Olsen 2003).

Moreover, it is unclear whether moving to a more advantaged neighborhood per se improves a child's academic outcomes. The most compelling evidence on this point comes from the U.S. Department of Housing and Urban Development's Moving to Opportunity (MTO) experiment, which, starting in 1994, randomly gave 4,600 mostly minority families living in public housing in five cities (Baltimore, Boston, Chicago, Los Angeles, and New York) the chance to use a housing voucher to move into private-market housing in a less disadvantaged neighborhood. MTO families offered the chance to move with a voucher wound up living in less economically disadvantaged neighborhoods compared to control group families, but the children in these families showed no statistically significant improvement on either reading or math test scores in the first five years following the move (Sanbonmatsu et al. 2006).[19]

Reducing the prevalence in the United States of either child poverty or the geographic concentration of poverty is difficult. As the editors note in their introduction to this volume, the United States has made little progress in reducing its poverty rate since the early 1970s. The concentration of poverty within census tracts increased substantially from 1970 to 1990, and despite a significant decline in the 1990s, the number of people living in high-poverty tracts was still substantially higher in 2000 than in 1970 (Jargowsky 2003). Although the well-being of children is not served by the persistence of these social problems, they do not undermine the potential to help poor children escape from poverty by improving their educational opportunities.

CONCLUSION

The release of the landmark Coleman Report in 1966 fostered pessimism about the ability of schools to improve the life chances of poor children. The report found that a variety of school "inputs" such as teacher educational attainment and per pupil spending were only weakly correlated with student test scores, and it raised questions about what schools could accomplish without broader changes in social policy. The Coleman Report and subsequent research pushed policymakers to consider outcome-based measures of success and spurred interest in reform strategies that focus on changing the incentives within the public school system.

A careful review of the empirical evidence has suggested, however, that a variety of policies are likely to improve substantially the academic performance of poor children. Importantly, we found examples of successful programs or policies within each of the three broad categories outlined at the beginning of this chapter. Targeted investment of additional resources in early childhood education, smaller class sizes, and bonuses for teachers in hard-to-staff schools and subjects are practices that are likely to pass a cost-benefit test, even without a fundamental reorganization of the existing public school system. At the same time, researchers have identified some ways of changing standard operating procedures within schools that can improve the outcomes of poor children even without large amounts of additional spending. Examples include the adoption of comprehensive school reform models like Success for All and Career Academies and the expansion of alternative certification opportunities. Finally, policies that seek to change incentives within schools, such as the accountability policies adopted by districts and states since the mid-1990s, offer some promise of improving schooling for poor children.

Given limited financial resources and perhaps even more limited political attention, it is unlikely that policymakers could adopt all of the "successful" practices discussed in this chapter. Based on our read of the empirical literature, we believe that the following should be the highest priorities for education policies to improve the academic achievement of poor children:

1. *Increase investments in early childhood education for poor children.* Even though short-term gains in IQ or achievement test scores diminish over time, there is evidence of long-term improvement in a variety of outcomes, such as educational attainment, that help children escape from poverty as adults. Increased investment in early childhood education is particularly important given the limited investment our society currently makes in the cognitive development of very young children. This should be the top priority for new spending in public education.

2. *Take advantage of the opportunity provided by No Child Left Behind to better utilize accountability reforms to improve outcomes for poor children.* NCLB was enacted in 2001 with bipartisan support, although it has received considerable criticism from all sides in recent years. In our view, the debate over the existence of NCLB misses a fundamental lesson we have learned about accountability in the past decade: the specific design of a program matters enormously. It would be a shame if the current (often legitimate) concerns with how NCLB has been implemented lead to a retreat from outcome-oriented accountability in education. Instead, we would recommend several changes to NCLB as well as coexisting state and district accountability systems: adopting common achievement standards across states, focusing accountability on student growth rather than proficiency levels, providing states and districts with the flexibility to focus limited resources on the neediest schools, and reconciling federal and state accountability systems.

3. *Give educators incentives to adopt practices with a compelling research base while expanding efforts (and increasing resources) to develop and identify effective instructional regimes.* One of the lessons from the accountability movement is that highly disadvantaged schools (and districts) often lack the capacity to change themselves. There is good evidence that certain comprehensive school reforms such as Success for All can raise achievement levels among poor children with little additional expenditures. Similarly, there is compelling evidence that alternative certification routes into teaching can expand the supply of teachers willing to work in hard-to-staff schools and subjects while maintaining, or perhaps even increasing, teacher quality. State and district officials should ensure that disadvantaged schools, particularly those that have continued to fail under recent accountability systems, adopt instructional practices and related policies that have a strong research base. There is no need to reinvent the wheel. At the same time, the federal government could help spur such advantages through more focused R&D spending (for example, through "design competitions," as suggested by Slavin 1997), and governments at all levels could help increase the supply of high-quality practices by requiring schools to use programs that have been rigorously evaluated (Jacob and Ludwig 2005).

4. *Continue to support and evaluate a variety of public school choice options.* The other noteworthy trend in output-based reform aside from NCLB is the spread of public school choice at the local level. Although we believe that the current evidence on the benefits of public school choice is limited, we also feel that the risk associated with these policies is small so long as they are implemented in ways that do not substantially exacerbate school segregation along race or class lines. Hence, we would encourage states to facilitate the expansion of magnet and charter schools and to evaluate carefully the impact of these schools on the students they serve and on the surrounding schools.

Most antipoverty policies focus on lifting adults out of poverty. These policies are often controversial because of an unavoidable tension between the desire to help people who have been unlucky and the motivation to encourage hard work and avoid rewarding socially unproductive behavior. In contrast, successful education policies can not only help reduce poverty over the long term by making poor children more productive during adulthood, but also foster economic growth that expands the "pie" for everyone. Educational interventions also benefit from a compelling moral justification as well: disadvantaged children should not be punished for the circumstances into which they were born. Improved education policy is one of the best ways to prevent this from happening.

Thanks to Helen Ladd, Betsey Stevenson, the editors, and conference participants at the University of Wisconsin's Institute for Research on Poverty and the Philadelphia Federal Reserve Bank and the University of Pennsylvania for helpful comments. All opinions and any errors are, of course, ours alone.

NOTES

1. Note that these disparities in schooling outcomes along race and class lines are not simply due to immigration into the United States by those with low initial levels of English or other academic skills, since, for example, reading and math disparities in NAEP scores are large among fourth- and eighth-graders even between non-Hispanic whites and non-Hispanic blacks; see U.S. Department of Education, National Center for Education Statistics, "NAEP Data Explorer," available at: www.nces.ed.gov/nationsreportcard/nde (accessed August 4, 2008).

2. The official evaluation of the program found impacts on elementary prereading and prewriting skills equal to about 0.3 and 0.2 of a standard deviation, respectively (Puma et al. 2005; Ludwig and Phillips 2007). If one calculates Head Start impacts by pooling together the three- and four-year-olds in the experiment, the increased statistical power leads to significant program impacts on math scores and on almost all of the other main cognitive skill outcomes in the report (Ludwig and Phillips 2007).

3. See Northwestern University, Institute for Policy Research Briefing, "Children's Achievement: What Does the Evidence Say About Teachers, Pre-K Programs, and Economic Policies," slide 16, "Irrelevant Difference 3: The Head Start Comparison Hurdle Is Higher," available at: http://www.northwestern.edu/ipr/events/briefing dec06-cook/slide16.html.

4. Some prior research has found that while prekindergarten programs improve cognitive outcomes, they may have adverse effects on noncognitive outcomes like self-control (see, for example, Magnuson, Ruhm, and Waldfogel 2004). The evidence on this issue is not yet available for the new state pre-K programs.

5. This section is based on the summary of Project STAR research by Diane Schanzenbach (2007).

6. Effects for outcomes such as criminal involvement or teen births yield point estimates that are in the direction of beneficial CSR impacts but are imprecisely estimated (Schanzenbach 2007).

7. There are three concerns with value-added measures of effectiveness. One involves the statistical precision of the measures and the possible biases inherent in such measures. Given the small number of students an individual teacher works with in any given year (that is, fifteen or twenty for many elementary school teachers) and the imperfect reliability of student achievement tests, teacher "value-added" measures are generally measured with considerable error (Kane and Staiger 2002a, 2002b). That is, the "confidence interval" around an estimate of a teacher's effectiveness is often quite large. A second concern is that students are not randomly assigned to classrooms, and hard-to-measure student characteristics may influence the rate of growth in their test scores, not just the levels of their scores. So value-added measures may partly confound the causal contribution of the teacher to student learning with those of the characteristics of their students (Rothstein 2007b). A third concern is that the impact of having an effective teacher may fade out over time (Jacob et al. 2008).

8. Several other elementary school models show promise, including Direct Instruction (CRSQ 2006). One of the only other reform models that has been rigorously evaluated is the Comer Schools program, although one problem identified by the research is the limited degree of difference between Comer treatment schools and control schools in the implementation of Comer-style school practices (Cook et al. 1999; Cook, Hunt, and Murphy 2000).

9. There has been little research on teacher "demand" policies. One reason is the perception that disadvantaged school districts are in a state of perpetual shortage and thus will hire anyone who walks through the door. In reality, although many disadvantaged districts often experience shortages in certain subjects and grade levels, they have an ample supply of teachers for most positions. For example, the Chicago Public Schools regularly receive ten applications for each position.

10. This discussion draws on Jacob (2007). Professional development, including mentoring for novice teachers, is another strategy for enhancing teacher ability. Such policies are complements to the policies discussed in this section. For a review, see Hill (2007).

11. As mentioned earlier, professional development is clearly an important complement to the dismissal of underperforming probationary teachers.

12. Personal communication with Jonah Rockoff, February 19, 2008.

13. Calculations by Brian Jacob from Chicago Public Schools administrative records.

14. Unlike more recent accountability reforms, the program in Chicago did not explicitly monitor the fraction of students who were tested so that placing students in special education would benefit a school rating.

15. A struggling student may benefit from placement in special education services. Similarly, teachers and administrators often believe that holding children back in an earlier grade provides them with additional opportunities to mature and to master basic skills before moving on to higher grades. Also, the focus on math and reading relative to science and social studies was one intended goal of the program.

16. If the administrators and teachers in a public school that loses half of its students to a nearby charter school continue teaching the smaller group of students who remain, or

are merely reassigned to other schools in the district, they may not change their practices despite the pressure exerted by the nearby charter.

17. For example, the back-to-basics, discipline-oriented "academy" may be a good fit for some students, while other children may be more likely to thrive in an environment that provides more flexibility and autonomy. Or a good "match" may reflect more mundane needs, including proximity to the parents' work or the availability of a particular elective.

18. For high school students, Cullen, Jacob, and Levitt (2005) find some evidence that winning a choice lottery improves certain non-academic outcomes such as the likelihood of getting into trouble with the police.

19. MTO itself was motivated by the quasi-experimental Gautreaux Program, which moved African American families in Chicago out of public housing to different parts of the metropolitan area. Follow-up surveys suggested that children in families who relocated to the suburbs had much better educational outcomes than those who moved to other parts of the city of Chicago (Rubinowitz and Rosenbaum 2000), although whether city and suburban movers were comparable at baseline remains unclear. There is evidence of positive academic effects for certain subgroups in the MTO experiment, mainly children in the nearly all-black MTO sites in Baltimore and Chicago; this is consistent with non-experimental evidence for African American children in the Project on Human Development in Chicago Neighborhoods (Sampson, Sharkey, and Raudenbush 2008). A ten-year follow-up study of MTO that is currently in progress should provide better evidence on the academic impacts of neighborhood environments.

REFERENCES

Achilles, C. M., Barbara A. Nye, Jayne B. Zaharias, and B. Dewayne Fulton. 1993. "The Lasting Benefits Study (LBS) in Grades 4 and 5 (1990–91): A Legacy from Tennessee's Four-Year (K–3) Class Size Study (1985–1989), Project STAR." Nashville: Tennessee State University.

Barnett, W. Steven, and Leonard Masse. 2007. "Comparative Benefit-Cost Analysis of the Abecedarian Program and Its Policy Implications." *Economics of Education Review* 26(1): 113–25.

Belfield, Clive R., Milagros Nores, Steve Barnett, and Lawrence Schweinhart. 2006. "The High/Scope Perry Preschool Program: Cost-Benefit Analysis Using Data from the Age-Forty Follow-up." *Journal of Human Resources* 41(1): 162–90.

Bifulco, Robert, and Helen Ladd. 2006. "The Impacts of Charter Schools on Student Achievement: Evidence from North Carolina." *American Education Finance Association* 1(1): 50–90.

Bloom, Howard S., Sandra Ham, Laura Melton, and Julieanne O'Brien. 2001. "Evaluating the Accelerated Schools Approach: A Look at Early Implementation and Impacts on Student Achievement in Eight Elementary Schools." New York: MDRC.

Borhnstedt, George W., and Brian M. Stecher. 2002. *What We Have Learned About Class Size Reduction in California.* Capstone Report (September). Palo Alto, Calif.: CSR Research Consortium. Available at: http://www.classize.org/techreport/CSRYear4_final.pdf.

Borman, Geoffrey D., and Gina M. Hewes. 2003. "The Long-Term Effects and Cost-Effectiveness of Success for All." *Educational Evaluation and Policy Analysis* 24(4): 243–66.

Borman, Geoffrey D., Robert E. Slavin, Alan C. K. Cheun, Anne M. Chamberlain, Nancy A. Madden, and Bette Chambers. 2007. "Final Reading Outcomes of the National Randomized Field Trial of Success for All." *American Educational Research Journal* 44(3): 701–31.

Boyd, Donald, Pamela Grossman, Hamilton Lankford, Susanna Loeb, and James Wyckoff. 2005. "How Changes in Entry Requirements Alter the Teacher Workforce and Affect Student Achievement." Working paper 11844. Cambridge, Mass.: National Bureau of Economic Research.

Calvo, Naomi. 2006. "How Parents Choose Schools: A Case Study of the Public School Choice Plan in Seattle." Working paper. Cambridge, Mass.: Harvard University Kennedy School of Government.

Campbell, Frances A., Craig T. Ramey, Elizabeth Puhn Pugnello, Joseph Sparling, and Shari Miller-Johnson. 2002. "Early Childhood Education: Young Adult Outcomes from the Abecedarian Project." *Applied Developmental Science* 6(1): 42–57.

Card, David, and A. Abigail Payne. 2002. "School Finance Reform, the Distribution of School Spending, and the Distribution of Student Test Scores." *Journal of Public Economics* 83(1): 49–82.

Carniero, Pedro, and James J. Heckman. 2003. "Human Capital Policy." In *Inequality in America: What Role for Human Capital Policies?* edited by James J. Heckman and Alan B. Krueger. Cambridge, Mass.: MIT Press.

Carnoy, Martin, and Susanna Loeb. 2003. "Does External Accountability Affect Student Outcomes? A Cross-State Analysis." *Education Evaluation and Policy Analysis* 24(4): 305–31.

Chakrabarti, Rajashri. 2008. "Impact of Voucher Design on Public School Performance: Evidence from Florida and Milwaukee Voucher Programs." Staff report 315. New York: Federal Reserve Bank.

Chiang, Hanley. 2007. "How Accountability Pressure on Failing Schools Affects Student Achievement." Unpublished paper, Harvard University, Cambridge, Mass.

Clotfelter, Charles T., Elizabeth Glennie, Helen Ladd, and Jacob Vigdor. 2006. "Would Higher Salaries Keep Teachers in High-Poverty Schools? Evidence from a Policy Intervention in North Carolina." *Journal of Public Economics* 92(April): 1352–70.

Clotfelter, Charles T., Helen F. Ladd, Jacob L. Vigdor. 2006. "Teacher-Student Matching and the Assessment of Teacher Effectiveness." *Journal of Human Resources* 41(April): 778–820.

Coleman, James S., et al. 1966. *Equality of Educational Opportunity*. Washington: U.S. Department of Health, Education, and Welfare, Office of Education, National Center for Education Statistics.

Comprehensive School Reform Quality (CRSQ). 2006. "Comprehensive School Reform Quality (CRSQ) Center Report on Elementary School Comprehensive School Reform Models." Washington, D.C.: American Institutes for Research (AIR).

Cook, Thomas D., Farah-Naaz Habib, Meredith Phillips, Richard A. Settersten, Shobha C. Shagle, and Serdar M. Degirmencioglu. 1999. "Comer's School Development Program in Prince George's County: A Theory-Based Evaluation." *American Educational Research Journal* 36(3): 543–97.

Cook, Thomas D., H. David Hunt, and Robert F. Murphy. 2000. "Comer's School Development Program in Chicago: A Theory-Based Evaluation." *American Educational Research Journal* 37(2): 535–97.

Cullen, Julie Berry, Brian A. Jacob, and Steven D. Levitt. 2005. "The Impact of School Choice on Student Outcomes: An Analysis of the Chicago Public Schools." *Journal of Public Economics* 89(5–6): 729–60.

———. 2006. "The Effect of School Choice on Student Outcomes: Evidence from Randomized Lotteries." *Econometrica* 74(5): 1191–1230.

Currie, Janet, and Duncan Thomas. 1995. "Does Head Start Make a Difference?" *American Economic Review* 85(3): 341–64.

Deming, David. 2007. "Early Childhood Intervention and Life-Cycle Skill Development." Working paper. Cambridge, Mass.: Harvard University.

Dynarski, Mark, Roberto Agodini, Sheila Heaviside, Timothy Novak, Nancy Care, Larissa Campuzano, Barbara Means, Robert Murphy, William Penuel, Hal Javitz, Deborah Emery, and Willow Sussex. 2007. *Effectiveness of Reading and Mathematics Software Products: Findings from the First Student Cohort.* U.S. Department of Education report to Congress, NCEE 2007-4005, prepared by Mathematica Policy Research (March). Available at: http://www.mathematica-mpr.com/publications/PDFs/effectread.pdf.

Figlio, David. 1997. "Did the 'Tax Revolt' Reduce School Performance?" *Journal of Public Economics* 65(3): 245–69.

Figlio, David N., and Cecilia Elena Rouse. 2006. "Do Accountability and Voucher Threats Improve Low-Achieving Schools?" *Journal of Public Economics* 90(1–2): 239–55.

Fiske, Edward B., and Helen F. Ladd. 2000. *When Schools Compete: A Cautionary Tale.* Washington, D.C.: Brookings Institution Press.

Garces, Eliana, Duncan Thomas, and Janet Currie. 2002. "Longer-Term Effects of Head Start." *American Economic Review* 92(4): 999–1012.

Glazer, Nathan. 1986. "Education and Training Programs and Poverty." In *Fighting Poverty: What Works and What Doesn't,* edited by Sheldon Danziger and Daniel Weinberg. Cambridge, Mass.: Harvard University Press.

Glazerman, Steven. 1998. "Determinants and Consequences of Parental School Choice." PhD diss., University of Chicago, Harris School of Public Policy.

Glazerman, Steven, Tom Silva, Nii Addy, Sarah Avellar, Jeffrey Max, Allison McKie, Brenda Natzke, Michael Puma, Patrick Wolf, and Rachel Ungerer Greszler. 2006. "Options for Studying Teacher Pay Reform Using Natural Experiments." Contract ED-04-CO-0112/0002. Washington, D.C.: Mathematica Policy Research, Inc.

Gordon, Nora E. 2004. "Do Federal Funds Boost School Spending? Evidence from Title I." *Journal of Public Economics* 88(9–10): 1771–92.

Gordon, Robert, Thomas J. Kane, and Douglas O. Staiger. 2006. "Identifying Effective Teachers Using Performance on the Job." Hamilton Project discussion paper 2006-01. Washington, D.C.: Brookings Institution.

Gormley, William T., and Ted Gayer. 2005. "Promoting School Readiness in Oklahoma: An Evaluation of Tulsa's Pre-K Program." *Journal of Human Resources* 40(3): 533–58.

Gormley, William T., Ted Gayer, Deborah Phillips, and Brittany Dawson. 2005. "The Effects of Universal Pre-K on Cognitive Development." Working paper. Washington, D.C.: Georgetown University, Center for Research on Children in the United States.

Guarino, Cassandra M., Lucrecia Santibañez, Glenn A. Daley. 2006. "Tescher Recruitment and Retention: A Review of the Recent Empirical Literature." *Review of Educational Research* 76(2): 173–208.

Guryan, Jonathan. 2004. "Desegregation and Black Dropout Rates." *American Economic Review* 94(4): 919–43.

Hanushek, Eric A. 1997. "Assessing the Effects of School Resources on Student Performance: An Update." *Educational Evaluation and Policy Analysis* 19(2): 141–64.

Hanushek, Eric A., John F. Kain, and Steven G. Rivkin. 2004. "Why Public Schools Lose Teachers." *Journal of Human Resources* 39(2): 326–54.

Hanushek, Eric, John F. Kain, Daniel M. O'Brien, and Steven G. Rivkin. 2005. "The Market for Teachers." Working paper 11154. Cambridge, Mass.: National Bureau of Economic Research.

Hanushek, Eric A., and Margaret E. Raymond. 2005. "Does School Accountability Lead to Improved Student Performance?" *Journal of Policy Analysis and Management* 24(2): 297–327.

Harris, Douglas N., and Tim R. Sass. 2007. "What Makes for a Good Teacher and Who Can Tell?" Unpublished paper. Florida State University, Tallahassee.

Hastings, Justine S., Thomas Kane, and Douglas Staiger. 2006a. "Preferences and Heterogeneous Treatment Effects in a Public School Choice Lottery." Working paper 12145. Cambridge, Mass.: National Bureau of Economic Research.

———. 2006b. "Parental Preferences and School Competition: Evidence from a Public School Choice Program." Working paper 11805. Cambridge, Mass.: National Bureau of Economic Research.

Hastings, Justine S., Richard van Weelden, and Jeffrey Weinstein. 2007. "Preferences, Information, and Parental Choice Behavior in Public School Choice." Working paper 12995. Cambridge, Mass.: National Bureau of Economic Research.

Herlihy, Corinne, and Janet Quint. 2006. "Emerging Evidence on Improving High School Student Achievement and Graduation Rates: The Effects of Four Popular Improvement Programs." National High School Center research brief. Available at: http://www.betterhighschools.org/docs/NHSC_EmergingEvidenceBrief_111606Final.pdf.

Hill, Heather C. 2007. "Learning in the Teaching Workforce." *The Future of Children* 17(1): 111–27.

Howell, William, Paul E. Peterson, and Patrick J. Wolf. 2002. *The Education Gap: Vouchers and Urban Schools*. Washington, D.C.: Brookings Institution Press.

Hoxby, Caroline. 2000. "The Effects of Class Size on Student Achievement: New Evidence from Population Variation." *Quarterly Journal of Economics* 115(4): 1239–85.

———. 2007. "Does Competition Among Public Schools Benefit Students and Taxpayers? Reply." *American Economic Review* 97(5): 2038–55.

Hoxby, Caroline M., and Sonali Murarka. 2007. "Charter Schools in New York City: Who Enrolls and How They Affect Their Students' Achievement." Working paper 14852. Cambridge, Mass.: National Bureau of Economic Research.

Hsieh, Chang-Tai, and Miguel Urquiola. 2006. "The Effects of Generalized School Choice on Achievement and Stratification: Evidence from Chile's Voucher Program." *Journal of Public Economics* 90(8–9): 1477–1503.

Imazeki, Jennifer. 2007. "Attracting and Retaining Teachers in High-Needs Schools: Do Financial Incentives Make Financial Sense?" Working paper. San Diego: San Diego State University, Department of Economics.

Jacob, Brian. 2005. "Accountability, Incentives, and Behavior: The Impact of High-Stakes Testing in the Chicago Public Schools." *Journal of Public Economics* 89(5–6): 761–96.

———. 2007. "The Challenges of Staffing Urban Schools with Effective Teachers." *The Future of Children* 17(1): 129–53.

———. 2008. "The Effect of Employment Protection on Productivity: Evidence from a Change in Teacher Dismissal Policy in the Chicago Public Schools." Working paper. Ann Arbor: University of Michigan, Ford School of Public Policy.

Jacob, Brian, Thomas Kane, Jonah Rockoff, and Douglas Staiger. 2008. "What Pre-employment Characteristics Predict Teacher Effectiveness: Evidence from New York City." Working paper. Ann Arbor: University of Michigan, Ford School of Public Policy.

Jacob, Brian, and Lars Lefgren. 2007. "What Do Parents Value in Education? An Empirical Investigation of Parents' Revealed Preferences for Teachers." *Quarterly Journal of Economics* 122(4): 1603–37.

Jacob, Brian, and Steven Levitt. 2003. "Rotten Apples: An Investigation of the Prevalence and Predictors of Teacher Cheating." *Quarterly Journal of Economics* 117(3): 843–78.

Jacob, Brian, and Jens Ludwig. 2005. "Can the Federal Government Improve Education Research?" In *Brookings Papers on Education Policy,* edited by Diane Ravitch. Washington, D.C.: Brookings Institution Press.

———. 2009. "The Effects of Housing Vouchers on Children's Outcomes." Working paper. Ann Arbor: University of Michigan.

Jargowsky, Paul A. 2003. "Stunning Progress, Hidden Problems: The Dramatic Decline of Concentrated Poverty in the 1990s." Report for the Living Cities Census Series. Washington, D.C.: Brookings Institution.

Jencks, Christopher. 1986. "Education and Training Programs and Poverty." In *Fighting Poverty: What Works and What Doesn't,* edited by Sheldon Danziger and Daniel Weinberg. Cambridge, Mass.: Harvard University Press.

Jencks, Christopher, and Meredith Phillips. 1998. *The Black-White Test Score Gap.* Washington, D.C.: Brookings Institution Press.

Jepsen, Christopher, and Steven G. Rivkin. 2002. "What Is the Trade-off Between Smaller Classes and Teacher Quality?" Working paper 9205. Cambridge, Mass.: National Bureau of Economic Research.

Kahlenberg, Richard D. 2001. "Review of Brown v. Board of Education, by James T. Patterson." *The American Prospect.* May 20, 2001.

Kane, Thomas J., Jonah Rockoff, and Douglas Staiger. 2006. "What Does Certification Tell Us About Teacher Effectiveness? Evidence from New York City." Working paper 12155. Cambridge, Mass.: National Bureau of Economic Research (April).

Kane, Thomas J., and Douglas Staiger. 2002a. "The Promise and Pitfalls of Using Imprecise School Accountability Measures." *Journal of Economic Perspectives* 16(4): 91–114.

———. 2002b. "Volatility in School Test Scores: Implications for Test-Based Accountability Systems." In *Brookings Papers on Education Policy,* edited by Diane Ravitch. Washington, D.C.: Brookings Institution Press.

Kemple, James J., Corinne M. Herlihy, and Thomas J. Smith. 2005. "Making Progress Toward Graduation: Evidence from the Talent Development High School Model." New York: MDRC.

Kemple, James J., and Judith Scott-Clayton. 2004. "Career Academies: Impacts on Labor Market Outcomes and Educational Attainment." New York: MDRC.

Kemple, James J., and Cynthia J. Willner. 2008. "Career Academies: Long-Term Impacts on Labor Market Outcomes, Educational Attainment, and Transitions to Adulthood." New York: MDRC.

Knudsen, Eric I., James J. Heckman, Judy L. Cameron, and Jack P. Shonkoff. 2006. "Economic, Neurobiological, and Behavioral Perspectives on Building America's Future Workforce." *Proceedings of the National Academy of Sciences* 103(27): 10155–62.

Koretz, Daniel, and Sheila Barron. 1998. "The Validity of Gains in Scores on the Kentucky Instructional Results Information System (KIRIS)." Santa Monica, Calif.: RAND Corporation.

Koretz, Daniel, Robert Linn, Stephen B. Dunbar, and Lorrie A. Shepard. 1991. "The Effects of High-Stakes Testing: Preliminary Evidence About Generalization Across Tests." Chicago: American Educational Research Association.

Krueger, Alan B. 2003. "Economic Considerations and Class Size." *Economic Journal* 113(485): 3–33.

Krueger, Alan B., and Diane M. Whitmore. 2001. "The Effect of Attending a Small Class in the Early Grades on College-Test Taking and Middle School Test Results: Evidence from Project STAR." *Economic Journal* 111(468): 1–28.

———. 2002. "Would Smaller Classes Help Close the Black-White Achievement Gap?" In *Bridging the Achievement Gap*, edited by John Chub and Tom Loveless. Washington, D.C.: Brookings Institute Press.

Krueger, Alan B., and Pei Zhu. 2004. "Another Look at the New York City School Voucher Experiment." *The American Behavioral Scientist* 47(5): 658.

Ladd, Helen F. 2002. "School Vouchers: A Critical View." *Journal of Economic Perspectives* 16(4): 3–24.

Ladd, Helen F., and Edward B. Fiske. 2001. "The Uneven Playing Field of School Choice: Evidence from New Zealand." *Journal of Policy Analysis and Management* 20(1): 43–63.

Levin, Henry. 1977. "A Decade of Policy Developments in Improving Education and Training for Low-Income Populations." In *A Decade of Federal Anti-Poverty Policy: Achievements, Failures, and Lessons*, edited by Robert Haveman. New York: Academic Press.

Levin, Jessica, Jennifer Mulhern, and Joan Schunck. 2005. "Unintended Consequences: The Case for Reforming the Staffing Rules in Urban Teachers Union Contracts." New York: The New Teacher Project. Available at: www.tntp.org.

Levin, Jessica, and Meredith Quinn. 2003. "Missed Opportunities: How We Keep High-Quality Teachers Out of Urban Classrooms." New York: The New Teacher Project. Available at: www.tntp.org.

Love, John M., Ellen Eliason Kisker, Christine M. Ross, Peter Z. Schochet, Jeanne Brooks-Gunn, Diane Paulsell, Kimberly Boller, Jill Constantine, Cheri Vogel, Allison Sidle Fuligni, and Christy Brady-Smith. 2002. "Making a Difference in the Lives of Infants and Toddlers and Their Families: The Impacts of Early Head Start." Research report. Princeton, N.J.: Mathematica Policy Research, Inc.

Ludwig, Jens. 2003. "The Great Unknown: Does the Black-White Test Score Gap Narrow or Widen Through the School Years? It Depends on How You Measure." *Education Next* (summer): 79–82.

Ludwig, Jens, and Douglas L. Miller. 2007. "Does Head Start Improve Children's Life Chances? Evidence from a Regression-Discontinuity Design." *Quarterly Journal of Economics* 122(1): 159–208.

Ludwig, Jens, and Deborah A. Phillips. 2007. "The Benefits and Costs of Head Start." Working Paper 12973. Cambridge, Mass.: National Bureau of Economic Research.

Ludwig, Jens, and Isabel Sawhill. 2007. "Success by Ten: Intervening Early, Often, and Effectively in the Education of Young Children." Hamilton Project discussion paper 2007-02. Washington, D.C.: Brookings Institution.

Magnuson, Katherine A., Christopher J. Ruhm, and Jane Waldfogel. 2004. "Does Pre-kindergarten Improve School Preparation and Performance?" Working paper 10452. Cambridge, Mass.: National Bureau of Economic Research.

Murnane, Richard, and David Cohen. 1986. "Merit Pay and the Evaluation Problem: Why Most Merit Pay Plans Fail and a Few Survive." *Harvard Educational Review* 56(spring): 1–17.

National Center for Education Statistics (NCES). 2007a. "The Nation's Report Card, Mathematics 2007: National Assessment of Educational Progress at Grades 4 and 8." NCES 2007-494. Washington: U.S. Department of Education, Institute of Education Sciences.

———. 2007b. "The Nation's Report Card, Reading 2007: National Assessment of Educational Progress at Grades 4 and 8." NCES 2007-496. Washington: U.S. Department of Education, Institute of Education Sciences.

Neal, Derek A. 2002. "How Vouchers Could Change the Market for Education." *Journal of Economic Perspectives* 16(4): 25–44.

Neal, Derek A., and Diane Schanzenbach. 2007. "Left Behind by Design: Proficiency Counts and Test-Based Accountability." Working paper 13293. Cambridge, Mass.: National Bureau of Economic Research.

Nye, Barbara, B. DeWayne Fulton, Jayne Boyd-Zaharias, and Van A. Cain. 1995. "The Lasting Benefits Study, Eighth Grade Technical Report." Nashville, Tenn.: Center of Excellence for Research in Basic Skills, Tennessee State University.

Olsen, Edgar O. 2003. "Housing Programs for Low-Income Households." In *Means-Tested Transfer Programs in the United States,* edited by Robert A. Moffitt. Chicago: University of Chicago Press.

Phillips, Meredith, James Crouse, and Ralph John. 1998. "Does the Black-White Test Score Gap Widen After Children Enter School?" In *The Black-White Test Score Gap,* edited by Christopher Jencks and Meredith Phillips. Washington, D.C.: Brookings Institution Press.

Puma, Michael, Stephen Bell, Ronna Cook, Camilla Heid, Michael Lopez, et al. 2005. "Head Start Impact Study: First-Year Findings." Report prepared for the U.S. Department of Health and Human Services. Washington: Westat.

Quint, Janet, Howard Bloom, Alison Rebeck Black, LaFleur Stephens, and Teresa Akey. 2005. "First Things First: The Challenge of Scaling Up Educational Reform." New York: MDRC.

Ramey, Craig T., and Frances A. Campbell. 1979. "Compensatory Education for Disadvantaged Children." *The School Review* 87(2): 171–89.

Rockoff, Jonah. 2004. "The Impact of Individual Teachers on Student Achievement: Evidence from Panel Data." *American Economic Review: Papers and Proceedings* 94(2): 247–52.

Rothstein, Jesse. 2007a. "Does Competition Among Public Schools Benefit Students and Taxpayers? A Comment on Hoxby (2000)." *American Economic Review* 97(5): 2026–37.

————. 2007b. "Do Value-Added Models Add Value? Tracking, Fixed Effects, and Causal Inference." Working paper. Princeton, N.J.: Princeton University Department of Economics.

Rouse, Cecilia E., Jane Hannaway, Dan D. Goldhaber, and David N. Figlio. 2007. "Feeling the Florida Heat? How Low-Performing Schools Respond to Voucher and Accountability Pressure." Working paper 13681. Cambridge, Mass.: National Bureau of Economic Research.

Rubinowitz, Leonard S., and James E. Rosenbaum. 2000. *Crossing the Class and Color Lines: From Public Housing to White Suburbia.* Chicago: University of Chicago Press.

Sampson, Robert J., Patrick Sharkey, and Stephen W. Raudenbush. 2008. "Durable Effects of Concentrated Disadvantage on Verbal Ability of African American Children." *Proceedings of the National Academy of Sciences* 105(3): 845–52.

Sanbonmatsu, Lisa, Jeffrey R. Kling, Greg J. Duncan, and Jeanne Brooks-Gunn. 2006. "Neighborhoods and Academic Achievement: Results from the MTO Experiment." *Journal of Human Resources* 41(4): 649–91.

Sass, Tim. 2006. "Charter Schools and Student Achievement in Florida." *Education Finance and Policy* 1(1): 91–122.

Scafidi, Benjamin, David L. Sjoquist, and Todd R. Stinebrickner. 2007. "Race, Poverty, and Teacher Mobility." *Economics of Education Review* 26(2): 145–59.

Schanzenbach, Diane Whitmore. 2007. "What Have Researchers Learned from Project STAR?" *Brookings Papers on Education Policy 2006–2007,* edited by Thomas Loveless and Frederick Hess. Washington, D.C.: Brookings Institution Press.

Schweinhart, Lawrence J., Jeanne Montie, Zongping Xiang, W. Steven Barnett, Clive R. Belfield, and Milagros Nores. 2005. *Lifetime Effects: The High/Scope Perry Preschool Study Through Age Forty.* Ypsilanti, Mich.: High/Scope Press.

Shonkoff, Jack, and Deborah Phillips, eds. 2000. *From Neurons to Neighborhoods: The Science of Early Childhood Development.* Washington, D.C.: National Academies Press.

Slavin, Robert E. 1997. "Design Competitions: A Proposal for a New Federal Role in Educational Research and Development." *Educational Researcher* 26(1): 22–28.

Snipes, Jason C., Glee Ivory Holton, Fred Doolittle, and Laura Sztejnberg. 2006. "Striving for Success: The Effect of Project GRAD on High School Student Outcomes in Three Urban School Districts." New York: MDRC.

Springer, Matthew G., Dale Ballou, and Art Peng. 2008. "Impact of the Teacher Advancement Program on Student Test Score Gains: Findings from an Independent Appraisal." Working paper 2008-19. Nashville: Vanderbilt University, National Center on Performance Incentives.

Steele, Jennifer, Richard Murnane, and John Willet. 2008. "Do Financial Incentives Help Low-Performing Schools Attract and Retain Academically Talented Teachers? Evidence from California." Working paper. Cambridge, Mass.: Harvard University Graduate School of Education.

Stinebrickner, Todd R. 2002. "An Analysis of Occupational Change and Departure from the Labor Force: Evidence of the Reasons That Teachers Leave." *Journal of Human Resources* 37(1): 192–216.

Teacher Advancement Program (TAP). 2009. "About Us." Available at: http://www.talentedteacher.org/about/about.taf (accessed May 2, 2009).

Urquiola, Miguel. 2005. "Does School Choice Lead to Sorting? Evidence from Tiebout Variation." *American Economic Review* 95(4): 1310–1326.

Van der Klaauw, Wilbert. 2008. "Breaking the Link Between Poverty and Low Student Achievement: An Evaluation of Title I." *Journal of Econometrics* 142(2): 731–56.

Vigdor, Jacob, and Jens Ludwig. 2008. "Segregation and the Black-White Test Score Gap." In *Stalled Progress,* edited by Katherine Magnuson and Jane Waldfogel. New York: Russell Sage Foundation.

Watson, Tara. 2006. "Metropolitan Growth, Inequality, and Neighborhood Segregation by Income." Unpublished paper, Williams College, Williamstown, Mass.

What Works Clearinghouse (WWC). 2007a. "Intervention Report: Everyday Mathematics." Washington: U.S. Department of Education.

Wong, Vivian C., Thomas D. Cook, W. Steven Barnett, and Kwanghee Jung. 2008. "An Effectiveness-Based Evaluation of Five State Prekindergarten Programs." *Journal of Policy Analysis and Management* 27(1): 122–54.

Chapter 11

Workforce Development as an Antipoverty Strategy: What Do We Know? What Should We Do?

Harry J. Holzer

O ver the past few decades, the gaps in earnings between more- and less-educated American workers have widened. The number of adult workers in low-wage jobs has risen, partly because of the growing *supply* of these workers, associated with welfare reform and immigration (among other forces), and partly because of growing *demand* for these workers in low-paying jobs (Autor, Katz, and Kearney 2006). And at least among less-educated and minority men, the numbers with criminal records and other characteristics that make them "hard to employ" has risen dramatically as well.

A consensus has developed among economists and policy analysts on the increasingly important role that workforce skills play in explaining the labor market problems of the disadvantaged. The lack of skills and educational credentials among disadvantaged groups, like racial and ethnic minorities and the poor, contributes to their low employment and earnings and inhibits their ability to advance in the labor market. As a result, many policymakers and researchers have suggested increased public investments in improving early education opportunities, reforming school practices in the K–12 years, and improving access to higher education (Heckman 2008; Jacob and Ludwig, this volume).

In contrast, there is no such consensus about the ability of workforce development (or job training programs) to raise employment and earnings for disadvantaged youth and adults. Federal funding of these efforts has greatly diminished over time, both in real terms and especially relative to the size of the economy, even though the economic rewards to skills have grown. Why has support for workforce development policies fallen so far as an antipoverty strategy? What are the most recent developments in the field, and what is the state of knowledge about their success? Is a resurgence of interest in workforce development for the poor merited? And for low-wage workers for whom workforce development is unlikely to be a successful option, what other policies might work?

In this chapter, I address these questions by reviewing trends in federal funding, the evolution of major workforce development programs, and the evaluation evidence about their cost-effectiveness. I then describe promising new approaches before concluding with some thoughts on what a workforce development agenda might include and what is needed for such an agenda to succeed.

TRENDS IN FEDERAL FUNDING AND THE EVOLUTION OF WORKFORCE DEVELOPMENT PROGRAMS

What do we mean by workforce development or employment and training programs? The latter might be defined as any kind of education or work experience that directly prepares workers for specific occupations or jobs. This definition potentially includes many types of activities, whether in the classroom or on the job, whether formal or informal, whether for workers currently employed or the unemployed.[1] The broader concept of workforce development might also include a range of employment services, including pre-employment assessments and job placement assistance as well as post-employment supports such as assistance with child care or transportation.

Training Programs at the Department of Labor

Since the early 1960s, and especially since the declaration of the "War on Poverty" in 1964, the U.S. Department of Labor (DOL) has funded employment and training services for the disadvantaged, along with other workers. Over the years these efforts have evolved through several major pieces of legislation: the Manpower Development Training Act (MDTA) of 1962 to 1973; the Comprehensive Employment and Training Act (CETA) of 1974 to 1984; the Job Training Partnership Act (JTPA) of 1984 to 1999; and the Workforce Investment Act (WIA) of 1999 to the present.[2] These legislative developments reflect the changes in priorities and perspectives on employment and training for the disadvantaged held by Congress during various presidential administrations. For instance, MDTA provided direct federal grants to local service providers and in 1965 began funding the Job Corps, which provides a year of education and training to disadvantaged youth at residential centers around the country.

With CETA, the federal government began to devolve responsibility for some employment and training to state and local advisory committees. Funding for employment and training increased dramatically in the late 1970s as employment levels among low-income and especially minority adults and youth deteriorated. Public-service employment was provided to 750,000 individuals in 1978 (Ellwood and Welty 2000), about 10 percent of all unemployed individuals, under the view that they would have difficulty obtaining employment on their own in the private sector.

With the passage of JTPA in 1984, the Reagan administration eliminated public-service employment, which it regarded as a wasteful substitution for employment that otherwise would exist in the private sector.[3] Funds were dispersed by private industry councils (PICs) that were expected to reflect local demand for labor. The notion of a "demand-driven" system was further implemented in 1999 with WIA: local workforce investment boards (WIBs) were to reflect the needs of local businesses, which now controlled the majority of seats on any board. Any remaining vestiges of public employment still available (in the summer youth programs, for example) were also eliminated.

Title I of WIA is now the primary vehicle for federal funding of job training and employment services. It focuses on three groups: adults, youth (mostly in-school), and dislocated workers. The last group includes adults who have permanently and involuntarily lost a job owing to plant closing or downsizing, regardless of skill level or wage. Title I still funds the Job Corps for disadvantaged youth and smaller programs for Native Americans, ex-offenders, veterans, and migrant and seasonal farmworkers, among others.[4]

Under WIA, workers have greater control over how to spend their training funds, particularly when they receive vouchers known as individual training accounts (ITAs). WIA created the "one-stop" offices at which workers gain access to all services funded by the Labor Department, including unemployment insurance and use of the Public Employment Service, the primary provider of public "labor exchange" services: unemployed workers can find out about available jobs by consulting job postings submitted to the government by private employers (O'Leary, Straits, and Wandner 2004).

WIA reflects a belief in empowering local employers and workers and providing services to a broader population that can be quickly matched to existing jobs. Importantly, adult services are no longer targeted only to the disadvantaged. This change was implemented in part to remove any stigma associated with publicly provided employment and training services from the perspective of employers.

There are three categories of employment services for adults: core, intensive, and training. Core services involve self-directed use of the Public Employment Service and other local employment listings as well as staff-assisted job search. Intensive services consist of assessments of job skills and counseling. Individuals must participate in core and intensive services before they can receive training, and many are diverted into the workforce without receiving any training. Thus, WIA reflects the "work-first" philosophy (embodied in "welfare reform") of getting as many people as possible into private-sector jobs as quickly as possible.

The goal of making services more universally available has been achieved: low-income individuals now make up only about 20 percent of nondislocated adult registrants and just over half of those receiving training. In contrast, the nondislocated adults served under CETA and JTPA were primarily disadvantaged until the late 1990s. Dislocated workers are less likely to have been low-

FIGURE 11.1   /   Worker Training in Primary Department of Labor Programs, 1963 to 2003

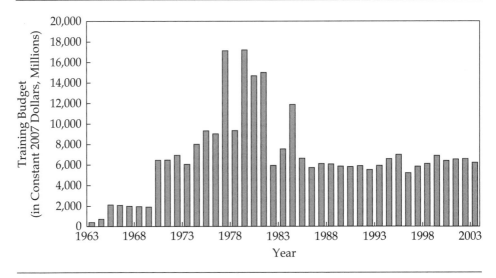

Source: Author's compilation based on Simonetta (2004).

income before their displacement, and the share of dislocated workers among training recipients has grown over time. The numbers and shares of all WIA participants receiving any training has declined, as has the average duration of such training; core and intensive services for the nondisadvantaged who take jobs without any new training now consume more resources than prior to WIA (Frank and Minoff 2005).[5]

What has happened to overall federal funding levels for employment and training programs at the Department of Labor? Total expenditures under Title I of WIA for the fiscal year 2008 were roughly $860 million, $1.2 billion, and $924 million for adult, displaced, and youth services, respectively, plus about $1.7 billion for the Job Corps. If funding for several smaller programs is included, total federal spending was about $5.5 billion. To compare current spending with that in earlier years, figure 11.1 plots annual expenditures on employment and job training from MDTA in 1963 through WIA in 2003 in constant dollars. After peaking in real terms in 1979 at about $17 billion, funding declined until 1985, and it has either remained flat or declined more since then. By 2003, inflation-adjusted funding had fallen by about 65 percent from its 1979 peak, and by nearly 70 percent by 2008. However, because the *real* economy has more than doubled in size since 1979, this funding has fallen by about 87 percent in *relative* terms—from roughly 0.30 percent to 0.04 percent of gross domestic product (GDP). Since 1985, funding in relative terms has declined from 0.08 to 0.04 percent of GDP. Because WIA now funds a broader range of services for a broader set of participants than it did thirty years ago, the decline in spending on the disadvantaged, especially for direct employment and training, has been even greater.

Other Workforce Development Programs

This picture of declining training over time would be inaccurate if funds for training in programs outside the Labor Department had increased sufficiently. In fact, a criticism of government programs for low-income individuals is the extent to which they appear in multiple agencies in the federal budget, with inefficiencies associated with overlapping clientele and jurisdictions.

A recent government report shows spending on about forty federal employment and training programs (Government Accountability Office [GAO] 2003).[6] These programs overall accounted for over $34 billion in spending, but actual expenditures on employment and training within these programs accounted for a much smaller amount—roughly $14 billion. These expenditures amount to just over 0.1 percent of GDP—a smaller fraction than is spent on training and workforce development virtually anywhere else in the industrial world (Heckman, Lalonde, and Smith 1999; O'Leary, Straits, and Wandner 2004).

As mentioned, much of this spending does not target the disadvantaged. About three-quarters of all training expenditures are accounted for by WIA Title I services for adults, youth, displaced workers, and the Job Corps, plus funds expended under state vocational rehabilitation services and Temporary Assistance for Needy Families (TANF). Vocational services target the disabled and not necessarily the disadvantaged; TANF training funds constitute a very small share of total TANF expenditures on welfare recipients or other needy families. Robin Spence and Brendan Kiel (2003) find that expenditures on education and training account for only about 2 percent of federal TANF expenditures, a major reduction relative to what was spent in the pre-TANF era on other employment programs for welfare recipients. This reflects the reorientation of welfare programs toward work-first approaches, generally to the exclusion of workforce training. Even if we add estimates of training expenditures funded by various block grants from the Department of Health and Human Services (HHS) to the states, like the Social Services Block Grant (SSBG) and the Community Services Block Grant (CSBG), this picture does not change fundamentally.[7]

The GAO report does not include expenditures by the Department of Education on vocational training (funded through the Perkins Act) or on college scholarships in the form of Pell grants (funded through the Higher Education Act of 1965). Perkins expenditures (of roughly $1.2 billion annually) accrue mainly to high schools and two-year technical colleges; thus, most funding goes to very young people. Funding for Perkins has been flat in nominal terms for many years and has declined in real terms.

Interest in career and technical education (CTE, formerly known as "vocational education") or in "school-to-career" programs that blend academic and occupational education with appropriate work experience for high school youth (both poor and nonpoor) has also dwindled over time. Modest federal funding for the School-to-Work Opportunities Act of 1994, which provided about $50 million each year in seed money to local school districts to develop new school-to-work programs with local employers between 1996 and 2001, has been eliminated.

Pell grants are the primary source of federal scholarship funds for college attendance among the poor—including those students receiving occupational training at community colleges.[8] Pell expenditures have risen in recent years, from $6.6 billion in 1990–1991 (or over $9 billion in 2008 dollars) to $14 billion in 2007–2008. These grants finance higher education among low-income youth or adults.

Nonetheless, the recent increases in Pell funding have fallen short of rising tuition costs and overall student needs.[9] Eligibility for Pell grant use is limited to those taking classes at accredited community colleges at least half-time, thereby excluding other training providers and students who are taking classes less than half-time; at community colleges, many short-term and remedial classes taken by poor students are not covered by Pell funding.[10]

In short, expenditures outside of the Department of Labor on employment and training have increased in some cases and decreased in others, but they have not fully offset the dramatic declines that have occurred in the former, especially relative to the growing needs of the low-income populations.

WHY HAS FUNDING FOR AND INTEREST IN TRAINING FALLEN?

Perceptions of Ineffectiveness: The Evaluation Literature

A major reason for the decline over time in public spending on and interest in workforce development has been a widespread perception that the programs are not cost-effective at raising future earnings of participants. There is little doubt about the large private and social returns to education and training in our economy. But why might training for *disadvantaged* adults or youth, in publicly funded programs, be less effective?

One reason might be that the basic cognitive skills of disadvantaged adults are too weak to be effectively increased by limited occupational training. Another might be that their motivation to participate in training is low, especially if the programs are time-consuming. This might be particularly true for working parents (especially single parents) who are already pressed for time, or for youth who are not yet ready to "settle down." Or perhaps prospective employers are not impressed by any government-sponsored training if an applicant's other educational and work experiences are weak.

Is the general perception of program ineffectiveness warranted by the evidence (Heckman, Lalonde, and Smith 1999; Lalonde 2003)? In the next section, I briefly summarize the evaluation literature and draw implications for workforce development policy. In this literature, the estimated impacts of training programs for disadvantaged workers on their later earnings vary considerably with demographic group: in general, *more positive impacts are observed for adult women than for men, and for adults more than for out-of-school youth.* The estimated impacts also vary with the following: (1) whether program participation was voluntary or mandatory; (2) whether participants were hard to employ because they had severe disabilities or because other barriers prevented them from working, such as a criminal record, substance abuse, or very poor skills; (3) the duration and intensity of the workforce development treatment; (4) the nature and content of the treatment—that is, whether it focused primarily on classroom training, on-the-job training, or work experience; (5) the scale of the program and whether it was a replication effort; and (6) whether the evaluation used survey or administrative data.

PROGRAMS FOR DISADVANTAGED ADULTS   The evidence on training programs for disadvantaged adults can be summed up as follows: modest expenditures usually produce modest positive impacts. The evidence derives from the experimental National JTPA Study (NJS) of the early 1990s, as well as from earlier non-experimental studies of CETA and more recent ones of WIA. Evaluations of various welfare-to-work programs lead to similar conclusions.

Estimates of the impacts on the annual earnings of adult men and women in the NJS within thirty months of random assignment are over $800 (10 percent and 16 percent, respectively, for men and women) for those who actually enrolled in the training program (or about $1,150 in 2007 dollars) and somewhat less for all those who were assigned but did not participate (Bloom et al. 1997).[11] Earnings gains were observed both for those engaged in classroom training and for those receiving on-the-job training. Although earnings gains were driven more by increases in employment rates than by hourly wages for enrollees, there was at least some modest evidence of both.[12]

These increases in annual earnings are modest and seem to fade somewhat over time (GAO 1996). However, these magnitudes need to be compared to program costs. Although the average cost of treatment was about $2,300, those in the control group also enrolled in other services. The net NJS costs per enrollee were about $1,000 for adult men and $1,300 for adult women for over two hundred hours of net increase in training (or $1,580 and $2,050 in 2007 dollars), and the net costs per assignee were roughly $650 and $850 (or $1,025 and $1,340 in 2007 dollars), respectively.[13] Thus, *the returns per net dollar spent in JTPA were quite impressive;* even with the fading out of positive impacts, the program paid for itself over five years. For instance, the sum of earnings impacts per assignee, after adjusting for inflation and discounting at 0.05, is well over double the net costs of the program (GAO 1996). Heckman, Lalonde, and Smith (1999) also report net social gains of up to $1,000 or more (or over $1,400 in 2007 dollars) for the five-year follow-up period for adult men and women each, even assuming annual discount rates up to 10 percent and various estimates of the "welfare cost" to the economy of each dollar of taxation.[14] Such gains represent a near-doubling of total benefits generated by the program, relative to its costs.

Recent training programs for poor adults have emphasized community college attendance paid for by Pell grants. The evidence suggests that these grants raise rates of college attendance among poor adults, though not necessarily for youth (Turner 2007). Whether attending community college generates significant earnings gains for disadvantaged adults is less clear. Statistical (but not experimental) studies show significant returns for disadvantaged individuals who attend community college for at least one year, especially when they gain a certificate or degree (Lerman 2007).

Evaluations of other programs, including mandatory welfare-to-work programs and voluntary work experience programs for women, involved a variety of different treatments (with more or less training) and led to mixed results. For instance, the mandatory GAIN program in Riverside, California, provided job search assistance but relatively little training, and it generated fairly sizable increases in subsequent employment rates (Riccio, Friedlander, and Freedman 1994). But Joseph Hotz, Guido Imbens, and Jacob Klerman (2000) find significant long-term returns to training at the Los Angeles and Oakland GAIN sites. The Saturation Work Initiative Model (SWIM) and Community Work Experience Program (CWEP) in San Diego, which combined job search assistance and some work supports with limited training and mandatory work experience, also generated fairly large impacts per dollar spent (Lalonde 2003).[15] However, other work experience programs that provided fewer supports and training services were less effective in generating lasting employment increases.

The National Evaluation of Welfare-to-Work Strategies (NEWWS), implemented in the mid-1990s, included both a human capital strategy and a labor market attachment strategy for welfare recipients, with the latter being less expensive than the former (Hamilton et al. 2001). The NEWWS evaluation found that the training programs were less effective than the labor market attachment programs, though impacts from both tended to fade with time. The Portland, Oregon, site generated large and lasting impacts, however, using a mixed strategy in which most participants faced pressure to seek work while case managers allowed access to job training at a community college for those who they thought would benefit from it.[16] Participants were also encouraged to search for higher-paying jobs at the outset, rather than accepting the first job they found. Mixed strategies that combine employment services (like job placement assistance) with other supports, such as earnings supplements, have also shown positive impacts elsewhere.[17] And some non-experimental evidence suggested that the NEWWS sites that provided occupational training rather than general adult education generated somewhat larger impacts at the "human capital" sites (Bos et al. 2001).

A quite different category of programs has targeted those generally considered hard to employ, such as long-term welfare recipients, those with physical or emotional disabilities or substance abuse problems, and those with criminal records. The number of individuals in the last category has grown enormously in recent years: over 2 million individuals are now incarcerated in the United States at any time, and about twice that many are on parole or probation (Travis 2005). These individuals generally had weak employment prospects before being incarcerated, and their experiences behind bars only further weaken those prospects; after they are released, employers are even more reluctant to hire them and their skills and labor market attachments are further attenuated (Holzer 2007b).

One effective treatment for harder-to-employ welfare recipients was the National Supported Work (NSW) demonstration. Participants were given twelve to eighteen months of paid work experience plus additional supports. Robert Lalonde (2003) reports sizable impacts for adult women that are cost-effective if they persist.[18] In contrast, the estimated impacts for adult men with criminal records and disadvantaged youth were not significant. A reexamination of the results for adult men (Uggen 2000), however, suggested significant reductions in recidivism for men above age twenty-seven, consistent with other evidence on offenders aging out of crime. On the other hand, we have little rigorous evidence to date of programs that raise their earnings.

Other examples of programs for disadvantaged adults deserve mention. An experimental evaluation of the Center for Employment Training (CET) in San Jose in the late 1980s showed large positive impacts on earnings.[19] This program represented a new approach to training in which the services were closely aligned with the needs of local employers, with whom the training providers were in close touch (Melendez 1996). An effort to replicate that model in other sites in the 1990s generated weaker impacts (Miller et al. 2005), partly because the control group members in high-fidelity sites (mostly in California) received unusually high amounts of community college training on their own.

Important questions remain about how to interpret these results. On the one hand, impact estimates from random experiments might be biased downward by the tendency of control group members to get services or training on their own—which apparently was the case in the CET replication and with JTPA (Heckman, Lalonde, and Smith 1999). This raises an important question: What exactly should be the counterfactual when judging the impact of specific training programs? Should outcomes for individuals in these programs be compared to outcomes for those with no training at all or for those who receive other forms of training already available (at least in some places)? On the other hand, positive impacts estimated for small programs might overstate the potential social benefits of replicating and expanding these efforts, especially if large-scale programs cause other workers to be displaced by program participants.

Also, the NJS study refers to training efforts around 1990; since then, JTPA has been transformed into WIA, which provides different training services (often shorter-term) to a different set of individuals. Unfortunately, there has been no randomized evaluation of WIA, though there is some positive non-experimental evidence (Mueser, Troske, and Gorislavsky 2005). Indeed, WIA cannot be considered a "program," as it is simply a set of funding streams that are locally dispersed in many different ways. We have little knowledge of which efforts are relatively more or less cost-effective for the disadvantaged, and especially for those who are harder to employ. Similar questions remain about how to interpret the results from welfare-to-work programs like Portland NEWWS and Riverside GAIN after the 1996 welfare reform dramatically changed welfare. And we know little about the effectiveness of other important kinds of services, such as adult basic education (including English-language instruction for immigrants).[20] Nonetheless, I conclude that many modest programs for disadvantaged adults in the past have worked reasonably well, as have a few intensive efforts for the harder-to-employ.

PROGRAMS FOR DISADVANTAGED YOUTH   If training programs for disadvantaged adults are at least modestly cost-effective, those for disadvantaged youth have been disappointing but somewhat better than the conventional wisdom would have it. For example, the short-term training provided by JTPA for disadvantaged youth was at best ineffective and at worst counterproductive (Bloom et al. 1997). More intensive programs, like the Job Corps, have seemed more promising. The Job Corps provides yearlong training to over sixty thousand disadvantaged youth each year at over one hundred residential centers nationwide; besides the education and training they receive, residence at the centers enables young people to escape their low-income family or neighborhood settings and what are likely for some to be negative parental or peer influences that might counteract the positive influences of training.[21]

The earliest experimental evaluations of the Job Corps showed positive impacts on youth wages and hours of work for up to thirty months after enrollment; there were also significant increases in the acquisition of general equivalency diplomas (GEDs) and vocational certificates and reductions in crime and incarceration. Program costs per participant (about $20,000 currently) were more than offset by social gains, since there was no early evidence that the positive impacts faded over time. A follow-up study (Schochet, McConnell, and Burghardt 2003) has found, however, that positive impacts of the Job Corps faded away by the fourth year after random assignment. For those who were age twenty to twenty-four while in the program, positive impacts persisted somewhat. But the notion that the Job Corps represents an effective intervention for out-of-school, disadvantaged youth in the long run has certainly been called into question.

Still, it is misleading and premature to infer that nothing works for disadvantaged youth, in part because recent training efforts for disadvantaged *in-school* youth seem promising. For example, career academies represent a new approach to career and technical education for young people in high school. Each academy is a "school within a school" that provides training and work experience within a particular sector of the economy. James Kemple (2008) shows that career academies raise earnings by 1 percent relative to the control group and that the impacts persist for at least eight years after high school graduation. These gains are larger for disadvantaged young men than for other young men, and stronger for young men than young women—a rare finding. Positive impacts were observed on wages as well as employment rates.[22] Despite concerns over whether career education "tracks" minority or low-income youth into noncollege trajectories, the experimental groups completed postsecondary education at the same rate as those in the control groups and suffered no loss (or gain) in academic achievement. Non-experimental evaluations of other school-to-work programs (Lerman 2007) indicate similar positive impacts on earnings and on high school graduation.

Attendance, retention, and achievement of at-risk youth at community colleges or four-year colleges can also be enhanced. Pell grants alone may not currently accomplish this goal for youth (Turner 2007), but the package of additional financial supports and services in the Opening Doors Project appear to be more successful in this regard (Richburg-Hayes 2008). A variety of proposals to simplify federal grants and student loan applications might also make Pell grants and other forms of aid more effective at raising college attendance for youth than they currently appear to be (Dynarski and Scott-Clayton 2007).

Even for *out-of-school* disadvantaged youth it is too soon to conclude that nothing works. A short-term experimental evaluation of the Youth Service and Conservation Corps (Jastrzab et al. 1997) showed strong positive impacts on a range of youth employment and behavioral outcomes, at least during the duration of the program; a longer-term evaluation of more sites is currently under way. Outcomes for Youth Build also suggest positive impacts on educational attainment and negative effects on recidivism, though no rigorous evaluations have yet been performed (Cohen and Piquero 2008). And other models, like the "military" approach of the National Guard's ChalleNGe program, a residential program based on a military model, has shown short-run success in raising the attainment of GEDs and diplomas among high school dropouts (Bloom, Gardenhire-Crooks, and Mandsager 2009).

Although employment programs for youth (both summer and year-round) have largely been eliminated from WIA, their short-term impacts might be more positive than have been appreciated. The Youth Incentive Employment Pilot Project (YIEPP) in the late 1970s, which guaranteed a publicly funded job to participating youth, had large positive impacts on employment and on school attendance and completion, suggesting that paid work experience tends to be successful in motivating disadvantaged youth to participate in schooling or training. It is unclear whether these employment efforts had long-term effects. However, even modest reductions in dropout rates (and accompanying criminal activity) for disadvantaged youth might be cost-beneficial.

Positive impacts have also been documented for mentoring and "youth development" programs like Big Brothers/Big Sisters (Herrera 1999) and, to some extent, for Quantum Opportunities.[23] Although these are not workforce development or job training programs, they can be viewed as complements rather than substitutes for workforce-type efforts. Finally, the Youth Opportunities Program earlier this decade was an attempt to saturate low-income neighborhoods (in thirty-six areas nationwide) with greater educational and employment opportunities for youth and to build "systems" that would better track these youth when they dropped out of school, left foster care, or became incarcerated. This program was eliminated before any evaluation results became available, though early descriptive evidence seemed promising (GAO 2006).

In sum, while much remains unknown about exactly which approaches are most successful for disadvantaged (especially out-of-school) youth, the successes noted in this chapter challenge the notion that "nothing works" for these youth.

Other Approaches, Other Problems, and a Changing Labor Market

The conclusion that job training programs for poor adults and youth are not cost-effective, while not very accurate, has been reinforced by several widely held perceptions, including:

- Other approaches for improving the earnings of the disadvantaged are more cost-effective than training and therefore are more worthy of scarce public dollars.

- Problems of the disadvantaged other than their lack of occupational skills and work experience are more serious.

- A changing labor market is rendering job training less relevant than it might have been in previous generations.

I review each of these arguments in the following section.

ARE OTHER APPROACHES MORE COST-EFFECTIVE?   For adults, the apparent success of welfare reform in raising employment and earnings among single mothers has been accompanied by a sense that "work-first" approaches are more cost-effective than education and training. But wages for former welfare recipients remain quite low, with little evidence of rapid labor market advancement. If wage growth is hard to achieve, then one option is to continue raising their employment levels in low-wage jobs through low-cost approaches such as job search assistance and then publicly supplementing their low earnings through extensions of the Earned Income Tax Credit (EITC) (Scholz, Moffitt, and Cowan, this volume) and expanding child care subsidies and other work supports.

But is it clear that these other efforts are more cost-effective than job training? My own calculations suggest that *moderately effective training for adults and youth might be at least as socially efficient as the EITC.* For instance, estimates suggest that every $1.00 of expenditure on the EITC raises the earnings of single mothers by about $0.25 and therefore raises their incomes by $1.25 (without accounting for any welfare cost of taxation).[24] This compares with the near-doubling of earnings generated per net dollar spent on JTPA over a five-year period that we noted earlier in this chapter. Of course, most training programs are not necessarily this successful. And the two approaches are not mutually exclusive. But given the high annual costs of the EITC relative to the very small sums now spent on training disadvantaged adults, I think that increased federal spending on WIA or Pell grants (in addition to some possible extensions of the EITC) is clearly warranted.[25]

ARE OTHER PROBLEMS MORE SERIOUS?   Recent efforts to improve skills and long-term earnings potential among the disadvantaged have focused not on adults and youth but on young children (Jacob and Ludwig, this volume). Many "high school reform" efforts (Quint 2006) also focus primarily on cognitive skills and academic achievement and are designed to promote greater college attendance and completion rather than training and work experience for high school students.

The current emphasis on younger children and academic skills reflects a growing awareness of:

- The large achievement gap between racial and income groups that develops very early in the lives of children (Jencks and Phillips 1998; Fryer and Levitt 2004)

- The ability of the achievement gap to account for large portions of the differences in college attendance and completion and earnings differences (Johnson and Neal 1998)

- Evidence that both relative and real wages of high school graduates have stagnated while the college–high school earnings gap has widened dramatically since the 1970s (Blank, Danziger, and Schoeni 2007)

Although the evidence on these three points is very solid, they do not necessarily imply an exclusive focus on early childhood preparation, test scores, and college outcomes. A strong proponent of primarily investing in early childhood education (perhaps at the expense of later efforts) is Nobel laureate James Heckman (see, for instance, Heckman 2008). He documents that cognitive skill formation occurs most easily at very early ages and that these early skills "beget" further cognitive skills over time. He also documents that noncognitive skills, which also affect the labor market outcomes of high school graduates, can be influenced at early (as well as somewhat later) ages. The importance of early cognitive skill-building leads Heckman to conclude that the social returns to human capital enhancement decrease strongly with age and that training programs beyond a certain age are not cost-effective. As a result, he advocates a major reorientation of resources away from the training of youth and adults and toward early childhood programs (along with some additional expenditures later in childhood that he views as complements with successful early childhood investment).

The empirical evidence on returns to education and training, however, does not always fit the predicted declining pattern over the life cycle (Karoly 2003).[26] In particular, evidence of very strong returns on pre-K is relatively limited to a few small and intensive programs (like the Abecedarian and Perry Preschool programs) that have never been replicated or scaled up, while rigorous evaluation evidence of positive impacts from efforts that have gone to scale (like Head Start) is more limited and often reflects the state of the program in the 1960s or 1970s rather than today (Jacob and Ludwig, this volume). Also, some newly popular statewide universal pre-K programs show highly varied short-term impacts on achievement (Wong et al. 2008) and quick fadeout of cognitive impacts (Hill 2007). And the strong returns per dollar spent in the estimated impacts of programs like the career academies, NSW, and JTPA for adults suggest that some training programs for youth and adults are quite effective.[27] Once again, I view the earlier investments in children and the later ones in youth and adults as complements, not substitutes, and support some expansion of both.

Similarly, I reject the notion that only test scores and cognitive achievement and ultimately college attendance merit public attention. Universal college attendance seems unachievable in the short term—especially when roughly one-quarter of our youth are not finishing high school on time (Heckman and LaFontaine 2007). The modest goal of "some postsecondary for all" seems more appropriate, especially because most analysts include a range of potential community college training options and certifications. The returns to one year or more of community college and to various kinds of CTE in secondary school (like career academies and Tech Prep, which provides strong career education programs that span high school and community college) are strong enough to justify some continued investment in these efforts (Lerman 2007).

A CHANGING LABOR MARKET   The declining interest in training programs for the disadvantaged has been reinforced by two economic developments that have negatively affected their employment and earnings. First, some analysts expect that continuing globalization leading to greater offshoring of service activities and more immigration (Freeman 2007) might enable employers to meet their future labor needs more easily with foreign (or foreign-born) labor than by training native-born, less-educated workers. Second, some authors have documented growth in both high-skill and low-skill jobs relative to those in the middle (Autor, Katz, and Kearney 2006). These developments imply that there may be little reason to train less-educated workers for relatively unavailable middle-level jobs.

I caution against overstating these trends. Regarding globalization, immigrants are heavily concentrated at the bottom and top of the skills distribution (Borjas 2007); it is in middle-skill jobs that the relative demand for labor may be least met by these workers.[28] Also, many economic sectors that use middle-skill labor, such as health care, construction, and retail trade, exhibit a strong "home bias"—the work will remain in the United States, where customers are located. Regarding labor market polarization, a recent study concludes that, while mildly shrinking, the middle of the labor market will continue to generate strong demands for hiring over the next decade and beyond (Holzer and Lerman 2007). This is especially true when we consider *gross* hiring, including "replacement" demand for retirees, rather than focus exclusively on net employment shifts across these categories. Thus, I see a need to continue training less-educated workers for jobs close to the middle of the skill spectrum.

SUMMARY   On close examination, the arguments that investments in workforce development for the poor should diminish because other approaches are more cost-effective, other problems are more serious, and the labor market is changing are, like the arguments of weak cost-effectiveness, not terribly convincing. Perhaps the real reasons why such investments have diminished so dramatically are *political* rather than substantive. In a world of scarce fiscal resources, advocates for the poor might concentrate their limited political capital on direct cash assistance, like welfare or child care, rather than on the more indirect and longer-term benefits that might accrue from job training. And as the resources have diminished over time, the interest in fighting for them has diminished as well.[29] Whether this interest might be restored over time, if a renewed commitment to public funding for workforce development becomes apparent, is unclear.

RECENT LABOR MARKET DEVELOPMENTS AND TRAINING APPROACHES

In recent years, some newer approaches to workforce development for the poor have been developed that might be more effective than those reviewed earlier in this chapter and that generate more enthusiasm among state and local policymakers. These approaches tend to emphasize the importance of linking education and training more closely to jobs on the *demand* side of the labor market—especially for sectors and employers that still offer well-paying and readily available jobs for less-educated workers and that cannot easily fill these jobs on their own. Targeting training for the disadvantaged to these sectors and jobs might serve a dual purpose of supporting *economic development* while also helping the poor and thus improving labor market efficiency as well as equity.[30]

For instance, many state agencies and employers in key industries are very concerned about potential shortages of workers in the middle-skill jobs as baby boomers retire. These concerns are greatest in sectors with well-paying jobs where future labor demand will be strong (as in health care and elder care) and where the need for specific skills (such as those of machinists, technicians, and construction workers) will not be easily met.

Many economists assume that these markets will equilibrate on their own as relative wages adjust and as private investments in training (by both employers and workers) rise in response to high returns. But these forces will not necessarily eliminate all shortages, even in the long run, and certainly will not do so without costs for employers and local economies. Various market forces and failures might also limit private expenditures on training, especially expenditures by small- and medium-sized employers and for disadvantaged workers.[31]

Thus, there are newer justifications for and some renewed interest in programs to help meet the needs of these workers as well as those of employers. Newer approaches to dealing with other populations, like at-risk youth and the hard to employ, have been developed as well.

New Approaches for Disadvantaged Adults

Table 11.1 lists some promising new approaches to meeting employer demands by training disadvantaged adult workers and some prominent programs around the country that apply these approaches, albeit on relatively small scales (Holzer and Martinson 2008). These approaches generally involve some combination of the following: (1) education and training (sometimes but not always at community colleges) that give workers a postsecondary credential; (2) direct ties to employers or industries that provide well-paying jobs in key sectors; and (3) a range of additional supports and services to help workers deal with problems that arise (such as child care and transportation), either during the training period or beyond.

In addition, labor market *intermediaries* often bring together the workers, employers, training providers and sources of supports needed to make this process work. The intermediaries might help overcome employer resistance to hiring workers (perhaps due partly to discrimination) by providing more information on positive worker skills and attributes and by carefully screening the applicants whom they refer to these employers. If the basic skills of the workers are not sufficient for their participation in the needed occupational training, remedial "bridge" programs are used at the community colleges. Intermediaries provide not only job placements with employers in well-paying jobs but also a range of post-employment services

TABLE 11.1 / New Training Approaches: Promising State and Local Programs

Sectoral Training Programs
- Cooperative Home Care Associates (CHCA)—Developed by the Paraprofessional Health Care Institute in the Bronx, CHCA is a worker-owned home health care cooperative that trains and employs home health care aides. Founded on the belief that higher quality jobs will lead to higher quality care, CHCA aims to restructure the long-term care industry by serving as a model employer that offers higher wages and benefits, supportive services, full-time work, opportunities for career growth, and reduced turnover. The program provides classroom training, on-the-job training, and peer mentorship. Employees of CHCA are guaranteed a paid wage for a minimum of 30 hours per week, receive free health insurance, and earn dividends. Internal career ladders offer employees the opportunity to move into higher-paying administrative positions. Over 900 workers are members of the cooperative, and over 200 per year join annually and receive training.
- AFSCME 1199c Training and Upgrading Fund—Funded through 1.5 percent of gross payroll by participating hospitals, nursing homes and other providers in Philadelphia, this program provides training and career ladders for certified nursing assistants (CNAs) and licensed practical nurses (LPNs). Each student is placed with a case manager to provide ongoing career and personal counseling. In 2005, the program provided training to over 4,000 individuals.
- Wisconsin Regional Training Partnership (WRTP)—WRTP is a nonprofit association of businesses and unions that has served employers, employees, job seekers, and unions in the Milwaukee area since 1996. WRTP works in several industries including manufacturing, health care, construction, and hospitality. Firms that join WRTP agree to develop education and training programs on-site or at community colleges and provide a payroll contribution. In return, they receive technical assistance to strengthen technology and workplace practices, improve the skills of incumbent workers, and recruit and train new workers. Nearly 100 employers with about 60,000 workers participate.

Career Ladder Programs
- Kentucky Career Pathways—Operating at all sixteen community and technical colleges in the state, this initiative generates partnerships with businesses and has developed "pathways" in health care, manufacturing, construction, and transportation. It mostly targets incumbent workers for training and upgrading with their companies. Participating institutions are encouraged to offer curriculums in modularized formats, at alternative times (such as evenings and weekends), and at alternative sites, such as at the workplace. Colleges are also encouraged to integrate intensive student support systems including improved advising, mentoring and career counseling strategies. Currently over 1,100 workers are participating.
- Arkansas Career Pathways—Instituted at 11 community colleges (out of 22) around the state, the program has created career pathways in a variety of sectors and has served about 2,000 workers in a short time period. The program features training programs that are clearly and closely linked to real local job opportunities upon graduation; "bridge," classes providing basic skills and workplace competencies that bring students to skill levels required for college entry; "fast track" two-semester developmental education programs that provide contextualized instruction to reach the skill level required for advanced college courses; and intensive support services offered by a case

TABLE 11.1   /   *Continued*

---

manager that provides academic advising and access to other supports, including child care and transportation.

- Massachusetts Extended Care Career Ladder Initiative (ECCLI)—ECCLI aims to improve the quality of nursing home care through instituting career ladders and promoting skill development and other supportive practices among nursing home staff. The program provides grants to nursing homes and home health agencies who may partner with other long-term care facilities, community colleges, WIBs, and others to create new career ladders for direct care staff and to address staff training, work environment, and quality of care issues. Partnerships involve 15 community colleges around the state and over 150 nursing homes (about 20 percent of the total). Over 7,500 workers have participated to date. Most are CNAs seeking to upgrade skills and perhaps become LPNs.

Incumbent Worker Programs

- New Jersey Workforce Development Program—Operated by the New Jersey Department of Labor and all nineteen community colleges in the state, the program funds incumbent worker training through grants to employers. It also includes the Supplemental Workforce Fund for Basic Skills, to finance basic education related to work. In fiscal year 2006 the latter program alone funded over 14,000 individuals. The program pays for the cost of the training, while employers pay workers' wages while they attend classes (usually at the worksite). The programs are financed by unemployment insurance (UI) taxes on both employers and workers.

- Pennsylvania Incumbent Worker Training Fund—The Incumbent Worker Training Fund is a large-scale statewide initiative to enhance the skills and earnings of incumbent workers in key targeted industries. The program provides grants to regional partnerships throughout the state between multiple employers, workforce development systems, and educational institutions and has trained over 4,000 individuals. Begun in 2005, the program is complemented by the Workforce and Economic Development Network of Pennsylvania that provides grants to twenty-eight community colleges to deliver basic skills to employees at their places of work.

Source: Holzer and Martinson (2008).

that are sometimes included to deal with the problems that frequently arise in new working contexts. The direct involvement of employers and the availability of jobs at the end of training help improve the match between the skills being acquired and the demand side of the labor market; in some cases, employers are even encouraged to change job structures and promotion ladders so that more "good jobs" are created to match the new skills of workers. The direct ties to available jobs at wages above their current level of earnings should also motivate the disadvantaged to undertake the training. Moreover, workers often receive some certification that indicates development of both general and specific occupational skills, thereby providing opportunities for mobility across employers and occupations in the future.

The best-known approaches that combine some or all of these elements include sectoral training, incumbent worker training, and the building of career ladders or career pathways. *Sectoral training* simply targets specific economic sectors at the local level where labor demand is strong and well-paying jobs are available for those without a four-year college degree (Conway, Dworak-Muñoz, and Blair 2004). *Incumbent worker training* programs sometimes use state funds to subsidize employer-sponsored training and upward mobility for entry-level workers in the firms that currently employ them. Efforts to build *career ladders* into low-skill jobs, like nursing aide positions, might enable low-wage workers to progress, either with their current employer or with other firms in the same industry. *Career pathway* programs have been built for particular industries in various states that reach into the high schools and community college populations and generate clear progressions to skilled jobs in these industries based on packages of education, training, and work experience (Jenkins 2006).

Because these are small-scale programs that have not been rigorously evaluated, we do not know the extent to which they can be successfully scaled up and whether they are cost-effective. But some sectoral programs—like the Massachusetts Extended Care Career Ladder Initiative and the Wisconsin Regional Training Partnership—have already achieved impressive scale. The Career Pathways and Ready to Work programs in Kentucky and Arkansas are statewide efforts to link community colleges to the working poor and to higher-wage jobs and employers in those states. As for evaluation evidence, much of what we have today are descriptive outcomes for small programs. But preliminary evidence from a random assignment evaluation of three sectoral programs shows large impacts on earnings for at least twenty-four months (Maguire et al. 2009).

Finally, some of the natural tensions between economic development and antipoverty efforts need to be addressed. Employers are often reluctant to become involved with antipoverty programs, which can tend to stigmatize the workers they are designed to help. The employers might well prefer to use public funding for others whom they might have hired and trained anyway. Targeting is needed to ensure that scarce public funds do not provide windfalls to such employers. At the same time, to maintain both employer interest and broader political support, some flexibility might be needed to provide funding to less-educated workers who are not necessarily poor.

New Programs for Ex-Offenders and At-Risk Youth

Among newer approaches to improving employment options for the hard to employ, transitional jobs (TJs) have recently gained some popularity. Much like National Supported Work (NSW), TJs generally provide adults who have little formal work history with six to twelve months of paid experience, in either a nonprofit or for-profit setting (Holzer 2003). This is particularly important for the ex-offender population, given its enormous growth in recent years and given the evidence of significant barriers to employment faced by ex-offenders (Travis 2005). Thus, the Center for Employment Opportunity (CEO) in New York provides every ex-offender leaving Rikers Island the opportunity to hold a TJ. CEO has been evaluated with a random assignment design, and preliminary results suggest a sizable drop in recidivism for those entering a TJ soon after release (Bloom et al. 2007). Other programs for ex-offenders, such as the Safer Foundation in Chicago, provide training and job placement services without the guarantee of a TJ; these programs are considerably less expensive, though we do not know how cost-effective their services are.[32] But whether any of these programs actually improve employment outcomes over the long term for ex-offenders, and for the hard to employ more generally, remains uncertain.

As for at-risk, out-of-school youth, a number of model programs are being investigated in a variety of settings. A variety of dropout prevention programs for youth in high school, both during school hours and afterwards, are being developed; some of these are programs within existing high schools, while others involve broader efforts at high school reform (Quint 2006). In addition, new dropout recovery models in alternative and charter schools now combine high school completion with the beginning of postsecondary education (Steinberg et al. 2003; Martin and Halperin 2006).

In all of these cases, more rigorous evaluation is necessary before we can draw firm conclusions about what works. In the meantime, it is clearly premature to conclude that "nothing works."

CONCLUSION

In a labor market that places a greater premium on skill development than ever before, we now spend dramatically fewer resources on the training of disadvantaged workers than we did in the 1970s. I have reviewed trends in workforce training for the poor, what we know and do not know about its cost-effectiveness, and some new strategies.

In general, the evidence for adults indicates that modest training and work experience programs can generate modest impacts that are cost-effective even though they do not dramatically improve the lives of the poor. A small number of more intensive efforts, like the National Supported Work program for hard-to-serve women (and for somewhat older men), have been quite effective as well. A few other programs, like the Portland site in NEWWS and the original CET, were quite successful but have not yet been widely replicated.

Pell grants do expand access to (community) college for poor adults, who are likely to benefit when they can attend for at least a year and gain a certification or degree. A new generation of programs for the working poor that are more closely tied to the demand side of the labor market and provide workers with marketable credentials and a range of supportive services—like sectoral models and career pathways—look promising, but these have mostly not been scaled up or rigorously evaluated.

Programs for youth who are still in school, like the career academies and Opening Doors, appear to be cost-effective. Others for out-of-school youth have not been as successful, though we do not yet have enough rigorous evidence on promising models such as YouthBuild, the Youth Conservation Corps, or the

National Guard ChalleNGe Program. For ex-offenders, some preliminary evidence on transitional jobs suggests a reduction in recidivism, though less impact on subsequent earnings.

Overall, the conventional wisdom that "nothing works" with regard to training disadvantaged youth and adults, or even that investments in other kinds of education (like early childhood programs) or in work supports (like the EITC) are more cost-effective than workforce development, is not clearly supported by the evidence. I thus reject the view that the dramatic declines in federal investments in workforce development for the poor can be justified by a lack of cost-effectiveness or by other labor market developments.

On the other hand, there is reason to be skeptical that workforce development for disadvantaged adults and out-of-school youth will ever be sufficient on its own to improve their life chances dramatically. Many of today's poor workers will probably never have access to additional training and might not benefit from it if they did. Perhaps workforce development is best seen as an important component of a broader strategy that also includes stronger income supplementation for the poor, like extensions of the EITC to childless adults and noncustodial fathers who do not now qualify for much; additional work supports, like child care and transportation, and benefits such as health insurance and parental leave; and a range of educational approaches that begin (but do not end) with high-quality early childhood and pre-K programs. And since so much remains unknown about exactly what is cost-effective in workforce development efforts for youth and adults, we need to generate a great deal more knowledge to guide policymakers in their choices.

Thus, I would argue for the following policy priorities in the area of workforce development:

1. *Greater funding should be available for Pell grants,* since these grants now finance much of the community college training at the core of our workforce development system and funding has not kept up with growing needs. These should be supplemented by additional reforms, like those suggested by Dynarski and Scott-Clayton (2007), to make Pell grants more effective and more accessible to low-income adults and youth.

2. *Funding for the federal workforce system for adults should be expanded* to restore at least some of what has been cut so dramatically in recent years. WIA now pays for a range of employment services and training not funded by Pell grants. The other elements of workforce development that are funded through WIA—such as core and intensive services, training for displaced workers, adult basic education (especially English instruction for immigrants), and administration of one-stop offices—are worth preserving and expanding. But when WIA is reauthorized (or replaced) in 2009 or beyond, greater emphasis should be put on building state-level workforce development systems that target good jobs in growing sectors for the disadvantaged, implementing the kinds of demand-oriented training programs plus support services described earlier in this chap-

ter. Additional funding for programs that reduce recidivism among ex-offenders and for other hard-to-employ workers is warranted as well.

3. *Funding should be increased for effective programs for at-risk youth*—such as high-quality career and technical education, efforts (like Opening Doors) to expand their access to higher education, and various kinds of youth development and mentoring programs. States should receive greater federal support as they experiment with new dropout prevention and recovery efforts and develop youth systems at the local level.

4. *An aggressive program of rigorous evaluation should accompany all of these expansions of funding.* The areas most in need of demonstration projects are those where our knowledge remains most limited—such as what works to improve earnings for out-of-school youth and for ex-offenders.

This list of priorities suggests that program expansion and rigorous evaluation should proceed simultaneously, and in ways that make it possible for the latter to continuously inform the former over time. At least some of the funding increases should be implemented by competitive rather than formula grants to states and cities so that renewal of these grants over time is conditional on strong observed performance and use of proven programs over time. Elsewhere (Holzer 2007a), I have outlined how the federal government could fund competitive grants for states to develop innovative programs. The federal government would provide states with substantial oversight and technical assistance and would also provide bonuses for performance.[33] Rigorous evaluation would be required. And renewal of grants to states in subsequent years would be conditional on the incorporation of the lessons learned through evaluation. Such a system could be designed as a complement to the current WIA system or as a major part of a new reform effort.

Whatever path is taken, we need to expand funding for a range of workforce development efforts for disadvantaged youth and adults. At the same time, some consolidation of the dozens of programs in the federal budget that now fund employment and training and some reforms aimed at improving system performance are also warranted.

I am grateful to Maria Cancian, Sheldon Danziger, Carolyn Heinrich, Karl Scholz, and other conference participants for helpful comments. Igor Kheyfets provided excellent research assistance.

NOTES

1. For a listing that includes remedial training in the classroom and that focuses on both basic academic skills and "soft" skills (such as language and communication),

"customized" training for particular employers and sectors, and post-employment training in classrooms or directly on the job, see O'Leary, Straits, and Wandner (2004). "Work experience" programs that try to increase the job-readiness of the hard to employ can also fit into this definition.

2. MDTA was preceded by the Area Redevelopment Act of 1961, a smaller effort that included at least some of the ideas contained in the later pieces of legislation.

3. The view that public-service jobs were wasteful and poorly managed was fed by a series of press reports in the late 1970s that highlighted workers who, under little oversight, were expending little effort on projects that produced little output (O'Leary, Straits, and Wandner 2004). David Ellwood and Elisabeth Welty (2000) discuss the conditions under which public jobs do or do not mostly substitute for production and employment in the private sector.

4. Other titles of WIA fund adult literacy programs and the labor exchange functions of the Employment Service. Other employment and training programs funded by DOL, such as those for workers displaced by trade (as part of the Trade Adjustment Assistance Program), the Community Service Employment Program for senior citizens, and the High Growth Job Training Initiative, are not included under WIA and do not target the disadvantaged.

5. According to Jonathan Simonetta (2004), most of the 200,000 to 300,000 disadvantaged adults receiving JTPA services each year in the 1990s received some training. Only about 100,000 now receive training in any year, and they constitute just one-fifth of all adult workers (excluding the dislocated) receiving WIA services. The fractions of dislocated workers receiving training have also fallen, from about 60 percent in the late 1990s to about 30 percent in 2005.

6. This list omits programs that provide tax credits for the employment of specified groups (like the Work Opportunity Tax Credit) or funds for labor exchange services only, since these do not qualify as "training." It also omits programs that primarily fund education, as opposed to labor market training, as I note in the following text.

7. Spence and Kiel (2003) estimate that less than 10 percent of CSBG funds are spent on employment programs, though these expenditures under SSBG have fluctuated over time.

8. Stafford loans and the Federal Work-Study Program are for students with "financial need," but they are not strictly limited to the poor and do not provide scholarships without repayment or work obligations.

9. Between fiscal year 1979 and 2002, the share of total average costs of attending a public four-year college covered by the maximum Pell grant fell from 77 percent to 41 percent (American Council on Education 2004). The maximum Pell grant will rise through 2012, and the share of the costs it covers is likely to rise as well, but not to anywhere close to the 1970s level.

10. Courses that are not part of a degree or certificate program are not covered by Pell grants.

11. The returns to training for those who actually enrolled in the program represent an estimate of the "treatment effect on the treated" (TOT), as opposed to the smaller "intent to treat" (ITT) effect for all those assigned (Heckman, Lalonde, and Smith 1999).

Under JTPA, the share of workers getting training was only 50 to 60 percent for the treatment group, as opposed to 20 to 30 percent for the control group.

12. James Heckman, Robert Lalonde, and Jeffrey Smith (1999) report wage gains of 2 to 3 percent for NJS adults, though these were not significant. Larger and more significant wage increases have been observed in other programs, like the career academies discussed later in the chapter.

13. Estimates of direct program expenditures do not include the opportunity cost of lost work time for those in training. But these costs are netted out of cumulative earnings gains, which are usually measured from the time at which the assignment to the experimental group or the control group is made.

14. The "welfare cost" of taxation refers to the economic value of the inefficiencies associated with taxation, above and beyond the actual dollar value of the tax. Assuming welfare costs of 0.50 per dollar of tax, the net social benefits estimated by James Heckman, Lalonde, and Smith (1999) are still over $1,000 (or over $1,500 in 2007 dollars) for both adult men and women. Assuming the high rate of $1.00 of welfare cost per dollar of tax still generates net social benefits of over $1,000 for men and over $600 to $800 for women (or $1,500 for men and $900 to $12,000 for women in 2007 dollars), depending on assumptions about the discount rate.

15. According to Robert Lalonde (2003), SWIM and CWEP generated earnings gains of $630 and $1,390, respectively, during the first two years after random assignment, while program costs were under $1,250 (all in 2007 dollars).

16. Gayle Hamilton (2008) reports annual earnings impacts averaging over $1,000 per year in years 2 through 5 (or over $1,200 in 2007 dollars), with little fadeout by the final year and with average costs per participant that were under $3,000 (or $3,600 in 2007 dollars).

17. For instance, the Jobs Plus demonstration combined employment services with rent subsidies in public housing projects and generated significant earnings impacts for participants (Riccio 2007). The emphasis at the Illinois site in the ERA project on assistance in placing low earners into better jobs also generated positive earnings impacts (Hamilton 2008).

18. Lalonde (2003) reports earnings impacts of over $740 annually in the first two years and over $1,240 annually in the next three, with costs per participant about $10,660 (in 2007 dollars).

19. Lalonde (2003) notes earnings impacts of about $1,825 per year during the first two years at a program cost of just over $6,000 (2007 dollars).

20. Cordelia Reimers (1983) shows that limited English-language facility contributes importantly to wage differences between native-born whites and immigrant Hispanics, but we have little evidence to date on the effectiveness of programs to remediate language proficiency for adults.

21. Job Start, a version of the Job Corps during the 1980s that did not include a residential component, had few significant impacts, even in the short run (Lalonde 2003).

22. Over the full follow-up period, monthly earnings impacts were 17 percent for young men and even higher for those considered at high risk. Impacts on hourly wages accounted for nearly half of the monthly earnings impact.

23. Quantum Opportunities provides four-year mentors to students, beginning in the ninth grade, and other financial incentives and educational supports. The most recent

evaluation (Schirm et al. 2003) showed positive short-term effects but smaller long-term effects on dropout rates and other outcomes.

24. Details of these calculations are available from the author.

25. Elsewhere (Carasso et al. 2008) I have argued for extending the EITC to childless adults, especially adult men who are noncustodial parents of children and who pay child support.

26. Lynn Karoly's (2003) findings were at least partly based on strong estimated impacts of the Job Corps and Quantum Opportunities, which faded out or failed to be fully replicated in subsequent evaluations. Nevertheless, her summary includes many interventions for youth and adults that appear fairly cost-effective.

27. In his 1999 paper with Robert Lalonde and Jeffrey Smith, James Heckman himself notes the quite positive impacts of JTPA, at least under some assumptions, and of NSW for disadvantaged adult women. In keeping with his view that positive noncognitive impacts on adolescents and teens are achievable, he praises youth development and mentoring programs for in-school youth in some of his writings as well.

28. "Middle-skill" jobs might be defined as those requiring something more than a high school diploma, in terms of education or training or work experience, but less than a bachelor's degree.

29. Indeed, the willingness of big-city mayors to fight for these funds has dropped off considerably since the late 1970s, when CETA expenditures on public-service jobs and other kinds of training were much more substantial.

30. Fredrik Andersson, Harry Holzer, and Julia Lane (2005) stress the importance of improving the access of the poor to well-paying jobs in high-wage firms and sectors to improve their advancement prospects in the labor market.

31. For instance, imperfect information or constraints that prevent workers from borrowing in credit markets might lead them to underinvest in their education and training. Employers might also underinvest in training their workers for the same reasons. Even in well-functioning markets, employers do not want to invest in training for general skills, since employees might leave before employers can reap the returns on these investments, and wage rigidities in some sectors might prevent employees from accepting the lower wages needed to pay for their training at these firms (see Lerman, McKernan, and Riegg 2004). In sectors like health care and elder care, third-party reimbursement rules (from insurers) might restrict the wage and salary adjustments that are necessary to attract and train enough workers to equilibrate supply and demand in the market.

32. These programs tend to focus on the labor market and provide little treatment for substance abuse or mental health issues (like post-traumatic stress disorder); thus, they are already targeted toward the relatively more job-ready portion of the offender population.

33. Since performance measures for program participants can be manipulated by the criterion for who is allowed to enter or exit the program, these measures should be supplemented or even replaced by statewide measures based on an expectation of improvement in employment outcomes. This would also encourage states to build greater scale into their efforts.

REFERENCES

American Council on Education. 2004. "Fact Sheet on Higher Education: Summary of Higher Education Institutions, by Enrollment and Degrees Conferred: Fall 2004" (revised February 2007). Available at: http://www.acenet.edu/AM/Template.cfm?Section=CPA&TEMPLATE=/CM/ContentDisplay.cfm&CONTENTID=22922.

Andersson, Fredrik, Harry J. Holzer, and Julia Lane. 2005. *Moving Up or Moving On: Who Advances in the Low-Wage Labor Market?* New York: Russell Sage Foundation.

Autor, David H., Lawrence F. Katz, and Melissa S. Kearney. 2006. "The Polarization of the U.S. Labor Market." Working paper 11986. Cambridge, Mass.: National Bureau of Economic Research. Available at: http://www.nber.org/papers/w11986.

Blank, Rebecca, Sheldon Danziger, and Robert Schoeni. 2007. *Working and Poor.* New York: Russell Sage Foundation.

Bloom, Dan, Cindy Redcross, Janine Zweig, and Gilda Azurdia. 2007. "Transitional Jobs for Ex-Prisoners: Early Impacts from a Random Assignment Evaluation of the Center for Employment Opportunities (CEO) Prisoner Reentry Program." Working paper. New York: MDRC (November). Available at: http://www.mdrc.org/publications/468/full.pdf.

Bloom, Dan, Alissa Gardenhire-Crooks, and Conrad Mandsager. 2009. "Reenergizing High School Dropouts: Early Results of the National Guard Youth ChalleNGe Program Evaluation." Working paper. New York: MDRC.(February). Available at: http://www.mdrc.org/publications/512/overview.html.

Bloom, Howard, Larry Orr, Stephen Bell, George Cave, Fred Doolittle, Winston Lin, and Johannes Bos. 1997. "The Benefits and Costs of JTPA Title II-A Programs." *Journal of Human Resources* 32(3): 549–76.

Borjas, George. 2007. "Immigration Policy and Human Capital." In *Reshaping the American Workforce in a Changing Economy,* edited by Harry Holzer and Demetra Nightingale. Washington, D.C.: Urban Institute.

Bos, Johannes, Susan Scrivener, Jason Snipes, and Gayle Hamilton. 2001. "Improving Basic Skills: The Effects of Adult Education in Welfare-to-Work Programs." Working paper. New York: MDRC.

Carasso, Adam, Harry J. Holzer, Elaine Maag, and Eugene Steuerle. 2008. "The Next Age for Social Policy: Encouraging Work and Family Formation Among Low-Income Men." Discussion paper 28. Washington, D.C.: Urban Institute. Available at: http://www.urban.org/UploadedPDF/411774_encouragingwork.pdf.

Cohen, Mark, and Alex Piquero. 2008. "Costs and Benefits of a Targeted Intervention Program for Youth Offenders: The Youth Build USA Ex-Offender Project." Unpublished paper, Vanderbilt University, Nashville.

Conway, Maureen, Linda Dworak-Muñoz, and Amy Blair. 2004. "Sectoral Workforce Development: Research Review and Future Directions." Washington, D.C.: Workforce Strategies Institute/Aspen Institute. Available at: http://www.aspenwsi.org/publications/05-WSI.pdf.

Dynarski, Susan M., and Judith E. Scott-Clayton. 2007. "College Grants on a Postcard: A Proposal for Simple and Predictable Federal Student Aid." Hamilton Project discussion paper 2007-01. Washington, D.C.: Brookings Institution (February). Available at: http://www.brookings.edu/~/media/Files/rc/papers/2007/02education_dynarski/200702dynarski%20scott%20clayton.pdf.

Ellwood, David, and Elisabeth Welty. 2000. "Public Service Employment and Mandatory Work: A Policy Whose Time Has Come and Gone and Come Again?" In *Finding Jobs: Work and Welfare Reform,* edited by David Card and Rebecca Blank. New York: Russell Sage Foundation.

Frank, Abbey, and Elisa Minoff. 2005. "Declining Share of Adults Receiving Training Under WIA Are Low-Income or Disadvantaged." Washington, D.C.: Center on Law and Social Policy (December 14). Available at: http://www.clasp.org/publications/decline_in_wia_training.pdf.

Freeman, Richard. 2007. "Is a Great Labor Shortage Coming? Replacement Demand in a Global Economy." In *Reshaping the American Workforce in a Changing Economy,* edited by Harry Holzer and Demetra Nightingale. Washington, D.C.: Urban Institute.

Fryer, Roland G., Jr., and Steven D. Levitt. 2004. "Understanding the Black-White Test Score Gap in the First Two Years of School." *Review of Economics and Statistics* 86(2): 447–64.

Government Accountability Office (GAO). 1996. *Job Training Partnership Act: Long-Term Earnings and Employment Outcomes.* Washington: U.S. Government Printing Office.

———. 2003. *Multiple Employment and Training Programs: Funding and Performance Measures for Major Programs.* Washington: U.S. Government Printing Office.

———. 2006. *Youth Opportunity Grants: Lessons Can Be Learned, But Labor Needs to Make Data Available.* Washington: U.S. Government Printing Office.

Hamilton, Gayle. 2008. "Promoting Stable Employment and Wage Progression: Findings from the Employment Retention and Advancement (ERA) Project." New York: MDRC.

Hamilton, Gayle, Stephen Freedman, Lisa Gennetian, Charles Michalopoulos, Johanna Walter, Diana Adams-Ciardullo, and Anna Gassman-Pines. 2001. "How Effective Are Different Welfare-to-Work Approaches? Five-Year Adult and Child Impacts for Eleven Programs." New York: MDRC. Available at: http://www.mdrc.org/publications/64/overview.html.

Heckman, James. 2008. "Schools, Skills, and Synapses." Working paper 14064. Cambridge, Mass.: National Bureau of Economic Research.

Heckman, James, and Paul LaFontaine. 2007. "The American High School Graduation Rate: Trends and Levels." Unpublished paper, University of Chicago.

Heckman, James, Robert Lalonde, and Jeffrey Smith. 1999. "The Economics and Econometrics of Active Labor Market Programs." In *Handbook of Labor Economics,* vol. 3A, edited by Orley Ashenfelter and David Card. Amsterdam: North-Holland.

Herrera, Carla. 1999. *School-Based Mentoring: A First Look into Its Potential.* Philadelphia: Private/Public Ventures.

Hill, Carolyn J. 2007. "The Longer-Term Effects of a Universal Prekindergarten Program." Working paper, Georgetown University, Washington, D.C.

Holzer, Harry J. 2003. "Can Work Experience Programs Work for Welfare Recipients?" Welfare Reform and Beyond brief 24. Washington, D.C.: Brookings Institution.

———. 2007a. "Better Workers for Better Jobs: Improving Worker Advancement in the Low-Wage Labor Market." Hamilton Project discussion paper 2007-15. Washington, D.C.: Brookings Institution.

———. 2007b. "Collateral Costs: The Effects of Incarceration on the Employment and Earnings of Young Workers." Discussion paper 3118. Bonn: Institute for the Study of Labor (IZA) (October). Available at: http://www.iza.org/index_html?lang=en&mainframe= http%3A//www.iza.org/en/webcontent/publications/papers/viewAbstract%3Fdp_id% 3D3118&topSelect=publications&subSelect=papers.

Holzer, Harry J., and Robert I. Lerman. 2007. "America's Forgotten Middle-Skill Jobs: Education and Training Requirements for the Next Decade and Beyond." Washington, D.C.: Workforce Alliance (November). Available at: http://www.urban.org/UploadedPDF/ 411633_forgottenjobs.pdf.

Holzer, Harry J., and Karin Martinson. 2008. "Helping Poor Working Parents Get Ahead: Federal Funds for New State Strategies and Systems." New Safety Net Paper 4. Washington, D.C.: Urban Institute (July). Available at: http://www.urban.org/UploadedPDF/ 411722_working_parents.pdf.

Hotz, V. Joseph, Guido Imbens, and Jacob Klerman. 2000. "The Long-Term Gains from GAIN: A Re-analysis of the Impacts of the California GAIN Program." NBER working paper no. 8007. Cambridge, Mass.: NBER.

Jastrzab, Joann, John Blomquist, Julie Masker, and Larry Orr. 1997. "Youth Corps: Promising Strategies for Young People and Their Communities." Studies in Workforce Development and Income Security Report 1-97. Cambridge, Mass.: Abt Associates (February). Available at: http://www.abtassoc.com/reports/Youth-Corps.pdf.

Jencks, Christopher, and Meredith Phillips, eds. 1998. *The Black-White Test Score Gap.* Washington, D.C.: Brookings Institution Press.

Jenkins, Davis. 2006. "Career Pathways: Aligning Public Resources to Support Individual and Regional Economic Advancement in the Knowledge Economy." White paper. New York: Workforce Strategies Center.

Johnson, William, and Derek Neal. 1998. "Basic Skills and the Black-White Earnings Gap." In *The Black-White Test Score Gap,* edited by Christopher Jencks and Meredith Phillips. Washington, D.C.: Brookings Institution Press.

Karoly, Lynn. 2003. "Caring for Our Children and Youth: An Analysis of Alternative Investment Strategies." Los Angeles: RAND Corporation.

Kemple, James. 2008. "Career Academies: Long-Term Impacts on Labor Market Outcomes, Educational Attainment and Transitions to Adulthood." New York: MDRC. Available at: http://www.mdrc.org/publications/482/overview.html.

Lalonde, Robert. 2003. "Employment and Training Programs." In *Means-Tested Transfer Programs in the United States,* edited by Robert A. Moffitt. Chicago: University of Chicago Press.

Lerman, Robert. 2007. "Career-Focused Education and Training for Youth." In *Reshaping the American Workforce in a Changing Economy,* edited by Harry Holzer and Demetra Nightingale. Washington, D.C.: Urban Institute Press.

Lerman, Robert I., Signe-Mary McKernan, and Stephanie Riegg. 2004. "The Scope of Employer-Provided Training in the United States: Who, What, Where, and How Much?" In *Job Training Policy in the United States,* edited by Christopher J. O'Leary, Robert A. Straits, and Stephen A. Wandner. Kalamazoo, Mich.: W. E. Upjohn Institute for Employment Research. Available at: http://www.upjohninst.org/publications/books/jtp/ch7_lerman_mckernan_ and_riegg.pdf.

Maguire, Sheila, Joshua Freely, Carol Clymer, and Maureen Conway. 2009. "Job Training That Works: Findings from the Sectoral Employment Impact Study." Philadelphia: Public/Private Ventures. Available at: http://ppv.org/publications/assets/294_publication.pdf.

Martin, Nancy, and Samuel Halperin. 2006. "Whatever It Takes: How Twelve Communities Are Reconnecting Out-of-School Youth." Washington, D.C.: American Youth Policy Forum.

Melendez, Edwin. 1996. *Working on Jobs: The Center for Employment Training.* Boston: Mauricio Gaston Institute.

Miller, Cynthia, Johannes Bos, Kristin Porter, Fannie Tseng, and Yasuyo Abe. 2005. "The Challenge of Repeating Success in a Changing World: Final Report on the Center for Employment Training Replication Sites." New York: MDRC.

Mueser, Peter, Kevin Troske, and Alexey Gorislavsky. 2005. "Using State Administrative Data to Measure Program Performance." Working paper. Columbia: University of Missouri.

O'Leary, Christopher, Robert Straits, and Stephen Wandner. 2004. "U.S. Job Training: Types, Participants, and History." In *Job Training Policy in the United States,* edited by Christopher J. O'Leary, Robert A. Straits, and Stephen A. Wandner. Kalamazoo, Mich.: W. E. Upjohn Institute for Employment Research. Available at: http://www.upjohninst.org/publications/titles/jtp.html.

Quint, Janet. 2006. "Meeting Five Critical Challenges of High School Reform." New York: MDRC.

Reimers, Cordelia. 1983. "Labor Market Discrimination Against Black and Hispanic Men." *Review of Economics and Statistics* 65(4): 570–79.

Riccio, James. 2007. "Subsidized Housing and Employment: Building Evidence of What Works to Improve Self-Sufficiency." New York: MDRC.

Riccio, James, Daniel Friedlander, and Stephen Freedman. 1994. "GAIN: Benefits, Costs, and Three-Year Impacts of a Welfare-to-Work Program." New York: MDRC.

Richburg-Hayes, Lashawn. 2008. "Helping Low-Wage Workers Persist in Educational Programs." New York: MDRC.

Schirm, Allen, Nuria Rodriguez-Planas, Myles Maxfield, and Christina Tuttle. 2003. "The Quantum Opportunities Demonstration: Short-Term Impacts." Princeton, N.J.: Mathematica Policy Research.

Schochet, Peter, Sheena McConnell, and John Burghardt. 2003. "National Job Corps Study: Findings Using Administrative Earnings Records Data." Princeton, N.J.: Mathematica Policy Research.

Simonetta, Jonathan. 2004. "Appendix A: Job Training Data." In *Job Training Policy in the United States,* edited by Christopher J. O'Leary, Robert A. Straits, and Stephen A. Wandner. Kalamazoo, Mich.: W. E. Upjohn Institute for Employment Research.

Spence, Robin, and Brendan Kiel. 2003. "Skilling the American Workforce 'on the Cheap': Ongoing Shortfalls in Federal Funding for Workforce Development." Washington, D.C.: Workforce Alliance.

Steinberg, Adria, Cheryl Almeida, Lili Allen, and Sue Goldberger. 2003. "Four Building Blocks for a System of Educational Opportunity: Developing Pathways to and Through College for Urban Youth." Boston: Jobs for the Future.

Travis, Jeremy. 2005. *But They All Come Back: Facing the Challenge of Prisoner Reentry.* Washington, D.C.: Urban Institute.

Turner, Sarah. 2007. "Higher Education Policies Generating the Twenty-First-Century Workforce." In *Reshaping the American Workforce in a Changing Economy*, edited by Harry Holzer and Demetra Nightingale. Washington, D.C.: Urban Institute Press.

Uggen, Christopher. 2000. "Work as a Turning Point in the Life Course of Criminals: A Duration Model of Age, Employment, and Recidivism." *American Journal of Sociology* 65(4): 529–46.

Wong, Vivian, Thomas Cook, Steven Barnett, and Kwanghee Jung. 2008. "An Effectiveness-Based Evaluation of Five State Prekindergarten Programs." *Journal of Policy Analysis and Management* 27(1): 122–54.

Chapter 12

Health Care for the Poor: For Whom, What Care, and Whose Responsibility?

Katherine Swartz

Americans' efforts to help poor people obtain medical care have evolved as the country has grown richer and as medicine has become capable of increasing life expectancy and improving quality of life. That evolution has not been a direct path of increased generosity toward poor people. Instead, it reflects a mix of philosophical beliefs, greater understanding of the links between health and ability to work, and swings in the economy that have made Americans alternately more and less willing to help pay for poor people's medical care.

Since the late 1940s, when the share of Americans with employer-sponsored, private health insurance started to grow rapidly, the primary approach to helping poor people obtain medical care has been to make public health insurance available to a growing share of the poor. Underlying this approach is the assumption that if poor people have health insurance, physicians and other providers of medical care will provide the same services to poor people as they do to middle-class people. But as experience with public insurance has grown, it has become clear that poor people face barriers to obtaining health care beyond simply their ability to pay for it. Many poor areas of the country have a shortage of physicians and nurses, and not all physicians and other medical care providers are willing to treat people with public insurance coverage. Many poor people are unaware of symptoms of medical need or do not know how to explain the symptoms to medical personnel. Others face language or cultural difficulties when seeking care. As understanding of these barriers has increased, efforts to help poor people with health care have expanded to include more funding for community health centers, public health clinics, language translators, and educational programs about health issues specifically targeted at groups of poor people. These public policy efforts, however, have been secondary to expanding health insurance coverage for low-income people.

The dramatic increase over the past fifty years in medicine's ability to increase life expectancy and improve quality of life (especially for people with chronic conditions) has made disparities in access to health care particularly troubling.

There is no doubt that poverty is a contributing factor to poor health outcomes. Poor people have lower life expectancies, a higher prevalence of chronic illnesses and health conditions, and more unmet health needs than do people with middle-class and high incomes. But the causal path between poverty and poor health out-comes is complex. Other factors correlated with low income, such as low education, the inability to speak English, and living in areas with high levels of pollution, also contribute to poor health (Lillie-Blanton et al. 1999; IOM 2003). Equally important, the link between poverty and poor health does not go in one direction (Smith 1999). Poor health is a contributing factor to low incomes and poverty. People with chronic medical conditions frequently are poor because they cannot work, and people who suffer a sudden decline in health—an accident, stroke, or cancer diagnosis—often become poor owing to a job loss. Moreover, people with such health problems often have problems accessing medical care because there are not enough medical providers nearby or they are not good advocates for themselves—and then they remain poor because they cannot work.

The fact that people in poor health often have low incomes as a result of their health problems is an increasingly important driver of efforts to expand eligibility for public insurance. This is especially the case in efforts to increase coverage of children. As we have come to appreciate how poor health can affect learning, which in turn is related to a person's productivity and earnings, awareness has grown that investing in improving access to health care pays off in areas beyond health outcomes. Thus, the recent history of public policies to help poor people obtain health care is an evolving mix of efforts to address the reasons why poor people have poor health. Some policies increase the availability of public insurance, and other initiatives are targeted at addressing language and cultural problems particular to the poor and increasing the supply of medical providers (especially those knowledgeable about the difficulties facing poor people).

This chapter focuses on the recent history of public policies intended to help the poor obtain health care, including the concerns now surrounding public insurance. The first half of the chapter provides a brief review of efforts to provide health care to the poor since 1900. That history shows a strong preference for helping poor children, the elderly, and disabled persons rather than all of the poor. In addition to describing what led up to the implementation of Medicaid in 1965 and how Medicaid eligibility expanded during the late 1980s, I review the State Children's Health Insurance Program (SCHIP) that was implemented in 1997 and reauthorized in 2009.[1] I also describe three innovative state insurance programs for the near-poor who are not eligible for Medicaid and the renewed interest in relying on community health centers to provide care to the poor rather than expanding public insurance programs.

The second half of the chapter shifts to examining current concerns with Medicaid and SCHIP and issues that should be addressed in continuing efforts to provide health care to the poor and near-poor. The chapter's third section focuses on recent efforts to control and slow spending for Medicaid and SCHIP. The rising cost of these programs is a major concern to policymakers. Although the public perception is that expanded eligibility for low-income children and nondisabled adults has driven up spending, it is the rising costs per person of caring for the poor aged and poor disabled that account for most of the recent growth in Medicaid's costs. In the fourth section, I examine four concerns with the current operation of Medicaid and SCHIP: the quality of care provided to elderly and disabled beneficiaries, poor people who are not eligible for Medicaid, the potential crowding out of private insurance by public programs, and efforts to increase the fraction of eligible people who enroll in public insurance. In the fifth section, I describe three issues that affect the future of our public insurance programs: disparities among the states in terms of eligibility for public insurance and their ability to fund such programs, how to slow the growth in Medicaid expenditures, and the role of public insurance in the country's system of financing health care. I conclude with observations about the inconsistency in our attitudes towards helping poor people with health care costs, and I offer three recommendations for improving health care outcomes for low-income people.

Health Insurance in the United States

A brief explanation of the broad types of health insurance now held by Americans is useful for understanding why the primary approach to helping poor people obtain medical care has been to expand eligibility for public health insurance. About 61 percent of people younger than sixty-five years old have employer-sponsored, private health insurance. Another 5 percent of the non-elderly have insurance policies that they buy themselves in the individual (or nongroup) insurance market from private insurance companies. Thus, about two-thirds of all non-elderly have private health insurance. In addition, about 3 percent have military coverage or coverage through the U.S. Department of Veterans Affairs, and 2 to 3 percent have Medicare (either because they have end-stage renal disease or are disabled and cannot work). Of the remaining non-elderly, about 13 percent are covered by Medicaid, and almost 18 percent have no insurance coverage at all. (Some people report more than one type of insurance during a year, so the numbers sum to more than 100 percent.) Medicaid covers about one-third of all people in poverty; most recipients are children and pregnant women, but about one-fourth of Medicaid recipients are disabled or elderly. Almost everyone sixty-five years of age and older is covered by Medicare.

Health insurance is available in many different forms. The most common forms are known as indemnity policies and managed care plans. Indemnity policies usually have a deductible (an amount of medical care expenses that a person has to pay all of before the insurance starts to pay anything) and a coinsurance rate (a percentage of the medical expenses that a person continues to

(Continues on p. 333.)

Health Insurance in the United States *(Continued)*

pay after the deductible is met). Catastrophic health plans are indemnity policies with quite large deductibles—generally $2,000 for an individual and $5,000 for a family policy. The deductible and coinsurance are intended to make people aware of the costs of medical care and restrain unnecessary demands for care. In contrast, most managed care plans usually do not have deductibles, although they require people to pay a co-payment when they obtain medical care. Co-payments are relatively modest amounts ($10 to $25 for a physician visit in 2008) and are independent of the full costs of the encounter (for example, the cost of the diagnostic tests ordered or the cost of a longer visit). Some managed care plans try to restrain health care spending by imposing tight restrictions on which physicians and hospitals their members can use; others have less restrictive networks of providers but create long waiting periods for certain types of specialists by not having many of them in their networks. Some managed care plans have strict guidelines on when further diagnostic testing or surgery is appropriate. Most of these managed care mechanisms for slowing health care spending also have been adopted by insurers that sell indemnity policies.

Health insurance provides the highly useful service of pooling millions of people's individual risks of needing expensive medical care. Since only a very small number of people will need expensive care during a year, insurance allows each enrolled individual to pay a relatively modest amount to avoid having to have a large amount of savings readily available in case of a medical emergency. But health insurance also creates what is known as moral hazard: because insurance pays most of the cost of care (above a deductible for those with indemnity policies), people are less hesitant to see a physician and request diagnostic and other services when something bothers them. Thus, health insurance is a double-edged sword—it protects us from catastrophic medical expenses, but it may also increase demand for medical care above medically justifiable levels.

Competition in the market for health insurance has caused insurers to negotiate the fees they pay physicians, hospitals, and other health care providers in local markets. Medicare and Medicaid also negotiate the fees they pay providers, but they pay rates that are below the private insurance fees. People without any health insurance are charged much higher fees than insured people. Thus, for low-income people without employer-sponsored insurance, Medicaid and other publicly funded insurance programs provide financial access to medical care that they could not otherwise afford.

A HISTORY OF MAJOR EFFORTS TO PROVIDE HEALTH CARE TO THE POOR SINCE 1900

Two themes are apparent when examining the last century of health care assistance for the poor. First, there has been a preference for state rather than federal control of how health care assistance is administered. Second, health care assistance for the poor has been administered more as a welfare program than as part of a national system of financing health insurance and medical care. Both themes have contributed to large disparities across states in who among the poor has access to what types of medical care.

The Origins of the Design Issues Embedded in Medical Assistance Programs

Until 1935 and the passage of the Social Security Act, medical care assistance for the poor generally came from ad hoc efforts by civic and religious groups to help some of the poor living in their communities. The poor who were most likely to receive such help were children with physical and mental health problems, pregnant women and infants, the blind, and the elderly—people who might be termed "deserving poor" because they were not responsible for their status (Stevens and Stevens 1974/2003; Engel 2006). The belief that state and local governments should have primary responsibility for providing health care to the poor stems from these earlier years.

One section of the Social Security Act set up federal funds to match state expenditures for income assistance for dependent children and their mothers (what became the Aid to Families with Dependent Children [AFDC] program), the poor elderly, the blind, and crippled children.[2] The states were in charge of administering the programs; they could set the income eligibility criteria. This was the precursor to the considerable variation in Medicaid eligibility criteria across states.

By the mid-1930s, public hospitals and clinics to care for the poor were common in urban areas of several states, particularly New York and California. These facilities contributed to the growth of a two-tiered system of medical care: private hospitals and physicians provided care to people who could afford it, while public hospitals and city or county health department physicians and nurses provided care to the poor. In areas where public hospitals did not exist, welfare departments reimbursed private hospitals for care provided to recipients—but at rates below what the hospitals charged private patients. The pattern of paying below-market rates for the care of the poor continued when Medicaid was implemented.

1945 to 1965: Private Insurance Coverage Expands, Setting the Stage for Medicaid

Few people had private health insurance before World War II. Commercial insurance companies did not want to sell policies to individuals because they feared that a disproportionate share of buyers would be people with high medical expenses—a problem known as "adverse selection." Although unions had tried for several decades to get large employers to pay for health insurance for workers, many employers did not want to pay for a benefit that would be controlled by the unions (Klein 2003). By the time the war was over, however, insurance companies had recognized that if employers provided policies to all of their workers, adverse selection was not an issue. And insurance companies could market the group policies to large employers by arguing that if an employer offered the policy, it was not a bargaining issue and the unions would not control it. As a result, most unionized blue-collar workers in manufacturing had hospitalization insurance by the late 1940s. Firms quickly added hospitalization insurance to the compensation packages of white-collar employees to recruit and retain them.

Thus, by the early 1950s, a large fraction of the workforce had hospitalization insurance. President Truman had tried to create national health insurance, but the fact that many people had employer-sponsored coverage dampened public demand for a change. Federal tax code changes in 1954 strengthened incentives for employers to offer health insurance by exempting employer-paid premiums from the payroll taxes paid by employers and workers and from worker income taxes. In 2007 the amount of foregone federal income and payroll taxes on employer payments for premiums was estimated to be greater than $200 billion—a significant subsidy for those who have employer-sponsored insurance (Burman 2006).

Because the expansion of health insurance occurred through employment, people who were uninsured were highly likely to be poor. They were poor because they could not work, had intermittent or seasonal jobs, or had low-wage jobs. Who was poor and left out of private health insurance has a bearing on how Medicaid developed and expanded, a point I return to later in the chapter.

1965 to 1983: The Implementation of Medicare and Medicaid

In 1965 Congress passed legislation intended to help people who were not likely to obtain employer-sponsored coverage. The legislation, which added Titles XIX and XX to the Social Security Act, created Medicare and Medicaid, respectively. Medicare provided health insurance for people age sixty-five and older and for disabled workers, while Medicaid was for some of the poor, such as children and disabled adults. Proponents of a single national health insurance system hoped that these programs would shift the United States onto such a path. However, the two programs are financed and administered in entirely different ways. Medicare is a federal program for all elderly and disabled people who contributed payroll taxes to the hospital trust fund. The program is financed by a combination of these payroll taxes, general revenue funds, and premiums paid by beneficiaries. Medicaid is a federal-state program available only to people who meet eligibility criteria based partly on who they are (what are known as categorical requirements, such as children under age six or pregnant women) and partly on whether their income is below some limit.[3] The federal government sets minimum eligibility criteria but also permits each state to cover other people at the state's option. The financing of

Medicaid is shared between the federal and state governments through a formula whereby every dollar of state expenditures is matched by federal dollars and states with the lowest per capita income receive more federal dollars per state dollar than higher-income states. Whereas Medicare was created as a national social insurance program for everyone, Medicaid from the beginning was operated like other welfare programs (Stevens and Stevens 1974/2003).

Medicaid's role as a payer of health care services has grown rapidly over the past four decades: in 2007 it paid for 40 percent of all births, covered about one-third of all children, paid for about two-thirds of all nursing home stays, and covered about one-third of all poor people. At the same time, not all poor people are eligible for Medicaid, and there are disparities in the ability of states to operate their programs.

1984 to 1990: The Expansion of Medicaid

Between 1984 and 1990, Congress expanded the eligibility criteria for Medicaid through seven different legislative acts.[4] The effect was increased equity in income eligibility rules across states. By 1990, all pregnant women, infants, and children under age six who had family incomes below 133 percent of the federal poverty level had to be covered, and all children between six and nineteen years of age with family incomes below the poverty level had to be covered by 2001. States also had the option of increasing the income eligibility ceiling to 185 percent of the poverty level for infants, children under age six, and pregnant women. By 1992, thirty-one states had opted to expand the income eligibility limit above 133 percent of the poverty level; twenty-four states plus the District of Columbia expanded the eligibility limit to 185 percent of the poverty level. John Holahan and his colleagues (1993) estimate that these changes alone added 2.5 million children and 1.0 million pregnant women to the Medicaid rolls between 1988 and 1992.

Congress also required the states to expand the "dual-eligible" categories of the elderly and disabled Medicare beneficiaries for whom Medicaid paid Medicare Part B premiums (Part B covers physician and outpatient services) and other cost-sharing required under Medicare (for example, the deductible for a hospital stay).[5] Before 1990, the only Medicare beneficiaries who were dually eligible for Medicaid were those who received Supplemental Security Income (SSI); to qualify for SSI, a person's income has to be below 74 percent of the poverty level. These dual-eligibles are entitled to all Medicaid benefits, such as nursing home care, in addition to having their Part B premiums and other Medicare cost-sharing paid by Medicaid. In 1990 Congress added two more dual-eligible categories: one for Medicare beneficiaries who do not receive SSI but have incomes below the poverty level, and the other for beneficiaries with incomes between 100 and 120 percent of the poverty level. The former are known as qualified Medicare beneficiaries (QMBs); Medicaid pays their Part B premium and other Medicare cost-sharing, but the QMBs are not eligible for other Medicaid benefits. The latter are known as special low-income Medicare beneficiaries (SLMBs); Medicaid pays only their Part B premium.

TABLE 12.1 / Minimum Required Income Eligibilty Ceilings by Medicaid Eligible
Group, 2008

Medicaid Eligible Group	Percent of Poverty Level
Pregnant women	133%
Children younger than six years	133
Children six to eighteen years	100
Aged and disabled persons	74
Working parents	65
Childless adults	0

Source: Centers for Medicare and Medicaid Services, U.S. Department of Health and Human
Services (CMS 2009b).

As a result of all of these eligibility criteria expansions, almost 50 million people
were covered by Medicaid for at least part of the year in fiscal year 2005 (the most
recent year for which we have data on Medicaid beneficiaries). This number
included people in nursing homes and institutional care. Half of the Medicaid
enrollees (25.2 million) were children, 22 percent (10.8 million) were nondisabled
adults, 18 percent were dual-eligibles (3.2 million were disabled and younger than
sixty-five, and 5.6 million were age sixty-five or older), and the remaining 10 percent (5.1 million) were other aged and disabled poor people who did not qualify
for Medicare (Holahan, Miller, and Rousseau 2009). Table 12.1 summarizes the minimum income eligibility ceilings that states must abide by for the different groups
covered by Medicaid; as noted earlier, states have the option to use higher income
ceilings for some groups.

The 1990s: Efforts to Slow Medicaid Spending Growth, Waivers, and Welfare Reform

The 1990s were marked by efforts both to control Medicaid spending growth
and to continue to expand access to public insurance for the poor and near-poor.
Medicaid spending more than doubled between 1988 and 1992. Holahan and his
colleagues (1993) estimated that just over two-fifths of this spending increase was
due to the eligibility expansions and the recession of 1990 to 1992. But it was the
particularly rapid growth in Medicaid spending for hospital services that caught
policy analysts' attention. The increased hospital spending had been observed by
1990 and was clearly related to financing strategies that a few states began to use
in the late 1980s to maximize federal matching funds: these states would collect
"donations" from private providers of medical care (mostly hospitals) to help pay
the states' share of Medicaid costs; with more "state" funds, the states were able
to obtain greater federal matching funds, which allowed the states to cover more
people with Medicaid. In turn, the hospitals could be reimbursed by Medicaid for
what otherwise might have been charity care provided to uninsured people. The

incentive to use this financing strategy was particularly strong in areas where hospitals provided care to a disproportionate share of Medicaid and uninsured patients. Congress had authorized higher Medicaid payments to such hospitals in 1981; such payments came to be known as DSH payments (pronounced "dish" payments; DSH is an acronym for "disproportionate share hospitals"). In 1986 Congress permitted states also to make DSH payments to hospitals that served a large number of low-income patients, not just Medicaid and uninsured patients. Between 1990 and 1992, the number of states engaged in these special financing strategies ballooned from six to thirty-nine—and the rapid growth in Medicaid spending on hospital services reflected this.

Medicaid analysts had recognized the impact of these financing strategies by 1991. Congress acted to restrict states' use of the strategies and placed a limit on higher payments to DSH hospitals, but the effects of these limits were not felt until after 1992. Holahan and his colleagues (1993) noted that after accounting for inflation in the prices of hospital services, 27 percent of the total Medicaid spending growth between 1990 and 1992 was due to greater use of hospital services and higher payments to DSH hospitals. Then, by the mid-1990s, Medicaid spending slowed down significantly—partly because the recession had ended and fewer people were enrolled in Medicaid and partly because the restrictions on how the states could provide matching funds had taken effect.

Expectations about health insurance reform that would cover the uninsured were high in 1993 and early 1994. In 1993, 39.3 million non-elderly people were uninsured, and almost half were poor or near-poor. Because the Clinton administration's health care reform proposal assumed that Medicaid would be the basis for covering the poor, it encouraged states to use Section 1115 waivers to shift Medicaid recipients into managed care plans.[6] The assumption was that managed care plans would manage recipients' care and save the states money that could then be used to cover the poor and near-poor uninsured. By 1995 one-third of all Medicaid recipients were in managed care plans (Holahan and Liska 1997). Medicaid became a purchaser of health insurance rather than a payer for health care services for these recipients (Holahan et al. 1995).

The 1996 welfare reform enacted under the Personal Responsibility and Work Opportunity Reconciliation Act (PRWORA) ended the AFDC program and its recipients' entitlement to Medicaid. However, an amendment allowed children and adults who *would* have been eligible for AFDC on the basis of the July 1996 criteria to remain eligible for Medicaid.[7] Nonetheless, the initial response to the welfare reform was a sharp decline in the number of Medicaid recipients (Holahan and Pohl 2002).

The Creation of the State Children's Health Insurance Program (SCHIP)

Legislation creating the State Children's Health Insurance Program (SCHIP), Title XXI of the Social Security Act, was passed in 1997—setting in motion the biggest effort to improve access to health care for the poor and near-poor since Medicaid was implemented. SCHIP enables states to expand health insurance coverage to near-poor uninsured children age eighteen and younger whose family incomes exceed the state's Medicaid eligibility ceiling. The original SCHIP legislation authorized the program for ten years. In 2007 and 2008, legislation to reauthorize and expand the program was vetoed twice by President George W. Bush, causing Congress to maintain it with continuing resolutions that provided the same funding as it had in 2007.

In early February 2009, Congress passed, and President Barack Obama signed, the Children's Health Insurance Program Reauthorization Act (CHIPRA), which reauthorized SCHIP until 2013. The reauthorization allows states to increase the income eligibility ceiling from 200 percent to 300 percent of the poverty level and cover children of legal immigrants.[8] It is projected that an additional 4 million children will be covered by the new rules governing SCHIP, bringing the total covered to about 11 million.

The federal matching rate for SCHIP is about 30 percent higher than it is for Medicaid. The rate is higher for SCHIP because in 1997 Congress wanted the states to establish the SCHIP programs quickly in order to reduce the number of uninsured children (Kenney and Chang 2004). The original SCHIP legislation gave each state a choice in how to set up SCHIP: they could cover all the newly eligible children under their Medicaid program; they could create a new program for children who did not qualify for Medicaid; or they could use their Medicaid programs to cover SCHIP children with incomes in a range between the state Medicaid eligibility ceiling and a higher income level (say, 150 percent of the poverty level) and establish a new program for children with higher but still eligible incomes. The advantage of a separate SCHIP program is that the states have greater freedom than under Medicaid to decide which medical services to cover, and they can use modest premiums and co-payments that are not permitted under Medicaid. As of 2007, only ten states (and the District of Columbia) used Medicaid as their SCHIP; the other forty used either a new SCHIP or a SCHIP with an expanded Medicaid (Kenney and Yee 2007).

Unlike Medicaid, SCHIP is not an entitlement program for all eligible children. It is a block grant program that distributes an annual allotment to each state based on the number of uninsured children with incomes below 200 (now 300) percent of the poverty level. Under the original SCHIP authorization, if a state spent its annual allotment, it could obtain more funds only if other states did not use up their allotments in that year. The original $40 billion allocation, however, did not anticipate the rapid increase in health care costs between 1997 and 2007. Some states exhausted their annual allocations by 2004 and 2005, not because they covered more children but because health costs rose faster than had been projected in 1997. Inequities in coverage across states were exacerbated by the fact that states could obtain additional funds only if other states did not use all of their allocations. The 2009 reauthorization of SCHIP increases federal funding for it by $32 billion over four and a half years, with the revenue to come from increased tobacco taxes.

In 2008, SCHIP covered almost 7 million poor and near-poor children, about 5 percent of all children, for some part of the year (Kaiser Family Foundation 2009). Its effects on poor and near-poor children's insurance coverage has been dramatic. Between 1998 and 2007, the percentage of children with incomes below 200 percent of the poverty level who were uninsured fell from 28 percent to 15 percent (Kaiser Family Foundation 2009).

The Early 2000s: Frustrated Efforts to Control Medicaid Spending Growth

Under George W. Bush's administration, there was a shift away from expanding Medicaid eligibility and toward efforts to control spending. The Bush administration's philosophy emphasized using public funds to provide care directly to the poor, for example, in community health care centers, instead of expanding eligibility limits and using public insurance to pay higher fees to providers. The administration's moves to limit Medicaid also were driven by rapid increases in spending. Between 2000 and 2002, Medicaid spending increased by an average 11.8 percent per year—a sharp acceleration from the 7.8 percent annual rate of growth between 1998 and 2000 (Holahan and Ghosh 2005).

The Bush administration initially proposed that Medicaid should change from a federal matching program to a block grant program. States objected because they might lose from such a shift if the number of poor people in their state increased more than anticipated by the proposed block grant formula. The recession of 2001 led states to argue for more federal funds to meet their increased Medicaid enrollments. In 2003, Congress provided $20 billion in additional funds; half were used to temporarily increase (through June 2004) each state's Medicaid matching rate. To obtain the additional funds, states could not reduce their eligibility criteria, but they were allowed to reduce reimbursement rates paid to health care providers and the kinds of benefits covered.[9] Although the additional funds were used to avoid major cuts in their Medicaid programs, every state and the District of Columbia began to implement cost containment strategies (Wachino, O'Malley, and Rudowitz 2005).

Data from the Medicaid Statistical Information System (MSIS) that became available in the early 2000s allow estimates of spending by Medicaid eligibility group. These estimates show that the growth in Medicaid spending in the early 2000s was due to rising enrollment—especially among the aged and disabled, who have higher costs of care. John Holahan and Arunabh Ghosh (2005) show that more than half of the growth in Medicaid spending between 2000 and 2003 was due to the aged and disabled, a finding confirmed by subsequent analyses of data through 2006 (Holahan, Cohen, and Rousseau 2007). It has become clearer in recent years that the driving force behind spending per Medicaid recipient is growth in prices of specific health care services and the intensity of services provided per recipient—factors that are more costly for the aged and disabled beneficiaries and beyond Medicaid's ability to control.

The Deficit Reduction Act of 2005: States Given the Option to Experiment with Medicaid

The Deficit Reduction Act of 2005 (DRA '05) provided states with greater latitude in the medical services that can be covered by their Medicaid programs and the beneficiaries to whom those services can be provided, and it allowed states to impose cost-sharing (premiums and co-payments for medical care) on enrollees. These options are particularly targeted at children and nondisabled adults. States no longer have to provide "mandatory" services and choose to offer additional "optional" services; instead, they can offer "benchmark equivalent" plans that cover different amounts of services for different groups of people based on their health status and where they live in the state. As of late 2008, however, only a few states had adopted such "tiered" benefits.[10] Beneficiaries with health care needs that are not covered have to bear the additional costs. This outcome is not consistent with Medicaid's mission and may explain why few states have adopted tiered benefits.

State Innovations with Insurance Programs for the Poor and Near-Poor

Between 2000 and 2006, the fraction of firms offering employer-sponsored insurance (ESI) fell from 69 percent to 61 percent (Claxton et al. 2006), and the fraction of the non-elderly population with ESI fell from 68.3 percent to 62.9 percent (Fronstin 2007). These trends were reflected in the uninsured population. As table 12.2 indicates, 55 percent of the non-elderly uninsured had incomes below 200 percent of the poverty level, and almost one-third of all non-elderly people with incomes below 200 percent of the poverty level were uninsured in 2007. Most of these uninsured near-poor and poor people are not eligible for Medicaid because they do not meet categorical eligibility requirements or they have incomes exceeding their state's eligibility ceiling.

In response to the growing numbers of uninsured working people, several states created innovative programs in the early and mid-2000s to encourage low-income people who were not eligible for Medicaid to buy private health insurance with state subsidies. The states did this not only to expand coverage but also to reduce pressures on hospitals and physicians who were providing more uncompensated care because there were more uninsured. Three such programs deserve attention—New York State's Healthy New York, Massachusetts's Commonwealth Care, and Wisconsin's BadgerCare Plus.

HEALTHY NEW YORK   Started in 2001, Healthy New York (HNY) is available for people who are not eligible for Medicaid but whose income is below 250 percent of the poverty level. People can apply as individuals or sole proprietors or as workers in small firms that do not sponsor health insurance and where at least

TABLE 12.2 / Family Income Relative to the Poverty Level for the Non-Elderly Uninsured, 2007

Family Income Relative to Poverty	Number Uninsured (Millions)	Percentage of Uninsured	Percentage of Cohort Uninsured
Below poverty level	11.404	25.4%	33.4%
1 to 1.49 times poverty	7.371	16.4	32.4
1.5 to 1.99 times poverty	5.777	12.9	27.1
2 to 2.99 times poverty	8.784	19.5	20.1
3 to 3.99 times poverty	4.594	10.2	12.5
4 times poverty and higher	7.026	15.6	6.8
Total	44.956	100	17.1

Source: Author's tabulations based on March 2008 Current Population Survey (U.S. Bureau of the Census 2008).

30 percent of the workers earn less than $38,000 (in 2009). All health maintenance organizations (HMOs) in the state must participate, and they cannot reject an applicant. Premiums are community-rated (the same for everyone in the same HMO regardless of age or health status) by county. The benefits covered and the cost-sharing required when people use care make the policies less generous than the standard policies sold in the individual market, contributing to lower premiums for Healthy New York. But the primary reason the premiums available in HNY are low (on average about half the premiums in the standard individual market) is that the state created a novel reinsurance program to reduce the risk of adverse selection. The state of New York provides reinsurance to the HMOs for any HNY enrollee whose annual expenses are between $5,000 and $75,000—the state pays 90 percent of an enrollee's expenses in this range. As of early 2008, about 150,000 people were enrolled in HNY. It appears to be serving two groups—those who cannot or do not expect to obtain employer-sponsored coverage, and those who needed coverage for a short period of time, either because they are between jobs with employer-sponsored coverage or because they have retired before age sixty-five and are not yet eligible for Medicare. The fact that the premiums have remained low relative to the private individual market suggests that HNY enrollees are relatively healthy.

COMMONWEALTH CARE Implemented in late 2006, Commonwealth Care provides a choice of four managed care plans (with some further choice of benefit plans depending on a person's income) to residents of Massachusetts who do not qualify for Medicaid but have incomes below 300 percent of the poverty level.[11] Participants receive subsidies that reduce their premium to $35 per person per month for those with incomes between 150 and 200 percent of the poverty level, $70 per month for incomes between 200 and 250 percent of poverty, and $105 per month for incomes between 250 and 300 percent of poverty. By April

2009, about 169,000 people were enrolled in Commonwealth Care, and about two-thirds did not have to pay premiums (Commonwealth Connector 2009). Although the program makes affordable health insurance available to low-income people who are not eligible for Medicaid, it does not cover people whose employers offer insurance that the workers consider unaffordable. In 2009 the primary problem facing Commonwealth Care was a shortfall in the state funds needed to pay for the subsidies. The shortfall arose because more people had enrolled needing full subsidies than had been predicted two years earlier.

BADGERCARE PLUS BadgerCare Plus began enrolling children under nineteen years of age in Wisconsin in early 2008. The program is open to all children, regardless of income, who do not have access to health insurance, as well as self-employed parents, pregnant women with annual incomes up to 300 percent of the poverty level, and farmers. The state subsidizes eligible people on a sliding scale: low-income families can enroll their children without paying anything, while families earning more than 300 percent of the poverty level can enroll their children at cost ($90.74 per child per month—or just under $1,100 in 2008). Children in families with incomes above 150 percent of the poverty level who have access to ESI can enroll in BadgerCare Plus only if the employer pays less than 81 percent of the premium. By the end of 2008, BadgerCare Plus had increased the enrollment in Wisconsin's public insurance program by almost 100,000 people (Wisconsin Department of Health Services 2008). Like Healthy New York, BadgerCare Plus has a less generous benefits package than Medicaid, and the state expects to enroll everyone in managed care plans to constrain costs.

Community Health Centers: An Alternative to Insurance Coverage for the Poor?

Since the "War on Poverty" was initiated in 1965, the federal government has funded community health centers (CHCs) to provide medical care to the poor and uninsured. Over the last four decades, there have been cycles of enthusiasm for and disillusionment with these public providers of medical care. Proponents of CHCs argue that they take better care of the health problems of low-income people because they know more about their clients' lives—their living conditions, reservations about discussing symptoms, tendency to not follow directions about prescriptions or nutrition—than medical personnel in physicians' offices or health plans. They argue that expanding public health insurance programs is less efficient than expanding CHCs.

President George W. Bush was an advocate of CHCs, in part because his home state of Texas has relied on them to provide care to the poor rather than expanding Medicaid. For fiscal year 2008, Congress approved just over $2 billion in funding of CHCs, almost double the amount spent in 2001. The National Association of CHCs (NACHC) estimates that in 2007 more than 17 million people were served in more than 1,000 federally qualified CHCs in more than 6,000 communities.

LeRoi Hicks and his colleagues (2006) estimate that one-quarter of the people served by CHCs are uninsured while the rest are covered by public insurance, and almost two-thirds are members of minority or immigrant groups.

In spite of the recent increase in funding for CHCs, there is a consensus of opinion that uninsured patients at CHCs who need specialty services, including diagnostic tests and medically necessary referrals to medical specialists and mental health and substance abuse services, face greater difficulties than do Medicaid enrollees (Gusmano, Fairbrother, and Park 2002; Hicks et al. 2006; Cook et al. 2007). Most analysts believe that CHCs need additional resources to provide better care. What is unresolved is whether it is more cost-effective to expand CHCs than to expand public insurance programs that pay for enrollees to receive care from all types of providers.

RECENT EFFORTS TO CONTROL MEDICAID AND SCHIP SPENDING[12]

Since 1970, when Medicaid was fully implemented in all the states except Arizona, the number of Medicaid enrollees has increased from 14.5 million in fiscal year 1970 (Stevens and Stevens 1974/2003, table 4) to 49.8 million in fiscal year 2005 (Holahan, Miller, and Rousseau 2009).[13] In those thirty-six years, Medicaid and SCHIP spending as a fraction of total national health spending more than doubled; Medicaid spending alone went from 6.9 percent to 14.8 percent (Catlin et al. 2008). As a fraction of the federal budget, federal Medicaid spending increased from 1.4 percent in 1970 to 6.6 percent in 2006, and as a share of all state expenditures, total Medicaid spending grew from 9.7 percent in fiscal year 1985 to 21.5 percent in fiscal year 2006.[14] The largest share of Medicaid spending in fiscal year 2005 (the most recent year for which we have Medicaid spending by category of beneficiary) was for dual-eligibles, who accounted for 46 percent ($131.9 billion) of Medicaid spending (Holahan, Miller, and Rousseau 2009). Other aged and disabled enrollees accounted for 27 percent ($78.2 billion) of Medicaid spending, non-aged adults for 10 percent ($28.6 billion), and children for 17 percent ($48.5 billion). The increase in the shares of the federal and state budgets devoted to Medicaid—and SCHIP—and the projected increases in future spending raise concerns about the ability of states to expand health insurance to more uninsured low-income people. States and the federal government are searching for ways to control spending, but the efforts to date have targeted children and nondisabled adults—in spite of the fact that these two groups accounted for just 27 percent of all Medicaid spending in fiscal year 2005.

Federal Efforts to Slow Spending

The Bush administration sought to reduce Medicaid spending through regulations (or rules) rather than legislation in 2007 and 2008 (Rudowitz 2008). These rules block state efforts to expand coverage to the uninsured poor and near-poor and limit payments to health care providers that serve a disproportionate share of low-income people. Since most of the rules involved estimated federal budget savings, they can be overturned by Congress only if it passes legislation that would "pay for" what would now be treated as increases in Medicaid costs.

The Bush administration also issued two directives in 2007 that limited states' ability to expand public coverage of poor and near-poor children. The first directive required states to cover 95 percent of all SCHIP-eligible children with incomes below 200 percent of the poverty level before they could use federal SCHIP funds for children with incomes above 250 percent of the poverty level.[15] This rule was widely interpreted as capping SCHIP coverage of children at 250 percent of the poverty level (Schwartz and McInerney 2008; Ross, Horn, and Marks 2008). Shortly after taking office, President Obama rescinded the directive. The second Bush directive restricted states' ability to expand their Medicaid income eligibility ceilings and transfer children covered by their SCHIP program to Medicaid. The directive affected only a few states that had not expanded Medicaid income limits when SCHIP was implemented, but it reinforced the current inequities across states in coverage of children. The Obama administration may move to rescind this rule as well.

State Efforts to Slow Spending

RAISING PREMIUMS AND CO-PAYMENTS   States have flexibility in setting SCHIP cost-sharing, although premiums and/or co-payments cannot exceed 5 percent of a child's family income for incomes at or above 150 percent of the poverty level (and a lower proportion of income for children with incomes below 150 percent of the poverty level). As a result, states have set very modest premiums and low co-payments. The Government Accountability Office (2004) reported that in August 2003 twenty-six states charged SCHIP premiums, compared to nine states doing the same in Medicaid, and that twenty-five states used some cost-sharing at the point of obtaining care in SCHIP, compared to six states for children in Medicaid. Twenty-five states used premiums for adults covered by Medicaid, and more than forty states required adults to share some costs when seeking care. States were most likely to use co-payments as the form of cost-sharing (as opposed to co-insurance rates or deductibles), and they were most often applied to physician services and prescription drugs for SCHIP children and all categories of adults who were not pregnant women or institutionalized beneficiaries.

Some states introduced premiums or raised existing SCHIP premiums because the recession of 2001–2002 reduced state tax revenues and caused more families to enroll their children in SCHIP after they lost their health insurance and/or income. Some states used premiums to discourage parents from dropping employer-sponsored coverage and enrolling the children in SCHIP (a phenomenon referred to as "crowd-out"); others used premiums to limit enrollment and reduce program costs because caseloads fall when low-income families face increases in premiums (Hadley et al. 2006/2007; Kenney, Hadley, and Blavin 2006/2007; Kenney et al. 2006/2007).

REDUCTIONS IN PAYMENTS TO PROVIDERS   States set the reimbursement rates paid to health care providers of services to Medicaid enrollees. As a result, reimbursement rates vary across the states. Most states reimburse physicians with relatively low fee-for-service (FFS) fees as a way of restraining costs. Stephen Zuckerman and his colleagues (2004) found that in 2003 Medicaid physician FFS fees were 69 percent of Medicare fees, and that the two states with the most Medicaid beneficiaries paid Medicaid physician fees that were even lower: California's were 59 percent and New York's were 45 percent of Medicare fees. Thus, states do not have a lot of room to save more by reducing physician payments.

Three out of five (61 percent) Medicaid beneficiaries are in managed care plans that do not pay physicians on an FFS basis.[16] States pay managed care plans capitated rates that are negotiated on the basis of historical averages of spending for services for beneficiaries.[17] The capitation rates are not easily renegotiated downward; the states cannot quickly shift beneficiaries from a plan that opts out of Medicaid if it feels the rate is too low. Here too, the states cannot easily reduce the payments to managed care providers.

Medicaid pays for almost half of total nursing home spending, which was $124.9 billion in 2006. Spending on nursing home care accounts for 17 percent of all Medicaid spending and is the largest spending category (O'Brien 2005). States do not have much leeway in controlling nursing home spending other than to maintain relatively low payment rates and restrict the supply of nursing home beds. States generally pay nursing homes on a prospective (per diem) cost basis or a combination of a prospective and retrospective cost basis. It does not appear that states are reducing nursing home per diem rates in an effort to reduce overall Medicaid spending. However, since nursing home residents are increasingly in need of more care (because they are sicker or more disabled by the time they enter nursing homes) than was the case before the early 1990s, the per diem rates per resident are declining de facto. This raises concerns about the quality of care provided to Medicaid beneficiaries in nursing homes.

CURRENT CONCERNS WITH PUBLIC HEALTH INSURANCE PROGRAMS

Beyond concerns about the rising costs of Medicaid, SCHIP, and other public health programs, there are four major concerns about how these programs collectively meet the needs of low-income people.

The Quality of Care for Elderly and Disabled Beneficiaries

Medicaid is the largest source of financing for long-term care; elderly and disabled beneficiaries account for 70 to 73 percent of all Medicaid spending, even though they are only 28 percent of the enrollees (Rowland 2008; Holahan, Miller, and Rousseau 2009). Recent efforts to limit Medicaid spending on elderly and disabled beneficiaries have focused on restricting the supply of nursing home beds and access to community and home care providers of long-term care (O'Brien 2005). Poor people needing long-term care also include children and non-elderly adults with cognitive and developmental disabilities, the severely mentally ill, people with traumatic brain or spinal cord injuries, children born with congenital impairments, and adults with illnesses such as Parkinson's disease or multiple sclerosis. Several studies (Grabowski et al. 2004; O'Brien 2005) have shown that there are large disparities in Medicaid spending on long-term care services across the states; these disparities, together with low payments, raise concerns about the quality of care provided to elderly and disabled Medicaid recipients. Given the aging of the population over the next two decades, pressures on states to expand the supply of long-term care services will increase (Stevenson 2008). Because elderly and disabled beneficiaries have far higher per capita costs than do children and nondisabled adults—$16,142 compared to $2,987, respectively, in 2006 (Holahan, Cohen, and Rousseau 2007)—the tension between improving quality of care and restraining spending will grow.[18]

The Poor Who Are Left Out of Medicaid

POOR ADULTS WHO DO NOT MEET CATEGORICAL ELIGIBILITY REQUIRE-MENTS   One-third of all non-elderly poor people were uninsured in 2007 (table 12.2). Some were eligible for Medicaid, but many were not because they were not members of the categorical groups of eligible people: children, pregnant women, some parents of children, elderly, and children and adults with physical or mental impairments. As table 12.3 shows, in 2007 between 41 and 52 percent of poor adults age nineteen to fifty-four were uninsured, as were 31 percent of adults age fifty-five to sixty-four. Among adults with incomes between 100 and 149 percent of the poverty level, the fractions who were uninsured are similar.

Low-wage workers are often employed by firms that do not sponsor employer-group health insurance. As table 12.4 shows, the fraction of people with private health insurance increases steadily with income; fewer than half of those with incomes below 200 percent of the poverty level have private coverage. One reason a majority of low-wage workers do not have employer-sponsored insurance (ESI) is that they work for small firms, and only about one-third of firms with fewer than fifty workers offer ESI (Swartz 2006). Further, there has been a decline in the number of employers that offer group coverage, from 69 percent in 2000 to 61 percent in 2006 (Claxton et al. 2006). This decline has been particularly prevalent among small firms. A second reason is that many low-wage workers may not be able to afford the employee share of the premium. While only about 3 percent of all workers who are offered ESI turn it down and remain uninsured (Haas and Swartz 2007), anecdotal indications that low-wage workers decline ESI due to the rising cost are increasing (Clemens-Cope and Garrett 2006).

The resistance of employers to paying for increases in health insurance premiums is a concern related to low-wage workers' ability to obtain insurance. They have little bargaining power in the labor market and cannot afford to pur-

TABLE 12.3 / The Uninsured, by Age Cohort and Income Relative to the Poverty Level, 2007

Age Cohort	Less Than Poverty Level	1.0 to 1.49 of Poverty Level	1.5 to 1.99 of Poverty Level	2.0 to 2.99 of Poverty Level	3.0 to 3.99 of Poverty Level	4.0 of Poverty Level or Higher	Total
Younger than nineteen	18.4%	18.6%	15.9%	11.8%	7.2%	4.0%	100%
Nineteen to twenty-four	45.1	45.2	38.3	31.2	25.1	15.4	100
Twenty-five to thirty-four	52.2	46.5	40.1	28.1	16.8	10.7	100
Thirty-five to forty-four	46.8	42.3	31.5	21.3	12.6	6.7	100
Forty-five to fifty-four	40.7	36.8	31.2	23.2	12.6	5.6	100
Fifty-five to sixty-four	31.5	30.1	21.6	16.2	9.9	5.1	100

Source: Author's tabulations based on March 2008 Current Population Survey (U.S. Bureau of the Census 2008).

TABLE 12.4 / Number of People Younger Than Age Sixty-Five by Health Insurance Type and Family Income Relative to the Poverty Level, and Distribution by Insurance Type Within Each Income Group, 2007 (Millions)

Insurance Status	Less Than Poverty Level	1.0 to 1.49 of Poverty Level	1.5 to 1.99 of Poverty Level	2.0 to 2.99 of Poverty Level	3.0 to 3.99 of Poverty Level	4.0 of Poverty Level or Higher
Uninsured	11.404	7.370	5.777	8.784	4.594	7.026
	32.4%	32.4%	27.1%	20.1%	12.5%	6.8%
Private[a]	6.993	8.320	11.413	30.243	30.035	93.717
	20.5%	36.6%	53.5%	69.3%	81.8%	90.4%
Medicare	1.717	1.107	0.740	0.760	0.376	0.490
	5.0%	4.9%	3.5%	1.7%	1.0%	0.5%
Medicaid	13.680	5.693	3.121	3.182	1.195	1.208
	40.1%	25.0%	14.6%	7.3%	3.3%	1.2%
CHAMPUS/ VA	0.322	0.260	0.286	0.695	0.538	1.176
	1%	1.1%	1.3%	1.6%	1.5%	1.1%
Total	34.115	22.750	21.337	43.665	36.739	103.617
	100%	100%	100%	100%	100%	100%

Source: Author's tabulations based on March 2008 Current Population Survey (U.S. Bureau of the Census 2008).
Note: Because people can have more than one insurance type during a year, a hierarchical assignment of insurance type was created: if a person had private coverage, he or she was assigned "private." If a person did not have private coverage but had Medicare, he or she was assigned "Medicare." If a person did not have private coverage or Medicare but had Medicaid, he or she was assigned "Medicaid." If a person did not have private coverage, Medicare, or Medicaid but had CHAMPUS/VA, he or she was assigned "CHAMPUS/VA." If a person had none of the above, he or she was assigned "uninsured."
a. Private includes employer- or union-sponsored coverage and self-purchased policies.

chase individual insurance policies (Swartz 2006). They need public assistance—either from Medicaid expansions or through subsidies to purchase quasi-private insurance—if they are to obtain insurance coverage.

IMMIGRANTS WHO ARE LEGAL RESIDENTS BUT NOT YET CITIZENS   People who reside legally in the United States but are not yet citizens accounted for 22 percent of all the uninsured in 2006 (Swartz 2008). Not quite half (47 percent) of non-elderly foreign-born residents who were not yet citizens were uninsured, in contrast with 15 percent of native citizens and 20 percent of naturalized citizens who were uninsured. A majority of foreign-born noncitizens are younger adults with low levels of formal education, low wages, and no employer-sponsored health insurance at their jobs. Among the 4 million foreign-born adults who were not yet citizens and were poor in 2007, between 55 and 70 percent were uninsured.[19]

Under the 1996 welfare reform, legal immigrants who are not citizens are not eligible for Medicaid (or SCHIP) until they have lived in the United States longer than five years. But CHIPRA, the 2009 SCHIP reauthorization legislation, removed this barrier for children who meet the income and categorical requirements for Medicaid and newly renamed CHIP (as of February 2009). The 2009 CHIPRA also overturned the DRA '05 requirement that Medicaid and CHIP applicants show proof of citizenship (or legal immigration status) and other identification papers. Now states can match a person's name and Social Security number with federal records to verify legal residency status.

Allowing children of legal immigrants to enroll in Medicaid and CHIP was done because not doing so was seen as creating more costly problems in the future. For example, immigrant children who do not receive recommended immunizations in a timely fashion, developmental screening exams, and prescription drugs for common childhood infections could be at risk for doing poorly in school, which in turn could affect their earnings capacity as adults.

LOW-INCOME PEOPLE WITH MENTAL HEALTH AND SUBSTANCE ABUSE PROBLEMS   Poor people who are disabled owing to mental health problems are categorically eligible for Medicaid. But low-income people who can work at least part-time do not qualify for disability status and therefore cannot obtain Medicaid coverage for their mental health problems. Medicaid enrollees who obtain coverage for mental health care services are those who meet the categorical requirements—for example, "traditionally" eligible poor adults in families with eligible children. Similarly, low-income people who have substance abuse problems are not likely to qualify for Medicaid. More to the point, most states do not cover health care services to address substance abuse problems.

Potential Crowding Out by Medicaid and CHIP of Employer-Sponsored Insurance

Ever since Medicaid was established, policy analysts and politicians have raised concerns about the possibility that low-income people will substitute public coverage for private insurance (Stevens and Stevens 1974/2003). This concern was raised again after the Medicaid eligibility criteria were expanded in the late 1980s, and the term for such substitution became known as "crowding out" in the mid-1990s. Crowd-out could occur, it was reasoned, because low-wage workers would find it cheaper to enroll their children in Medicaid than to pay the additional premium for dependent coverage; moreover, if wives of low-income workers became pregnant, the pregnancy costs would be covered by Medicaid. Another explanation for crowd-out was that firms that employed mostly low-wage workers would no longer feel that they needed to offer ESI since Medicaid would be available for more children and pregnant women. As we saw in the second section of this chapter, enrollment of children and pregnant women increased substantially during the economic recession of the early 1990s when many low-wage workers lost their jobs—further raising concerns about the magnitude of public insurance's potential to crowd out ESI. Although the first three decades' experience with Medicaid did not confirm these fears, the 1997 law establishing SCHIP required states to take measures to prevent SCHIP from substituting for ESI. As a result, most states do not allow children who have access to ESI to enroll in CHIP even if their family income makes them eligible.

Estimating the effects of the income eligibility expansions of Medicaid and the implementation of SCHIP is confounded by simultaneous changes in the economy and rising health care costs, both of which have caused employers to stop offering ESI. Depending on how these factors are accounted for, estimates are that between 10 and 70 percent of children covered by SCHIP might have had ESI if SCHIP did not exist (Kenney and Yee 2007). Studies that focus on children with family incomes between 100 and 200 percent of the poverty level estimate that between one-third and one-half of such children would have had ESI if SCHIP had not been available (Lo Sasso and Buchmueller 2004; Cunningham, Hadley, and Reschovsky 2002). All of these estimates, however, are quite sensitive to the estimating model and the data used to estimate the models. Also, other studies suggest that fewer than one-third of all SCHIP-eligible children have at least one parent with ESI (Kenney and Yee 2007). Some of these studies suggest that instead of children moving from ESI to SCHIP, they shifted from an uninsured status to SCHIP and would have remained uninsured if SCHIP had not been available. Thus, it appears that SCHIP and Medicaid have not crowded out private coverage to the extent predicted by some econometric studies.

Nonetheless, the potential for crowd-out continues to be cited by opponents of further expansions of Medicaid and CHIP. These concerns reflect fears about shifting the costs of health insurance from the private sector to taxpayers. However, with the growing number of employers—especially new small employers—that do not offer ESI, there is a growing fraction of adults who have low incomes and are uninsured.

Increasing the Enrollment and Reenrollment of Eligible People

As noted, policymakers concerned about providing access to medical care for low-income people have grappled with whether it is more effective to create public insurance programs or to expand clinics and community health centers where poor people live. One problem with creating programs with eligibility criteria is that not everyone who is eligible enrolls. This "take-up" problem is evident in other public programs, such as food stamps, as well as in Medicaid and SCHIP. Thomas Selden, Julie Hudson, and Jessica Banthin (2004) estimate that not quite three-fourths of the children eligible for either Medicaid or SCHIP were enrolled in 2002.[20]

Efforts to raise take-up rates and retain people in the programs once they enroll have grown in recent years as evidence has mounted that people (children and older people especially) who lack continuity of care often have avoidable health problems (Olson, Tang, and Newacheck 2005; Lave et al. 1998; Bermudez and Baker 2005). Over the course of a year or longer, it is not uncommon for low-income people to have periods of time with Medicaid or ESI coverage or no insurance. One reason for these dynamics is that families' incomes often are not stable from month to month. A change in jobs or hours worked during a month can cause a family to experience an increase or drop in income. For children whose family incomes are close to the income eligibility ceilings for SCHIP or the income eligibility interface between Medicaid and SCHIP, income dynamics can cause "churning" in and out of enrollment in SCHIP or Medicaid (Sommers 2007; Sommers et al. 2007). Benjamin Sommers (2007) estimates that one-third of all uninsured children in 2006 were enrolled in Medicaid or SCHIP in 2005, and that among uninsured children eligible for public coverage in 2006, more than two out of five were in Medicaid or SCHIP in 2005. He argues that the issue of uninsured children who are eligible for Medicaid or SCHIP is as much a problem of retaining enrolled children as it is a take-up problem. The retention problem has grown since 2000 as policymakers concerned about the rising costs of Medicaid and SCHIP have moved to make it more difficult to enroll and reenroll.

Take-up rates have increased when there have been greater and more imaginative outreach efforts to reach communities with high numbers of eligible people and simplified enrollment and renewal processes have been implemented. SCHIP showed this in its early years with a wide variety of efforts that also raised Medicaid take-up rates (Kenney and Chang 2004; Dubay et al. 2007). Expanding eligibility for public programs cannot be an effective policy to help poor people unless there is also sufficient funding for efforts that raise take-up and retention rates.

ISSUES THAT AFFECT THE FUTURE OF PUBLIC HEALTH INSURANCE

Inequities in Eligibility Across States and by Type of Person

The current set of state-administered public insurance programs for low-income people—Medicaid, CHIP, and programs financed only by the states—create two kinds of inequities. One inequity occurs across states: uninsured people with the same income and family circumstances who live in different states often do not have the same publicly financed coverage. A person may be ineligible for either

Medicaid or CHIP in one state while the same person would be eligible for one of the programs in another state. Similarly, a person enrolled in Medicaid (or CHIP) might be able to receive some health care services that are covered in some states but not in others because of the options that states have in setting up their programs. The second inequity occurs across persons: Medicaid and CHIP eligibility criteria do not allow people who have access to ESI to enroll. This prevents low-income people who cannot afford the employee share of the ESI premium from enrolling in the public programs even though their incomes are the same as those of other people who are eligible.

The variation in state income eligibility ceilings for categorically eligible groups does not fully reveal the extent of the differences across states in income eligibility for Medicaid. States can elect to deduct or disregard certain amounts of income when determining income eligibility, especially for children. As Sonya Schwartz and John McInerney (2008, 3) note, "As of January 2008, 46 states (including the District of Columbia) applied at least one of the following disregards or deductions when determining income eligibility for children's Medicaid: earnings disregards, deductions for child care expenses, and deductions for child support received and paid." The extent of the second inequity is difficult to estimate, but a lower-bound estimate is suggested by one study that finds that about 3 percent of the uninsured are low-income people who were offered ESI and turned it down (Haas and Swartz 2007).

Disparities in States' Ability to Fund Public Programs and Spending per Enrollee

The inequities in income eligibility limits are largely due to differences in states' ability to fund public insurance programs even though the federal matching rates under Medicaid and CHIP are highest for the states with low per capita incomes. For example, in fiscal year 2008, California, New York, and Massachusetts, with high per capita incomes, received one federal dollar for each state dollar spent on Medicaid, whereas Arkansas, Louisiana, and Mississippi, with low per capita incomes, received from $2.64 to $3.22 in federal funds for each dollar spent by the state. As noted earlier, the CHIP matching formula is more generous than the Medicaid formula: the states with higher per capita income received $1.86, and the states with lower per capita income received up to $5.00 per state dollar spent on CHIP in fiscal year 2008.

A primary reason for the disparity in the generosity of programs across states is that a state has to spend its own funds to obtain the federal matching dollars, and the poorer states are not able to—or choose not to—spend as much on Medicaid and CHIP as the higher-income states. Holahan (2007) reports that Medicaid spending per enrollee in 2004 varied from about $10,200 in New Jersey and New York to $4,100 in Alabama and $3,700 in California. The variation in per enrollee spending is affected by differences in the reimbursement rates paid to providers, the health care services that are covered, the supply of long-term care services compared to the number of elderly in the state, and the proportions of a state's enrollees who are aged and disabled relative to children and nondisabled adults. For example, states with higher proportions of costly enrollees (the aged and disabled) have higher spending per enrollee (everything else being equal).

State differences in Medicaid and CHIP spending depend on the differences in per enrollee spending as well as the income eligibility maximums set for each categorically eligible group and the proportions of their populations who are low-income and uninsured. States with higher proportions of low-income uninsured people (due to a lower proportion of ESI coverage) have relatively more people who could be eligible for public programs. Of course, if states set the income eligibility ceilings at lower levels, they can limit Medicaid or CHIP spending.

The disparities in the ability of states to pay for Medicaid and CHIP and the differences across states in spending per enrollee raise questions about the wisdom of the state-federal structure of these programs. There is a strong association between the level of state Medicaid spending and lower levels of access to medical care as well as health care outcomes (Holahan 2003). A design structure that provides benefits to some poor people and not to other poor people simply because of where they live is not equitable.

The American Recovery and Reinvestment Act of 2009 (better known as "the economic stimulus bill") acknowledges the severe fiscal difficulties that states are having in the economic recession that started in 2008. The stimulus package provides an estimated $87 billion over two years for additional federal matching funds to help states maintain their Medicaid programs as they face declining tax revenues and increasing inability to raise state funds to obtain the federal Medicaid dollars. Details of how these funds will be distributed to the states were scarce as this book was going to press, but the expectation is that the additional federal dollars will go to states with larger numbers of poor uninsured people. This could be the first step in revising the matching formula that has favored states with higher per capita incomes.

How to Slow the Growth in Spending on Medicaid

The growth in spending on Medicaid over the past forty years has been driven to varying degrees by increases in enrollment and increases in health care costs.[21] Enrollment has grown in response to downturns in the economy and expansions of eligibility criteria as well as stepped-up efforts to enroll eligible people and a general increase in the U.S. population. The increases in the costs of health care provided to Medicaid beneficiaries are related to the services that are covered and the costs of different types of services.[22] In turn, the costs of specific services (for example, inpatient hospital care, diagnostic tests, physician visits, nursing facility and mental health institutional care) depend on changes in norms regarding the intensity of care provided with such services and the reimbursement rates paid to providers.

For policymakers, the fact that expenditures for the elderly and disabled have accounted for a majority of the spending growth in recent years makes it difficult to rein in spending on Medicaid. This is particularly true in the current environment of rising concerns about the quality of care provided in nursing facilities compounded by the expected rapid growth in need for long-term care as the baby boomers retire. Reversing the past two decades' expansions of eligibility criteria for children and nondisabled adults will not radically slow the growth in overall Medicaid spending. Further, although Medicaid spending per enrollee grew more slowly than spending per privately insured person (Holahan, Cohen, and Rousseau 2007), policymakers realize that this has resulted in part from Medicaid paying providers less than they receive from private insurers.

Given concerns about ensuring access to care by physicians and other health care providers (for example, for mental health care), policymakers cannot cut Medicaid payments much below what they are now. Thus, unless policymakers cut Medicaid eligibility, Medicaid spending growth is unlikely to fundamentally change without changes in the underlying medical care system that sets norms for the intensity of care provided for different diagnoses.

The Role of Medicaid and CHIP in the System of Financing Health Care

Medicaid now covers 20 percent of the total population, and CHIP covers about 5 percent of all children at any point in time. Together, these programs covered roughly one in six people in 2006 (Kenney and Yee 2007; Ellis et al. 2008). Equally significant, CHIP covers almost 30 percent of all the children who meet the program's income eligibility requirements (Kenney and Yee 2007), and Medicaid covers almost 40 percent of the non-elderly poor and 25 percent of the non-elderly who have incomes between 100 and 150 percent of the poverty level and are not living in institutions.[23]

Medicaid has a particularly important role in providing access to health care for the low-income people who are most likely to have high medical expenses: disabled and elderly people and pregnant women. Without Medicaid, private insurance markets (especially the individual market) would use many more mechanisms than they do now to avoid insuring potentially high-cost people, and there would be more uninsured (Swartz 1996/1997). Thus, because Medicaid insures people deemed high-risk for needing high-cost medical care, everyone who has private insurance gains by having lower premiums and easier access to insurance.

However, Medicaid cannot control the growth in its own costs caused by the rising intensity of medical services provided when someone is sick. Medicaid now accounts for almost 15 percent of total health spending, but this share of total spending is too small to have any great influence on the costs of medical care services (except for long-term care services). Moreover, because states set the payment rates for Medicaid health care providers and there is great variation in what states pay providers, Medicaid lacks sufficient coherence to influence the norms for the intensity of services provided for diagnoses. Changes in these norms, particularly the increase in the use of new technologies and pharmaceuticals, are believed by most policy analysts to explain most of the growth in spending for health care since 1960 (Weisbrod 1991; Newhouse 1992).

Because Medicaid by itself cannot control the share of spending growth that is due to greater intensity of services and use of new technologies, and because many poor people remain uninsured, questions can be raised about how financing health care for the poor might change in the future. A national system of health care financing that includes everyone could be based on a combination of individual payments (premiums) and payroll-based premiums (taxes). This financing structure could ensure a progressive payment system that subsidizes low-income people. Further, a national system would reduce the expenses for administrative procedures that are in place now to verify a person's eligibility for Medicaid or SCHIP and that have discouraged eligible people from enrolling in both programs.[24]

CONCLUSION

For at least the past century, Americans have charted an inconsistent course to providing health care assistance to poor people. When economic times have been good, the country has expanded the groups of low-income people who are eligible for assistance. When the costs of providing care have increased more rapidly than the economy or tax revenues, governments have either paid providers of health care less or made it more difficult for eligible people to enroll. Some of this inconsistency reflects our federalist system of government. Under Medicaid, the federal government provides at least half of Medicaid funding to states and sets general guidelines about which poor people are eligible, and the states have flexibility over optional services, people who are covered, and payment rates to providers. Similarly, the federal government pays more of the CHIP costs but states have control over the income eligibility criteria. Some of the inconsistency reflects tensions in our views of different subgroups of the poor. Poor children and pregnant women have fared well compared to poor childless adults. Access to medical care for children is viewed as a good investment because healthier people are more productive members of society. In the case of pregnant women, this view extends to concern for the unborn child's health. The disabled poor and the poor elderly are viewed as deserving of our help because they cannot earn more income. In contrast, there is far less sympathy for nondisabled adults without children; many people believe that these adults should be able to find a job with health insurance. There is little acknowledgment that the fraction of employers sponsoring ESI has been declining over the past decade and that many people cannot obtain ESI (Swartz 2006). Also, most people do not know how expensive individual health insurance is and how difficult it is for anyone with an income below 300 percent of the poverty level to afford individual coverage.

The state of the economy and the distribution of gains in national income across income cohorts clearly affect our attitudes about who among the poor deserves health care assistance. This is reflected in concerns about the tax consequences of rising spending on Medicaid and CHIP (and other state programs), especially when we are in a deep recession. There also is growing concern about the costs of long-term care and the expected growth in the demand for such care as the baby boomers retire and swell the ranks of the poor elderly needing Medicaid. Similarly, recent state initiatives to expand health insurance coverage to more of their low-income populations, such as those in Massachusetts and Wisconsin, will succeed or fail depending on the states' ability to control health care costs.

Although there is antipathy to paying higher taxes to fund Medicaid and CHIP, middle-class people view Medicaid as a program to which their elderly relatives are entitled when they need long-term care services. Those who have elderly relatives in nursing homes realize that the quality of care often needs improvement. Demands to improve the quality of long-term care services collide with the fact that the middle class and people in lower income deciles did not see their real incomes rise over the past decade (Mishel, Bernstein, and Allegretto 2007). They do not want to pay more in taxes, and yet their elderly relatives often are Medicaid beneficiaries.

Thus, we return to the fundamental question of how medical assistance should be provided to the poor: should they be included in any health insurance program we have, or should assistance with medical care be provided as a welfare program and only to deserving groups of poor? Answering this question involves examining our system of health insurance for everyone. Currently, about 60 percent of Americans rely on employer-sponsored coverage. For the last decade, however, employers have been backing away from offering ESI and increasingly requiring workers to pay a higher share of the costs for medical care services. The recession that started in 2008 will accelerate this trend, increasing the number of uninsured workers. This should be a catalyst to consider our options for restructuring how we pay for health insurance and health care for all (Swartz 2008). Among the issues that must be considered are two that particularly affect the poor: How much should higher-income people and companies be taxed in order to provide subsidies to low-income people? And what package of health care services will be considered the minimum to which everyone is entitled regardless of income? How we answer these questions will determine how we share the responsibility for providing the poor with access to health care in the coming decades.

Recommendations

The United States should move to a national system of health insurance so that everyone, regardless of income, would have access to a minimum set of medical services that are covered, in much the same way as Medicare covers a minimum set of services. A national insurance system would achieve three other objectives related to the poor and the country's ability to provide medical care to the poor. First, it would eliminate the current inequities in eligibility criteria for Medicaid and CHIP and in the states' ability to fund assistance programs for the poor. Second, it would provide a mechanism for slowing the rate of growth in health care spending; without a slowdown, the disparities in the medical care available to high- and lower-income people in this country will only increase. Finally, a national system of health insurance would efficiently and quickly redistribute income to poor people when they get sick.

The federal government should provide funding to expand the number of primary care medical personnel. Funding should be devoted particularly to increasing the number of registered nurses (RNs), nurse-practitioners, and physicians who are knowledgeable about issues that affect low-income people's health and their ability to articulate symptoms and concerns. Community health centers are one mechanism for providing medical care in poor areas, but they are not a substitute for increasing the number of primary care providers.

Finally, greater attention should be paid to providing information about health issues to low-income people. Public health campaigns on the importance of brushing teeth and smoking cessation worked to increase oral health and reduce smoking in poor areas. Targeting understandable information about the links between obesity and diabetes and cardiac problems, for example, would help lower-income people avoid some of the health issues that restrict their ability to earn more. Moreover, given the fact that a large share of the poor are foreign-born, health information specifically developed for low-income people should reflect greater sensitivity to cultural nuances related to health care.

NOTES

1. The Children's Health Insurance Program Reauthorization Act caused the SCHIP to be known simply as CHIP. I will refer to the program as SCHIP when discussing events through 2008.

2. The Social Security Act also included matching federal funds (that is, a state would have to spend its own revenues to obtain federal matching funds) that could be used for medical care if the money was an allowance in the monthly cash amount paid to recipients. This did not work well.

3. See Kaiser Commission on Medicaid and the Uninsured (2009b) for many current details about the Medicaid program.

4. These included six annual budget acts and the short-lived Medicare Catastrophic Act of 1989. The budget acts were the Deficit Reduction Act of 1984 (DEFRA), the Combined Omnibus Budget Reconciliation Act of 1985 (COBRA), the Omnibus Budget Reconciliation Acts of 1986 (OBRA '86) and 1987 (OBRA '87), and the Omnibus Budget Reconciliation Acts of 1989 (OBRA '89) and 1990 (OBRA '90).

5. The Medicare deductible for a stay in the hospital in 2008 was $1,024.

6. Section 1115 of the Social Security Act was enacted in 1962 (before Medicaid) and authorizes the secretary of Health and Human Services to permit demonstration projects that modify aspects of state grant programs under the Social Security Act (not just Medicaid) without congressional approval. A number of states used the Section 1115 waivers for small demonstrations before the early 1990s. Among these demonstrations

were some that moved nondisabled adults and children into managed care plans—
in part to see if managed care would reduce spending per recipient and in part to obtain
greater access to care for the recipients. Evaluations of the demonstrations were confounded by the lack of randomized control trials, but the popular consensus was that
the managed care plans saved money. The Clinton administration promoted the use
of Section 1115 waivers for statewide (rather than small) demonstrations that moved
more recipients (initially nondisabled adults and children) into managed care plans
and expanded Medicaid eligibility to low-income individuals and families who previously were not eligible (Lambrew 2001). See also Kaiser Commission on Medicaid
and the Uninsured (2009a).

7. The amendment was sponsored by Senators John Chafee (R-RI) and John Breaux
(D-LA).

8. By 2007 all but eight states had increased the SCHIP income eligibility ceiling up to
200 percent of the poverty level (Kenney and Yee 2007), and seventeen states had limits at or above 250 percent of the poverty line (Kaiser Commission on Medicaid and
the Uninsured 2007).

9. States also were permitted to restrict enrollment rates among eligible poor people by,
among other actions, reducing the number of months between recertification of eligibility and increasing the types of documents required when applying for Medicaid.

10. Kentucky, Idaho, and West Virginia created tiered benefits by dividing enrollees
into groups and offering each group somewhat different benefits packages (covered
services). Beneficiaries who are healthier have more limited benefits. This approach
limits a state's Medicaid costs (and federal matching funds) because it is the benefits
package that restricts the costs rather than a person's medical needs.

11. Commonwealth Care was part of legislation that requires Massachusetts residents to
have insurance unless they are exempted. The state also obtained a Section 1115 waiver
to be able to use federal Medicaid funds to help cover more uninsured adults with
incomes up to 150 percent of the poverty level. Medicaid enrollment and expenditure information is available in the annual Statistical Supplement to the Health Care
Financing Review (CMS various years, 2009a, 2009b).

12. See the conference version of this chapter for a more detailed discussion of federal and
state efforts to control expenditures for Medicaid and SCHIP.

13. Estimates of how many people received Medicaid and SCHIP at any time during 2006
range from 55 million to 59 million (Centers for Medicare and Medicaid Services [CMS],
various years, see http://www.cms.hhs.gov/MedicareMedicaidStatSupp/LT/list.asp;
Kaiser Family Foundation [KFF], "Kaiser State Health Facts," statehealthfacts.org). One
reason for the difference in estimates is that some low-income people who are not
eligible for Medicaid can receive some Medicaid-financed special services (for example, family planning).

14. Estimates based on author's calculations using data from Catlin et al. (2008); the *Statistical
Abstract of the United States* (U.S. Census Bureau 2008) for federal expenditures and
budgets; and data from the National Association of State Budget Officers for state
expenditures and budgets (1987 and 2007).

15. In 2006, 91 percent of SCHIP children had incomes below 200 percent of the poverty
level (Kaiser Commission on Medicaid and the Uninsured 2007).

16. See Centers for Medicare and Medicaid Services (2009c). Available at: http://www.cms.hhs.gov/MedicaidManagCare.

17. A capitated rate is simply a per person (per capita) amount. It is based on the average costs of providing care to an "average" person.

18. The per capita costs have been adjusted to exclude all prescription drug spending for dual-eligibles.

19. Author's calculations based on analyses of the March 2008 Current Population Survey. For more information about immigrants' lack of health insurance and use of health care, see Kaiser Commission on Medicaid and the Uninsured (2008).

20. The Medicaid take-up rates among dual-eligibles are similar for poor elderly, but the rate for those with incomes just above the poverty level is very low. Marilyn Moon, Niall Brennan, and Misha Segal (1998) estimate that 78 percent of QMBs enrolled in Medicaid while only 16 percent of SLMBs enrolled.

21. Policy analysts' understanding of the different periods when Medicaid's growth in spending was driven by increases in enrollment by different groups versus increases in health care costs is due primarily to the analyses conducted by John Holahan and various colleagues. The conference version of this chapter contains a long reference list that includes many papers by Holahan and his coauthors.

22. Two examples illustrate the effects of changes in the services covered. The costs of prescription drugs for Medicare-Medicaid dual-eligibles were shifted to Medicare Part D in 2005, causing a first-time-ever decline in Medicaid spending between 2005 and 2006. In contrast, states have increased their use of waivers to expand home- and community-based long-term care (LTC) services, which has caused spending on these services to be almost as large as spending on nursing homes. While home- and community-based LTC is less expensive per person than nursing facility care, states are struggling with how to respond to the growing number of people whose preference for home- and community-based care (and who might not go to a nursing facility) is driving such spending close to that for nursing home care.

23. Author's analyses of March 2008 Current Population Survey.

24. Checking people's incomes could be done through annual filing of income statements, which would require a change in who has to file income tax statements.

25. The conference version of the chapter has a longer list of references that were helpful to the author.

REFERENCES[25]

Bermudez, Dustin, and Laurence C. Baker. 2005. "The Relationship Between SCHIP Enrollment and Hospitalizations for Ambulatory Care Sensitive Conditions in California." *Journal of Health Care for the Poor and Underserved* 16(1): 96–110.

Burman, Len. 2006. "Taking a Check Up on the Nation's Health Care Tax Policy: A Prognosis." Statement before the U.S. Senate Committee on Finance, March 8.

Catlin, Aaron, Cathy Cowan, Micah Hartman, Stephen Heffler, and the National Health Expenditure Accounts Team. 2008. "National Health Spending in 2006: A Year of Change for Prescription Drugs." *Health Affairs* 27(1): 14–29.

Centers for Medicare and Medicaid Services (CMS). Various years. Annual Statistical Supplement to the Health Care Financing Review. Baltimore, Md.: CMS. The 2008 Statistical Supplement Medicaid Figures are available at: http://www.cms.hhs.gov/Medicare MedicaidStatSupp/LT/list.asp

———. 2009a. CHIP Enrollment Data. Available at: http://www.cms.hhs.gov/National CHIPPolicy.

———. 2009b. Medicaid Information. Available at: http://www.cms.hhs.gov/home/medicaid.asp.

———. 2009c. Medicaid Managed Care Information. Available at: http://www.cms.hhs.gov/MedicaidManagCare.

Claxton, Gary, Isadora Gil, Benjamin Finder, Bianca DiJulio, Samantha Hawkins, Jeremy Pickreign, Heidi Whitmore, and J. Gabel. 2006. *Employer Health Benefits: 2006 Annual Survey.* Menlo Park, Calif.: Kaiser Family Foundation.

Clemens-Cope, Lisa, and Bowen Garrett. 2006. "Changes in Employer-Sponsored Health Insurance Sponsorship, Eligibility, and Participation: 2001 to 2005." Washington, D.C.: Kaiser Commission on Medicaid and the Uninsured.

Commonwealth Connector. 2009. "Commonwealth Care Quarterly Update." Report prepared for Commonwealth Connector board meeting of April 9, 2009. Available at: http://www.mahealthconnector.org/portal/site/connector.

Cook, Nakela L., LeRoi S. Hicks, A. James O'Malley, Thomas Keegan, Edward Guadagnoli, and Bruce E. Landon. 2007. "Access to Specialty Care and Medical Services in Community Health Centers." *Health Affairs* 26(5): 1459–68.

Cunningham, Peter J., Jack Hadley, and James Reschovsky. 2002. "The Effects of SCHIP on Children's Health Insurance Coverage: Early Evidence from the Community Tracking Study." *Medical Care Research and Review* 59(4): 359–83.

Dubay, Lisa, Jocelyn Guyer, Cindy Mann, and Michael Odeh. 2007. "Medicaid at the Ten-Year Anniversary of SCHIP: Looking Back and Moving Forward." *Health Affairs* 26(2): 370–81.

Ellis, Eileen R., Dennis Roberts, David M. Rousseau, and Karyn Schwartz. 2008. "Medicaid Enrollment in 50 States: December 2006 Data Update." Washington, D.C.: Kaiser Commission on Medicaid and the Uninsured.

Engel, Jonathan. 2006. *Poor People's Medicine: Medicaid and American Charity Care Since 1965.* Durham, N.C.: Duke University Press.

Fronstin, Paul. 2007. "Sources of Health Insurance and Characteristics of the Uninsured: Analysis of the March 2007 Current Population Survey." Issue brief 310. Washington, D.C.: Employee Benefit Research Institute.

Government Accountability Office (GAO). 2004. "Medicaid and SCHIP: States' Premium and Cost-Sharing Requirements for Beneficiaries." GAO-04-491. Washington: GAO.

Grabowski, David C., Zhanlian Feng, Orna Intrator, and Vincent Mor. 2004. "Recent Trends in State Nursing Home Payment Policies." *Health Affairs* (web exclusive, June 16): W4-363–73.

Gusmano, Michael K., Gerry Fairbrother, and Heidi Park. 2002. "Exploring the Limits of the Safety Net: Community Health Centers and Care for the Uninsured." *Health Affairs* 21(6): 188–94.

Haas, Jennifer, and Katherine Swartz. 2007. "The Relative Importance of Worker, Firm, and Market Characteristics for Racial-Ethnic Disparities in Employer-Sponsored Health Insurance." *Inquiry* 44(3): 280–302.

Hadley, Jack, James D. Reschovsky, Peter Cunningham, Genevieve Kenney, and Lisa Dubay. 2006/2007. "Insurance Premiums and Insurance Coverage of Near-Poor Children." *Inquiry* 43(4): 362–77.

Hicks, LeRoi S., A. James O'Malley, Tracy A. Lieu, Thomas Keegan, Nakela L. Cook, Barbara McNeil, Bruce E. Landon, and Edward Guadagnoli. 2006. "The Quality of Chronic Disease Care in U.S. Community Health Centers." *Health Affairs* 25(6): 1712–23.

Holahan, John. 2003. "Variation in Health Insurance Coverage and Medical Expenditures: How Much is Too Much?" In *Federalism and Health Policy*, edited by John Holahan, Alan Weil, and Joshua M. Wiener. Washington, D.C.: Urban Institute.

Holahan, John. 2007. "State Variation in Medicaid Spending: Hard to Justify." *Health Affairs* (web exclusive, September 18): W667–9.

Holahan, John, Mindy Cohen, and David Rousseau. 2007. "Why Did Medicaid Spending Decline in 2006? A Detailed Look at Program Spending and Enrollment, 2000–2006." Washington, D.C.: Kaiser Commission on Medicaid and the Uninsured.

Holahan, John, Teresa Coughlin, Leighton Ku, Debra J. Lipson, and Shruti Rajan. 1995. "Insuring the Poor Through Section 1115 Medicaid Waivers." *Health Affairs* 14(1): 199–216.

Holahan, John, and Arunabh Ghosh. 2005. "Understanding the Recent Growth in Medicaid Spending, 2000–2003." *Health Affairs* (web exclusive, January 26): W5-52–62.

Holahan, John, and David Liska. 1997. "The Slowdown in Medicaid Spending Growth: Will It Continue?" *Health Affairs* 16(2): 157–63.

Holahan, John, Dawn M. Miller, and David Rousseau. 2009. "Dual-Eligibles: Medicaid Enrollment and Spending for Medicare Beneficiaries in 2005." Washington, D.C.: Kaiser Commission on Medicaid and the Uninsured.

Holahan, John, and Mary Beth Pohl. 2002. "Changes in Insurance Coverage: 1994–2000 and Beyond." *Health Affairs* (web exclusive, April 3): W162–71.

Holahan, John, Diane Rowland, Judith Feder, and David Heslam. 1993. "Explaining the Recent Growth in Medicaid Spending." *Health Affairs* 12(3): 177–93.

Institute of Medicine (IOM). 2003. *Unequal Treatment: Confronting Racial and Ethnic Disparities in Health Care*, edited by Brian D. Smedley, Adrienne Y. Stich, and Alan R. Nelson. Washington, D.C.: National Academies Press.

Kaiser Commission on Medicaid and the Uninsured. 2007 (revised August 29). "SCHIP Reauthorization: Key Questions in the Debate and a Description of New Administrative Guidance and the House and Senate Proposals." Washington, D.C.: Kaiser Commission on Medicaid and the Uninsured.

———. 2008. "Summary: Five Basic Facts on Immigrants and Their Health Care." Washington, D.C.: Kaiser Commission on Medicaid and the Uninsured.

———. 2009a. "The Role of Section 1115 Waivers in Medicaid and CHIP: Looking Back and Looking Forward." Washington, D.C.: Kaiser Commission on Medicaid and the Uninsured.

———. 2009b. *Medicaid: A Primer*. Washington, D.C.: Kaiser Commission on Medicaid and the Uninsured.

Kaiser Family Foundation. 2009. "Enrolling Uninsured Low-Income Children in Medicaid and SCHIP" (January). Available at: http://www.statehealthfacts.org.

Kenney, Genevieve, R. Andrew Allison, Julia F. Costich, James Marton, and Joshua McFeeters. 2006/2007. "Effects of Premium Increases on Enrollment in SCHIP: Findings from Three States." *Inquiry* 43(4): 378–92.

Kenney, Genevieve, and Debbie I. Chang. 2004. "The State Children's Health Insurance Program: Successes, Shortcomings, and Challenges." *Health Affairs* 23(5): 51–62.

Kenney, Genevieve, and Justin Yee. 2007. "SCHIP at a Crossroads: Experiences to Date and Challenges Ahead." *Health Affairs* 26(2): 356–69.

Kenney, Genevieve, Jack Hadley, and Fredric Blavin. 2006/2007. "Effects of Premiums on Children's Health Insurance Coverage: Evidence from 1999 to 2003." *Inquiry* 43(4): 345–61.

Klein, Jennifer. 2003. *For All These Rights: Business, Labor, and the Shaping of America's Public-Private Welfare State*. Princeton, N.J.: Princeton University Press.

Lambrew, Jeanne. 2001. "Section 1115 Waivers in Medicaid and the State Children's Health Insurance Program: An Overview." Washington, D.C.: Kaiser Commission on Medicaid and the Uninsured.

Lave, Judith R., Christopher R. Keane, Chyongchiou J. Lin, Edmund M. Ricci, Gabriele Amersbach, and Charles P. LaVallee. 1998. "Impact of a Children's Health Insurance Program on Newly Enrolled Children." *Journal of American Medical Association* 279(22): 1820–5.

Lillie-Blanton, Marsha, Rose Marie Martinez, Barbara Lyons, and Diane Rowland, eds. 1999. *Access to Health Care: Promises and Prospects for Low-Income Americans*. Washington, D.C.: Kaiser Commission on Medicaid and the Uninsured.

Lo Sasso, Anthony T. and Thomas C. Buchmueller. 2004. "The Effect of the State Children's Health Insurance Program on Health Insurance Coverage." *Journal of Health Economics* 23(5): 1059–82.

Mishel, Lawrence, Jared Bernstein, and Sylvia Allegretto. 2007. *The State of Working America 2006–2007*. Ithaca, N.Y.: Cornell University Press.

Moon, Marilyn, Niall Brennan, and Misha Segal. 1998. "Improving Coverage for Low-Income Medicare Beneficiaries." Policy brief. New York: Commonwealth Fund.

Newhouse, Joseph P. 1992. "Medical Care Costs: How Much Welfare Loss?" *Journal of Economic Perspectives* 6(3): 3–21.

O'Brien, Ellen. 2005. "Long-Term Care: Understanding Medicaid's Role for the Elderly and Disabled." Washington, D.C.: Kaiser Commission on Medicaid and the Uninsured.

Olson, Lynn M., Suk-Fong S. Tang, and Paul W. Newacheck. 2005. "Children in the United States with Discontinuous Health Insurance Coverage." *New England Journal of Medicine* 353(4): 382–91.

Ross, Donna Cohen, Aleya Horn, and Caryn Marks. 2008. "Health Coverage for Children and Families in Medicaid and SCHIP: State Efforts Face New Hurdles: A Fifty-State Update on Eligibility Rules, Enrollment and Renewal Procedures, and Cost-Cutting Practices in Medicaid and SCHIP in 2008." Washington, D.C.: Kaiser Commission on Medicaid and the Uninsured.

Rowland, Diane. 2008. "Medicaid's Role for People with Disabilities." Testimony before the U.S. House of Representatives, Committee on Energy and Commerce, Subcommittee on Health, January 16.

Rudowitz, Robin. 2008. "Medicaid: Overview and Impact of New Regulations." Washington, D.C.: Kaiser Commission on Medicaid and the Uninsured.

Schwartz, Sonya, and John McInerney. 2008. "Examining a Major Policy Shift: New Federal Limits on Medicaid Coverage for Children." *State Health Policy Briefing.* Washington, D.C.: National Academy for State Health Policy.

Selden, Thomas M., Julie L. Hudson, and Jessica S. Banthin. 2004. "Tracking Changes in Eligibility and Coverage Among Children, 1996–2002." *Health Affairs* 23(5): 39–50.

Smith, James P. 1999. "Healthy Bodies and Thick Wallets: The Dual Relation Between Health and Economic Status." *Journal of Economic Perspectives* 13(2): 145–66.

Sommers, Anna S., Lisa Dubay, Linda J. Blumberg, Fredric E. Blavin, and John L. Czajka. 2007. "Dynamics in Medicaid and SCHIP Eligibility Among Children in SCHIP's Early Years: Implications for Reauthorization." *Health Affairs* (web exclusive, August 7): W598–607.

Sommers, Benjamin D. 2007. "Why Millions of Children Eligible for Medicaid and SCHIP Are Uninsured: Poor Retention Versus Poor Take-Up." *Health Affairs* (web exclusive, July 26): W560–67.

Stevens, Robert, and Rosemary Stevens. 2003. *Welfare Medicine in America: A Case Study of Medicaid,* with a new introduction by Rosemary Stevens. New Brunswick, N.J.: Transaction Publishers. (Originally published in 1974 by Free Press.)

Stevenson, David G. 2008. "Planning for the Future: Long-Term Care and the 2008 Election." *New England Journal of Medicine* 358(19): 1985–87.

Swartz, Katherine. 1996–97. "Let's Not Neglect Medicaid's Vital Role in Insurance Markets." *Inquiry* 33(4): 301–3.

———. 2006. *Reinsuring Health: Why More Middle-Class People Are Uninsured and What Government Can Do.* New York: Russell Sage Foundation.

———. 2008. "Uninsured in America: New Realities, New Risks." In *Health at Risk: America's Ailing Health System—and How to Heal It,* edited by Jacob S. Hacker. New York: Columbia University Press.

U.S. Bureau of the Census. 2008. *Statistical Abstract of the United States.* Available at: http://www.census.gov/compendia/statab/2008/2008edition.html.

U.S. Bureau of the Census. Various years. Current Population Survey. Available at: http://www.census.gov/cps.

Wachino, Victoria, Molly O'Malley, and Robin Rudowitz. 2005. "Financing Health Coverage: The Fiscal Relief Experience." Washington, D.C.: Kaiser Commission on Medicaid and the Uninsured.

Weisbrod, Burton. 1991. "The Health Care Quadrilemma: An Essay on Technological Change, Insurance, Quality of Care, and Cost Containment." *Journal of Economic Literature* 29(2): 523–52.

Wisconsin Department of Health Services. 2008. "BadgerCare Plus Enrollment Report" (December). Monthly statewide enrollment data available at: http://www.badgercareplus.org/enrollmentdata/enrolldata.htm.

Zuckerman, Stephen, Joshua McFeeters, Peter Cunningham, and Len Nichols. 2004. "Changes in Medicaid Physician Fees, 1998–2003: Implications for Physician Participation." *Health Affairs* (web exclusive, June 23): W4-374–84.

Part 4

The Politics of Poverty and Its Meaning in a Rich Country

Chapter 13

Poverty Politics and Policy

Mary Jo Bane

In 1992, "ending welfare as we know it" was an important theme in Bill Clinton's presidential campaign. It polled well and was consistent with other aspects of the New Democrat agenda that Clinton was campaigning on, an agenda that also included "making work pay" and "reinventing government." Candidate Clinton talked a good deal about welfare in the context of an approach to poverty that emphasized work and responsibility.

In May 2008, when Hillary Clinton and Barack Obama were neck and neck for the Democratic nomination, neither of their campaign websites mentioned welfare. Both had issue papers on poverty: Clinton's was a subtopic under the broad issue of "Strengthening the Middle Class," and Obama's was one of twenty issue areas. John McCain, the Republican nominee, included neither poverty nor welfare in his list of important issues, though he did have an economic plan that included proposals directed at the struggling middle class. He began his general election campaign with a "poverty tour," but abandoned that strategy quite quickly. Barack Obama's campaign and post-election rhetoric focused on the middle class and working families.

Much has happened in politics and policy around poverty and welfare in the years since—and to some extent because of—Clinton's 1992 campaign agenda. In this chapter, I address three questions:

1. What has changed in policy, practice, and the lives of the poor since 1992?

2. What has changed, if anything, in public opinion and the political context around poverty and welfare?

3. What are the prospects and best political strategies for improvement in the lives of the poor going forward from 2009?

WHAT CHANGED IN POLICY, PRACTICE, AND THE LIVES OF THE POOR?

The End of Welfare

Welfare as we know it has indeed ended. The importance and magnitude of this change cannot be overemphasized. John Karl Scholz, Robert Moffitt, and Benjamin Cowan (this volume) provide data on both the number of recipients of Aid to Families with Dependent Children (AFDC) and Temporary Assistance for Needy Families (TANF) and the amount of federal spending on TANF relative to other poverty programs. They show that the number of recipients of AFDC/TANF fell by 68 percent between 1994 and 2006 and that constant dollar spending on AFDC/TANF fell by 48 percent over the same period. These are dramatic changes indeed. A survey conducted by the *New York Times* in early 2009 suggested that even the recession of 2008 led to only small increases in caseloads between 2007 and 2008.

The changes look even more dramatic if we look behind the gross spending numbers and examine how the states are spending their block grant money. Data on spending are reported to the federal Administration for Children and Families (ACF) and compiled and reported on that agency's website.[1] In 2005 the states reported spending $20.6 billion in state and federal TANF funds. Of this, $10.7 billion was for basic cash assistance; most of the rest was spent on child care. The WELPAN study, conducted in seven midwestern states (Illinois, Indiana, Iowa, Michigan, Minnesota, Ohio, and Wisconsin), was able to account for spending more precisely. This study found that in 1996 the seven states spent 72 percent of their AFDC-TANF budgets on cash assistance; in 2003 they spent 30 percent on cash assistance. In addition, in 2003 these seven states spent 35 percent of their budgets on child care and 23 percent on family-related programs and services (Members of the WELPAN Network 2002, 2005). These are substantial shifts in the nature of the program.

The TANF caseload numbers also underestimate the extent of the change in welfare because a large proportion of cases now are child-only cases. The number of adults receiving cash payments under TANF in September 2007 was only 896,000, down from 4.4 million in 1992.[2] The number of adult welfare recipients, the object of so much concern in the 1990s, is now a trivial proportion of the population, and only a very small proportion of the adult poor (20.2 million in 2006).[3] Of course, because of the shift in the type of services provided under TANF, cash assistance recipients are not the only group served, and it would improve the accuracy of our caseload descriptions if they were better counted (Swartz 2002).

In claiming that "welfare as we know it" has ended, I have thus far defined "welfare" as cash assistance received through AFDC or TANF. I believe that this is the correct way to characterize what candidate Clinton and the voters who supported him were determined to reform. But it is worth noting that the food stamp program as we know it has not ended. Food stamp receipt declined quite dramatically after welfare reform, but it has been rising since about 2000 and is now above its 1996 level (Scholz, Moffitt, and Cowan, this volume). It appears that potential recipients are making the distinction between welfare and food stamps and are applying for and receiving food stamps even as they have been removed or deterred from cash assistance. The Food and Nutrition Service certainly makes the distinction.[4]

The Structure and Operation of Poverty Policy

A second big change, running in parallel with the first, is that the structure of antipoverty policy shifted quite dramatically, away from AFDC-TANF and toward supports for work. The most impressive change is the increase in the number of recipient filing units of the Earned Income Tax Credit (EITC), from 19,017 in 1994 to 22,752 in 2005, and in spending on the EITC, from $29.5 billion to $45 billion over the same period (Scholz, Moffitt, and Cowan, this volume).

Spending on child care assistance has also increased. In 2005 a reasonable estimate is that the states spent $11.1 billion in state and federal funds on child care.[5] In addition, 30 percent of the households receiving food stamps in 2006 reported earned income; the increase from 19 percent in 1990 made food stamps more of a work support program.[6] (And the percentage of food stamp recipients reporting welfare income declined from 42 percent to 13 percent.) Spending for work supports now dwarfs spending for cash and food assistance for the non-elderly.

An important implication of the change in the structure of poverty policy is that the operation of poverty programs—the practice—has shifted somewhat to differently conceptualized welfare offices, to different government agencies, and to nongovernmental organizations (NGOs). State and county welfare departments now play a smaller role and a different role. The EITC, now the most important poverty program, is administered by the Internal Revenue Service (IRS). Potential recipients file for the tax credit with the IRS, often with the help (necessary or not) of commercial tax preparers. Applying for and receiving the EITC does not require interaction with state or county welfare agencies, though these agencies may help recipients document their eligibility and fill out the forms. Applying for food stamps can now be done online in seventeen states.[7] In most states, however, applicants must go to the local welfare office to turn in their applications and to be interviewed.

Welfare offices in many states, however, are different places than they used to be. In some states, welfare bureaucracies have been reinvented or at least renamed as temporary assistance, work-oriented operations.[8] In some places they have been merged with workforce development agencies, which deal with employment and training programs more generally. These changes seem to have been accompanied by a change in the culture of the agencies toward a much greater emphasis on working and moving toward independence (Lurie 2006). Larry Mead (2004) has documented the extensive changes made in Wisconsin in organization, culture, worker practices, and results, and he has also documented the variation among other states in the extent to which welfare reform has been implemented, noting perhaps half a dozen more (out of his sample of twenty-four states) that exhibited real excellence in carrying out a new, work-oriented mission. In her detailed study of worker practices in four very different states, Irene Lurie (2006, 253) concluded that in contrast to earlier welfare reform efforts, "TANF's goals regarding employment did reach the front lines." Her analyses found that in a majority of encounters between workers and clients, in all four states, both employment and child care were discussed (Lurie 2006, 62–63), a finding that would not have been expected if this study had been done before 1996. Mead, Lurie, and other researchers who have looked at welfare reform implementation note that the change in the culture and operations of welfare offices has been unprecedented.

Another change in the ways in which the poor interact with government programs is the increasingly large and diverse networks of providers through which services are offered. Child care assistance appears to be administered by the states through a variety of agencies—sometimes the state social services agency, sometimes the education department, sometimes an independent child care agency.[9] Child care is provided by an incredible variety of private and nonprofit organizations, some schools, and a few government providers. With the growing importance of subsidized child care, this network assumes increasing salience in the lives of the poor.

Work-related services, including job search, placement, and job training, are increasingly being delivered by broader networks of providers, both for-profit and nonprofit, including faith-based organizations (Martinson and Holcomb 2002). An examination of the implementation of the 2002 Workforce Investment Act in eight states found that all of the states had indeed integrated their workforce services into one-stop career centers and that these centers worked with a wide variety of private, nonprofit, and governmental providers. In some of the states studied, though not all, TANF was a full partner in the one-stop centers (Barnow and King 2005). In these states, clients interacted with the workforce development system for most of what they needed.

The role of faith-based service providers has been much discussed. It is indeed the case that the 1996 welfare reform legislation included provisions for "charitable choice," which were meant to increase the opportunity for religious organizations to apply for and receive state and federal grants for providing services such as job placement and training, mentoring, and child care.

The Bush administration established a well-publicized Office of Faith-Based and Community Initiatives in the White House and similarly named offices within a number of federal agencies. Grant and contract funding to these organizations increased modestly. But the changes should not be exaggerated—in 2004 only 8 percent of Department of Health and Human Services (HHS) grant funds went to faith-based organizations (Montiel and Wright 2006).[10] It is also worth noting that the services that are often talked about as important components of the poverty agenda—workforce and training program—reach relatively small proportions of the poor.

These are all important if not exactly earth-shattering changes in the organizational landscape through which the poor interact with public programs. They are part of a changed landscape of organizational culture and capacity that may have implications for what is possible in the future.

The Lives of the Poor

In the fall of 1996, after President Clinton signed the welfare reform bill, three senior officials in the Department of Health and Human Services, including myself, resigned in protest.[11] We believed that the abolishment of the entitlement to assistance, the five-year hard time limit, and the block granting of funds would increase poverty among children to an unacceptable degree. Our belief was shared by Senator Daniel Patrick Moynihan—who predicted on the Senate floor on September 6 that passage of the bill would lead to "children sleeping on grates" (Fisher 1995; see also DeParle 2004)—and supported by a study done by the Urban Institute, which estimated that one million children would be thrown into poverty if welfare reform was enacted (Zedlewski et al. 1996).[12]

Our predictions were wrong, at least for the period between 1996 and December 2007, the beginning of a severe recession. The overall poverty rate fell between 1994 and 2001 from 14.5 percent to 11.3 percent. The poverty rate for children in female-headed families, the group most likely to be affected by welfare reform, fell from 52.9 percent in 1994 to 38.2 percent in 2001.[13] This is not a heart-warming number, to be sure, but it is certainly not an increase in poverty. In 2007, already worse times economically, the poverty rate for children in female-headed families was 42.9 percent, still well below the 1994 number.

A minor academic industry has developed around trying to explain both the changes in poverty and the changes in caseloads during the 1990s and early 2000s. The general consensus is that a very good economy, the expansion of work supports, and welfare reform all combined to bring about these changes. Whatever the explanation, it seems clear that poverty rates went down, not up, after welfare reform, though they still remain distressingly high.

It is also clear that the income sources of the poor have changed. The Congressional Budget Office (CBO) published an analysis in May 2007 of "Changes in the Economic Resources of Low-Income Households with Children."[14] In its analysis of female-headed families with children in the bottom fifth of the income distribution, the CBO found that overall income went up from $10,100 in 1992 to $13,000 in 2005, all in constant 2005 dollars. Earnings went from 35 percent of income to 54 percent. AFDC-TANF decreased from 39 percent of income to 7 percent, and the EITC increased from 4 percent of income to 11 percent. (Social Security, SSI, child support, and other income made up the difference.) Consistent with other analyses, the CBO report shows that welfare essentially ended, work increased a lot, and the EITC made up for some though by no means all of the decrease in AFDC-TANF. The report also shows that average income for these families went up, consistent with the decline in poverty rates. Here too, the direction of the movement is reassuring, though the income level itself remains too low to provide very much satisfaction.

Assessing the effects of overall income, different sources of income, and work on families, and especially on children, has been attempted by many researchers (Duncan, Gennetian, and Morris 2007–2008). Employment certainly places a family more in the American mainstream; parents' work provides an important model for children. Employment also provides a platform for income growth and asset building, which welfare surely does not. At the same time, employment brings with it new expenses (child care, transportation, work-appropriate clothing), some new stress, and perhaps more time when children are not adequately supervised. On net, it is probably a benefit for low-income adults and their children when the adults are firmly in the labor market. At the same time, their low income levels and the high poverty rates among single-parent families make it clear that the poverty problem has not been solved for them, however much the public and political candidates push it to the sidelines.

Nor has the poverty problem been solved for other groups. In 2007 persons in female-headed families with children made up 33 percent of the total poor. Persons in married-couple families with children made up 23 percent of the poor. Like female-headed families, their income improved between 1992 and 2005, but to a still quite low level. The same CBO analysis referred to earlier found that the income of families with children in the bottom fifth of the income distribution who were not female-headed (overwhelmingly married-couple families) rose from $15,500 in 1992 to $20,300 in 2005, again in constant 2005 dollars. (The poverty line for a family of four with two children in 2005 was $19,806.) These families, too, were affected by the decline of AFDC-TANF, which went from contributing 11.6 percent of their income in 1992 to 1.5 percent in 2005, and by the expansion of the EITC, which contributed 6 percent of income in 1992 and 11.8 percent in 2005.

Forty-five percent of the poor in 2007 were not living in families with children.[15] About half of these were non-elderly individuals living alone ("unrelated individuals" in census parlance). It is hard to assess the changes for this largely forgotten though large group. It appears from Current Population Survey (CPS) tables as though the average income of unrelated individuals has gone down in real terms since 1992.[16] For this group, the percentage of income that came from Social Security fell from 43 percent to 36 percent, and the percentage from means-tested cash assistance from 15 percent to 13 percent. Only 15 percent of all unrelated individuals reported receiving any Social Security income or any means-tested cash assistance.

The period between welfare reform and the 2008 recession was characterized by marginal improvements in the material well-being of the poor, almost entirely because of increased earnings, presumably helped by the very good economy of the 1990s. Government played a lesser role: the expansion of the EITC did not quite make up for the decline of AFDC, even among married-couple families. Large groups among the poor have been largely neglected by policy. All of these changes in the structure and operation of programs and in the lives of the poor set part of the stage for meeting the challenges of poverty in the next decade.

WHAT CHANGED IN PUBLIC OPINION AND THE POLITICAL CONTEXT?

Public Attitudes

In the years prior to the welfare reform legislation of 1996, the politics around poverty was dominated by rancorous discussion of welfare. Simultaneously with the "end of welfare as we know it," described earlier in this chapter, public concern with welfare fell as well. Welfare hardly shows up when poll respondents in the years around 2007 were asked to name the major issues facing the country or the issues that gave them concern about parties or candidates. This was no doubt partly because other issues, like the economy, war, and terror, had become much more salient, but also presumably because of welfare reform and the restructuring of poverty policy.[17]

Attitudes about government help for the needy seem to have become slightly more positive since 1994, when they were relatively more negative compared to previous periods. An analysis by the Pew Research Center for the People and the Press reports that the percentage of poll respondents who agreed with the statement, "It is the responsibility of the government to take care of people who can't take care of themselves" rose from 57 percent in 1994 to 69 percent in 2007. The percentage who agreed that the government should "guarantee food and shelter for all" rose from 59 percent in 1994 to 69 percent in 2007. The percentage who agreed that the government should "help more needy people even if debt increases" rose from 41 percent in 1994 to 54 percent in 2007 (Pew Research Center 2007, 12–13).

In contrast, negative stereotypes about the poor and about welfare persist. For example, Joe Soss and Sanford Schram (2007, 16) report from their analysis of poll data that a near-majority of Americans in the early 2000s agreed that "poor people today do not have an incentive to work because they can get government benefits without doing anything in return." The same Pew analysis quoted earlier found that 71 percent of respondents in 2007 agreed that "poor people have become too dependent on government assistance programs"—down from 87 percent in 1994, but still very high. The complexity, or confusion, of public attitudes is illustrated by the fact that 63 percent of those who say the poor are too dependent also agree that the government should take care of people who cannot take care of themselves (Pew Research Center 2007).

These data paint a mixed picture: the disappearance of welfare as a contentious issue; increased approval of government help for the needy; and continued stereotypes (now demonstrably inaccurate) about the dependence of the poor on government handouts.

It would be helpful to know how these attitudes play out in people's lives—that is, in the way folks see themselves, their neighbors, and their fellow citizens. The polls ask about "the poor" and about "people who can't take care of themselves." In people's characterizations of themselves and their neighbors, who fits into these categories? Does the head of a family who is poor under the standard income definition and who both works and receives food stamps see herself as a struggling member of the working class? How is she seen by her neighbors? What about the family now receiving unemployment benefits because one or more workers have been laid off? Perhaps these families are seen not as the "poor" who have become too dependent on government assistance, but instead as ordinary Americans who are getting an appropriate helping hand through hard times.

Poll respondents may interpret the questions they are asked as being about two distinct groups of people. The first is the "poor," people who are too dependent on government, who are unwilling to work, and who receive "welfare"—a group that is now extremely small. Even for those who do not work, however, a majority of poll respondents seem to believe that the government has a responsibility to guarantee food and shelter, presumably through food pantries and homeless shelters, though public approval may extend to food stamps.

The second implicit group is "people who can't care for themselves" or people who have been laid low through no fault of their own by hard economic times and who deserve government help and ought to get more: the elderly, the disabled, the sick, and the unemployed. I suspect that neither category includes, in the minds of poll respondents, what we might call struggling workers. We know little about public attitudes toward them, though we can hypothesize that they would be at least somewhat positive and supportive.

If these distinctions are important and are indeed behind the poll responses, then the findings may be neither as contradictory nor as depressing as they first appear. And they may reflect a public and political climate in which it is possible to build support for recognizing and addressing the problems that are still with us, after the end of welfare as we knew it.

Political Rhetoric

Despite persistent negative public attitudes about the overdependence of the poor on the government, there has not been much recent nasty talk about welfare by politicians and public officials. There has not been very much constructive talk about poverty either. Recent State of the Union speeches have spoken little about poverty. George W. Bush used the word "poverty" three times in State of the Union addresses; each time the reference was to poverty in Africa and other developing countries.[18] State of the State speeches barely mention poverty, though they do contain a lot of discussion of health care and education. Even, interestingly, in Louisiana post-Katrina, the State of the State speech did not discuss poverty.[19]

Recently there have been some breaks in this silence; for example, John Edwards's presidential campaign had a strong antipoverty theme. That the poverty theme was dismissed by some of his opponents as class warfare is telling. As noted in my opening paragraph, candidates Clinton and Obama both had issue papers on poverty, but they were not prominently displayed or highlighted.[20] Barack Obama's inaugural address did not speak of poverty, though it did address "poor nations." It seems fair to conclude that politicians in 2009 do not see a poverty agenda as important politically, either as a potential positive aspect of their campaigns or as something to be attacked—at least not under the label of "poverty."

State- and Local-Level Activity

There has recently been some interesting activity, however, at the state and local levels directed explicitly at poverty alleviation. (It remains to be seen whether these efforts will survive the state budget crises generated by the recession.) In April 2008, the Center for Law and Social Policy and the organization Spotlight on Poverty and Opportunity issued a joint report on "State Governments and the New Commitment to Reduce Poverty in America" (Levin-Epstein and Gorzelany 2008). Their survey of the states found that twelve states have set up poverty initiatives of one sort or another and that three additional states have initiatives pending. In eight states, poverty commissions have been set up, and two states have new legislative caucuses. One state has scheduled a state summit. Five states have established poverty reduction targets, and four states have issued recommendations. The report sees this activity as a very promising development.

None of the states with poverty initiatives are large. The states with poverty reduction targets are Connecticut, Delaware, Minnesota, Oregon, and Vermont. The states that have issued recommendations are Alabama, Connecticut, Iowa, and Washington. As of the date of the report, it appears that Connecticut has made the most progress.[21] It has specified a target of cutting child poverty in half by 2014. It has established a child poverty and prevention council, which has had several meetings and come up with a report that includes sixty-seven policy recommendations. These were considered by an expert committee, which in December 2007 reviewed them and made thirteen more specific recommendations in four areas: family income and earnings potential, education, income safety nets, and family structure and support. The council also recommended a change in the definition of the poverty line to ensure that progress made on initiatives like child care and housing benefits would show up in progress against poverty. And the council took note of the fact that its recommendations on education would not have any effect on poverty numbers in the short run. Also noteworthy in Connecticut's approach is the emphasis placed by the council and the expert committee on evidence of impact, cost-effectiveness, and the likelihood that a particular policy will indeed lead to progress toward the poverty reduction target. The Connecticut approach is in many ways a model.

The National League of Cities and the Institute for Youth, Education, and Families surveyed cities in 2007 to identify poverty initiatives at the city level (National League of Cities 2007). Twenty-nine cities (32 percent of responding cities) indicated that they had a poverty initiative. Among the most interesting are the initiatives in New York City and Providence, Rhode Island. Mayor Michael Bloomberg of New York established the Commission on Economic Opportunity, which issued recommendations in the fall of 2006. This led to the establishment of the Center for Economic Opportunity, whose mission is "to reduce the number of people living in poverty in New York City through the implementation of result-driven and innovative initiatives."[22] One of the Center's programs is an experimental conditional cash transfer modeled on Mexico's Oportunidades program—the first such program to be tried in the United States.[23] The Center has also formulated a new poverty measure to be used in tracking poverty in New York City and assessing the effectiveness of the new initiatives.[24] Both of these steps suggest that the New York effort is both serious and practical and that it will be contributing to knowledge about poverty alleviation as it proceeds.

In Providence, Mayor David Cicilline established the Poverty, Work, and Opportunity Task Force in January 2007; the group issued a report called *Pathways to Opportunity* in November 2007. Its recommendations aim to "help low-wage workers to improve skills and obtain quality jobs; connect youth to jobs and college; make work pay; reduce the high cost of being poor; and prevent poverty in future generations" (Poverty, Work, and Opportunity Task Force 2007, 6). The task force recommendations are directed at the city, state, and federal governments. Because the task force included a range of stakeholders, and also because the mayor seems committed to the effort, there is reason for hope that some of the recommendations will indeed be taken up.

THE CURRENT CONTEXT

The changes described earlier provide some grounds for modest optimism about the prospects for future progress in improving the lives of the poor. The positive changes include:

- The end of the rancorous welfare debates in the media and in political campaigns
- A relatively supportive public opinion climate regarding the needy
- A restructuring of cash assistance policies toward work support and as a result greater consistency with generally held values
- A restructuring of program operations such that programs for the poor are more integrated into programs for the working class and for families more generally
- Some activity at the state and local levels that is evidence-based and pragmatic, with the potential for demonstrating that government programs for the poor can be both effective and efficient
- Inclusion of expansions of many programs important to the poor in the stimulus and recovery packages of early 2009

At the same time, other contextual factors may limit the prospects for new efforts to address the problems of the substantial number of poor Americans:

- The severe recession that began in December 2007 and is predicted, as of the time of this writing, to last several years

- The impact of the recession on state revenues and spending ability

- The huge federal budget deficit, dramatically increased by the financial bailouts and stimulus spending, which will at some point limit the ability of any presidential administration, Republican or Democrat, to increase spending on social programs

- The combination of high and growing economic inequality in the United States and the increased influence of affluent Americans in politics

- The potentially contentious effects of immigration policy on debates about poverty

Inequality and Political Influence

The growth of economic inequality in the United States is well documented. The interactions of growing inequality with politics and policy have been explored recently by some political scientists (Soss, Hacker, and Mettler 2007; Bartels 2008; Hacker and Pierson 2007). They argue that politics has developed in ways that increase the importance of money in electoral politics and decrease the potential influence of the less affluent. They also argue that the political preferences of the median voter are now less important than the preferences of better-off voters, because of their higher rates of voting and their importance as campaign contributors. Less affluent citizens vote less, contribute less to campaigns, and have lost much of the organizational infrastructure, especially labor unions, that once amplified their voices. At the same time, the influence of the better-off has grown as campaigns have changed to be more dependent on money than on grassroots mobilization. To the extent that this analysis of American politics is correct (and remains correct in 2009), it suggests that any social policy opportunities will be constrained by a politics shaped by economic inequality. It also suggests that the politically well organized groups that represent the interests of the affluent will continue to be effective in preserving and perhaps even enlarging tax cuts that benefit the wealthy and thus constraining the opportunity for pro-poor policy at the federal level even further.

Immigration: A Potentially Rancorous Complication

In 2006 about 16 percent of the officially counted poor were foreign-born, and three-quarters of these foreign-born poor were not citizens (see Raphael and Smolensky, this volume). Between one-fifth and one-quarter of all poor children are either immigrants themselves or children of immigrants. A large majority of these immigrants are Hispanic; an unknown but probably large number are undocumented.

A 2006 survey of attitudes toward immigration by the Pew Research Center revealed considerable ambivalence in American attitudes toward immigration and immigration policy (Pew Research Center 2006). For example, respondents were asked to choose between these two statements: "Immigrants today are a burden on our country because they take our jobs, housing, and health care" and "Immigrants today strengthen our country because of their hard work and talents." Fifty-two percent of respondents chose the former statement, and 41 percent the latter (Pew Research Center 2006, 60). When asked whether "recent immigrants pay their fair share of taxes," 56 percent of respondents said no. At the same time, when asked whether immigrants mostly take jobs away from Americans or mostly take jobs Americans do not want, 65 percent responded that immigrants mostly take jobs that Americans do not want (72).

When asked about immigration policy, 40 percent agreed that legal immigration levels should be decreased; 53 percent thought that illegal immigrants should be required to go home. Sixty-seven percent thought that illegal immigrants should not be eligible for social services, but 71 percent said that the children of illegal immigrants should be permitted to attend public schools (Pew Research Center 2006, 76).

Despite the ambivalence of Americans about immigrants and immigration policy, these attitudes toward immigrants are sufficiently negative that political support for "struggling working families" or "people who cannot take care of themselves" would be seriously diminished if these groups were perceived as including large numbers of immigrants—which is in fact the case.

POSSIBLE STRATEGIES

Given this background, I turn now to the more speculative topic of general strategies for addressing the continuing problems related to poverty.

Changing Language

Trying to make sense of the public opinion results suggests that the word "poor" in the U.S. context connotes unwillingness to work and dependence on government. This is an inaccurate description, especially post–welfare reform, of those who are defined as poor in the official measures and by most academics. It is worth asking whether attempting to change public perceptions about the American "poor" is a battle worth having, or whether using different language might be a more productive strategy.

The public appears to be quite sympathetic to "people who can't take care of themselves," presumably the elderly, the disabled, the involuntarily unemployed, and perhaps some groups of children. There is public and political support for programs that help struggling working families make ends meet—for example, child care and the Earned Income Tax Credit. There is also a surprisingly high level of public support, as noted earlier, for "guaranteeing food and shelter for all." Using the language of "people who can't take care of themselves," "struggling working families," and "guaranteeing food and shelter" may make little difference in terms of actual policies, but a big difference in public perception and public support.

This language does reflect and continue the distinction between the deserving and the undeserving poor that has long characterized American public opinion and policy, often to the detriment of those left behind. But another way to think about this distinction is that it appropriately incorporates the values of work and responsibility that Americans hold so dear and that they want government policy to reward and reinforce. Accepting these values and distinctions, and using language that speaks to them, may be the most effective strategy for moving beyond the stereotypes of the poor that get in the way of constructive policies. A side benefit of this change in language could be a more accurate designation of the global poor and global poverty.

Recognizing the Importance of State, Local, and Nongovernmental Actors

Because of the constraints of the federal deficit and the nature of American politics in an age of inequality, opportunities for large-scale antipoverty initiatives at the federal level are limited. Health care is the most likely candidate for significant change and new investments. Some expansion of the EITC and of unemployment benefits may be possible, and other smaller programs may be part of a new president's agenda.

As noted earlier, however, considerable antipoverty innovation is going on at the state and local levels. Some of these efforts are located in large and challenging environments, like that in New York City, and are taking a very practical, evidence-based, problem-solving approach to the problems. They tend to involve partnerships with business, the nonprofit sector, and communities. Because state and local efforts are necessarily directed at locality-specific manifestations of the poverty problem, they are more likely than federal programs to be concrete and innovative. If these efforts are in fact successful, they may spread to other states, perhaps to the large states where the majority of the poor live. Encouraging these developments is likely to be a quite promising strategy.

Changing Specifications of the Problem and Measures of Progress

The more practical and promising of the current state and local initiatives build on some basic principles of good management, which are sometimes forgotten in academic policy development exercises and Washington-based policy shops. They recognize that, for goals to be achieved, the goals have to be specified, plans with time frames have to be developed, and realistic measures of progress or lack thereof toward the goals have to be used to hold accountable those with responsibility for achieving them. Plans and activities need to be continually updated as evidence is gathered and as learning takes place about what is and is not working.

This requirement of good management makes the specification of "poverty" very important and also recognizes that goals defined in other ways may be more appropriate for addressing specific problems. Some states have set a percentage reduction in income poverty, either for children or for the overall population, as a goal. Some of these states recognize—and all of them should—that the official federal poverty definition, which excludes noncash benefits and any distributional effects of the tax system, is inappropriate as a management tool. This is true even when the goal is framed in terms of reducing income poverty, since noncash benefits and tax credits are among the tools that states frequently use.

Goals specified in other terms might, however, be more appropriate than a goal tied to the reduction of income poverty. For a locality where hunger, for example, is a serious concern, increased food security might be a good goal. This goal can be specified using measures developed by the Food and Nutrition Service (Nord, Andrews, and Carlson 2007). Different approaches to increasing food security, from expanding food stamp participation to educating families about food budgeting, can be developed, tried out, and assessed as to their effectiveness. Another specific goal might be increasing the employment rate of young minority men, which has obvious implications for poverty more generally. An analysis in a specific state or community of the barriers to employment could lead to program experimentation and modifications of programs as progress toward the goal, or lack thereof, is assessed.

Part of the reason that the public, both in general and among the elite, is skeptical of a new "War on Poverty" is that they have seen no evidence that such efforts actually work. Making sure that goals are specified appropriately and that both learning and accountability are built into program efforts can help change both the perception and the reality.

Recognizing That Operational Improvements Are Possible and Important

Policymakers often forget, or never knew, the impact of operational choices on whether programs are seen as useful in people's lives and whether interactions with programs are experienced as positive or negative. It really does make a difference whether it is easy or hard, pleasant or unpleasant, time-consuming or efficient, to apply for, say, food stamps, child care, or the EITC. It really does make a difference whether it is easy or hard, pleasant or unpleasant, to avail oneself of, say, educational or training opportunities. There are many opportunities for improving services and improving the lives of the poor by changing application and service delivery processes. This is all more likely to happen in communities and NGOs than in federal or state legislation or regulation. It is a vastly underused and underappreciated strategy that requires more attention.

A LARGE STRATEGIC QUESTION: GLOBALIZATION AND POVERTY BEYOND OUR BORDERS

Globalization—increased trade, freer movements of capital, the growth of increasingly sophisticated and increasingly competitive industries in China, India, and other developing countries—is thought by some to be exacerbating the plight of the American poor, or at least making it more difficult to address American poverty. There is controversy among experts about the effects of globalization, trade, and immigration on the American poor. Overall, the effects appear to be beneficial for Americans, but there is some evidence that some low-wage workers are hurt by global competition, and certainly there is a perception by some Americans, as noted earlier, that immigrants and outsourcing are taking "good jobs" away from Americans.

These facts tempt some who worry about the American poor to advocate or at least flirt with protectionist and exclusivist policies. Candidates for the Democratic presidential nomination and some left-leaning think tanks discuss limitations on both trade and immigration. In the spring of 2008 it seemed that the two democratic candidates were trying to outdo each other in denouncing NAFTA (North American Free Trade Agreement).

Protectionist and nativist policies, however, are unlikely to work. The low cost of goods produced in China, India, and other developing countries has not escaped the attention of American consumers and American retailers. The combination of a long porous border and a wage differential of a factor of five or six means that the U.S. economy exercises an irresistible draw for Mexican workers. Mexican immigrants, both legal and illegal, now make up about 30 percent of the very low-skilled (education less than high school) workforce. No number of border guards can overcome these facts: 85 percent of Mexicans are poor by American standards; their economic well-being is vastly improved by migration; remittances make a large contribution to the Mexican economy; and American employers need a larger low-wage, low-skill workforce for some jobs than they can recruit from native-born workers (Bane and Zenteno 2005).

There is another reason that protectionist and exclusivist impulses are unfortunate: Americans should be—and to at least some extent are—concerned about poverty in the world, not just in the United States. Interestingly, when public officials or reporters use the word "poverty," they are as likely—indeed, more likely—to be referring to sub-Saharan Africa or other regions of the developing world as to the United States. There is increased interest in world poverty from the World Bank, the United Nations, the G-8, and the governments of many developed countries.

"Poverty," of course, means quite different things in the developed world, the middle-income countries, and what Collier (2007) calls the "bottom billion." Even when poverty is defined solely in terms of income or consumption (rather than incorporating the broader notions of capability deprivation), the cutoff lines below which a person is defined as poor range from $1 or $2 per person per day (World

Bank, for the world) through about $6 per person per day (Mexico), to about $16 per person per day (the Census Bureau line) in the United States. These differences reflect much more than differences in the cost of living and indeed are adjusted (imperfectly to be sure) to reflect purchasing power parity. If being poor means not having electricity, safe drinking water, indoor plumbing, a house with a roof and floor, or a minimally adequate diet, very, very few in the United States are "poor" and a billion or so people in the world are.

The main reason to avoid increased protectionism and to continue to reduce our trade barriers is that exporting to the United States and other industrialized countries has been crucial in fueling development in Asia and will also be crucial for development in Africa, if such is ever to occur. And not only trade with but investment in Mexico is crucial for addressing poverty in North America. Since North America, including Mexico, is in our neighborhood, our policy ought to be responsive to poverty in the entire region.

Suppose North America—Canada, the United States, and Mexico—were one country of 443 million people. Suppose poverty were defined using the current U.S. income poverty line, with regional cost-of-living adjustments. In this world, we would find that about 100 million or 110 million people were counted as poor, with about two-thirds of them living below the Rio Grande. We would also find that poverty was much more concentrated geographically than it is in the current United States, with the largest concentrations occurring in the southern states of Mexico.

How would we think about economic and social policy in this world? We would think very hard about how to encourage economic development in areas of concentrated poverty, especially in what are now the southern states of Mexico; we would build physical infrastructure and perhaps design incentives for firms to locate in those regions. We would think about education, health, and human capital development more generally in all the areas of concentrated poverty. We might focus on how to build decent but affordable housing in all of the places where the poor live. We would worry about how best to deliver nutrition assistance to those who need it and how best to structure social insurance and safety net programs to support economic development. We might be less obsessed with whether government programs were creating dependency.

CONCLUSION: CHANGING POVERTY

The title of this volume is apt in two ways. Poverty is changing, and poverty policy has changed, and continues to change, quite dramatically. The end of welfare has been accompanied by a shift in the income sources of the poor and in the programs and policies through which government assists the poor. At the same time, poverty and poverty policy need changing to address the fact that the incidence of poverty in the United States and more generally in North America and the world remains distressingly high. Poverty policy in the next decade should build on, rather than attempt to reverse, the end of welfare. And perhaps, in this country, it should not be "poverty policy" at all.

NOTES

1. See U.S. Department of Health and Human Services, Administration for Children and Families, TANF financial data, especially "Table F: Combined Federal and State Spending on Basic Assistance," available at: http://www.acf.hhs.gov/programs/ofs/data/index.html.
2. Data from the ACF website: http://www.acf.hhs.gov/programs/ofa/data-reports/caseload/caseload_recent.html#2007
3. Calculated using data from the U.S. Census Bureau, Current Population Survey, "Annual Social and Economic (ASEC) Supplement: Age and Sex of All People, Family Members, and Unrelated Individuals Iterated by Income-to-Poverty Ratio and Race: 2006, Below 100% of Poverty—All Races," available at: http://pubdb3.census.gov/macro/032007/pov/new01_100_01.htm.
4. In late 2008, the food stamp program was renamed SNAP—Supplemental Nutrition Assistance Program—partly to emphasize the nutrition mission of the program in contrast to the income support mission.
5. These numbers include spending from the Child Care Development Block Grant (CCDBG) (see ACF, "Child Care and Development Fund [CCDF] Expenditure Data," available at: http://www.acf.hhs.gov/programs/ccb/data/index.htm), TANF spending on child care, and state TANF-MOE (maintenance of effort) spending on child care. To avoid double-counting, state MOE spending on child care in the CCDBG data is not included. States are permitted to transfer TANF money to the CCDF as well as to spend straight TANF money on child care, both of which they do. For comparison purposes, the Government Accountability Office (GAO) reported that federal and state spending on child care in 1997 was $4.1 billion; see GAO, "Child Care: States Increased Spending on Low-Income Families" (February 2001), GAO-01-293, available at: http://www.gao.gov/new.items/d01293.pdf.
6. Data from the Food and Nutrition Service website: http://www.fns.usda.gov/pd/snapmain.htm.
7. The Food and Nutrition Service website provides links for the states in which applications can be made online: http://www.fns.usda.gov/fsp/applicant_recipients/apply.htm.
8. The website for the American Public Human Services Association gives the names and links for all state-level human services agencies: http://www.aphsa.org/Links/links-state.asp.
9. For information on state child care agencies, see ACF, National Child Care Information and Technical Assistance Center (NCCIC): http://nccic.acf.hhs.gov/statedata/dirs/display.cfm?title=ccdf.
10. See also the interesting, insightful, and humorous discussion of faith-based initiatives in DiIulio (2007).
11. I was at the time assistant secretary for children and families. The others who resigned were Peter Edelman, then assistant secretary for planning and evaluation, and Wendell Primus, deputy assistant secretary.
12. It is worth noting that much of the increase in poverty predicted by the Urban Institute analysis resulted from the exclusion of most immigrants from public programs. This aspect of the legislation was changed soon after passage.

13. Data from U.S. Census Bureau, "Poverty: Historical Poverty Tables: Table 10: Related Children in Female Householder Families as a Proportion of All Related Children, by Poverty Status: 1959 to 2006," available at: http://www.census.gov/hhes/www/poverty/histpov/hstpov10.html.

14. Backup data, which I used in calculating some of the numbers in the text, are available at Congressional Budget Office, "Figure 1: Sources of Income for Low-Income Households with Children," http://www.cbo.gov/ftpdocs/81xx/doc8113/8113_Data.xls.

15. All of the calculations of the composition of the poor in 2006 were made from data available through the detailed tables posted at U.S. Census Bureau, Current Population Survey, "2006 Poverty," http://pubdb3.census.gov/macro/032007/pov/toc.htm.

16. Average income in current dollars in 1992 for unrelated individuals in the CPS was $3,840; in 2006 it was $4,780.

17. For recent data on the issues most important to the country, see PollingReport.com, "Problems and Priorities," available at: http://www.pollingreport.com/prioriti.htm. The time-series data have been analyzed and are reported in Soss and Schram (2007).

18. The results of my search of "poverty" in State of the Union addresses can be replicated at State of the Union, available at: http://stateoftheunion.onetwothree.net/index.shtml.

19. The text of the 1996 Louisiana State of the State speech is available at Stateline.org, available at: http://www.stateline.org/live/details/speech?contentId=101167.

20. For Barack Obama's statements on poverty, see Organizing for America, "Poverty," available at: http://www.barackobama.com/issues/poverty; Hillary Clinton's campaign Web site is no longer available.

21. Information on the Connecticut initiative is available at Connecticut Commission on Children, "Poverty," http://www.cga.ct.gov/coc/poverty.htm.

22. See New York City Center for Economic Opportunity, http://www.nyc.gov/html/ceo/home/home.shtml. For a 2007 report on the Center's activities, see: http://www.nyc.gov/html/ceo/downloads/pdf/ceo_2007_report_small.pdf.

23. A description of New York's conditional cash transfer program is available at New York City Center for Economic Opportunity, "Opportunity NYC," http://www.nyc.gov/html/ceo/html/programs/opportunity_nyc.shtml.

24. For the mayor's press release on the new poverty measure, see NYC.gov, "News from the Blue Room: New York City Mayor Bloomberg Announces New Alternative to Federal Poverty Measure" (July 13, 2008), available at: http://nyc.gov/portal/site/nycgov/menuitem.c0935b9a57bb4ef3daf2f1c701c789a0/index.jsp?pageID=mayor_press_release&catID=1194&doc_name=http%3A%2F%2Fnyc.gov%2Fhtml%2Fom%2Fhtml%2F2008b%2Fpr271-08.html&cc=unused1978&rc=1194&ndi=1.

REFERENCES

Bane, Mary Jo, and Rene Zenteno. 2005. "Poverty and Place in North America." Faculty research working paper RWP05-035. Cambridge, Mass.: Harvard University, John F. Kennedy School of Government.

Barnow, Burt S., and Christopher T. King. 2005. *The Workforce Investment Act in Eight States.* Report to the U.S. Department of Labor, Employment and Training Administration. Albany, N.Y.: Nelson A. Rockefeller Institute of Government (February).

Bartels, Larry M. 2008. *Unequal America: The Political Economy of the New Gilded Age.* New York: Russell Sage Foundation.

Collier, Paul. 2007. *The Bottom Billion.* New York: Oxford University Press.

Congressional Budget Office (CBO). 2007. *Changes in the Economic Resources of Low-Income Households with Children.* Washington: CBO (May).

DeParle, Jason. 2004. *American Dream: Three Women, Ten Kids, and a Nation's Drive to End Welfare.* New York: Viking Penguin.

———. 2009. "Welfare Aid Isn't Growing as Economy Drops Off." *New York Times,* February 2.

DiIulio, John J. 2007. *Godly Republic.* Berkeley: University of California Press.

Duncan, Greg J., Lisa Gennetian, and Pamela Morris. 2007–2008. "Effects of Welfare and Antipoverty Programs on Participants' Children." *Focus* 25(2, fall–winter). Madison: University of Wisconsin, Institute for Research on Poverty.

Fisher, Ian. 1995. "Moynihan Stands Alone in Welfare Debate." *New York Times,* September 27. Available at: http://www.nytimes.com/1995/09/27/nyregion/moynihan-stands-alone-in-welfare-debate.html.

Hacker, Jacob S., and Paul Pierson. 2007. "Winner-Take-All Politics: Organizations, Policy, and the New American Political Economy." Paper presented to the annual meeting of the American Political Science Association. Chicago (September).

Levin-Epstein, Jodie, and Kirsten Michelle Gorzelany. 2008. *Seizing the Moment: State Governments and the New Commitment to Reduce Poverty in America.* Washington, D.C.: Center for Law and Social Policy and Spotlight on Poverty and Opportunity (April).

Lurie, Irene. 2006. *At the Front Lines of the Welfare System: A Perspective on the Decline in Welfare Caseloads.* Albany, N.Y.: Rockefeller Institute Press.

Martinson, Karin, and Pamela Holcomb. 2002. "Reforming Welfare: Institutional Change and Challenge." Assessing the New Federalism Occasional Paper 60. Washington, D.C.: Urban Institute.

Mead, Lawrence M. 2004. *Government Matters: Welfare Reform in Wisconsin.* Princeton, N.J.: Princeton University Press.

Members of the WELPAN Network. 2002. "Welfare Then, Welfare Now: Expenditures in Some Midwestern States." *Focus* 22(1): 11–14. Madison: University of Wisconsin, Institute for Research on Poverty.

———. 2005. Unpublished data. Madison: University of Wisconsin, Institute for Research on Poverty.

Montiel, Lisa M., and David J. Wright. 2006. *Getting a Piece of the Pie: Federal Grants to Faith-Based Social Service Organizations.* Washington, D.C.: Roundtable on Religion and Social Welfare Policy (February). Available at: http://www.religionandsocialpolicy.org/docs/research/federal_grants_report_2-14-06.pdf.

National League of Cities. 2007. *Combating Poverty: Emerging Strategies from the Nation's Cities.* Washington, D.C.: National League of Cities and Institute for Youth, Education, and Families.

Nord, Mark, Margaret Andrews, and Steven Carlson. 2007. *Household Food Security in the United States, 2006.* Economic Research Report 48. Washington: U.S. Department of Agriculture, Economic Research Center (November).

Pew Research Center for the People and the Press. 2006. *America's Immigration Quandary.* Washington, D.C.: Pew Research Center.

———. 2007. *Trends in Political Values and Core Attitudes: 1987–2007.* Washington, D.C.: Pew Research Center.

Poverty, Work, and Opportunity Task Force. 2007. *Pathways to Opportunity: Building Prosperity in Providence.* Providence, R.I.: Providence City Government.

Soss, Joe, Jacob S. Hacker, and Suzanne Mettler. 2007. *Remaking America: Democracy and Public Policy in an Age of Inequality.* New York: Russell Sage Foundation.

Soss, Joe, and Sanford F. Schram. 2007. "A Public Transformed? Welfare Reform as Policy Feedback." *American Political Science Review* 101(1): 111–27.

Swartz, Rebecca. 2002. "Redefining a Case in the Postreform Era: Reconciling Caseload with Workload." *Focus* 22(1): 16–21. Madison: University of Wisconsin, Institute for Research on Poverty.

Zedlewski, Sheila, Sandra J. Clark, Eric Meier, and Keith Watson. 1996. "Potential Effects of Congressional Welfare Reform Legislation on Family Incomes." Washington, D.C.: Urban Institute.

Chapter 14

What Does It Mean to Be Poor in a Rich Society?

Robert Haveman

In 2007, Mollie Orshansky, whose contributions led to the nation's official poverty measure, passed away. Given the data available in the early 1960s, the Orshansky poverty measure—based on family money income and an absolute poverty threshold—made perfect sense. President Lyndon Johnson had declared a War on Poverty in 1964, and the nation needed a statistical picture of the poor. Although she recognized the criticisms of her measure,[1] the concept of absolute income poverty as well as the nation's official measure of poverty can be directly traced to her contributions.[2]

Since that time, the U.S. official poverty measure has stood nearly unchanged (see Smeeding 2006; Citro and Michael 1995; Jencks, Mayer, and Swingle 2004; Blank 2008), in spite of extensive efforts designed to improve the measurement of both financial means (for example, extensions of the income concept to include the value of in-kind transfers and tax liabilities) and the poverty threshold (for example, alternative equivalence scales and revised needs standards).[3]

In this chapter, I attempt to broaden the discussion of poverty and poverty measurement. I first discuss the broad question of "what is poverty?" and describe various poverty concepts that have been proposed. Then, I describe the official U.S. poverty measure, highlight its main characteristics, and note some of the criticisms directed toward it. I compare this official, absolute income poverty measure to a relative measure, as well as to alternative concepts of economic poverty that rely on indicators of permanent income (such as consumption or the ability to secure income) and a family's own assessment of its well-being; the pros and cons of these measures are also noted. Finally, I examine broader conceptions of poverty and deprivation and discuss proposals for a comprehensive measure of poverty that takes into consideration indicators of material deprivation and "social exclusion." Most of the research on this approach has occurred in the European Union and the United Kingdom. The chapter ends with a modest proposal for the development of a broader measure of poverty and social exclusion for the United States.

CONCEPTS OF POVERTY

Improving the well-being of deprived people is a nearly universal goal among policymakers in all nations. However, there is no commonly accepted way of identifying who is deprived or who has an unacceptably low level of well-being.

Economists tend to prefer a concept of hardship that reflects "economic position" or "economic well-being," which is typically measured by an indicator of *command over resources,* typically annual income.[4] These economic poverty measures seek to identify those families whose command over resources (income) falls below some minimally acceptable level. This economic approach requires precise definitions of both available economic resources and the minimum level of economic "needs," both of which must be measured in the same units.

Such economic poverty measures do not impose any norm on people's preferences among goods and services (for example, necessities versus luxuries) or between work and leisure. They also allow for differentiation according to household size and composition. By focusing on command over resources, however, they ignore many non-economic considerations that may affect individual "utility" or "well-being." To the extent that such factors—for example, living in unsafe surroundings, being socially isolated, or experiencing adverse health or living arrangements not remediable by spending money—are neglected by these measures, policy efforts designed to reduce economic poverty may also overlook these other aspects of what it means to be poor.

Because of such concerns, income-based poverty measures are increasingly challenged, particularly in other Western industrialized countries. Critics argue for a *multidimensional poverty concept.* For example, people deprived of social contacts (with friends, family, and neighbors) are described as "socially isolated" and hence poor in this dimension, people living in squalid housing are "housing poor," and people with health deficits are "health poor." However, those who prefer to take a broader approach to the measurement of poverty face a difficult task in changing the official U.S. measure. Dimensions of well-being beyond income need to be identified and agreed upon, indicators that accurately reflect these dimensions need to be defined, the data necessary to accurately measure these dimensions for individual living units need to be collected, and the several indicators need to be weighted to produce an index of the size of the poor population and its composition.

While debates over the appropriate concept of poverty seem unlikely to cease, a basic question lurks over the discussion: does the measure of poverty chosen matter? As with the debates over the poverty concept, there are differences of opinion on this question. Nearly all observers believe, however, that the concept and measure of poverty does matter. Because all poverty measures seek to identify the most economically "hardshipped" in society, different measures imply a different size and composition of the target poverty population, different patterns of change in the extent of poverty over time, and hence a different set of antipoverty policies. Policymakers and citizens react to information on these patterns. Reported increases in the poverty rate trigger concerns regarding inequality in the distribution of income and elicit calls for changes in taxation and public spending policies and in the provisions covering the impact of these policies on various groups in the population. Such changes in poverty over time lead to questions regarding the direction of the nation and the effectiveness of social policies. It is difficult to imagine a political debate that fails to touch on these questions.[5]

MEASURING ECONOMIC POVERTY

Even among those who prefer income-based or command-over-resources poverty measures, there are substantial differences of opinion regarding which is the best measure. For example, the official U.S. measure relies on the *annual cash income* of a family and compares this to a minimum income standard or "poverty line." An alternative position is that *annual consumption* better reflects a family's level of living, or that some measure of a family's *ability to secure income* identifies a nation's truly needy population. Others advocate reliance on families' *own assessment of their economic well-being*. Even if the measure of economic position has been chosen, poverty measures can be either *absolute* or *relative*. The indicator is absolute if the definition of "needs" is fixed, so that the poverty threshold does not change with the standard of living of the society. A relative measure uses a poverty line that increases along with the general standard of living of the society.

The Official U.S. Measure of Absolute Income Poverty

The official U.S. poverty measure seeks to identify those families who do not have sufficient annual cash income—from either government support or their own efforts—to meet the official poverty threshold. It compares two numbers for each living unit—the unit's annual cash income and the poverty threshold for a unit of its size and composition. It is an absolute measure because it is adjusted each year only for changes in prices, not for changes in living standards.

This official measure assumes that (1) money can buy those things the absence of which makes people feel deprived, (2) money income is a good proxy for welfare (or utility), and (3) a particular year's income is an acceptable indicator of longer-run income. Although people may experience hardship in many dimensions—education, housing, food, social contacts, security, environmental amenities—only a low level of money income matters in determining who is poor.

The U.S. Census Bureau performs the official poverty measurement each year, and each year it presents a public report on the level of poverty in the prior year and on changes in the level and composition of the poor from year to year. All major news media carry the story and reflect on who is winning, who is losing, and how the nation is doing in fighting poverty.

This annual news story also provokes a barrage of commentary on the nature of the official measure and whether the message it conveys is reliable. Although the cash income numerator of the measure may reflect the extent to which a family can meet its immediate needs, this value may fluctuate substantially from year to year owing to unemployment, job changes, health considerations, and especially income flows from farming and self-employment. For this reason, some claim that the measure conveys an unreliable picture of who is poor over the longer run.

It is also argued that even as an indicator of a family's ability to meet its immediate needs, the measure is flawed. The income reported by families to census surveyors tends to be artificially low, and often income from various nonstandard sources is not reported at all. As a result, the overall poverty rate tends to be higher than it should be. Importantly, the annual income measure reflects neither the value of in-kind transfers (for example, food stamps or Medicaid) nor taxes paid nor tax credits received, including the Earned Income Tax Credit (EITC). Indeed, virtually all actual reforms since the 1960s have been in the form of giving families benefits, such as food, health care, and child care, that do not count in the poverty statistics. Similarly, the assets available to families are not counted, nor is the value of leisure (or voluntary nonwork) time reflected in the measure. As a result, the consumption spending of a family in any given year may differ substantially from the family's reported income.[6] Although there may be major differences in the needs of workers and nonworkers, of those with and without serious medical care needs, and of those living in high-cost areas relative to those in low-cost areas, none of these considerations are reflected in the official measure.

The family-size specific denominator of the poverty ratio—the poverty line threshold—also comes under fire. Critics claim that this needs indicator has little conceptual basis and rests on empirical evidence about food consumption in the mid-1950s (Ruggles 1990). The same criticism applies to the equivalence scales used to adjust needs for differences in family size.

In addition to these criticisms, conservative commentators also emphasize that many of those who are poor by the official measure do not live in destitute circumstances, own color television sets, automobiles, refrigerators, stoves, and in some cases homes, and are not undernourished. Their estimates of the poverty rate are much lower than the official estimate. Given the annual income measure on which official poverty rests, these commentators emphasize the low level of earnings of adults in poor families and claim that major reductions in official poverty could be achieved if the adults in these families would work more and if there were two parents rather than one living in the family. However, the easy conclusions regarding work and marriage fail to reflect the high incidence of low education, mental and physical disabilities, unsafe neighborhoods, and lack of health and child care facilities confronting low-income families. Analysts at the other end of the political spectrum find that in order to meet "basic needs" income needs to be substantially greater than the current poverty thresholds; they find a much higher poverty rate than the official measure (see Renwick and Bergmann 1993). These critiques do highlight the complex nature of American poverty and emphasize the need for improvements in the official poverty measure.

Given this litany of concerns regarding the nation's official poverty measure, it should not be assumed that nothing has been done to improve the measure. Indeed, in 1995 the National Research Council of the National Academy of Sciences reported the results of a comprehensive study of the strengths and weaknesses of the official measure and proposed a major revision designed to address many of the criticisms that had been levied against it (see Citro and Michael 1995). The reform proposed would involve a new threshold based on budget studies of food, clothing, shelter (including utilities), and amounts that would allow for other needs to be met, such as household supplies, personal care, and non-work-related transportation. The thresholds would reflect geographic differences in housing costs, and the income measure would also be reworked to include the value of the near-money benefits that are available to buy goods and services (for example, food stamps) and would subtract from income those required expenses that cannot be used to buy these goods and services (for example, income and payroll taxes, child care and other work-related expenses, child support payments to another household, and out-of-pocket medical care costs, including health insurance premiums).

Since that report, the Census Bureau and other governmental statistical agencies have developed a variety of improved poverty measures reflecting the recommendations of the 1995 report. Two extensive reports by the Census Bureau present estimates of these alternative measures since 1990; in addition, the Bureau has released a number of alternative poverty measure estimates in materials that accompany the annual official poverty report.[7] Unfortunately, none of these improved alternatives has been adopted to replace the existing official poverty measure.[8]

Alternative Measures of Economic Poverty

In addition to the official U.S. absolute income poverty measure (and extensions of it), a wide range of other indicators of economic poverty have been proposed and implemented. In this section, we briefly describe a few of these and indicate some of their pros and cons.

RELATIVE INCOME POVERTY   Many accept the access-to-resources (income) basis for measuring poverty but reject an absolute poverty threshold. Instead, poverty is viewed as a matter of *economic and social distance*. These measures compare the income of a family to a norm reflecting the economic position of the overall society (say, the income of the median family), adjusted for price-level changes. Because overall measures of social well-being, such as median income, tend to increase over time, the poverty standard also tends to increase. Both the United Kingdom and countries in the European Union measure income poverty using such a relative definition. Currently, the EU considers those with "equivalized" incomes of less than 60 percent of median income to be in poverty.[9]

Relative poverty measures also have their weaknesses. For example, when an absolute poverty standard is used, antipoverty efforts are judged by their ability to move families above the fixed standard; relative poverty declines only if the income of families in the bottom tail of the distribution increases relative to that of the median family.[10]

CONSUMPTION POVERTY   One of the main criticisms of measures of income poverty is that an annual income measure of resources is highly transitory. For many households, income may temporarily dip below the poverty line because of something that happened that year, such as unemployment or a bad harvest. Critics urge the use of a more permanent indicator of resources or well-being, such as annual family consumption spending.[11]

The use of annual family consumption in the poverty measure reflects the view that consumption is a better proxy for permanent income than is annual income. Daniel Slesnick (1993) estimates such a consumption-based poverty measure and advocates its superiority to income poverty measures.[12] Measuring the level of family economic resources as household real consumption expenditure per equivalent adult, he compares it to a set of poverty lines designed to be "conceptually consistent" with the U.S. official poverty standard. The resulting consumption poverty rate is much lower than the official rate, reflecting the overrepresentation of families experiencing a transitory income reduction in the official poverty rate.

Although Slesnick's consumption poverty measure probably does better reflect the "permanently poor" population, it has been criticized. One criticism points out that Slesnick's family size adjustments seem quite out of line with others in the literature, and that largely because of this, Slesnick's poverty measure has declined over time; in contrast, other consumption-based indicators have increased over the last two decades (Cutler and Katz 1991). Other critics have noted that the difficulty of obtaining accurate and complete family expenditure data is a large impediment to adopting a consumption-based index. Furthermore, consumption may not fully reflect a family's true well-being; it is possible that simple frugality may be mistaken for poverty (Triest 1998).

"CAPABILITY" POVERTY   Poverty indicators based on income or consumption presume that families should have *actual* resources to meet some minimum standard. An alternative objective would identify the poor to be those who do not have the *capability* to secure a sufficient level of resources to meet this standard.

Amartya Sen (1995), among others, has presented the basic argument for a poverty measure based on capabilities. He argues that "the basic failure that poverty implies is one of having minimally adequate capabilities" (111) and that "poverty is better seen in terms of capability failure than in terms of the failure to meet the 'basic needs' of specified commodities" (109).[13] Hence, a poverty measure should seek to identify those people who do not possess the capability of generating sufficient income to meet basic needs.

There is also a *policy-related reason* for a capability (or self-sufficiency) measure of poverty. To many analysts and policymakers, policy interventions should seek to provide a pathway to self-sufficiency. Such measures are preferred to income-conditioned in-kind support and cash support, which are viewed as encouraging "dependence." A capability measure of poverty focuses attention on policies that foster economic independence.[14]

Robert Haveman and Andrew Bershadker (1999, 2001) have proposed an "earnings capacity" self-sufficiency poverty measure based on a family's earnings capacity, a concept similar to one suggested earlier by Gary Becker (1965).[15] Their measure of earnings capacity adjusted the full-time, full-year earnings of all adults in a family to account for health issues and other constraints on full-time work and for the required expenses (largely child care) associated with full-time work. The resulting net family earnings capacity value is compared to the official U.S. poverty line.

This measure rests on several norms and assumptions. First, it assumes that full-time, full-year work indicates the full (or capacity) use of human capital. Second, the adjustments to family earnings capacity reflecting the constraints on and the costs of working full-time are assumed to be accurate. Finally, the measure captures only those capabilities that are reflected in market work and earnings; the potential services of other valuable, though nonmarketed, capabilities are neglected.

ASSET POVERTY   There has been much interest recently in the role of asset (wealth) holdings in understanding the level and composition of poverty in the United States (Oliver and Shapiro 1997; Sherraden 1991). In the words of Melvin Oliver and Thomas Shapiro, "Wealth is . . . used to create opportunities, secure a desired stature and standard of living, or pass class status along to one's children. In this sense the command over resources that wealth entails is more encompassing than is income or education, and closer in meaning and theoretical significance to our traditional notions of economic well-being and access to life chances" (1997, 2).

Robert Haveman and Edward Wolff (2005) have estimated the level and composition of asset poverty in 2001, presuming that net worth equal to less than one-fourth of the official poverty line (reflecting the ability to live for three months at the poverty line by drawing down assets) indicates asset poverty. In 2001 one-fourth of American families were asset-poor; among blacks and Hispanics, the asset poverty rate was 62 percent, among those with less than a high school degree it was 60 percent, and among non-aged female heads with children the asset poverty rate stood at 71 percent. From 1983 to 2001, the rate of asset poverty grew by over 9 percent, much faster than the growth of income poverty.

SUBJECTIVE POVERTY   Some researchers have measured poverty by relying on the subjective responses of individuals to questions about their perceptions of economic position or well-being, relative to some norm. Because the norms applied by people are likely to change over time (as their incomes change), subjective poverty measures are relative poverty indicators. These measures survey households and ask them to specify the minimum level of income or consumption they consider to be "just sufficient" to allow them to live a minimally adequate lifestyle. If respondents indicate that their own level of living either exceeds or falls short of what they consider to be the "minimally adequate" monetary poverty line, a poverty rate can be estimated from observations of actual income.[16]

While attractive, subjective measures are based on individual opinions of what constitutes "minimally adequate" or "enough to get by." Hence, establishing an overall poverty rate requires an assumption that individual perceptions of these notions reflect the same level of real welfare for all respondents. The effectiveness of subjective measures is limited by the small sample sizes on which they are based;

most estimates show wide variation around the mean (Citro and Michael 1995, 135), impeding the setting of a reliable and generally accepted poverty threshold.

MEASURING OTHER DIMENSIONS OF DEPRIVATION

In both the United States and Europe, social scientists and policymakers have expressed concerns about using dollar-valued indicators to assess the well-being of citizens and to evaluate the effect of policy changes on various groups of people. These concerns have also been registered with respect to measures of poverty based on annual cash income.

In the 1960s, these concerns led to substantial efforts by U.S. and European government and university researchers to develop a wide variety of indicators to both measure the social and economic performance of society and serve in evaluating the effectiveness of policy efforts. These efforts resulted in a number of prominent government and other reports that presented a variety of social indicators promising improved policy monitoring, policymaking, and policy management.[17] Although this "social indicator" movement faded during the 1980s and 1990s, especially in the United States, interest in the development of such indicators has been renewed in recent years on both sides of the Atlantic (van Dooren and Aristigueta 2005).

In the context of measuring poverty, this interest in broader measures of well-being was strongest in the European Union countries. Until recently, these countries had limited their measurement of poverty to a relative annual income measure, using a poverty line equal to 50 percent of median equivalized income; in recent years, this was increased to 60 percent of median income. An increasing number of European social scientists and policymakers, however, view this economic approach to poverty measurement as too narrow.

A basic argument in support of a broader, multidimensional concept of poverty contends that because markets fail and are incomplete, money income cannot always be readily transformed into the fundamental goods and services necessary for the attainment of well-being. If this is the case, then the measure of poverty must explicitly recognize these shortfalls. A policy judgment provides a second argument in support of a multidimensional approach to the measurement of poverty. If one believes that antipoverty policies should target those with multiple disadvantages, it follows that the poverty measure should also be multidimensional.[18]

Recently, the EU countries and the United Kingdom, emphasizing this multidimensional nature of deprivation, have developed supplementary indicators of poverty based on indicators of material hardship and a broad concept of "social exclusion."[19] The earliest writings urging a multidimensional measure originated in France in the 1970s (Lenoir 1974), where the term "social exclusion" was first used to refer to those who were administratively excluded from the receipt of social benefits. Later, the term was expanded to emphasize the importance of long-term unemployment, or exclusion from work (Paugam 1995).

There are a variety of interpretations of the term "social exclusion"; some use the term to refer to concepts such as marginalization, ghettoization, and the underclass, and others use the term to refer to a broader concept of poverty, encompassing polarization, discrimination, and inequality.[20] In recent discussions of social exclusion, it is argued that broader dimensions of well-being should be included in identifying who is poor, including education, health, employment, housing, access to public benefits, and social contacts. For those who emphasize that poverty is a multidimensional concept, a national poverty measure must reflect these non-income aspects of well-being.

Measuring Poverty and Social Exclusion in the United Kingdom

British social scientists have advanced this multidimensional approach to poverty measurement, including Amartya Sen (1983, 1997) and Anthony Atkinson (1989, 1998). Their work builds on Peter Townsend's pioneering study in 1979 urging attention to lack of access to important goods or services rather than only a lack of income. Their writings implicitly accept the proposition that, because of lack of information and other market failures, important dimensions of well-being cannot be purchased in markets with money and hence require independent measurement.

Even if this proposition is accepted, any proposal for including non-income aspects of well-being in a formal poverty measure has to confront difficult questions. One concerns how to deal with persons with substantial amounts of money income who voluntarily choose low levels of certain non-income dimensions of well-being (for example, housing or vehicle access). A second concerns the selection of appropriate indicators and how to weight them.

ATKINSON'S APPROACH TO MULTIDIMENSIONAL POVERTY   These concerns are reflected in Atkinson's (1998) analysis of the concept of social exclusion. In his view, there are three key issues in thinking about social exclusion—*relativity* (one must indicate the element of society that has excluded an individual, as well as at what time and in what place); *agency* (being excluded requires an act, either by the person excluded or by others); and *dynamics* (being excluded implies a lack of long-term prospects).

In this framework, being long-term unemployed because of lack of aggregate demand or changing technology (leading to feelings of powerlessness and loss of personal control) may be classified as social exclusion, but being long-term unemployed because of an unwillingness to accept an available job is not. Similarly, voluntarily living in poor housing would exclude one from being socially excluded. However, failure to receive public benefits for which one is eligible (owing, for instance, to lack of information, the time costs of applying, or the stigma associated with receipt) or failure to be employed (through, say, the market power held by employers) or failure to consume certain goods and services such as housing, health care, credit, or insurance (through, say, explicit discriminatory practices by property owners or banks) may all be classified as social exclusion. In these cases, it is the acts of others that lead to the exclusion of some from benefits, work, or consumption. Hence, "agency" must be established if a non-economic component of well-being is to be considered in defining poverty.

EMPIRICAL STUDIES OF MULTIDIMENSIONAL POVERTY IN THE UNITED KINGDOM   Atkinson's perspective is reflected in several U.K. empirical studies that have attempted to use "deprivation indicators" to measure poverty and deprivation. Tania Burchardt, Julian Le Grand, and David Piachaud (1999, 2002) have constructed a multidimensional poverty measure; it is summarized in the appendix to this chapter. Matthew Barnes (2002) combines multiple indicators of hardship into a single multidimensional poverty measure. He concludes that about 8 percent of working-age individuals experienced six or more observations of multidimensional disadvantage (out of ten) and that about 6 percent experienced long-term persistent disadvantage on two or more indicators. Only about 5 percent of the U.K. population was found to experience long-term disadvantage on two or more indicators in each of three integral elements of social exclusion (economic deprivation, personal civic exclusion, and personal health exclusion). These studies have been greatly facilitated by relatively new surveys designed to facilitate these efforts—the British Household Panel Survey (BHPS) and the 1999 Poverty and Social Exclusion (PSE) Survey.[21]

POLITICAL SUPPORT IN THE UNITED KINGDOM FOR A MULTI-DIMENSIONAL APPROACH TO POVERTY MEASUREMENT   Efforts to include dimensions beyond income were supported by the government of Prime Minister Tony Blair, who described social exclusion as "the greatest social crisis of our time" (Mandelson 1997). In 1997 the New Labour government set up the Social Exclusion Unit (SEU) as a cabinet office headed by a minister. In 2006 the SEU was replaced by the Social Exclusion Task Force, also headed by a minister.[22]

Since 1999, reports presenting measures of social exclusion in the United Kingdom have been published under the title *Opportunity for All*, the most recent of which appeared in 2007 (United Kingdom Department for Work and Pensions 2007).[23] These reports indicate the government's commitment to annually monitor the state of poverty and social exclusion through a set of quantitative indicators.

Measuring Poverty and Social Exclusion in the European Union

The European Commission recently developed a formal protocol for measuring poverty and social exclusion in the EU countries. The protocol has been called the "Laeken Indicators" because it was established at the European Council of December 2001 in Laeken, Belgium.[24] The Laeken indicators, and their measurement, include:

- At-risk-of-poverty rate—share of persons age zero or older with an equivalized disposable income below 60 percent of the national equivalized median income

- Persistent at-risk-of-poverty rate—share of persons age zero or older with an equivalized disposable income below the at-risk-of-poverty threshold in the current year and in at least two of the preceding three years

- Relative median poverty risk gap—difference between the median equivalized income of persons age zero or older below the at-risk-of-poverty threshold and the threshold itself, expressed as a percentage of the at-risk-of-poverty threshold

- Long-term unemployment rate—total long-term unemployed population (per ILO definition of unemployed as out of work for twelve months or more) as a proportion of total active population age fifteen or older

- Population living in jobless households—proportion of people living in jobless households, expressed as a share of all people in the same age group

- Early school leavers not in education or training—share of persons age eighteen to twenty-four who have only lower secondary education

- Employment gap of immigrants—percentage-point difference between the employment rate for non-immigrants and that for immigrants

- Material deprivation—to be developed

- Housing—to be developed

- Unmet need for care—to be developed

- Child well-being—to be developed

A 2006 EU report (European Commission 2006a, 2006b) indicates that since 2000 the list of country-specific indicators of poverty and social exclusion has been modified and streamlined into a list of eleven primary indicators. Currently, Eurostat publishes country-specific information on the first six of these eleven indicators of poverty and deprivation.[25]

TOWARD MEASURING THE MANY DIMENSIONS OF LOW WELL-BEING IN THE UNITED STATES: A MODEST PROPOSAL

Researchers and policymakers in the United Kingdom and the European Union have adopted a broader concept of poverty than have their U.S. counterparts. The European developments reflect the view that rich societies require officially recognized measures that track progress in meeting many dimensions of the needs of their least well off citizens and that income alone fails to capture the complex situation in which the most deprived citizens find themselves. These developments also reflect the judgment that as societies become more affluent, the nonmoney aspects of well-being take on increased salience. While the Western nations were well served by an income poverty measure a half-century ago, today a variety of additional considerations—including the level of cognitive and noncognitive skills, access to important social institutions (for example, the labor market), the ability to attain minimum standards of food and shelter, and having sufficient time for home production and child care—need to be taken into account.

The European developments also reflect the fact that, today, rich societies possess vastly improved data sources on individual living units than in the 1960s. In the 1960s, when the first efforts to measure poverty were undertaken in the United States, cash income was one of the few accurately recorded indicators of well-being available in survey or census-type data. Today numerous continuing cross-section and longitudinal data sets with large and nationally representative samples are available. Many data sets reveal multiple aspects of the well-being of living units beyond their annual cash income. It follows that official poverty indicators should reflect this improved information.

U.S. academic and policy discussions should move beyond the concept of income poverty, and additional statistical measures of U.S. poverty and deprivation should be developed and published as supplements to an improved set of official income poverty measures.[26]

Any proposal for additional, formal measures of "disadvantage" encounters the issue of whether to combine or weight these measures. As studies in Europe have demonstrated, techniques are available for either developing a single measure based on the "weighting" of multiple indicators of deprivation (Burchardt et al. 1999, 2002, summarized in the appendix; Barnes 2002) or describing deprivation by using counts of the presence of "disadvantage" in multiple dimensions.[27]

The latter approach requires the setting of minimum standards in each dimension, determining if a living unit meets each standard, and then determining for any living unit the number and the standards it fails to meet. With this way of proceeding, one could envision an ongoing tabulation of the number and composition of living units that fail to meet any one (or two, or n) of the minimum standards of a multifaceted concept of disadvantage or deprivation. For example, such a measure could identify as "disadvantaged" the number and composition of living units that fall below the income standard and below the standard in any one or more of the additional dimensions of well-being.

To perform a multidimensional poverty measurement analysis, a large-scale, detailed survey including information on a wide range of living conditions is needed; ideally, the survey would be longitudinal in nature. Indeed, advances in poverty measurement in Europe have been accompanied by extensive data collection efforts designed to implement a reliable multidimensional measure.

Currently, such information is not available for the U.S. population. What is possible, however, is to make use of annual survey data from the U.S. Census Bureau's American Community Survey (ACS) to develop an illustrative, multidimensional measure of deprivation in the United States.[28] The ACS includes many indicators of the living circumstances of American households in addition to incomes that are not reflected in the Current Population Survey (CPS), on which the current official U.S. poverty measure rests. In addition to indicators of educational attainment (for example, less than a high school diploma) and labor force and employment status (for example, living in a jobless household) that are included in the CPS, the ACS also includes information on the quality of housing (for example, crowding, lacking plumbing or kitchen facilities), health and disability status (for example, number of disabling conditions, presence of a mental health problem), vehicle availability, and being linguistically isolated.

A research study that made use of the ACS data could illustrate the many-faceted nature of need and demonstrate the possibility of a U.S. poverty measure that reflects dimensions of disadvantage beyond cash income. Both researchers and policymakers would be well served by complementary measures of poverty that reveal the complexity and multifaceted nature of disadvantage. Such an illustration of the extent of multiple forms of need in the United States would incorporate the 1995 proposed reforms and highlight the many other dimensions of what it means to be poor in a rich society. It would also accelerate debate on needed changes in the official poverty measure.[29]

CONCLUSION

In this chapter, I have sought to broaden the discussion of poverty and poverty measurement by introducing additional concepts of poverty, describing their conceptual basis, and assessing their pros and cons. Following a discussion of the nature and shortcomings of the official U.S. poverty measure (and the revisions of it proposed in 1995), I discuss a number of alternative concepts of economic poverty. These include measures based on family consumption, family potential income (or earnings capacity), assets or wealth, and families' own assessments of their well-being. Relative income poverty measures such as those used in European countries are also described.

The chapter focuses, however, on broader conceptions of the meaning of poverty and deprivation. Some theoretical contributions to this approach are noted, and studies implementing broader, multidimensional measures are described. Most of these studies have taken place in the European Union and the United Kingdom. Finally, I make a modest proposal for implementing a broader measure of hardship and social exclusion that makes use of information available in the recently developed American Community Survey.

Any poverty measure is an indicator of a nation's performance in improving social conditions, and as such it serves many functions. The poverty measure documents the size and composition of the disadvantaged population within a country, and it allows citizens and policymakers to assess the nation's "progress against poverty." The measure also provides guidance for policymakers in assessing the potential of proposed measures for reducing poverty and for evaluating the impact of the social policy measures already in effect. I have argued that moving toward broader measures of poverty and deprivation than simply income has a number of advantages.

First, measures of material hardship or social exclusion capture intrinsic elements of the underlying hardship that people face, and they complement income-based measures by providing "important insights into different dimensions of people's well-being" (Iceland 2005, 220).[30]

Moreover, because antipoverty policy measures are often directed at increasing access to particular goods, services, or environments (for example, policies designed to increase access to food, housing, transportation, medical care, education or train-ing, and employment, among others), it is important to use measures of need that reflect these dimensions. Ongoing reports detailing how many citizens of work-ing age are excluded from health, disability, or unemployment insurance cover-age, how many families fail to live in adequate housing, and how many families are excluded from employment because of health problems or disabling conditions could be influential in policy discussions and choices.

Finally, measures that reflect the lack of access to various non-income dimen-sions of need also indicate different patterns of hardship by sociodemographic groups (for example, single mothers, the aged, and the disabled) more than do measures of income poverty, and these measures point to the gains that could be secured by effective targeting of policies among demographic groups.

Some analysts emphasize the inherent difficulties in developing meaningful mea-sures of material hardship or social exclusion. Although these obstacles are formida-ble, they need to be weighed alongside the benefits of a more full-bodied picture of poverty in a rich society. Progress in tackling these issues would also advance the agenda for extending the current national measure of income poverty.[31]

APPENDIX: BURCHARDT, LE GRAND, AND PIACHAUD'S EMPIRICAL MEASURE OF SOCIAL EXCLUSION POVERTY

Burchardt, Le Grand, and Piachaud (1999) adopt a definition of social exclusion that reflects the elements emphasized by Atkinson, for whom an individual is socially excluded if (a) he or she is geographically resident in a society, but (b) for reasons beyond his or her control, he or she cannot participate in the normal activ-ities of citizens in that society, and (c) he or she would like to so participate.[32] The authors' definition states that: "An individual is socially excluded if (a) he or she is geographically resident in a society and (b) he or she does not participate in the normal activities of citizens in that society" (230).[33]

Measuring social exclusion consistent with this definition covers the following four dimensions of well-being, with the specified thresholds:

1. *Consumption activity of a minimum level of goods and services.* A person is socially excluded if he or she has income less than half of mean equivalized household income.

2. *Engagement in an economically or socially productive activity.* A person is socially excluded if he or she is not in paid work, in full-time education or training, retired if of retirement age, or caring for children.

3. *Engagement in political activity.* A person is socially excluded if he or she did not vote in a recent election and is not a member of a political organization.

4. *Engagement in social interaction with family or friends.* A person is socially excluded if he or she lacks someone who offers support in any one of these five dimensions: listening, helping in a crisis, and being someone the person can relax with, feel really appreciated by, and count on for comfort.

These empirical characteristics were then measured using the British Household Panel Survey (BHPS), and the results were used to reveal the extent of and trends in exclusion on each dimension, the exclusion of the same people on multiple dimensions, the overlap between being income-poor and poor in the other dimensions, and the number of dimensions of exclusion for those who were poor in terms of this multidimensional measure of poverty.

The authors found that in Britain in 1995, of those in income poverty, 20 percent fell below the social productivity threshold, 19 percent fell below the political activity threshold, and 16 percent fell below the social interaction threshold. Conversely, of those below the social productivity (political activity, social interaction) threshold, 39 (31, 32) percent were income-poor.

NOTES

1. At one point, Orshansky stated: "The best that can be said of the measure is that at a time when it seemed useful, it was there."
2. Her first paper on the measurement of poverty was published in the 1963 volume of the *Social Security Bulletin,* where she first described her income poverty concept and applied it to only families with children. In her central paper (Orshansky 1965), she presented a refined version of her measure—expanded to include all types of family units—and described how she had developed the thresholds and analyzed the population shown to be in poverty by the thresholds. Four months later, the Office of Economic Opportunity (OEO) adopted her thresholds as a working or quasi-official definition of poverty.
3. The official definition of poverty has played a special role in the development of social policy. James Tobin (1970, 83) made the case that because of the official adoption of this measure, the nation had committed itself to producing an annual report on its progress toward poverty reduction and, as a result, "no politician will be able to . . . ignore the repeated solemn acknowledgments of society's obligation to its poorer members."
4. As discussed later, this economic concept underlies the official U.S. poverty measure and measures of relative income poverty as implemented in the United Kingdom and western Europe. It also underlies the proposed revisions of the U.S. measure by the National Research Council's (NRC) Panel on Poverty and Family Assistance (Citro and Michael 1995). See also U.S. Bureau of the Census (2007).
5. Within each perspective, there is a wide range of definitions and concepts. For example, if income is taken to be the best indicator of economic status, is annual, multiyear, or lifetime income the appropriate measure? Should we examine pretax, pretransfer income, or income after accounting for taxes and/or transfers? Should means-tested in-kind income or refundable tax credits be counted or not?

6. See Mayer and Jencks (1992), Slesnick (1993), Meyer and Sullivan (2003, 2006), and the discussion later in this chapter. This pattern is especially true for those households in the tails of the distribution of annual income in a particular year. For example, in 1994 consumer units in the Labor Department's annual Consumer Expenditure Survey (CES) reported average pretax income of about $6,800, but average consumption expenditures of about $14,000.

7. Kathleen Short and her colleagues (1999) discuss the implementation of the recommended poverty measures and present estimates of them for the decade of the 1990s; see also Short (2001) and Short (2005).

8. Rebecca Blank (2008) extensively discusses the weaknesses of the official poverty measure and analyzes why adoption of a more reliable measure of poverty has been so difficult to achieve.

9. In the mid-1960s, when the U.S. official poverty measure was adopted, the poverty line was about one-half of median income for a family of four (Ruggles 1990, 19). Today, however, the official income threshold stands at about 30 percent of median income.

10. Robert Lampman (1971, 53) emphasized this weakness of the relative standard as an indicator of the effectiveness of antipoverty policies in reducing poverty: "While income poverty is a relative matter, I do not think we should engage in frequent changes of the poverty lines, other than to adjust for price change. As I see it, the elimination of income poverty is usefully thought of as a one-time operation in pursuit of a goal unique to this generation."

11. Slesnick (1993, 2) argued that annual income measures are "severely biased": "Households in the lower tail of the income distribution are disproportionately represented by those with temporary reductions in income."

12. Following Slesnick's paper, Mayer and Jencks (1989, 1992) and Meyer and Sullivan (2003, 2006) made important contributions to the discussion of consumption expenditure in assessing the level, trend, and prevalence of economic deprivation.

13. Development of the philosophical and value basis for this viewpoint can be found throughout Sen's many writings on inequality and poverty, especially his 1979 Tanner Lecture (Sen 1980), his 1982 Geary Lecture (Sen 1983), and Sen (1997).

14. One of the earliest proponents of this view was Charles Murray (1984). He argued that government policy should stop assisting the destitute and start emphasizing individual self-reliance.

15. Becker's concept of family capability relies on a measure of family "full income," which includes both income realized through market work and the value of leisure time.

16. This approach to poverty measurement is often called the Leyden School; see van Praag (1968), Hagenaars (1986), and van Praag, Hagenaars, and van Weeren (1982). The "minimum income" question approach to poverty measurement is employed in Goedhart and others (1977).

17. In the United States, the earliest such report was published in 1974 by the Office of Management and Budget (OMB). This report was followed by even more comprehensive efforts by the U.S. Bureau of the Census (1977, 1981). Similar studies and publications were sponsored by the United Nations (1975) and the Organization for Economic Cooperation and Development (OECD 1973, 1976, 1982). See also Sawhill (1969).

18. For example, Lesley Turner, Sheldon Danziger, and Kristen Seefeldt (2006) suggest that welfare programs be targeted on women who are *both* income-poor and "chronically disconnected" (without work or benefits for long periods of time), a group largely comprising those with physical or learning disabilities and alcohol or drug dependency.

19. Several "Laeken indicators" (after the European Council meeting in Laeken, Belgium, in 2001) were designed to measure a broad concept of poverty. See http://epp.eurostat.ec.europa.eu/cache/ITY_SDDS/EN/ilc_base.htm. Anthony Atkinson and others (2002) and Eric Marlier and others (2007) discuss concepts and measurement proposals of the 2001 Laeken European Council for securing national multidimensional indicators designed to monitor progress in reducing poverty and social exclusion.

20. For example, British prime minister Tony Blair spoke of social exclusion as being "shut out from society" (Tony Blair, November 23, 1997, cited in Atkinson 1998).

21. The BHPS is a nationally representative survey of about ten thousand adults who have been interviewed each year, beginning in 1991; fifteen waves of data are now available to researchers. The survey contains questions on topics related to social exclusion, including possession of durable goods, housing quality, social relationships, and health. The PSE survey was designed by senior academics from the Universities of Bristol, Loughborough, and York, carried out in 1999 by the Office for National Statistics, and funded by the Joseph Rowntree Foundation. It was designed to be a comprehensive national survey emphasizing issues of poverty, deprivation, and exclusion in Britain.

22. The website of the task force defines social exclusion as follows: "Social exclusion is about more than income poverty. It is a short-hand term for what can happen when people or areas have a combination of linked problems, such as unemployment, discrimination, poor skills, low incomes, poor housing, high crime and family breakdown. These problems are linked and mutually reinforcing. Social exclusion is an extreme consequence of what happens when people don't get a fair deal throughout their lives, often because of disadvantage they face at birth, and this disadvantage can be transmitted from one generation to the next." See Social Exclusion Task Force, "Context for Social Exclusion Work," available at: http://www.cabinetoffice.gov.uk/social_exclusion_task_force/context.aspx.

23. The 2007 report included forty-one primary indicators and fifty-nine total indicators of low income, access to services, health, education, and social isolation.

24. See Marlier and others (2007) for a full listing of the measures.

25. See European Commission, Eurostat, "Data Navigation Tree," available at: http://epp.eurostat.ec.europa.eu/portal/page?_pageid=1996,45323734&_dad=portal&_schema=PORTAL&screen=welcomeref&open=/sd_sc&language=en&product=REF_SD_SC&root=REF_SD_SC&scrollto=0. See also Barnes (2005).

26. Lampman (1971) argued that income poverty is the most fundamental indicator of low well-being and hence should serve as the basis of national measures of poverty. He suggested that, until rich societies eliminate income poverty, there is little to be gained from introducing "new economic and social goals" (53); see also Danziger (2007) and Danziger and Gottschalk (2005), who echo this point of view. While recognizing the weakness of existing income-based poverty measures, John Iceland (2005, 220) argues that "there continues to be a vital place for income-based measures of poverty . . . [as they] . . . are the most conceptually and, especially, operationally advanced measures of

poverty available, and they are broadly understood and accepted by researchers, policy makers, and the public."

27. See also Desai and Shah (1988), Gordon and others (2000), Whelan and others (2001), Bradshaw (2004), Saunders and Adelman (2004), Levitas (2006), Pantazis, Gordon, and Levitas (2006), Cappellari and Jenkins (2006), and Levitas and others (2007). Richard Berthoud and Mark Bryan (2007) have studied the dynamics of social deprivation in a longitudinal context.

28. For a description of the American Community Survey, see U.S. Census Bureau, "American Community Survey," http://www.census.gov/acs/www/index.html.

29. The U.S. NRC report of 1995 (Citro and Michael 1995) stated: "Many other dimensions of impoverishment can exist, from anxiety and fear about one's personal safety when living in a high-crime neighborhood or with abusive family members to suffering from inadequate medical care and from homelessness to loneliness and helplessness. These, too, need to be conceptualized, measured, and their prevalence recorded across groups and over time. . . . In describing the extent of impoverishment in the United States, these nonmonetary indices would provide important added information" (314–15).

30. John Iceland and Kurt Baumann (2007) have studied the correspondence of income poverty and material hardship. They conclude that "both [income] poverty and material hardship are multifaceted, and this needs to be better recognized by those who would treat either as a single concept or measure" (391). Maya Federman and her colleagues (1996) also examine the relationship between income poverty and material hardship.

31. Daniel Lichter (2005) examines issues related to the growing immigrant population and the effect of cohabitation on poverty. See also Smeeding (2005, 2006). Blank (2008) proposes a set of concrete steps designed to advance revisions of the official poverty measure.

32. The following summary draws from Burchardt, Le Grand, and Piachaud (1999). The version of the analysis in Burchardt, Le Grand, and Piachaud (2002) extends the analysis to make use of additional years of data.

33. Burchardt, Le Grand, and Piachaud (1999) have particular difficulty with (b). For example, groups faced with persistent hostility might voluntarily choose to withdraw, or individuals who are raised in very narrow or countercultural circumstances might "choose," say, gang membership and hence should perhaps be considered socially excluded. Also presenting problems is (c), in that if real acts by others to exclude a person are met with indifference by the excluded person, should such a person be considered socially excluded?

REFERENCES

Atkinson, Anthony. 1989. "How Should We Measure Poverty? Some Conceptual Issues." In *Poverty and Social Security*, edited by Anthony B. Atkinson. Hemel Hempstead, U.K.: Harvester-Wheatsheaf.

———. 1998. "Social Exclusion, Poverty, and Unemployment." In *Exclusion, Employment, and Opportunity*, edited by Anthony Atkinson and John Hills. CASE paper 4. London: London School of Economics, Centre for Analysis of Social Exclusion.

Atkinson, Anthony B., Bea Cantillon, Eric Marlier, and Brian Nolan. 2002. *Social Indicators: The EU and Social Inclusion.* Oxford: Oxford University Press.

Barnes, Matthew. 2002. *Poverty and Social Exclusion in Europe.* Northampton, Mass.: Edward Elgar.

———. 2005. *Social Exclusion in Great Britain: An Empirical Investigation and Comparison with the EU.* Ashgate, U.K.: Aldershot.

Becker, Gary S. 1965. "A Theory of the Allocation of Time." *Economic Journal* 75(299): 493–517.

Berthoud, Richard, and Mark Bryan. 2007. "Income, Deprivation, and Poverty: A Longitudinal Analysis." Working paper. Essex, U.K.: University of Essex.

Blank, Rebecca. 2008. "How to Improve Poverty Measurement in the United States." *Journal of Policy Analysis and Management* 27(2): 233–54.

Bradshaw, Jonathan. 2004. "How Has the Notion of Social Exclusion Developed in the European Discourse?" *Economic and Labor Relations Review* 14(2): 168–86.

Burchardt, Tania, Julian Le Grand, and David Piachaud. 1999. "Social Exclusion in Britain 1991–1995." *Social Policy and Administration* 33(3): 227–44.

———. 2002. "Degrees of Exclusion: Developing a Dynamic Multidimensional Measure." In *Understanding Social Exclusion,* edited by John Hills, Julian Le Grand, and David Piachaud. New York: Oxford University Press.

Cappellari, Lorenzo, and Stephen Jenkins. 2006. "Summarizing Deprivation Indicators." Working paper 2006-40. Colchester: University of Essex, Institute for Social and Economic Research.

Citro, Constance F., and Robert T. Michael, eds. 1995. *Measuring Poverty: A New Approach.* Washington, D.C.: National Academies Press.

Cutler, David M., and Lawrence F. Katz. 1991. "Macroeconomic Performance and the Disadvantaged." *Brookings Papers on Economic Activity* (pt. 2): 1–61.

Danziger, Sheldon. 2007. "Fighting Poverty Revisited: What Did Researchers Know Forty Years Ago? What Do We Know Today?" *Focus* 25(1, spring–summer): 3–11.

Danziger, Sheldon, and Peter Gottschalk. 2005. "Diverging Fortunes: Trends in Poverty and Inequality." In *The American People: Census 2000,* edited by Reynolds Farley and John Haaga. New York: Russell Sage Foundation.

Desai, Meghnad, and Anup Shah. 1988. "An Econometric Approach to the Measurement of Poverty." *Oxford Economic Papers* 40(3): 505–22.

European Commission. Employment, Social Affairs, and Equal Opportunities. 2006a. *Joint Report on Social Protection and Social Inclusion.* Brussels: European Commission (April).

———. 2006b. "Portfolio of Overarching Indicators and Streamlined Social Inclusion, Pensions, and Health Portfolios." Brussels: European Commission (June).

Federman, Maya, Thesia I. Garner, Kathleen Short, W. Boman Cutter IV, John Kiely, David Levine, Duane McGough, and Marilyn McMillen. 1996. "What Does It Mean to Be Poor in America?" *Monthly Labor Review* 119(5, May): 3–17.

Goedhart, Theo, Victor Halberstadt, Arie Kapteyn, and Bernard van Praag. 1977. "The Poverty Line: Concept and Measurement." *Journal of Human Resources* 12(4): 503–20.

Gordon, David, Laura Adelman, Karl Ashworth, Jonathan Bradshaw, Ruth Levitas, Sue Middleton, Christina Pantazis, Demi Patsios, Sarah Payne, Peter Townsend, and Julie Williams. 2000. *Poverty and Social Exclusion in Britain.* York, U.K.: Joseph Rowntree Foundation.

Hagenaars, Aldi J. M. 1986. *The Perception of Poverty.* Amsterdam: North-Holland.

Haveman, Robert, and Andrew Bershadker. 1999. "Self-Reliance and Poverty: Net Earnings Capacity Versus Income for Measuring Poverty." Public policy brief. Annandale-on-Hudson, N.Y.: Bard College, Jerome Levy Economics Institute.

———. 2001. "The 'Inability to Be Self-Reliant' as an Indicator of Poverty: Trends for the U.S., 1975–1997." *Review of Income and Wealth* 47(3): 335–60.

Haveman, Robert, and Edward Wolff. 2005. "The Concept and Measurement of Asset Poverty: Levels, Trends, and Composition for the U.S., 1983–2001." *Journal of Economic Inequality* 2(2): 145–69.

Iceland, John. 2005. "Measuring Poverty: Theoretical and Empirical Considerations." *Measurement* 3(4): 199–235.

Iceland, John, and Kurt J. Baumann. 2007. "Income Poverty and Material Hardship: How Strong Is the Association?" *Journal of Socio-Economics* 36(3): 376–96.

Jencks, Christopher, Susan Mayer, and Joseph Swingle. 2004. "Can We Fix the Federal Poverty Measure So It Provides Reliable Information About Changes in Children's Living Conditions?" Paper presented to an American Enterprise Institute seminar on "Reconsidering the Federal Poverty Measure." Washington (September 14).

Lampman, Robert. 1971. *Ends and Means of Reducing Income Poverty.* New York: Academic Press.

Lenoir, Re'mi. 1974. *Les Exclus: Un français sur dix,* 2d ed. Paris: Éditions du Seuil, 1989.

Levitas, Ruth. 2006. "The Concept and Measurement of Social Exclusion." In *Poverty and Social Exclusion in Britain: The Millennium Survey,* edited by Christina Pantazis, David Gordon, and Ruth Levitas. Bristol, U.K.: Policy Press.

Levitas, Ruth, Christina Pantazis, Eldin Fahmy, David Gordon, Eva Lloyd, and Demi Patsios. 2007. *The Multidimensional Analysis of Social Exclusion.* Bristol, U.K.: University of Bristol, Department of Sociology and the School for Social Policy.

Lichter, Daniel. 2005. "In Search of the 'Best' Poverty Measure." *Measurement* 3(4): 253–58.

Mandelson, Peter. 1997. *Labour's Next Steps: Tackling Social Exclusion.* Fabian Pamphlet 581. London: Fabian Society.

Marlier, Eric, Anthony Atkinson, Bea Cantillon, and Brian Nolan. 2007. *The EU and Social Inclusion: Facing the Challenges.* Bristol, U.K.: Policy Press.

Mayer, Susan E., and Christopher Jencks. 1989. "Poverty and Distribution of Material Hardship." *Journal of Human Resources* 24(1): 88–114.

———. 1992. "Recent Trends in Economic Inequality in the United States: Income vs. Expenditures vs. Material Well-Being." In *Poverty and Prosperity in the USA in the Late Twentieth Century,* edited by Dimitri Papadimitriou and Edward Wolff. New York: St. Martin's Press.

Meyer, Bruce D., and James X. Sullivan. 2003. "Measuring the Well-Being of the Poor Using Income and Consumption." *Journal of Human Resources* 38(supp.): 1180–1220.

———. 2006. "Three Decades of Consumption and Income Poverty." Working Paper 04.16. Chicago: University of Chicago, Harris School. Available at: http://harrisschool.uchicago.edu/About/publications/working-papers/pdf/wp_04_16.pdf.

Murray, Charles A. 1984. *Losing Ground: American Social Policy, 1950–1980.* New York: Basic Books.

Office of Management and Budget (OMB). 1974. *Social Indicators 1973: Selected Data on Social Conditions and Trends in the United States.* Washington: U.S. Government Printing Office.

Oliver, Melvin L., and Thomas M. Shapiro. 1997. *Black Wealth/White Wealth: A New Perspective on Racial Inequality.* New York: Routledge.

Organization for Economic Cooperation and Development (OECD). 1973. *The OECD Social Indicator Program: List of Social Concerns Common to Most OECD Countries.* Paris: OECD.

———. 1976. *Measuring Social Well-Being: A Progress Report on the Development of Social Indicators.* Paris: OECD.

———. 1982. *The OECD List of Social Indicators: OECD Social Indicator Development Program.* Paris: OECD.

Orshansky, Mollie. 1963. "Children of the Poor." *Social Security Bulletin* 26(1): 3–13.

———. 1965. "Counting the Poor: Another Look at the Poverty Profile." *Social Security Bulletin* 28(1, January): 3–29. (Reprinted in *Social Security Bulletin* 51[10, October 1988]: 25–51.)

Pantazis, Christina, David Gordon, and Ruth Levitas, eds. 2006. *Poverty and Social Exclusion in Britain: The Millennium Survey.* Bristol, U.K.: Policy Press.

Paugam, Serge. 1995. "The Spiral of Precariousness: A Multidimensional Approach to the Process of Social Disqualification in France." In *Beyond the Threshold: The Measurement and Analysis of Social Exclusion,* edited by Graham Room. Bristol, U.K.: Policy Press.

Renwick, Trudi J., and Barbara R. Bergmann. 1993. "A Budget-Based Definition of Poverty, with an Application to Single-Parent Families." *Journal of Human Resources* 28(1): 1–24.

Ruggles, Patricia. 1990. *Drawing the Line: Alternative Poverty Measures and Their Implications for Public Policy.* Washington, D.C.: Urban Institute.

Saunders, Peter, and Laura Adelman. 2004. "Resources, Deprivation, and Exclusion Approaches to Measuring Well-Being: A Comparative Study of Australia and Britain." Paper presented to the twenty-eighth general conference of the International Association for Research in Income and Wealth. Cork, Ireland (August 22–28).

Sawhill, Isabel. 1969. "The Role of Social Indicators and Social Reporting in Public Expenditure Decisions." In U.S. Joint Economic Committee, *The Analysis and Evaluation of Public Expenditures: The PPB System.* Washington: U.S. Government Printing Office.

Sen, Amartya. 1980. "Equality of What?" In *Tanner Lectures on Human Values,* edited by S. M. McMurrin. New York: Cambridge University Press.

———. 1983. "Poor, Relatively Speaking." *Oxford Economic Papers* 35(2): 153–69.

———. 1995. *Inequality Reexamined.* Cambridge, Mass.: Harvard University Press.

———. 1997. *On Economic Inequality.* Oxford: Clarendon Press.

Sherraden, Michael. 1991. *Assets and the Poor: A New American Welfare Policy.* Armonk, N.Y.: M. E. Sharpe.

Short, Kathleen, Thesia Garner, David Johnson, and Patricia Doyle. 1999. *Experimental Poverty Measures: 1990 to 1997.* Current Population Reports P60-205. Washington: U.S. Department of Commerce, U.S. Census Bureau.

Short, Kathleen. 2001. "Experimental Poverty Measures: 1999." Current Population Reports P60-216. Washington: U.S. Department of Commerce, U.S. Census Bureau.

———. 2005. "Material and Financial Hardship and Alternative Poverty Measures in the USA." *Journal of Social Policy* 34(1): 21–38.

Slesnick, Daniel T. 1993. "Gaining Ground: Poverty in the Postwar United States." *Journal of Political Economy* 101(1): 1–38.

Smeeding, Timothy M. 2005. "Poor People in Rich Nations: The United States in Comparative Perspective." Luxembourg Income Study working paper 419 (October). Available at: http://ssrn.com/abstract=835506.

———. 2006. "Measuring Poverty and Deprivation in a U.S. Context: Some Additional Considerations." *Measurement* 3(4): 258–60, and *Wealth* 25: 429–40.

Tobin, James. 1970. "Raising the Incomes of the Poor." In *Agenda for the Nation*, edited by Kermit Gordon. Washington, D.C.: Brookings Institution Press.

Townsend, Peter. 1979. *Poverty in the United Kingdom: A Survey of Household Resources and Standards of Living.* Harmondsworth, U.K.: Penguin.

Triest, Robert K. 1998. "Has Poverty Gotten Worse?" *Journal of Economic Perspectives* 12(1): 97–114.

Turner, Lesley J., Sheldon Danziger, and Kristen S. Seefeldt. 2006. "Failing the Transition from Welfare to Work: Women Chronically Disconnected from Employment and Cash Welfare." *Social Science Quarterly* 87(2): 227–49.

United Kingdom Department for Work and Pensions. 2007. *Opportunity for All: Indicators Update 2007.* London (October). Available at: http://www.dwp.gov.uk/ofa/reports/2007/OpportunityforAll2007.pdf.

U.S. Bureau of the Census. 1977. *Social Indicators 1976: Selected Data on Social Conditions and Trends in the United States.* Washington: U.S. Government Printing Office.

———. 1981. *Social Indicators III: Selected Data on Social Conditions and Trends in the United States.* Washington: U.S. Government Printing Office.

———. 2007. Current Population Survey, Annual Social and Economic Supplements. Washington: U.S. Government Printing Office.

United Nations. 1975. *Towards a System of Social and Demographic Statistics.* New York: United Nations.

Van Dooren, Wouter, and Maria Aristigueta. 2005. "The Rediscovery of Social Indicators in Europe and the USA: An International Comparison." Paper presented to the annual meeting of the European Group for Public Administration. Berne, Switzerland (March 8–9). Available at: http://soc.kuleuven.be/io/egpa/qual/bern/vanDooren_Aristigueta.pdf.

Van Praag, Bernard M. S. 1968. *Individual Welfare Functions and Human Behavior.* Amsterdam: North-Holland.

Van Praag, Bernard M. S., Aldi J. M. Hagenaars, and Hans van Weeren. 1982. "Poverty in Europe." *Review of Income and Wealth* 28(3): 345–59.

Whelan, Christopher T., Richard Layte, Bertrand Maître, and Brian Nolan. 2001. "Income, Deprivation, and Economic Strain: An Analysis of the European Community Household Panel." *European Sociological Review* 17(4): 357–72.

Index

Boldface numbers refer to figures and tables.